ENCYCLOPEDIA OF THE WARS OF THE ROSES

ENCYCLOPEDIA OF THE WARS OF THE ROSES

John A. Wagner

ABC ❧ CLIO

Santa Barbara, California   Denver, Colorado   Oxford, England

Library of Congress Cataloging-in-Publication Data
Wagner, J. A. (John A.)
    Encyclopedia of the Wars of the Roses / John A. Wagner
       p.   cm.
    Includes bibliographical references and index.
    ISBN 1-85109-358-3 (alk. paper) — ISBN 1-57607-575-3 (e-book)
    1. Great Britain—History—Wars of the Roses,
1455–1485—Encyclopedias.   I. Title.
DA250.W34   2001
942.04—dc21

                                                                              2001001605

06   05   04   03   02   01   10 9 8 7 6 5 4 3 2 1

This book is also available on the World Wide Web as an e-book. Visit abc-clio.com for
details.

ABC-CLIO, Inc.
130 Cremona Drive, P.O. Box 1911
Santa Barbara, California 93116–1911

This book is printed on acid-free paper ∞.
Manufactured in the United States of America

To the women who have made a difference:
my mother,
Dolores Burmahln Wagner;
my grandmothers,
Olivia Gruhle Burmahln and Dorothy Stephanie Wagner;
my mother-in-law,
Mary Schultz Bronski;
my great-aunt,
Elizabeth Butler Burmahln;
and, of course, my wife,
Donna Bronski

Contents

Encyclopedia of the Wars of the Roses

Guide to Related Topics

Battles and Campaigns
Alnwick Castle
Bamburgh Castle
Barnet, Battle of
Battles, Nature of
Blore Heath, Battle of
Bosworth Field, Battle of
Castillon, Battle of
Dunstanburgh Castle
Edgecote, Battle of
Edward IV, Overthrow of
Edward IV, Restoration of
Ferrybridge, Battle of
Harlech Castle
Hedgeley Moor, Battle of
Heworth, Battle of
Hexham, Battle of
Losecote Field, Battle of
Ludford Bridge, Battle of
March on London
Military Campaigns, Duration of
Mortimer's Cross, Battle of
Nibley Green, Battle of
Northampton, Battle of
St. Albans, Battle of (1455)
St. Albans, Battle of (1461)
Stamford Bridge, Battle of
Stoke, Battle of
Tewkesbury, Battle of
Towton, Battle of
Twt Hill, Battle of
Wakefield, Battle of

Brittany
Brittany
Burgundy
France
Francis II, Duke of Brittany

Henry VII, King of England
Landais, Pierre

Burgundy
Brittany
Burgundy
Charles, Duke of Burgundy
France
Gruthuyse, Louis de, Seigneur de la
    Gruthuyse, Earl of Winchester
Hanseatic League
Margaret of York, Duchess of Burgundy
Memoirs (Commines)
Philip, Duke of Burgundy
Recueil des Croniques et Anchiennes Istories de la
    Grant Bretaigne, a present nomme Engleterre
    (Waurin)
Simnel, Lambert
Warbeck, Perkin

Castles and Fortresses
Alnwick Castle
Bamburgh Castle
Caister Castle, Siege of
Dunstanburgh Castle
Harlech Castle
Tower of London

Church and Churchmen
Booth, Lawrence, Archbishop of York
Bourchier, Thomas, Cardinal Archbishop of
    Canterbury
Coppini Mission
Courtenay, Peter, Bishop of Winchester
English Church and the Wars of the Roses
Kennedy, James, Bishop of St. Andrews
Langstrother, Sir John, Prior of the Hospital of
    St. John of Jerusalem

Neville, Richard, Earl of Warwick
Neville, Sir Thomas
Neville-Percy Feud
Nibley Green, Battle of
Percy, Henry, Earl of Northumberland
    (d. 1455)
Percy, Henry, Earl of Northumberland
    (d. 1461)
Percy, Thomas, Lord Egremont
Plantagenet, Richard, Duke of York (d. 1460)
Radford, Nicholas
Stamford Bridge, Battle of

France

Angers Agreement
Brézé, Pierre de, Seneschal of Normandy
Brittany
Burgundy
Calais
Castillon, Battle of
Charles VII, King of France
Charles VIII, King of France
Chinon Agreement
France
Hanseatic League
Hundred Years War
Louis XI, King of France
Manner and Guiding of the Earl of Warwick at
    Angers
Memoirs (Commines)
Warbeck, Perkin

Gentry

Brackenbury, Sir Robert
Bray, Sir Reginald
Catesby, William
Fortescue, Sir John
Gentry
Hungerford, Sir Thomas
Hungerford, Sir Walter
Malory, Sir Thomas
Neville, Sir Humphrey
Neville, Sir Thomas
Neville, Thomas, Bastard of Fauconberg
Paston Letters
Plumpton Letters and Papers
Radford, Nicholas
Ratcliffe, Sir Richard
Rhys ap Thomas

Stanley, Sir William
Stonor Letters and Papers
Tailboys, Sir William
Thomas ap Gruffydd
Trollope, Sir Andrew
Tudor, Owen
Tunstall, Sir Richard
Tyrell, Sir James
Vaughan, Sir Thomas

Government, Politics, and Parliament

Accord, Act of
Attainder, Act of
Clarence, Execution of
Council, Royal
Council Meeting of 13 June 1483
Court, Royal
Coventry Parliament
De Facto Act
First Protectorate
Fortescue, Sir John
Henry VI, Illness of
Henry VI, Murder of
Hundred Years War
Love-Day of 1458
Parliament
Prerogative
Propaganda
Readeption
Retaining, Acts against
Richard II, Deposition of
Sanctuary
Second Protectorate
Titulus Regius
Usurpation of 1483
Wars of the Roses, Causes of

Henry VI, Reigns of (1422–1461, 1470–1471)

Accord, Act of
Castillon, Battle of
"Compilation of the Meekness and Good
    Life of King Henry VI" (Blacman)
Coppini Mission
Courtenay-Bonville Feud
Coventry Parliament
Dartford Uprising
First Protectorate

Henry VI, King of England
Henry VI, Illness of
Henry VI, Murder of
Hundred Years War
Jack Cade's Rebellion
Love-Day of 1458
March on London
Neville-Percy Feud
Northampton, Battle of
Readeption
St. Albans, Battle of (1455)
St. Albans, Battle of (1461)
Second Protectorate
Stamford Bridge, Battle of
Wakefield, Battle of

Henry VII, Reign of (1485–1509)

Anglica Historia (Vergil)
Beaufort, Margaret, Countess of Richmond
    and Derby
Bosworth Field, Battle of
Bray, Sir Reginald
Charles VIII, King of France
De Facto Act
Elizabeth of York, Queen of England
Grey, Thomas, Marquis of Dorset
Henry VII, King of England
Lovell-Stafford Uprising
Morton, John, Cardinal Archbishop of
    Canterbury
Plantagenet, Edward, Earl of Warwick
Rhys ap Thomas
Richard III, Historical Views of
Simnel, Lambert
Stanley, Thomas, Earl of Derby
Stanley, Sir William
Stoke, Battle of
Tudor, House of
Tudor, Jasper, Earl of Pembroke and Duke of
    Bedford
Urswick, Christopher
Vere, John de, Earl of Oxford
Warbeck, Perkin
Wars of the Roses, Naming of
Yorkist Heirs (after 1485)

Historical Sources and
Literary Works

Anglica Historia (Vergil)

The Ballad of Bosworth Field
Cely Letters and Papers
Chronicle of the Rebellion in Lincolnshire
"Compilation of the Meekness and Good
    Life of King Henry VI" (Blacman)
Croyland Chronicle
Hardyng's Chronicle
Henry VI, Part 1 (Shakespeare)
Henry VI, Part 2 (Shakespeare)
Henry VI, Part 3 (Shakespeare)
The History of King Richard III (More)
History of the Arrival of Edward IV
London Chronicles
Manner and Guiding of the Earl of Warwick at
    Angers
Memoirs (Commines)
Paston Letters
Plumpton Letters and Papers
Recueil des Croniques et Anchiennes Istories de la
    Grant Bretaigne, a present nomme Engleterre
    (Waurin)
Richard III, Historical Views of
Richard III (Shakespeare)
The Rose of England
Rous, John
Shakespeare and the Wars of the Roses
The Song of Lady Bessy
Stonor Letters and Papers
The Union of the Two Noble and Illustrious
    Families of Lancaster and York (Hall)
The Usurpation of Richard III (Mancini)
Warkworth's Chronicle
Whethamstede, John, Abbott of St. Albans

Ireland

Butler, James, Earl of Wiltshire and Ormond
Fitzgerald, Gerald, Earl of Kildare
Fitzgerald, Thomas, Earl of Desmond
Fitzgerald, Thomas, Earl of Kildare
Ireland
Scotland
Simnel, Lambert
Wales
Warbeck, Perkin

Lancaster, House of, Members
and Partisans of

Beaufort, Edmund, Duke of Somerset
    (d. 1455)

Bourchier, Henry, Earl of Essex
Butler, James, Earl of Wiltshire and Ormond
Clifford, John, Lord Clifford
Clifford, Thomas, Lord Clifford
Courtenay, Henry, Earl of Devon (Lancastrian)
Courtenay, John, Earl of Devon (Lancastrian)
Courtenay, Thomas, Earl of Devon (d. 1458)
Courtenay, Thomas, Earl of Devon (d. 1461)
Devereux, Walter, Lord Ferrers of Chartley
Dinham, John, Lord Dinham
Fitzgerald, Gerald, Earl of Kildare
Fitzgerald, Thomas, Earl of Desmond
Fitzgerald, Thomas, Earl of Kildare
Grey, Edmund, Earl of Kent
Grey, Thomas, Marquis of Dorset
Gruthuyse, Louis de, Seigneur de la Gruthuyse, Earl of Winchester
Hastings, William, Lord Hastings
Herbert, William, Earl of Pembroke
Holland, Henry, Duke of Exeter
Howard, John, Duke of Norfolk
Howard, Thomas, Earl of Surrey and Duke of Norfolk
Hungerford, Robert, Lord Hungerford
Jacquetta of Luxembourg, Duchess of Bedford
Lovell, Francis, Viscount Lovell
Mowbray, John, Duke of Norfolk (d. 1461)
Mowbray, John, Duke of Norfolk (d. 1476)
Neville, Cecily, Duchess of York
Neville Family
Neville, Isabel, Duchess of Clarence
Neville, John, Earl of Northumberland and Marquis of Montagu
Neville, John, Lord Neville
Neville, Richard, Earl of Salisbury
Neville, Richard, Earl of Warwick
Neville, William, Lord Fauconberg and Earl of Kent
Peerage
Percy, Henry, Earl of Northumberland (d. 1455)
Percy, Henry, Earl of Northumberland (d. 1461)
Percy, Henry, Earl of Northumberland (d. 1489)
Percy, Thomas, Lord Egremont
Plantagenet, Edmund, Earl of Rutland
Plantagenet, Edward, Earl of Warwick

Plantagenet, George, Duke of Clarence
Plantagenet, Richard, Duke of York (d. 1460)
Plantagenet, Richard, Duke of York (d. c. 1483)
Pole, John de la, Duke of Suffolk
Pole, John de la, Earl of Lincoln
Pole, William de la, Duke of Suffolk
Roos, Thomas, Lord Roos
Scales, Thomas, Lord Scales
Stafford, Henry, Duke of Buckingham
Stafford, Humphrey, Duke of Buckingham
Stafford, Humphrey, Earl of Devon
Stanley, Thomas, Earl of Derby
Tiptoft, John, Earl of Worcester
Touchet, James, Lord Audley
Tudor, Edmund, Earl of Richmond
Tudor, Jasper, Earl of Pembroke and Duke of Bedford
Vere, John de, Earl of Oxford
Wenlock, John, Lord Wenlock
Woodville, Anthony, Earl of Rivers
Woodville Family
Woodville, Richard, Earl Rivers

North of England

Alnwick Castle
Bamburgh Castle
Berwick-on-Tweed
Booth, Lawrence, Archbishop of York
Clifford, John, Lord Clifford
Clifford, Thomas, Lord Clifford
Dunstanburgh Castle
Ferrybridge, Battle of
Hedgeley Moor, Battle of
Heworth, Battle of
Hexham, Battle of
Lovell, Francis, Viscount Lovell
Neville Family
Neville, George, Archbishop of York
Neville, Sir Humphrey
Neville Inheritance Dispute
Neville, John, Earl of Northumberland and Marquis of Montagu
Neville, John, Lord Neville
Neville, Richard, Earl of Salisbury
Neville, Richard, Earl of Warwick
Neville, Sir Thomas
Neville, William, Lord Fauconberg and Earl of Kent

Hungerford, Sir Walter
Morton, John, Cardinal Archbishop of
    Canterbury
Rhys ap Thomas
Stanley, Thomas, Earl of Derby
Stanley, Sir William
Tudor, Edmund, Earl of Richmond
Tudor, House of
Tudor, Jasper, Earl of Pembroke and Duke of
    Bedford
Tudor, Owen
Urswick, Christopher
Vere, John de, Earl of Oxford

Wales

Devereux, Walter, Lord Ferrers of Chartley
Edward of Lancaster, Prince of Wales
Harlech Castle
Herbert, William, Earl of Pembroke
Ireland
Ludford Bridge, Battle of
Mortimer's Cross, Battle of
Rhys ap Thomas
Scotland
Stafford, Henry, Duke of Buckingham
Thomas ap Gruffydd
Tudor, Edmund, Earl of Richmond
Tudor, House of
Tudor, Jasper, Earl of Pembroke and Duke of
    Bedford
Tudor, Owen
Twt Hill, Battle of
Vaughan, Sir Thomas
Wales

Wars of the Roses, First Phase (1459–1461)

Accord, Act of
Blore Heath, Battle of
Coppini Mission
Coventry Parliament
Ferrybridge, Battle of
Ludford Bridge, Battle of
March on London
Mortimer's Cross, Battle of
Northampton, Battle of
St. Albans, Battle of (1461)
Sun in Splendor/Sunburst Badge

Towton, Battle of
Twt Hill, Battle of
Wakefield, Battle of
Wars of the Roses, Causes of

Wars of the Roses, Second Phase (1469–1471)

Angers Agreement
Barnet, Battle of
Caister Castle, Siege of
Chronicle of the Rebellion in Lincolnshire
Edgecote, Battle of
Edward IV, Overthrow of
Edward IV, Restoration of
Henry VI, Murder of
History of the Arrival of Edward IV
Losecote Field, Battle of
*Manner and Guiding of the Earl of Warwick at
    Angers*
Nibley Green, Battle of
Readeption
Tewkesbury, Battle of
Welles Uprising
Wars of the Roses, Causes of

Wars of the Roses, Third Phase (1483–1487)

Bosworth Field, Battle of
Buckingham's Rebellion
Butler Precontract
Council Meeting of 13 June 1483
The History of King Richard III (More)
Princes in the Tower
Richard III, Northern Affinity of
Shaw's Sermon
Stoke, Battle of
Titulus Regius
Usurpation of 1483
The Usurpation of Richard III (Mancini)
Wars of the Roses, Causes of
Wars of the Roses, Naming of
Yorkist Heirs (after 1485)

Weapons

Archers
Armor
Artillery
Weaponry

Women

Beaufort, Margaret, Countess of Richmond and Derby
Elizabeth of York, Queen of England
Jacquetta of Luxembourg, Duchess of Bedford
Margaret of Anjou, Queen of England
Margaret of York, Duchess of Burgundy
Mary of Gueldres, Queen of Scotland
Neville, Anne, Queen of England
Neville, Cecily, Duchess of York
Neville, Isabel, Duchess of Clarence
Shore, Elizabeth (Jane)
Woodville, Elizabeth, Queen of England

York, House of, Members and Partisans of

Blount, Walter, Lord Mountjoy
Bonville, William, Lord Bonville
Bourchier, Henry, Earl of Essex
Bourchier, Thomas, Cardinal Archbishop of Canterbury
Brackenbury, Sir Robert
Catesby, William
Courtenay, Peter, Bishop of Winchester
Devereux, Walter, Lord Ferrers of Chartley
Dinham, John, Lord Dinham
Edward IV, King of England
Edward V, King of England
Elizabeth of York, Queen of England
Fitzgerald, Gerald, Earl of Kildare
Fitzgerald, Thomas, Earl of Desmond
Fitzgerald, Thomas, Earl of Kildare
Grey, Edmund, Earl of Kent
Grey, Thomas, Marquis of Dorset
Hastings, William, Lord Hastings
Herbert, William, Earl of Pembroke
Howard, John, Duke of Norfolk
Howard, Thomas, Earl of Surrey and Duke of Norfolk
Jacquetta of Luxembourg, Duchess of Bedford
Lovell, Francis, Viscount Lovell
Margaret of York, Duchess of Burgundy
Mowbray, John, Duke of Norfolk (d. 1461)

Mowbray, John, Duke of Norfolk (d. 1476)
Neville, Anne, Queen of England
Neville, Cecily, Duchess of York
Neville Family
Neville, George, Archbishop of York
Neville, John, Earl of Northumberland and Marquis of Montagu
Neville, Richard, Earl of Salisbury
Neville, Richard, Earl of Warwick
Neville, Sir Thomas
Neville, William, Lord Fauconberg and Earl of Kent
Percy, Henry, Earl of Northumberland (d. 1489)
Plantagenet, Edmund, Earl of Rutland
Plantagenet, Edward, Earl of Warwick
Plantagenet, George, Duke of Clarence
Plantagenet, House of
Plantagenet, Richard, Duke of York (d. 1460)
Plantagenet, Richard, Duke of York (d. c. 1483)
Pole, John de la, Duke of Suffolk
Pole, John de la, Earl of Lincoln
Ratcliffe, Sir Richard
Richard III, King of England
Rotherham, Thomas, Archbishop of York
Russell, John, Bishop of Lincoln
Stafford, Henry, Duke of Buckingham
Stafford, Humphrey, Earl of Devon
Stanley, Thomas, Earl of Derby
Stanley, Sir William
Stillington, Robert, Bishop of Bath and Wells
Tiptoft, John, Earl of Worcester
Tyrell, Sir James
Vaughan, Sir Thomas
Wenlock, John, Lord Wenlock
Woodville, Anthony, Earl Rivers
Woodville, Elizabeth, Queen of England
Woodville Family
Woodville, Lionel, Bishop of Salisbury
Woodville, Richard, Earl Rivers
York, House of
Yorkist Heirs (after 1485)

Preface

The *Encyclopedia of the Wars of the Roses* provides its users with clear, concise, and basic descriptions and definitions of people, events, and terms relating in some significant way to the series of civil conflicts that disturbed English politics and society in the second half of the fifteenth century, and that later came to be known as the Wars of the Roses. Because the book focuses exclusively on the Wars of the Roses themselves—what caused them, how they were fought, and what effects they had on English life and government—it is not a general overview of fifteenth-century England but a specialized treatment of one of the most important aspects of English history during that century.

The *Encyclopedia* was written primarily for students and other nonspecialists who have an interest—but little background—in this period of British history. Besides providing a highly usable resource for quickly looking up names and terms encountered in reading or during study, the *Encyclopedia* offers an excellent starting point for classroom or personal research on subjects relating to the course, causes, and consequences of the Wars of the Roses. The entries provide the basic information needed to choose or hone a research topic, to answer small but vital questions of fact, and to identify further and more extensive information resources. The *Encyclopedia* also serves as a handy guide for those interested in re-creating the military and social aspects of the wars, as well as a useful reader's companion for those whose reading on the period—whether of fiction or nonfiction—is more for enjoyment than for study.

Scope of the Book

In chronological terms, the *Encyclopedia of the Wars of the Roses* concerns itself largely with the most active phases of civil conflict in the late fifteenth century, primarily the years 1459–1461, 1469–1471, and 1483–1487, the periods when politics was most disordered, society was most disrupted, and military activity was most intense. Some entries, such as those on the Neville-Percy Feud and the Yorkist pretender Perkin Warbeck, cover the political turmoil that preceded civil war in the 1450s or the dynastic uncertainty that lingered after the fighting in the 1490s. Other entries, such as those describing the deposition of Richard II in 1399 or the Hundred Years War of the fourteenth and fifteenth centuries, cover broader topics or issues related to the long-term causes of the Wars of the Roses.

In geographical terms, the *Encyclopedia* is concerned not only with the course of political and military events in England, but with how the English civil wars both affected and were influenced by people and happenings in neighboring states. Readers will find entries that relate the Wars of the Roses to relevant contemporary events in the other states of the British Isles (Ireland, Scotland, and Wales) and in the most important states on the continent (Brittany, Burgundy, and France). Also included are foreign rulers and leaders whose actions and decisions affected the civil wars, such as France's Louis XI, Scotland's Mary of Gueldres, and Burgundy's Charles the Bold.

Criteria for Inclusion

To be included in the *Encyclopedia,* a topic, event, or person had to have a role in some significant aspect of the Wars of the Roses. Nonbiographical entries relate mainly to military issues (e.g., the raising of armies, the nature of combat, and the use of naval forces), to political terms and events (e.g., the employment of attainder, the Readeption government, and the usurpation of 1483), to the major battles of the Wars of the Roses (e.g., Towton, Barnet, and Bosworth Field), and to the chief historical sources for the civil wars (e.g., Sir Thomas More's *History of King Richard III,* Philippe de Commines's *Memoirs,* and the continuations of the *Croyland Chronicle*).

Because the Wars of the Roses were dynastic struggles concerned with who should exercise the powers of the Crown, the great majority of biographical entries cover the most active participants in the conflicts, that is, noblemen and members of the English royal family. Also included are entries on the contending branches of the royal family, such as the houses of Lancaster, York, and Tudor; on key magnate families, such as the Nevilles and the Woodvilles; on important members of the gentry, such as Sir John Fortescue and William Catesby; on politically active members of the clergy, such as Bishop John Morton and Prior John Langstrother; and on broad social classes, such as the peerage, gentry, and commons.

Structure of Entries

The *Encyclopedia*'s 281 entries, 130 of which are biographical, average about 500 words in length. Each entry opens with a sentence or brief paragraph that carefully places its subject, whether a person, event, or term, within the context of the Wars of the Roses, explaining the subject's significance for the emergence, course, or impact of the civil wars. Each entry also contains numerous cross-references to related entries (which appear in SMALL CAPITALS) and concludes with one or more recommendations for additional reading. These reading recommendations include both scholarly works and popular treatments. In a few cases, older books have been included if no more recent study has been published or if the older work remains the accepted scholarly

standard on the subject, as is the case, for instance, with biographies of some lesser-known figures. Also included in the readings are important essays and papers published in book form in collections of articles. All works appearing at the ends of entries as further reading are listed in the general bibliography, which also contains numerous other worthwhile books not found among the entry recommendations. A reader interested in further reading on a particular person or topic should check both the general bibliography and the further reading listings at the ends of relevant entries.

All biographical entries provide the person's title or office. For titles of nobility, only the highest title attained is given; thus, Anthony Woodville is noted as Earl Rivers, the title he acquired on his father's death, and not as Lord Scales, the title he had held previously. In a few cases, such as Jasper Tudor, who was earl of Pembroke throughout the Wars of the Roses and only became duke of Bedford later, both titles are given. Except in cases where birth dates are unknown, as is often the case with fifteenth-century figures, life dates are also supplied for all biographical entries. When exact birth or death years are uncertain, the *c.* notation, meaning "circa," or "at about that time," precedes the date to indicate that the year given is approximate. When a single year is preceded by *d.,* the year given is the death date, and the birth date is totally unknown. The date ranges supplied for ruling monarchs are birth and death dates, not the years of their reign, which are given in the text of the entry. Finally, the spelling for all titles of fifteenth- and sixteenth-century publications has been modernized.

Additional Features

Preceded by a brief, general introduction that describes the historiography of the Wars of the Roses, the entries are augmented by a map of battlefield sites, a detailed chronology, and five genealogical tables depicting the royal houses and important noble families. Appendixes also include a listing of fifteenth-century monarchs in England and neighboring countries, a quick reference table showing the (sometimes shifting) dynastic allegiances of important noblemen, a table showing the consequences of involvement in the wars for the higher peerage, and an annotated listing of useful Wars of the Roses Web sites. Besides an extensive general bibliography, which is divided by broad topics, the *Encyclopedia* also includes a bibliography of historical fiction with Wars of the Roses characters and settings and a detailed subject index. When used with the cross-references in the entries, the Guide to Related Topics will allow readers to trace broad themes—such as the north of England, local feuds, or foreign affairs—through all their most important events, ideas, and personalities and so will help to provide users with a sound basic understanding of the Wars of the Roses.

Acknowledgments

I want to thank the photo archive staffs of the following institutions for the illustrations they helped provide for this volume: the British Library; the British Museum; the Public Record Office, London; the National Portrait Gallery, London; the Birmingham Art Gallery; the University of Ghent; the Brooklyn Museum; and the Bibliothèque Municipale d'Arras.

At Arizona State University, I wish to thank the staff of Hayden Library for assisting me in obtaining necessary and sometimes obscure research materials, and the members of my British history classes for helping me hone ideas and definitions with their questions, comments, and interest.

At ABC-CLIO, I wish to thank Bob Neville for his help in getting this book under way and for keeping it on track; Michelle Trader for carefully shepherding it through the production process; Liz Kincaid for handling the illustrations; and Silvine Marbury Farnell for expert copyediting.

I also want to thank all the members of my family in Phoenix—Gene, Fran, Michael, Mary, Courtney, Mary, and Kerby—and my family in Wisconsin—Karen, Fred, Paul, Katie, Patrick, Peter, Charles, Debbie, Scott, Tammy, Haley, and my dad, Joe—for supporting me in the long and sometimes tedious process of putting together a good reference book. And, for keeping me quiet company through long hours at the computer, I thank my little button-nosed friend, Midnight. Finally, I must express my gratitude and love to my wife, Donna, without whose unfailing support nothing of any value is ever possible.

Introduction

Until the mid-twentieth century, the nature and consequences of the series of civil conflicts fought in England in the late fifteenth century were not in doubt. These civil wars, which in the nineteenth century were termed the "Wars of the Roses," were a time of political chaos, economic disorder, social disruption, cultural stagnation, and even moral decline. The royal family was torn apart, and the politically influential classes, the nobility and gentry, destroyed themselves in a series of bloody battles fought to determine who would wear the Crown and control the royal government. The detrimental effects of this prolonged warfare severely damaged not only the English polity, but also the whole of England's economy and society.

Reflecting this accepted view of the late fifteenth century, the 1911 edition of the *Encyclopaedia Britannica* described the Wars of the Roses as a series of civil wars characterized "by a ferocity and brutality which are practically unknown in the history of English wars before or since" (Pollard, p. 13). Two decades earlier, William Denton, a fellow of Worcester College, had written that the Wars of the Roses caused "the baronage of England" to be "almost extirpated," and that the common people, although slaughtered in greater numbers "than in any former war on English soil," suffered even more grievously from the "want, exposure and disease" that the wars engendered. "The standard of morality," concluded Denton, "could not have been lower than it was at the end of the fifteenth century" (Denton, pp. 118–119). This horrific view of the late fifteenth century, which had slowly but steadily developed throughout the sixteenth century, was largely uncontested for over 300 years, from 1600 to the first decades of the twentieth century.

Although the actual term "Wars of the Roses" was unknown in the fifteenth and sixteenth centuries, the concept of the warring roses was familiar to anyone who lived under the rule of the Tudors between 1485 and 1603. Within months of winning the throne in August 1485, Henry VII ordered the blending of the red rose emblem (symbolizing his own Lancastrian lineage) with the white rose emblem (symbolizing his wife's Yorkist blood) to form the two-color Tudor rose, a new royal emblem to signify for all the peace and unity that Henry's accession and marriage had brought to England. Because the size and importance of Henry's accomplishment were directly related to the disorder and destructiveness of what had gone before, histories of the fifteenth century written under the Tudors in the sixteenth century tended to magnify the horrors of the civil war and vilify the actions of Henry's defeated predecessor, just as that predecessor had sought to justify his own usurpation by denouncing the actions of those who had ruled before him. In *Titulus Regius,* the parliamentary declaration of his title to the throne, Richard III had listed in lurid detail the failings of his brother's administration, which, the document concluded, had brought "great sorrow and heaviness [to] all true Englishmen." And Edward IV, in 1461, had portrayed his seizure of the Crown as making right the terrible crime "against God's law [and] man's liegance" committed by the Lancastrians when they deposed Richard II in 1399 (Pollard, pp. 8, 9).

By the mid-sixteenth century, the propaganda of a succession of usurpers of the English Crown had become the commonly accepted framework for explaining the course and consequences of fifteenth-century English history. Developed by such early Tudor historians as Sir Thomas More in his *History of King Richard III* (c.1513) and Polydore Vergil in his *Anglica Historia* (1534), the outlines of this framework were picked up and widely disseminated by Edward Hall's *The Union of the Two Noble and Illustrious Families of Lancaster and York* (1548), a chronicle that by its very title proclaimed the benefits of Tudor rule. For Hall, the Wars of the Roses encompassed not only the battles fought between the 1450s and the 1480s, but the entire sweep of English history from 1399 to 1485, a period defined by the deposition of a rightful king, the divine punishment of the whole realm for this unlawful act, and the restoration of divine order and favor as symbolized by the accession of Henry VIII, a descendant of both warring houses. Such were the "misery . . . murder and . . . execrable plagues" that England had suffered before Henry VII that Hall wrote, "my wit cannot comprehend nor my tongue declare neither yet my pen fully set forth" all the terrible consequences of that time (Ellis, p. 1).

In 1561, at the start of the reign of Elizabeth I, Henry VIII's daughter, Sir Thomas Smith wrote a pamphlet that elaborated on what Hall could not describe. According to Smith, the civil wars of the fifteenth century were a time when "blood pursued blood and ensued blood till all the realm was brought to great confusion" and England in the last years of Henry VI "was almost a very chaos" (Aston, pp. 282–283). Thus, the Elizabethans, then some seventy years removed from the civil wars, and well aware of the political upheavals that disturbed their own times, could be secure in the knowledge that their troubles in no way approached the "chaos" that had reigned before Henry VII.

This notion of chaos before the coming of the Tudors was reinforced in the sixteenth century by the spread of humanism, a movement that saw the Middle Ages as a long barren period standing between the glorious achievements of the classical world and the re-

vival of classical learning in contemporary times. Henry VII's accession was well suited to serve as the initiating event of this classical renewal, and the Wars of the Roses served equally well as the period of most intense darkness before the humanist dawn. Thus, the humanist view of the Middle Ages fit well with the official view of the fifteenth century being developed by Tudor propaganda and historiography. Humanism also encouraged the writing of English history and the use of that history as a moral yardstick for critiquing contemporary politics and society. And no period was more fraught with moral lessons than the Wars of the Roses.

In the 1590s, William Shakespeare, making use of Holinshed's *Chronicles* and other histories deriving from Hall, More, and other early Tudor sources, applied his genius to the rapidly solidifying historiography of the Wars of the Roses. Basing no less than eight plays on fifteenth-century English history, Shakespeare dramatized, sharpened, and darkened the conventional view of the period, and explored broader themes that connected it to the political concerns of his own times. The plays, from *Richard II* to *Richard III,* presented a unified explanation of the fifteenth century that warned anyone in their Elizabethan audiences to refrain from active opposition to the lawful monarch, lest the horrors of the Wars of the Roses descend again upon England. By 1600, few English subjects questioned that the fifteenth-century civil wars were a time of political, social, and economic chaos unleashed by the deposition of one king in 1399 and ended by the accession of another in 1485.

Except for occasional attempts to rehabilitate the reputation of Richard III, such as the efforts of Sir George Buck in the seventeenth century, Horace Walpole in the eighteenth century, and Caroline Halsted in the nineteenth century, the traditional view of the Wars of the Roses continued unchallenged almost into the twentieth century. By encouraging the publication and study of fifteenth-century documents, whether public records or private papers, the development of modern historical research in the mid-nineteenth century confirmed the prevailing interpretation of the period. The Paston Letters, which first became available in an edition published between 1787 and 1823, and the ongoing publications of the Deputy Keeper of Public Records and the Camden Society provided historians with an accumulating mass of evidence that the fifteenth century had indeed been a time of turbulence and disorder. Stories of corruption, violence, and lawlessness emerged from such sources as the records of the Court of King's Bench and the proceedings of royal councils and local commissions. Such evidence convinced the medieval historian Bishop William Stubbs "that all that was good and great in [late medieval life] was languishing even unto death" (Stubbs, p. 632) and persuaded Charles Plummer, as he wrote in the introduction to his edition of Sir John Fortescue's *Governance of England,* that the scourge of a social system he called "bastard feudalism" was responsible for a total breakdown of law and order in late fifteenth-century England.

However, certain records seemed to tell another story, and a few historians in the late nineteenth and early twentieth centuries began to cautiously suggest that perhaps the Wars of the Roses had not been as widely disruptive as had been thought. In 1874, in his *Short History of the English People,* J. R. Green agreed that there were few periods in English history "from which we turn with such weariness and disgust as from the Wars of the Roses" (Green, p. 288), but he also proposed that the worst aspects of the conflict were largely confined to the nobility and their retainers. The merchants of the towns and the peasants of the countryside suffered less from the civil wars because they largely avoided participation in them. In 1886, Thorold Rogers, thanks to his detailed study of fifteenth-century economic documents, supported Green's dissent by declaring that the agricultural classes "must have had only a transient and languid interest in the faction fight" (Rogers, p. 240), for the evidence was that the fifteenth century was for them a period of general prosperity. In 1923, C. L.

Kingsford, drawing upon the Stonor family archives and other legal documents, expanded this notion by arguing that the Wars of the Roses were not nearly as destructive as had been thought, and that many members of the fifteenth-century gentry, such as the Stonors, had thrived, while taking little or no part in the conflict.

These first stirrings of revisionism became a transforming movement through the scholarship of K. B. McFarlane, who, for more than thirty years before his death in 1966, conducted studies that ranged widely over the late medieval period. McFarlane refuted Plummer's thesis that bastard feudalism was a structurally corrupt social system and the root cause of the disorder and lawlessness that plagued fifteenth-century society. Bastard feudalism, argued McFarlane, was a generally effective response to the needs of late medieval society and the basis of English political interaction from the thirteenth to the sixteenth centuries, not simply an aberration of the late fifteenth century. McFarlane also believed that the disorder caused by the Wars of the Roses was limited and arose mainly from the inability of Henry VI to function effectively.

Although he published little on the civil wars themselves, McFarlane inspired through his teaching a great many historians who thoroughly reinvigorated and transformed the study of the Wars of the Roses after 1960. By revising, expanding, and refining McFarlane's basic ideas, a host of scholars working in the last third of the twentieth century questioned not only the effects of the Wars of the Roses, but their causes and their chronology. In the 1970s, J. R. Lander and Charles Ross both concluded that the Wars of the Roses saw little real fighting, caused little real destruction, and had little real effect on trade and agriculture. Ross declared that the late fifteenth century supported a "rich, varied and vigorous civilization [that] . . . was a product of political violence which did nothing to hinder its steady development" (Ross, p. 176). By the early 1980s, when John Gillingham described fifteenth-century England as "a society organized for peace" and "the most peaceful country in Europe (Gillingham, pp. 14, 15), some historians had taken the traditional view to the opposite extreme and argued that the Wars of the Roses were hardly wars at all and had exercised almost no influence on most aspects of fifteenth-century society. Although this view has been much revised and largely rejected, the received tradition of a horrific series of devastating civil wars has also been largely dismissed.

Stripped of the certainty of the past, the Wars of the Roses are currently among the most controversial events in English political history. Most historians now agree that the term "Wars of the Roses," no matter how unsatisfactory it may be in any number of ways, can be used to describe a period of about four decades in the second half of the fifteenth century during which England experienced ongoing political instability and intermittent open warfare. Beyond that, historians working at the start of the twenty-first century are in disagreement over such fundamental issues as when these periods of warfare started and ended, and even over how many such wars actually occurred.

McFarlane described three wars, covering the years 1450–1464, 1464–1471, and 1483–1487, while John Gillingham identified three wars dated 1455–1464, 1469–1471, and 1483–1487. Ross talked about three periods of warfare, but only two wars, arguing that the conflicts of 1460–1464 and 1469–1471 were two parts of the one war between Lancaster and York, while the 1483–1487 episode was really a separate struggle between York and Tudor. Meanwhile, in the 1980s, Anthony Goodman characterized the Wars of the Roses as merely a related series of military eruptions occurring between 1452 and 1497, whereas in the 1990s Christine Carpenter sought to understand the civil wars within the broader context of a period running from the commencement of the personal rule of Henry VI in 1437 to the peaceful accession of Henry VIII in 1509. As these widely differing views illustrate, the study and interpretation of the Wars of the Roses is today one of the most engaging and dynamic subfields in English history.

References

Aston, M. E. "Richard II and the Wars of the Roses," in F. R. H. DuBoulay and C. M. Barron, eds. *The Reign of Richard II: Essays in Honour of May McKisack.* London: Athlone, 1971.

Buck, Sir George. *The History of King Richard III.* Edited by A. N. Kincaid. Stroud, Gloucestershire, UK: Sutton Publishing, 1982.

Carpenter, Christine. *The Wars of the Roses: Politics and the Constitution in England, c. 1437–1509.* Cambridge: Cambridge University Press, 1997.

Denton, William. *England in the Fifteenth Century.* London: George Bell, 1888.

Ellis, Henry, ed. *Hall's Chronicle.* London, 1548; reprinted New York: AMS Press, 1965.

Gillingham, John. *The Wars of the Roses: Peace and Conflict in Fifteenth-Century England.* Baton Rouge: Louisiana State University Press, 1981.

Goodman, Anthony. *The Wars of the Roses: Military Activity and English Society, 1452–97.* New York: Dorset Press, 1981.

Green, J. R. *A Short History of the English People.* 3d ed. London: Macmillan, 1916.

Halsted, Caroline A. *Richard III as Duke of Gloucester and King of England.* 2 vols. London, 1844; reprinted Stroud, Gloucestershire, UK: Sutton Publishing, 1977.

Kingsford. C. L. *Prejudice and Promise in Fifteenth Century England.* Ford Lectures of 1923. Oxford: Oxford University Press, 1925.

Lander, J. R. *Crown and Nobility, 1450–1509.* Montreal: McGill-Queen's University Press, 1976.

McFarlane, K. B. "The Wars of the Roses," in *England in the Fifteenth Century.* London: Hambledon Press, 1981.

Plummer, Charles. Introduction to Sir John Fortescue, *The Governance of England,* edited by Charles Plummer. Oxford: Oxford University Press, 1885.

Pollard, A. J. *The Wars of the Roses.* New York: St. Martin's Press, 1988.

Rogers, J. E. Thorold. *Six Centuries of Work and Wages.* London: Sonnenschein, 1886.

Ross, Charles. *The Wars of the Roses.* London: Thames and Hudson, 1987.

Stubbs, William. *The Constitutional History of England.* vol. 3. 5th ed. Oxford: Clarendon Press, 1897.

Walpole, Horace. *Historic Doubts on the Life and Reign of Richard III.* Edited by P. W. Hammond. Stroud, Gloucestershire, UK: Sutton Publishing, 1987.

Chronology: Wars of the Roses

1399   *29 September.* Deposition of Richard II; accession of Henry of Bolingbroke as Henry IV, first king of the house of Lancaster.

1411   *22 September.* Birth of Richard Plantagenet, future duke of York.

1413   *20 March.* Death of Henry IV; uncontested accession of Henry V, second king of the house of Lancaster.

1415   *25 October.* Battle of Agincourt—Henry V wins major victory over the French.

1417– 1420   Henry V conquers Normandy.

1420   *22 May.* Treaty of Troyes recognizes Henry V as heir to Charles VI of France, disinherits the Dauphin Charles, future Charles VII.
2 June. Henry V marries Catherine of Valois, daughter of Charles VI of France.

1421   *6 December.* Prince Henry, son of Henry V and future Henry VI, is born at Windsor.

1422   *31 August.* Death of Henry V; uncontested accession of nine-month-old Henry VI, third king of the house of Lancaster.
21 October. Death of Charles VI of France; Charles VII accepted as king in areas of France outside Anglo-Burgundian control.

1428   *28 November.* Birth of Richard Neville, future earl of Warwick.

1429   *8 May.* English abandon siege of Orleans in France.
17 July. Charles VII is crowned king of France at Rheims.

6 November. Henry VI is crowned king of England at Westminster.

1430   *23 May.* Joan of Arc is captured by Burgundian forces.

1431   *30 May.* Joan of Arc is burned at the stake for heresy in Rouen.
16 December. Henry VI is crowned king of France at Paris.

1435   *15 September.* Death of John, duke of Bedford, uncle of Henry VI and regent of France.
21 September. Burgundians abandon English alliance and conclude treaty with France.

1436   *17 April.* Paris falls to the forces of Charles VII.
8 May. York appointed lord lieutenant of France.

1437   *3 January.* Death of Catherine of Valois, mother of Henry VI.
12 November. The minority of Henry VI, now almost sixteen, formally ends.

1440   *2 July.* York appointed lord lieutenant of France for a second time.
12 September. Henry VI founds Eton College.

1441   *12 February.* Henry VI founds King's College, Cambridge.

1442   *28 April.* Birth of Edward, earl of March, eldest son of the duke of York and future Edward IV.

1443   *30 March.* Henry VI appoints John Beaufort, duke of Somerset, captain-general of France and Gascony.
31 May. Birth of Margaret Beaufort, future mother of Henry VII.

1445	*23 April.* Henry VI marries Margaret of Anjou.		*c. 1 August.* Onset of Henry VI's first bout of mental illness.
1447	*23 February.* Death of Humphrey, duke of Gloucester, uncle and former lord protector of Henry VI. *9 December.* York appointed lord lieutenant of Ireland.		*24 August.* Percy and Neville families clash at Heworth. *13 October.* Birth of Edward of Lancaster, son of Henry VI and Margaret of Anjou.
1448	*16 March.* English surrender Le Mans, the capital of Maine, to the French.	1454	*27 March.* York is named lord protector during the king's illness. *c. 31 October.* Percy and Neville families clash at Stamford Bridge. *c. 25 December.* Henry VI recovers.
1449	*21 October.* Birth of George, son of duke of York, and future duke of Clarence. *29 October.* English surrender Rouen, the capital of Normandy, to the French.	1455	*January.* York surrenders the office of protector. *22 May.* First Battle of St. Albans— York and his allies, the Neville earls of Salisbury and Warwick, win control of the king and kill their chief enemies: Somerset, Northumberland, and Clifford. *19 November.* York is appointed lord protector for the second time.
1450	*15 April.* English defeat at the Battle of Formigny allows French to overrun much of Normandy. *2 May.* William de la Pole, duke of Suffolk, after being impeached by Parliament and banished by Henry VI, is murdered by sailors when trying to leave the kingdom. *June–July.* Jack Cade rebels occupy London. *12 August.* French capture Cherbourg and end English rule in Normandy.	1456	*25 February.* York resigns as lord protector. *August.* Court travels to Coventry and the Midlands.
1451	*12 June.* French capture Bordeaux in Gascony.	1457	*28 January.* Birth of Henry Tudor, earl of Richmond, the future Henry VII.
1452	*2 March.* York ends his opposition to the court and submits to the king at Dartford. *2 October.* Birth of Richard, youngest son of the duke of York and future Richard III. *23 October.* English recapture Bordeaux. *November.* Henry VI ennobles his uterine half brothers, Edmund and Jasper Tudor, as earls of Richmond and Pembroke, respectively.	1458	*25 March.* Henry VI mediates the love-day of 1458, a negotiated settlement between York and his Neville allies and the heirs of their victims at first Battle of St. Albans.
1453	*17 July.* French victory at Castillon ends English rule in Gascony; Calais is only remaining English possession in France.	1459	*23 September.* Battle of Blore Heath—Richard Neville, earl of Salisbury, defeats a Lancastrian force trying to block his junction with York. *12–13 October.* Heavily outnumbered, the Yorkist lords abandon their men and flee from the royal army at Ludford Bridge; York goes to Ireland and Warwick, Salisbury, and March go to Calais. *20 November.* Lancastrian-controlled Parliament opens at Coventry.

1460 *26 June.* Yorkist earls of Warwick, Salisbury, and March land in England from Calais.
10 July. Battle of Northampton—Warwick captures Henry VI and control of the government.
3 August. James II of Scotland killed by a cannon fired to celebrate the arrival of his wife, Mary of Guelders, at the siege of Roxburgh; accession of eight-year-old James III.
30 December. Battle of Wakefield—defeat and death of York, Salisbury, and York's second son, Edmund Plantagenet, earl of Rutland.

1461 *2 February.* Battle of Mortimer's Cross—Yorkist victory in Wales.
17 February. Second Battle of St. Albans—Margaret of Anjou defeats Warwick and reunites herself and her son with Henry VI.
4 March. Edward, earl of March, York's eldest son, takes coronation oath and is proclaimed king as Edward IV at Westminster.
27–28 March. Battle of Ferrybridge—Lancastrian attempts to prevent a Yorkist crossing of the River Aire.
29 March. Battle of Towton—Edward IV wins throne and Henry VI and his family flee into Scotland.
28 June. Official coronation of Edward IV.
22 July. Charles VII of Frances dies; accession of Louis XI.
16 October. Battle of Twt Hill—Yorkist victory in Wales.
4 November. Opening of Edward IV's first Parliament.

1462–1463 Led by Margaret of Anjou, Lancastrians based in Scotland several times seize and lose the Northumbrian castles of Alnwick, Bamburgh, and Dunstanburgh.

1464 *25 April.* Battle of Hedgeley Moor—Yorkist victory in the north.

1 May. Edward IV secretly marries Elizabeth Woodville.
15 May. Battle of Hexham—Yorkist victory leads to the execution of Henry Beaufort, the Lancastrian duke of Somerset.
25 December. Elizabeth Woodville is publicly introduced to the court as queen.

1465 *13 July.* Henry VI is captured in Lancashire and imprisoned in the Tower of London.

1467 *15 June.* Death of Philip the Good, duke of Burgundy; accession of Charles the Bold.

1468 *3 July.* Margaret of York, sister of Edward IV, marries Charles the Bold, duke of Burgundy.
3 August. Edward IV concludes an alliance with Burgundy, agreeing to send English troops to support the duke against France.
14 August. Lancastrian defenders of Harlech Castle in Wales surrender.

1469 *April–July.* Robin of Redesdale's Rebellion is fomented by Warwick.
11 July. Clarence marries Warwick's daughter, Isabel Neville, at Calais.
26 July. Battle of Edgecote Moor—William Herbert, earl of Pembroke, and other Yorkist lords are defeated and executed by Warwick.
29 July. Deserted by most of his supporters, Edward IV is taken into custody by Warwick's brother, George Neville, archbishop of York, who places the king under the earl's "protection."
c. 10 September. Warwick is forced by rebellion to release Edward IV from custody.

1470 *12 March.* Battle of Losecote Field—Edward IV defeats rebels operating under the direction of Warwick and Clarence.
early April. Warwick and Clarence flee England.
22 July. Warwick and Margaret of Anjou meet in Angers to conclude

a formal accord known as the Angers Agreement.

25 July. Prince Edward of Lancaster is formally betrothed to Warwick's daughter, Anne Neville.

c. 15 September. Warwick and Clarence land in West Country and declare for Henry VI.

1 October. Elizabeth Woodville, wife of Edward IV, takes sanctuary with her children at Westminster.

2 October. Isolated in the north, Edward IV and a small party of supporters, including Richard, duke of Gloucester, flee England for Burgundy.

6 October. Warwick enters London in triumph.

2 November. Birth in sanctuary of Prince Edward, eldest son of Edward IV and future Edward V.

26 November. Readeption Parliament meets at Westminster.

c. 13 December. Prince Edward of Lancaster marries Anne Neville.

1471	*14 March.* Edward IV lands in England at Ravenspur, Henry of Bolingbroke's landing site in 1399.

3 April. Clarence abandons Warwick and is reconciled with his brothers, Edward IV and Gloucester.

14 April. Battle of Barnet— Warwick is defeated and killed; Margaret of Anjou and Prince Edward of Lancaster land in England at Weymouth.

4 May. Battle of Tewkesbury— Prince Edward of Lancaster is killed on the field.

7 May. Margaret of Anjou is captured and taken to the Tower of London.

21 May. Edward IV enters London in triumph; Henry VI is murdered in the Tower of London.

2 June. Jasper Tudor, earl of Pembroke, escapes from England with his nephew, Henry Tudor, earl of Richmond.

c. 1472	Richard, duke of Gloucester, marries Anne Neville, daughter of Warwick and widow of Prince Edward of Lancaster.

1473	*c. 17 August.* Birth of Richard, second son of Edward IV and future duke of York.

30 September. John de Vere, the Lancastrian earl of Oxford, seizes St. Michael's Mount on the tip of Cornwall.

1474	*May.* An act of Parliament attempts to settle the long-running dispute between Edward IV's brothers, the dukes of Clarence and Gloucester, over the division of their wives' Neville inheritance.

25 July. Treaty of London concludes a formal alliance between England and Burgundy against France.

1475	*4 July.* Edward IV crosses to Calais to begin invasion of France.

29 August. Edward IV concludes Treaty of Picquigny with Louis XI, ending the English invasion of France.

1476	*21 December.* Death of Isabel, duchess of Clarence.

1477	*5 January.* Death in battle of Charles the Bold, duke of Burgundy, ally and brother-in-law of Edward IV.

1478	*18 February.* George, duke of Clarence, is executed in the Tower of London.

1482	*27 March.* Death of Mary, duchess of Burgundy, begins ultimate division of Burgundy between France and Maximilian Habsburg of Austria, Mary's husband and eventual ruler of the Netherlands.

11 June. Treaty of Fotheringhay is concluded between Edward IV and the duke of Albany, brother of James III of Scotland.

29 August. Death of Margaret of Anjou, widow of Henry VI, in France.

1483 *9 April.* Death of Edward IV; accession of Edward V.

30 April. Richard, duke of Gloucester, takes charge of his nephew, Edward V, at Stony Stratford on the road to London.

13 June. Summary execution of William Hastings, Lord Hastings.

17 June. Richard, duke of York, leaves sanctuary at Westminster to join his brother, Edward V, at the Tower of London.

22 June. Dr. Ralph Shaw delivers a public sermon at Paul's Cross in London setting forth Richard of Gloucester's claim to the throne.

26 June. At an assembly of political notables at Baynard's Castle in London, Henry Stafford, duke of Buckingham, presents Richard of Gloucester with a petition requesting him to take the throne.

6 July. Coronation of Richard III.

30 August. Death of Louis XI of France; accession of Charles VIII.

July–September? Probable deaths of Edward V and his brother Richard, duke of York, in the Tower of London.

October. Buckingham's Rebellion fails; Henry Tudor, earl of Richmond, aborts planned landing in England.

2 November. Buckingham is executed at Salisbury.

25 December. Henry Tudor, earl of Richmond, takes oath to marry Elizabeth of York, eldest daughter of Edward IV.

1484 *23 January.* Richard III's only Parliament opens at Westminster—the members attaint the Buckingham rebels, including Henry Tudor, and embody the petition of June 1483, which asked Richard III to take the Crown, in the statute *Titulus Regius.*

1 March. With her daughters, Elizabeth Woodville, widow of Edward IV, leaves sanctuary at Westminster.

April. Death of Edward of Middleham, only child of Richard III.

September. Three-year truce is concluded between England and Scotland; Henry Tudor, earl of Richmond, flees from Brittany to France.

1485 *16 March.* Death of Anne Neville, wife of Richard III.

30 March. Richard III is forced by rumor to publicly deny any intention of marrying his niece Elizabeth of York, eldest daughter of Edward IV.

7 August. Henry Tudor, earl of Richmond, lands with an invasion force at Milford Haven in Wales.

22 August. Battle of Bosworth Field—Richard III is defeated and killed; accession of Henry Tudor, earl of Richmond, as Henry VII.

30 October. Coronation of Henry VII.

7 November. Henry VII's first Parliament opens at Westminster.

1486 *18 January.* Henry VII marries Elizabeth of York, daughter of Edward IV.

19 September. Birth of Prince Arthur, first child of Henry VII.

1487 *24 May.* Lambert Simnel, who claims to be a nephew of Edward IV, is crowned king of England in Dublin.

16 June. Battle of Stoke—Henry VII defeats Yorkist supporters of Lambert Simnel.

1488 *11 June.* Death of James III of Scotland after Battle of Sauchieburn; accession of James IV.

1489 *28 March.* Treaty of Medina del Campo is concluded with Spain.

1491 *28 June.* Birth of Prince Henry, future Henry VIII.

November. Perkin Warbeck, another pretended son of Edward IV, appears in Ireland.

1492   *8 June.* Death of Elizabeth Woodville, widow of Edward IV, at Bermondsey Abbey.

3 November. Treaty of Etaples is concluded with France, forcing Warbeck to leave France for Burgundy. Warbeck spends most of 1492 in France and Burgundy, where he is supported by Margaret, duchess of Burgundy and sister of Edward IV.

1495   *23 July–3 August.* Warbeck launches unsuccessful invasion of Kent.

November. Warbeck is given shelter in Scotland by James IV.

21 December. Death of Jasper Tudor, duke of Bedford and uncle of Henry VII.

1496   *February.* The treaty called *Intercursus Magnus* is concluded with the Netherlands.

1497   *17 June.* Henry VII crushes Cornish rebels at the Battle of Black Heath.

7 September. Warbeck lands in Cornwall.

30 September. The truce leading to the Treaty of Ayton is concluded with Scotland, ending Scottish support for Warbeck.

5 October. Warbeck surrenders and confesses his imposture of Richard, duke of York, second son of Edward IV.

1499   *16 November.* Execution of Warbeck.

29 November. Execution of Edward Plantagenet, earl of Warwick, son of George, duke of Clarence, and nephew of Edward IV.

1501   *14 November.* Prince Arthur, eldest son of Henry VII, marries the Spanish princess Catherine of Aragon.

1502   *2 April.* Death of Prince Arthur.

6 May. Execution of Sir James Tyrell for allegedly murdering Edward V and his brother on Richard III's orders in 1483.

1503   *11 February.* Death of Elizabeth of York, wife of Henry VII and daughter of Edward IV.

23 June. Prince Henry, heir to the English throne, is betrothed to his former sister-in-law, Catherine of Aragon.

8 August. Princess Margaret, eldest daughter of Henry VII, marries James IV of Scotland.

1506   *30 April.* The treaty *Intercursus Malus* is concluded with Duke Philip of Burgundy; the treaty leads to the expulsion of the Yorkist pretender, Edmund de la Pole, earl of Suffolk, from the Netherlands.

1509   *21 April.* Death of Henry VII; uncontested accession of Henry VIII as second king of the house of Tudor.

29 June. Death of Margaret Beaufort, mother of Henry VII.

ENCYCLOPEDIA OF THE WARS OF THE ROSES

Accord, Act of (1460)

Although meant to end the political instability caused by the rival claims of the royal houses of LANCASTER and YORK, the Act of Accord of October 1460 helped transform a dynastic dispute into a civil war. By disinheriting EDWARD OF LANCASTER, Prince of Wales, and vesting the succession to the throne in Richard PLANTAGENET, duke of York, and his heirs, the act compelled Queen MARGARET OF ANJOU and her followers to take arms against the settlement as the only way to ensure the future of the prince and the Lancastrian dynasty.

The Lancastrian defeat at the Battle of NORTHAMPTON in July 1460 left both HENRY VI and the government in the hands of Richard NEVILLE, earl of Warwick, York's most prominent supporter. In exile in IRELAND since the Battle of LUDFORD BRIDGE in late 1459, York returned to England in September. By moving across the country in leisurely state and settling himself in the royal apartments at Westminster, York left no doubt that he intended to claim the throne. In LONDON, Warwick; his father, Richard NEVILLE, earl of Salisbury; and York's son Edward, earl of March (see EDWARD IV), established a Yorkist regime, calling a PARLIAMENT to meet at Westminster in early October. On 10 October, York entered the Parliament chamber and made to seat himself on the throne; when this action elicited silence rather than acclaim, Archbishop Thomas BOURCHIER asked the duke if he wished to see the king. Although York replied that the king should rather come to see him, the lords' obvious disapproval of his actions caused York to withdraw.

On 16 October, York formally laid his claim to the Crown before Parliament. Supported by a pedigree that detailed York's royal descent, the claim sought to prove the Lancastrians usurpers. After a week of debate, the lords crafted the Act of Accord, which disinherited the Prince of Wales and gave the succession to York and his heirs. On 25 October, both Henry VI and York accepted the settlement. Given immediate approval by Parliament, the act avoided the unwanted deposition of Henry VI, while giving York an interest in maintaining the political stability of the realm, even though it lessened the likelihood of his accession, the duke being ten years older than the king.

The act assigned York and his two eldest sons 10,000 marks from the revenues of the prince's earldom of Chester, thus depriving the prince of income as well as status. York was given powers similar to those he enjoyed during his two protectorates in the 1450s. On 31 October, the lords swore to accept York as heir and the duke swore to accept Henry VI as king for life. The act was then publicly proclaimed throughout the realm. The great weakness of the Act of Accord was its disregard of the queen and her commitment to her son's right to the Crown. The act quickly drove Lancastrians, who considered Henry VI a prisoner acting under duress, into the field to overthrow the Yorkist regime.

See also First Protectorate; Second Protectorate; Wakefield, Battle of
Further Reading: Griffiths, Ralph A., *The Reign of King Henry VI* (Berkeley: University of California Press, 1981); Johnson, P. A., *Duke Richard of York* (Oxford: Clarendon Press, 1988); Wolffe, Bertram, *Henry VI* (London: Eyre Methuen, 1981).

Act of Accord. *See* Accord, Act of

Act of Attainder. *See* Attainder, Act of.

Affinity

In fifteenth-century England, an affinity was a web of political and social connections constructed by a nobleman, either on the basis of royal favor and personal political standing or on the basis of family and territorial influence.

A noble created an affinity by assembling a band of followers, known as RETAINERS, who were sworn to provide their lord with legal, political, or military service in return for money. Retainers also expected that the lord's influence would be exercised on their behalf in legal proceedings and in pursuit of office and other rewards. Retainers signaled their attachment to a lord's affinity by wearing his livery (i.e., uniform) or his BADGE or emblem. The dispersal of fees and wages by a magnate to the members of his affinity was the heart of the social system known as BASTARD FEUDALISM. Although individual retainers could be household servants or legal or financial advisors, a large affinity above all provided its lord with a military force that could be used both to support and threaten the Crown. Although not private armies because they were rarely kept under arms for long, noble affinities formed the core of royal forces sent to FRANCE or used to crush internal rebellion. During the WARS OF THE ROSES, such affinities constituted the bulk of the military forces raised by both parties. Although attempts were made through PARLIAMENT to limit retaining, the Crown, dependent on noble affinities for military strength, sought only to control such groupings.

An example of an affinity created on the basis of personal influence was the one constructed by William HASTINGS, Lord Hastings, whose peerage and estates derived from his close friendship with EDWARD IV. Hastings's influence with the king attracted many members of the GENTRY to his affinity, which was soon extensive and therefore a valuable resource for the house of YORK in military emergencies. During his 1471 campaign to regain the Crown, Edward's initially thin forces were soon swollen by the arrival of loyal members of Hastings's affinity (see EDWARD IV, RESTORATION OF). In 1483, control of such military potential made Hastings a danger to Richard, duke of Gloucester (see RICHARD III); when he began to fear that Hastings might mobilize his affinity on behalf of EDWARD V, Gloucester ordered Hastings's summary execution (see COUNCIL MEETING OF 13 JUNE 1483).

A powerful and extensive connection based on family loyalty and landholding, as well as on personal political influence, was the Neville affinity, controlled after 1460 by Richard NEVILLE, earl of Warwick. The most influential subject in the realm during the early years of Edward IV, and possessing a mighty military reputation (see GENERALSHIP), Warwick could also draw on a deeply engrained loyalty to his family among the gentry of the north, where the Neville lands were concentrated. When Warwick brought this affinity into alliance with the house of LANCASTER in 1470, he was able to restore HENRY VI to the throne. After Warwick's death in 1471, Edward IV ensured that his brother Gloucester, the husband of Warwick's daughter Anne NEVILLE, became heir to the family loyalty and territorial power upon which the Neville affinity was based.

> **See also** Livery and Maintenance; Neville Family; North of England and the Wars of the Roses; Peerage
> **Further Reading:** Hicks, Michael, *Bastard Feudalism* (London: Longman, 1995); Walker, S., *The Lancastrian Affinity, 1361–1399* (Oxford: Oxford University Press, 1989).

Alnwick Castle (1461–1464)

Along with the other Northumberland fortresses of BAMBURGH and DUNSTANBURGH, Alnwick Castle demonstrated the insecurity of EDWARD IV's throne by falling several times into Lancastrian hands between 1461 and 1464.

After the Yorkist victory at the Battle of TOWTON in March 1461, Alnwick was one of several northern strongholds that remained under the control of RETAINERS loyal to the Lancastrian Percy family (see entries under PERCY). The castle fell to Richard NEVILLE, earl of Warwick, in September, but was lost again in November to a Lancastrian raiding party from SCOTLAND under Sir William TAILBOYS. Realizing that the Northumberland fortresses were vulnerable so long as the Lancastrians could cross the border, Edward IV negotiated a three-month truce with Scotland to begin in June 1462. Edward used the cease-fire to retake the lost castles, with Alnwick falling in July after a short siege conducted by William HASTINGS, Lord Hastings, and Sir John HOWARD. Once again, Yorkist control of the fortress was short-lived, for in late October Alnwick capitulated to MARGARET OF ANJOU and her newly landed force of French MERCENARIES under Pierre de BRÉZÉ. The Lancastrian royal family and de Brézé retired to Scotland in November upon receiving news of an approaching Yorkist army. By early December 1462, Warwick was coordinating sieges of all three castles, with the Alnwick operation under the command of William NEVILLE, earl of Kent; Anthony WOODVILLE, Lord Scales; and John TIPTOFT, earl of Worcester.

On 5 January 1463, a Scottish relief force under de Brézé and the Scottish earl of Angus appeared at Alnwick. Warwick, perhaps conscious of the low morale of his men, who had been maintaining a difficult siege in midwinter, declined to fight. Robert HUNGERFORD, Lord Hungerford, commander of the Alnwick garrison, marched his men out of the castle and withdrew into Scotland with de Brézé's force. Warwick installed a Yorkist garrison in Alnwick, but Hungerford retook the castle in March when the Yorkist commander, Sir Ralph Grey, defected and allowed the Lancastrians to enter the fortress unopposed. By June, Warwick and his brother John NEVILLE, Lord Montagu, were again marching north. The Nevilles surprised a large Scottish army as it was besieging Norham Castle; the Scots force, which included not only JAMES III and

his mother MARY OF GUELDRES, but also the Lancastrian royal family, fled in panic before the Yorkist army. This defeat cooled Scottish support for the Lancastrians and allowed the negotiation of a ten-month Anglo-Scottish truce in December.

With Scotland thus neutralized, the Yorkists began a campaign to end Lancastrian activity in Northumberland once and for all. In April 1464, Montagu defeated a Lancastrian force under Henry BEAUFORT, duke of Somerset, at the Battle of HEDGELEY MOOR west of Alnwick. The Lancastrian survivors of that battle gathered at Alnwick, where, under the nominal leadership of HENRY VI himself, they reformed and marched out to again face Montagu. At the Battle of HEXHAM on 15 May, Montagu defeated and captured Somerset, while the demoralized remnants of Somerset's force retreated to Alnwick, which they surrendered to Warwick on 23 June. Alnwick was henceforth Yorkist, and the Northumberland phase of the civil wars was over.

Further Reading: Haigh, Philip A., *The Military Campaigns of the Wars of the Roses* (Stroud, Gloucestershire, UK: Sutton Publishing, 1995); Pollard, A. J., *North-Eastern England during the Wars of the Roses* (Oxford: Clarendon Press, 1990).

Angers Agreement (1470)

By forging an alliance between Richard NEVILLE, earl of Warwick, and Queen MARGARET OF ANJOU, the Angers Agreement of July 1470 made possible the overthrow of EDWARD IV and the restoration of HENRY VI and the house of LANCASTER.

In April 1470, after the failure of their attempt to dethrone Edward IV, Warwick and his ally, George PLANTAGENET, duke of Clarence, Edward's younger brother, took ship with their wives for CALAIS, where Warwick was captain. Denied entrance to the town by a garrison loyal to Edward, Warwick turned to piracy, preying on Burgundian shipping with a squadron of vessels that had defected from the royal NAVY under the command of the earl's kinsman, Thomas NEVILLE, the Bastard of Fauconberg.

In May, Warwick's booty-laden flotilla anchored in the Seine, providing LOUIS XI with an ideal opportunity to strike at both England and BURGUNDY. If Warwick and Queen Margaret could be persuaded to bury their considerable differences, they might, with Louis's aid, overthrow Edward and establish a Lancastrian regime that would gratefully support the French king against Burgundy. For both Warwick and Margaret, Louis's plan, though personally distasteful, was their only political option. Having failed to control Edward IV in 1469, and to replace him with Clarence in 1470, Warwick's only hope for power in England was the restoration, under his auspices, of Henry VI. For Margaret, alliance with Warwick and his supporters represented her only hope of ever seeing her son on the English throne.

After conferring privately with both parties, and paying for Margaret to come to Angers, Louis brought the two principals together in that town on 22 July. Although the basic outline of the agreement had probably already been accepted by all parties, Margaret, upon meeting Warwick, made a show of rejecting the earl and supposedly kept him on his knees in supplication for twenty minutes before granting him pardon for his Yorkist past. The settlement that followed called for Warwick to lead an invasion of England, financed by Louis, to overthrow the house of YORK and restore Henry VI. In return, Margaret agreed to the marriage of her son, Prince EDWARD OF LANCASTER, to Anne NEVILLE, Warwick's younger daughter. The betrothal was formalized in Angers Cathedral on 25 July and the wedding was celebrated in the following December. For Louis, the centerpiece of the agreement was the new allies' promise to bring a restored Lancastrian regime into an offensive alliance with FRANCE against Burgundy. The odd man out was Clarence. Although honorably treated, for Warwick needed his support, he was obliged to renounce his claim to the throne in return for the lands and title of duke of York and a promise of the succession should the house of Lancaster fail of heirs.

Although she accepted the marriage, Margaret refused to allow her son to return to England until Warwick had recovered the kingdom for Henry VI, a decision that was to cost Warwick dearly in terms of Lancastrian support. The earl and Clarence issued a proclamation, which was widely distributed in England, promising to end Edward's "tyranny." Warwick was probably also responsible for the production of a PROPAGANDA tract entitled the *MANNER AND GUIDING OF THE EARL OF WARWICK AT ANGERS,* a document, written by someone privy to the Angers discussions, that describes the agreement and the reasons for its conclusion. Fortified by the French and Lancastrian aid acquired under the Angers Agreement, Warwick returned to England in September; by early October, he was master of the kingdom and leader of the newly established READEPTION government of Henry VI.

See also Edward IV, Overthrow of
Further Reading: Hicks, Michael, *Warwick the Kingmaker* (Oxford: Blackwell Publishers, 1998); Kendall, Paul Murray, *Louis XI* (New York: W. W. Norton, 1971).

Anglica Historia (Vergil)

Although commissioned by HENRY VII, and therefore favorable to the house of TUDOR, Polydore Vergil's *Anglica Historia* (*English History*) is an important, if controversial, source for the WARS OF THE ROSES, and especially for the reign of RICHARD III.

Polydore Vergil (c.1470–1555) was an Italian humanist who came to England on a papal mission in 1502. He spent most of the rest of his life in England and became a naturalized English subject. Persuaded by Henry VII to write a history of England, Vergil spent twenty-six years on the project, which was published in 1534 and dedicated to Henry VIII. Running to twenty-six books in total, the *Anglica Historia* covers the Wars of the Roses in Books 23–25. Although he interpreted history in a manner flattering to his Tudor patrons, Vergil was not simply a royal apologist writing whatever he was told. He was a classically trained Renaissance historian who carefully based his work on a wide variety of available sources—both oral and written—and who was willing to present and evaluate conflicting viewpoints from those sources. Genuinely seeking to provide an accurate account of events, Vergil tried to strip away myth and to understand motives, causes, and effects.

For the reign of EDWARD IV, the *Anglica Historia* is reasonably balanced, describing the king's virtues as well as his faults. Vergil also provided incisive political analyses for important events of the reign, such as the king's marriage to Elizabeth WOODVILLE in 1464 and his execution of his brother, George PLANTAGENET, duke of Clarence, in 1478 (see CLARENCE, EXECUTION OF). The *Anglica Historia* also offers detailed accounts of the 1469–1471 phase of the civil war and of Edward's reign thereafter.

Although Vergil condemned Richard III as ambitious, devious, and wicked, his critical view likely derived from his sources, which probably included former opponents of Richard who were prominent at the Tudor COURT, and written sources unfriendly to Richard, such as various LONDON CHRONICLES and the Second Continuation of the *CROYLAND CHRONICLE*. Although conceding that Richard had courage, Vergil otherwise depicted the king as cruel and tyrannous, seeing even his most innocent actions as calculated attempts to conceal his desire to seize the Crown from his nephew, EDWARD V, for whose murder Vergil held Richard responsible. Vergil was also the first to claim that Richard personally murdered HENRY VI in the TOWER OF LONDON and that Richard poisoned his own queen, Anne NEVILLE. Because Vergil's portrait contains the outlines of the monstrous Richard later depicted by William Shakespeare in his influential play *RICHARD III,* modern defenders of Richard have sometimes dismissed the *Anglica Historia* as mere Tudor PROPAGANDA.

See also *The History of King Richard III* (More); Shakespeare and the Wars of the Roses
Further Reading: Ellis, Sir Henry, ed., *Three Books of Polydore Vergil's English History, Comprising*

the Reigns of Henry VI, Edward IV, and Richard III (London: Camden Society, 1844); Hay, Denys, *Polydore Vergil: Renaissance Historian and Man of Letters* (Oxford: Clarendon Press, 1952); Vergil, Polydore, *The Anglica Historia of Polydore Vergil* (London: Royal Historical Society, 1950); the text of Books 23–25 covering the Wars of the Roses is available on the Richard III Society Web site at <http://www.r3.org/bookcase/polydore.html>.

Anne, Queen of England. *See* Neville, Anne, Queen of England

Archers

Having themselves learned the lessons they taught the French during the HUNDRED YEARS WAR, the English during the WARS OF THE ROSES adopted equipment and tactics that nullified the power and effectiveness of the longbow, which, during the civil wars, was never the decisive weapon it had been in FRANCE. Nonetheless, a sizable contingent of archers was an important component of almost every civil war army.

English victories over the French at Crécy (1346), Poitiers (1356), and Agincourt (1415), as well as thirteenth- and fourteenth-century English triumphs in WALES and SCOTLAND, derived in large part from the superiority in firepower that the six-foot longbow conferred on English armies. Able to fire ten to twelve arrows a minute, a rate of fire five to six times that of continental crossbowmen, English archers decimated French cavalry charges over an effective range of 165 yards. By the late fifteenth century, both English and continental armies had learned to attack with foot soldiers who employed curved plate ARMOR, which arrows could not penetrate, or other types of lighter protection, such as leather jerkins, which lessened an arrow's impact. Also, because both sides in the civil wars had bodies of archers, the two contingents often canceled each other out. As a result, most battles were decided by the course of hand-to-hand combat between struggling lines of dismounted MEN-AT-ARMS. Two exceptions were the Battle of EDGECOTE in 1469 and the Battle of STOKE in 1487; in both cases, the eventual winning side enjoyed a distinct superiority in numbers of archers.

Although archers did not decide most civil war battles, they could significantly shape the course of the fighting. Volleys of arrows and ARTILLERY opened most civil war encounters, and occasionally forced an opponent to abandon a strong defensive position and launch an unplanned attack. At the Battle of TOWTON, fought on a blustery day in March 1461, William NEVILLE, Lord Fauconberg, used an advantageous wind to neutralize the Lancastrian archers. He ordered his own archers, who were shooting with the wind, to fire one volley and then stand still. Stung by the Yorkist arrows, the Lancastrians responded in kind, only to find that the wind caused their missiles to fall short of the Yorkist line, where Fauconberg's men picked them up and fired them back. Under a hail of arrows, and unable to respond effectively, the Lancastrian troops suffered both heavy casualties and falling morale. To halt the damage inflicted on his lines by the Yorkist archers, Henry BEAUFORT, duke of Somerset, the Lancastrian commander, ordered his men to attack, thus opening the close-quarter combat that characterized the rest of the battle. Seeing the enemy advance, Fauconberg realized that his archers were becoming vulnerable; he ordered them to withdraw behind the Yorkist lines, but also told them to leave some of the Lancastrian arrows in the snow where they would obstruct the enemy attack.

See also Battles, Nature of
Further Reading: Boardman, Andrew W., *The Medieval Soldier in the Wars of the Roses* (Stroud, Gloucestershire, UK: Sutton Publishing, 1998); Bradbury, Jim, *The Medieval Archer* (Woodbridge, Suffolk: Boydell Press, 1985).

Armies, Recruitment of

Because fifteenth-century England had no standing armies, WARS OF THE ROSES military forces had to be raised anew each time a campaign was undertaken. Surviving records, although fragmentary, indicate that these armies mainly comprised contingents of RETAINERS that the PEERAGE and GENTRY supplied to the king or party leader they supported, groups of tenants who held land of the peer or gentleman who called them to take arms on behalf of his party, and bodies of men who were summoned to service by official COMMISSIONS OF ARRAY, which the party in power used to mobilize the local county and town militias.

The best-documented armies of the fifteenth century are not civil war forces, but the armies English kings raised for overseas expeditions, such as the force EDWARD IV recruited for his invasion of FRANCE in 1475. Composed of almost 200 contingents provided by noblemen or gentlemen who had contracted with the king to supply specific numbers and kinds of troops, this expeditionary force was an army of indentured retainers, men who had contracted to supply paid military service to a lord so he could, in turn, fulfill his contract (or indenture) with the king. For example, Sir Richard TUNSTALL contracted to provide 10 spears and 100 archers to serve for one year. Civil war armies were probably raised in a similar fashion. In 1455, Humphrey STAFFORD, duke of Buckingham, paid ninety men 6s 8d per head to serve with the royal army at the Battle of ST. ALBANS. These wages were likely based on the rates the king paid to the contingent leaders with whom he contracted.

Because we know that in the 1450s Buckingham had less than 130 paid retainers, including serving women and nonmilitary household officers, his 1455 contingent of ninety men was clearly recruited from other sources. A wealthy landed noble like Buckingham, and powerful noble families like the Nevilles and the Percies, had extensive territorial influence that gave them a wide network or AFFINITY of political and military support on which to draw. Such magnates could summon their tenant farmers to service, as the Percy family did during the NEVILLE-PERCY FEUD of the 1450s. Of the 710 persons we know to have been part of the Percy army at the Battle of HEWORTH in 1453, the largest group (about 330) were Percy tenants.

The last major method of recruitment was the issuance of commissions of array, whereby the party in power used its control of the government to call upon men to perform their public duty and assist their lawful king in defending the realm from invasion or rebellion. By law, the Crown could summon all able-bodied men between sixteen and sixty to serve for forty days at the expense of their town or county. During the Wars of the Roses, the question of who the lawful king was severely complicated the use of commissions of array. From 1458 to 1460, the Lancastrian regime of MARGARET OF ANJOU controlled the administrative machinery of government and issued commissions in the name of HENRY VI. Late in 1460, the ACT OF ACCORD made Richard PLANTAGENET, duke of York, heir to the throne and head of the government, allowing the duke to issue commissions in Henry's name. However, the followers of Margaret either ignored these orders or employed them to raise troops that were eventually used to defeat and kill York at the Battle of WAKEFIELD. After March 1461, when there existed both a Lancastrian and a Yorkist monarch, counties and towns either sent troops to both armies or followed the allegiance of the most powerful local lord or noble family.

See also Armies, Size of; Armies, Supplying of; Battles, Nature of; Casualties; Commons (Common People) and the Wars of the Roses; Military Campaigns, Duration of; Neville Family; Towns and the Wars of the Roses
Further Reading: Boardman, Andrew W., *The Medieval Soldier in the Wars of the Roses* (Stroud, Gloucestershire, UK: Sutton Publishing, 1998); Gillingham, John, *The Wars of the Roses* (Baton Rouge: Louisiana State University Press, 1981); Goodman, Anthony, *The Wars of the Roses* (New York: Dorset Press, 1981); Ross, Charles, *The Wars of the Roses* (New York: Thames and Hudson, 1987).

Armies, Size of

Aside from the fantastically large estimates of contemporary chroniclers and commentators, little evidence survives to support the realistic calculation of the size of WARS OF THE ROSES armies. However, the pay records for English armies sent to FRANCE in the fifteenth century are more plentiful and do permit historians to make educated guesses as to the sizes of most civil war forces.

English claims for the numbers engaged were disbelieved even in the fifteenth century. In 1461, the Milanese ambassador in BURGUNDY confessed to his master, Francesco Sforza, duke of Milan, that he was ashamed to speak of the huge numbers of men (about 300,000) who were reported to have participated in the recent campaign and Battle of ST. ALBANS. Such numbers, observed the ambassador, resembled "the figures of bakers" (Gillingham, p. 43). For the Battle of TOWTON in March 1461, the bishop of Salisbury, writing one week after the battle, and the LONDON merchant who likely wrote *Gregory's Chronicle* (see LONDON CHRONICLES) both claimed that EDWARD IV's army numbered 200,000. Because all accounts of Towton agree that the Lancastrian force was larger than Edward's, accepting the chronicle figures means accepting that almost a half million men fought at Towton. For these numbers to be accurate, almost every adult fighting man in mid-fifteenth-century England—perhaps 600,000 out of an estimated total population of less than 3 million—must have been present at the battle. Given the size and extent of contemporary problems of supply and transport, such figures are clearly incredible (see ARMIES, SUPPLYING OF).

Although few such documents exist for Wars of the Roses armies, the surviving pay records of various other fifteenth-century military forces allow for more believable size estimates. For instance, the accounts of the Exchequer, the ancient royal financial office, show that Edward IV transported 11,500 fighting men to France in 1475. In 1415, when Henry V crossed the Channel to launch the Agincourt campaign, he took with him an army of about 9,000. The largest English army of the century was the force of 20,000 men with which Richard, duke of Gloucester (see RICHARD III), invaded SCOTLAND in 1482. Because no English king or commander had the full military resources of the realm at his disposal during the civil wars, the armies of the Wars of the Roses are unlikely to have exceeded the 1482 force in size. A reasonable estimate is that the largest armies at the largest battles, such as the Battles of St. Albans (1461), BARNET, and TEWKESBURY, did not number more than 10,000 to 15,000 men. At most other battles, and especially later in the wars, when enthusiasm for actively taking sides waned among the PEERAGE and GENTRY, the armies may have been half or less this size. The one possible exception is the Battle of Towton, for which exact figures are elusive, but which clearly was the largest, longest, and bloodiest battle of the conflict.

One possible way to explain chronicle figures is to make a distinction between fighting men and the large numbers of noncombatants who supported them. Besides its ARCHERS and MEN-AT-ARMS, a fifteenth-century army might include chaplains, grooms, bakers, carpenters, physicians, fletchers, and servants and hangers-on (both male and female) of all kinds. If such noncombatants were counted as part of the army, an actual fighting force of 10,000 could be a much larger aggregation of human beings. The counting of noncombatants may explain why, for instance, the force with which Edward IV left Burgundy in March 1471 was given as 2,000 in the *HISTORY OF THE ARRIVAL OF EDWARD IV,* the official Yorkist account of the invasion, but was recorded as 1,200 in Jean de Waurin's *RECUEIL DES CRONIQUES ET ANCHIENNES ISTORIES DE LA GRANT BRETAIGNE.*

See also Armies, Recruitment of; Battles, Nature of; Casualties; Commons (Common People) and the Wars of the Roses; Military Campaigns, Duration of
Further Reading: Boardman, Andrew W., *The Medieval Soldier in the Wars of the Roses* (Stroud, Gloucestershire, UK: Sutton Publishing, 1998); Gillingham, John, *The Wars of the Roses* (Baton Rouge: Louisiana State University Press, 1981); Goodman, Anthony, *The Wars of the Roses* (New York: Dorset Press, 1981); Ross, Charles, *The Wars of the Roses* (New York: Thames and Hudson, 1987).

Armies, Supplying of

Supplying a fifteenth-century army with food, clothing, and other necessary items was a difficult task that often limited the size of the force, affected its mobility, and influenced the strategy of its leaders. Three different methods were employed, usually in combination, to supply WARS OF THE ROSES armies—the troops carried their own supplies, purchased supplies from merchants accompanying the army, or lived off the land.

Records for the armies EDWARD IV raised in the early 1480s to invade SCOTLAND indicate that huge quantities of mutton, bacon, beef (on the hoof), fish, grain, beans, and salt were collected at Newcastle, the army's base. Large numbers of carts and horses were gathered to carry the food and such cooking supplies as kettles, ladles, and dishes, as well as such other necessary tools and equipment as axes, shovels, and sickles. Although most civil war armies were half or less the size of the 20,000-man force that Richard, duke of Gloucester (see RICHARD III), led northward in 1482, they still required lengthy wagon trains even to carry only a few days' worth of supplies. Thus, even for brief campaigns—and most during the Wars of the Roses lasted for only days or weeks—troops quickly exhausted their food reserve and had to turn for supplies to merchants following the army or to foraging in their area of operations. Merchants and their vital supply trains could limit movement, especially when their numbers were added to the already large number of noncombatants who accompanied an army—servants (male and female), fletchers, carpenters, grooms, physicians, chaplains, cooks and bakers, and general laborers. The presence of merchants also required that a troop of soldiers—a contemporary military manual suggests no less than 400—be deployed to protect them and their wares.

In a civil war, the practice of living off the country posed serious political risks. Taking supplies from the people of the countryside, even upon promise of payment, could easily degenerate into looting and turn friendly or neutral towns or regions into hostile territories disposed to favor the other side. The plundering that characterized the southward march of MARGARET OF ANJOU's army in 1461 cost the Lancastrians much support in LONDON and southern England and gave a boost to Yorkist PROPAGANDA. Because only London, with perhaps 40,000 inhabitants, was larger than an army of 10,000, living off the land also limited movement into sparsely populated areas and encouraged operations near a larger town or in a richer agricultural area. Speed of movement was also affected by the problem of supply. In March 1470, Edward IV marched quickly northward to quell the uprisings instigated by Richard NEVILLE, earl of Warwick. However, before engaging the rebels, Edward had to spend four days in York collecting supplies; the food his troops carried with them had been exhausted on the march, and Warwick's men, through their own foraging, had exhausted the supplies available in the countryside. The problem of supplying a large army in the field may have been the main reason civil war commanders tended to seek rather than avoid battle, so as to quickly end campaigns and disband armies.

See also Armies, Recruitment of; Armies, Size of; Battles, Nature of; Casualties; Harbingers; March on London; Military Campaigns, Duration of; Towns and the Wars of the Roses
Further Reading: Boardman, Andrew W., *The Medieval Soldier in the Wars of the Roses* (Stroud, Gloucestershire, UK: Sutton Publishing, 1998); Gillingham, John, *The Wars of the Roses* (Baton Rouge: Louisiana State University Press, 1981); Goodman, Anthony, *The Wars of the Roses* (New York: Dorset Press, 1981); Ross, Charles, *The Wars of the Roses* (New York: Thames and Hudson, 1987).

Armor

During the WARS OF THE ROSES, English MEN-AT-ARMS, and especially members of the PEERAGE and GENTRY, entered battle encased in a defensive body covering of metal plate armor, which was designed to deflect blows from heavy weapons in close combat and to ward off arrows shot from a distance. Because most civil war battles were decided by

hand-to-hand combat between men fighting on foot, full or partial sets of armor of any available quality were worn by any soldier able to buy or otherwise procure them.

By the late fifteenth century, the making of plate armor was a fine art, and new methods of forging iron allowed for the production of lighter, stronger, more flexible suits that could better protect a larger portion of the body and allowed for greater mobility and endurance. Although a complete set of armor, or "harness," was expensive, and might only be available to wealthy nobles and knights, most men went into combat at least partially harnessed, even if with older, lower-quality pieces. The finest armor had curved and fluted design elements, which gave it strength and allowed it to deflect blows more easily. Totally encased in metal, a knight in full harness had greater confidence in battle, and by the late fifteenth century many discarded the shields of earlier times and opted instead to wield the heavy two-handed weapons, such as poleaxes, which were, ironically, designed to crush the new, stronger body armor (see WEAPONRY). Although they also employed two-handed, shafted weapons, such as the bill and glaive, more lightly armored men-at-arms continued to carry a small, round shield known as a buckler, which could be easily slung from a belt or strap worn around the waist.

Full harness was worn over a heavy padded doublet that was slit for ventilation. Gussets (i.e., metal or mail inserts) were sewn to the doublet to protect vulnerable areas such as the arms, elbows, and armpits, where metal joints would have been too restrictive of movement. Wax cords (arming points) were attached to the doublet to allow the plate armor to be secured to the body. Other undergarments included heavy, padded hose and leather shoes. The main body armor comprised upper and lower breastplates, which were hinged vertically on one side, back plates, a metal skirt, and tassets, which hung from straps on the skirt and protected the lower body. The feet were encased in plate shoes called sabatons, which were attached to lower leg coverings called greaves. The greaves and the upper leg cover-

Two fifteenth-century knights in full armor engage in the kind of hand-to-hand combat that characterized Wars of the Roses battles. (Cotton Jul. E VI Art. 6 f. 7, British Library)

ings, known as cuisseis, had two halves that hinged on the side and were secured by buckles and straps. A special knee piece, attached by rivets or pins, protected the gap between greaves and cuisseis. Arms were protected by two similar coverings, the vambraces (for the lower arm) and rerebraces (for the upper arm), with special pieces called cowters and pauldrons attached by straps to protect, respectively, the elbows and the shoulders. Gauntlets fitted over the vambrace protected the hands and wrists. The sallet, a visored metal helmet worn over a padded arming cap, protected the head, while the bevor, a triangular metal plate worn below the sallet, protected the neck.

Although most knights dismounted for battle, the grand cavalry charge, as RICHARD III proved at the Battle of BOSWORTH FIELD, could still be employed to retrieve desperate situations. During the HUNDRED YEARS WAR, unarmored horses had been extremely vulnerable to ARCHERS. Thus, many noblemen armored their mounts during the Wars of the Roses. Horse armor involved protective pieces for the head, neck, chest, rump, and flank, and might even include armor-plated reins to prevent an enemy from cutting them and depriving the rider of control. Nonetheless, the weight and expense of horse armor limited its use to the wealthiest combatants, who generally used their mounts only to ride to or escape from the battlefield.

See also Badges; Battles, Nature of; Generalship; Military Campaigns, Duration of
Further Reading: Ayton, Andrew, "Arms, Armour, and Horses," in Maurice Keen, ed., *Medieval Warfare* (Oxford: Oxford University Press, 1999); Boardman, Andrew W., *The Medieval Soldier in the Wars of the Roses* (Stroud, Gloucestershire, UK: Sutton Publishing, 1998); DeVries, Kelly, *Medieval Military Technology* (Peterborough, Ontario: Broadview Press, 1992); Prestwich, Michael, *Armies and Warfare in the Middle Ages: The English Experience* (New Haven, CT: Yale University Press, 1996).

Artillery

By the start of the WARS OF THE ROSES in the late 1450s, artillery had been in use in northern Europe for over a century, and most civil war armies included at least a small artillery force.

The pace of advancement in European gun technology had quickened in the 1370s, when the small, inaccurate, and unreliable artillery used early in the HUNDRED YEARS WAR gave way to larger, more powerful weapons able to breach the high stone walls of towns and castles. Although the new artillery could still be unpredictable—JAMES II of SCOTLAND was killed in 1460 when one of his siege cannons exploded—the English began using such guns with great effect in WALES and on the Scottish border in the early fifteenth century. The new guns came in many types and sizes, ranging from massive bombards, which could batter down walls with huge balls of stone or iron, through a variety of intermediate-sized serpentines, orgues, and ribaudequins, to the smaller culverins, which could be fired from tripods or used as handguns. Fifteenth-century cannon were made of iron or bronze, although cast bronze weapons

were most common because techniques for casting iron did not reach a similar level of expertise until the late sixteenth century. Because weapons were nonstandard and each large gun fired projectiles made especially for it, the gun makers usually also served as gunners. This uniqueness in projectile size caused individual large guns to be given their own names, such as Mons Meg, now in Edinburgh Castle, a 14,000-pound cannon with a caliber of twenty inches.

Firing a fifteenth-century artillery piece was a slow and difficult process. The larger siege guns threw stone and iron projectiles that could weigh hundreds of pounds. To fire the weapon, the gunner used a firing iron—an iron bar heated in a pan of charcoal that was kept hot and near at hand. Because one pound of powder was required to throw nine pounds of shot, and because the barrel had to be washed with a mixture of water and vinegar after every firing, ten shots per hour was considered a good rate of fire. During the Wars of the Roses, this slow rate meant that cannon were used mainly on the eve or at the start of a battle, firing one volley at the enemy before the hand-to-hand combat commenced. During the night before the Battle of BARNET, Richard NEVILLE, earl of Warwick, fired his cannon continuously, hoping to create fear and disorder in the Yorkist ranks; however, Warwick was unaware of how close the enemy was and his guns overshot. To keep Warwick from learning his error, EDWARD IV ordered his own guns to refrain from revealing their position by returning fire. A few weeks later at the Battle of TEWKESBURY, Edward drew the Lancastrians out of an excellent defensive position with an opening artillery salvo.

Nonetheless, artillery pieces were much less of a factor in the Wars of the Roses than they were in contemporary campaigns on the continent. Able to fire a ball about 2,000 to 2,500 paces, cannon could be used with devastating effect against massed immobile troop concentrations, such as at river crossings, or against town or castle walls during a siege, situations where the slow rate of fire did not matter. But the art of fortification was less advanced in

Artillery pieces are used to batter the walls of a castle in this fifteenth-century depiction of siege warfare. (Royal MS 14 E IV f. 281, British Library)

England than elsewhere, and the English civil wars were therefore characterized by pitched battles, not by sieges; during the Wars of the Roses, the enemy's towns or castles usually surrendered soon after the enemy's field armies had been defeated.

Still, both sides recognized the growing importance of artillery and took measures to ensure a good supply of guns. Since about 1415, the English Crown had appointed a master of ordnance to supervise the king's artillery. In 1456, John Judde, a LONDON merchant, won appointment to the post by offering to supply HENRY VI with guns and powder at his own expense. Judde's ambitious program of collecting and manufacturing guns for the Lancastrians so alarmed the Yorkists that they ambushed and killed him in June 1460 as he was supervising delivery of a new shipment of weapons. Edward IV also appreciated the importance of artillery, and his Masters of Ordnance (like John Wode, who held office from 1463 to 1477) were trusted members of the royal household. Edward was said to frequently inspect his ordnance, and his campaigns usually included a sizable artillery train. Thus, by HENRY VII's reign, the English Crown housed a large and growing collection of ordnance in the TOWER OF LONDON.

See also Archers; Battles, Nature of; Military Campaigns, Duration of; Weaponry
Further Reading: DeVries, Kelly, *Medieval Military Technology* (Peterborough, Ontario: Broadview Press, 1992); Gillingham, John, *The*

Wars of the Roses (Baton Rouge: Louisiana State University Press, 1981); Norris, John, *Artillery: An Illustrated History* (Stroud, Gloucestershire, UK: Sutton Publishing, 2000); Rogers, H. C. B., *Artillery through the Ages* (London: Seeley, 1971); Ross, Charles, *The Wars of the Roses* (New York: Thames and Hudson, 1987).

Attainder, Act of

During the WARS OF THE ROSES, attainder developed as an act of PARLIAMENT whereby the faction in power could convict its political opponents of treason without bringing them to trial. By passing a bill of attainder, Parliament simply declared anyone named in the act to be guilty of treason and subject to the loss of all civil rights and the forfeiture to the Crown of all property. Because attainder declared anyone so convicted to be "corrupt of blood," all heirs and descendants of attainted persons were disinherited, thus allowing the confiscated property to be parceled out among members and supporters of the winning faction.

Although attainder was originally used to supplement the conviction of persons found guilty of a capital offence in a court of law, Queen MARGARET OF ANJOU and the victorious Lancastrians used it in the COVENTRY PARLIAMENT of 1459 to extinguish the rights and seize the property of the exiled Yorkist leaders. When the Yorkists won control of HENRY VI and the royal administration in 1460, they used the Lancastrian precedent of the previous year to reverse their own attainders and to convict and dispossess their enemies. Between 1459 and 1500, Parliament attainted over 400 persons in the various reversals of political and military fortune that marked the Wars of the Roses. Most acts of attainder were reversed in subsequent Parliaments, either because attainted individuals or their heirs belonged to the party then in power or because they submitted to the ruling party.

Further Reading: Bellamy, John G., *The Law of Treason in England in the Later Middle Ages* (Cambridge: Cambridge University Press, 1970); Lander, J. R., *Crown and Nobility, 1450–1509* (Montreal: McGill-Queens University Press, 1976).

Audley, Lord. *See* Touchet, James, Lord Audley

Badges

In the fifteenth century, badges were personal or familial emblems adopted by noblemen and distributed as part of the distinctive livery, or uniform, given to RETAINERS who were part of their AFFINITY of sworn followers. These badges proclaimed their wearer's political allegiance and helped combatants distinguish friend from foe during battle. The red and white roses that came to symbolize, and later to describe, the English civil wars of the fifteenth century were among the family badges of the contending houses of LANCASTER and YORK.

The royal family, and such important noble families as the Courtenays, Percies, and Nevilles, collected numerous badges reflecting the lineages and titles inherited from various ancestors (see NEVILLE FAMILY). For instance, HENRY VII employed the portcullis, a symbol inherited from his maternal relatives, the BEAUFORT FAMILY; the red dragon of Cadwallader, an emblem deriving from WALES and his paternal ancestors; and a dun cow, which represented his earldom of Richmond.

The white boar, the favorite badge of Richard III. (British Library)

Besides family emblems, individuals adopted badges and mottoes to symbolize their own particular ideals, claims, or associations. As visual PROPAGANDA to secure the house of TUDOR on the throne and to illustrate the union of Lancaster and York achieved by his marriage to ELIZABETH OF YORK, Henry VII devised the Tudor rose, a combination of the red rose of Lancaster and the white rose of York. In preparation for a visit to the city of York in 1486, Henry instructed the civic magistrates to construct displays that contained "a royal, rich, red rose conveyed by a vice, unto which rose shall appear another rich white rose" (Pollard, p. 7).

Although the red rose was one Lancastrian (and perhaps Beaufort) emblem, HENRY VI's personal badge was an antelope, while MARGARET OF ANJOU gave her retainers a swan badge, and the men recruited in the name of her son, Prince EDWARD OF LANCASTER, received the prince's ostrich plume emblem. Although the white rose, which was inherited from the Mortimer earls of March, was a well-known symbol of the house of York, and may have become the personal badge of Elizabeth of York, EDWARD IV favored the SUN IN SPLENDOR/SUNBURST BADGE as his personal emblem. Edward's father, Richard PLANTAGENET, duke of York, used the falcon and fetter lock, while Edward's brothers, George PLANTAGENET, duke of Clarence, and RICHARD III, chose, respectively, the black bull and the white boar. While duke of Gloucester, Richard distributed the white boar widely among his northern retainers (see RICHARD III, NORTHERN AFFINITY OF), many of whom had formerly worn the bear and ragged staff of Richard NEVILLE, earl of

Warwick, an emblem long associated with the Warwick title. Gloucester also adopted a personal motto—*loyaulté me lie* (loyalty binds me)—which took on ironic overtones after the duke usurped the throne of his nephew EDWARD V in 1483.

See also Bastard Feudalism; Livery and Maintenance; Retaining, Acts Against
Further Reading: Bean, J. M. W., *From Lord to Patron: Lordship in Late Medieval England* (Manchester: Manchester University Press, 1989); Bellamy, J. G., *Bastard Feudalism and the Law* (Portland, OR: Areopagitica Press, 1989); Hicks, Michael, *Bastard Feudalism* (London: Longman, 1995); Pollard, A. J., *The Wars of the Roses* (New York: St. Martin's Press, 1988).

The Ballad of Bosworth Field

The Ballad of Bosworth Field is one of the fullest poetic retellings of the 1485 Battle of BOSWORTH FIELD, and may possibly provide authentic details concerning the battle itself.

The earliest surviving copy of the ballad dates to the mid–seventeenth century, although a sixteenth-century prose summary of the poem also exists. Like THE SONG OF LADY BESSY and THE ROSE OF ENGLAND, *The Ballad of Bosworth Field* was composed by someone connected with the Stanley family, for Thomas STANLEY, Lord Stanley, and his brother Sir William STANLEY are central characters. The author may also have been an eyewitness to the battle, for the poem gives an extensive listing of the noblemen and gentlemen whom RICHARD III summoned to meet the invasion of Henry Tudor, earl of Richmond (see HENRY VII).

After describing Richmond's landing in WALES and his appeal for aid to the Stanleys, the poem recounts Richard's arrest and near execution of Stanley's son Lord Strange, an element common to all major Bosworth ballads. After detailing the mutual determination of the king and Lord Stanley to destroy each other, the poem uses the long list of Richard's supporters to enhance the gallantry of the Stanley-dominated shires of Lancashire and Cheshire, which are portrayed as standing alone against the mighty royal host.

The account of the battle itself tells of the fearsome strength of the king's ARTILLERY. Although the numbers of royal cannon are likely exaggerated, their detailed description is another story element that points to the poet's actual presence on the field. Like the other Bosworth ballads, this poem describes Richard's defiant refusal to flee when the battle seems lost.

> "One foot will I never flee
> Whilst the breath is my breast within!"
> As he said, so did it be;
> If he lost his life, if he were King. (Bennett,
>   p. 173)

The ballad closes with a listing of the most important nobles and gentlemen to die in the battle, including, on the king's side, John HOWARD, duke of Norfolk; Sir Richard RATCLIFFE; and Sir Robert BRACKEN-BURY, and, on Richmond's side, William Brandon, the earl's standard-bearer, who was slain by Richard III himself. *The Ballad of Bosworth Field* ends with the crowning of Richmond on the battlefield and the public display of Richard's corpse in Leicester. The value of the *Ballad* and the other Bosworth poems as sources for the battle itself has been questioned by modern historians, with one even suggesting that the poems may be works of fiction. However, other researchers have made cautious use of the *Ballad* and its companion pieces to elucidate certain aspects of the battle.

Further Reading: Bennett, Michael, *The Battle of Bosworth* (New York: St. Martin's Press, 1985); Hammond, P. W., and Anne F. Sutton, *Richard III: The Road to Bosworth Field* (London: Constable, 1985); Rowse, A. L., *Bosworth Field* (Garden City, NY: Doubleday, 1966); Williams, D. T., *The Battle of Bosworth* (Leicester: Leicester University Press, 1973); the text of *The Ballad of Bosworth Field* is available on the Richard III Society Web site at <http://www.webcom.com/r3/bosworth/ballad2.html>.

Bamburgh Castle (1461–1464)

Along with the other Northumberland fortresses of ALNWICK and DUNSTAN-

BURGH, Bamburgh Castle demonstrated the insecurity of EDWARD IV's throne by falling several times into Lancastrian hands between 1461 and 1464.

After the Yorkist victory at the Battle of TOWTON in March 1461, Bamburgh was one of several northern strongholds controlled by RETAINERS loyal to the Lancastrian Percy family (see entries under PERCY). The fortress fell to Edward IV's men in July 1462, but the Yorkist garrison surrendered the castle to MARGARET OF ANJOU in October, when she landed nearby with HENRY VI and a body of French MERCENARIES under Pierre de BRÉZÉ. The Lancastrian royal family and de Brézé withdrew into SCOTLAND in November, leaving a garrison under Henry BEAUFORT, duke of Somerset, and Sir Ralph Percy to defend Bamburgh against an approaching Yorkist army. In early December, Richard NEVILLE, earl of Warwick, began coordinated siege operations of all three Northumberland castles, giving direction of the Bamburgh effort to his brother, John NEVILLE, Lord Montagu. On 26 December 1462, Somerset surrendered the fortress; the garrison was allowed to depart, and Somerset and Percy were pardoned upon swearing allegiance to Edward IV.

Accepting Percy's pledge of loyalty, Edward placed both Bamburgh and Dunstanburgh in his charge, but in March 1463 Percy reverted to his Lancastrian allegiance and yielded both fortresses to Margaret, who arrived from Scotland at the head of a joint Scottish-Lancastrian army. In June, another Scottish force, accompanied by both JAMES III and his mother MARY OF GUELDRES, as well as by the Lancastrian royal family, laid siege to Norham Castle, where it was surprised in July by a Yorkist force under Warwick and Montagu. The invading army disintegrated in panic before the Yorkist troops, leading to a rout that destroyed Scottish enthusiasm for the Lancastrian cause. In December, Edward IV concluded a ten-month truce with the Scottish government as a prelude to a final Yorkist campaign in Northumberland. However, before this effort could begin, Somerset returned to Bamburgh, where Henry VI was holding

court, and openly declared himself for the house of LANCASTER. From Bamburgh, Somerset launched a campaign that captured several neighboring towns and castles and brought most of the shire under Lancastrian control. Montagu's victories at the Battles of HEDGELEY MOOR and HEXHAM in April and May 1464 led to Somerset's capture and restored all Northumberland outside the three castles to Yorkist control. Alnwick and Dunstanburgh surrendered on terms in June, but Bamburgh, commanded by the Yorkist turncoat Sir Ralph Grey, refused and stood siege. When Grey was knocked senseless by falling masonry during a bombardment by royal ARTILLERY, his second-in-command surrendered Bamburgh to Warwick in July, thus securing the shire for Edward IV and the house of YORK.

Further Reading: Haigh, Philip A., *The Military Campaigns of the Wars of the Roses* (Stroud, Gloucestershire, UK: Sutton Publishing, 1995); Pollard, A. J., *North-Eastern England during the Wars of the Roses* (Oxford: Clarendon Press, 1990).

Barnet, Battle of (1471)

Fought on Easter Sunday, 14 April 1471, the Battle of Barnet began EDWARD IV's restoration to the throne and destroyed Richard NEVILLE, earl of Warwick, and his political faction.

On 11 April, one month after his landing in England, Edward entered LONDON unopposed. Warwick was at Coventry awaiting the arrival from the north of the forces of his brother, John NEVILLE, marquis of Montagu, while Edmund BEAUFORT, duke of Somerset, and other Lancastrian leaders were on the south coast awaiting the arrival from FRANCE of Queen MARGARET OF ANJOU and her son EDWARD OF LANCASTER, Prince of Wales. After taking custody of HENRY VI, whom he eventually dispatched to the TOWER OF LONDON, Edward went to Westminster Abbey, where he reunited with his wife, Elizabeth WOODVILLE, and saw for the first time the son (see EDWARD V) who had been born in SANCTUARY in the Abbey

This portrayal of the Battle of Barnet illustrates a French version of the History of the Arrival of Edward IV, *the official Yorkist account of Edward IV's restoration in 1471. (MS 236, University of Ghent)*

during the previous November. The next day, as Yorkist supporters flooded into the capital, Edward learned that Warwick had joined forces with Montagu and was marching on the city. To meet this threat, a Yorkist army of almost 10,000 left London on 13 April heading northwest on the road to St. Albans.

Accompanied by Henry VI and over thirty magnates, including his newly reconciled brother George PLANTAGENET, duke of

Clarence, Edward learned that evening that Warwick had deployed north of the town of Barnet, which lay midway between London and St. Albans. Edward advanced through Barnet and halted his troops only a short distance from Warwick's larger force, although the onset of darkness meant neither army was aware of the other's exact position. Warwick ordered his ARTILLERY to harass the Yorkist army that he knew was somewhere on his front. Because the two armies were so close, Warwick overshot the Yorkist position, which Edward refused to reveal by ordering his artillery not to respond.

The battle began about 4 A.M. in a swirling fog, when the Yorkist army advanced in response to a barrage from Warwick's ARCHERS and artillery. Only when the lines clashed did the commanders on each army's right wing realize that the two forces were misaligned, with each right wing overlapping the enemy's left. John de VERE, earl of Oxford, in command on Warwick's right, quickly collapsed the Yorkist left, but then had trouble controlling his men, who streamed off the field to plunder Barnet. When Warwick's left was similarly overrun by the troops of Edward's brother, Richard, duke of Gloucester (see RICHARD III), in command on the Yorkist right, the entire battlefront shifted at right angles. This change of position, unrealized because of the fog, meant that when Oxford got part of his force back into the battle, he fell upon the rear of Montagu's men. Mistaking Oxford's badge of a star with streams for the Yorkist emblem of a sun with streams, Montagu ordered his archers to fire on the surprised attackers, who then threw Warwick's whole line into confusion with shouts of "treason" (see SUN IN SPLENDOR/SUNBURST BADGE). Seeing the enemy in distress, Edward pressed his advantage; when Montagu was killed in this onslaught, Warwick's line broke and the rout began. With his entire front collapsing, Warwick, who had been fighting on foot, tried to reach his horse, which, due to the shifting lines, was now far to the rear. Before Edward could intervene, Warwick was overtaken by Yorkist foot soldiers, who beat him to the ground and slew him. Shortly after Warwick met this end, Margaret of Anjou and her son landed at Weymouth. Met by Somerset and other old-line Lancastrians who had never trusted Warwick, the queen was persuaded to continue the fight.

See also Battles, Nature of; Edward IV, Restoration of; Military Campaigns, Duration of
Further Reading: Haigh, Philip A., *The Military Campaigns of the Wars of the Roses* (Stroud, Gloucestershire, UK: Sutton Publishing, 1995); Hammond, P. W., *The Battles of Barnet and Tewkesbury* (New York: St. Martin's Press, 1990).

Bastard Feudalism

The term "bastard feudalism" refers to a society in which titled noblemen, and some members of the GENTRY, developed networks or affinities of sworn RETAINERS who provided political, legal, domestic, and military service in return for money, office, and influence. Because the system allowed the raising of large bands of armed men, bastard feudalism enabled wealthy members of the PEERAGE to disrupt law and order and conduct private feuds in their localities, and even to contend for control of the national government. For these reasons, bastard feudalism was once considered a primary cause of the WARS OF THE ROSES, although most historians today view it as a useful and neutral social system that merely became susceptible to abuses during periods of royal weakness, such as occurred during the personal rule of HENRY VI and the first reign of EDWARD IV.

Charles Plummer coined the term bastard feudalism in 1885 to describe what he believed was a degeneration of feudalism, the early medieval social system that was based on a lord's granting of land (by heritable tenure) to a vassal in return for military or other services. Plummer blamed bastard feudalism for the disorder and instability that for him characterized the late fifteenth century. Plummer's phrase came into wide use in the 1940s when the influential historian K. B. McFarlane employed it to describe the functioning of English political society between the thirteenth and sixteenth centuries. McFarlane viewed bastard feudalism not as an illegitimate off-shoot of an earlier, purer system but as a natural response to societal changes that was, through individual abuses and royal incapacity, employed for disruptive and illegal purposes.

Because they were rarely kept under arms for long periods, noble retinues were not private armies. Although it could be seriously threatened by the military forces of dissident noblemen, as occurred to Henry VI in the 1450s, the Crown never sought to abolish retaining, only to control it through statutes passed by PARLIAMENT (see RETAINING, ACTS AGAINST). Lacking standing armies, kings relied on noble retinues for the military forces they required to conduct foreign wars or crush internal rebellions. Once Edward IV destroyed the house of LANCASTER and secured himself on the throne, armed forces raised by bastard feudal relationships tended to support rather than threaten the Crown. However, under an inept monarch like Henry VI, or an insecure one like Edward IV before 1471, ambitious or disaffected magnates, like Richard PLANTAGENET, duke of York, in the 1450s and Richard NEVILLE, earl of Warwick, in the 1460s, could use their networks of retainers to defy or even control the Crown. Although bastard feudalism did not cause the disorder and instability of these decades, it did provide powerful men with the means to take advantage of royal weakness and their own ambition.

Men recruited under the bastard feudal system were not exclusively employed for military purposes; many were household servants, while others bound themselves by indenture (contract) to supply various services. Only those recruited in emergencies, as when Warwick summoned retainers to repel Edward IV in 1471, were meant solely for military employment. In return for money and "good lordship," which might mean using influence to obtain an office or bribing or intimidating a judge or jury in a lawsuit (known as embracery), retainers often wore their lord's BADGE or livery (uniform) and took their lord's part (except, technically, against the king) in any political or military dis-

pute. Although both Edward IV and HENRY VII limited retaining, bastard feudalism continued as the basis of English political society until the late sixteenth century.

See also Affinity; Livery and Maintenance
Further Reading: Bean, J. M. W., *From Lord to Patron: Lordship in Late Medieval England* (Manchester, UK: Manchester University Press, 1989); Bellamy, J. G., *Bastard Feudalism and the Law* (Portland, OR: Areopagitica Press, 1989); Hicks, Michael, *Bastard Feudalism* (London: Longman, 1995); McFarlane, K. B., "Bastard Feudalism," in *England in the Fifteenth Century: Collected Essays* (London: Hambledon Press, 1981).

Bastard of Fauconberg. *See* Neville, Thomas, Bastard of Fauconberg

Bath and Wells, Bishop of. *See* Stillington, Robert

Battle Casualties. *See* Casualties

Battles, Nature of

Although involving the deployment of ARCHERS and ARTILLERY, most battles during the WARS OF THE ROSES were relatively brief hand-to-hand mêlées fought by bodies of armored foot soldiers.

Because the wars were civil conflicts, with Englishmen fighting Englishmen, neither side possessed any great technical advantage. Both armies had the same components and WEAPONRY, usually an artillery contingent, complements of archers and cavalry, and a core of similarly equipped footmen. Battles usually opened with an exchange of bow and gun fire, but neither weapon had much effect on the fighting once hand-to-hand combat was joined. The great English victories of the HUNDRED YEARS WAR, in which ranks of longbowmen had decimated enemy cavalry charges, had taught armored cavalry to fight on foot as heavy infantry wielding swords, battle-axes, maces (heavy, spiked staffs or clubs), or flails (a mace with a spiked ball attached to

The straight, regular lines of men shown in this fifteenth-century battle scene give no hint of the confusion and disorder that characterized a Wars of the Roses battle once the men-at-arms engaged. (Royal MS 16 G VIII f. 189, British Library)

it by a chain). These latter weapons were devised to counter fluted ARMOR, which could deflect sword or arrow but might be crushed by the impact of mace or flail. Unlike the Battles of Crécy (1346) and Agincourt (1415), English victories in FRANCE that were won by the army on the defensive, most Wars of the Roses battles were won by the attacking force—the impact of the charge giving the attackers an advantage at the clash of battle lines.

Because armor was heavy, and a fighting man encased within it quickly grew hot and weary, few battles continued more than a few hours—the momentous Battle of BOSWORTH FIELD in 1485 may have lasted little more than one hour. The Battle of TOWTON, fought throughout the length of a March day in 1461, was altogether exceptional in its duration. Because most cavalry fought on foot, the longbow was not a decisive weapon in civil war battles. After discharging a series of opening volleys to draw the enemy from his position, the lightly armored archers were at a severe disadvantage against heavily armored infantry. Battles were decided by the experience and morale of the infantry, who slugged it out with one another until one side gained an advantage. Thus, the heart of any army consisted of the retinues of the PEERAGE and GENTRY, men better trained and equipped in arms than the local levies of peasants and townsmen who comprised the bulk of most civil war forces (see ARMIES, RECRUITMENT OF). The RETAINERS of a lord or gentleman tended to be more disciplined and steadier in battle, less likely to break and run when heavily engaged. For instance, at the Battle of TEWKESBURY in 1471, EDWARD IV may have been victorious because he had a higher proportion of nobility and their retainers in his army than the Lancastrians, who were relying on hastily recruited shire and town levies from the West Country (see COMMISSIONS OF ARRAY).

In terms of morale, a final factor in the outcome of civil war battles was the quality of leadership (see GENERALSHIP). Commanders were expected to lead their armies into combat and to inspire their men with their own deeds of valor. In this regard, the Yorkists had a distinct advantage, for Edward IV was a skilled and confident soldier and leader, while HENRY VI never led an army into battle. Richard NEVILLE, earl of Warwick, was also an inspiring commander, whose leadership greatly benefited the house of YORK in the early stages of the wars, and the house of LANCASTER during the READEPTION of 1470–1471.

See also Armies, Size of; Casualties; Men-at-Arms; Mercenaries; Military Campaigns, Duration of; entries for each battle listed in the table below
Further Reading: Boardman, Andrew W., The Medieval Soldier in the Wars of the Roses (Stroud, Gloucestershire, UK: Sutton Publishing, 1998); Haigh, Philip A., The Military Campaigns of the Wars of the Roses (Stroud, Gloucestershire, UK: Sutton Publishing, 1995); Ross, Charles, The Wars of the Roses (London: Thames and Hudson, 1987).

Table 1 Chronological Listing of the Battles of the Wars of the Roses

Battle	Date
St. Albans	22 May 1455
Blore Heath	23 September 1459
Ludford Bridge	12–13 October 1459
Northampton	10 July 1460
Wakefield	30 December 1460
Mortimer's Cross	2 February 1461
St. Albans	17 February 1461
Ferrybridge	27–28 March 1461
Towton	29 March 1461
Twt Hill	16 October 1461
Hedgeley Moor	25 April 1464
Hexham	15 May 1464
Edgecote	26 July 1469
Losecote Field	12 March 1470
Barnet	14 April 1471
Tewkesbury	4 May 1471
Bosworth Field	22 August 1485
Stoke	16 June 1487

Beaufort, Edmund, Duke of Somerset (c. 1406–1455)

Through his quarrel with Richard PLANTAGENET, duke of York, Edmund Beaufort, second duke of Somerset, helped initiate the political conflicts that eventually escalated into the WARS OF THE ROSES.

Edmund Beaufort was a younger son of John Beaufort, earl of Somerset (d. 1409), eldest of the legitimate children of John of Gaunt, duke of Lancaster (1340–1399), by his mistress Katherine Swynford (d. 1403). As a branch of the house of LANCASTER, the BEAUFORT FAMILY held a claim to the Crown that could possibly rival the claim of the house of YORK. Beaufort succeeded his elder brother John as earl of Somerset in 1444 and as duke of Somerset in 1448. He served in FRANCE from the 1420s, recapturing Harfleur in 1440 and relieving CALAIS in 1442. In 1446, he succeeded York as lieutenant of France, but his failure to hold Normandy against French assaults, though not entirely his fault, earned him great unpopularity.

In 1450, anger over the defeats in France sparked JACK CADE'S REBELLION, which in turn led to the overthrow and murder of HENRY VI's chief minister, William de la POLE, duke of Suffolk. Despite his unpopularity and his military failures, Somerset enjoyed Henry's confidence and assumed leadership of the royal government. York, angered by Somerset's appointment to the French governorship and believing him to be ambitious for the throne, attacked the duke as an obstacle to needed reforms and as a traitor responsible for the loss of France.

Holding few lands of his own, Somerset was staunchly loyal to Henry VI, upon whom he depended for favor and office. The king frustrated all York's attempts to remove Somerset from power until 1453, when the onset of Henry's mental illness initiated York's FIRST PROTECTORATE and allowed the duke to commit Somerset to the TOWER OF LONDON. Released immediately upon Henry's recovery in early 1455, Somerset was acquitted of all charges and restored to office. Fearing perhaps that Somerset meant to destroy him, York and his noble allies, Richard NEVILLE, earl of Salisbury, and his son Richard NEVILLE, earl of Warwick, took arms against the COURT. After failing to achieve Somerset's surrender, York and his allies attacked a royal party at the Battle of ST. ALBANS in May 1455. The battle ended when York's forces slew Somerset. Considering his father's death a murder, Henry BEAUFORT, third duke of Somerset, intensified his family's rivalry with the house of York, thereby ensuring the continuance of civil strife.

See also Dartford Uprising; Henry VI, Illness of; Hundred Years War; other entries under Beaufort
Further Reading: Allmand, C. T., *Lancastrian Normandy, 1415–1450* (Oxford: Clarendon Press, 1983); "Edmund Beaufort," in Michael Hicks, *Who's Who in Late Medieval England* (London: Shepheard-Walwyn, 1991), pp. 285–287; Griffiths, Ralph A., *The Reign of King Henry VI* (Berkeley: University of California Press, 1981); Storey, R. L., *The End of the House of Lancaster,* 2d ed. (Stroud, Gloucestershire, UK: Sutton Publishing, 1999); Wolffe, Bertram, *Henry VI* (London: Eyre Methuen, 1981).

Beaufort, Edmund, Duke of Somerset (1439–1471)

Edmund Beaufort, younger son of Edmund BEAUFORT, second duke of Somerset, led the Lancastrian cause during the second phase (1469–1471) of the WARS OF THE ROSES.

Although deprived of his title and property by a Yorkist act of ATTAINDER in January 1465, seven months after the execution of his elder brother Henry BEAUFORT, third duke of Somerset, Edmund Beaufort was regarded as fourth duke of Somerset by the Lancastrians and later by his cousin, the first TUDOR king, HENRY VII. In July 1460, Beaufort was captured by the Yorkists and imprisoned at CALAIS and in the TOWER OF LONDON, where he remained in confinement until 1463. By 1464, Beaufort was in exile in FRANCE with Queen MARGARET OF ANJOU and her son, Prince EDWARD OF LANCASTER. Beaufort, now calling himself duke of Somerset, had no part in the restoration of HENRY VI engineered by Richard NEVILLE, earl of Warwick, in the autumn of 1470. After spending the first weeks of 1471 in BURGUNDY seeking aid for the READEPTION government from Duke CHARLES, Somerset returned to England in February. He gave little support to Warwick, and was not present at the Battle of BARNET in April, preferring to wait on the south coast for the arrival of Queen Margaret and her son.

After receiving news of Warwick's defeat and death, Somerset urged the queen to continue the fight, convincing her that the Lancastrian cause was stronger without Warwick and his adherents. Given command of the Lancastrian army that gathered around the queen in the West Country, Somerset met EDWARD IV at the Battle of TEWKESBURY on 4 May 1471. The battle was a disaster for the house of LANCASTER because Prince Edward was killed on the field, destroying any hope of the dynasty's restoration. Before taking refuge in Tewkesbury Abbey, Somerset was said to have slain his fellow commander, John WENLOCK, Lord Wenlock, for not properly supporting his troops during the battle. Hauled out of SANCTUARY, Somerset was executed in Tewkesbury on 6 May. With the duke's younger brother John Beaufort dead on Tewkesbury field, Somerset's execution ended the direct male line of the BEAUFORT FAM-

Only days after the Battle of Tewkesbury, Edward IV witnesses the beheading of Edmund Beaufort, the Lancastrian Duke of Somerset. Sir John Langstrother (right, with hands bound) awaits his turn to be executed. (MS 236, University of Ghent)

ILY and transmitted the family's claim to the throne to Henry Tudor, then earl of Richmond, the son of Somerset's cousin, Margaret BEAUFORT, Countess of Richmond.

See also Edward IV, Restoration of; other entries under Beaufort

Further Reading: Haigh, Philip A., *The Military Campaigns of the Wars of the Roses* (Stroud, Gloucestershire, UK: Sutton Publishing, 1995); Hammond, P. W., *The Battles of Barnet and Tewkesbury* (New York: St. Martin's Press, 1990); Ross, Charles, *Edward IV* (New Haven, CT: Yale University Press, 1998).

Beaufort Family

A branch of the house of LANCASTER, the Beaufort family transmitted the Lancastrian claim to the Crown to the house of TUDOR.

The family sprang from the 1396 marriage of John of Gaunt, duke of Lancaster (1340–1399), to his longtime mistress Katherine Swynford (d. 1403). Gaunt was the third son of Edward III (r. 1327–1377) and the uncle of Richard II (r. 1377–1399). Although Gaunt's four children by Swynford were all adults when their parents married, Richard II legitimized them in 1397 under the name Beaufort, which was drawn from the French castle in which they were born. The Beauforts were thus half siblings of Henry IV (r. 1399–1413), Gaunt's eldest son by his first marriage, who became the first king of the house of Lancaster in 1399 when he usurped the throne of his childless cousin Richard (see RICHARD II, DEPOSITION OF). Although Henry confirmed the Beauforts' legitimation in 1407, he added a proviso barring the family from the succession.

The Beauforts prospered under Lancastrian rule. One of Gaunt's sons, Henry Beaufort, cardinal-bishop of Winchester (c.1376–1447), was chancellor under both Henry IV and Henry V (r. 1413–1422), and a prominent member of the minority COUNCIL of HENRY VI. In the 1420s, Beaufort served as chancellor again and fell frequently at odds with the nominal leader of Henry VI's council, Humphrey, duke of Gloucester (1390–1447), the king's uncle. During the royal minority, the hostility between the two men was mainly personal, but in the 1440s they began to disagree over French policy, with Beaufort advocating peace and Gloucester preferring more vigorous prosecution of the war (see HUNDRED YEARS WAR). By his death in 1447, Beaufort, who held one of the wealthiest bishoprics in England, had lent the Crown over £200,000.

During the WARS OF THE ROSES, the Beauforts were represented by the cardinal's nephew, Edmund BEAUFORT, second duke of Somerset; by Somerset's two sons, Henry and Edmund (see both under BEAUFORT); and by their cousin, Margaret BEAUFORT, daughter of John Beaufort (1404–1444), first duke of Somerset. The rivalry between Edmund, the second duke, and Richard PLANTAGENET, duke of York, was a major cause of the civil wars. Edmund was killed at the Battle of ST. ALBANS in 1455. Henry, the third duke, commanded the Lancastrian army at the Battle of TOWTON in 1461 and was executed by EDWARD IV in 1464. Edmund, considered the fourth duke by the Lancastrians, commanded the Lancastrian army at the Battle of TEWKESBURY in 1471. His execution after the battle ended the direct male line of Beaufort only weeks before the murder of Henry VI ended the direct male line of Lancaster (see HENRY VI, MURDER OF). The Lancastrian claim therefore devolved on Margaret Beaufort, who in 1455 had married Edmund TUDOR, earl of Richmond, half brother of Henry VI. Margaret transmitted the claim to her only child, Henry Tudor, earl of Richmond, who in 1485 overthrew RICHARD III and the house of YORK at the Battle of BOSWORTH FIELD. Thanks to the Beaufort blood inherited from his mother, Richmond became HENRY VII, first king of the house of Tudor.

> **See also:** Appendix 1, "Genealogies"
> **Further Reading:** Griffiths, Ralph A., and Roger S. Thomas, *The Making of the Tudor Dynasty* (New York: St. Martin's Press, 1985); Harriss, G. L., *Cardinal Beaufort* (Oxford: Clarendon Press, 1988); Jones, Michael K., and Malcolm G. Underwood, *The King's Mother: Lady Margaret Beaufort, Countess of Richmond and Derby* (Cambridge: Cambridge University Press, 1992); Simon, Linda, *Of Virtue Rare: Margaret Beaufort, Matriarch of the House of Tudor* (Boston: Houghton Mifflin Company, 1982).

Beaufort, Henry, Duke of Somerset (1436–1464)

The son and heir of Edmund BEAUFORT, second duke of Somerset, Henry Beaufort, third duke of Somerset, was one of the chief military leaders of the Lancastrian cause during the first phase (1459–1461) of the WARS OF THE ROSES.

In May 1455, Beaufort was severely wounded at the Battle of ST. ALBANS, where he witnessed his father's death at the hands of troops commanded by his father's rival, Richard PLANTAGENET, duke of York. Both dynastic and personal considerations made the new duke a staunch supporter of HENRY VI—the BEAUFORT FAMILY was a branch of the house of LANCASTER, and Somerset considered York guilty of his father's murder. In early 1458, Somerset and the sons of the other noblemen slain at St. Albans brought large retinues to LONDON, where they demanded revenge against York and his chief allies, Richard NEVILLE, earl of Salisbury, and his son Richard NEVILLE, earl of Warwick. After attempting to ambush York and Salisbury, Somerset and his allies agreed to a reconciliation brokered by Henry VI and sealed by the LOVE-DAY of March 1458.

When that settlement collapsed in civil war in 1459, Henry VI appointed Somerset captain of CALAIS. But being unable to dislodge Warwick from the town, Somerset returned to England in October 1460. In December, the duke led the army that defeated and killed York and Salisbury at the Battle of WAKE-FIELD, and in February 1461 he commanded the victorious Lancastrians at the Battle of ST. ALBANS. Somerset commanded again at the Battle of TOWTON in late March, but fled into SCOTLAND with the Lancastrian royal family when EDWARD IV won the day. In March 1462, after failing to win help from FRANCE, Somerset returned to England where Queen MARGARET OF ANJOU entrusted him with the Lancastrian-held castle of BAMBURGH, which he surrendered in December. Edward IV pardoned Somerset in March 1463, and later reversed his ATTAINDER and restored him to his lands and titles. In late 1463, the duke reverted to his old allegiance, fleeing to the Lancastrian-held castles of Bamburgh and ALNWICK, from which he conducted a spring campaign that wrested much of northeastern England from Yorkist control. Defeated at the Battle of HEDGELEY MOOR in April 1464, Somerset regrouped and, placing Henry VI at the head of his army, marched south, encountering the forces of John NEVILLE, Lord Montagu, on 15 May.

Defeated and captured at the subsequent Battle of HEXHAM, Somerset was executed shortly thereafter. Because Somerset was unmarried, the Lancastrians conferred his title on his younger brother, Edmund BEAUFORT.

See also other entries under Beaufort
Further Reading: Haigh, Philip A., *The Military Campaigns of the Wars of the Roses* (Stroud, Gloucestershire, UK: Sutton Publishing, 1995); "Henry Beaufort," in Michael Hicks, *Who's Who in Late Medieval England* (London: Shepheard-Walwyn, 1991), pp. 313–315; Pollard, A. J., *North-Eastern England during the Wars of the Roses* (Oxford: Clarendon Press, 1990); Ross, Charles, *Edward IV* (New Haven, CT: Yale University Press, 1998).

Beaufort, Margaret, Countess of Richmond and Derby (1443–1509)

After RICHARD III's usurpation of the Crown revived dynastic strife in the mid-1480s, Margaret Beaufort, Countess of Richmond, worked secretly to ensure that her son, Henry Tudor, earl of Richmond, made good the BEAUFORT FAMILY's claim to the throne.

Margaret was the only child of John Beaufort, first duke of Somerset (1404–1444), who died when his daughter was little more than a year old. A wealthy heiress with a claim to the Crown, Margaret was only twelve when HENRY VI married her to his half brother Edmund TUDOR, earl of Richmond, in 1455. Three months after Richmond's death in November 1456, Margaret, now under the protection of her brother-in-law, Jasper TUDOR, earl of Pembroke, gave birth to a son named Henry. Seeking a husband who could protect her rights and those of her son, Margaret married Sir Henry Stafford, younger son of Humphrey STAFFORD, duke of Buckingham, in early 1458. However, after the Yorkist victory at the Battle of TOWTON in 1461, EDWARD IV granted the wardship of Henry Tudor, earl of Richmond, to Sir William HERBERT, Edward's chief supporter in WALES.

After the restoration of Henry VI in 1470, Margaret was reunited briefly with her son (see READEPTION). However, the deaths at

Lady Margaret Beaufort, the mother of Henry VII, transmitted to her son the Beaufort family's claim to the Crown. (National Portrait Gallery: NPG 551)

the Battle of TEWKESBURY of Prince EDWARD OF LANCASTER and Edmund BEAUFORT, fourth duke of Somerset, ended the direct male lines of both LANCASTER and Beaufort, and made Richmond the surviving holder of the Lancastrian claim to the Crown. To save himself from prison or worse, Richmond fled to BRITTANY with Pembroke, his Lancastrian uncle. After her husband died of wounds received at the Battle of BARNET, Margaret made peace with the Yorkists by marrying Thomas STANLEY, Lord Stanley, in 1472. Although she kept in contact with her son, Margaret, as the wife of Stanley, enjoyed the favor of Edward IV. In 1483, when Richard III usurped the throne of his nephew, EDWARD V, Margaret worked with Queen Elizabeth WOODVILLE to plan an uprising that would put their children, Richmond and ELIZABETH OF YORK, on the throne. The rebellion, which eventually encompassed Henry STAFFORD, duke of Buckingham, and therefore became known as BUCKINGHAM'S REBELLION, failed, and the PARLIAMENT of 1484 deprived Margaret of her lands, which

were given, along with custody of her person, to her husband. Although Stanley maintained a careful neutrality when Richmond invaded England in 1485, his growing sympathy for the earl allowed Margaret the freedom to again involve herself in the planning of her son's enterprise.

When Richmond achieved the throne as HENRY VII at the Battle of BOSWORTH FIELD in August 1485, Margaret withdrew from politics and thereafter came rarely to COURT. She continued, however, to have a strong influence on her son, for Henry never forgot that his right to the Crown came from his mother's family. Margaret devoted her later years to religion, separating from her husband before his death in 1504 and taking monastic vows. She also became a great patron of the universities, endowing the "Lady Margaret" chairs in divinity at Oxford and Cambridge in 1502. Margaret died in June 1509, two months after the death of Henry VII.

See also Tudor, House of, and other entries under Beaufort
Further Reading: Jones, Michael K., and Malcolm G. Underwood, *The King's Mother: Lady Margaret Beaufort, Countess of Richmond and Derby* (Cambridge: Cambridge University Press, 1992); Simon, Linda, *Of Virtue Rare: Margaret Beaufort, Matriarch of the House of Tudor* (Boston: Houghton Mifflin Company, 1982).

Beaumont, William, Lord Beaumont (1438–1507)

A staunch adherent of the house of LANCASTER, William Beaumont, Lord Beaumont, continued to resist Yorkist rule even after the destruction of the Lancastrian male line in 1471.

After his father John Beaumont, Lord Beaumont, died fighting for HENRY VI at the Battle of NORTHAMPTON in July 1460, William Beaumont was courted by the Yorkist regime and allowed to take possession of his family estates. However, he maintained his father's Lancastrian allegiance and in March 1461 fought against EDWARD IV at the Battle of TOWTON, where he was taken prisoner. In November, when Edward's first PAR-

LIAMENT included Beaumont in a bill of AT-TAINDER, the king pardoned him, but granted the Beaumont estates to William HASTINGS, Lord Hastings, and to John NEVILLE, Lord Montagu, both loyal Yorkists. Beaumont did not regain his lands until November 1470, when they were restored to him by the READEPTION government of Henry VI, whose leader, the former Yorkist Richard NEVILLE, earl of Warwick, was desirous of winning the support of all former Lancastrians.

Beaumont fought with Warwick at the Battle of BARNET in April 1471, escaping after that defeat into SCOTLAND with John de VERE, earl of Oxford. Although the death of Prince EDWARD OF LANCASTER at the Battle of TEWKESBURY on 4 May 1471 and the murder of his father, Henry VI, in the TOWER OF LONDON (see HENRY VI, MURDER OF) some weeks later seemed to end forever all hopes of a Lancastrian restoration, Beaumont and Oxford remained implacably hostile to the house of YORK.

In September 1473, they seized the small fortress on the island of St. Michael's Mount off the Cornish coast. Unable to do any real damage, Beaumont and Oxford were nonetheless sore irritants to a Yorkist government seeking to finally secure its hold on power. After a lengthy siege, the two lords surrendered in February 1474, and Beaumont remained in prison until after the fall of the house of York in 1485, when the new king, HENRY VII of the house of TUDOR, released him and restored him to his lands and titles.

In 1487, Beaumont suffered a mental breakdown that rendered him incapable of caring for himself and his property. Custody of Beaumont's estates was transferred to Oxford, who, in 1495, also received custody of Beaumont's person. Beaumont spent the rest of his life as Oxford's guest, dying at the earl's house in Essex in December 1507.

Further Reading: Gillingham, John, *The Wars of the Roses* (Baton Rouge: Louisiana State University Press, 1981); Ross, Charles, *Edward IV* (New Haven, CT: Yale University Press, 1998).

Bedford, Duchess of. *See* Jacquetta of Luxembourg, Duchess of Bedford

Bedford, Duke of. *See* Tudor, Jasper, Earl of Pembroke and Duke of Bedford

Berwick-on-Tweed

An important town and castle on the Anglo-Scottish border, Berwick served as a base for Lancastrian and Scottish raids into northern England in the 1460s, and remained a complicating factor in Anglo-Scottish relations throughout the WARS OF THE ROSES.

After the capture of HENRY VI at the Battle of NORTHAMPTON in July 1460, Queen MARGARET OF ANJOU and her son Prince EDWARD OF LANCASTER fled into SCOTLAND, where they were honorably received by the regency government of young JAMES III. In January 1461, after negotiations with Queen MARY OF GUELDRES, mother of the Scottish king and leader of his regency council, Margaret agreed to surrender Berwick to the Scots in return for Scottish military assistance against the Yorkists. The agreement was to be sealed by a marriage between the Prince of Wales and Mary, the sister of James III. Although the Yorkist victory at the Battle of TOWTON in March 1461 won the throne for EDWARD IV, the north of England remained loyal to Henry VI, and Edward was unable to prevent the Lancastrian surrender of Berwick to the Scots on 25 April 1461.

The loss of Berwick infuriated Edward IV, but he could do little about it beyond using Margaret's surrender of an English town as a PROPAGANDA weapon against the Lancastrians. Prince Edward's marriage to the Scottish princess never occurred, but a Scottish-held Berwick became an ideal staging point for repeated Lancastrian and Scottish military efforts, which kept northern England unsettled for most of the 1460s. Although the Lancastrian threat to the region ended with Edward IV's restoration in 1471, continued Scottish possession of Berwick irritated the Yorkist government, and Anglo-Scottish relations remained poor (see EDWARD IV, RESTORA-TION OF).

Having unsuccessfully besieged Berwick since the previous year, Edward IV concluded the Treaty of Fotheringhay with Alexander, duke of Albany, estranged brother of James III, in June 1482. In return for the surrender of Berwick and certain other concessions, Edward IV agreed to support Albany's claim to his brother's throne. In fulfillment of the treaty, Richard, duke of Gloucester (see RICHARD III), led a large army northward in July. The town of Berwick capitulated immediately, but the castle held out. Gloucester then invaded Scotland, where the political opposition to James III prevented any real resistance and allowed the duke to enter Edinburgh on 1 August. With no help coming from the Scottish king, the Berwick garrison surrendered the castle to Gloucester on 24 August 1482. After twenty-one years in Scottish hands, Berwick was once again an English town.

See also North of England and the Wars of the Roses
Further Reading: Haigh, Philip A., *The Military Campaigns of the Wars of the Roses* (Stroud, Gloucestershire, UK: Sutton Publishing, 1995); Macdougall, Norman, *James III: A Political Study* (Edinburgh: J. Donald, 1982); Nicholson, Ranald, *Scotland: The Later Middle Ages*, vol. 2 of *The Edinburgh History of Scotland* (New York: Barnes and Noble, 1974); Ross, Charles, *Richard III* (Berkeley: University of California Press, 1981).

Blacman, John. *See* "Compilation of the Meekness and Good Life of King Henry VI" (Blacman)

Blore Heath, Battle of (1459)

Fought on 23 September 1459 near the village of Mucklestone in northwestern Staffordshire, the Battle of Blore Heath initiated a period of open civil war that lasted until the Battle of TOWTON in March 1461.

In June 1459, Queen MARGARET OF ANJOU convened a Great Council at Coventry to consider charges of treason against Richard PLANTAGENET, duke of York, and

his chief allies Richard NEVILLE, earl of Salisbury, and Richard NEVILLE, earl of Warwick, all three of whom were excluded from the council summons. Seeking to repeat his success of 1455, when he had destroyed his enemies and taken custody of HENRY VI at the Battle of ST. ALBANS, York began raising an army and called the Nevilles to meet him with their own forces at Ludlow in southern Shropshire.

Warwick eluded Lancastrian efforts to intercept him and reached Ludlow with a contingent from the CALAIS garrison, but Salisbury, coming from his seat at Middleham Castle in Yorkshire, encountered a Lancastrian force under James TOUCHET, Lord Audley, on Blore Heath about halfway between the towns of Newcastle-under-Lyme and Market Drayton. Charged by the queen with arresting Salisbury and preventing his army from joining York's, Audley, who had the larger force, led two unsuccessful cavalry charges against the hastily entrenched Yorkist position in hopes of overrunning the enemy line and seizing Salisbury before he could withdraw. When Audley died in the second assault, the Lancastrian command fell to John Dudley, Lord Dudley.

Because almost no accounts of the battle have survived, the exact course of the fighting thereafter is unclear. Dudley seems to have dismounted some of his cavalry and brought them into action on foot. By late afternoon, after three or four hours of combat, the remaining Lancastrian cavalry, seeing their infantry give ground, left the field. This loss of expected cavalry support and the possible defection of some of its members to the Yorkists caused the Lancastrian line to break. In the flight and pursuit that followed, Lord Dudley was captured and various other Lancastrian gentlemen were killed. With two other Lancastrian armies still in the field, Salisbury quickly recalled his scattered force and resumed the march to Ludlow, which he reached without further incident.

See also Ludford Bridge, Battle of
Further Reading: Haigh, Philip A., *The Military Campaigns of the Wars of the Roses* (Stroud,

Gloucestershire, UK: Sutton Publishing, 1995); Swynnerton, Brian, and William Swinnerton, *The Battle of Blore Heath, 1459* (Nuneaton: Paddy Griffith Associates, 1995).

Blount, Walter, Lord Mountjoy (d. 1474)

Walter Blount, Lord Mountjoy, was a member of the loyal circle of nobles and gentlemen who supported EDWARD IV and the house of YORK throughout the WARS OF THE ROSES.

Born into a Derbyshire GENTRY family, Blount was a servant of Richard PLANTA-GENET, duke of York, in the 1450s, and probably fled to CALAIS in 1459 with York's son Edward, earl of March, and the duke's chief allies, Richard NEVILLE, earl of Salisbury, and his son Richard NEVILLE, earl of Warwick. In 1461, after York's death at the Battle of WAKE-FIELD, Blount fought for March, now Edward IV, at the Battle of TOWTON, where Blount was knighted. He was also rewarded with the treasurership of Calais in 1461 and the treasurership of England in 1464. In 1461, he was co-commander at the siege of Hammes, a Calais fortress that held out for HENRY VI until 1462. Raised to the peerage as Lord Mountjoy in 1465 and appointed to the royal COUNCIL, he had previously been allowed to marry the king's aunt, Anne, the dowager duchess of Buckingham. He was also granted lands formerly belonging to Thomas COURTENAY, the Lancastrian earl of Devon, who had died at Towton in 1461.

In 1468, the king appointed Mountjoy to command a campaign against FRANCE, although the expedition never sailed. In 1469, he was one of the first peers Edward summoned to his presence after the king freed himself from the custody of the rebellious Warwick; Mountjoy then accompanied Edward on his public reentry into LONDON. Mountjoy also rode with the king in March 1470 during the campaign that defeated Warwick's second coup attempt at the Battle of LOSECOTE FIELD. Upon Edward's flight to the continent in October 1470, Mountjoy was one of the Yorkist peers who was arrested and briefly imprisoned by the READEPTION government of Henry VI. Although soon released, he was dismissed from all his offices, including all commissions of the peace. Mountjoy rejoined Edward upon the king's return in the spring of 1471 and probably fought for the Yorkists at the Battles of BARNET and TEWKESBURY. His eldest son William died fighting for Edward IV at Barnet. Honored with a Garter Knighthood (i.e., membership in the highest order of English chivalry) in 1472, Mountjoy died in 1474.

See also Edward IV, Overthrow of; Edward IV, Restoration of; Peerage

Further Reading: Hicks, Michael, *Warwick the Kingmaker* (Oxford: Blackwell Publishers, 1998); Ross, Charles, *Edward IV* (New Haven, CT: Yale University Press, 1998).

Bones of 1674

The term "bones of 1674" refers to two skeletons found in the TOWER OF LONDON in 1674 and believed to be the remains of ED-WARD V and his younger brother, Richard PLANTAGENET, duke of York, who both disappeared in the Tower in 1483 during the last phase of the WARS OF THE ROSES. Examined by forensic experts in the twentieth century, the bones have become another element in the ongoing controversy over how and by whose hand the sons of EDWARD IV met their end.

In 1674, while engaged in clearing away some ruinous structures adjacent to the White Tower, workmen discovered a wooden chest at a depth of about ten feet under the bottom step of an old staircase. The chest contained the skeletons of two children, with the taller one lying on its back and the smaller one lying face down on top of it. Because the well-known account of the princes' murders in Sir Thomas More's *HISTORY OF KING RICHARD III* stated that the bodies were, at least initially, buried "at the stair foot, meetly deep in the ground" (More, p. 88), the skeletons were immediately assumed to be the sons of Edward IV. In 1678, Charles II commissioned Sir

Christopher Wren to design a marble urn to serve as a more fitting repository for royal remains. Thus encased, the bones were reinterred in Westminster Abbey in the Chapel of HENRY VII.

In 1933, the urn was opened, and the bones were examined by several medical experts. Their report, published in 1934, stated that the elder child stood about four feet ten inches tall and the younger about four feet six and a half inches. Although unable to determine the sex of the children, the examiners concluded from the development of the vertebrae and jawbones that the elder child was about twelve at the time of death and the younger about ten. Because these ages corresponded well with the ages of the princes in July 1483—Edward V and his brother would have been twelve years and eight months and nine years and eleven months, respectively—the examiners believed that death occurred in 1483 and that Henry VII, who had no access to the boys until August 1485, could therefore be absolved of any responsibility for their fate. The examiners also determined that the older child suffered from a painful and chronic infection of the lower jaw and that a discoloration of the facial bones of the elder child might indicate death by strangulation. In general, the 1934 report seemed to strengthen the argument that RICHARD III had murdered his nephews in 1483.

In the 1950s, when Richard III biographer Paul Murray Kendall submitted the findings of the original examination to a new team of experts, they concluded that the elder child might not be as old as originally thought and that the mark on the facial bones was not a bloodstain resulting from strangulation. Because of these new findings, and because the sex and overall age of the remains—the burial could have occurred well before or well after 1483—are uncertain, the Tower skeletons cannot be definitely identified as those of the princes, and their value in determining what happened to the princes remains problematic.

See also Princes in the Tower
Further Reading: Fields, Bertram, *Royal Blood: Richard III and the Mystery of the Princes* (New York:

Regan Books, 1998); Jenkins, Elizabeth, *The Princes in the Tower* (New York: Coward, McCann and Geoghegan, 1978); More, Sir Thomas, *The History of King Richard III and Selections from the English and Latin Poems,* edited by Richard S. Sylvester (New Haven, CT: Yale University Press, 1976); Pollard, A. J., *Richard III and the Princes in the Tower* (New York: St. Martin's Press, 1991); Weir, Alison, *The Princes in the Tower* (New York: Ballantine Books, 1992); Williamson, Audrey, *The Mystery of the Princes* (Chicago: Academy Chicago Publishers, 1986); see also the many materials on the fate of the princes available on the Richard III Society Web site at <http://www.r3.org/bookcase>.

Bonville, William, Lord Bonville (1393–1461)

Through his long and violent feud with Thomas COURTENAY, fifth earl of Devon, William Bonville, Lord Bonville, helped form the factions of rival nobles that ignited the WARS OF THE ROSES.

Born into a Devonshire gentry family, Bonville rose to local and national prominence through talent, ambition, and two shrewd marriages. He was knighted in about 1417 while serving in FRANCE under Henry V. In 1423, Bonville was sheriff of Devonshire and in 1424 he again fought in France. By the mid-1430s, Bonville was widely active in West Country government, serving as justice of the peace for various counties and sitting on numerous royal commissions. In the late 1430s, Bonville came into conflict with Devon, who perhaps saw Bonville's growing influence as a threat to the Courtenays' traditional dominance in the region, or who possibly had some grievance over land arising out of Bonville's 1427 marriage to his aunt. The dispute intensified in 1437 when Bonville obtained the lucrative office of steward of the royal Duchy of Cornwall. In 1438, Devon petitioned the king for the stewardship; HENRY VI, ignoring the previous grant to Bonville, assented to the request. Although the government sought to cancel Devon's appointment, violence quickly erupted in the West Country between the adherents of both men.

The COUNCIL intervened and imposed arbitration, but disorders continued until Bonville left for France in 1444 to become seneschal of Gascony. Returning to England in 1447, he was raised to the PEERAGE in 1449 as Lord Bonville of Chewton, a promotion that made Bonville an even greater threat to Devon. After 1450, the COURTENAY-BONVILLE FEUD merged into the national rivalry developing between the COURT party led by Edmund BEAUFORT, duke of Somerset, and the opposition faction led by Richard PLANTAGENET, duke of York. To counter Bonville's alliance with James BUTLER, earl of Wiltshire, another royalist courtier with interests in the West Country, Devon associated himself with York.

In 1451, Devon raised an army and besieged Bonville in Taunton Castle, but York intervened, and Bonville used his influence at court to escape without punishment for his role in the earlier disorders. With the support of the government, Bonville was predominant in the West Country until 1454, when the king's illness and the establishment of York's FIRST PROTECTORATE weakened the court party and strengthened Devon (see HENRY VI, ILLNESS OF). However, in 1455, York's alliance with the NEVILLE FAMILY alienated Devon, who drew closer to the king's party, while Bonville, having lost his old patrons Somerset and Wiltshire in the aftermath of the Battle of ST. ALBANS, sealed his new loyalty to the house of YORK by marrying his grandson to a daughter of Richard NEVILLE, earl of Salisbury, York's closest ally.

In the autumn of 1455, Devon and his sons launched an assault on Bonville's servants and property throughout the West Country. The Courtenays murdered NICHOLAS RADFORD for his association with Bonville, ransacked Bonville's residences, and robbed the homes of his supporters. On 15 December, Bonville, having gathered a large force of RETAINERS, was defeated by the Courtenays in a bloody battle at Clyst. However, Bonville retrieved his position by appealing to York, who was then in control of the government (see SECOND PROTECTORATE). Devon was imprisoned, and Bonville was restored to dominance in the West, his own transgressions being once more overlooked by the party in

power. The Courtenay-Bonville feud subsided after 1456, thanks in part to Devon's death in 1458 and to the aged Bonville's semiretirement from public life.

After the Lancastrian victory at the Battle of LUDFORD BRIDGE in 1459, Bonville muted his Yorkist allegiance, but rejoined the Yorkists after their victory at the Battle of NORTHAMPTON in 1460. Having escorted Henry VI to the Battle of ST. ALBANS in February 1461, Bonville stayed with him after the Yorkist defeat on the king's promise that he would not be harmed. But Queen MARGARET OF ANJOU, encouraged by Thomas COURTENAY, sixth earl of Devon, ignored her husband's pledge and ordered Bonville's execution.

Further Reading: Cherry, Martin, "The Struggle for Power in Mid-Fifteenth-Century Devonshire," in Ralph A. Griffiths, ed., *Patronage, the Crown and the Provinces in Later Medieval England* (Atlantic Highlands, NJ: Humanities Press, 1981), pp. 123–144; Griffiths, Ralph A., *The Reign of King Henry VI* (Berkeley: University of California Press, 1981); Storey, R. L., *The End of the House of Lancaster,* 2d ed. (Stroud, Gloucestershire, UK: Sutton Publishing, 1999).

Bonville-Courtenay Feud. *See* Courtenay-Bonville Feud

Booth, Lawrence, Archbishop of York (d. 1480)

Lawrence Booth (or Bothe) was the only bishop appointed under the house of LANCASTER to later secure ecclesiastical advancement and high political office under the house of YORK.

Educated at Cambridge, Booth obtained his first political office in March 1451, succeeding his half brother William Booth as MARGARET OF ANJOU's chancellor. In September 1456, he became keeper of the privy seal, his appointment signaling a general purge of Yorkist sympathizers from the government. In January 1457, the queen's influence won Booth appointment to the COUNCIL of Prince EDWARD OF LANCASTER, a body used by Margaret to encourage Lancastrian loyalty throughout the prince's lordships in Wales and Chester. In 1457, when the king nominated his confessor to be bishop of Durham, the queen instead promoted Booth for the office, which he duly obtained in September. At Durham, Booth supported the Lancastrian branch of the NEVILLE FAMILY, favoring its members over their Yorkist cousins for offices in his gift.

In October 1459, Booth swore loyalty to HENRY VI at the COVENTRY PARLIAMENT, where Queen Margaret attainted Richard PLANTAGENET, duke of York, and his allies; as a result of the ATTAINDER of Richard NEVILLE, earl of Warwick, Booth seized Barnard Castle, possession of which bishops of Durham had disputed with earls of Warwick since the thirteenth century. In 1460, Booth left the royal army before the Battle of NORTHAMPTON, and was shortly thereafter replaced as keeper of the privy seal by a Yorkist appointee, Bishop Robert STILLINGTON. In 1461, EDWARD IV tried to conciliate Booth by appointing him to a royal chaplaincy. The bishop responded in June by defeating a Lancastrian invasion force led out of SCOTLAND by Thomas ROOS, Lord Roos. However, Booth lost favor in December 1462, when he was suspended from office, perhaps for suspected dealings with Queen Margaret. Restored in April 1464, Booth spent the rest of the 1460s quietly administering his diocese.

Little is known of Booth's activities during the READEPTION in 1470–1471, but his rapid reemployment by Edward IV after the king's restoration in 1471 argues against any strong support for the Lancastrian regime (see EDWARD IV, RESTORATION OF). In 1473, Booth led an embassy to Scotland to conclude a treaty with JAMES III, whereby the future JAMES IV was to marry Edward's daughter Cecily. From July 1473 to May 1474, Booth served as chancellor of England, and in 1476 Edward nominated him for the archbishopric of York, the office earlier held by his half brother. Booth's elevation may have been partially due to Richard, duke of Gloucester (see RICHARD III), who found the bishop an ob-

stacle to his assumption of the influence once exercised across the north by Warwick. Booth died in May 1480.

See also North of England and the Wars of the Roses
Further Reading: Davies, Richard G., "The Church and the Wars of the Roses," in A. J. Pollard, ed., *The Wars of the Roses* (New York: St. Martin's Press, 1995), pp. 143–161; Griffiths, Ralph A., *The Reign of King Henry VI* (Berkeley: University of California Press, 1981); Reeves, A. Compton, "Lawrence Booth: Bishop of Durham (1457–76), Archbishop of York (1476–80)," in Sharon D. Michalove and A. Compton Reeves, eds., *Estrangement, Enterprise and Education in Fifteenth-Century England* (Stroud, Gloucestershire, UK: Sutton Publishing, 1998), pp. 63–88.

Bosworth Field, Battle of (1485)

Fought on 22 August 1485 near the Leicestershire village of Market Bosworth, the Battle of Bosworth Field overthrew the house of YORK and initiated the rule of the TUDOR dynasty.

By early 1485, RICHARD III knew that Henry Tudor, earl of Richmond (see Henry VII), the remaining Lancastrian claimant to the throne, intended to invade England. Not knowing where Richmond would land, the king based himself in Nottingham, from where he could strike quickly in any direction. On 1 August, Richmond, having finally persuaded the government of CHARLES VIII to back his enterprise, left FRANCE with a force of about 600 English exiles and about 2,000 French and Scottish MERCENARIES. Hoping to take advantage of his Welsh ancestry and the local influence of his uncle, Jasper TUDOR, earl of Pembroke, and anxious to contact his stepfather, Thomas STANLEY, Lord Stanley, whose base was in the northwest, Richmond landed in WALES at Milford Haven on 7 August.

The earl collected some reinforcements in Wales, but upon entering England at Shrewsbury received a message from Stanley that offered encouragement but no support. Suspicious of Stanley, who was the husband of Richmond's mother, Margaret BEAUFORT,

Richard had demanded that he leave his son, Lord Strange, as a hostage when he withdrew from COURT. Upon Richmond's landing, the king interrogated Strange, who confessed that his uncle, Sir William STANLEY, was plotting to join Richmond. In receipt of a letter from his son begging him to join Richard, Stanley remained cautiously aloof from both armies.

On 17 August, Richmond met with Sir William Stanley, whom Richard had denounced as a traitor. Three days later, the earl met both Stanleys, but, fearing for Strange's life, neither would openly join Richmond. Doubting the loyalty of some of his supporters, such as Henry PERCY, earl of Northumberland, and relying mainly on his trusted northern adherents, Richard marched west to the town of Sutton Cheney, which he reached on 21 August (see RICHARD III, NORTHERN AFFINITY OF). That same evening, Richmond camped about four miles away at a place called Whitemoors, while the Stanleys, with about 8,000 men between them, remained at a distance from both armies. Next morning, the king, who had the larger force, was on or near Ambien Hill, high ground above Richmond's position. As the two armies maneuvered for battle, the Stanleys arrived within sight of the field, but joined neither army, leaving both Richmond and the king to guess their intentions. After barrages of ARCHER and ARTILLERY fire, the two armies clashed, with John de VERE, earl of Oxford, leading Richmond's van, and John HOWARD, duke of Norfolk, commanding the royal van. Tradition placed the fighting on the slope of Ambien Hill, but recent research suggests that the battle occurred a half mile to the south in the plain between Ambien Hill and the village of Dadlington.

The course of the battle is also in doubt. Richmond, seeking to persuade Stanley to commit his forces, may have started toward his stepfather's position, thus providing the king an opportunity to catch and destroy his opponent in the open field. Or Richard, sensing that the Stanleys were about to join Richmond, may have decided to descend rapidly on either the earl or Stanley before this conjunction could occur. Whatever his thinking,

Richard led a charge of his mounted RETAINERS and became heavily engaged with Richmond's men, the king himself slaying the earl's standard-bearer, Sir William Brandon. Before Richard could bring his charge to a successful conclusion, Sir William Stanley's men overwhelmed his small retinue and the king was unhorsed and killed.

The death of Richard ended the fighting. Richmond was immediately proclaimed king as Henry VII, while Richard's body was slung on a horse and paraded naked through Leicester. Dead on the field were Norfolk, Sir Robert BRACKENBURY, and Sir Richard RATCLIFFE, all Yorkists, and 3,000 soldiers, mostly Yorkists. Three other Yorkists were taken prisoner—William CATESBY, who was executed several days later; Thomas HOWARD, earl of Surrey, Norfolk's son, who was imprisoned; and Northumberland, who was detained only briefly. Tradition says that Richard had entered battle wearing a gold circlet, which Stanley retrieved from beneath a hawthorn bush and placed on Henry's head. While possible, this story cannot be confirmed.

See also *The Ballad of Bosworth Field; The Rose of England; The Song of Lady Bessy*
Further Reading: Bennett, Michael, *The Battle of Bosworth* (New York: St. Martin's Press, 1985); Foss, Peter J., *The Field of Redemore: The Battle of Bosworth, 1485,* 2d ed. (Newtown Linford, UK: Kairos, 1998); Hammond, P. W., and Anne F. Sutton, *Richard III: The Road to Bosworth Field* (London: Constable, 1985); Rees, David, *The Son of Prophecy: Henry Tudor's Road to Bosworth,* 2d ed. (Ruthin, UK: John Jones, 1997); Richmond, Colin, "Bosworth Field and All That," in P. W. Hammond, ed., *Richard III: Loyalty, Lordship and Law* (London: Richard III and Yorkist History Trust, 1986); Rowse, A. L., *Bosworth Field* (Garden City, NY: Doubleday, 1966); Williams, D. T., *The Battle of Bosworth* (Leicester: Leicester University Press, 1973); see also the Richard III Society Web site at <http://www.r3.org> for various sources relating to the Battle of Bosworth Field.

Bourchier, Henry, Earl of Essex (d. 1483)

Although a political moderate who followed a general policy of reconciliation in the 1450s,

Henry Bourchier was, after 1460, a loyal supporter of the house of YORK.

A maternal half brother of Humphrey STAFFORD, duke of Buckingham, Bourchier was also married to the sister of Richard PLANTAGENET, duke of York. Bourchier traveled to CALAIS with HENRY VI in 1430, and served in FRANCE under York in the 1440s, winning appointment as captain of Crotoy in 1443. On 29 May 1455, only a week after York won custody of the king and control of the government at the Battle of ST. ALBANS, Henry VI appointed Bourchier lord treasurer, a post he continued to hold even after the dismissal of York's SECOND PROTECTORATE in February 1456. Despite their association with York, Bourchier and his brother Thomas BOURCHIER, archbishop of Canterbury, were still identified with Buckingham, their half sibling, as moderates not clearly attached to either the Yorkist or Lancastrian factions. Dismissed from office in October 1456, probably on the initiative of Queen MARGARET OF ANJOU, Bourchier and his brother, who was removed as chancellor, gradually drifted toward York.

By July 1460, when he fought with Richard NEVILLE, earl of Warwick, at the Battle of NORTHAMPTON, Bourchier was a declared partisan of York. In June 1461, three months after winning the throne at the Battle of TOWTON, EDWARD IV, York's son, created Bourchier earl of Essex, appointed him lord treasurer, and granted him numerous estates. Quietly acquiescing in the READEPTION of Henry VI in October 1470, Essex was among the first noblemen to raise troops for Edward IV upon the Yorkist king's return in the following spring (see EDWARD IV, RESTORATION OF). Essex also helped mediate the reconciliation of Edward with his brother, George PLANTAGENET, duke of Clarence. Reappointed lord treasurer after Edward's resumption of the throne in April 1471, Essex helped defeat the invasion of Cornwall launched by John de VERE, the Lancastrian earl of Oxford, in May 1473. Thereafter, Essex served loyally as lord treasurer until his death

on 4 April 1483, only days before Edward IV's own death.

Further Reading: Griffiths, Ralph A., *The Reign of King Henry VI* (Berkeley: University of California Press, 1981); Ross, Charles, *Edward IV* (New Haven, CT: Yale University Press, 1998); Wolffe, Bertram, *Henry VI* (London: Eyre Methuen, 1981).

Bourchier, Thomas, Cardinal Archbishop of Canterbury (c. 1404–1486)

As archbishop of Canterbury throughout the WARS OF THE ROSES, Cardinal Thomas Bourchier participated in most of the conflict's major events.

The brother of Henry BOURCHIER, earl of Essex, and half brother of Humphrey STAFFORD, duke of Buckingham, Bourchier was descended through his mother from Edward III (r. 1327–1377). As a third son, he was destined for an ecclesiastical career, and obtained his first clerical office in 1424. He became bishop of Worcester in 1434 and bishop of Ely in 1443. In 1454, during the FIRST PROTECTORATE of Richard PLANTAGENET, duke of York, Bourchier was appointed archbishop of Canterbury. Although his promotion owed much to York's influence, Bourchier was also acceptable to HENRY VI; in March 1455, after recovering his health and authority, the king named Bourchier chancellor of England. Following the Battle of ST. ALBANS in May 1455, Bourchier tried to act as a peacemaker, but was unsuccessful and resigned the chancellorship in October 1456. However, in March 1458, he worked closely with the king to promote the ultimately unsuccessful LOVE-DAY peace settlement.

In June 1460, when York's Neville allies returned from exile in CALAIS, Bourchier met them at their landing and followed them to LONDON, where he took their oaths of loyalty to Henry VI. The archbishop agreed to accompany the army of Richard NEVILLE, earl of Warwick, to try and arrange a settlement. The peace effort failed, and Warwick captured the king at the Battle of NORTH-

AMPTON. In the autumn, Bourchier participated in the PARLIAMENT that answered
York's demand for the Crown with the compromise Act of ACCORD, which left Henry
on the throne but disinherited Prince ED-
WARD OF LANCASTER in favor of the duke.
In March 1461, with York dead and Queen
MARGARET OF ANJOU's unruly army
threatening the capital (see MARCH ON
LONDON), Bourchier acquiesced in the elevation of York's son to the throne as EDWARD
IV. The archbishop formally crowned Edward
in the following June, and performed the like
ceremony for Queen Elizabeth WOODVILLE
in 1465.

In 1471, the archbishop raised troops to
support the restoration of Edward IV and
helped convince Edward's brother, George
PLANTAGENET, duke of Clarence, to abandon Warwick (see EDWARD IV, RESTORA-
TION OF). In 1473, the pope made Bourchier a cardinal in response to a royal
petition. In June 1483, two months after Edward's death, the archbishop led a delegation
to Westminster to persuade Queen Elizabeth
to release her second son, Richard PLANTA-
GENET, duke of York, from SANCTUARY
and into the keeping of her brother-in-law,
Richard, duke of Gloucester. Whether the
queen's acquiescence to this request was due
to Bourchier's entreaties or to Gloucester's
threats is now unclear. Most historians accept
that the archbishop was sincere in his guar-
antees of the boy's safety and that he was not
privy to Gloucester's plans to usurp the
throne from the duke's brother, EDWARD V.
Nonetheless, within weeks, Bourchier was
obliged to officiate at Gloucester's coronation as RICHARD III, and within months
both boys disappeared forever into the
TOWER OF LONDON. Whether as a result
of this experience the aging archbishop participated in the later conspiracies against
Richard III is uncertain (see BUCKING-
HAM'S REBELLION).

Bourchier closed his career by crowning
HENRY VII in October 1485 and by symboli-
cally uniting the houses of LANCASTER and
YORK by marrying Henry to ELIZABETH
OF YORK, daughter of Edward IV, in January
1486. Bourchier died in March 1486.

Further Reading: Davies, Richard G., "The
Church and the Wars of the Roses," in A. J.
Pollard, ed., *The Wars of the Roses* (New York: St.
Martin's Press, 1995), pp. 143–161; Ross, Charles,
Edward IV (New Haven, CT: Yale University
Press, 1998); Ross, Charles, *Richard III* (Berkeley:
University of California Press, 1981).

Brackenbury, Sir Robert (d. 1485)

A loyal supporter of RICHARD III during the
last phase of the civil wars (1483–1487), Sir
Robert Brackenbury had custody of the
TOWER OF LONDON during the confinement there in 1483 of EDWARD V and his
brother Richard PLANTAGENET, duke of
York.

The younger son of a minor GENTRY
family from Durham, Brackenbury became
treasurer of the duke of Gloucester's household in about 1476. Upon Gloucester's assumption of the throne as Richard III in July
1483, Brackenbury was given a lifetime appointment as constable of the Tower, a position of great trust, for it gave Brackenbury
charge of important royal prisoners and of
the royal mint. Although Brackenbury was a
northerner, Richard made him a power in
the key southern county of Kent, placing him
in charge of all royal manors in the southeast
and granting him the Kentish estates of Anthony WOODVILLE, Earl Rivers, and other
defeated opponents (see RICHARD III,
NORTHERN AFFINITY OF). In 1484, the
king knighted Brackenbury, appointed him
sheriff of Kent, and named him to the admi-
ralty commission. Invested with numerous
duties and offices, Brackenbury soon found it
necessary to exercise many by deputy. By
1485, Brackenbury's annual income from
royal service approached £500, a substantial
sum that made him one of the most heavily
rewarded of Richard's servants.

According to the account of the deaths of
EDWARD IV's sons in Sir Thomas More's
HISTORY OF KING RICHARD III, Richard
ordered Brackenbury to kill the princes, who

were in his charge as Tower prisoners. Brackenbury refused, but did comply with Richard's subsequent order to temporarily deliver the keys of the Tower to Sir James TYRELL, another highly favored royal servant, who then murdered the boys with the aid of several accomplices. Whether or not Brackenbury was involved in or aware of the murder of the princes is now unclear. What is certain is that he served Richard III loyally throughout his reign, actively assisting in the suppression of BUCKINGHAM'S REBELLION in 1483 and dying with Richard at the Battle of BOSWORTH FIELD in 1485.

See also Bones of 1674; North of England and the Wars of the Roses; Princes in the Tower
Further Reading: Horrox, Rosemary, *Richard III: A Study in Service* (Cambridge: Cambridge University Press, 1991); More, Sir Thomas, *The History of King Richard III and Selections from the English and Latin Poems,* edited by Richard S. Sylvester (New Haven, CT: Yale University Press, 1976); Ross, Charles, *Richard III* (Berkeley: University of California Press, 1981).

Bray, Sir Reginald (1440–1503)

Sir Reginald Bray played a vital role in organizing BUCKINGHAM'S REBELLION against RICHARD III during the last phase of the civil wars (1483–1487) and later became one of the most active and trusted ministers of HENRY VII.

Born into an ancient Hampshire family, Bray began his career as receiver-general for Sir Henry Stafford, second husband of Margaret BEAUFORT, mother of the future Henry VII. After Stafford's death in 1471, Bray continued to serve Lady Margaret as steward. In 1483, Bray acted as go-between for Margaret and John MORTON, bishop of Ely, who was then engaged in drawing his jailer, Henry STAFFORD, duke of Buckingham, into the conspiracy being formed to dethrone Richard III in favor of Margaret's son, Henry Tudor, earl of Richmond. Bray also raised much-needed funds for Richmond and won several key gentlemen to the earl's cause, including Giles Daubeney and Richard Guildford.

After the failure of Buckingham's Rebellion in October 1483, Bray was pardoned by Richard III, but continued to support Richmond and may have gone into exile with the earl in FRANCE. Knighted after the Battle of BOSWORTH FIELD in 1485, Bray was quickly named chancellor of the Duchy of Lancaster and knight of the body. Appointed a member of the COUNCIL, Bray held various financial and administrative positions, sat in numerous PARLIAMENTS, and served on over 100 commissions. Bray's record of loyal service to Margaret Beaufort made him a member of Henry VII's inner circle of advisors, especially in matters of finance. Bray was responsible for the financial provisions that made possible construction of Henry VII's chapel at Westminster and his renovations of St. George's chapel at Windsor. Bray died in August 1503.

Further Reading: Chrimes, S. B., *Henry VII* (New Haven, CT: Yale University Press, 1999); Gill, Louise, *Richard III and Buckingham's Rebellion* (Stroud, Gloucestershire, UK: Sutton Publishing, 1999); Guth, DeLloyd J., "Climbing the Civil-Service Pole during the Civil War: Sir Reynald Bray," in Sharon D. Michalove and A. Compton Reeves, eds., *Estrangement, Enterprise and Education in Fifteenth-Century England* (Stroud, Gloucestershire, UK: Sutton Publishing, 1998), pp. 47–62.

Brézé, Pierre de, Seneschal of Normandy (c. 1408–1465)

A friend of Queen MARGARET OF ANJOU, Pierre de Brézé, seneschal of Normandy, fought for the Lancastrians in the northern campaigns of the early 1460s.

A vassal of Margaret's father, de Brézé became one of the chief ministers and military commanders of CHARLES VII, and took part in the negotiations that led to Margaret's marriage to HENRY VI in 1445. The queen's connections with de Brézé led to rumors that Margaret had instigated the seneschal's raid on Sandwich in August 1457 to help her win her power struggle with Richard PLANTAGENET, duke of York. This charge has been dismissed by modern historians, but Margaret did appeal to de Brézé for French naval assistance in 1460 to prevent York's ally, Richard NEVILLE, earl of Warwick, from returning to England from his base at CALAIS. After the Lancastrian defeat at the Battle of TOWTON in March 1461, Charles VII allowed de Brézé, who had been advocating French support for the house of LANCASTER since 1459, to assemble a fleet and attack the English Channel Islands.

De Brézé seized Jersey in May, but the death of Charles VII in July ended the Seneschal's efforts on Margaret's behalf, for LOUIS XI, the new French king, stripped de Brézé of his offices and imprisoned him in Loches Castle. Never on good terms with his father, Louis distrusted de Brézé for his past loyalty to Charles. In April 1462, Margaret secured de Brézé's release as part of the Franco-Lancastrian CHINON AGREEMENT, whereby Louis lent money to the queen in return for her surrender of Calais. Although Louis's enthusiasm for the alliance faded when the Burgundians denied him access to Calais, he allowed de Brézé to accompany Margaret and her son Prince EDWARD OF LANCASTER to SCOTLAND in October. Commanding 800 French troops in his own pay, the seneschal and the Lancastrian royal family landed near BAMBURGH CASTLE in Northumberland on 25 October. Although Bamburgh and the neighboring castles of ALNWICK and DUNSTANBURGH quickly submitted to Henry VI, Margaret and de Brézé, believing themselves too weak to face the army EDWARD IV was bringing against them, retreated to Scotland in November. The royal family and de Brézé arrived safely in BERWICK only after a local fisherman rescued them from their foundering vessel. De Brézé's troops were less fortunate, being forced ashore on Lindisfarne, where most were killed or captured by the local inhabitants.

In January 1463, de Brézé and the Scottish earl of Angus led a mainly Scots force that surprised Warwick as he besieged the Lancastrian garrison in Alnwick Castle. Perhaps unwilling to give battle because of the low morale of his troops, Warwick allowed the garrison to withdraw into Scotland with de Brézé's army. In June, de Brézé returned to England as part of a Scottish invasion force that included not only Henry VI and Queen Margaret, but also JAMES III of Scotland and his mother MARY OF GUELDRES. The invaders besieged Norham Castle until surprised by a Yorkist force under Warwick and his brother John NEVILLE, Lord Montagu. The Scots army disintegrated in panic, and de Brézé, Margaret, and Prince Edward escaped to Berwick, while Henry VI fled into Scotland. In early August, de Brézé accompanied Margaret and the prince to FRANCE. Restored to his offices in 1464, de Brézé was killed while leading Louis XI's forces against the Burgundians at the Battle of Montlhéry in July 1465.

Further Reading: Haigh, Philip A., *The Military Campaigns of the Wars of the Roses* (Stroud, Gloucestershire, UK: Sutton Publishing, 1995); Kendall, Paul Murray, *Louis XI* (New York: W. W. Norton, 1971); Vale, M. G. A., *Charles VII* (Berkeley: University of California Press, 1974).

Brittany

As a potential ally with naval resources, and, after 1471, as the place of exile for Henry Tudor, earl of Richmond (see HENRY VII), the last royal claimant of the house of LANCASTER, the French Duchy of Brittany played an important role in the WARS OF THE ROSES.

Although FRANCIS II, duke of Brittany from 1458 to 1488, held his title of the king of FRANCE, the duchy in the fifteenth century was an independent state, with its own administrative and ecclesiastical structure and its own legislative and judicial bodies. Breton dukes had achieved political autonomy by playing off the French against the English during the HUNDRED YEARS WAR. Breton independence served English interests, for a French Brittany threatened English security. Lying across the Channel from England, the Breton peninsula had a long coastline, and the duchy was strong in ships and experienced seamen; in French hands, Brittany was a potential base for invading England. Alternatively, England could employ an autonomous Brittany to trouble France in the same way France encouraged SCOTLAND to threaten England, while the Breton fleet was a useful addition to any anti-French alliance.

To maintain Breton independence from France, Francis sought to establish close relations with England and BURGUNDY without unnecessarily alienating the French. Thus, in the early 1460s, Francis, following his own inclinations and the lead of LOUIS XI, provided assistance to Lancastrian exiles within his borders, such as Jasper TUDOR, earl of Pembroke. However, in 1465, Francis took Brittany into the League of the Public Weal, a coalition of French princes led by CHARLES of Burgundy that forced Louis to concede privileges and territories. By 1468, growing threats of French invasion and a thriving trade with England persuaded Francis to conclude formal treaties of commerce and alliance with EDWARD IV. In 1471, Channel storms drove Pembroke and his nephew Richmond, the last Lancastrian claimant of consequence, onto the Breton coast. This literal windfall provided Francis with the means for pressuring Edward IV, now secure on his throne, into maintaining English support for Brittany.

In 1472, Edward sent English ARCHERS under Anthony WOODVILLE, Earl Rivers, to help the Bretons repel a French invasion; in 1480, Edward betrothed his son (see EDWARD V), to Francis's only child, Anne. In 1483, after RICHARD III destabilized English politics by usurping his nephew's throne, Richmond, who was kept in increasingly rigorous confinement, became a serious threat to the house of YORK. Because Richard was too insecure to materially assist Brittany, Francis provided Richmond with men and ships and allowed him to join BUCKINGHAM'S REBELLION in October 1483. After the failure of that uprising, a band of English exiles formed around Richmond in Brittany, and the pro-English faction at the Breton court, led by Pierre LANDAIS, the treasurer, used the duke's illness to secretly negotiate with Richard for Richmond's surrender. Warned of the plot by Bishop John MORTON, Richmond and his followers fled into France, from where they launched a successful invasion of England in 1485.

Francis II died in 1488 in the midst of a French invasion that only ended in 1491 with the conclusion of a marriage treaty between Duchess Anne and CHARLES VIII. Because the settlement laid out terms for Brittany's incorporation into France, Henry VII led an English army to Anne's assistance in 1492. However, the invasion ended in the Treaty of Etaples, whereby Henry acquiesced in the takeover of Brittany in return for a French pension and an agreement to expel Perkin WARBECK and other Yorkist pretenders from France. Although the Breton Estates (a legislative assembly) did not formally vote for perpetual union with France until 1532, the duchy was effectively under French control after 1491.

See also Urswick, Christopher
Further Reading: Davies, C. S. L., "The Wars of the Roses in European Context" in A. J. Pollard, ed., *The Wars of the Roses* (New York: St. Martin's Press, 1995), pp. 162–185; Galliou, Patrick, and Michael Jones, *The Bretons* (Oxford: Basil Blackwell, 1991); Jones, Michael, *The Creation of Brittany: A Late Medieval State* (London: Hambledon, 1988).

Brittany, Duke of. *See* Francis II, Duke of Brittany

Buckingham, Duke of. *See* entries under Stafford

Buckingham's Rebellion (1483)

Buckingham's Rebellion is the name given to a series of uprisings that occurred in England in the autumn of 1483 in reaction to RICHARD III's seizure of his nephew's throne, to the disappearance of that nephew and his brother, and to the growing belief that both boys were dead.

Buckingham's Rebellion comprised two independently organized conspiracies against Richard III that, despite some incompatibilities of purpose, joined together to achieve their shared goal of overthrowing the king. The first conspiracy was planned and led by

Henry STAFFORD, duke of Buckingham, heretofore Richard's chief ally. The exact reasons for Buckingham's desertion of the king he had helped to make are unclear. The traditional reason, used by William Shakespeare in his play *RICHARD III,* is the king's refusal to keep a promise to restore to Buckingham certain lands to which he had a claim. Most modern historians discount this theory, for Richard restored the lands in question in July 1483. More likely theories are that Buckingham, aware of the ruthless methods Richard was willing to use to hold power, and perhaps aware of the fate of EDWARD V and his brother, Richard PLANTAGENET, duke of York, feared that Richard would turn on him whenever it suited the king's purposes. Buckingham may also have been driven by ambition, for along with Richard III and the exiled Henry Tudor, earl of Richmond (see HENRY VII), the duke was one of only three surviving adult males of the royal house of PLANTAGENET. If Richard were eliminated, the throne would be Buckingham's.

Hatched probably at Brecon Castle in August and September 1483, the duke's plot was encouraged by Bishop John MORTON, who had been arrested by Richard and placed in Buckingham's custody. In his *HISTORY OF KING RICHARD III,* Sir Thomas More claimed that Morton persuaded the duke to betray Richard, but in his *ANGLICA HISTORIA,* the Tudor historian Polydore Vergil stated that Buckingham first suggested rebellion to the bishop, who initially suspected that the suggestion was a ruse to entrap him. However, once convinced of Buckingham's sincerity, Morton readily cooperated. Morton probably put Buckingham in contact with Margaret BEAUFORT, the mother of Richmond, and with Queen Elizabeth WOODVILLE, the widow of EDWARD IV and the mother of the missing princes. The two women were the central figures in a conspiracy that was forming around former Lancastrians, adherents of the WOODVILLE FAMILY, and former servants of Edward IV. Assuming that Queen Elizabeth's sons were dead, these plotters planned to overthrow Richard in favor of Richmond, who would then marry ELIZABETH OF YORK, eldest daughter of Edward IV, and thereby unite the houses of LANCASTER and YORK.

On 24 September, Buckingham wrote to Richmond, then in BRITTANY, inviting the earl to join his uprising, which would begin on 18 October. The duke did not acknowledge Richmond's claim to the Crown, nor did he speak of the proposed marriage with Elizabeth of York. Although later Tudor writers claimed that Buckingham supported the effort to make Richmond king, it is more likely that he sought the throne for himself. In September 1483, he was probably interested only in gaining the support of the pro-Richmond forces in overthrowing the king and was willing to leave the question of who was to be Richard's successor until later. In any event, a series of connections were soon established between the principal figures in both plots. The Welsh physician Lewis Caerleon was the main contact between Margaret Beaufort and Queen Elizabeth, while Reginald BRAY, a servant of Margaret's who was known to Buckingham, kept the Beaufort-Woodville conspirators apprised of what the duke and Morton were planning. To inform her son of events in England, Margaret had planned to send the priest Christopher URSWICK to Brittany, but instead later dispatched Hugh Conway (a servant of her husband, Henry STANLEY, Lord Stanley) to Richmond with a large sum of money raised by Margaret in LONDON.

Thanks to spies and the premature outbreak of rebellion in southern England, Richard was aware of Buckingham's betrayal by 11 October. While the king hastily gathered an army, Buckingham marshaled his forces in WALES, and various gentlemen attached to the Beaufort-Woodville conspiracy led uprisings in their home counties. Hampered by the disloyalty of his Welsh RETAINERS, who were unwilling to rebel against a Yorkist king, and attacked by Welsh royalists, Buckingham was on the run by late October. Most of the other uprisings were also quickly suppressed, their leaders fleeing to Brittany to join Richmond. Betrayed by an old servant with whom he had sought shelter, Buckingham was in custody by 31 October. Taken to Salisbury by Richard's servant, Sir James TYRELL, the duke was executed there on 2 November.

Richmond, meanwhile, did not leave Brittany until about 31 October. Given ships, money, and men by Duke FRANCIS II, the earl anchored off Plymouth harbor in the first week of November, his fleet having been scattered by storms. Unsure of what success Buckingham might have enjoyed, Richmond sent a boat to reconnoitre the coast, which was lined by Richard's men, who urged Richmond to land by claiming to be followers of Buckingham. Exercising a lifesaving caution, Richmond refused to come ashore until he had more certain news. When word arrived of Buckingham's execution, the earl and his flotilla recrossed the Channel, landing in FRANCE in mid-November. Although seeming to harm Richmond's prospects, Buckingham's Rebellion revealed the breadth of the opposition to Richard III, destroyed the rival claim of Buckingham, and created a large and talented group of exiles around Richmond in Brittany—such men as Morton, Urswick, Bray, and many former servants of Edward IV. By 1485, Richmond was ready to try again to win the throne.

Further Reading: Gill, Louise, *Richard III and Buckingham's Rebellion* (Stroud, Gloucestershire, UK: Sutton Publishing, 1999); Horrox, Rosemary, *Richard III: A Study in Service* (Cambridge: Cambridge University Press, 1991).

Burgundy

Burgundy was the wealthiest and most powerful state in fifteenth-century Europe. During the WARS OF THE ROSES, the principality was the chief rival of FRANCE, and thus always a possible ally for whichever English faction lacked French support. Burgundy was also England's chief trading partner and an important influence on English art, music, and COURT ceremonial during the Yorkist and early Tudor periods.

Burgundy comprised a patchwork of territories stretching from the English Channel to western Germany. The heart of the principality was the Duchy of Burgundy, an appanage (territorial grant to a younger son) in northeastern France given by John II to his son Philip the Bold in 1363. By marriage, Philip also acquired the County of Burgundy (Franche-Comté), which lay east of the duchy in the Holy Roman Empire, and the County of Flanders, which lay across the Channel from England. In the fifteenth century, Philip's successors became rulers of Luxembourg, most of the modern states of Belgium and the Netherlands, and parts of northern France. Because each province jealously guarded its own laws, privileges, and language, Burgundy's Valois dukes had difficulty imposing a centralized administration on their far-flung territories. However, by the early fifteenth century, the dukes of Burgundy were effectively independent of either the king of France or the Holy Roman Emperor.

In 1419, while contending for control of the French government during the rule of his deranged cousin Charles VI, Duke John the Fearless (1371–1419) was murdered by servants of the future CHARLES VII. This act drove the new duke, PHILIP the Good (1396–1467), into an alliance with Henry V that allowed the English to seal their conquest of Normandy and portions of northern France. Although he broke with the English in 1435, Philip remained at odds with his royal cousin. Thus, when Charles VII and his son LOUIS XI supported the house of LANCASTER in the early 1460s, Philip assisted the house of YORK, pressing his kinswoman, Queen MARY OF GUELDRES, to deny the Lancastrians asylum in SCOTLAND, sending Burgundian handgunners to fight for EDWARD IV at the Battle of TOWTON, and nullifying the Franco-Lancastrian CHINON AGREEMENT by refusing French troops permission to attack CALAIS across Burgundian territory. Although wary of any permanent ties with the insecure Edward IV and involved in commercial disputes with the English government, Philip, by his death in 1467, was being drawn into alliance with the house of York by a mutual distrust of France and the vital Anglo–Burgundian trade relationship.

Philip's son, CHARLES the Bold (1433–1477), having inherited Lancastrian blood from his Portuguese mother, was personally inclined to the cause of HENRY VI. However, being more anti-French than his father, Charles concluded a commercial agreement with Yorkist England in 1467 and a formal alliance in 1468, the latter sealed by the duke's marriage to MARGARET OF YORK, Edward IV's sister. This Burgundian connection was one of the grievances of Richard NEVILLE, the pro-French earl of Warwick, who overthrew Edward in 1470 (see EDWARD IV, OVERTHROW OF). The ANGERS AGREEMENT of 1470, which created Warwick's alliance with MARGARET OF ANJOU and the house of Lancaster, was brokered by Louis XI, who won Warwick's promise that a Lancastrian England would wage war against Burgundy as France's ally. When Warwick fulfilled his promise in January 1471, Charles dropped his refusal to assist Edward IV, who had fled to Burgundy the previous October, and allowed Edward to obtain men, money, and ships for the March 1471 invasion of England that ultimately restored him to power (see EDWARD IV, RESTORATION OF).

In the 1470s, Burgundian cultural influences permeated Yorkist England; Edward IV adopted the elaborate ceremony of the Burgundian court, and English music, art, and architectural design borrowed heavily from Burgundian developments. By 1475, Charles, seeking to establish a Kingdom of Burgundy between France and the empire, began forcibly expanding his domains in the east. When the duke died in battle against the Swiss in 1477, Burgundy passed to his only child, Mary, whose husband, Maximilian of Habsburg, heir to the Holy Roman Emperor, contended with Louis XI for control of the principality. The Duchy of Burgundy was reabsorbed into the French state, and the county returned to imperial control, but the Netherlands remained in Habsburg hands and continued its diplomatic and commercial part-

nership with England. Also, from 1485 until her death in 1503, Duchess Margaret remained hostile to HENRY VII and the house of TUDOR and gave valuable assistance to numerous Yorkist pretenders, including both Lambert SIMNEL and Perkin WARBECK.

> **See also** Yorkist Heirs (after 1485)
> **Further Reading:** Davies, C. S. L., "The Wars of the Roses in European Context" in A. J. Pollard, ed., *The Wars of the Roses* (New York: St. Martin's Press, 1995), pp. 162–185; Vaughan, Richard, *Valois Burgundy* (Hamden, CT: Archon Books, 1975).

Burgundy, Duke of. *See* Charles, Duke of Burgundy; Philip, Duke of Burgundy

Butler, James, Earl of Wiltshire and Ormond (1420–1461)

James Butler, the Irish earl of Ormond, was one of the most ambitious and politically disruptive favorites of HENRY VI, and a committed adherent of the House of LANCASTER.

Although several times lord lieutenant of IRELAND, Butler spent most of his career in England, where he built a substantial body of estates through marriage, inheritance, and royal favor. Created earl of Wiltshire in 1449, Butler's attempt to increase his political influence in the West Country, challenged the traditional dominance there of the earls of Devon and aggravated the violent feud between Thomas COURTENAY, earl of Devon, and William BONVILLE, Lord Bonville, another royal favorite. By the early 1450s, Butler was strongly identified with the COURT and with opposition to Richard PLANTAGENET, duke of York.

Knighted in 1426, Butler accompanied Henry VI to FRANCE, and served there again during York's French regency in 1441. He was York's deputy in Ireland in 1449, but supplanted York as lord lieutenant in 1453, by which time he was also a royal councilor. He succeeded his father as earl of Ormond in 1452. In 1454, during York's FIRST PROTECTORATE, Ormond lost the Irish lieutenancy and was briefly imprisoned for his role in the worsening COURTENAY-BONVILLE FEUD. Upon regaining his senses in early 1455, Henry VI restored Ormond to favor and appointed him lord treasurer. Part of the king's army at the Battle of ST. ALBANS, Ormond is said to have saved himself by fleeing the field disguised as a monk. York's SECOND PROTECTORATE cost Ormond the treasurership, but the king's resumption of power in 1456 led to the earl's appointment as councilor to Prince EDWARD OF LANCASTER in 1457 and to reappointment as lord lieutenant of Ireland in 1459.

When the Yorkist earls of Warwick, Salisbury, and March landed in England in the summer of 1460, Ormond fled abroad, but returned by December to take part in the Lancastrian victory at the Battle of WAKEFIELD, which led to the defeat and death of York. Demonstrating a pronounced ability to survive, Ormond twice more escaped from Lancastrian defeats—at the Battle of MORTIMER'S CROSS in February 1461 and at the Battle of TOWTON in March. The Yorkists finally captured him at Cockermouth in Cumberland in the month after Towton, and executed him at Newcastle on 1 May 1461. He and his brothers were attainted by EDWARD IV's first PARLIAMENT, although his brother John eventually succeeded to the earldom of Ormond. Because Ormond was childless, his earldom of Wiltshire lapsed at his death.

See also Attainder, Act of; Neville, Richard, Earl of Warwick; Neville, Richard, Earl of Salisbury **Further Reading:** Griffiths, Ralph A., *The Reign of King Henry VI* (Berkeley: University of California Press, 1981); "James Butler" in Michael Hicks, *Who's Who in Late Medieval England* (London: Shepheard-Walwyn, 1991), pp. 301–303; Storey, R. L., *The End of the House of Lancaster*, 2d ed. (Gloucestershire: Sutton Publishing, 1999).

Butler Precontract (1483)

The Butler precontract, the claim that EDWARD IV was betrothed to Lady Eleanor Butler prior to his marriage to Elizabeth WOODVILLE, was used by RICHARD III in 1483 to justify his usurpation of his nephew's throne, an act that revived the WARS OF THE ROSES in the mid-1480s.

In June 1483, Robert STILLINGTON, bishop of Bath and Wells and former chancellor of England under Edward IV, informed the duke of Gloucester that EDWARD V was a bastard and therefore not legally qualified to rule. According to the bishop, Edward V's illegitimacy resulted from a legally and spiritually binding betrothal or precontract of marriage that Edward IV had entered into with another woman some time before his 1464 marriage to Elizabeth Woodville. This exchange of vows with Eleanor Butler, widow of Sir Thomas Butler and daughter of John Talbot, earl of Shrewsbury, was unknown until Stillington supposedly divulged it to Gloucester. Because the precontract meant that Edward was considered already married by church and state, the Woodville union was invalid, and all children born to it were illegitimate and thereby barred from the throne. Immediately after Stillington's revelation, the precontract story appeared in a petition asking Gloucester to take the throne; this document, which was presented to the duke by his supporters in late June 1483, was later embodied in *TITULUS REGIUS,* the 1484 statute that formally presented Richard III's reasons for accepting the Crown.

The authenticity of the Butler story is much in doubt. Most modern historians believe the precontract to be a fabrication devised to give Richard III's usurpation a veneer of legitimacy. The betrothal cannot be documented beyond the account rehearsed in *Titulus Regius,* and Richard never attempted to have the precontract authenticated by a church court, the proper venue for such a case. The timing of the story's appearance—after the death of both parties and just in time to forestall Edward V's coronation—is suspicious, as is the fact that the tale never surfaced in the PROPAGANDA of Edward IV's former enemies. It is unlikely that either Queen MARGARET OF ANJOU or Richard NEVILLE, earl of Warwick, would have ignored the story had they known of it. Also, even if the story were true, the precontract would have barred neither Edward V nor his brother, Richard PLANTAGENET, duke of York, from the

Crown, since both were born after 1468, when the death of Eleanor Butler would have invalidated the betrothal. Many contemporary writers also rejected the precontract story, including the normally pro-Yorkist CROYLAND chronicler, who considered the Butler betrothal "colour" for an "act of usurpation" (Levine, p. 30).

Modern supporters of Richard III accept the Butler precontract as genuine, arguing that the exchange of vows may have occurred shortly after Edward's seizure of the throne in 1461, when Eleanor Butler was newly widowed and seeking (successfully, as it turned out) to regain family manors confiscated by the Crown. The story of the beautiful older widow in distress who contrived to meet the young king, a tale often told of Edward's first encounter with Elizabeth Woodville, may actually have been a memory of his first meeting with Eleanor Butler. Supporters of Richard also argue that Stillington's arrest in 1478, when he was fined for speaking in a manner prejudicial to the king, was a result of the bishop having once incautiously told the recently executed George PLANTAGENET, duke of Clarence, of the precontract. Although these arguments are often dismissed as unsupported speculation, the truth of the Butler precontract cannot now be conclusively determined.

See also English Church and the Wars of the Roses

Further Reading: Kendall, Paul Murray, *Richard the Third* (New York: W. W. Norton, 1956); Levine, Mortimer, *Tudor Dynastic Problems 1460–1571* (London: George Allen and Unwin, 1973); Ross, Charles, *Richard III* (Berkeley: University of California Press, 1981).

Cade, Jack. *See* Jack Cade's Rebellion

Cade's Rebellion. *See* Jack Cade's Rebellion

Caister Castle, Siege of (1469)

In July 1469, Richard NEVILLE, earl of Warwick, seized control of the royal government by capturing and confining EDWARD IV. The king's detention created a leadership vacuum that allowed great noblemen to act as they pleased in their areas of influence. Because it is described in detail in the PASTON LETTERS, the siege of Caister Castle in Norfolk is the best-known consequence of the local lawlessness that flowed from Warwick's coup. The violence at Caister is a prime example of the disorder that afflicted some parts of the country during the WARS OF THE ROSES.

On 21 August 1469, less than a month after Warwick took the king into custody, John MOWBRAY, fourth duke of Norfolk, laid siege to Caister Castle, a fortified manor house in the possession of a Norfolk GENTRY family named Paston. Since 1459, Norfolk's family had disputed possession of the house with the Pastons, who claimed it by right of inheritance from Caister's wealthy builder, Sir John Fastolf. John MOWBRAY, the third duke of Norfolk, had contested Fastolf's will and briefly held Caister in 1461, until compelled by Edward to restore it to the Pastons. The two families continued the dispute in the courts until the fourth duke took advantage of royal weakness to resolve the issue by force.

Sir John Paston, the head of his family in 1469, was in LONDON when his younger brother, also named John, found himself surrounded at Caister by a force said to number 3,000. With only twenty-seven defenders armed with crossbows and a few small guns, Paston was able to hold out for five weeks against the duke's ARCHERS and ARTILLERY pieces. Although everyone was anxious to avoid bloodshed and damage to the house, the duke lost two men and Paston one. The elder Paston appealed to George PLANTAGENET, duke of Clarence, the king's brother and Warwick's ally, to help mediate a settlement. Thanks to Clarence's intervention, Norfolk agreed to terms of surrender on 26 September, several weeks before the disorders in the kingdom (like the Caister siege) forced Warwick to release the king. Paston marched his men out of the house under a safe-conduct that allowed them to keep their ARMOR and horses, but forced them to abandon their arms, the castle's furnishings, and all Sir John Paston's private possessions.

Because he needed Norfolk's support, Edward IV failed to bring the duke to account for the siege. As a consequence, the Pastons became retainers of John de VERE, the Lancastrian earl of Oxford, and, in 1470, supported the restoration of HENRY VI; both brothers fought for Warwick at the Battle of BARNET in 1471. However, Edward IV's victory ensured that Caister, which had been briefly returned to the Pastons during the READEPTION, remained in Norfolk's possession until his death in 1476.

See also Edward IV, Overthrow of; Edward IV, Restoration of
Further Reading: Bennett, H. S., *The Pastons and Their England: Studies in an Age of Transition*, 2d ed. (Cambridge: Cambridge University Press, 1990);

Davis, Norman, ed., *The Paston Letters and Papers of the Fifteenth Century,* 2 vols. (Oxford: Oxford University Press, 1971, 1976); Gies, Frances, and Joseph Gies, *A Medieval Family: The Pastons of Fifteenth-Century England* (New York: HarperCollins, 1998).

Calais

An English possession since 1347, the French Channel town of Calais was of immense military importance during the WARS OF THE ROSES. Whoever held Calais controlled the town's 1,000-man garrison, the largest permanent military establishment under the English Crown, and also possessed a secure, fortified base and refuge from which it was possible to prey on Channel shipping or harry the coasts of England.

By 1453, Calais was all that remained of the English empire in FRANCE. Maintenance of the town's garrison and fortifications was expensive, consuming almost a quarter of the Crown's annual revenues by the 1450s. Since 1363, the government had funneled the export of English wool through Calais; this practice allowed the Crown to collect customs duties more easily and concentrated the wool trade in the hands of the Company of the Staple, an association of wool merchants whose privileged position made them more willing to lend money to the king. Although the government used the Calais customs to pay the garrison, the fifteenth century witnessed a decline in the export of raw wool in relation to the export of woolen cloth. Because cloth merchants could trade where they pleased, the subsequent drop in the wool customs created a gap between revenues and expenses in Calais. Frequently unable to make up the difference, the government of HENRY VI faced recurring mutinies by the unpaid garrison.

Edmund BEAUFORT, duke of Somerset, became captain of Calais in 1451. In 1454, after Somerset's imprisonment and the establishment of the FIRST PROTECTORATE, nominal control of Calais passed to Richard PLANTAGENET, duke of York. However, the garrison denied York entry to the town until they were paid or given license to sell the wool in their custody. Occupied elsewhere, York never addressed the Calais issue, and the garrison remained defiant when Henry regained his senses and restored Somerset to the captaincy in 1455. After Somerset's death at the Battle of ST. ALBANS in May 1455, York instituted his SECOND PROTECTORATE and handed the Calais captaincy to Richard NEVILLE, earl of Warwick. The earl finally entered the town in 1456 after negotiating a loan from the Staplers that allowed the garrison to be paid. By 1458, Queen MARGARET OF ANJOU, then in control of the English government, sought to undermine Warwick by denying him funds. The earl promptly built a fleet of ten vessels and began plundering foreign shipping in the Channel; his exploits paid his men, won him a heroic national reputation, and deeply embarrassed the Lancastrian regime.

Summoned to LONDON, Warwick was attacked by royal guards during a fight between his servants and those of the king. He escaped and returned to Calais, where he openly defied the government. In September 1459, the earl took part of the Calais garrison to England to rendezvous with York's forces at Ludlow. Led by Andrew TROLLOPE, the Calais contingent defected to the king, forcing the Yorkists to flee the Battle of LUDFORD BRIDGE. Warwick; his father, Richard NEVILLE, earl of Salisbury; and York's son, Edward, earl of March (see EDWARD IV) took refuge in Calais. Appointed captain by Queen Margaret, Henry BEAUFORT, duke of Somerset, captured the Calais fortress of Guisnes, but failed to take the town. Swayed both by his reputation and by the fruits of his Channel piracy, the garrison remained loyal to Warwick. In January 1460, Warwick's Calais fleet captured a Lancastrian flotilla in preparation at Sandwich, carrying off Richard WOODVILLE, Earl Rivers, and his son. In June, after returning from a conference with York in IRELAND, Warwick sent John DINHAM to seize Sandwich; possession of the town gave the Yorkists the bridgehead they needed to invade England from Calais and allowed Warwick to capture the king at the Battle of NORTH-

AMPTON in July. By depriving him of any possible assistance from England, Northampton forced Somerset to surrender Guisnes in return for his own freedom. Calais was thus secured for Warwick.

After 1461, Edward IV, realizing Calais's importance, spent heavily to modernize the town's defenses. As part of the 1462 CHINON AGREEMENT, Queen Margaret agreed to cede Calais to LOUIS XI in return for French assistance. The plan collapsed when Louis, who had to seize the town from the Yorkists, was denied access to Calais by Duke PHILIP of BURGUNDY, whose territory bordered the English enclave. In 1469, Warwick, who retained the captaincy, launched his coup against Edward IV from Calais, where George PLANTAGENET, duke of Clarence, married the earl's daughter, Isabel NEVILLE, and joined the earl in issuing a manifesto denouncing Edward's government. In 1470, Warwick, in flight after the failure of his second coup, tried to enter Calais, but his deputy, John WENLOCK, Lord Wenlock, warned him that the garrison was loyal to Edward and advised him to land in France.

In 1471, Thomas NEVILLE, the Bastard of Fauconberg, led part of the Calais garrison to England to support the Lancastrian READEPTION government headed by Warwick. In May, a month after Warwick's death at the Battle of BARNET, Fauconberg unsuccessfully attacked London, and most of the garrison soon returned to Calais and to their Yorkist allegiance. In the 1470s, Edward IV gave the Calais captaincy only to his most trusted supporters—Anthony WOODVILLE, Earl Rivers, and William HASTINGS, Lord Hastings. In 1473, Edward imprisoned the diehard Lancastrian, John de VERE, earl of Oxford, at Calais. In 1484, part of the Calais garrison defected to Henry Tudor, earl of Richmond (see HENRY VII), and allowed Oxford to escape. To ensure his control of the town, RICHARD III gave the captaincy to his bastard son, John of Gloucester, and installed a new garrison under his loyal servant James TYRELL. Because Gloucester was only a boy, his appointment made the king the effective captain of Calais.

After Richard's death at the Battle of BOSWORTH FIELD in 1485, Calais readily submitted to Henry VII. The town remained an English possession until captured by the French in 1558.

Further Reading: Gillingham, John, *The Wars of the Roses* (Baton Rouge: Louisiana State University Press, 1981); Hicks, Michael, *Warwick the Kingmaker* (Oxford: Blackwell Publishers, 1998); Ross, Charles, *The Wars of the Roses* (New York: Thames and Hudson, 1987).

Campaigns, Duration of. *See* Military Campaigns, Duration of

Canterbury, Archbishop of. *See* Bourchier, Thomas; Morton, John

Castillon, Battle of (1453)

Fought on 17 July 1453, the Battle of Castillon ended the HUNDRED YEARS WAR and stripped England of all its holdings in FRANCE except the town of CALAIS.

After their conquest of Normandy in 1450, the French focused their energy and resources on Gascony, a province of southwestern France that had been an English possession for almost 300 years. As an army of 7,000 marched south from Normandy, other French forces besieged the fortresses protecting Bordeaux, the Gascon capital, while a joint French, Spanish, and Breton fleet blockaded the mouth of the Gironde to prevent the English from relieving the city. Isolated and outnumbered, the English garrison in Bordeaux surrendered on 29 June 1451. A severe blow to English national pride and to the popularity of HENRY VI's government, the loss of Bordeaux was reversed in October 1452, thanks to the English sympathies of some of the Gascon nobility and the military skill of John Talbot, earl of Shrewsbury (c. 1384–1453), the most famous and successful English soldier of the time. Within months of reentering Bordeaux on 23 October, Shrewsbury had restored English control to most of Gascony.

The military victory in France, followed by news of Queen MARGARET OF ANJOU's pregnancy, placed Henry VI and his chief minister, Edmund BEAUFORT, duke of Somerset, in the strongest political position they had enjoyed since 1450. On the other hand, Somerset's chief rival, Richard PLANTAGENET, duke of York, already humiliated by the failure of his uprising at DARTFORD in February 1452, was further isolated by the government's newfound success and popularity. However, CHARLES VII was determined to retake and hold Gascony, and by the early summer of 1453 he had reestablished the naval blockade of the Gironde, thereby threatening Bordeaux with starvation. The English government realized the precariousness of Shrewsbury's position, and undertook feverish efforts to collect men, money, and shipping. However, French ARTILLERY made all this activity unavailing. On 17 July near Castillon east of Bordeaux, Shrewsbury attacked a strong French position protected by cannon. The enemy guns cut the English to pieces, killing Shrewsbury and his son and ending English rule in Gascony forever. News of the battle not only left Somerset's government saddled with blame for losing the province, it may also have triggered Henry VI's mental collapse, for the king's illness descended upon him in early August 1453, about the time he would have been informed of the disaster (see HENRY VI, ILLNESS OF). The king's incapacity revived York's political fortunes, further depressed those of Somerset, and dangerously intensified the rivalry between the two dukes, which, in turn, fostered the violence and political instability that led to the WARS OF THE ROSES.

Further Reading: Griffiths, Ralph A., *The Reign of King Henry VI* (Berkeley: University of California Press, 1981); Pollard, A. J., *John Talbot and the War in France, 1427–1453* (London: Royal Historical Society, 1983); Wolffe, Bertram, *Henry VI* (London: Eyre Methuen, 1981).

Casualties

As with the overall size of armies during the WARS OF THE ROSES, figures for the casual-ties suffered in civil war battles are difficult to calculate and often seriously inflated by contemporary commentators.

Because Wars of the Roses armies probably rarely numbered more than 10,000 to 15,000 men, with perhaps some smaller battles counting their combatants in the hundreds, chronicle accounts such as the one claiming that over 3,000 Lancastrians died at the Battle of MORTIMER'S CROSS in February 1461 are highly suspect. The figure 3,000 probably exceeds the entire strength of the Lancastrian force engaged at Mortimer's Cross, which was not a major battle but a regional encounter between the Welsh and Marcher (i.e., borderland) supporters of the houses of LANCASTER and YORK.

The one possible exception to the untrustworthiness of contemporary casualty figures is the number given for those killed in March 1461 at the Battle of TOWTON, the largest and longest battle of the Wars of the Roses. Various chroniclers claimed that between 30,000 and 38,000 men lay dead on the field after the battle. Although modern historians estimate that between 50,000 and 75,000 men participated in the fighting at Towton, the chronicle figures would still strain belief, except that a letter written immediately after the battle states that the heralds counted 28,000 slain, and the same figure was shortly thereafter reported by both EDWARD IV and by several other contemporary observers. Clearly, the magnitude of the slaughter at Towton was unprecedented during the wars, even if one accepts later estimates that only about 9,000 died in the battle.

In many battles, the number of dead was small. At the Battle of ST. ALBANS in May 1455 only a few thousand men were engaged and the fighting ended abruptly on the death of Edmund BEAUFORT, duke of Somerset, and his noble allies. At the Battle of NORTHAMPTON in July 1460, the armies involved were larger, but the fighting was brief, and the casualties were highest among the Lancastrian noblemen who fought to defend the person of HENRY VI, for Richard NEVILLE, earl of Warwick, the Yorkist commander, told his men to spare the king and commons and to concentrate their efforts on killing the peers and gentlemen who led the Lancastrian force. At the Battle of EDGECOTE in July 1469, the slaughter of Welsh gentry in the royalist force was particularly high, with one account claiming that 168 Welsh gentlemen fell on the field. About 2,000 Welsh commons were said to have died at Edgecote, but that figure is again probably high for the number of men engaged (see COMMONS [COMMON PEOPLE] AND THE WARS OF THE ROSES).

Other encounters, such as the Battle of LUDFORD BRIDGE in 1459 or the Battles of HEDGELEY MOOR and HEXHAM in 1464, were mere skirmishes or involved small forces and few casualties. At the Battle of Hexham, the executions of captured Lancastrians after the battle may have rivaled the number of men killed during the actual fighting. Warwick and his brother John NEVILLE, Lord Montagu, who were rarely hesitant to dispatch captured opponents, executed over two dozen Lancastrian leaders after Hexham, including Henry BEAUFORT, duke of Somerset; Robert HUNGERFORD, Lord Hungerford; and Thomas ROOS, Lord Roos. Although the number of noble and GENTRY dead, both in the fighting and through execution afterward, was high in many battles, the number of casualties among the commons probably was counted in the hundreds for all battles except the largest, such as the Battles of Towton, BARNET, and TEWKESBURY.

See also Armies, Size of; Battles, Nature of; Military Campaigns, Duration of; Peerage
Further Reading: Boardman, Andrew W., *The Medieval Soldier in the Wars of the Roses* (Stroud, Gloucestershire, UK: Sutton Publishing, 1998); Goodman, Anthony, *The Wars of the Roses* (New York: Dorset Press, 1981); Ross, Charles, *The Wars of the Roses* (New York: Thames and Hudson, 1987).

Catesby, William (1450–1485)

In 1483, when RICHARD III's usurpation of his nephew's throne revived dynastic conflict and political instability, William Catesby served as one of Richard's closest advisors and confidants.

One of the few southern members of the king's inner circle, Catesby was born into an obscure Northamptonshire GENTRY family and trained as a lawyer. A councilor of William HASTINGS, Lord Hastings, who later acquired some of Hastings's offices, Catesby's rapid rise to power and influence under Richard III led to later charges that he had connived at Hastings's death in 1483. In his *HISTORY OF KING RICHARD III,* Sir Thomas More suggested that Catesby sounded out Hastings about Richard's decision to claim the throne, and that his unfavorable report of Hastings's response led to Hastings's summary execution.

After Richard's accession, Catesby was appointed chancellor of the Exchequer and chancellor of the earldom of March. He was also made a squire of the body (i.e., a close personal servant of the king) and was given lands worth more than £300 a year, an income that made Catesby wealthier than many knights and brought him much unpopularity as an undeserving parvenu. He was sent on embassy to SCOTLAND in September 1484 and to BRITTANY in February 1485. Catesby served as Speaker of the PARLIAMENT of 1484, in which he sat as member for Northamptonshire. His speakership indicated the position of trust he held with the king, for it was unusual for a member to be Speaker in his first Parliament.

Along with Sir Richard RATCLIFFE and Francis LOVELL, Lord Lovell, Catesby became widely known as a member of Richard's inner circle of advisors. A popular satirical couplet of the time declared that "The cat [Catesby], the rat [Ratcliffe], and Lovell our dog [Lovell's emblem], / Rule all England under a hog [referring to Richard III's white boar emblem]." In March 1485, Catesby and Ratcliffe were said to have opposed Richard's plan to wed his niece, ELIZABETH OF YORK. Catesby was taken prisoner at the Battle of BOSWORTH FIELD on 22 August 1485 and executed three days later at Leicester.

See also Richard III, Northern Affinity of
Further Reading: Horrox, Rosemary, *Richard III: A Study in Service* (Cambridge: Cambridge

University Press, 1991); Roskell, John S., *William Catesby, Counselor to Richard III* (Manchester: John Rylands Library, 1959) [reprinted from the *Bulletin of the John Rylands Library,* vol. 42, no. 1, September, 1959]; Ross, Charles, *Richard III* (Berkeley: University of California Press, 1981); "William Catesby," in Michael Hicks, *Who's Who in Late Medieval England* (London: Shepheard-Walwyn, 1991), pp. 366–369.

Causes of the Wars of the Roses.
See Wars of the Roses, Causes of

Caxton, William (c. 1421–1491)

Commencing operations after EDWARD IV had seemingly ended the WARS OF THE ROSES, cloth merchant William Caxton introduced printing to England in 1477. With the patronage of courtiers and members of the royal houses of YORK and TUDOR, Caxton produced English works of history, philosophy, religion, and romance.

Born in Kent, Caxton was apprenticed to a LONDON mercer (i.e., cloth merchant) in 1438. When his apprenticeship ended in 1446, he was already engaged in trade at Bruges in BURGUNDY. In 1462, the membership of the Merchant Adventurers, an association of English merchants, appointed Caxton their governor at Bruges, thereby giving him oversight of the group's continental operations. Because he ceased to function as governor in 1470, Caxton may have been dismissed from office by the READEPTION government of HENRY VI, which probably objected to Caxton's close association with Edward IV's sister, MARGARET OF YORK, duchess of Burgundy. Because the king later employed him as a commercial diplomat, Caxton may have met Edward IV when he was in exile in Burgundy over the winter of 1470. In 1471, having completed an English translation of a French *History of Troy,* Caxton traveled to Cologne to learn about the new printing technology. Published in Bruges in 1474, Caxton's *History of Troy* was the first book ever printed in English.

Returning home in 1476, Caxton established the first printing press in England near the center of royal government in Westminster. His first printed works in England—*The Dictes and Sayings of the Philosophers* (1477) and the *Moral Proverbs* of Christine de Pisan (1478)—were translations from the French by Caxton's chief patron, Anthony WOODVILLE, Earl Rivers, the king's brother-in-law. Although Edward IV directly commissioned none of Caxton's works, the printer sought and probably obtained the patronage of members of the house of York. Two books printed in 1481—*Tully of Old Age* and *Godefroy of Bologne*—were dedicated to Edward IV, while the *Life of Jason* (1477) and *The Order of Chivalry* (1484) were dedicated, respectively, to Prince Edward (see EDWARD V) and to RICHARD III. Because Edward IV, who had an extensive library, may have preferred colorful hand-illuminated manuscripts to plainer print publications, he was probably never more than a passive patron of Caxton's press.

A Woodcut illustrating William Caxton's Fables of Aesop. *(North Wind Picture Archives)*

The trademark and initials of the English printer William Caxton. (British Library)

However, both Margaret BEAUFORT, countess of Richmond, and Henry BOURCHIER, earl of Essex, actively favored Caxton, while HENRY VII commanded Caxton to print his English translation of Christine de Pisan's *Feats of Arms and Chivalry* in 1489.

Caxton printed some eighty different titles, including twenty-one of his own translations and the first editions of Geoffrey Chaucer's *Canterbury Tales* and Sir Thomas MALORY's *Le Morte d'Arthur*. Caxton's concentration on chivalric romances, histories, and religious works reflected the tastes of his aristocratic patrons and of the wealthy London merchants who purchased his books in growing numbers. By the 1480s, the government, thanks in part to Caxton, was becoming increasingly aware of the PROPAGANDA potential of the printing press. After 1485, the Crown appointed a royal printer to publish all the king's proclamations and began to take steps to ensure that no politically or religiously subversive works issued from English presses, although real censorship did not appear until Lutheran works entered England in the 1520s. After Caxton's death in 1491, his press continued to operate under his apprentice, Wynkyn de Worde.

See also English Economy and the Wars of the Roses
Further Reading: Blake, N. F., *Caxton: England's First Publisher* (New York: Barnes and Noble, 1976); Blake, N. F., *William Caxton and English Literary Culture* (London: Hambledon Press, 1991); Hindley, Geoffrey, *England in the Age of Caxton* (New York: St. Martin's Press, 1979); Painter, George D., *William Caxton: A Biography* (New York: Putnam, 1977).

Cely Letters and Papers

The letters and papers of the Cely (or Sely) family, a series of documents describing the lives and business activities of a family of LONDON wool merchants in the 1470s and 1480s, are primary sources of information on English society and the English economy at the end of the WARS OF THE ROSES.

The letters, accounts, and memoranda in the collection concern the family of Richard Cely (d. 1482), who, with his wife Agnes (d. 1483), raised three sons—Robert (d. 1485), Richard (d. 1493), and George (d. 1489). The senior Richard Cely was a prominent member of the London merchant community in the 1460s, and in 1481 ran unsuccessfully for the office of sheriff of London. The Celys were wool traders, buying wool in England and shipping it to CALAIS for sale to cloth makers in BURGUNDY. Until his death, the elder Richard handled the London end of the operation—the purchase, inspection, sorting, and shipping of wool—while his sons Richard and George (mainly the latter in the 1480s) handled the Calais end of the business—the negotiation of terms for sale of the wool. After their father's death, Richard and George continued the business as a true partnership, with Richard conducting operations in London. Besides wool, the brothers also occasionally traded in other commodities and purchased ships to engage in the carrying trade, that is, to transport the goods of other merchants. The eldest brother, Robert, seems to have been a rather unstable character who had a poor relationship with his father; he apparently dropped out of the family business and largely disappears from the correspondence after 1479.

Now found in the Public Record Office, the Cely papers survived because they were submitted to the Court of Chancery in 1489 as evidence in a court case involving a dispute over debts between Richard Cely and the widow of his brother George. The collection comprises 247 letters and over 200 other documents that cover the period from 1472 to 1488, although the bulk of the correspondence begins in 1474 and no letters have survived for 1475 and the greater part of the years 1483, 1485, and 1486. The letters shed little direct light on the politics of the period, but they are full of concerns about how political and military events might affect trade. This urban merchant perspective distinguishes the Cely collection from the other surviving family archives from the fifteenth century; the PASTON, PLUMPTON, and STONOR letters were all written from the perspective of rural, landholding GENTRY. The Celys and their correspondents had some landed interests, but their main concerns focused on London and on trade, an outlook that makes the Cely documents an important source for the social and economic history of England in the later years of the civil wars.

See also English Economy and the Wars of the Roses
Further Reading: Hanham, Alison, ed., *The Cely Letters 1472–1488* (Oxford: Oxford University Press, 1975); Hanham, Alison, *The Celys and Their World: An English Merchant Family of the Fifteenth Century* (Cambridge: Cambridge University Press, 1985); selections of the Cely letters are available online through the Richard III Society Web site at <http://www.r3.org/bookcase/cely/>.

Charles VII, King of France (1403–1461)

Although his reign was spent reconquering the Lancastrian-controlled areas of FRANCE, Charles VII gave cautious support to the house of LANCASTER during the first phase of the WARS OF THE ROSES.

In 1411, the violent and intermittent insanity of Charles VI led to civil war between the houses of Orleans and BURGUNDY for control of the French government. After both sides appealed to him for assistance, Henry V of England invaded France in 1415 and within five years controlled Normandy and large areas of northern France. A leader of the anti-Burgundian party, Prince Charles assumed the regency in 1418, but was soon driven from Paris by John the Fearless, duke of Burgundy. In 1419, an attempted reconciliation with Burgundy ended with the duke's assassination by some of Charles's companions, an act that drove PHILIP, the new duke of Burgundy, into alliance with Henry V. The Treaty of Troyes of 1420 disinherited Charles in favor of the English king, who was declared heir to the French throne.

However, on his father's death in 1422, the prince assumed the title of king, even though his capital and much of his kingdom were beyond his control. In England, the infant HENRY VI, who had come to the English throne two months earlier on the unexpected death of his father, was proclaimed king of France under the terms of the Treaty of Troyes. With the help of Joan of Arc, Charles was crowned at Reims in 1429. In 1435, he made peace with Burgundy and reentered Paris in the next year. After a period of truce in the 1440s, Charles's campaign of reconquest drove the English from Normandy in 1450 and from Gascony in the southwest in 1453. By the end of the reign, only CALAIS remained in English hands.

On the outbreak of civil war in England in 1459, Charles gave surreptitious diplomatic and military aid to the Lancastrians. Queen MARGARET OF ANJOU was Charles's niece, and her marriage to Henry VI had been Charles's instrument for improving Anglo-French relations and for persuading the English to surrender the county of Maine. Also, the leaders of the house of YORK, seeking to highlight Lancastrian military failures, spoke frequently of England's past triumphs in France, a tendency that alarmed Charles with the prospect of renewed English invasions should the Yorkists come to power. Believing that Margaret could win without French aid, and that too much foreign assistance could cost the Lancastrians support in England, Charles remained largely aloof from English affairs until after EDWARD IV's victory at the Battle of TOWTON in March 1461. In the remaining months before his death in July, Charles funded a successful attack on the Channel Islands, which Margaret had ceded to France, and provided more open and substantial diplomatic, financial, and military support to the Lancastrian cause.

See also Castillon, Battle of; Hundred Years War; Louis XI
Further Reading: Vale, M. G. A., *Charles VII* (Berkeley: University of California Press, 1974).

Charles VIII, King of France (1470–1498)

In 1485, the regency government of Charles VIII of FRANCE supplied money and men for the invasion that placed HENRY VII and the house of TUDOR on the English throne. In 1492, after having assumed personal direction of the government, Charles VIII threatened the Tudor dynasty by supporting Perkin WARBECK, a Yorkist pretender to the English Crown.

Because Charles was only thirteen when his father, LOUIS XI, died in 1483, control of the French government fell to the new king's sister, Anne of Beaujeau. When a coalition of French nobles sought to overthrow the regent by forging alliances with foreign princes, including RICHARD III of England and FRANCIS II of BRITTANY, the government responded by encouraging internal opposition in those states. To distract the English king, the French offered financial assistance to Henry Tudor, earl of Richmond, the remaining Lancastrian claimant to the English Crown. On 1 August 1485, Richmond sailed from France with a fleet of seven vessels paid for by the French Crown and led by a French vice admiral. Most of the 2,000-man force that embarked with the earl consisted of French and Scottish veterans provided by the regency government. Because these troops formed the core of the army that won Richmond the Crown at the Battle of BOSWORTH FIELD

on 22 August, the French later claimed that Henry VII had become king of England "by the grace of Charles VIII" (Davies, p. 177).

Anglo-French relations deteriorated in 1491, when Charles married Anne of Brittany, a match that threatened absorption of the Duchy of Brittany into France. To counter Henry's opposition to his Breton designs, Charles invited Perkin Warbeck to travel from IRELAND to Paris, where the king promised to fund Warbeck's attempt to overthrow Henry VII. Warbeck claimed to be EDWARD IV's younger son, Richard PLANTAGENET, duke of York, who had disappeared in the TOWER OF LONDON in 1483 with his brother EDWARD V. Recognizing Warbeck as "Richard IV," rightful king of England, Charles granted him a generous pension and allowed him to live in comfort at the French COURT.

In October 1492, Henry led an army across the Channel to the defense of Brittany. However, by early November, he and Charles had concluded the Treaty of Etaples. In return for Henry's acquiescence in the French takeover of Brittany, Charles, who was anxious to undertake a campaign in Italy, covered Henry's campaign expenses and paid the arrears of the pension promised to Edward IV in 1475. Charles also agreed to give no shelter to Henry's rebels, a clause that forced Warbeck to end his ten-month stay in France and remove to BURGUNDY. Having divorced himself from Warbeck's enterprise, Charles was freed to launch his Italian adventure, which, after initial successes, ended in failure in 1495. Charles died childless in April 1498.

Further Reading: Antonovics, A. V., "Henry VII, King of England, By the Grace of Charles VIII of France," in Ralph A. Griffiths and James Sherborne, eds., *Kings and Nobles in the Later Middle Ages* (New York: St. Martin's Press, 1986), pp. 169–184; Commines, Philippe de, *The Memoirs of Philippe de Commynes,* edited by Samuel Kinser, translated by Isabelle Cazeaux, 2 vols. (Columbia: University of South Carolina Press, 1969–1973); Davies, C. S. L., "The Wars of the Roses in European Context," in A. J. Pollard, ed., *The Wars of the Roses* (New York: St. Martin's Press, 1995), pp. 162–185; Potter, David, *A History of France, 1460–1560: The Emergence of a Nation State* (London: Macmillan, 1995).

Charles, Duke of Burgundy (1433–1477)

By supplying a safe place of exile and vital material assistance, Charles "the Bold" (or "the Rash"), duke of BURGUNDY, enabled EDWARD IV to mount a successful campaign to retake the English throne in 1471.

In 1467, Charles succeeded his father, Duke PHILIP the Good, who since the late 1450s had followed a generally pro-Yorkist policy toward England. Having inherited Lancastrian blood from his mother, a princess of Portugal, Charles personally favored the house of LANCASTER and befriended such staunch adherents of HENRY VI as Henry BEAUFORT, duke of Somerset. After Somerset's execution in 1464, Charles sheltered numerous Lancastrian exiles at the Burgundian COURT, including the late duke's brother, Edmund BEAUFORT. However, Charles was also more hostile to LOUIS XI of FRANCE than Philip had been, a stance that forced Charles into a closer alignment with the anti-French house of YORK.

In 1465, Charles, who had assumed direction of the Burgundian government from his increasingly ill father, took Burgundy into the League of the Public Weal, an alliance of French nobles, including FRANCIS II of BRITTANY, that defeated Louis in battle and forced him to make important concessions to his feudal vassals. When Charles also became a widower in 1465, he opened negotiations with Yorkist England that led by 1467 to a commercial treaty and by 1468 to a formal alliance sealed by Charles's marriage to Edward IV's sister, MARGARET OF YORK. Because the marriage was a political defeat for Richard NEVILLE, earl of Warwick, who favored a pro-French foreign policy, the alliance with Charles aggravated the growing rift between Warwick and the king and forced Warwick to turn to Louis of France when he fled England after the failure of his rebellion in early 1470.

When French assistance allowed Warwick to drive him from the kingdom in October 1470, Edward IV fled to Burgundy, where he was warmly received by the Burgundian nobleman Louis de GRUTHUYSE, Seigneur de la Gruthuyse, although denied an audience by his pro-Lancastrian brother-in-law. However, when Warwick, acting in accordance with the ANGERS AGREEMENT, which he had concluded in 1470 with MARGARET OF ANJOU and Louis XI, declared war on Burgundy in early 1471, Charles determined to support Edward and provided him with funds to hire ships and recruit men.

After Edward's restoration in April 1471, England's newfound stability meant that both Charles and Louis were eager to win Edward's friendship; like Louis, Charles paid handsome pensions to important English courtiers, who then exercised their influence with Edward on the duke's behalf. By 1475, Charles's attention had turned to accomplishing the eastward expansion of Burgundy as part of a plan to establish a Burgundian kingdom between France and Germany. As he pursued this plan, Charles suffered several severe defeats at the hands of the Swiss, who finally slew the duke in battle at Nancy in January 1477.

See also Edward IV, Overthrow of; Edward IV, Restoration of

Further Reading: Vaughan, Richard, *Charles the Bold: The Last Valois Duke of Burgundy* (London: Longman, 1973); Vaughan, Richard, *Valois Burgundy* (Hamden, CT: Archon Books, 1975).

Chinon Agreement (1462)

The Chinon Agreement of June 1462 was a largely unsuccessful attempt by Queen MARGARET OF ANJOU to create an alliance with FRANCE that could supply her with the men, money, and supplies required to overthrow EDWARD IV and the house of YORK and restore HENRY VI and the house of LANCASTER to the English throne.

In April 1462, Margaret left SCOTLAND, where she and her family had been in exile for the past year, and sailed for France, where she hoped to convince her kinsman, LOUIS XI, to support the Lancastrian cause. Willing to cede CALAIS to France for a substantial loan, Margaret induced the French king to conclude a secret agreement with her at Chinon on 24 June. Four days later, the Franco-Lancastrian alliance was publicly proclaimed in the Treaty of Tours, which, to protect Margaret's reputation in England and deprive Edward IV of a PROPAGANDA weapon, made no mention of the provisions concerning Calais. As a favor to Margaret, Louis also released her friend Pierre de BRÉZÉ from prison and allowed him to assist her in recruiting men.

When Louis informed Duke PHILIP of BURGUNDY and Duke FRANCIS II of BRITTANY of the alliance, the former refused permission for French troops to cross Burgundian territory to attack Calais, while the latter gave modest support to a Lancastrian naval squadron being prepared in Normandy. With his designs on Calais stymied by the Burgundians, Louis failed to provide Margaret with much of the promised support. Upon her departure for Scotland in October, Margaret took with her only about 800 men, who may have been largely paid for by de Brézé. Yet, despite her lack of men and money, Margaret's return to northern England in late October was sufficient to cause the surrender to her forces of ALNWICK and BAMBURGH Castles, and the renewal of Lancastrian resistance in northeastern England.

Further Reading: Griffiths, Ralph A., *The Reign of King Henry VI* (Berkeley: University of California Press, 1981); Kendall, Paul Murray, *Louis XI* (New York: W. W. Norton, 1971); Ross, Charles, *Edward IV* (New Haven: Yale University Press, 1998).

Chronicle of the Rebellion in Lincolnshire (1470)

The *Chronicle of the Rebellion in Lincolnshire* is a brief account of EDWARD IV's campaign against the Lincolnshire uprising led by Sir Robert Welles in March 1470.

Cast in the form of a journal or day-by-day listing of events, the *Chronicle* is an important source of information for the second coup launched against Edward by Richard NEVILLE, earl of Warwick, and George PLANTAGENET, duke of Clarence. The narrative traces the king's movements between 7 and 26 March, and provides details of the Battle of LOSECOTE FIELD, fought on 12 March. The Lincolnshire uprising grew out of a feud between Richard Welles, Lord Welles, and Sir Thomas Burgh, Edward's master of Horse (see WELLES UPRISING). By coming to Burgh's aid, Edward drove Welles and his son Sir Robert to seek assistance from Warwick, who, since the failure of his 1469 coup, had awaited another opportunity to seize power. Warwick encouraged Sir Robert Welles to raise Lincolnshire by claiming that the king was coming north to exact retribution for the shire's involvement in the ROBIN OF REDESDALE REBELLION in the previous July, an uprising that had accompanied Warwick's first coup attempt. Although as yet unaware of Warwick and Clarence's involvement, Edward left LONDON on 6 March to suppress Welles's fast-growing rebellion.

The *Chronicle* was written by someone traveling in the king's party and is thus largely an eyewitness account of the events described. Because the chronicler was particularly well informed as to the documents and letters issued under the privy seal during the campaign, modern historians have speculated that the writer was one of the royal privy seal clerks. The *Chronicle* is clearly an officially sanctioned PROPAGANDA effort, for its author took great pains to show that Warwick and Clarence were traitors and the instigators of the uprising. The chronicler also stressed the magnitude of Edward's success in crushing the rebellion, claiming that Welles brought 30,000 rebels to Losecote Field and emphasizing how dangerous the king's situation would have been had Welles successfully rendezvoused with Warwick. Although its official nature and its obvious exaggerations and biases require it to be used with caution, the *Chronicle* is valuable because it was composed within days of the end of the campaign. The narrative stops on 26 March, and the *Chronicle* may have been completed before the end of the month, or at least by mid-April, before the writer knew how Warwick's rebellion would conclude.

Further Reading: Gillingham, John, *The Wars of the Roses* (Baton Rouge: Louisiana State University Press, 1981); *Three Chronicles of the*

Reign of Edward IV, introduction by Keith Dockray (Stroud, Gloucestershire, UK: Alan Sutton Publishing, 1988).

Church. *See* English Church and the Wars of the Roses

Clarence, Duchess of. *See* Neville, Isabel, Duchess of Clarence

Clarence, Duke of. *See* Plantagenet, George, Duke of Clarence

Clarence, Execution of (1478)

As punishment for the duke's betrayal of his brother in 1469–1471, the 1478 trial and execution of George PLANTAGENET, duke of Clarence, younger brother of EDWARD IV, terminated the political turmoil of the second phase of the WARS OF THE ROSES; as an act that unintentionally eased Richard, duke of Gloucester's (see RICHARD III), path to the throne, the death of Clarence contributed to the eruption of the final phase of the civil wars in 1483.

Although Clarence had been pardoned in 1471 for helping Richard NEVILLE, earl of Warwick, overthrow Edward in 1470, the duke continued to antagonize his brother (see EDWARD IV, OVERTHROW OF). After the death of his wife, Isabel NEVILLE, in 1476, Clarence sought to wed Mary, daughter and heiress of Duke CHARLES of BURGUNDY. Edward forbade the match, fearing that Clarence, backed by the resources of Burgundy, might again attempt to seize the English throne. The king also rejected Clarence's proposed match with a sister of JAMES III of SCOTLAND. The duke accepted these disappointments with ill grace, withdrawing from COURT and COUNCIL and refusing to dine with the king as if he feared poison. The duke's enemies, particularly LOUIS XI of FRANCE, who welcomed any chance to destabilize the English state, and Queen Elizabeth WOODVILLE and her family, who saw Clarence as a threat to Prince Edward (see EDWARD V), informed the king of anything provocative that the duke said or did.

In May 1477, the king arrested Thomas Burdett, a member of Clarence's household, for attempting to destroy the king and the prince through black magic. Burdett, who was also charged with inciting rebellion, was convicted and executed, his fate an obvious warning to the duke. Clarence's response was to burst into a council meeting and have Burdett's statement of his innocence read out by a preacher who was notorious for publicly expounding HENRY VI's right to the throne in September 1470. An infuriated king summoned Clarence to his presence and charged him with usurping royal authority by arresting and summarily trying Ankarette Twynho, a servant of the late duchess, whom Clarence's men had executed in April for allegedly poisoning her mistress. For this perversion of the judicial process, Clarence was committed to the TOWER OF LONDON in June.

In January 1478, PARLIAMENT arraigned the duke on charges of treason. The king himself introduced a bill of ATTAINDER against his brother; Edward's unusual action was instigated in part by his belief that Clarence had openly declared that Burdett had been unjustly executed and that the king was a bastard with no right to the Crown. Although Clarence was allowed to deny the charges, no one else would speak in his defense, and little attempt was made to prove the accusations. After a Parliament filled with royal servants passed the bill, Edward hesitated for ten days before ordering that the sentence be carried out. To spare both the duke and the house of YORK a public execution, Clarence was put to death inside the Tower on 18 February, probably, as later rumor claimed, by being drowned in a butt (i.e., a large cask) of malmsey wine. Although Tudor propagandists later accused Gloucester of engineering his brother's death, responsibility for the execution rests with Edward IV, who by 1478 had come to see Clarence's death as a political necessity.

See also Usurpation of 1483; Woodville family
Further Reading: "George, Duke of Clarence,"
in Michael Hicks, *Who's Who in Late Medieval England* (London: Shepheard-Walwyn, 1991), pp. 331–333; Hicks, Michael, *False, Fleeting, Perjur'd Clarence: George, Duke of Clarence, 1449–78,* rev. ed. (Bangor, UK: Headstart History, 1992); Lander, J. R., "The Treason and Death of the Duke of Clarence," in J. R. Lander, *Crown and Nobility, 1450–1509* (Montreal: McGill-Queen's University Press, 1976), pp. 242–266; Ross, Charles, *Edward IV* (New Haven, CT: Yale University Press, 1998).

Clifford, John, Lord Clifford (c. 1435–1461)

Motivated by the slaying of his father by the Yorkists at the Battle of ST. ALBANS in May 1455, John CLIFFORD, ninth Lord Clifford, committed such violent acts of battlefield vengeance against his opponents that he won the epithets "butcher" and "black-hearted Clifford." His most notorious deed was the slaying, after the Battle of WAKEFIELD, of seventeen-year-old Edmund PLANTAGENET, earl of Rutland, second son of Richard PLANTAGENET, duke of York, as the earl knelt before Clifford imploring mercy.

In February 1458, Clifford, Henry BEAUFORT, duke of Somerset, and Henry PERCY, third earl of Northumberland, two other noblemen whose fathers had been killed by the Yorkists at the Battle of St. Albans, came to LONDON "with a great power," clamoring for compensation for the deaths of their fathers. Clifford was described as being so bitter about his father's fate that "the sight of any of the house of York was as a fury to torment his soul" (Haigh, p. 80). HENRY VI and the COUNCIL temporarily mollified the three men by ordering York and his chief allies at St. Albans, Richard NEVILLE, earl of Salisbury, and his son Richard NEVILLE, earl of Warwick, to fund masses for the souls of the slain men and to pay an indemnity to their heirs (see LOVE-DAY OF 1458).

In November 1459, Clifford was present at the Lancastrian-controlled COVENTRY PARLIAMENT, where he took an oath of allegiance to Henry VI, who shortly thereafter named him commissary-general of the Scottish marches (i.e., borderlands) and conservator of the truce with SCOTLAND. After the Act of ACCORD of October 1460 disinherited EDWARD OF LANCASTER, Prince of Wales, and recognized York as heir to the throne, Clifford was one of the Lancastrian nobles who took the field against the Yorkist regime on the prince's behalf, and was a leader of the Lancastrian force that defeated and killed York at the Battle of Wakefield in December 1460.

At some point after the battle, Clifford overtook the fleeing Rutland, probably somewhere on or near Wakefield Bridge, and slew the young man while he knelt in supplication and his chaplain begged for his life. The best-known account, that of the Tudor chronicler Edward Hall, has Clifford refuse all entreaties by saying: "By God's blood, thy father slew mine, and so I will do thee and all thy kin" (Haigh, p. 75). Although the exact location and circumstances of Rutland's death are uncertain, all accounts agree that Clifford was the earl's killer. Hall and other sources also charge Clifford with having York's head struck from his dead body and topped with a derisive paper crown (see *THE UNION OF THE TWO NOBLE AND ILLUSTRIOUS FAMILIES OF LANCASTER AND YORK* [HALL]).

In February 1461, Clifford participated in the Lancastrian victory at the Battle of ST. ALBANS. He was slain at the Battle of FERRYBRIDGE on 28 March 1461, one day before the Yorkist victory at the Battle of TOWTON gave the throne to EDWARD IV. The first PARLIAMENT of the new reign attainted Clifford, and his estates were divided among various Yorkists, including Richard, duke of Gloucester (see RICHARD III).

See also Attainder, Act of; Clifford, Thomas, Lord Clifford; North of England and the Wars of the Roses
Further Reading: Boardman, Andrew W., *The Battle of Towton* (Stroud, Gloucestershire, UK: Sutton Publishing, 1996); Haigh, Philip A., *The Battle of Wakefield, 1460* (Stroud, Gloucestershire, UK: Sutton Publishing, 1996).

Clifford, Thomas, Lord Clifford (1414–1455)

An ally of the Percy family in the NEVILLE-PERCY FEUD, which helped instigate the civil disturbances of the 1450s, Thomas Clifford, eighth Lord Clifford, was slain by the Yorkists at the Battle of ST. ALBANS in 1455. His death turned his son into an implacable foe of the house of YORK and was the cause of one of several feuds among the English PEERAGE that embittered political relations on the eve of the WARS OF THE ROSES.

Thomas Clifford came of age and was first summoned to PARLIAMENT as Lord Clifford in 1436. He was one of the lords who accompanied William de la POLE, earl of Suffolk, to FRANCE in 1444 to escort MARGARET OF ANJOU to England for her marriage to HENRY VI. As one of the leading magnates of the north, Clifford, along with the Nevilles and Percies, was excused attendance in Parliament in 1449 to defend the border from possible invasion by the Scots. In 1451, Clifford was part of an embassy to JAMES II of SCOTLAND, and he also served in the 1450s as sheriff of Westmorland.

Clifford accompanied the royal army that confronted Richard PLANTAGENET, duke of York, at DARTFORD in 1452, and he supported Henry PERCY, earl of Northumberland, and his sons in their ongoing quarrel with Richard NEVILLE, earl of Salisbury, and his sons in the mid-1450s. When the Nevilles allied themselves with York and took up arms against the king in 1455, Clifford naturally supported Henry VI and led the defense of the barricades against the Yorkist attack at the Battle of St. Albans on 22 May. Like Northumberland and Edmund BEAUFORT, duke of Somerset, who were also slain in the fighting, Clifford was likely marked as a special enemy and targeted for death by the Yorkist forces. Clifford's death at the hands of the Yorkists had an important effect on the WARS OF THE ROSES, for it turned his son, John CLIFFORD, ninth Lord Clifford, into a staunch supporter of the house of Lancaster and a bitter personal enemy of York and the NEVILLE FAMILY.

See also North of England and the Wars of the Roses

Further Reading: Griffiths, Ralph A., *The Reign of King Henry VI* (Berkeley: University of California Press, 1981); Haigh, Philip A., *The Military Campaigns of the Wars of the Roses* (Stroud, Gloucestershire, UK: Sutton Publishing, 1995); Storey, R. L., *The End of the House of Lancaster*, 2d ed. (Stroud, Gloucestershire, UK: Sutton Publishing, 1999).

Commines, Philippe de. *See Memoirs* (Commines)

Commissions of Array

A commission of array was a written grant of authority from the king to certain named individuals (commissioners) to gather all able-bodied men within a particular town or shire for military service, usually to resist foreign invasion or quell internal rebellion. The issuance of commissions of array was one of the chief methods for recruiting armies during the WARS OF THE ROSES (see ARMIES, RECRUITING OF).

Under the Statute of Winchester, promulgated by Edward I in 1285, all men between the ages of sixteen and sixty who were fit to bear arms could be summoned annually for forty days of military service. Twice each year, royal commissioners, who were usually members of the GENTRY, were given authority under their commissions of array to inspect and report on the military readiness of the county or town in their charge. In times of military emergency, the commissioners mustered these local levies for service with the royal army. During the Wars of the Roses, the party in power used commissions of array to call men to perform their public duty to provide military service to the king, even if they lived in a region dominated by a nobleman then in rebellion against the monarch, and even if they were RETAINERS or tenants of a magnate or noble family supporting the opposition party.

Because the Wars of the Roses forced men to choose whether to obey a royal commission or the summons of an opposing magnate to whom they were attached, or, after 1461, whether to obey the commission of the Lancastrian or the Yorkist monarch, the operation of commissions of array became extremely complicated. For instance, in 1460, Richard PLANTAGENET, duke of York, having been recently declared heir to the throne by the Act of ACCORD, was governing the realm in the name of HENRY VI. To counter increasing Lancastrian activity in Yorkshire, the duke issued a commission of array to John NEVILLE, Lord Neville, who was to gather troops from York's northern estates for a forthcoming campaign in the region. Neville raised the men as ordered, but then marched them into the Lancastrian encampment at Pontefract, where most became part of the army that defeated and killed York at the Battle of WAKEFIELD on 30 December. Those of Neville's recruits who did not fight with the Lancastrian army probably returned home and so were also lost to York, whose campaign was troubled from the start by lack of manpower. How Neville's men made the decision to fight against rather than for York is uncertain. Loyalty to Henry VI, local pride, Lancastrian PROPAGANDA, Neville's presence, York's absence, and the respect accorded a royal commissioner probably all played a part. Thanks to the clash of loyalties engendered by civil war, recruitment by commissions of array became very haphazard during the Wars of the Roses.

See also Bastard Feudalism
Further Reading: Boardman, Andrew W., *The Medieval Soldier in the Wars of the Roses* (Stroud, Gloucestershire, UK: Sutton Publishing, 1998); Hicks, Michael, *Bastard Feudalism* (London: Longman, 1995).

Commons (Common People) and the Wars of the Roses

The vast majority of English men and women held no titles, owned little or no land, and had little or no political influence. Except for the residents of LONDON and a few larger towns, the common people of England lived and worked in the countryside, where over 90 percent of the English population resided in the fifteenth century. Although comprising the bulk of most civil war armies, these countrymen were generally little affected in their daily lives by the WARS OF THE ROSES, which for them meant brief, intermittent campaigns and little material destruction (see MILITARY CAMPAIGNS, DURATION OF).

The common soldiers who fought in civil war armies were usually conscripts, countrymen thrust into battle not by their own political convictions but by the social conventions of the day. The PEERAGE and GENTRY expected that able-bodied men living within their spheres of influence or on their estates would follow them into combat when summoned. Accustomed both to bearing arms and to a certain level of violence in their lives, commoners could usually be persuaded by a local magnate or gentleman, or by a popular preacher, to take arms in a particular political cause. In 1485, for example, John HOWARD, duke of Norfolk, recruiting troops to support RICHARD III against Henry Tudor, earl of Richmond (see HENRY VII), expected to raise 1,000 men from the towns and villages on his East Anglian estates.

Common men had much less stake in the wars than their social superiors did, and common soldiers usually had much less to lose by taking sides. While the noble and gentry leadership of civil war armies was often targeted for death, as the Yorkists likely targeted Edmund BEAUFORT, duke of Somerset, at the Battle of ST. ALBANS in 1455, victorious commanders, such as Richard NEVILLE, earl of Warwick, at the Battle of NORTHAMPTON in 1460, ordered their men to spare the opposing commons. The common soldiers also avoided the executions and bills of ATTAINDER that consumed noble and gentry lives and property after most battles.

During the HUNDRED YEARS WAR, English armies operating in FRANCE had systematically devastated the countryside, killing villagers, burning buildings, and destroying crops and livestock. During the Wars of the Roses, the English countryside saw very little destruction. In 1461, when the northern army of Queen MARGARET OF ANJOU plundered Yorkist towns and strongholds during its

MARCH ON LONDON, the great terror that swept over the southern shires was in part due to the novelty of such pillaging in England. Attacks on or sieges of towns were also rare, with the 1471 assault on London by Thomas NEVILLE, the Bastard of Fauconberg, being the major example during the wars.

The great social evils of the civil war period were the violence, disorder, and corruption of justice inflicted on the countryside by the RETAINERS and servants of noblemen. In some parts of the country, riots, murders, assaults, and forcible dispossessions were common, especially in the 1450s and 1460s. Although these evils arose chiefly from feeble royal government, especially under HENRY VI, and from abuses in the system of BASTARD FEUDALISM, the Wars of the Roses aggravated the problem, at least during the periods 1459–1461 and 1469–1471. EDWARD IV's preoccupation with the uprisings precipitated by Warwick allowed the five-week siege of CAISTER CASTLE to occur in Norfolk in 1469 and the bloody Battle of NIBLEY GREEN to erupt in Gloucestershire in 1470. However, the political security achieved by Edward IV in 1471 seemed to end the wars and allowed a strengthened Crown to reduce the level of violence in the countryside thereafter.

See also Battles, Nature of; Towns and the Wars of the Roses
Further Reading: Gillingham, John, *Wars of the Roses* (Baton Rouge: Louisiana State University Press, 1981); Goodman, Anthony, *The Wars of the Roses* (New York: Dorset Press, 1981); Harvey, I. M. W., "Was There Popular Politics in Fifteenth-Century England?" in R. H. Britnell and A. J. Pollard, eds., *The McFarlane Legacy: Studies in Late Medieval Politics and Society* (Stroud, Gloucestershire, UK: Alan Sutton, 1995), pp. 155–174; Ross, Charles, *The Wars of the Roses* (London: Thames and Hudson, 1987).

"Compilation of the Meekness and Good Life of King Henry VI" (Blacman)

An account of the character and personal life of HENRY VI ostensibly written by the king's chaplain John Blacman, the "Compilation of the Meekness and Good Life of King Henry VI" is the basis of later depictions of Henry as a holy and innocent man, whose neglect of government was a result of his great piety and sanctity.

John Blacman was associated with two of Henry VI's educational foundations, being a fellow of Eton in the 1440s and warden of King's Hall, Cambridge, in the 1450s. Blacman may also have served as Henry's chaplain or confessor during these decades. The date of Blacman's death is uncertain, as is his authorship of the "Compilation," which may simply have once been in his possession. The manuscript was unknown until 1919, when it was discovered and published by M. R. James, the provost of Eton College. The "Compilation" is a collection of first-person anecdotes that illustrates the saintly nature of Henry VI. The hagiographic tone and certain internal evidence suggest that the manuscript was written about 1500 at the court of HENRY VII, who was then attempting to persuade the pope to canonize his Lancastrian uncle.

Any campaign to make a saint of Henry VI, and thereby transform him into an illustrious forebear of the house of TUDOR, could not base its argument on the quality of Henry's kingship. However, by relating a series of stories that illustrated Henry's otherworldliness, simplicity, and lack of deceit, and that made no mention of his mental illness, a case could be made for his canonization (see HENRY VI, ILLNESS OF). The "Compilation" turned Henry's well-known failings as a king into the virtues of a saint. For instance, after describing Henry as much given to prayer and private meditation, the compiler related the king's annoyance when he was roused one day from his devotions by a duke demanding an audience. The anecdotes also displayed Henry's high morals, recounting his shock at seeing men enjoying the waters of Bath in the nude and at women appearing at COURT bare breasted.

Besides his own firsthand knowledge, the compiler also claimed to have interviewed others who knew the king, including Henry's chamberlain, Sir Richard TUNSTALL, who lived until 1492 and would have been present in the early Tudor court, and Henry's friend, Bishop William WAINFLEET, who died in 1486. Whatever the origins of the "Compilation," which Polydore Vergil probably consulted for his ANGLICA HISTORIA, it could not have appeared before 1485, when such a laudatory account of Henry VI would have been considered treasonous by the ruling house of YORK. The work must therefore be used with caution as a source for Henry VI's reign and personality.

Further Reading: James, M. R., ed., *Henry the Sixth: A Reprint of John Blacman's Memoir* (Cambridge: Cambridge University Press, 1919); Lovatt, R., "John Blacman: Biographer of Henry VI," in R. H. C. Davis and J. M. Wallace-Hadrill, eds., *The Writing of History in the Middle Ages* (Oxford: Clarendon Press, 1981), pp. 415–444; Lovatt, R., "A Collector of Apocryphal Anecdotes: John Blacman Revisited," in A. J. Pollard, ed., *Property and Politics: Essays in Later Medieval English History* (Stroud, Gloucestershire, UK: Alan Sutton, 1984), pp. 172–197; Wolffe, Bertram, *Henry VI* (London: Eyre Methuen, 1981).

Cook, Sir Thomas (1420–1478)

A former Lord Mayor of London and one of the wealthiest merchants in the city, Sir Thomas Cook was prosecuted for treason in 1468 in a famous episode that was later used by RICHARD III to illustrate the ambition and avarice of the WOODVILLE FAMILY.

Apprenticed to a LONDON cloth merchant as a child, Cook so prospered in that profession that by the 1460s his London mansion contained tapestries, plates (of precious metals), and art objects worth almost £1,400. He also owned various properties in and around London, including a country home at Gidea Park, and he lent money to EDWARD IV. Cook served as an alderman of London from 1456 to 1468 and as mayor in 1462–1463. For his financial services to the Crown, he was knighted at Elizabeth WOODVILLE's coronation in 1465.

In 1468, Cook was implicated in the CORNELIUS PLOT. He was accused of failing to inform the government that he had been contacted, in about 1466, by agents of the exiled Lancastrian queen, MARGARET OF ANJOU. According to the traditional account of Cook's case, the merchant declined the agents' request for financial assistance, but, because he was a former Lancastrian customs officer, aroused enough suspicion to be arrested and imprisoned. During Cook's confinement, agents of Richard WOODVILLE, Earl Rivers, Queen Elizabeth's father, ransacked the merchant's house, carrying off cloth and other valuables, including an £800 arras coveted by Rivers's wife, JACQUETTA, duchess of Bedford. Brought to trial for treason, Cook was acquitted of that charge by a London jury, but convicted of misprision of treason (i.e., being aware of treason but failing to report it). Although the court imposed a huge fine of over £8000, which effectively ruined Cook, the Woodvilles were so dissatisfied with the verdict that Rivers persuaded the king to dismiss the presiding judge, John Markham. Meanwhile, Queen Elizabeth revived an ancient privilege called "Queen's gold" to demand a further £500 from Cook.

Several modern historians (e.g., see Hicks, below) have disputed this view. They argue that Cook's alleged victimization by the Woodvilles was largely the product of anti-Woodville PROPAGANDA, which was initially employed in the late 1460s by Richard NEVILLE, earl of Warwick, to attack the king and the COURT party, and was then taken up again after 1485 by historians writing in support of the house of TUDOR. The modern view also suggests that Cook was actively working for the house of LANCASTER and was, as the jury found him, guilty of misprision of treason. Thus, as regards the Cook case, the conduct of Edward IV and of the Woodvilles was far less reprehensible than tradition would have it.

Whatever the facts of the case, Cook supported the READEPTION of HENRY VI in 1470 (see EDWARD IV, OVERTHROW OF). He secured election to PARLIAMENT and reappointment as alderman and sought compensation for his losses of 1468. Upon Edward's return in 1471, Cook strove to keep

London solidly behind the Lancastrian government, even exercising the office of mayor when the incumbent feigned illness to avoid taking sides. Upon Edward's restoration, Cook fled the country but was captured and returned to London, where he was again tried, stripped of his offices, and fined (see EDWARD IV, RESTORATION OF). Released in 1472, Cook died a relatively poor man in May 1478.

In 1483, while seeking to convince London citizens of the desirability of replacing the Woodville-dominated kingship of EDWARD V with that of his uncle, Richard, duke of Gloucester, Henry STAFFORD, duke of Buckingham, reminded them of the sufferings supposedly inflicted on Cook by the Woodvilles.

Further Reading: Hicks, Michael, "The Case of Sir Thomas Cook, 1468," in *Richard III and His Rivals: Magnates and Their Motives in the Wars of the Roses* (London: Hambledon Press, 1991); Ross, Charles, *Edward IV* (New Haven, CT: Yale University Press, 1998).

Coppini Mission (1459–1461)

Although charged by the pope with reconciling the warring English factions, Francesco Coppini, bishop of Terni, sided openly with the Yorkists during their invasion of England in 1460. By appearing to give papal sanction to the Yorkists' demands, Coppini generated much support for the Yorkist cause.

In 1459, Pope Pius II sent Coppini to England to persuade HENRY VI to join a crusade against the Turks. To achieve this goal, Coppini was instructed to help the English peacefully resolve their internal quarrels. The bishop was also acting as an informal agent for Francesco Sforza, duke of Milan, whose patronage had helped Coppini obtain his bishopric in 1458. The duke wanted Coppini to promote an English invasion of FRANCE, which would prevent CHARLES VII from intervening in Italy. Although respectfully received at court, Coppini was largely ignored by Queen MARGARET OF ANJOU and her advisors, who were busy preparing for the coming struggle with Richard PLANTA-

GENET, duke of York. When Coppini suggested that the queen consider an accommodation with York, Margaret offended the bishop by curtly dismissing his proposal. Ambitious for promotion to the cardinalate and filled with self-importance, Coppini angrily withdrew to BURGUNDY in early 1460.

Hoping to make use of a friendly papal legate, York's ally, Richard NEVILLE, earl of Warwick, who had been headquartered at CALAIS since being driven from England in the previous autumn, began to play on the bishop's vanity. He assured Coppini that the Yorkists shared his desire for an invasion of France and declared to him their loyalty to Henry VI. After coming to Calais at Warwick's invitation, Coppini was treated with great deference and urged to accompany the Yorkists to England, where he could bring peace by pleading their cause to the king. Swept away by Warwick's charm and flattery, Coppini embarked for England with the Yorkists on 25 June. Once in LONDON, the legate addressed the convocation of English bishops on Warwick's behalf and wrote to Henry urging him to give the Yorkists a hearing.

On 5 July, the legate accompanied Warwick's army northward. Prior to the Battle of NORTHAMPTON on 10 July, Coppini announced to the Yorkist camp that all who fought for Warwick would have remission of sins, while the earl's opponents risked excommunication. After Warwick defeated the Lancastrian army and captured the king, Coppini returned with them to London, where the earl persuaded him that an invasion of France was possible, encouraged his ambition for a cardinal's hat, and licensed him to hold an English bishopric. However, after York was killed at the Battle of WAKEFIELD in December, the Lancastrians began spreading rumors that the pope had repudiated his legate, and Coppini's growing pretensions—he had even begun offering military advice to Warwick—damaged his credibility among the Yorkists. In February 1461, after the failure of a clumsy attempt to negotiate with Margaret, and with a Lancastrian army advancing on London, the legate announced his intention to retire to the continent (see MARCH ON LONDON). Coppini spent the next year angling for promotion and touting himself as an expert on English affairs, but the pope, now fully informed of his legate's pro-Yorkist activities, stripped him of his bishopric and confined him to an abbey for life. Although of great service to the Yorkist cause, Coppini's English mission destroyed his own career.

See also English Church and the Wars of the Roses
Further Reading: Harvey, Margaret, *England, Rome and the Papacy, 1417–1464* (Manchester: Manchester University Press, 1993); Hicks, Michael, *Warwick the Kingmaker* (Oxford: Blackwell Publishers, 1998); Kendall, Paul Murray, *Warwick the Kingmaker* (New York: W. W. Norton, 1987).

Cornelius Plot (1468)

Uncovered in June 1468, the Cornelius plot was a shadowy Lancastrian conspiracy that sought to persuade former supporters of HENRY VI to again become active in his cause.

The plot came to light when EDWARD IV's agents in Kent arrested a shoemaker named John Cornelius, who was caught carrying letters from Lancastrian exiles in FRANCE to secret Lancastrian sympathizers in England. Cornelius was brought before Edward IV, who committed the courier to the TOWER OF LONDON and authorized the use of torture to extract from the prisoner the names of the intended letter recipients. This authorization reveals how nervous the government was at the time about Lancastrian activities, for the Cornelius case is the only example of officially sanctioned torture in England before the time of Henry VIII.

Before succumbing to his harsh treatment, Cornelius implicated several people, including John Hawkins, a servant of John WENLOCK, Lord Wenlock, a former Lancastrian then serving Edward IV as a trusted diplomat. Hawkins, who in his turn implicated several others, was executed, but any suspicions about Wenlock were suppressed so that he could conduct the king's sister, MARGARET OF YORK, to BURGUNDY for her wedding to Duke CHARLES. Unhappy with the Burgundian alliance that the marriage cemented, Wenlock later abandoned Edward and supported Richard NEVILLE, earl of Warwick, in securing the restoration of Henry VI (see EDWARD IV, OVERTHROW OF).

Several other persons implicated by Cornelius and Hawkins were arrested, including the LONDON merchant Sir Thomas COOK and, most likely, Sir Thomas MALORY, the author of *Le Morte d'Arthur*, who was specifically exempted from a 1468 pardon along with several other men known to have been involved in the Cornelius enterprise. The first of several Lancastrian plots uncovered in 1468, the Cornelius conspiracy revealed a rising dissatisfaction with Edward IV and his government, which helped sweep the king from his throne in 1470.

Further Reading: Field, P. J. C., *The Life and Times of Sir Thomas Malory* (Cambridge: D. S. Brewer, 1993); Hicks, Michael, "The Case of Sir Thomas Cook, 1468," in *Richard III and His Rivals: Magnates and Their Motives in the Wars of the Roses* (London: Hambledon Press, 1991); Ross, Charles, *Edward IV* (New Haven, CT: Yale University Press, 1998).

Council, Royal

All medieval English kings required expert advice and administrative assistance to effectively govern the kingdom. The great nobles of the realm considered themselves the monarch's natural advisors, and the political conflict of the 1450s arose in part from the belief of Richard PLANTAGENET, duke of York, that he and other magnates were being improperly excluded from their rightful roles as advisors to HENRY VI. However, the king had the right to seek advice from whomever he wished, and prior to the outbreak of the WARS OF THE ROSES, the king's council was largely an informal body of advisors selected by the monarch to give counsel on topics, at times, and in places of the monarch's choosing. After 1461, the emergency of civil war and the subsequent need to rebuild the authority of the Crown led EDWARD IV and his successors to give their councils more permanent, formal status and to enlarge the role of the council in the daily administration of the realm.

Before the Wars of the Roses, royal councils assumed institutional form only during royal minorities, such as occurred during Henry VI's childhood in the 1420s, or during times of royal incapacity, such as the onset of Henry VI's mental illness in 1453 (see HENRY VI, ILLNESS OF). When the king came of age or demonstrated his fitness to resume ruling, the council again became dependent on him for its membership and the scope of its activities. Medieval kings had always drawn their councilors from various sources—the PEERAGE, the GENTRY, and both the greater and lesser clergy. Under Edward IV and HENRY VII, all three groups were still represented, although gentlemen and peers recently raised from the gentry, such as William HASTINGS, Lord Hastings, formed a higher percentage of Yorkist and early Tudor councils.

Although councilors were sworn and salaried, they were not required to attend meetings. The greater use of gentry councilors may in part have been a result of the inability of busy nobles to regularly appear at council; most magnates had their own estates to run, and many had public offices that kept them from Westminster; for example, in the 1470s, Richard, duke of Gloucester (see RICHARD III), was too occupied with governing the north to attend many council sessions. On fragmentary evidence, we know of 105 councilors appointed by Edward IV, although council meetings during the reign were normally attended by a working group of nine to twelve persons, consisting mainly of the chief officers of state (e.g., the chancellor and treasurer); experienced clerical administrators like John RUSSELL, bishop of Lincoln, and John MORTON, bishop of Ely; and favored gentlemen of the royal household, such as Thomas VAUGHAN.

In the late fifteenth century, the council advised the king on a variety of matters, from the formulation of policy to the answering of petitions and the appointment of royal officials. Except perhaps in the late 1460s, when Richard NEVILLE, earl of Warwick, led a sort of opposition to the WOODVILLE FAMILY

and to the interests of a newly risen group of "King's men" such as William HERBERT, earl of Pembroke, the Yorkist council was not a forum for contending factions to compete for influence, as it had become for a time in the last years of Henry VI; under Edward IV and Henry VII, men of whatever social status were summoned to council to advise and support the king, not to oppose his wishes or criticize his government.

Meeting usually in the Star Chamber at Westminster, the Yorkist and Tudor councils discussed questions of war and peace, addressed issues of foreign and economic policy, conducted daily administration, and helped the king dispense justice. For instance, the decision to retaliate against the HANSEATIC LEAGUE, which led to a costly trade war, was reached in council in 1468. The council also assisted with such tasks as administering CALAIS, maintaining trade relations with BURGUNDY, and suppressing Channel piracy. However, all this was done, as it had been under earlier monarchs, at the direction and under the authority of the king. What was different, especially after 1471, was the widening scope of the council's executive activity and the institutional continuity given to the royal board by the development of a large group of experienced clerical and non-noble lay councilors who served throughout the rule of the house of YORK and into the first decades of the house of TUDOR.

Further Reading: Baldwin, James F., *The King's Council in England during the Middle Ages* (Gloucester, MA: P. Smith, 1965); Chrimes, S. B., *Henry VII* (New Haven, CT: Yale University Press, 1999); Guy, John A., "The King's Council and Political Participation," in J. A. Guy and A. Fox, eds., *Reassessing the Henrician Age* (Oxford: Blackwell, 1986), pp. 121–147; Ross, Charles, *Edward IV* (New Haven, CT: Yale University Press, 1998); Watts, John, *Henry VI and the Politics of Kingship* (Cambridge: Cambridge University Press, 1996).

Council Meeting of 13 June 1483

The meeting of EDWARD V's regency COUNCIL that convened at the TOWER OF

LONDON on Friday, 13 June 1483, was used by Richard, duke of Gloucester, to destroy possible opponents to his forthcoming usurpation of his nephew's Crown. By easing the duke's path to the throne, this council meeting became an important factor in the revival of dynastic warfare in the mid–1480s.

On 12 June, Gloucester summoned two meetings of royal councilors to convene the following day. One group, headed by Chancellor John RUSSELL, was to meet at Westminster to discuss the king's coronation. The second group, led by Gloucester, was to meet at the Tower to discuss more urgent political issues. Besides Gloucester, the group that gathered at ten o'clock in the council chamber in the White Tower included William HASTINGS, Lord Hastings; Thomas ROTHERHAM, archbishop of York; John MORTON, bishop of Ely; Thomas STANLEY, Lord Stanley; John HOWARD, Lord Howard; and Henry STAFFORD, duke of Buckingham. During the course of the meeting, Gloucester surprised his colleagues by accusing Hastings of plotting his destruction with Queen Elizabeth WOODVILLE and with EDWARD IV's former mistress, Jane SHORE. The two near contemporary chroniclers of this council meeting, Polydore Vergil in his *ANGLICA HISTORIA,* and Sir Thomas More, in his *HISTORY OF KING RICHARD III,* both believed that Gloucester's charge was pure invention. Hastings was a known opponent of the WOODVILLE FAMILY and had helped Gloucester frustrate the family's attempt to control the government, while the queen was considered most unlikely to plot with her late husband's former lover.

Although Hastings, having grown suspicious of Gloucester's intentions, may have begun to talk with his rivals, the only declaration of such a plot comes from Gloucester himself. More likely is that Gloucester, having decided to take the throne, realized that Hastings would have to be eliminated because he was unshakably loyal to the son of Edward IV and would never accept Gloucester's usurpation. According to More, whose information, like Vergil's, probably came from

Morton, Gloucester charged the two women with witchcraft and, in a scene made famous by William Shakespeare in *RICHARD III,* displayed his withered left arm as proof of their sorcery. Everyone in the chamber, wrote More, "knew that his arm was ever such since his birth." Vergil, meanwhile, said nothing of the arm and stated simply that the witchcraft had made the duke weak and unable to sleep or eat. Whatever his claims, Gloucester then pounded the table and cried "treason," a signal for Thomas HOWARD, who waited outside with armed men, to invade the chamber and seize Hastings, Rotherham, Morton, and Stanley.

Morton and Rotherham were confined in the Tower, and Stanley was detained in his lodgings, but Hastings was hauled outside to Tower Green and summarily executed on a block of wood; he was given no trial and only a few minutes to confess to a priest. Although Hastings was the most influential, and therefore the most dangerous to Gloucester's plans, all four men were old servants of Edward IV and were thus unlikely to accept Edward V's deposition. By striking quickly, and before his intentions were clear, Gloucester was able to prevent his most dangerous opponents from acting against him. Within two weeks, the duke had made himself king as RICHARD III, and within two months, rumors began circulating that Richard had murdered Edward V and his younger brother, Richard PLANTAGENET, duke of York. Given the king's willingness to use violence to attain his ends, many once loyal adherents of the house of YORK believed the rumors and began plotting with former Lancastrians to overthrow Richard and replace him with Henry Tudor, earl of Richmond (see HENRY VII), the surviving Lancastrian heir.

See also Princes in the Tower; Usurpation of 1483

Further Reading: Kendall, Paul Murray, *Richard the Third* (New York: W. W. Norton, 1956); Ross, Charles, *Richard III* (Berkeley: University of California Press, 1981); Wood, Charles T., "Richard III, William, Lord Hastings, and Friday the Thirteenth," in Ralph A. Griffiths and James Sherborne, eds., *Kings and Nobles in the Later*

Middle Ages (New York: St. Martin's Press, 1986), pp. 155–168; the text of More's *History of King Richard III,* which contains an account of the 13 June council meeting, is available on the Richard III Society Web site at <www.r3.org/bookcase/more/moretext.html>.

Court, Royal

As the center of power and influence, the source of favor and patronage, and the means of access to the king and his most important magnates and councilors, the fifteenth-century court was the birthplace of the political tensions that initiated and fostered the WARS OF THE ROSES. Besides a constant throng of suitors and petitioners, the court consisted of the royal household and its officers, all government ministers and officials, foreign envoys, and the monarch's personal servants. The court served the personal and political needs of the monarch and his family, displayed the wealth and power of the Crown to the kingdom and to foreign courts, and provided an arena for Englishmen to obtain redress or to pursue political and economic advancement through royal favor.

Because fifteenth-century monarchy was personal, access to the king or to someone who had influence with the king was vital, especially for the PEERAGE and the GENTRY, who, as the politically conscious landowning classes, often required favorable royal intervention for the furtherance of their private interests. The PASTON LETTERS, which describe the Paston family's long feud with unscrupulous neighboring magnates, clearly illustrate the importance of having friends and influence at court. The letters are a catalogue of the Pastons' constant attempts to find patrons whose standing at court could win the family effective royal protection. Besides approaching Richard NEVILLE, earl of Warwick, and various members of the WOODVILLE FAMILY, the Pastons in the 1460s lobbied William HASTINGS, Lord Hastings; Henry BOURCHIER, earl of Essex; and George NEVILLE, archbishop of York. By 1470, after EDWARD IV had frustrated all their efforts, the family abandoned the house of YORK, welcomed the READEPTION of HENRY VI and the house of LANCASTER, and, in 1471, fought for Warwick at the Battle of BARNET. With the Yorkist restoration (see EDWARD IV, RESTORATION OF), the Pastons had to renew their suits to Edward IV, even turning in 1479 to several gentlemen of the royal household.

In the 1440s and 1450s, the personal deficiencies of Henry VI allowed a group of favored courtiers to gain an unusual hold on power and patronage. By seeming to divert the grace and favor of the Crown to the benefit of themselves and their supporters, nobles like William de la POLE, duke of Suffolk, and Edmund BEAUFORT, duke of Somerset, fueled the discontent of rivals like Richard PLANTAGENET, duke of York, who enjoyed noble birth and royal blood but lacked access to the king and standing at court. By the start of the civil war in 1459, the court party that had been created by Henry's favor became the nucleus of the Lancastrian party that formed around Queen MARGARET OF ANJOU. For these courtiers, Yorkist rule threatened the end of their ability as favored courtiers to obtain special favors from the monarch.

The renewal of civil war in 1469 was at least partially due to a changing dynamic at the Yorkist court. The rise of the Woodvilles and of a party of "King's men" like Hastings and William HERBERT, earl of Pembroke, caused the slow erosion of Warwick's special standing with the king, and drove the ambitious earl to seek new ways to exercise his former dominance. By 1470, Warwick allied himself with the Lancastrians in an effort to recreate for himself the favored position that his one-time enemies had enjoyed under the easily manipulated Henry VI.

In the 1470s, the English court was given a more formal structure by Edward IV's adoption of some of the elaborate ceremonial of the ducal court of BURGUNDY. Edward (and later HENRY VII) also reinforced the court's role as the political and administrative center of the kingdom by requiring courtiers to earn royal favor by serving as councilors, administrators, diplomats, and soldiers.

Further Reading: Griffiths, Ralph A., "The King's Court during the Wars of the Roses," in Ralph A. Griffiths, ed., *King and Country: England and Wales in the Fifteenth Century* (London: Hambledon Press, 1991), pp. 11–32; Loades, David, *The Tudor Court* (Totowa, NJ: Barnes and Noble Books, 1987); Myers, A. R., *The Household of Edward IV* (Manchester: Manchester University Press, 1959); Starkey, David, et al., *The English Court: From the Wars of the Roses to the Civil War* (London: Longman, 1987).

Courtenay, Henry, Earl of Devon (Lancastrian) (c. 1435–1469)

Although rewarded by EDWARD IV for his neutrality during the fighting of 1460–1461, Henry Courtenay, younger brother of Thomas COURTENAY, sixth earl of Devon, was unable to restore Courtenay dominance in the West Country and remained under suspicion of harboring his family's Lancastrian sympathies.

Unlike his brothers, who fought for HENRY VI at the Battles of WAKEFIELD, ST. ALBANS, and TOWTON, Henry Courtenay took no sides in the civil war and escaped mention in the bill of ATTAINDER passed against prominent Lancastrians in the PARLIAMENT of November 1461. Because his elder brother the earl had been executed after the Battle of Towton and his younger brother Sir John COURTENAY had gone into exile with Henry VI, Henry Courtenay was left to make the family's peace with the new Yorkist regime and salvage the family's position in the West Country.

Deprived by the attainder of the Courtenay lands and of his rightful title as seventh earl of Devon, Courtenay was nonetheless cultivated by Edward IV with a partial grant of his two brothers' former properties. Although the king employed him on various minor commissions, Courtenay was not allowed to revive his family's influence in the West Country, which passed instead to Humphrey STAFFORD, Lord Stafford, who was given many former Courtenay lands and offices. Perhaps as a result of Stafford's rise, or, as was later rumored, as a result of Stafford's ambition to be earl of Devon,

Courtenay and Sir Thomas HUNGERFORD were arrested in November 1468 on a charge of plotting to depose Edward in favor of Henry VI. Convicted of treason in January 1469, both men were hanged, drawn, and quartered, an unusual mode of execution for persons of their rank.

See also all entries under Courtenay
Further Reading: Cherry, Martin, "The Struggle for Power in Mid-Fifteenth-Century Devonshire," in Ralph A. Griffiths, ed., *Patronage, the Crown and the Provinces in Later Medieval England* (Atlantic Highlands, NJ: Humanities Press, 1981), pp. 123–144; Ross, Charles, *Edward IV* (New Haven, CT: Yale University Press, 1998); Storey, R. L., *The End of the House of Lancaster*, 2d ed. (Stroud, Gloucestershire, UK: Sutton Publishing, 1999).

Courtenay, John, Earl of Devon (Lancastrian) (c. 1440–1471)

A staunch partisan of the house of LANCASTER, John Courtenay was instrumental in convincing Queen MARGARET OF ANJOU to continue the war against EDWARD IV in 1471.

In October 1460, Courtenay joined his elder brother Thomas COURTENAY, sixth earl of Devon, when the earl took the field against the Yorkist regime established by the Act of ACCORD. He fought at the Battle of WAKEFIELD in December 1460, where he was later accused by the widow of Richard NEVILLE, earl of Salisbury, of participating after the battle in the unlawful execution of her husband. In March 1461, when Devon was executed after the Battle of TOWTON, Courtenay fled into SCOTLAND with HENRY VI. In 1463, he joined Queen Margaret in exile in FRANCE.

Recognized by the Lancastrians as the eighth earl of Devon after Edward IV's execution of his brother Henry COURTENAY in 1469, John Courtenay was among the first wave of Lancastrian exiles to return to England with Richard NEVILLE, earl of Warwick, in the autumn of 1470 (see EDWARD IV, OVERTHROW OF). He regained possession of the Courtenay lands in the West Country when the PARLIAMENT called by the READEPTION government reversed the ATTAINDER of the sixth earl. In March 1471, Devon traveled north with Warwick to oppose the landing of Edward IV, but soon returned to LONDON to await the arrival of the queen and thus was not present when Warwick met defeat and death at the Battle of BARNET on 14 April 1471 (see EDWARD IV, RESTORATION OF). When Queen Margaret and her son EDWARD OF LANCASTER, Prince of Wales, landed late on the day of Barnet, Devon encouraged them to continue the fight and persuaded them to withdraw into the West Country, where Devon used his family's influence to raise substantial forces for the Lancastrian army. The queen's decision to follow the earl's advice led on 4 May to the Battle of TEWKESBURY, where Devon was slain.

See also all entries under Courtenay
Further Reading: Cherry, Martin, "The Struggle for Power in Mid-Fifteenth-Century Devonshire," in Ralph A. Griffiths, ed., *Patronage, the Crown and the Provinces in Later Medieval England* (Atlantic Highlands, NJ: Humanities Press, 1981), pp. 123–144; Ross, Charles, *Edward IV* (New Haven, CT: Yale University Press, 1998); Storey, R. L., *The End of the House of Lancaster*, 2d ed. (Stroud, Gloucestershire, UK: Sutton Publishing, 1999).

Courtenay, Peter, Bishop of Winchester (1432–1492)

Although part of the Yorkist branch of his prominent West Country family, Peter Courtenay, bishop of Winchester, was an active member of the political opposition to RICHARD III during the dynastic struggles of the 1480s.

Educated at Oxford and at the University of Padua in Italy, Courtenay rose steadily through the church hierarchy, becoming archdeacon (i.e., a diocesan official under the bishop) of Exeter in 1453 and of Wiltshire in 1464; dean (i.e., head of a community of clergy resident at a cathedral) of Windsor in 1476 and of Exeter in 1477, and bishop of Exeter in 1478. A member of the Courtenays of Powderham, cousins of the Lancastrian earls of Devon and clients of George PLANTAGENET, duke of Clarence, Courtenay was secretary to Clarence and, during the READEPTION in

1470–1471, to HENRY VI. After 1471, the Powderham Courtenays returned with Clarence to their Yorkist allegiance, which they continued after the duke's execution in 1478 (see CLARENCE, EXECUTION OF). In July 1483, Bishop Peter Courtenay followed his father and brothers in supporting Richard III's usurpation of his nephew's throne. However, in the autumn of 1483, for reasons that remain obscure, Courtenay abandoned the house of YORK, joined the uprising led by Henry STAFFORD, duke of Buckingham, and assisted various of his Courtenay kinsmen in encouraging opposition to Richard across the West Country.

After the failure of BUCKINGHAM'S REBELLION, Courtenay was attainted and fled to BRITTANY to join the growing group of exiles surrounding Henry Tudor, earl of Richmond. The bishop returned to England in 1485, after Richmond won the Crown at the Battle of BOSWORTH FIELD on 22 August. Courtenay acted as seneschal at Richmond's coronation as HENRY VII in October 1485, and the bishop's ATTAINDER was reversed in the first PARLIAMENT of the reign. Appointed keeper of the privy seal in 1485, Courtenay was elevated to the wealthy bishopric of Winchester in 1487. Until his death in September 1492, Courtenay continued to serve Henry VII in various capacities.

See also all entries under Courtenay
Further Reading: Chrimes, S. B., *Henry VII* (New Haven, CT: Yale University Press, 1999); Gill, Louise, *Richard III and Buckingham's Rebellion* (Stroud, Gloucestershire, UK: Sutton Publishing, 1999); Ross, Charles, *Richard III* (Berkeley: University of California Press, 1981).

Courtenay, Thomas, Earl of Devon (1414–1458)

Through his long and violent feud with William BONVILLE, Lord Bonville, Thomas Courtenay, fifth earl of Devon, contributed significantly to the rising disorder in the shires that helped initiate civil war in the 1450s.

Courtenay became the premier nobleman in the West Country when he succeeded his father as earl of Devon in 1422. In 1441, Devon was appointed to the lucrative stewardship of the Duchy of Cornwall, an office HENRY VI had already conferred on Sir William Bonville in 1437. Bonville was a West Country gentleman whose growing influence at COURT threatened Courtenay dominance in the region. In 1442, after violence had repeatedly erupted in the West Country between the Courtenay and Bonville affinities (see AFFINITY), the COUNCIL intervened, stripping both men of the stewardship and putting both under large bonds to ensure good behavior.

With Bonville serving in FRANCE between 1443 and 1447, and Devon restored to the Cornwall stewardship in 1444, the COURTENAY-BONVILLE FEUD lapsed until 1450, when Bonville, now raised to the PEERAGE as Lord Bonville, strengthened his standing at court by attaching himself to James BUTLER, earl of Wiltshire, a royal favorite who was also seeking to enhance his western influence at Devon's expense. To compensate for his own lack of influence at court, Devon allied himself with Richard PLANTAGENET, duke of York, the leading opponent of the court party. In 1452, Devon instigated pro-York riots and assemblies across the West Country and was one of the few noblemen to side with York against the court at DARTFORD, an armed confrontation at which the duke and his allies were forced to submit to Henry VI.

Imprisoned and stripped of his offices after Dartford, Devon was released by York in late 1453, when the king's illness restored the duke's political position (see HENRY VI, ILLNESS OF). During York's FIRST PROTECTORATE in 1454, Devon resumed his attacks on Bonville, forcing the council to again intervene with warnings and bonds. During 1455, Devon's alliance with York dissolved. In May, Devon was with the royal army at the Battle of ST. ALBANS, where York and his new allies, Richard NEVILLE, earl of Salisbury, and Richard NEVILLE, earl of Warwick, destroyed their enemies and took custody of the king. Having watched York achieve his goals

through direct action, Devon threw the West Country into an uproar in October 1455 by leading a force of several thousand in attacks on Bonville's property and servants and by instigating the murder of Nicholas RADFORD. On 1 November, Devon seized Exeter, holding the city for six weeks. Although compelled to surrender by York and imprisoned in the TOWER OF LONDON for murder and riot, Devon was released in 1456 and pardoned in 1457 by a government now controlled by Queen MARGARET OF ANJOU, who looked upon Devon as an enemy of York and thus a friend of hers. Devon died shortly thereafter in February 1458, leaving his sons as committed supporters of the house of LANCASTER.

See also all entries under Courtenay
Further Reading: Cherry, Martin, "The Struggle for Power in Mid-Fifteenth-Century Devonshire," in Ralph A. Griffiths, ed., *Patronage, the Crown and the Provinces in Later Medieval England* (Atlantic Highlands, NJ: Humanities Press, 1981), pp. 123–144; Griffiths, Ralph A., *The Reign of King Henry VI* (Berkeley: University of California Press, 1981); Storey, R. L., *The End of the House of Lancaster,* 2d ed. (Stroud, Gloucestershire, UK: Sutton Publishing, 1999).

Courtenay, Thomas, Earl of Devon (1432–1461)

A firm adherent of the house of LANCASTER, Thomas Courtenay, sixth earl of Devon, was, like his father, Thomas COURTENAY, fifth earl of Devon, a violent man whose vigorous pursuit of the COURTENAY-BONVILLE FEUD helped shape the political alignments that fueled the civil war.

In October 1455, Courtenay led the party of 100 men that invaded the Devonshire home of Nicholas RADFORD, a former Courtenay associate who had fallen afoul of the family for his recent support of William BONVILLE, Lord Bonville, the Courtenays' chief rival for dominance in the West Country. The subsequent despoliation and murder of Radford were part of a regionwide campaign of violence conducted by the earl of Devon and his sons against the friends, servants, and property of Bonville. Indicted with his father and brothers for these crimes, Courtenay was pardoned, along with his family, in 1457, after control of the government had passed from Richard PLANTAGENET, duke of York, to Queen MARGARET OF ANJOU, who sought to lure the fifth earl, a former supporter of York, to the Lancastrian cause.

Upon succeeding his father as earl of Devon in 1458, Courtenay continued the family's recent support of HENRY VI, receiving two sizable annuities as rewards. When passage of the Act of ACCORD in October 1460 disinherited the queen's son, EDWARD OF LANCASTER, Prince of Wales, Devon raised a force in the West Country and joined various other Lancastrian lords at the Battle of WAKEFIELD, where York was defeated and slain. In February 1461, Devon fought at the Battle of ST. ALBANS, where he had the satisfaction of seeing his enemy, Lord Bonville, beheaded after the Lancastrian victory. Six weeks later, Devon received the same summary justice, when he was executed by order of EDWARD IV after the Yorkist triumph at the Battle of TOWTON.

See also all entries under Courtenay
Further Reading: Cherry, Martin, "The Struggle for Power in Mid-Fifteenth-Century Devonshire," in Ralph A. Griffiths, ed., *Patronage, the Crown and the Provinces in Later Medieval England* (Atlantic Highlands, NJ: Humanities Press, 1981), pp. 123–144; Griffiths, Ralph A., *The Reign of King Henry VI* (Berkeley: University of California Press, 1981); Storey, R. L., *The End of the House of Lancaster*, 2d ed. (Stroud, Gloucestershire, UK: Sutton Publishing, 1999).

Courtenay-Bonville Feud (1450s)

The feud between Thomas COURTENAY, fifth earl of Devon, and William BONVILLE, Lord Bonville, spread violence and disorder across the West Country in the 1450s and helped create the political alignments that made civil war possible.

Although the quarrel may have originated in a land dispute arising out of the marriage of Bonville to Devon's aunt, Elizabeth Courtenay, its underlying cause was the growth of Bonville's influence at COURT, which enhanced his political position in the West Country and made him a threat to the traditional Courtenay dominance in the region. The two sides had already clashed by 1441, when HENRY VI aggravated the dispute by granting Devon the stewardship of the Duchy of Cornwall, a lucrative office that the king had already given to Bonville in 1437. To end the resulting tumults, the COUNCIL deprived both men of the appointment and placed both under large bonds to prevent further disorder.

Because Bonville was in FRANCE between 1443 and 1447, and Devon reacquired the Cornwall stewardship in 1444, the West Country remained quiet until 1450, when Devon, seeking to nullify his rival's influence at court, allied himself with Richard PLANTAGENET, duke of York, a powerful opponent of the court party. Devon's actions caused Bonville to associate himself with another court favorite with ambitions in the West Country, James BUTLER, earl of Wiltshire. In August 1451, Devon, provoked by Wiltshire's involvement in the quarrel, raised a sizable force and besieged Bonville in Taunton Castle. To save his ally from imprisonment, York intervened to end the siege. Devon then supported York at his armed confrontation with the king at DARTFORD in 1452. The failure of this effort led to Devon's confinement and Bonville's unchallenged dominance in the West Country. However, the king's illness restored York's political position, and the duke arranged Devon's release in November 1453 (see HENRY VI, ILLNESS OF). Devon immediately began harassing Bonville's followers and attacking his property, although a further intervention by the council restored order for a time.

By 1455, York's alliance with the NEVILLE FAMILY again isolated Devon, and he accompanied the king's army in May, when Henry VI was defeated and taken into custody by York at the Battle of ST. ALBANS. Encouraged to take direct action by the example of York's success at St. Albans, Devon and his sons launched a series of assaults on Bonville's West Country servants and property in October

1455. The most notorious episode in this campaign of violence was the murder on 23 October of Nicholas RADFORD, a former Courtenay associate who had earned Devon's hatred with his recent support of Bonville. On 1 November, Devon seized Exeter and held it for six weeks, his men garrisoning the walls and questioning the allegiance of anyone who sought to leave or enter the town. After a victorious confrontation with Bonville's forces at Clyst on 15 December, Devon withdrew from Exeter and soon after surrendered himself to York, who committed him to the TOWER OF LONDON.

Indicted for the murder of Radford and the occupation of Exeter, Devon and his sons were saved from trial by the end of York's SECOND PROTECTORATE in February 1456. Queen MARGARET OF ANJOU, who now dominated the royal government, saw Devon as a valuable ally against York, and arranged the earl's release and pardon. The Courtenay-Bonville feud now merged fully into the national political struggle. In the civil war that began in 1459, Devon's sons—the earl having died in 1458—became firm supporters of the house of LANCASTER, while Bonville fought and eventually died for the house of YORK.

See also all entries under Courtenay
Further Reading: Cherry, Martin, "The Struggle for Power in Mid-Fifteenth-Century Devonshire," in Ralph A. Griffiths, ed., *Patronage, the Crown and the Provinces in Later Medieval England* (Atlantic Highlands, NJ: Humanities Press, 1981), pp. 123–144; Griffiths, Ralph A., *The Reign of King Henry VI* (Berkeley: University of California Press, 1981); Storey, R. L., *The End of the House of Lancaster*, 2d ed. (Stroud, Gloucestershire, UK: Sutton Publishing, 1999).

Coventry Parliament (1459)

The PARLIAMENT that opened in the royalist stronghold of Coventry on 20 November 1459 was a staunchly Lancastrian body, which gave statutory expression to Queen MARGARET OF ANJOU's desire for the political and economic destruction of Richard PLANTAGENET, duke of York, and his allies, the

men who had dared to exclude her from the exercise of royal power.

With elections to the Coventry Parliament called for and controlled by the queen and her supporters, the 260 members of the Commons were almost to a man Lancastrian in their sympathies. The central business of the session was consideration and passage of a bill of ATTAINDER against York; his eldest sons, Edward, earl of March (see EDWARD IV), and Edmund PLANTAGENET, earl of Rutland; his chief noble allies, Richard NEVILLE, earl of Salisbury, and his son Richard NEVILLE, earl of Warwick; and certain other knights and gentlemen who had conspicuously supported York's cause.

Passed without difficulty, the act of attainder proclaimed the named parties rebels and traitors, declared them legally dead, and placed their vast estates and incomes in the hands of the king. York, his sons, and the Nevilles were in overseas exile, having fled the country for IRELAND and CALAIS after their defeat at the Battle of LUDFORD BRIDGE in October. Because the Yorkists were beyond the government's control and could not be brought to trial, the Lancastrians decided to proceed against them through Parliament—extinguishing their power and position, and the threat they presented, through legislative action. By handing most of the confiscated lands to royal officers appointed for life, the Crown indicated its intention that the extinction of rights be permanent, and not merely a temporary measure to be reversed should the Yorkists submit and seek pardon. The duke and his supporters were thus left with few options but continuing the fight.

On 11 December, the lords assembled in Parliament swore a solemn oath in the royal presence to support HENRY VI and the eventual succession of his son, Prince EDWARD OF LANCASTER, and to preserve and honor the queen. Having achieved Margaret's main goals, the Coventry Parliament ended on 20 December. In October 1460, with Warwick in control of the king and the government after his victory in July at the Battle of NORTHAMPTON, a Yorkist-dominated assembly at Westminster reversed the decisions of the Coventry Parliament and restored the duke and the Nevilles to control of their lands. The Coventry Parliament, which became known as the Parliament of Devils for the severity with which it treated the Yorkists, had clearly shown how the party in power could use the national assembly to crush its defeated enemies.

Further Reading: Griffiths, Ralph A., *The Reign of King Henry VI* (Berkeley: University of California Press, 1981).

Crowland Chronicle. *See Croyland Chronicle*

Croyland Chronicle

For the period 1459 to 1485, the two accounts known as the First and Second Continuations of the *Croyland Chronicle* are valuable sources of information. While the First Continuation supplies details for events in the 1460s, the Second Continuation is the single most important source for the period of Yorkist rule.

The Benedictine abbey of Crowland (or Croyland) in Lincolnshire produced a medieval chronicle for which the two fifteenth-century works were contemporary continuations. The First Continuation, written by an anonymous prior of Crowland, concludes in January 1470 and pertains mainly to the history of the abbey. Its relevance to the struggle between the houses of LANCASTER and YORK is therefore limited, although the author adopted a more national perspective when writing about the 1460s. The chronicler detested northerners, and he particularly castigated their behavior during Queen MARGARET OF ANJOU's MARCH ON LONDON in 1461. This prejudice resurfaces in the description of the ROBIN OF REDESDALE REBELLION and other northern uprisings in 1469, a year when EDWARD IV's capture in Lincolnshire by Richard NEVILLE, earl of Warwick, brought national events to the vicinity of Crowland. Although the tone of the First Continuation is moderately Yorkist, the

author was critical of the influence exercised on the king by Queen ELIZABETH WOODVILLE and the WOODVILLE FAMILY.

The Second Continuation was, according to its author, written at Crowland in April 1486. It is the only continuous, contemporary political narrative of the Yorkist years, overlapping the First Continuation by covering the period from October 1459 to 1485. It is also not Yorkist PROPAGANDA, but a sophisticated historical narrative that was intended to be an accurate and objective account of events. The author described himself as a doctor of canon law, a member of Edward IV's COUNCIL, and an ambassador to BURGUNDY in 1471. He was clearly familiar with the workings of English government, personally acquainted with Edward IV and RICHARD III, and an eyewitness to many of the events described. Although generally friendly to Edward IV, the writer was critical of the king's financial exactions; of his destruction of his brother, George PLANTAGENET, duke of Clarence; and of his aggressive policy toward SCOTLAND in the 1480s.

The writer was far more critical of Richard III, disapproving of the USURPATION OF 1483; of the execution of William HASTINGS, Lord Hastings; and of the king's behavior after the death of his wife, Anne NEVILLE, especially in regard to his niece, ELIZABETH OF YORK. The author also applauded the victory of HENRY VII at the Battle of BOSWORTH FIELD in 1485. Given what the writer reveals about himself, a possible (but by no means the only) candidate for authorship of the Second Continuation is John RUSSELL, bishop of Lincoln, who was keeper of the privy seal for Edward IV and chancellor under Richard III.

See also North of England and the Wars of the Roses
Further Reading: Pronay, Nicholas, and John Cox, eds., *The Crowland Chronicle Continuations: 1459–1486* (London: Richard III and Yorkist History Trust, 1986); the text of the Second Continuation of the *Croyland Chronicle* is available on the Richard III Society Web site at <http://www.r3.org/bookcase/croyland/croy1.html>.

Dartford Uprising (1452)

The unsuccessful armed uprising that culminated at Dartford in Kent in March 1452 was the first attempt by Richard PLANTAGENET, duke of York, to use force to achieve his political ends.

In January 1452, York, seeking to secure recognition of himself as heir to the childless HENRY VI and eager to increase his influence in the royal government, issued a public declaration of allegiance to the king and a statement of regret that Henry did not currently look upon him with favor. In February, the duke issued a condemnation of Edmund BEAUFORT, duke of Somerset, who was York's rival both for political power and for the succession, the BEAUFORT FAMILY having as compelling a claim to the throne as the house of YORK. The duke charged Somerset with responsibility for the recent English military collapse in FRANCE and with plotting the destruction of York and his family. Backed by Thomas COURTENAY, earl of Devon, who was seeking allies against his courtier rival, William BONVILLE, Lord Bonville, and relying on public support born of anger over Somerset's perceived failures in France, York began raising an armed force to march on LONDON and compel the king to dismiss Somerset. When several deputations from the king failed to deflect York from his purpose, Henry ordered the London authorities to refuse York admittance to the city, which they did in late February, forcing the duke to march into Kent to his property at Dartford.

Because Kent had been the heart of JACK CADE'S REBELLION in 1450, York hoped to increase his support by tapping into any lingering antigovernment sentiment. On 1 March, Henry entered Kent at the head of a large army. Although York's own forces were sizable, and he had several ships in the Thames loaded with ARTILLERY, the English PEERAGE, with the exception of Devon and Lord Cobham, backed the king. As the two armies advanced toward each other, a team of mediators led by the bishops William WAINFLEET and Thomas BOURCHIER, and including Richard NEVILLE, earl of Salisbury, and his son, Richard NEVILLE, earl of Warwick, moved back and forth between the king and the duke. According to some sources, an agreement was concluded on 2 March whereby York would lay down his arms in return for being allowed to present his petition against Somerset to the king. Somerset was then to be imprisoned in the TOWER OF LONDON pending an investigation into York's charges against him. However, when York came before Henry, he found Somerset at the king's side and himself in custody. Other sources simply say that York came and knelt before the king, presented his petition, and then returned to London with Henry.

Finding the commons of Kent hesitant to follow him, and lacking any significant support from other peers, York probably realized the futility of his position and submitted. Nonetheless, the same nobles who refused to support his armed rising were also unwilling to see him too severely punished. York was detained at his London residence, compelled to make a public oath of loyalty to Henry at St. Paul's Cathedral, and then released. He was also forced to submit to an arbitration of his dispute with Somerset, which was conducted by a panel dominated by friends of Somerset. Although a pardon was issued to encourage

York's supporters to disperse, the king sought to warn the duke's RETAINERS against future armed demonstrations by leading a series of judicial commissions into areas of Yorkist influence. The king's liberal imposition of fines and imprisonments impressed York's supporters with royal authority and left the duke powerless and politically isolated.

Further Reading: Griffiths, Ralph A., *The Reign of King Henry VI* (Berkeley: University of California Press, 1981); Johnson, P. A., *Duke Richard of York* (Oxford: Clarendon Press, 1988).

De Facto Act (1495)

Passed by PARLIAMENT in October 1495, the De Facto Act sought to heal the lingering divisions of the WARS OF THE ROSES by encouraging former adherents of RICHARD III and the house of YORK to support HENRY VII against any current and future Yorkist attempts to retake the throne. The act was designed to reassure those fighting for the king against his rivals that they would suffer no loss of property as a result of their military service.

Entitled "An Act that No Person Going with the King to the Wars Shall be Attainted of Treason," the statute declared that it would be unreasonable and illegal to deprive any subject of his property for serving the person who was "for the time being" king of England. Although service to Richard III had been treated as treason since the Battle of BOSWORTH FIELD in 1485—Henry had even dated his reign from the day before Bosworth to more clearly extend the penalties of treason to those who had fought for Richard—the De Facto Act reassured former Yorkists that they would not henceforth suffer forfeiture or ATTAINDER for treason for their past allegiance. The act prohibited loyal military servants of the king from losing life, lands, income, or possessions on account of such service. It did not absolve anyone from providing military service to Henry VII, since he was, "for the time being," king. However, it did safeguard anyone who served Henry in any of his wars, foreign and domestic, from being convicted of treason should Henry himself be overthrown by a Yorkist pretender, such as Perkin WARBECK, who was threatening the security of the house of TUDOR in 1495. Although the act sought to invalidate any future statutes that might punish a subject for military service to the king, it was generally understood that no Parliament could limit the actions of a future Parliament. The De Facto Act was thus not a proclamation of constitutional principle, but a practical expedient designed to pacify any remaining hostility from the late civil wars and to unite the country around the king who had emerged from those wars.

See also Yorkist Heirs (after 1485)
Further Reading: Chrimes, S. B., *Henry VII* (New Haven, CT: Yale University Press, 1999).

Derby, Countess of. *See* Beaufort, Margaret, Countess of Richmond and Derby

Derby, Earl of. *See* Stanley, Thomas, Earl of Derby

Desmond, Earl of. *See* Fitzgerald, Thomas, Earl of Desmond

Devereux, Walter, Lord Ferrers of Chartley (1432–1485)

Walter Devereux, Lord Ferrers of Chartley, was a loyal adherent of the house of YORK and one of EDWARD IV's chief lieutenants in WALES.

Born into a Herefordshire GENTRY family, Devereux was a councilor of Richard PLANTAGENET, duke of York, and served as steward of many of the duke's Welsh lordships in the 1450s. When war erupted in 1459, Devereux took up arms for York and was with the duke's forces at the Battle of LUDFORD BRIDGE. After York's flight to IRELAND, Devereux was included in the bills of ATTAINDER passed against leading Yorkists in the COVENTRY PARLIAMENT, but he saved his life by submitting to HENRY VI. He resumed his Yorkist allegiance in 1460 and fought with York's son, Edward, earl of March, at the Battle of MORTIMER'S CROSS in February 1461. He was also present at the LONDON assembly that proclaimed March king as Edward IV. Devereux fought for Edward at the Battle of TOWTON in late March, being knighted on the field, and was one of the commanders of the Yorkist forces at the Battle of TWT HILL in October. In 1462, Devereux was elevated to the PEERAGE as Lord Ferrers of Chartley, a title that he held by right of his wife. With his home at Weobley in Herefordshire, Ferrers had interests in the Welsh marches (i.e., borderlands). Edward strengthened these connections in the 1460s by naming Ferrers to numerous Welsh commissions, granting him lands in the marches and in Berkshire, and appointing him captain of Aberystwyth Castle.

In the spring of 1470, Ferrers assisted the king in suppressing the rebellion raised by Richard NEVILLE, earl of Warwick, and his ally, George PLANTAGENET, duke of Clarence, the king's brother. As a prominent Yorkist, Ferrers was dismissed from all county commissions of the peace by the READEPTION government of Henry VI. When Edward IV returned from exile in March 1471, Ferrers fought for him at the Battles of BARNET and TEWKESBURY. He also helped drive Jasper TUDOR, earl of Pembroke, and his nephew, Henry Tudor, earl of Richmond, into exile in BRITTANY, thereby restoring Yorkist authority in Wales. In 1473, Edward appointed Ferrers to the COUNCIL, and in 1475, Ferrers raised a troop of MEN-AT-ARMS and ARCHERS to accompany the king on his French expedition.

Although a long-time Yorkist who might have been expected to support EDWARD V, Ferrers acquiesced in RICHARD III's usurpation of the throne in 1483 (see USURPATION OF 1483). Richard rewarded Ferrers's loyalty with a grant of lands and an annuity of £146 per year. Ferrers died fighting for Richard at the Battle of BOSWORTH FIELD in August 1485. He was attainted in the first PARLIAMENT of HENRY VII, and his estates were confiscated by the Crown.

Further Reading: Boardman, Andrew W., *The Medieval Soldier in the Wars of the Roses* (Stroud, Gloucestershire, UK: Sutton Publishing, 1998); Evans, H. T., *Wales and the Wars of the Roses* (Stroud, Gloucestershire, UK: Alan Sutton Publishing, 1995); Ross, Charles, *Edward IV* (New Haven, CT: Yale University Press, 1998).

Devon, Earl of. *See* entries under Courtenay; Stafford, Humphrey, Earl of Devon

Dinham, John, Lord Dinham (d. 1501)

A capable administrator and military commander, John Dinham (or Dynham), Lord Dinham, was a loyal adherent of the house of YORK and a trusted servant of the house of TUDOR.

Born into a Devonshire GENTRY family, Dinham rendered vital service to the Yorkist cause in October 1459, when, after guiding them from the Battle of LUDFORD BRIDGE, he sheltered Richard NEVILLE, earl of Warwick; Richard NEVILLE, earl of Salisbury; and Edward, earl of March (see EDWARD IV) in the Dinham family home at Newton Abbot. Dinham also hired a vessel to carry himself and the Yorkist lords to safety at CALAIS. In the early morning of 15 January 1460, Dinham raided Sandwich, capturing a Lancastrian fleet being readied there for an attack on Calais and carrying off its commander, Richard WOODVILLE, Earl Rivers, as well as Rivers's wife, JACQUETTA OF LUXEMBOURG, and his son, Anthony WOODVILLE. In early June, Dinham, accompanied by William NEVILLE, Lord Fauconberg, and John WENLOCK, again descended on Sandwich, defeating a Lancastrian force of ARCHERS and MEN-AT-ARMS and seizing the town as a Yorkist bridgehead.

Named to the royal COUNCIL in 1462 and raised to the PEERAGE in 1467, Dinham became the chief Yorkist peer in the West Country after the death of Humphrey STAFFORD, earl of Devon, in 1469. Loyal to Edward IV, Dinham was one of only seven nobles not summoned to the READEPTION session of PARLIAMENT in 1470. After Edward's restoration in 1471, Dinham became deputy at Calais to William HASTINGS, Lord Hastings. In May 1473, Dinham helped repel the landing in Essex of John de VERE, the Lancastrian earl of Oxford, and in 1475 he commanded a fleet charged with holding the Channel while Edward IV's army sailed to FRANCE.

After the USURPATION OF 1483, Dinham supported RICHARD III, who rewarded him with the stewardship of the royal Duchy of Cornwall. Dinham also received extensive land grants in the autumn after remaining loyal to Richard during BUCKINGHAM'S REBELLION. In December 1484, Dinham recaptured the Calais fortress of Hammes from its turncoat garrison, which had defected to Henry Tudor, earl of Richmond (see HENRY VII). Perhaps because he allowed the Hammes garrison to march away, Dinham was superseded in the Calais command in 1485 by John of Gloucester, the king's bastard son. Because Dinham remained in Calais as one of Gloucester's deputies, he was not present at the Battle of BOSWORTH FIELD in August 1485. Dinham was almost immediately favored by Henry VII, who appointed him treasurer of England, an influential office that Dinham held until his death in January 1501. One of Henry's most active councilors, Dinham served on many royal commissions and received numerous rewards, including election to the prestigious Order of the Garter.

Further Reading: Gillingham, John, *The Wars of the Roses* (Baton Rouge: Louisiana State University Press, 1981); Ross, Charles, *Edward IV* (New Haven, CT: Yale University Press, 1998); Ross, Charles, *Richard III* (Berkeley: University of California Press, 1981).

Dorset, Marquis of. *See* Grey, Thomas, Marquis of Dorset

Dunstanburgh Castle (1461–1464)

Along with the other Northumberland fortresses of ALNWICK and BAMBURGH,

Dunstanburgh Castle demonstrated the insecurity of EDWARD IV's throne by falling several times into Lancastrian hands between 1461 and 1464.

After the Yorkist victory at the Battle of TOWTON in March 1461, Dunstanburgh was one of several northern strongholds controlled by RETAINERS loyal to the Lancastrian Percy family (see entries under PERCY). Beginning in August, Richard NEVILLE, earl of Warwick, campaigned to reduce Lancastrian outposts across the north, with Sir Ralph Percy surrendering the coastal fortress of Dunstanburgh in October. Edward IV ordered Warwick to leave Percy in command of the castle, a decision that proved disastrous in the following month when Percy yielded Dunstanburgh to a Lancastrian force from SCOTLAND under Sir William TAILBOYS.

In October 1462, when MARGARET OF ANJOU recaptured Bamburgh and Alnwick with a troop of French MERCENARIES commanded by Pierre de BRÉZÉ, Percy was still holding Dunstanburgh for the house of LANCASTER. But the Lancastrian royal family and de Brézé withdrew to Scotland in November, leaving the Northumberland garrisons to face Warwick's approaching army. Throughout December, Warwick coordinated siege operations, placing the effort at Dunstanburgh under the command of Lords Scrope, Greystoke, and Powis. When the castle surrendered on 28 December, the king's desire to reconcile the rival parties led him to again show an unwise generosity to Percy, who, upon swearing allegiance to Edward, was given custody of Dunstanburgh and Bamburgh. Percy's Yorkist loyalty evaporated a second time in March 1463, when he handed both fortresses to Margaret upon her return to England at the head of a Lancastrian-Scottish force.

In June 1463, a Scottish army accompanied by JAMES III and his mother MARY OF GUELDRES, as well as by the Lancastrian royal family, crossed the border and laid siege to Norham Castle. Warwick and his brother, John NEVILLE, Lord Montagu, hurried north and surprised the Scots in July, driving the panicked invaders out of the kingdom and dampening Scottish enthusiasm for the Lancastrian cause. Edward IV concluded a ten-month truce with the Scottish government in December, and in early 1464, the Yorkists prepared to suppress Lancastrian activity in Northumberland once and for all. In April, Percy left Dunstanburgh to fight with Henry BEAUFORT, duke of Somerset, against Montagu at the Battle of HEDGELEY MOOR. Percy's death there and Somerset's defeat and capture at the Battle of HEXHAM in May cleared all Northumberland outside the three castles of Lancastrian resistance. On 25 June, the Dunstanburgh garrison surrendered to Warwick on terms that granted all its members pardons. With the fall of Bamburgh a few weeks later, the war in Northumberland ended.

See also North of England and the Wars of the Roses
Further Reading: Haigh, Philip A., *The Military Campaigns of the Wars of the Roses* (Stroud, Gloucestershire, UK: Sutton Publishing, 1995); Pollard, A. J., *North-Eastern England during the Wars of the Roses* (Oxford: Clarendon Press, 1990).

Economy. *See* English Economy and the Wars of the Roses

Edgecote, Battle of (1469)

Fought on 26 July 1469 near Banbury in Oxfordshire, the Battle of Edgecote allowed Richard NEVILLE, earl of Warwick, to seize temporary control of EDWARD IV and thereby initiate a new phase of the WARS OF THE ROSES.

In the spring of 1469, Warwick, angered by the growing wealth and political influence of Edward IV's in-laws, the WOODVILLE FAMILY, and certain of the king's favorites, such as William HERBERT, earl of Pembroke, forged an alliance with George PLANTAGENET, duke of Clarence, Edward's equally disgruntled younger brother. The pact, which was sealed on 11 July with Clarence's unauthorized marriage to Warwick's daughter, Isabel NEVILLE, aimed at separating the offending courtiers from the king and making Warwick and Clarence the premier peers of the realm. The allies issued a manifesto calling for loyal Englishmen to support them in reforming Edward's corrupt government and expressed support for an ongoing northern rebellion led by someone calling himself Robin of Redesdale, who had issued a similar call for reform in mid-June. In reality, the ROBIN OF REDESDALE REBELLION was directed by Warwick, and probably led by Sir William Conyers, a Neville retainer. By drawing Edward into the north, the Redesdale uprising sought to give Warwick time to secure LONDON and raise an army (see NORTH OF ENGLAND AND THE WARS OF THE ROSES).

When Edward marched north in June to confront the Redesdale rebels, he was unaware of their connection to Warwick and Clarence. By mid-July, he was in Nottingham awaiting the arrival of forces from WALES under the command of Pembroke and Humphrey STAFFORD, earl of Devon. Although he was by this time probably aware of Warwick's activities, the king made no move, and the Redesdale rebels bypassed Nottingham to hasten their meeting with Warwick, who was marching north from London. On the evening of 25 July, Pembroke and Devon argued over billeting arrangements. As a result of the quarrel, Devon withdrew toward Banbury with the ARCHERS, leaving Herbert with only the Welsh footmen. Shortly afterward, Pembroke encountered the Redesdale rebels, who attacked him vigorously the next morning. Although Pembroke's men offered fierce resistance, they were hampered by lack of archers and forced to retreat with heavy losses. When advance elements of Warwick's army arrived later in the day, a second rebel attack broke Pembroke's force before Devon could engage his men.

With Conyers and many others dead on the field, Pembroke and his brother were taken prisoner and executed the next day at Northampton in Warwick's presence. Devon was killed some weeks later in Somerset and Richard WOODVILLE, Earl Rivers, and his son Sir John Woodville, whom the king had sent away from him for their safety, were captured and executed at Coventry in August on Warwick's orders. Hearing of the disaster at Edgecote, Edward, now deserted by most of his RETAINERS, was on the road to Northampton when he was taken into Warwick's "protection" by the earl's brother, Archbishop George NEVILLE. For the moment, the king and the royal government were in the hands of Warwick and Clarence. Although Edward soon regained his freedom, he lacked the political strength to proceed against the earl and the duke, who extorted a royal pardon and remained free to resume their rebellion in 1470.

See also Robin of Holderness Rebellion
Further Reading: Haigh, Philip A., *The Military Campaigns of the Wars of the Roses* (Stroud, Gloucestershire, UK: Sutton Publishing, 1995).

Edmund, Earl of Rutland. *See* Plantagenet, Edmund, Earl of Rutland

Edward IV, King of England (1442–1483)

Edward IV, first king of the house of YORK, was a central figure in the WARS OF THE ROSES. Only eighteen when he overthrew HENRY VI and the house of LANCASTER, Edward, despite personal flaws and political misjudgments that briefly cost him the Crown, was a strong and successful monarch who reduced disorder and lawlessness and reversed the deterioration of royal authority.

The eldest son of Richard PLANTAGENET, duke of York, and his wife, Cecily NEVILLE, Edward was born on 28 April 1442 at Rouen in English-held Normandy, where his father was then serving as lord lieutenant. By 1454, twelve-year-old Edward had been created earl of March, a title formerly belonging to the Mortimers, the family of Edward's paternal grandmother, from whom the house of York derived its claim to the throne. In 1459, when civil war erupted between the supporters of York and the king, Edward, now seventeen, was with his father at the Battle of LUDFORD BRIDGE, where the defection of Andrew TROLLOPE and his men forced the duke and his adherents to flee the country. York sailed for IRELAND, while Edward made for CALAIS with his father's chief allies, Richard NEVILLE, earl of Salisbury, and his son, Richard NEVILLE, earl of Warwick.

Edward IV, the first king of the house of York. (National Portrait Gallery: NPG 3542)

Although separated from his father, Edward began in 1460 to emerge as an important political figure in his own right as he acted in concert with the vigorous Warwick to advance his family's cause. Having frustrated all Lancastrian attempts to dislodge them from Calais, the three Yorkist earls invaded England in June 1460. After securing LONDON, the earls marched north and, on 10 July, captured Henry VI at the Battle of NORTHAMPTON. In October, York returned to lay claim to the Crown. PARLIAMENT, being unwilling to depose Henry, fashioned the compromise Act of ACCORD, which disinherited Henry's son, Prince EDWARD OF LANCASTER, and vested succession to the Crown in York and his sons. In December, when York marched north to suppress Lancastrian uprisings against the new regime, Edward set out to raise troops on the Welsh border. At Gloucester, in early January 1461, Edward learned of the death of his father at the Battle of WAKEFIELD.

Now leader of the Yorkist cause and, for the first time, in independent command of a military force, Edward confronted the army of

Jasper TUDOR, earl of Pembroke, who was advancing against him from WALES. Edward crushed Pembroke at the Battle of MORTIMER'S CROSS on 2 February, but two weeks later Queen MARGARET OF ANJOU defeated Warwick and took custody of Henry at the Battle of ST. ALBANS. Aided by southern fears of the northerners in Margaret's army (see MARCH ON LONDON), whose acts of plunder had been magnified by Warwick's PROPAGANDA efforts, Edward boldly entered London in late February. Handsome and confident, the very antithesis of Henry VI, Edward, though only eighteen, looked and acted like a king and was therefore hailed as a deliverer by the frightened Londoners. Proclaimed king on 4 March, Edward began immediately to gather an army. On 29 March, Edward secured his throne by winning the bloody, daylong Battle of TOWTON, his personal leadership helping to steady his troops at several crucial junctures during the fighting (see GENERALSHIP). Although the Lancastrian royal family fled into SCOTLAND, from where their supporters raided the north for the next three years, Edward was firmly in power by 1465, when Henry VI was in the TOWER OF LONDON and Queen Margaret and her son were in exile in FRANCE.

During the 1460s, Edward's political inexperience led him to pardon opponents too easily, to reward supporters too richly, and to delegate authority too freely, especially to Warwick and the NEVILLE FAMILY. Although he never abdicated ultimate control, and never allowed his mistresses political power, Edward was also pleasure loving and much given to sexual dalliance. In 1464, he created enormous political problems for himself and his heirs by secretly marrying a subject, Elizabeth WOODVILLE, who brought to COURT a host of ambitious relatives. Although the WOODVILLE FAMILY eventually formed a powerful political connection in support of the Yorkist throne, their avid pursuit of wealth and power alienated Warwick and the king's brother, George PLANTAGENET, duke of Clarence, who in 1469 launched a coup that briefly placed Edward in their custody. When a sec-

ond coup failed in the spring of 1470, Warwick and Clarence fled to France, where the earl, through the self-interested mediation of LOUIS XI, concluded the ANGERS AGREEMENT with Margaret of Anjou. Realizing that Edward had grown too independent and politically astute to allow him to continue to dominate the government, Warwick agreed to restore the weak-minded Henry VI, who could never be more than a figurehead. Given to indolence and self-indulgence, Edward had been caught unprepared in 1469, and was again in 1470, when the Neville defection to Lancaster found him in the north without sufficient forces to make a stand. On 2 October, Edward fled to BURGUNDY with his brother Richard, duke of Gloucester (see RICHARD III), and a small band of supporters (see EDWARD IV, OVERTHROW OF).

Over the winter of 1470–1471, Edward convinced the previously hostile HANSEATIC LEAGUE to supply him with ships, while Warwick's alliance with France persuaded Duke CHARLES of Burgundy to allow Edward to recruit men and raise money. Landing in England in March 1471, Edward began a bold and energetic two-month campaign that permitted him to retake London, defeat and kill Warwick at the Battle of BARNET, and defeat and kill Prince Edward of Lancaster at the Battle of TEWKESBURY. When Henry VI was murdered in the Tower on 21 May, undoubtedly on Edward's orders, the house of York was secure and the Wars of the Roses were over (see EDWARD IV, RESTORATION OF).

In the 1470s, Edward began the process, which was continued and extended by HENRY VII, of restoring royal authority, of making the king once more the powerful and respected arbiter of noble disputes, rather than merely the leader of one faction of the PEERAGE. As the power of the Crown grew in relation to that of the nobility, noblemen found themselves no longer able to conduct private feuds or disrupt local courts, although, as the PASTON LETTERS indicate, the Crown still required the military and political support of great magnates (see BASTARD FEUDALISM) and Edward was occasionally willing to overlook their transgressions to retain their cooperation. Edward also reorganized Crown finances, becoming one of the few medieval English kings to die solvent, and developed a loyal and capable body of councilors and household servants, often drawn from former opponents, who worked to improve royal administration and implement royal policy (see COUNCIL, ROYAL). However, Edward was also willing to allow his closest supporters to build regional political interests that had serious consequences in the reign of his son. His brother Gloucester governed the north as heir to Warwick, while William HASTINGS, Lord Hastings, dominated the Midlands, and the Woodville family developed powerful support in the south and Wales, where Anthony WOODVILLE, Earl Rivers, supervised the household of Prince Edward.

In 1475, Edward invaded France in concert with the duke of Burgundy, who had been a formal ally of the house of York since his marriage to Edward's sister, MARGARET OF YORK, in 1468. However, no fighting occurred, for, after a personal meeting with Louis XI, Edward agreed to the Treaty of Picquigny, whereby he withdrew his army in return for an annual pension and a promise of marriage between Louis's heir and Edward's daughter, ELIZABETH OF YORK. In 1478, Edward preferred a bill of ATTAINDER against his brother Clarence, whose long history of treasonous and provocative behavior, perhaps magnified in the king's mind by Woodville hostility, determined Edward to destroy him (see CLARENCE, EXECUTION OF). In the late 1470s, Edward revived claims to English hegemony over Scotland, an ill-advised policy that achieved the recapture of BERWICK but otherwise led only to costly and futile campaigns by Gloucester.

By 1483, Edward's power was unquestioned, and his dynasty was recognized across Europe and unchallenged in England, although many of his subjects were beginning to see him as increasingly arbitrary and avaricious. Edward died unexpectedly on 9 April 1483, just short of his forty-first birthday; given to corpulence in later years, the king was said to be the victim of a life given to excess and self-indulgence. He was succeeded by his son EDWARD V, who within three months of his father's death had lost his Crown to his uncle and disappeared into the Tower.

Further Reading: Ross, Charles, *Edward IV* (New Haven, CT: Yale University Press, 1998).

Edward IV, Overthrow of (1470)

Outmaneuvered by his former ally Richard NEVILLE, earl of Warwick, EDWARD IV was compelled to flee the realm in October 1470. Besides allowing the restoration of HENRY VI, Edward's overthrow and flight demonstrated the depth of support commanded by the NEVILLE FAMILY and the house of LANCASTER, exposed the unpopularity of the Yorkist government, and ensured the continuation of the WARS OF THE ROSES.

With the failure of his second coup attempt in April 1470, Warwick fled to FRANCE with his family and his chief ally, Edward IV's brother, George PLANTAGENET, duke of Clarence. Having failed either to control Edward or to replace him with Clarence, Warwick sought to restore a king whom he could control—Henry VI. In July, the earl, with assistance from LOUIS XI of France, convinced a hostile MARGARET OF ANJOU to accept the ANGERS AGREEMENT, a pact whereby Warwick undertook to overthrow Edward and restore Henry in return for the marriage of his daughter, Anne NEVILLE, to Henry's son, Prince EDWARD OF LANCASTER. In early August, after the prince and Anne were solemnly betrothed in Angers Cathedral, Warwick began fulfilling his part of the bargain by directing supporters in northern England to initiate a series of uprisings. Just as he had used the ROBIN OF REDESDALE REBELLION to draw Edward away from LONDON in 1469, so Warwick hoped to again use a northern uprising to draw Edward's attention (and perhaps his person) away from the English Channel (see NORTH OF ENGLAND AND THE WARS OF THE ROSES).

Although unaware of Warwick's Lancastrian alliance, Edward spent the early summer preparing to repel an invasion. He ordered the English NAVY to blockade the French ports where Warwick's fleet lay at anchor. In the Lancastrian north, Henry PERCY, earl of Northumberland, newly restored to his title by Edward, guarded the coasts along with John NEVILLE, marquis of Montagu, Warwick's brother. Although compelled to surrender the earldom of Northumberland to Percy, Montagu appeared content with his elevation to a marquisate. However, when Warwick's uprisings erupted in August, neither Northumberland nor the usually capable Montagu seemed able to handle the situation. With his fleet still holding the Channel, Edward made the risky decision to march north himself to crush the rebellions. By 16 August, Edward was in Yorkshire, where the mysterious rebels dispersed as quickly as they had gathered. The king then made what proved to be a serious blunder; rather than return to London, he remained with his army in the north.

In early September, a storm swept the Channel and scattered the English fleet, breaking the blockade and allowing Warwick to put to sea. Accompanied by Clarence and such longtime Lancastrians as Edmund BEAUFORT, duke of Somerset; Jasper TUDOR, earl of Pembroke; and John de VERE, earl of Oxford, Warwick landed in the West Country in mid-September. Immediately proclaiming for Henry VI, Warwick attracted wide support, and a large force had rallied to him by the time he reached Coventry. Edward started to march south, but halted at Doncaster when he received word that Montagu, who was expected to join the king, had declared for Henry VI and was moving to trap Edward between his force and Warwick's army. With public opinion running in Warwick's favor, Edward's support melted away, leaving him unable to face Montagu and with few options but flight. Edward rode southeast to King's Lynn, which he reached only after almost drowning in the Wash. Accompanied by his brother Richard, duke of Gloucester (see RICHARD III); William HASTINGS, Lord Hastings; Anthony WOODVILLE, Earl Rivers; and several other lords and their RETAINERS,

a party of some 500 persons, the king procured three ships and set sail for BURGUNDY on 2 October. Having no money, Edward was forced to pay for his passage with a fur-lined gown.

In England, the Yorkist government collapsed on the flight of the king. Queen Elizabeth WOODVILLE, only weeks away from giving birth to Edward's first son (see EDWARD V), fled into SANCTUARY at Westminster. On 6 October, Warwick entered London, where, after removing Henry VI from the TOWER OF LONDON, he began organizing the Lancastrian READEPTION government and taking steps to prevent the return of the house of YORK. To the surprise of almost everyone, it had taken only three weeks to overthrow Edward IV and restore Henry VI to the throne.

See also Edward IV, Restoration of
Further Reading: Gillingham, John, *The Wars of the Roses* (Baton Rouge: Louisiana State University Press, 1981); Goodman, Anthony, *The Wars of the Roses* (New York: Dorset Press, 1981); Ross, Charles, *Edward IV* (New Haven, CT: Yale University Press, 1998); Ross, Charles, *The Wars of the Roses* (London: Thames and Hudson, 1987).

Edward IV, Restoration of (1471)

In the spring of 1471, only six months after being driven from the throne, EDWARD IV returned to England, overthrew the READEPTION government of HENRY VI, defeated and killed Richard NEVILLE, earl of Warwick, and destroyed the male line of the house of LANCASTER.

Funded by his brother-in-law, Duke CHARLES of BURGUNDY, Edward IV departed the Dutch port of Flushing on 11 March 1471. Leading a fleet of 36 ships and 1,200 men, both Englishmen and Burgundians, Edward sought first to land in East Anglia, where he hoped for assistance from John MOWBRAY, duke of Norfolk, and John de la POLE, duke of Suffolk. However, when agents sent ashore learned that the dukes were in custody and John de VERE, earl of Oxford, was keeping close watch on the coast, Edward turned north to land at Ravenspur. As he marched through a hostile Yorkshire that provided few recruits, Edward was menaced by John NEVILLE, marquis of Montagu, and unsupported by Henry PERCY, the sympathetic earl of Northumberland, who could not persuade his Lancastrian followers to join the king who had slain so many of their relatives ten years earlier at the Battle of TOWTON. Still, Northumberland did good service by keeping his men from taking an active part in resisting Edward and by preventing an uncertain Montagu from attacking the Yorkist force while it was still small and vulnerable.

Denied entry to several towns, Edward announced that he had come not to reclaim the throne but merely to secure his inheritance as duke of York. At York, he gained admission to the city only by agreeing to leave his army outside the walls. Nonetheless, Montagu's failure to attack allowed Edward to survive, which increased his chances of gaining support. As Edward marched south into the Midlands, men loyal to such Yorkist lords as William HASTINGS, Lord Hastings, joined his force, which now grew to sufficient size to convince Warwick to withdraw before it into Coventry. Rejoined by his wayward brother, George PLANTAGENET, duke of Clarence, and unable to coax Warwick to give battle, Edward left Coventry and marched on LONDON, which he entered unopposed on 11 April. After taking custody of Henry VI and releasing Queen Elizabeth WOODVILLE and his newborn son (see EDWARD V) from SANCTUARY at Westminster, Edward led his rapidly growing army northward. On 14 April, he slew both Warwick and Montagu at the Battle of BARNET.

On the same day as Barnet, Queen MARGARET OF ANJOU and her son Prince EDWARD OF LANCASTER landed in southern England. Greeted by Edmund BEAUFORT, duke of Somerset, and other staunch Lancastrians, the queen marched into the West Country, where she raised a large force. Edward followed quickly and on 4 May defeated the Lancastrians at the Battle of TEWKESBURY, where Prince Edward was slain and Somerset was captured and executed. With a captive Queen Margaret in tow, Edward returned to London, where Anthony WOODVILLE, Earl Rivers, and other Yorkist lords had beaten back an assault on the city by Thomas NEVILLE, the Bastard of Fauconberg. With all significant resistance crushed, Edward entered London on 21 May. That night, Henry VI was murdered in the TOWER OF LONDON, thus ending the Lancastrian cause and completing the restoration of the house of YORK.

See also Edward IV, Overthrow of
Further Reading: Gillingham, John, *The Wars of the Roses* (Baton Rouge: Louisiana State University Press, 1981); Goodman, Anthony, *The Wars of the Roses* (New York: Dorset Press, 1981); Ross, Charles, *Edward IV* (New Haven, CT: Yale University Press, 1998); Ross, Charles, *The Wars of the Roses* (London: Thames and Hudson, 1987).

Edward V, King of England (1470–c. 1483)

The eldest son of EDWARD IV and second monarch of the house of YORK, Edward V was the uncrowned king of England from April to June 1483, when he was dethroned by his uncle RICHARD III in an act of usurpation that reignited the WARS OF THE ROSES (see USURPATION OF 1483).

At Edward's birth in November 1470, his family's cause was in disarray. In the previous month, his father had been overthrown and forced into exile in BURGUNDY by a former ally, Richard NEVILLE, earl of Warwick, who restored HENRY VI to the throne (see EDWARD IV, OVERTHROW OF; READEPTION). Edward was born at Westminster, where his mother, Queen Elizabeth WOODVILLE, had taken SANCTUARY after her husband's flight. However, by May 1471, Edward was heir to a Yorkist throne made secure by his father's destruction of the rival house of LANCASTER and by his own birth (see EDWARD IV, RESTORATION OF).

In 1473, the three-year-old prince was given his own household at Ludlow, a Yorkist stronghold in Shropshire. Supervised by his maternal uncle Anthony WOODVILLE, Earl Rivers, the household included twenty-five

EDWARDVS V

Edward V, the eldest son of Edward IV, was deposed and likely murdered by his uncle Richard III. (National Portrait Gallery: NPG 4980[11])

councilors, a large staff of servants, and numerous schoolfellows and playmates drawn from the sons of English noblemen. Directed by Bishop John Alcock of Worcester, the prince's formal educational program involved training in Latin, music, religion, and archery and other physical recreations. The prince was eventually made the nominal head of a Council of Wales, which included Rivers, Alcock, and other experienced royal administrators, and which was charged with maintaining order on the chronically disordered Welsh border.

After his father's death on 9 April 1483, the prince, now recognized as Edward V, was escorted to LONDON by Rivers. In late April, Richard, duke of Gloucester, Edward's paternal uncle, intercepted the royal party at Stony Stratford, arrested Rivers, and took custody of the king. Over the next two months, Gloucester, fearing the young king was dominated by his mother's family and unsure of his own future in a Woodville-controlled monarchy, had Edward V declared illegitimate and engineered his own usurpation of the throne,

which was completed with his coronation as Richard III on 6 July. Edward V and his younger brother Richard PLANTAGENET, duke of York, were lodged together in the TOWER OF LONDON, where they disappeared from view by late summer. By the autumn of 1483, the country was awash with rumors that Richard III had murdered the princes.

Although the exact fate of Edward V and his brother has never been resolved, and the role of Richard III in their disappearance is still vigorously debated, by September 1483 most people believed the princes were dead, and Richard's responsibility for their fate was sufficiently accepted to undermine support for his regime. In the autumn of 1483, many Yorkists transferred their allegiance to Edward V's elder sister, ELIZABETH OF YORK. When Henry Tudor, earl of Richmond (see HENRY VII), the Lancastrian pretender to the throne, agreed to take Elizabeth as his queen, the Yorkist and Woodville interests supported BUCKINGHAM'S REBELLION as the first step in an eventually successful effort to win the Crown for Richmond. Thus, Edward V's removal from the throne reopened the dynastic wars and ultimately destroyed the house of York.

See also Princes in the Tower; Woodville Family
Further Reading: Fields, Bertram, *Royal Blood: Richard III and the Mystery of the Princes* (New York: Regan Books, 1998); Jenkins, Elizabeth, *The Princes in the Tower* (New York: Coward, McCann and Geoghegan, 1978); More, Sir Thomas, *The History of King Richard III,* edited by Richard S. Sylvester (New Haven, CT: Yale University Press, 1976); Pollard, A. J., *Richard III and the Princes in the Tower* (New York: St. Martin's Press, 1991); Ross, Charles, *Richard III* (Berkeley: University of California Press, 1981); Weir, Alison, *The Princes in the Tower* (New York: Ballantine Books, 1992); Williamson, Audrey, *The Mystery of the Princes* (Chicago: Academy Chicago Publishers, 1986); the text of More's *History of King Richard III* is also available on the Richard III Society Web site at <http://www.r3.org/bookcase/more/moretext.html>.

Edward, Earl of Warwick. *See* Plantagenet, Edward, Earl of Warwick

Edward of Lancaster, Prince of Wales (1453–1471)

The birth of Edward of Lancaster, the only child of HENRY VI and MARGARET OF ANJOU, enormously complicated the political crisis of the 1450s. Occurring on 13 October 1453, during Henry VI's first period of mental incapacity, Edward's birth removed Richard PLANTAGENET, duke of York, from his position as heir apparent to the throne and thrust the queen into leadership of an anti-York court party on her son's behalf. With the birth of the prince, the easiest political solution to the problems of Henry's inability to rule and York's dissatisfaction with his lack of influence—that is, the naming of York as the king's heir—could no longer be undertaken without risking war and political upheaval.

In March 1454, York and the queen maneuvered against one another for the right to exercise royal authority during the king's illness (see HENRY VI, ILLNESS OF). The lords in PARLIAMENT named the infant Prince of Wales and heir to the throne, but appointed York protector of the realm during the king's pleasure or until the prince came of age. Edward's early years were marked by his father's continuing mental illness and by the increasingly violent struggle for power between his mother's party and the Yorkists. Having spent the first years of his life largely in his mother's company, the prince by 1459 was closely identified with her struggle against York and became the subject of Yorkist rumors questioning his paternity.

The Yorkist victory at the Battle of NORTHAMPTON in July 1460 resulted in the capture of the king and the flight of the prince and his mother to HARLECH CASTLE in WALES. In October, York claimed the throne by right of hereditary succession. A compromise Act of ACCORD allowed Henry to retain the Crown but disinherited the prince in favor of York and his heirs. To win support for their cause, Margaret and the prince took ship for SCOTLAND, where the queen agreed in January 1461 to give BERWICK to the Scots in return for military assistance and a marriage between the prince and a sister of JAMES III. The death of York at the Battle of WAKE-FIELD in December 1460 and the queen's victory over a Yorkist army under Richard NEVILLE, earl of Warwick, at the Battle of ST. ALBANS in February 1461 restored Lancastrian fortunes. Reunited with his wife and son on the battlefield, Henry VI knighted the prince, who in turn knighted ANDREW TROLLOPE. At his mother's instigation, the seven-year-old prince then pronounced a death sentence upon several captured Yorkists and witnessed their executions.

After EDWARD IV's victory at the Battle of TOWTON in March 1461, the prince fled with his parents to Scotland. In 1462, he was with the Lancastrian force with which his mother recaptured BAMBURGH and DUNSTANBURGH castles in Northumberland. At the approach of a Yorkist army, the prince and his mother escaped, but were shipwrecked and wandered for weeks along the coast; the two were eventually captured by robbers and escaped only with the help of one of their captors. From 1463, the prince and his mother lived in FRANCE at the castle of St. Michel-en-Barrois. Under the tutelage of Sir John FORTESCUE and the strong influence of his mother, Edward grew into a handsome and intelligent young man with a warlike turn of mind. A 1467 letter to the duke of Milan described the thirteen-year-old as talking of "nothing but cutting off heads or making war" (Seward, p. 129). Fortescue himself described how fiercely the prince applied himself to feats of arms.

In 1470, after his estrangement from Edward IV, Warwick agreed to restore Henry VI in return for a marriage between the prince and the earl's younger daughter, Anne NEVILLE (see ANGERS AGREEMENT). Although the two sixteen-year-olds were betrothed at Angers in July, the queen refused to allow her son to go to England until Warwick had secured the kingdom for the house of LANCASTER. The queen's decision weakened Warwick's regime and cost the earl vital Lancastrian support. The prince finally landed in England with his mother on 14 April 1471, within hours of the death of Warwick at the Battle of BARNET. The queen and prince then based themselves in the friendly western counties, where they came to ruin at the Battle of TEWKESBURY on 4 May. The seventeen-year-old prince, in nominal command of the Lancastrian army, was slain while fleeing the field. The prince's death sealed the fate of Henry VI, who was murdered in the TOWER OF LONDON on 21 May 1471, thus ending the direct male line of Lancaster (see HENRY VI, MURDER OF).

Further Reading: Griffiths, Ralph A., *The Reign of King Henry VI* (Berkeley: University of California Press, 1981); Seward, Desmond, *The Wars of the Roses* (New York: Viking, 1995); Wolffe, Bertram, *Henry VI* (London: Eyre Methuen, 1981).

Egremont, Lord. *See* Percy, Thomas, Lord Egremont

Elizabeth of York, Queen of England (1465–1503)

Through her marriage to HENRY VII, Elizabeth of York, eldest daughter of EDWARD IV, sealed a union of the houses of LANCASTER and YORK that came to symbolize the end of the WARS OF THE ROSES and the legitimacy of the house of TUDOR.

In 1469, four-year-old Elizabeth was betrothed to George Neville, son of John NEVILLE, marquis of Montagu, and nephew of Richard NEVILLE, earl of Warwick. The match evaporated in 1470, when the Nevilles overthrew Edward IV, and forced Elizabeth to accompany her mother, Queen Elizabeth WOODVILLE, into SANCTUARY at Westminster Abbey until Edward's return in April 1471 (see NEVILLE FAMILY). In 1475, the king betrothed Elizabeth to the son of LOUIS XI of FRANCE as part of the Treaty of Picquigny, but the French king broke off that match in the early 1480s (see CHARLES VIII).

After Edward IV's death in April 1483, the queen, fearing her brother-in-law, Richard, duke of Gloucester, again fled into SANCTUARY at Westminster, taking her five daughters and her younger son, Richard PLANTA-

Elizabeth, the eldest daughter of Edward IV, married Henry VII, first king of the House of Tudor, in 1486. (National Portrait Gallery: NPG 311)

GENET, duke of York, with her. Gloucester secured custody of the duke in June, and by the autumn of 1483 York and his elder brother, EDWARD V, were commonly believed to have been murdered by Gloucester, who had taken the throne as RICHARD III in July. Now Edward IV's heir, Elizabeth became an important element in BUCKINGHAM'S REBELLION, an uprising planned in part by her mother and in part by Margaret BEAUFORT, Countess of Richmond, and involving Henry STAFFORD, duke of Buckingham, heretofore an ally of Richard III. The rebels intended to enthrone Margaret Beaufort's son, Henry Tudor, earl of Richmond, the surviving Lancastrian claimant to the Crown, and to marry him to Elizabeth.

After the failure of the rebellion, Elizabeth remained in sanctuary with her mother and sisters until March 1484, when Richard III, in an effort to divorce the ex-queen from Richmond's cause, agreed to find his nieces good marriages and to provide for them financially. Even though the PARLIAMENT of 1484 had bastardized the children of Edward IV, Elizabeth was so warmly welcomed at COURT that rumors soon claimed Richard was planning to replace his ailing queen, Anne NEVILLE, with his nineteen-year-old niece. The rumors intensified at Christmas 1484, when the queen and Elizabeth wore similar gowns at the court festivities, and in March 1485, when Queen Anne died. These reports were so persistent and so damaging to the king's reputation that his chief advisors successfully urged him to take the unprecedented step of publicly repudiating the union. Although some later writers have claimed that Elizabeth was eager to marry Richard, the contemporary ballad, *THE SONG OF LADY BESSY,* described her loathing for her uncle, whom she blamed for her brothers' deaths. Nothing can now be said with certainty about Elizabeth's opinion of her uncle, who underscored his disavowal of the match by sending her to Sheriff Hutton.

She was still at this Yorkshire castle in late August 1485, when Richmond defeated Richard at the Battle of BOSWORTH FIELD and took the throne as Henry VII. Because he was unwilling to have it appear he owed his Crown to his wife, Henry delayed his marriage to Elizabeth until January 1486, after Parliament had recognized his right to the throne. Elizabeth bore seven children, four of whom survived infancy. The eldest, Prince Arthur, preceded Elizabeth in death in 1502, but her second son became king as Henry VIII in 1509. Elizabeth died in February 1503 at the age of thirty-eight.

Further Reading: Harvey, Nancy Lenz, *Elizabeth of York* (New York: Macmillan, 1973).

Elizabeth, Queen of England. *See* Woodville, Elizabeth, Queen of England

Embracery. *See* Livery and Maintenance

English Church and the Wars of the Roses

Because of a lack of political talent among its leaders, the English Church took little part in the WARS OF THE ROSES, and few bishops were strong or consistent advocates for either the house of LANCASTER or the house of YORK. Thus, the various changes in dynasty brought the church neither great harm nor great benefit. Also, the brief and intermittent nature of civil war campaigns caused the church to suffer little material damage during the conflict (see MILITARY CAMPAIGNS, DURATION OF).

Because HENRY VI made bishops of the pious and scholarly men who served him as confessors and spiritual advisors, the outbreak of civil war in 1459 found his government deficient in the practical, politically experienced bishops who had formed the core of previous royal administrations. Thomas BOURCHIER, the archbishop of Canterbury, had been appointed during the FIRST PROTECTORATE of Richard PLANTAGENET, duke of York, and supported the Yorkists in 1460 after having accommodated both sides during the 1450s. William Booth, archbishop of York, and his brother Lawrence BOOTH, bishop of Durham, were Lancastrians, but neither gave sufficient support to Henry's cause to suffer any consequences when EDWARD IV won the throne in 1461, although Lawrence was suspended briefly from office in 1462 for his Lancastrian sympathies. The most vigorous ecclesiastical involvement in the conflict in 1459–1461 was by a foreign bishop, Francesco Coppini, bishop of Terni (see COPPINI MISSION), who used his position as papal legate to actively promote the Yorkist cause. Although some historians have argued that the church demanded redress of its grievances in return for sanctioning the Yorkist usurpation in 1461, the bishops made few complaints, Edward IV granted few concessions, and the house of York based its claim to the Crown on hereditary right, thus avoiding any need for the church to legitimize the family's position.

In 1470–1471, the most political bishop was George NEVILLE, archbishop of York, who abandoned Edward IV (whom he had served as chancellor) to actively support his brother, Richard NEVILLE, earl of Warwick, the head of the Lancastrian READEPTION government. After Warwick's death and the Yorkist restoration, Edward IV imprisoned the archbishop in the TOWER OF LONDON. In 1472, after being pardoned and released, Neville was re-arrested and confined at CALAIS until 1475. Besides Neville, no other bishops were so harshly treated, and politically talented Lancastrian clerics, such as John MORTON, the future archbishop of Canterbury, were pardoned and admitted to Edward's COUNCIL. Unlike those of Henry VI, most of Edward's ecclesiastical appointees tended to be men of humble origins who displayed a talent for secular government, such as Thomas ROTHERHAM as archbishop of York, John RUSSELL as bishop of Lincoln, and Morton as bishop of Ely.

In 1483, Morton was one of the few bishops to oppose RICHARD III's usurpation of the throne. Arrested at the infamous COUNCIL MEETING OF 13 JUNE 1483, Morton later participated in BUCKINGHAM'S REBELLION and, after the failure of that uprising, fled to BURGUNDY to support Henry Tudor, earl of Richmond, the future HENRY VII. Meanwhile, Richard III employed various ecclesiastical servants to successfully complete his seizure of the throne (see USURPATION OF 1483). He sent aging Archbishop Bourchier to persuade Queen Elizabeth WOODVILLE, then in SANCTUARY at Westminster, to surrender her younger son, Richard PLANTAGENET, duke of York, into Richard's custody. To justify his usurpation, Richard commissioned the respected preacher Ralph Shaw to deliver a sermon extolling Richard's merits as king to the citizens of LONDON (see SHAW'S SERMON). Richard also used Bishop Robert STILLINGTON's revelation of the BUTLER PRECONTRACT to declare EDWARD V illegitimate and unfit for the Crown. While the English Church largely acquiesced in Richard's reign, both the papacy and the English bishops readily accepted Henry VII and the house of TUDOR after the Battle of BOSWORTH FIELD in 1485. The new dynasty, like its Lancastrian and Yorkist predecessors, faced few demands from the bishops and

in return largely left the English Church as it found it.

Further Reading: Davies, Richard G., "The Church and the Wars of the Roses," in A. J. Pollard, ed., *The Wars of the Roses* (New York: St. Martin's Press, 1995), pp. 143–161; Dunning, Robert W., "Patronage and Promotion in the Late-Medieval Church," in Ralph A. Griffiths, ed., *Patronage, the Crown and the Provinces in Later Medieval England* (Atlantic Highlands, NJ: Humanities Press, 1981); Harvey, Margaret, *England, Rome and the Papacy, 1417–1464* (Manchester: Manchester University Press, 1993).

English Economy and the Wars of the Roses

Although the WARS OF THE ROSES caused political instability and, at least among the governing classes, some social disruption, the conflict had little direct effect on the English economy. Military campaigns were brief, and incidents of plunder and deliberate destruction of property were few and localized (see MILITARY CAMPAIGNS, DURATION OF). Except for members of the PEERAGE and GENTRY whose involvement in the wars led to confiscation of their estates through acts of ATTAINDER, the livelihoods of most English people were unaffected by the civil wars.

Because it reduced the overall wealth of the kingdom and alienated the people the contending houses of LANCASTER and YORK sought to rule, military action that damaged or destroyed the resources or economic well-being of any area of the country was rarely in the best interest of either party. Most such destruction occurred during the first phase of the civil wars, during the years 1460 and 1461. In the north in 1460, supporters of the family of Henry PERCY, third earl of Northumberland, looted estates owned by the rival NEVILLE FAMILY and by the Nevilles' ally, Richard PLANTAGENET, duke of York (see NEVILLE-PERCY FEUD). In the first weeks of 1461, the army of Queen MARGARET OF ANJOU, marching southward after the Battle of WAKEFIELD (see MARCH ON LONDON), plundered property and towns belonging to or associated with York or his ally Richard

NEVILLE, earl of Salisbury. Although fear and Yorkist PROPAGANDA likely exaggerated the destructiveness of the advancing Lancastrians in the minds of southern residents and LONDON citizens, such unrestrained pillaging was rarely seen again during the conflict. Even areas that saw numerous campaigns and battles, such as northeastern England in the early 1460s, suffered little material damage. Despite frequent Lancastrian incursions from SCOTLAND; sustained campaigning around ALNWICK, BAMBURGH, and DUNSTANBURGH castles; and the pitched battles of HEDGELEY MOOR and HEXHAM, surviving monastic and estate accounts for northeastern England between 1461 and 1464 indicate little economic disruption and give only slight evidence that the area was an ongoing war zone (see NORTH OF ENGLAND AND THE WARS OF THE ROSES).

One cause of economic distress during the Wars of the Roses was the lingering demographic effect of epidemic disease, both the devastating depopulation caused by visitations of the Black Death in the fourteenth century and the more localized depopulations caused by smaller disease outbreaks in the fifteenth century. The resulting labor shortages undermined the unfree status of rural peasants (villeins), who by manorial custom were to remain on the land on which they were born, paying customary dues in labor or produce to their customary landlords. Competition for scare labor often meant better terms for peasants but declining rents for landlords. Another cause of economic hardship arose from fluctuations in foreign trade. Many English people were involved in some aspect of the wool and cloth trades—noble or gentle landowners raised sheep and town or peasant families produced woolen cloth, either for the domestic market or for export to the cloth-making towns of BURGUNDY. Foreign wars; trade embargoes, such as those undertaken by the HANSEATIC LEAGUE; shrinking demand in foreign markets; or the restrictive or retaliatory trade policies of the English or Burgundian governments could affect the health of the English export trade in wool, cloth, or grain, the three major English exports. A recession in continental markets in the early 1460s spread to England by 1465, forcing EDWARD IV to devalue the coinage and causing more economic distress in the country than was ever caused by the civil wars themselves. By the 1480s, improvement in European markets helped the English market rebound, even though RICHARD III's 1483 usurpation of his nephew's throne revived the Wars of the Roses at about the same time (see USURPATION OF 1483).

Further Reading: Bolton, J. L., *The Medieval English Economy, 1150–1500* (London: J. M. Dent and Sons, 1980); Britnell, R. H., "The Economic Context," in A. J. Pollard, ed., *The Wars of the Roses* (New York: St. Martin's Press, 1995), pp. 41–64; Hatcher, John, *Plague, Population and the English Economy, 1348–1530* (London: Macmillan, 1994); Munro, J. H., *Wool, Cloth and Gold* (Toronto: University of Toronto Press, 1972).

English History (Vergil). *See Anglica Historia* (Vergil)

Essex, Earl of. *See* Bourchier, Henry, Earl of Essex

Execution of George Plantagenet, Duke of Clarence. *See* Clarence, Execution of

Exeter, Duke of. *See* Holland, Henry, Duke of Exeter

Fabyan, Robert. *See* London Chronicles

Fauconberg, Lord. *See* Neville, William, Lord Fauconberg and Earl of Kent

Fauconberg, Thomas, Bastard of Fauconberg. *See* Neville, Thomas, Bastard of Fauconberg

Ferrers of Chartley, Lord. *See* Devereux, Walter, Lord Ferrers of Chartley

Ferrybridge, Battle of (1461)

Occurring on 27 and 28 March 1461, the encounters at the Ferrybridge crossing of the River Aire in Yorkshire were the final moves in the campaign that culminated in the Battle of TOWTON, the largest and bloodiest battle of the WARS OF THE ROSES.

On 27 March, while still south of the Aire, EDWARD IV learned that a large Lancastrian army commanded by Henry BEAUFORT, duke of Somerset, had deployed on a plateau north of the river between the villages of Towton and Saxton. Later in the day, Richard NEVILLE, earl of Warwick, commanding the Yorkist vanguard, reached the river at Ferrybridge only to find the bridge destroyed and a small Lancastrian force on the other side ready to dispute any crossing. By bridging the gaps in the damaged span with planks, Warwick's troops crossed the river, drove off the Lancastrians, and secured a bridgehead on the north bank, although not without losing many men on the bridge to enemy ARCHERS. By evening, Warwick had repaired the bridge and positioned a small force across the river to hold the crossing until the rest of the army could arrive next day.

At dawn, an enemy force under John CLIFFORD, Lord Clifford, and John NEVILLE, Lord Neville, one of Warwick's Lancastrian cousins from the Westmorland branch of the NEVILLE FAMILY, surprised the Yorkist camp on the north bank and drove its occupants across the river in confusion. When the survivors of Warwick's force reached the main Yorkist army, their panic caused Edward's men to fear that a Lancastrian horde was upon them. To restore morale, Warwick, who had been wounded in the leg by an arrow during the morning's fight at the bridge, cried out, "Flee if you want but I will tarry with he who will tarry with me" (Haigh, pp. 58–59), and then dramatized his resolve by killing his own horse. Although Warwick did not know it at the time, Clifford and Neville were content to hold the crossing and never came south of the river.

By noon, the Yorkist army reached Ferrybridge to find the bridge again destroyed and a Lancastrian force again holding the north bank. To avoid the casualties of the previous day, Warwick sent his uncle, William NEVILLE, Lord Fauconberg, to ford the river three miles upstream with a band of mounted archers. This force fell upon the Lancastrians as they were retreating toward Somerset's position. The Yorkist archers killed both Clifford and Neville, and Edward IV brought his army safely across the river by nightfall. Encamped less than a mile from each other, the two armies waited in the cold for morning, when the Battle of Towton began.

Further Reading: Boardman, Andrew W., *The Battle of Towton* (Stroud, Gloucestershire, UK: Sutton Publishing, 1996); Haigh, Philip A., *The Military Campaigns of the Wars of the Roses* (Stroud, Gloucestershire, UK: Sutton Publishing, 1995).

First Protectorate (1454–1455)

Lasting from March 1454 until February 1455, the first protectorate was an attempt to solve the constitutional crisis created by the mental illness of HENRY VI (see HENRY VI, ILLNESS OF). Realizing that the king was unable to govern for the foreseeable future, and being unwilling to name Queen MARGARET OF ANJOU regent, the English PEERAGE, acting through PARLIAMENT, vested limited royal authority in the king's cousin, Richard PLANTAGENET, duke of York. Named protector of the realm and chief councilor, York, supported by a COUNCIL of nobles, assumed temporary control of the royal administration on the same terms granted to Henry's uncles during his minority in the 1420s and 1430s. Although York's appointment restored his political position, which had been damaged by the failure of the DARTFORD UPRISING in 1452, it also saddled him with the undying enmity of Queen Margaret, whose efforts to protect the future of her infant son promoted the political factionalization that helped fuel the WARS OF THE ROSES.

In November 1453, after three months of royal incapacity, the king's COUNCIL summoned a great council of nobles to meet at Westminster. Acting for York, John MOWBRAY, duke of Norfolk, accused Edmund BEAUFORT, duke of Somerset, Henry's chief minister and York's chief rival, of treasonously mishandling the war in FRANCE. With no king to protect him, Somerset was arrested and imprisoned in the TOWER OF LONDON, although no attempt was made to try him. Hoping that the king would improve, or that York and the queen would come to some accommodation, the Lords postponed Parliament for three months. However, by March,

Henry was no better and the appointment of a royal stand-in could no longer be delayed. To discourage the view that his new office implied any challenge to the house of LANCASTER, York demanded that the parliamentary act creating the protectorate clearly declare that he assumed the position only at the request and on the authority of the Lords. The act also specified that York served at the king's pleasure or until Prince EDWARD OF LANCASTER came of age, a clause that protected the prince's position as heir.

York tried to rule with the support of a broad-based coalition of magnates; however, his position as leader of a faction of nobles who had opposed the former regime was incompatible with his new responsibility to maintain order throughout the kingdom. When he intervened in local disputes, he could not avoid charges of being biased in favor of his own supporters. Thus, when the duke involved himself in the NEVILLE-PERCY FEUD, he appeared to back the NEVILLE FAMILY, while intervention in the COURTENAY-BONVILLE FEUD made him seem a partisan of William BONVILLE, Lord Bonville. Feeling aggrieved, the Percies and the Courtenays approached the queen, who began forming her own faction around York's personal and political foes. York also made enemies by using his powers of patronage to appoint his ally, Richard NEVILLE, earl of Salisbury, lord chancellor, and to take for himself the important captaincy of CALAIS, an office that had belonged to Somerset and that gave York control of England's only standing military force.

Henry's sudden recovery at Christmas 1454 led to York's formal resignation of his protectorship in February 1455. The king's resumption of power gave the queen and York's enemies their chance to retaliate. Somerset was released from the Tower, and York's charges against him were rejected, while new appointments filled the council with the queen's friends. Feeling themselves threatened, York, Salisbury, and Salisbury's son, Richard NEVILLE, earl of Warwick, who had also quarreled with Somerset, armed themselves, an action that raised political tensions and led in May to the first military encounter of the civil wars, the Battle of ST. ALBANS.

See also Second Protectorate
Further Reading: Griffiths, Ralph A., *The Reign of King Henry VI* (Berkeley: University of California Press, 1981); Johnson, P. A., *Duke Richard of York* (Oxford: Clarendon Press, 1988).

Fitzgerald, Gerald, Earl of Kildare (1456–1513)

The dominant political figure in IRELAND during the last phase of the Wars of the Roses, Gerald Fitzgerald, eighth earl of Kildare, continued his family's Yorkist allegiance and maintained Ireland as a haven for Yorkist political activity.

The son of Thomas FITZGERALD, seventh earl of Kildare, the eighth earl served as lord deputy of Ireland from 1478 to 1492 and again from 1496 until his death in 1513. As lord deputy to Richard PLANTAGENET, duke of York, EDWARD IV'S younger son, Kildare enjoyed great power and influence in the early 1480s. After 1483, RICHARD III, seeking to maintain Yorkist dominance in Ireland, appointed his son, Prince Edward, lord lieutenant, but left the government of Ireland in Kildare's hands as the young Prince's deputy.

In 1485, after the death of Richard III and the accession of HENRY VII, Kildare remained loyal to the house of YORK. He welcomed Lambert SIMNEL to Ireland in 1487, accepting the young man's claim to be Edward PLANTAGENET, earl of Warwick, the surviving Yorkist claimant to the English throne. In May 1487, Kildare allowed John de la POLE, earl of Lincoln and nephew to Richard III, to land in Dublin with 2,000 men provided by Lincoln's aunt, MARGARET OF YORK, duchess of BURGUNDY. On 24 May, Kildare attended the Dublin coronation of Simnel as "Edward VI," and governed Ireland in "King Edward's" name in defiance of Henry VII. However, in 1488, a year after Simnel and Lincoln invaded England from Ireland and came to ruin at the Battle of STOKE, Kildare submitted to Henry VII and was pardoned. He

lost the deputyship and again fell out of favor in the mid-1490s when he was suspected of supporting Perkin WARBECK, a Yorkist pretender who claimed to be the duke of York, the younger son of Edward IV.

Attainted by the Irish PARLIAMENT of 1494, Kildare spent two years in the TOWER OF LONDON before being restored as lord deputy in 1496. To prevent Ireland from again becoming a launchpad for Yorkist invasions, Henry VII made a concerted effort to win Kildare's support. To enhance his position with the English landowners resident in Ireland, Kildare was given many marks of royal favor, including being allowed to marry the king's kinswoman, Elizabeth St. John. In 1504, the king rewarded Kildare with a Garter knighthood (i.e., membership in a prestigious chivalric order) for his victory over Irish rebels at the Battle of Knockdoe. Having made his peace with the house of TUDOR, Kildare remained lord deputy into Henry VIII's reign, dying in September 1513.

See also Yorkist Heirs (after 1485)
Further Reading: Bryan, Donough, *Gerald Fitzgerald, the Great Earl of Kildare, 1456–1513* (Dublin: Talbot Press, 1933); Cosgrove, Art, *Late Medieval Ireland, 1370–1541* (Dublin: Helicon, 1981); Lydon, James, *Ireland in the Later Middle Ages* (Dublin: Gill and Macmillan, 1973); Otway-Ruthven, A. J., *A History of Medieval Ireland* (New York: Barnes and Noble Books, 1980).

Fitzgerald, Thomas, Earl of Desmond (c. 1426–1468)

An adherent of the house of YORK, Thomas Fitzgerald, the eighth earl of Desmond, served as EDWARD IV's lord deputy of IRELAND in the mid-1460s.

With the execution of James BUTLER, the staunchly Lancastrian earl of Ormond, in May 1461, political dominance in Ireland passed to the Fitzgerald family, whose leaders had attached themselves in the 1450s to the cause of Richard PLANTAGENET, duke of York. Succeeding his father as earl of Desmond in 1462, the eighth earl maintained his family's Yorkist allegiance by crushing a Lancastrian invasion of Ireland led by Ormond's brothers, John and

Thomas Butler, both of whom had been attainted by Edward IV's first PARLIAMENT. In 1463, the king rewarded Desmond by appointing him lord deputy. Governing in close association with his kinsman, Thomas FITZGERALD, earl of Kildare, Desmond, like earlier Anglo-Irish deputies, used the authority and financial resources attached to his official position to advance his own and his family's interests.

Desmond's quarrels with other Anglo-Irish nobles, his friendliness with native Irish leaders, and his attempts to impose new exactions on the landowners in the Pale (i.e., the most Anglicized region of Ireland around Dublin) led to uprisings and complaints that cost him the favor of the king. By 1468, Edward had replaced him as lord deputy with John TIPTOFT, the English earl of Worcester. In the Irish Parliament of that year, Worcester secured a bill of ATTAINDER against both Desmond and Kildare, although only the former suffered execution. His effectiveness destroyed by his actions against his predecessors, Worcester was recalled in 1470. The attainders of Desmond and Kildare were reversed, and the latter assumed the deputyship. Although Desmond's heir was allowed to succeed to his father's lands and title, relations between the English Crown and the Desmond Fitzgeralds were strained for decades.

See also Fitzgerald, Gerald, Earl of Kildare
Further Reading: Cosgrove, Art, *Late Medieval Ireland, 1370–1541* (Dublin: Helicon, 1981); Lydon, James, *Ireland in the Later Middle Ages* (Dublin: Gill and Macmillan, 1973); Otway-Ruthven, A. J., *A History of Medieval Ireland* (New York: Barnes and Noble Books, 1980).

lieutenant, Richard PLANTAGENET, duke of York. When York fled England after the Battle of LUDFORD BRIDGE in October 1459, he withdrew to Ireland, where he was warmly welcomed by Kildare. Although the government of HENRY VI strove over the next year to weaken Kildare's Yorkist connection, the earl remained loyal to York. In 1461, he was handsomely rewarded by EDWARD IV, who granted Kildare various long-lost family lands and named the earl lord deputy (to Edward's brother George PLANTAGENET, duke of Clarence).

Kildare served as lord deputy or as chancellor of Ireland for most of the 1460s and 1470s, but in 1468, Kildare and his cousin, Thomas FITZGERALD, earl of Desmond, lost favor with the new English lord deputy, John TIPTOFT, earl of Worcester. When landowners in the Pale (i.e., the most Anglicized region of Ireland around Dublin) complained of the exactions imposed upon them by the earls for the maintenance of their troops, Worcester had both men attainted, and had Desmond executed. However, because Edward IV soon found Ireland difficult to govern without Fitzgerald support, Kildare's ATTAINDER was reversed and he was restored as lord deputy in 1470. The earl was thereafter secure in the royal favor and governed Ireland for Edward IV until 1475. Kildare died in March 1478.

See also Fitzgerald, Gerald, Earl of Kildare
Further Reading: Cosgrove, Art, *Late Medieval Ireland, 1370–1541* (Dublin: Helicon, 1981); Lydon, James, *Ireland in the Later Middle Ages* (Dublin: Gill and Macmillan, 1973); Otway-Ruthven, A. J., *A History of Medieval Ireland* (New York: Barnes and Noble Books, 1980).

Fitzgerald, Thomas, Earl of Kildare (d. 1478)

The dominant political figure in IRELAND from the mid-1450s until his death, Thomas Fitzgerald, seventh earl of Kildare, closely allied himself and his family with the house of YORK and made Ireland a Yorkist stronghold.

Between 1455 and 1459, Kildare served as lord deputy of Ireland for the English lord

Fortescue, Sir John (c. 1394–1476)

A loyal adherent of the house of LANCASTER, Sir John Fortescue was also chief justice of the Court of King's Bench and the preeminent constitutional and legal theorist of medieval England.

The second son of a Devonshire gentleman, Fortescue was educated at Oxford and trained in the common law at Lincoln's Inn.

He became serjeant-at-law (i.e., a senior attorney who specialized in pleading cases in common law courts) in 1430, and was appointed chief justice of King's Bench in 1442. Fortescue fought for HENRY VI at the Battle of TOWTON in March 1461, and afterward fled into SCOTLAND with the Lancastrian royal family. Over the next two years of Scottish exile, Fortescue wrote several treatises defending the Lancastrian title to the throne and refuting the claim of the house of YORK. The best known of these works, *De Natura Legis Naturae (On the Nature of Law)*, dismisses the Yorkist claim because of its descent through the female line. In 1463, Fortescue followed Queen MARGARET OF ANJOU and her son Prince EDWARD OF LANCASTER to FRANCE. At the queen's court in exile at St. Michel-en-Barrois, Fortescue tutored the prince and probably also acted as the Lancastrian chancellor. Exile gave Fortescue time to write his *De Laudibus Legum Angliae (In Praise of the Laws of England)*, which may have been intended, in part, to familiarize the prince with his future kingdom. *De Laudibus* compares English and French law by way of explaining that England, unlike France, was a mixed monarchy in which the Crown (i.e., the king in PARLIAMENT) governed with the consent of the people.

In 1470, Fortescue supported the ANGERS AGREEMENT, the alliance that Queen Margaret concluded with Richard NEVILLE, earl of Warwick. After the Lancastrian restoration, while waiting to return to England, Fortescue drafted a series of proposals to advise Henry VI's READEPTION government on how to avoid the errors that had caused Henry's earlier downfall. Fortescue landed in England with Margaret and the prince on 14 April 1471, the day of Warwick's death at the Battle of BARNET. Captured in May after the Battle of TEWKESBURY, Fortescue acknowledged Lancastrian defeat and submitted to EDWARD IV, who pardoned him and restored his estates on condition that he refute his own earlier arguments in favor of the Lancastrian claim. Achieving this in his *Declaration upon Certain Writings Sent Out of Scotland,* Fortescue successfully petitioned for reversal of his ATTAINDER. Fortescue's last work, *On the Governance of the Kingdom of England,* summarized portions of *De Laudibus* and was the first work of constitutional theory in English and the first book of English law written specifically for laypersons. Appointed to the COUNCIL in the 1470s, Fortescue served until his death in 1476.

Further Reading: Fortescue, Sir John, *De Laudibus Legum Angliae,* edited and translated by S. B. Chrimes (Holmes Beach, FL: William W. Gaunt and Sons, 1986); Fortescue, Sir John, *Sir John Fortescue: On the Laws and Governance of England,* edited by Shelley Lockwood (Cambridge: Cambridge University Press, 1997); Gross, Anthony, *The Dissolution of the Lancastrian Kingship: Sir John Fortescue and the Crisis of Monarchy in Fifteenth-Century England* (Stamford, UK: Paul Watkins, 1996).

France

Although the HUNDRED YEARS WAR had made France the traditional enemy of England, the French monarchy became the chief potential source of foreign assistance for both sides during the WARS OF THE ROSES. French kings viewed perpetuation of civil war in England as a means for preventing further English military intervention in France and for weakening English support for the independent principalities of BURGUNDY and BRITTANY, the incorporation of which into France was a cornerstone of French royal policy throughout the fifteenth century.

CHARLES VII, who was king of France when the English civil war erupted in 1459, tended to favor the house of LANCASTER, even though he had spent most of his reign reconquering the Lancastrian-controlled areas of France. Not only was Queen MARGARET OF ANJOU Charles's niece, but the Yorkist tendency to emphasize the military inadequacies of the Lancastrian regime by recalling the lost glories of England's French empire convinced Charles that the house of YORK, once in power, would launch new invasions of France. However, Charles cautiously avoided involvement in English affairs until EDWARD IV overthrew the house of Lancaster at the Battle of TOWTON in March 1461. In the four months between the battle and his death in July, Charles provided the Lancastrian cause with substantial assistance, including financing a successful attack on the English Channel Islands.

Although he had been estranged from his father, the new French king, LOUIS XI, seeking both to weaken England and enlarge France, continued Charles's pro-Lancastrian policies. In the 1462 CHINON AGREEMENT, Louis agreed to provide Margaret of Anjou with French MERCENARIES commanded by Pierre de BRÉZÉ in return for her surrender of CALAIS, the last remaining English possession in France. When Burgundian intervention prevented a French attack on Calais, and military defeats seemed to doom the Lancastrian cause in England, Louis sought instead to negotiate a marriage alliance with Edward IV. However, Edward's preference for a Burgundian alliance, which was sealed in 1468 by the marriage of Edward's sister, MARGARET OF YORK, to Duke CHARLES of Burgundy, turned Louis against the Yorkist regime.

An opportunity to strike at Edward IV arose in 1470 when Richard NEVILLE, earl of Warwick, fled to France after the failure of his second coup attempt. Arranging for Warwick to meet Margaret of Anjou, Louis guided the two former enemies through the difficult negotiations that resulted in the ANGERS AGREEMENT, whereby Margaret agreed to marry her son Prince EDWARD OF LANCASTER to Warwick's daughter Anne NEVILLE in return for Warwick's promise to restore HENRY VI to the throne. For his part, Louis pledged financial and military assistance to Warwick, whose pro-French stance had been partially responsible for his break with Edward, in return for Warwick's agreement to bring England into war with Burgundy as France's ally.

Warwick toppled Edward in October 1470, but his declaration of war on Burgundy in January 1471 convinced Duke Charles to support Edward's attempt to regain the Crown, and in April Warwick's short-lived READEPTION government collapsed when the earl

was slain at the Battle of BARNET. With Warwick dead and the house of Lancaster destroyed, the English civil wars and French opportunities to exploit them were over. In the early 1470s, Louis, like Duke Charles, paid English courtiers to use their influence on his behalf with their king, but in 1475 Edward launched the long-threatened Yorkist invasion of France. However, Edward's willingness to withdraw his army in return for a large French pension convinced Louis that he had little to fear from England and led him to aggressively reabsorb large parts of the Burgundian state after 1477, when the death of Duke Charles gave the rule of the duchy to the duke's daughter Mary.

The deaths of both Louis XI and Edward IV in 1483 left both countries with unstable regimes. In England, RICHARD III sought support for his usurpation of EDWARD V's Crown, while in France the regency government of thirteen-year-old CHARLES VIII faced a coalition of disaffected nobles. To prevent Richard from supporting its own rebels and in pursuit of the traditional policy of weakening England, the French government provided men and ships for an invasion of England launched in 1485 by Henry Tudor, earl of Richmond, the remaining heir to the Lancastrian claim. Leading an army composed largely of French and Scottish veterans provided by the king of France, Richmond (thereafter HENRY VII) defeated and killed Richard III at the Battle of BOSWORTH FIELD in August.

Henry VII fell at odds with his former benefactor in 1491, when Charles's marriage to Duchess Anne of Brittany signaled the eventual incorporation of that duchy into France, an event that threatened English economic and security interests. Henry's opposition to French designs on Brittany led Charles to invite the Yorkist pretender Perkin WARBECK to France. Because Warbeck claimed to be Richard PLANTAGENET, duke of York, the younger son of Edward IV who had disappeared in the TOWER OF LONDON in 1483, Charles publicly acknowledged him as "Richard IV," granting him a large pension and comfortable lodgings at the French court. In 1492, Henry led an invasion force across the Channel, but neither side wanted war with the other—France was now too powerful for England to face alone, and Charles was more interested in Italy than in northwestern Europe. As a result, Henry and Charles agreed to the Treaty of Etaples in November. In return for payment of English campaign costs and the arrears of Edward IV's 1475 pension, and for a promise to expel Warbeck and all other Yorkist conspirators from France, Henry agreed to withdraw his army and tacitly accept the French takeover of Brittany. By 1500, a stronger, larger, more unified France, having recognized the legitimacy of the house of TUDOR, was no longer fearful of English invasion and increasingly interested in achieving political and military dominance in Europe.

Further Reading: Davies, C. S. L., "The Wars of the Roses in European Context," in A. J. Pollard, ed., *The Wars of the Roses* (New York: St. Martin's Press, 1995), pp. 162–185; Kendall, Paul Murray, *Louis XI* (New York: W. W. Norton, 1971); Potter, David, *A History of France, 1460–1560: The Emergence of a Nation State* (London: Macmillan, 1995); Tyrrell, Joseph M., *Louis XI* (Boston: Twayne, 1980); Vale, M. G. A., *Charles VII* (Berkeley: University of California Press, 1974).

Francis II, Duke of Brittany (d. 1488)

After 1471, Francis II, ruler of the French Duchy of BRITTANY, held custody of Henry Tudor, earl of Richmond (see HENRY VII), the surviving Lancastrian claimant to the English throne.

Becoming duke of Brittany in 1458, Francis's goal was to maintain Breton independence, which was threatened by the growing power of his feudal overlord, the king of FRANCE. To achieve this end, Francis, a weak and irresolute man, conducted a complex foreign policy that sought to preserve the friendship of England and BURGUNDY without unduly alienating France. Personally favorable to the house of LANCASTER, Francis allowed Jasper TUDOR, earl of Pembroke, to hire Breton men and ships for an invasion of WALES

in 1464. However, the expedition never sailed, in part because Francis withdrew his support when LOUIS XI of France became less friendly to the Lancastrian cause. Nonetheless, Francis remained cool to diplomatic overtures from Yorkist England until 1468, when the growing threat of French invasion and Brittany's thriving English trade forced the duke to conclude formal treaties of commerce and alliance with EDWARD IV.

After 1471, Francis had custody of Pembroke and his nephew Richmond, who had been driven ashore in Brittany after the restoration of the house of YORK forced them to flee Wales (see EDWARD IV, RESTORATION OF). Francis used his possession of Richmond, the remaining Lancastrian heir, to pressure Edward IV into supporting Brittany against France. In 1472, a force of 1,000 English ARCHERS under Anthony WOODVILLE, Earl Rivers, helped the Bretons repel a French invasion. In 1476, after persistent lobbying by Bishop Robert STILLINGTON, the English envoy, and by the pro-English faction at his own COURT, Francis agreed to surrender Richmond to Edward. However, before the English could sail, Richmond's friends among the duke's advisors persuaded Francis to change his mind, and Richmond eventually returned safely to the Breton court.

In 1480, Francis betrothed his only child, Anne, to Edward IV's heir, the future EDWARD V. When RICHARD III usurped the throne in 1483, he ended the marriage and so damaged the duke's hopes for the future independence of Brittany. After failing in an attempt to use his continued possession of Richmond to extort military assistance from Richard, Francis supplied Richmond with ships and men and allowed him to participate in BUCKINGHAM'S REBELLION in October 1483. After the failure of that uprising, a growing band of English exiles formed around Richmond in Brittany. In 1484, Richard, working through Francis's treasurer, Pierre LANDAIS, who had temporary direction of the Breton government while the duke was ill, secured an agreement to hand Richmond over to the king's agents. Warned of the plot by Bishop John MORTON, Richmond fled to France. Francis died in 1488, three years before his daughter's marriage to CHARLES VIII of France effectively ended Breton independence.

Further Reading: Griffiths, Ralph A., and Roger S. Thomas, *The Making of the Tudor Dynasty* (New York: St. Martin's Press, 1985); Jones, Michael, *The Creation of Brittany: A Late Medieval State* (London: Hambledon, 1988).

Generalship

Because most civil war armies comprised the same types of troops, wielding the same types of WEAPONRY and wearing similar ARMOR, the battles of the WARS OF THE ROSES rarely offered much opportunity for the exercise of creative or resourceful generalship by army commanders. However, the personal bravery, martial prowess, and military reputation of a commander, whether a king, prince, or nobleman, could give an army a decided edge in the hand-to-hand combat that characterized most civil war encounters (see BATTLES, NATURE OF).

Because fifteenth-century commanders were expected to personally lead their men into battle and to inspire them with deeds of valor, the house of YORK enjoyed a distinct leadership advantage early in the war, for it possessed the two most vigorous and inspiring leaders of the conflict—EDWARD IV and Richard NEVILLE, earl of Warwick. Young and strong, Edward, as his 1471 campaign showed (see EDWARD IV, RESTORATION OF), was capable of speed and decision, and possessed boldness, self-confidence, and an ability to inspire men. Never defeated in battle, Edward was also blessed with good luck, a reputation for which could itself greatly boost morale among such a commander's troops. In 1471, for instance, Edward was fortunate that Queen MARGARET OF ANJOU and her son Prince EDWARD OF LANCASTER did not arrive in England until after Warwick had been defeated and killed at the Battle of BARNET.

Although not the battlefield commander that Edward IV was, being more conservative and defensively minded, Warwick knew how to inspire men and possessed a great reputation for military success. His elaborate defensive preparations before the Battle of ST. ALBANS in 1461 proved useless, but his political/factional leadership was largely responsible for the Yorkist successes of 1460 and for the Lancastrian restoration a decade later (see EDWARD IV, OVERTHROW OF). Until Warwick joined them, the Lancastrians' most vigorous leader was Queen Margaret, who could inspire men but who could not, as a woman, lead them into combat. HENRY VI was present on numerous battlefields, but never as a commander. Captured no less than three times (NORTHAMPTON and the two battles at St. Albans) and held captive on a fourth occasion (Barnet), Henry apparently lacked the wit to flee a losing field. With his son too young to command, Henry left the leadership of his armies to prominent Lancastrian noblemen like the Dukes of Somerset and Humphrey STAFFORD, duke of Buckingham. By the Battle of HEXHAM in 1464, the Lancastrians no longer brought Henry to the field, but deposited him some miles away at Bywell Castle from which he could be quickly spirited away.

Because commanders themselves engaged in combat, many were killed in battle or taken and executed later. Three Dukes of Somerset (see under BEAUFORT), two earls of Northumberland (see under PERCY), two earls of Devon (see under COURTENAY), a Lancastrian Prince of Wales, and a king of England (see RICHARD III) all died in battle or on the block afterward. Between 1459 and 1487, combat and execution claimed the lives of forty-two noblemen, excluding Richard III and Edward of Lancaster. Many battles ended when the commander of an army was slain. Henry VI's men laid down their arms upon the death of Edmund BEAUFORT, duke of Somerset, at the 1455 Battle of ST. ALBANS, while royal troops quickly scattered or surrendered upon Richard III's death at the Battle of BOSWORTH FIELD. Although civil war commanders usually had little scope for imaginative generalship, their presence and conduct on the field were of great importance to the outcome of battles.

> **See also** Armies, Supplying of; Military Campaigns, Duration of
> **Further Reading:** Gillingham, John, *The Wars of the Roses* (Baton Rouge: Louisiana State University Press, 1981); Goodman, Anthony, *The Wars of the Roses* (New York: Dorset Press, 1981); Ross, Charles, *The Wars of the Roses* (London: Thames and Hudson, 1987).

Gentry

Other than the PEERAGE, no social class in fifteenth-century England was more actively involved in the WARS OF THE ROSES than the gentry.

The English gentry consisted of nontitled landholders who exercised extensive political and social influence in their localities. Although they stood below the peerage in terms of political power, social position, and economic resources, they formed the backbone of the military forces that titled peers led into battle. The gentry were subdivided into knights, esquires, and mere gentry—categories based roughly on income and social status. As knights of the shire, and increasingly as representatives for the towns, the gentry comprised the greater part of the House of Commons. As the century progressed, the gentry served more frequently on the royal COUNCIL and in important COURT and household offices. By the late fifteenth century, the total number of gentlemen of all subclasses probably stood at 2,000 to 3,000 persons.

As the natural leaders in their counties, the gentry usually could not avoid participation in the civil wars. Almost all gentlemen were linked by family ties or long traditions of service to the king or a local nobleman. Many gentlemen holding offices in the household of HENRY VI, or in the households of Queen MARGARET OF ANJOU or Prince EDWARD OF LANCASTER, fought for the house of LANCASTER, while many members of families that had long served the house of YORK, like William HASTINGS, Lord Hastings, fought for Richard PLANTAGENET, duke of York, and his sons. Gentlemen who were paid RETAINERS of a particular nobleman (see BASTARD FEUDALISM), or who hailed from a region where a particular noble or family was dominant, as the NEVILLE FAMILY was in parts of the north, risked losing their income, or worse, by refusing their lord's call to arms.

However, self-interest and ambition led some gentlemen to ignore ties of kinship or service and switch sides or refuse to fight. The retainers of George PLANTAGENET, duke of Clarence, grew increasingly reluctant to follow the duke through his frequent changes of coat, and otherwise loyal Percy retainers ignored the summons of Henry PERCY, fourth earl of Northumberland, to fight for EDWARD IV in 1471—too many of their male relatives had died fighting against Edward at the Battle of TOWTON in 1461. The severe penalties that accompanied defeat also persuaded gentlemen to refuse, delay, or limit participation. Almost 200 Welsh gentlemen fell at the Battle of EDGECOTE in 1469, and the Yorkists executed ten gentlemen after the Battle of MORTIMER'S CROSS in 1461 and almost thirty after the Battle of HEXHAM in 1464. Besides death in battle or execution afterward, gentlemen also risked confiscation of their estates. Under Edward IV, PARLIAMENT passed bills of ATTAINDER against ninety-three gentlemen, and under RICHARD III seventy gentlemen were attainted for involvement in BUCKINGHAM'S REBELLION in 1483. The wars inflicted heavy losses on the gentry, especially among wealthier members of the class.

> **Further Reading:** Carpenter, Christine, *Locality and Polity: A Study of Warwickshire Landed Society, 1401–1499* (Cambridge: Cambridge University Press, 1992); Pollard, A. J., "The Richmondshire Community of Gentry during the Wars of the Roses," in Charles Ross, ed., *Patronage, Pedigree and*

Power in Later Medieval England (Stroud, Gloucestershire, UK: Alan Sutton, 1979), pp. 37–59; Pugh, T. B., "The Magnates, Knights and Gentry" in S. B. Chrimes, C. D. Ross, and Ralph A. Griffiths, eds., Fifteenth-Century England, 1399–1509, 2d ed. (Stroud, Gloucestershire, UK: Alan Sutton, 1995), pp. 86–128; Ross, Charles, The Wars of the Roses (London: Thames and Hudson, 1987).

George, Duke of Clarence. See Plantagenet, George, Duke of Clarence

Gloucester, Duke of. See Richard III

The Great Chronicle of London. See London Chronicles

Gregory's Chronicle. See London Chronicles

Grey, Edmund, Earl of Kent (c. 1420–1489)

In the summer of 1460, Edmund Grey, future earl of Kent, helped alter the course of the WARS OF THE ROSES and revitalize the Yorkist cause by switching sides at the Battle of NORTHAMPTON.

Grey served in FRANCE in the late 1430s and was knighted in October 1440, only two weeks after succeeding his grandfather as fourth Lord Grey of Ruthyn. He generally supported HENRY VI during the 1450s, and declared himself the king's man at the 1459 COVENTRY PARLIAMENT that attainted Richard PLANTAGENET, duke of York, and his Neville allies. In July 1460, Grey commanded the right flank of the royal army at the Battle of Northampton; but when the Yorkist troops approached his part of the line, Grey ordered his men to lay down their arms and allow the Yorkists to enter the king's camp. This betrayal of Henry VI was apparently preplanned, for Richard NEVILLE, earl of Warwick, the Yorkist commander, had told his men

to spare anyone wearing Grey's BADGE, the black ragged staff. Thanks to Grey's treachery, the Yorkists overwhelmed the royal army, slew such important Lancastrian lords as Humphrey STAFFORD, duke of Buckingham, and Thomas PERCY, Lord Egremont, and seized control of the king and the government.

After he won the Crown in 1461, EDWARD IV rewarded Grey for his services to the house of YORK by naming him lord treasurer in 1463 and creating him earl of Kent in May 1466. In the mid-1460s, Grey's son married a sister of Queen Elizabeth WOODVILLE. After about 1469, Kent seems to have withdrawn from politics and to have played little part either in the READEPTION of Henry VI in 1470 or the restoration of Edward IV in 1471 (see EDWARD IV, RESTORATION OF). In 1483, Kent participated in the coronation of RICHARD III and in 1484 won confirmation of his titles from the new king. However, Kent received no other rewards from Richard, who perhaps considered the support of the aging and long inactive earl not worth buying. In 1487, two years after HENRY VII had overthrown Richard III, Kent again had his titles confirmed. The earl died in 1489.

Further Reading: Haigh, Philip A., The Military Campaigns of the Wars of the Roses (Stroud, Gloucestershire, UK: Sutton Publishing, 1995); Ross, Charles, Edward IV (New Haven, CT: Yale University Press, 1998).

Grey, Thomas, Marquis of Dorset (1451–1501)

A half brother of EDWARD V, Thomas Grey, marquis of Dorset, participated in the final phase of the civil wars by supporting efforts to overthrow RICHARD III.

The eldest son of John Grey and Elizabeth WOODVILLE, Grey became the stepson of EDWARD IV when his widowed mother married the king in 1464. Although his father had died fighting for HENRY VI in 1461, Grey fought for his Yorkist stepfather at the Battle of TEWKESBURY in May 1471, and was raised to the PEERAGE as earl of Huntingdon three months later. In 1475, only weeks before accompanying the king to FRANCE, he was created marquis of Dorset. Although acquiring a reputation as a licentious courtier, Dorset, by the 1480s, was also a royal councilor and an emerging political figure. His feud with William HASTINGS, Lord Hastings, disturbed the peace of the COURT during the last months of Edward IV.

On Edward V's accession in April 1483, Dorset became constable of the TOWER OF LONDON and sought to secure the royal NAVY for the Woodville interest. When Richard, duke of Gloucester, Edward V's paternal uncle, seized custody of the young king, and arrested Lord Richard Grey, Dorset's brother and one of the king's governors, the marquis fled into SANCTUARY at Westminster with his mother. He escaped from sanctuary in June, only weeks before Gloucester took the Crown as Richard III. In October 1483, with a price on his head, and with rumors claiming that Edward V and his brother were dead, Dorset joined BUCKINGHAM'S REBELLION. When that uprising on behalf of Henry Tudor, earl of Richmond, failed, Dorset joined Richmond in exile in BRITTANY. In early 1484, Richard III reconciled with Queen Elizabeth Woodville, who left sanctuary and convinced her son by letter to abandon Richmond and submit to the king. Dorset quit Paris secretly, but Richmond sent two of his men to retrieve the marquis, who was privy to all Richmond's plans. Overtaken near Compiègne, Dorset was either persuaded or compelled to return to Paris, where a mistrustful Richmond left him when he embarked for England in August.

After his victory at the Battle of BOSWORTH FIELD, Richmond, now HENRY VII, recalled Dorset to England and confirmed him in his titles and offices. However, in 1487, the king committed Dorset to the Tower. Henry's reasons for this action are uncertain. Perhaps he still distrusted Dorset for his attempted defection in 1485, but more likely he believed Dorset was somehow involved with Lambert SIMNEL or with some other conspiracy that claimed the sons of Edward IV were still alive. In any event, Dorset was re-leased and restored to favor shortly after Simnel's uprising collapsed at the Battle of STOKE in June 1487. The marquis died in September 1501.

Further Reading: Chrimes, S. B., *Henry VII* (New Haven, CT: Yale University Press, 1999); Ross, Charles, *Richard III* (Berkeley: University of California Press, 1981).

Gruthuyse, Louis de, Seigneur de la Gruthuyse, Earl of Winchester (c. 1427–1492)

In late 1470, the Burgundian nobleman, Louis de Gruthuyse, Lord of Gruthuyse, provided the newly exiled EDWARD IV with vital material and political support.

Louis succeeded his father as Lord of Gruthuyse in 1438, and became cupbearer to Duke PHILIP of BURGUNDY by 1449. The duke appointed him captain of Bruges in 1452 and knighted him at the Battle of Gavre in July 1453. By 1461, Gruthuyse was the duke's chamberlain and a member of his COUNCIL. As Burgundian ambassador to both SCOTLAND and England in 1460, Gruthuyse displayed his friendship for the house of YORK by persuading the Scottish regent, Queen MARY OF GUELDRES, to refrain from aiding Queen MARGARET OF ANJOU until after the death of Richard PLANTAGENET, duke of York, at the Battle of WAKEFIELD in December. In 1466–1467, while again serving as ambassador to England, Gruthuyse became familiar with the Yorkist COURT and personally known to Edward IV.

On 2 October 1470, after being isolated and outmaneuvered by Richard NEVILLE, earl of Warwick, Edward and a small band of followers fled England and landed on the Dutch coast (see EDWARD IV, OVERTHROW OF). As governor of Holland since 1463, Gruthuyse welcomed the weary and destitute exiles to Burgundy. After escorting the Englishmen to his house in The Hague, Gruthuyse supplied them with food, clothes, and money, and worked to secure Edward an interview with Duke CHARLES, whose Lancastrian inclinations made him unwilling to receive the ex-king. Edward had to rely on the unfailing hospitality of Gruthuyse until January, when the friendship that HENRY VI's READEPTION government displayed for FRANCE forced the duke to meet with Edward and begin quietly assisting him. As a consequence, Edward sailed for England in March, defeated and killed Warwick at the Battle of BARNET in April, and secured his Crown after the Battle of TEWKESBURY in May (see EDWARD IV, RESTORATION OF).

In October 1472, Duke Charles sent Gruthuyse to England to discuss an Anglo-Burgundian alliance. To express his gratitude for the ambassador's assistance in 1470, Edward gave Gruthuyse a lavish welcome to the English court, creating him earl of Winchester, granting him an annuity of £200, and presenting him with such gifts as a bejeweled cup, a fine crossbow, and one of the royal horses. Edward also employed Winchester as a negotiator for England with the HANSEATIC LEAGUE, a powerful association of German merchants, and granted the earl special trading rights in English ports. Winchester spent most of the rest of his life in service to the dukes of Burgundy, dying at Bruges in November 1492. A noted bibliophile, with one of the largest private libraries in Europe, Winchester is often credited by historians with encouraging Edward IV to begin collecting manuscripts, a pursuit that the king began only after his return from Burgundy in 1471.

Further Reading: Ross, Charles, *Edward IV* (New Haven, CT: Yale University Press, 1998); Vaughan, Richard, *Valois Burgundy* (Hamden, CT: Archon Books, 1975).

Hanseatic League

Established to control the activities and protect the privileges of German merchants trading in northern Europe, the Hanseatic League (or Hansa) was by the late fourteenth century a loose association of almost one hundred north German and Baltic towns. By the fifteenth century, Hansa merchants (known as Easterlings) enjoyed extensive trading privileges in England and operated trading posts in various English ports, including LONDON. A power at sea capable of organizing economic blockades and naval campaigns to support its members' interests, the league, through its hostility toward the commercial policies of EDWARD IV, affected the course of the WARS OF THE ROSES in 1470–1471.

By the 1460s, Hansa traders had largely frozen English merchants out of direct participation in trade with North Germany, the Baltic, Scandinavia, and Iceland. Meanwhile, league merchants had achieved a privileged position in England—their headquarters in London (known as the Steelyard) enjoyed extraterritorial status, and they were exempt from the poundage customs duty that all English merchants were required to pay. These privileges made the league highly unpopular in England, and especially in London, and explain the great national reputation won by Richard NEVILLE, earl of Warwick, when he preyed upon Hansa shipping from his CALAIS base in 1460.

In 1468, league involvement in the seizure of four English vessels led Edward IV and his COUNCIL to authorize the arrest and imprisonment of all Hansa merchants in London. This action, which was condemned even by English traders as arbitrary and counterproductive, initiated a damaging commercial and naval war that virtually halted English trade with Germany and the Baltic. In 1470, after Warwick concluded the ANGERS AGREEMENT with MARGARET OF ANJOU, Hanseatic naval attacks forced Edward IV to divert the English fleet from keeping watch for the earl's return from FRANCE. In October, when Warwick's landing forced Edward to flee the realm, a Hanseatic vessel pursued and almost caught Edward's ship as it made for BURGUNDY. Although Warwick had been invested in the captured English ships, and had thus been a strong advocate of the 1468 decision to retaliate against the league, the earl, on his return to England in 1470, reaped the benefits of the unpopularity that decision had earned for Edward IV among the English merchant community (see EDWARD IV, OVERTHROW OF).

In early 1471, Edward obtained Hanseatic vessels to convey him to England in exchange for a promise to restore all the league's trading privileges when he regained the throne (see EDWARD IV, RESTORATION OF). However, once in power, the king reneged on the agreement, and the Hansa resumed the naval war. Edward's attitude changed when he realized that peace with the league was necessary if he was to secure the English Channel in preparation for his intended invasion of France. Anglo-Hanseatic negotiations collapsed in 1472 when England rejected the league's demands for full compensation for all ships and goods seized in 1468 and for complete restoration of all trading privileges formerly held in England. In 1474, Edward, anxious to begin the French campaign, put political interests before commercial ones and agreed to all the league's terms in the Treaty of Utrecht. The agreement was a complete surrender on Edward's part; aside from an end to the naval war, he achieved no improvement in the status of English merchants trading in Hanseatic territories, where the tax exemptions extended to Easterlings in England were not reciprocated. As a result of the treaty, English trade with Germany and the Baltic declined drastically, while Hansa trade with England reached record levels by the 1480s.

See also English Economy and the Wars of the Roses
Further Reading: Lloyd, T. H., *England and the German Hanse, 1157–1611* (Cambridge: Cambridge University Press, 1991).

Harbingers

Harbingers were a special corps of men who rode before an army on the march and arranged for the billeting, or lodging, of the troops.

Harbingers generally came under the command of the army's marshal, the officer responsible for keeping the troops well fed and supplied. Because the WARS OF THE ROSES were civil wars, harbingers usually had to maintain friendly relations with the local people on whom troops were billeted while also providing suitable accommodations for the men. Uncomfortable sleeping quarters could damage army morale, and quarrels over who got choice billets could destroy an army's cohesion and seriously divide its leadership. The Yorkists lost the Battle of EDGECOTE in 1469 largely because EDWARD IV's commanders, William HERBERT, earl of Pembroke, and Humphrey STAFFORD, earl of Devon, argued over lodging the night before. When Devon led most of the ARCHERS to distant billets, Pembroke had mainly footmen when he was confronted next day by the ROBIN OF REDESDALE insurgents.

Harbingers could also act as foragers and information gatherers, since they often made first contact with the enemy force by clashing with its harbingers. Because encountering opposing harbingers could reveal a foe's location

and direction, commanders sometimes ordered their own harbingers to ride away from the army's line of march, thereby deceiving the enemy as to the army's position and the commander's intentions. Richard NEVILLE, earl of Warwick, used this tactic during his coup attempt in 1470, as did Edmund BEAUFORT, duke of Somerset, the Lancastrian commander during the western campaign in 1471. In an effort to reach the Severn fords before Edward IV, Somerset sent harbingers southeast from Bristol when the army moved north. Although Edward eventually caught and defeated his enemies at the Battle of TEWKESBURY, the ploy almost delayed the king sufficiently to allow MARGARET OF ANJOU's army to reach WALES.

See also Armies, Supplying of
Further Reading: Boardman, Andrew W., *The Medieval Soldier in the Wars of the Roses* (Stroud, Gloucestershire, UK: Sutton Publishing, 1998); Gillingham, John, *The Wars of the Roses* (Baton Rouge: Louisiana State University Press, 1981).

Hardyng, John. *See Hardyng's Chronicle*

Hardyng's Chronicle

Written by John Hardyng (1378–c. 1465), a soldier and antiquarian, *Hardyng's Chronicle* is an English verse account of the history of England from its beginnings to 1461. Although *Hardyng's Chronicle* is of value for the reign of HENRY VI, historians of the WARS OF THE ROSES use the work cautiously because it exists in different versions and was rewritten at each change of regime to reflect the interests of the party in power.

A northerner, Hardyng spent part of his youth in service to the Percy family (see NORTH OF ENGLAND AND THE WARS OF THE ROSES). He fought against the Scots in 1402 and in FRANCE at the Battle of Agincourt in 1415. From 1418 to 1421, he traveled through SCOTLAND collecting evidence to prove that the Scots owed homage to England. The death of Henry V in 1422 ended the project, until Hardyng resumed his search for

Henry VI in 1439. Hardyng eventually received grants totaling £30 per year for his services, even though the six documents relating to the matter that Hardyng gave to the Crown in 1457 were proven in the nineteenth century to be forgeries. The documents were probably created by Hardyng, whose antiquarian knowledge would have allowed him to produce convincing fakes.

Hardyng's Chronicle consists of seven-line verse stanzas rhyming according to the scheme *ababbcc*. In 1457, Hardyng, in an unsuccessful attempt to obtain a royal grant, dedicated his *Chronicle* to Henry VI; to the king's wife, Queen MARGARET OF ANJOU; and to the king's son, Prince EDWARD OF LANCASTER. Although favorable to the house of LANCASTER, this initial version obliquely criticizes Henry VI by informing the king of instances of civil unrest and local injustice. A second version, suitably revised to win the favor of the house of YORK, was dedicated to Richard PLANTAGENET, duke of York, some time between 1458 and 1460. While the first version contains no judgment on the abilities of Henry VI, the second questions the king's wits and moral reasoning.

> He could little within his breast conceive,
> The good from evil he could not perceive.
> (Ellis, p. 394)

Shortly before his death in about 1465, Hardyng presented yet another version of his chronicle to EDWARD IV. Although this version ends with the flight of the Lancastrian royal family into Scotland after the Battle of TOWTON in 1461, mention of Queen Elizabeth WOODVILLE dates completion of the manuscript to 1464, the year of Elizabeth's marriage to the king. The best-known edition of *Hardyng's Chronicle* was printed in 1543 by the Tudor chronicler Richard Grafton, who updated the work to his own time. Although his poetry is poor and his partisan purposes are clear, Hardyng is still a useful source for events of the 1450s that led up to the Wars of the Roses.

See also Rous, John

Further Reading: Ellis, Henry, ed., *The Chronicle of John Hardyng Together with the Continuation of Richard Grafton* (London, 1812); Hardyng, John, *The Chronicle of John Hardyng,* reprint ed. (New York: AMS Press, 1974); see the online Catholic Encyclopedia at <http://www.newadvent.org/cathen/07136a.htm> for a brief biography of John Hardyng.

Harlech Castle (1461–1468)

By holding out for most of the 1460s, the Lancastrian garrison in the Welsh castle at Harlech prevented the establishment of effective Yorkist government in WALES and encouraged Lancastrian resistance throughout England.

Harlech Castle was one of the massive fortresses built by Edward I in the late thirteenth century to overawe the newly subdued Welsh. Like Edward's other Welsh strongholds, Harlech was designed and built to be supplied by sea. After EDWARD IV's victory at the Battle of TOWTON in March 1461, HENRY VI's half brother, Jasper TUDOR, earl of Pembroke, placed Lancastrian garrisons in Harlech and various other Welsh fortresses in an effort to hold Wales against the Yorkists. Sir William HERBERT, the leading Yorkist in Wales, defeated Pembroke at the Battle of TWT HILL in October 1461, forcing the earl to flee to IRELAND. By the end of 1462, Herbert had captured all the Lancastrian strongholds in Wales except Harlech Castle, which remained in the hands of a garrison commanded by the Welshman David ap Eynon and including such prominent English Lancastrians as Sir Richard TUNSTALL.

Far from LONDON on the remote coast of northwest Wales, Harlech remained largely unmolested for seven years. The garrison kept North Wales in disorder for the whole time, periodically sallying forth to seize cattle, wheat, and other supplies and loudly proclaiming their allegiance to Henry VI and the house of LANCASTER. Harlech became a safe point of entry and exit for Lancastrian agents and a link to Ireland and SCOTLAND. The fortress also became a center of Lancastrian intrigue. In early 1462, the garrison helped foment a conspiracy to bring Pembroke back to Wales to coordinate Lancastrian attacks there and in England. The Yorkists discovered the plot and executed two Englishmen implicated in it, John de Vere, earl of Oxford, and his eldest son Aubrey, thereby making John de VERE, the earl's second son, an implacable foe of the house of YORK (see OXFORD CONSPIRACY). In 1461, Edward IV promised a pardon to the garrison leaders if they surrendered and an ATTAINDER if they did not. The garrison ignored the offer. In 1464, PARLIAMENT called upon the garrison to submit, and Edward issued a proclamation giving the garrison until 1 January 1465 to surrender. Harlech's defenders again ignored the king.

In June 1468, Pembroke returned to Harlech. After attracting large numbers of Welsh Lancastrians to his banner, the earl launched a campaign of destruction across central Wales, eventually seizing and plundering the town of Denbigh. These new disorders convinced Edward IV that Harlech had to be taken, and he issued COMMISSIONS OF ARRAY to Herbert to raise an army in the English border counties. Dividing his force of 9,000 into two parts, Herbert sent his brother, Richard Herbert, to devastate the coast north of the castle while he advanced on Harlech from the south. After the northern force defeated and scattered Pembroke's men, the two wings of the army reunited and forced the surrender of Harlech on 14 August 1468. Although David ap Eynon was pardoned, Sir Richard Tunstall and the other Englishmen in the garrison were conveyed to the TOWER OF LONDON, where some were eventually executed. The king pardoned the rest of the garrison in December. Pembroke once again escaped Wales, but his earldom was awarded to Herbert in September. With the fall of Harlech, all England and Wales were for the first time under Yorkist control.

Further Reading: Davies, John, *A History of Wales* (London: The Penguin Group, 1993); Evans, H. T., *Wales and the Wars of the Roses* (Stroud, Gloucestershire, UK: Sutton Publishing, 1998); Griffiths, Ralph A., "Wales and the Marches," in

S. B. Chrimes, C. D. Ross, and Ralph A. Griffiths, eds., *Fifteenth-Century England, 1399–1509,* 2d ed. (Stroud, Gloucestershire, UK: Alan Sutton, 1995); Williams, Glanmor, *Renewal and Reformation: Wales, c. 1415–1642* (Oxford: Oxford University Press, 1993).

Harness. *See* Armor

Hastings, William, Lord Hastings (c. 1430–1483)

William Hastings, Lord Hastings, was a personal friend and loyal supporter of EDWARD IV, and, as the most important supporter of EDWARD V in 1483, was summarily executed by Richard, duke of Gloucester (see RICHARD III).

Born into a Leicestershire GENTRY family that had long served the house of YORK, Hastings, like his father, was a RETAINER of Richard PLANTAGENET, duke of York. He was with the Yorkist army at the Battle of LUDFORD BRIDGE in 1459 and joined the forces of York's son, Edward, earl of March, after the earl's victory at the Battle of MORTIMER'S CROSS in 1461. Present in LONDON when March was proclaimed king as Edward IV, Hastings was several weeks later knighted by Edward on the field of TOWTON. Quickly rewarded with lands and offices, Hastings was soon known to be high in the king's confidence, a personal friend of unshakable loyalty who shared Edward's tastes. He was a member of the COUNCIL by April 1461 and a member of the PEERAGE by the following June. In the same year, he was appointed master of the mint and lord chamberlain. The latter office was highly lucrative, for it allowed Hastings to control access to the king. Many important people, including both Elizabeth WOODVILLE, on her first appearance at COURT, and Richard NEVILLE, earl of Warwick, paid him to exercise his influence with Edward on their behalf. By the 1470s, Hastings was receiving handsome pensions from both LOUIS XI of FRANCE and Duke CHARLES of BURGUNDY. The king also granted Hastings extensive estates in the Mid-

The lion badge of William Hastings, Lord Hastings, the loyal Yorkist executed by Richard III in 1483. (Add. MS 40742 f. 11, British Library)

lands, a traditionally Lancastrian region that Edward was anxious to pacify. Thanks largely to the position of trust that he enjoyed at court, Hastings soon became so influential in the Midlands that he could retain men simply on the promise of "good lordship" without the usual monetary payment (see BASTARD FEUDALISM).

In 1470, Hastings fled with Edward to Burgundy. On their return to England in 1471, Hastings quickly raised 3,000 men on his Midland estates, the first significant body of reinforcements to join Edward. Hastings commanded the Yorkist left at the Battle of BARNET and the right wing at the Battle of TEWKESBURY. After Edward's restoration,

Hastings served on various diplomatic missions, becoming well known at foreign courts, especially Burgundy, where he had helped negotiate the duke's 1468 marriage to Edward's sister, MARGARET OF YORK. He accompanied Edward on the French expedition of 1475 and was named governor of CALAIS in 1471, an appointment that angered the queen, who wanted that important post for her brother, Anthony WOODVILLE, Earl Rivers. The queen also disliked Hastings because he was, in the words of Dominic MANCINI, "the accomplice and partner of [the king's] privy pleasures" (Ross, *Edward IV,* p. 74). Although Hastings seems, for one of his position, to have had few enemies—in his *HISTORY OF KING*

RICHARD III, Sir Thomas More called him "an honourable man, a good knight and . . . passing well-beloved" (Ross, *Edward IV,* p. 73)—his rivalry with the WOODVILLE FAMILY, and especially with the queen's son, Thomas GREY, marquis of Dorset, so intensified in the early 1480s that Edward IV tried to reconcile the two on his deathbed.

After the king's death in April 1483, Hastings's antipathy toward the Woodvilles made him an early ally of Richard, duke of Gloucester, Edward's brother. However, Hastings's loyalty to Edward V, his late master's son, was deep, and when Gloucester realized that the influential peer would not countenance Edward's removal from the throne, the duke struck Hastings down. At the famous COUNCIL MEETING OF 13 JUNE 1483 in the TOWER OF LONDON, Gloucester accused Hastings of plotting treason with the queen and Jane SHORE, a former mistress of Edward IV with whom Hastings may have recently begun a relationship. Seized by Thomas HOWARD who led armed men into the council chamber on Gloucester's command, Hastings was summarily executed on Tower Hill without trial. Although no evidence of any Hastings-Woodville conspiracy exists beyond Gloucester's accusation, such a plot is not impossible given Hastings's well-known loyalty to Edward IV and his sons.

See also Usurpation of 1483
Further Reading: Hicks, Michael, "Lord Hastings' Indentured Retainers?" in *Richard III and His Rivals: Magnates and Their Motives in the Wars of the Roses* (London: Hambledon Press, 1991); Ross, Charles, *Edward IV* (New Haven, CT: Yale University Press, 1998); Ross, Charles, *Richard III* (Berkeley: University of California Press, 1981); Seward, Desmond, *The Wars of the Roses* (New York: Viking, 1995); "William Lord Hastings," in Michael Hicks, *Who's Who in Late Medieval England* (London: Shepheard-Walwyn, 1991), pp. 345–346.

Hedgeley Moor, Battle of (1464)

The Battle of Hedgeley Moor, fought in Northumberland on 25 April 1464, checked the growth of Lancastrian insurgency in the far north and allowed the continuation of peace talks between SCOTLAND, a former Lancastrian refuge, and the Yorkist government of EDWARD IV.

Early in 1464, Henry BEAUFORT, the Lancastrian duke of Somerset, whom Edward IV had pardoned in the previous year, left his post in WALES and fled into the Lancastrian north, where he declared openly for HENRY VI. After a failed attempt to seize the Yorkist supply base at Newcastle, Somerset appeared at the Northumbrian castle of BAMBURGH, then in Lancastrian hands. Joining forces with Sir Ralph Percy and other recently pardoned Lancastrians, Somerset launched a two-month campaign that by late March had turned northeastern England into a Lancastrian enclave. With Norham Castle and the towns of Bywell, Hexham, Langley, and Prudhoe all in Somerset's hands, the Anglo-Scottish talks that were set to resume in Newcastle on 6 March had to be rescheduled for late April in York. To safely escort the Scottish commissioners from the border to York, Edward IV dispatched John NEVILLE, Lord Montagu, into Northumbria.

Collecting strength as he moved north, Montagu evaded a Lancastrian ambush and came safely to Newcastle. Resuming his march to the Scottish border, Montagu encountered a force under Somerset about nine miles northwest of ALNWICK on Hedgeley Moor. Although accounts of the battle are sketchy, fighting seems to have begun with the usual exchange of ARCHER fire. But before the two armies could engage, the left wing of Somerset's force suddenly broke and ran, perhaps because of poor morale. Montagu shifted his position to attack the remaining Lancastrians, who were quickly overwhelmed by the larger Yorkist army. At some point during the fighting, Somerset and most of the Lancastrian army disengaged and scattered, leaving Sir Ralph Percy and his household RETAINERS on the field to be slaughtered. After the battle, Montagu reformed his army and continued his march to the border, where he met the Scottish envoys and conducted them safely to York to resume their talks with Edward IV's commissioners.

See also Dunstanburgh Castle; Hexham, Battle of; North of England and the Wars of the Roses
Further Reading: Haigh, Philip A., *The Military Campaigns of the Wars of the Roses* (Stroud, Gloucestershire, UK: Sutton Publishing, 1995).

Henry VI, King of England (1421–1471)

Through his favoritism and inability to function effectively as king, Henry VI, third monarch of the house of LANCASTER, became a chief cause of the WARS OF THE ROSES.

Born at Windsor in December 1421, the only child of Henry V (r. 1413–1422) and Catherine of Valois (d. 1437), Henry was less than a year old when he succeeded his father as king of England and his maternal grandfather, Charles VI (r. 1380–1422), as king of FRANCE. Having reopened the HUNDRED YEARS WAR, Henry V had conquered large areas of northern France and had won official recognition as heir to the French throne. However, Henry VI's maternal uncle, CHARLES VII, rejected this settlement, and maintenance of England's French possessions required a continuous military effort. Henry's eldest paternal uncle, John, duke of Bedford (1389–1435), directed the English administration in France, while the king's younger uncle, Humphrey, duke of Gloucester (1390–1447), presided in England over a minority COUNCIL composed of experienced noble and ecclesiastical councilors. Acting in the child king's name, though unable to make any permanent decisions affecting his Crowns, the minority administration preserved the French domain and provided generally effective government.

Crowned at Westminster in 1429 and at Paris in 1431, Henry was declared of full age in 1437. He was eager to exercise his office and to have his will in matters that interested him, such as the royal foundations of Eton College and King's College, Cambridge, which the king planned in minute detail and to which he diverted funds that were urgently needed elsewhere. However, he had little un-

Henry VI, third and last king of the house of Lancaster, was overthrown by Edward IV of the house of York in 1461, and murdered, probably on Edward's order, in the Tower of London in 1471. (National Portrait Gallery: NPG 2457)

derstanding of the workings of government, and was easily persuaded by self-interested courtiers to grant titles, lands, offices, pardons, and monetary rewards without any thought to the merits or the consequences of the request. An exceptionally pious man, Henry had no interest in leading armies and in the 1440s allowed England's military position in France to deteriorate. He actively if ineffectively pursued a peace policy that led in 1445 to a truce with Charles VII and to his marriage with Charles's kinswoman, MARGARET OF ANJOU. Pressed by his wife, and anxious to achieve a final settlement in France, Henry fulfilled a rash promise to surrender Maine, thereby buying much ill will in England for his chief minister, William de la POLE, duke of Suffolk. When the French overwhelmed a poorly defended Normandy in 1449–1450, public dissatisfaction with government policy fell upon Suffolk, who was driven from office. Suffolk's fall was followed by JACK CADE'S REBELLION, which protested military failure in France and the breakdown of royal justice in England, and which gave voice to the frustration of noblemen who felt themselves excluded from royal patronage by a clique of favored courtiers.

Chief among these disaffected magnates was Richard PLANTAGENET, duke of York, who was heir presumptive to the childless king. The duke's anger grew when Henry replaced Suffolk with Edmund BEAUFORT, duke of Somerset, who had his own claim to the throne. York made several abortive attempts to force his way into the royal counsels (see DARTFORD UPRISING) but did not succeed until 1453, when Henry suffered a serious mental breakdown that left him completely incapacitated (see HENRY VI, ILLNESS OF). With Henry unable to communicate, and even unaware of the birth of his son, Prince EDWARD OF LANCASTER, PARLIAMENT appointed York protector, and the duke committed Somerset to the TOWER OF LONDON. Henry's recovery in early 1455 ended the FIRST PROTECTORATE and effected Somerset's release. Meanwhile, lack of an effective king had allowed noble quarrels, such as the NEVILLE-PERCY FEUD, to flourish, and these feuds began to merge into the growing national rivalry between York and Somerset. With Henry unable to play the traditional royal role of arbiter, factions developed around York and around Somerset and the queen, who entered the political fray out of fear that York's ambition might threaten her son. Violence erupted in May 1455, when York, fearing arrest, took up arms against the COURT with his new allies, Richard NEVILLE, earl of Salisbury, and his son Richard NEVILLE, earl of Warwick.

At the Battle of ST. ALBANS, Somerset died and York used custody of the king to establish his short-lived SECOND PROTECTORATE. Soon after, Henry suffered a relapse from which he never fully recovered. For the rest of his life, Henry was a symbol of monarchy rather than a functioning monarch; political factions fought to control his person, seeking to use custody of the king to legitimize their control of the king's government. In 1459,

after the failure of Henry's LOVE-DAY peace effort, the queen drove York and the Nevilles from England. Warwick returned in 1460 and captured Henry at the Battle of NORTHAMPTON, thereby allowing York to lay his claim to the Crown before Parliament, an act that transformed a political dispute into a dynastic war between the houses of Lancaster and YORK. Henry made no protest, and his deposition was prevented only by the unwillingness of Parliament, which imposed a settlement— the Act of ACCORD—that disinherited Prince Edward in favor of York. Henry passively accepted this agreement, although the queen continued the war. Lancastrian victories at the Battles of WAKEFIELD in December 1460 and ST. ALBANS in February 1461 led to York's death and Henry's reunion with his wife and son.

Having lost control of Henry, the Yorkists needed a king of their own, and in March 1461 they elevated York's son to the throne as EDWARD IV. After the Battle of TOWTON on 29 March, Henry fled into SCOTLAND with his family. He spent the next four years there or, after his family left for France, in hiding in northern England, where he was captured in 1465. He remained in the TOWER OF LONDON until October 1470, when Warwick's defection to Lancaster restored Henry to the throne (see EDWARD IV, OVERTHROW OF). The READEPTION government was directed by Warwick, and Henry served merely as a means for rallying Lancastrians to the new regime. When Edward IV reentered LONDON in April 1471, he returned Henry to the Tower (see EDWARD IV, RESTORATION OF). Warwick's death at the Battle of BARNET in April and Prince Edward's death at the Battle of TEWKESBURY in May ended any need to keep Henry alive, and the ex-king was murdered in the Tower on 21 May 1471 (see HENRY VI, MURDER OF).

See also "Compilation of the Meekness and Good Life of Henry VI" (Blacman)
Further Reading: Griffiths, Ralph A., *The Reign of King Henry VI* (Berkeley: University of California Press, 1981); Storey, R. L., *The End of the House of Lancaster,* 2d ed. (Stroud,

Gloucestershire, UK: Sutton Publishing, 1999); Watts, John, *Henry VI and the Politics of Kingship* (Cambridge: Cambridge University Press, 1996); Wolffe, Bertram, *Henry VI* (London: Eyre Methuen, 1981).

Henry VI, Illness of

HENRY VI's inability to function as an effective monarch, which became total in 1453 with the onset of chronic mental illness, was a main cause of the WARS OF THE ROSES.

In early August 1453, while staying at the royal hunting lodge at Clarendon, Henry fell suddenly into a stupor that rendered him unable to communicate. Because we have no eyewitness accounts of the start of Henry's illness, the exact cause and nature of his ailment remain mysterious. One contemporary chronicler claimed that it commenced when the king suffered a sudden shock, a suggestion that has led modern historians to speculate that Henry fell ill when he received the devastating news of the destruction in July of an English army at the Battle of CASTILLON, a defeat that ended the English presence in FRANCE. Although rumors that the king was childish or simple had been whispered about the kingdom before 1453, Henry showed no signs of mental illness until that date. However, he may have inherited a genetic predisposition to such illness from his maternal grandfather, Charles VI of France, who suffered recurring bouts of violent madness.

In March 1454, a deputation from PARLIAMENT visited the king at Windsor. Instructed to ascertain Henry's wishes as to the filling of several important offices that had fallen vacant in recent months, the deputation could get no response from Henry, who seemed unaware of their presence. He could not stand or walk and required round-the-clock care from his grooms and chamber servants. He displayed none of the frenzy that had characterized his grandfather's illness but neither recognized nor understood anyone or anything. When he finally recovered around Christmas 1454, Henry remembered nothing of the previous seventeen months, including the birth of his son, Prince EDWARD OF LANCASTER. Henry was again unwell after the Battle of ST. ALBANS in May 1455, when the unaccustomed shock of combat may have triggered another episode.

From 1456, the few surviving accounts of Henry's condition show him as weak-minded, requiring inordinate amounts of sleep, and given almost entirely to a routine of religious devotions. After 1457, the king found seclusion attractive, and his wife, Queen MARGARET OF ANJOU, often housed him in monasteries, away from any but loyal courtiers. Although the king had periods of lucid activity, such as his personal direction of the LOVE-DAY peace effort in 1458, he was largely a cipher during the last fifteen years of his life; the political factions that coalesced around the queen and Richard PLANTAGENET, duke of York, fought to control his person and thereby his government. Because his illness rendered him unable to function as an arbiter of noble disputes, and because the queen's partisanship made him the figurehead for one political faction, Henry's mental incapacity was instrumental in overthrowing royal authority and bringing about the dynastic war between the houses of LANCASTER and YORK.

See also "Compilation of the Meekness and Good Life of Henry VI" (Blacman); Henry VI, Murder of

Further Reading: Griffiths, Ralph A., *The Reign of King Henry VI* (Berkeley: University of California Press, 1981); Wolffe, Bertram, *Henry VI* (London: Eyre Methuen, 1981).

Henry VI, Murder of (1471)

The death of HENRY VI, which occurred under mysterious circumstances in the TOWER OF LONDON in May 1471, ended the direct male line of the house of LANCASTER and thrust the family's claim to the Crown upon Henry Tudor, earl of Richmond, the surviving male heir of Henry's cousins, the BEAUFORT FAMILY.

Confined to the Tower after his capture in July 1465, Henry remained there until October 1470, when Richard NEVILLE, earl of Warwick, restored him to the throne (see EDWARD IV, OVERTHROW OF). Warwick's READEPTION government, in which the befuddled Henry (see HENRY VI, ILLNESS OF) took no active part, collapsed in April 1471, when EDWARD IV returned from BURGUNDY to reclaim his Crown. As Edward neared LONDON, Warwick's brother, George NEVILLE, archbishop of York, paraded Henry through the streets in an unsuccessful attempt to generate enthusiasm for the Lancastrian regime. Entering London on 11 April, Edward immediately secured possession of Henry, who embraced his rival and said: "Cousin of York, you are very welcome. I hold my life to be in no danger in your hands" (Wolffe, p. 345). Edward then had Henry travel under guard with the Yorkist army to the Battle of BARNET, where Warwick was killed on 14 April. After the battle, Edward returned Henry to the Tower and then marched west, where he defeated Henry's wife, MARGARET OF ANJOU, and killed Henry's son, Prince EDWARD OF LANCASTER, at the Battle of TEWKESBURY on 4 May (see EDWARD IV, RESTORATION OF).

Edward returned to London on 21 May, and some time during that night, Henry died in the Tower. The *HISTORY OF THE ARRIVAL OF EDWARD IV,* a pro-Yorkist account, claims that Henry died of "pure displeasure and melancholy" (*Three Chronicles,* p. 184) at the news of Tewkesbury. WARKWORTH'S *CHRONICLE,* written in the 1480s, suggests that Richard, duke of Gloucester, Edward's brother, was at the Tower that night and was responsible for murdering Henry. Gloucester's involvement cannot be proven, but the widespread contemporary belief that murder had occurred was confirmed in 1910 when an exhumation of Henry's body indicated violence to the skull. With the death of Prince Edward, a living Henry could serve only as a symbol to rally surviving Lancastrian malcontents. To prevent this, Edward almost surely ordered Henry's death. The ex-king's body was publicly displayed at St. Paul's in London and then buried at Chertsey Abbey, where Henry's reputation for saintliness led to pilgrimages to his tomb and claims of miracles worked in his name. Edward IV discouraged such devotions, but RICHARD III sought to benefit from them by removing Henry's remains to St. George's Chapel at Windsor, where Henry lay across the altar from Edward IV. HENRY VII, first king of the house of TUDOR, who based his claim to the Crown on his relationship to Henry VI, went even further, appealing unsuccessfully to three different popes for Henry's canonization.

See also "Compilation of the Meekness and Good Life of Henry VI" (Blacman)
Further Reading: Griffiths, Ralph A., *The Reign of King Henry VI* (Berkeley: University of California Press, 1981); *Three Chronicles of the Reign of Edward IV,* introduction by Keith Dockray (Stroud, Gloucestershire, UK: Alan Sutton Publishing, 1988); Wolffe, Bertram, *Henry VI* (London: Eyre Methuen, 1981).

Henry VI, Part 1 (Shakespeare)

Written probably in early 1590, *Henry VI, Part 1,* is the first work in William Shakespeare's tetralogy (i.e., series of four plays) depicting the people and events of the WARS OF THE ROSES. The play is probably Shakespeare's first attempt at historical drama, and it is considered by most Shakespeare scholars to be one of the playwright's least successful efforts.

The play covers the period from the death of Henry V in 1422 until the marriage of his son HENRY VI in 1445, although, because Shakespeare alters actual chronology for dramatic effect, some events that occurred after 1445 are included. *Henry VI, Part 1,* is concerned with the end of the HUNDRED YEARS WAR in FRANCE and with the beginnings of the Wars of the Roses in England. The play portrays a series of major disputes among nobles, thus painting a picture of mounting internal disorder that presages the outbreak of actual civil war in the following plays. While most of these disputes were historical, Shakespeare intensifies the political conflict and its likely consequences by compressing decades

Painting by Henry A. Payne (1868–1939) depicting the most famous scene in Shakespeare's Henry VI, Part 1, *the choosing of the red and white roses. (Birmingham Art Gallery)*

into a quick succession of scenes and by altering the order of events to build tension.

For example, the struggle between Humphrey, duke of Gloucester, and Cardinal Henry Beaufort over the conduct of the French war, which extended from the 1420s to the 1440s, is immediately followed by the quarrel between Richard PLANTAGENET, duke of York, and Edmund BEAUFORT, duke of Somerset, rivals for command in France and influence in England, whose real feud extended from the late 1440s to 1455. By compressing and intensifying these disputes,

Shakespeare reinforces the main theme underlying all his fifteenth-century history plays, namely, that the deposition of Richard II by the house of LANCASTER in 1399 disrupted the divinely ordained order and cost England decades of war and suffering.

The most famous scene in the play occurs in act 2, when Richard Plantagenet (who in the play has not yet been recognized as duke of York) and Somerset argue in the Temple garden. Plantagenet plucks a white rose and calls upon all who favor his cause to do the same. Somerset picks a red rose and invites his supporters to do likewise. Richard NEVILLE, earl of Warwick, takes up a white rose, while William de la POLE, earl of Suffolk, claims a red one. Because a majority of the remaining characters choose white flowers, Somerset reneges on an agreement to let the dispute be settled by a vote of the roses. When the party breaks up with mutual threats, the coming of civil war is assured. Although the plucking of rose emblems is a visually powerful image that played an important role in the development of the term "Wars of the Roses" to describe the fifteenth-century civil wars, the scene is entirely fictional.

See also *Henry VI, Part 2; Henry VI, Part 3;* Richard II, Deposition of; *Richard III;* Shakespeare and the Wars of the Roses; *The Union of the Two Noble and Illustrious Families of Lancaster and York* (Hall)

Further Reading: Norwich, John Julius, *Shakespeare's Kings* (New York: Scribner, 1999); Saccio, Peter, *Shakespeare's English Kings,* 2d ed. (Oxford: Oxford University Press, 2000); the text of *Henry VI, Part 1* can be found on-line at <http://shakespeare.about.com/arts/shakespeare/library/bl1kh6scenes.htm>.

Henry VI, Part 2 (Shakespeare)

Henry VI, Part 2, is the second play in William Shakespeare's tetralogy (i.e., four-play series) depicting the characters and events of the WARS OF THE ROSES.

If the traditional belief that the four plays were written in chronological order is correct, *Henry VI, Part 2,* may be dated to late 1590. Extending from the 1440s to the Battle of ST. ALBANS in 1455, *Henry VI, Part 2,* reinforces the main theme of the tetralogy, which is the inexorable tragedy that England must suffer because of the Lancastrian usurpation of 1399, an act that disrupted the divine order of things (see RICHARD II, DEPOSITION OF). By compressing and rearranging the actual chronology of events in the 1440s and 1450s, Shakespeare portrays the ambitious house of YORK as the agency by which retribution is visited upon the house of LANCASTER.

As he does in *HENRY VI, PART 1,* Shakespeare in this play distorts and omits actual his-

torical events to serve his dramatic purposes. Shakespeare's greatest misrepresentation is his depiction of Richard PLANTAGENET, duke of York, as plotting deliberately to seize the throne of his Lancastrian cousin, HENRY VI. Although the real York claimed the Crown in 1460, he did so only after years of seeking to govern as Henry's chief minister and only after the sustained opposition of Queen MARGARET OF ANJOU (whom Shakespeare depicts as a strong-willed villain) effectively blocked all other paths to power. In the play, York is portrayed as instigating JACK CADE'S REBELLION, although the involvement of the real duke in that 1450 uprising is highly questionable. In his sharply drawn depiction of York's ambition, Shakespeare ignores Henry VI's mental breakdowns in the 1450s (see HENRY VI, ILLNESS OF); the king is portrayed as well-meaning but weak and ineffectual. The playwright is also silent about York's two periods of relatively effective rule during Henry's bouts of illness in 1454 (see FIRST PROTECTORATE) and 1455 (see SECOND PROTECTORATE).

The play is also notable as the first appearance of York's sons Edward (see EDWARD IV) and Richard (see RICHARD III). The latter, who will become the central character of the last play in the tetralogy (see *RICHARD III*) and one of the great villains in the Shakespearean canon, is depicted in *Henry VI, Part 2,* as ruthlessly slaying Edmund BEAUFORT, duke of Somerset, at the Battle of St. Albans, which was fought when the real Richard was only two. Although he is only a minor character in this play, the ready wit and enthusiastic evil that Shakespeare's Richard will display in the two remaining plays of the series are foreshadowed by the words he speaks over the dead Somerset.

Sword, hold thy temper; heart, be wrathful still:
Priests pray for enemies, but princes kill.
(5.2.70–71)

See also *Henry VI, Part 3;* Shakespeare and the Wars of the Roses; *The Union of the Two Noble and Illustrious Families of Lancaster and York* (Hall)

Further Reading: Norwich, John Julius, *Shakespeare's Kings* (New York: Scribner, 1999); Saccio, Peter, *Shakespeare's English Kings,* 2d ed. (Oxford: Oxford University Press, 2000); the text of *Henry VI, Part 2* can be found online at <http://shakespeare.about.com/arts/shakespeare/library/bl2kh6scenes.htm>.

Henry VI, Part 3 (Shakespeare)

Probably written early in 1591, *Henry VI, Part 3* is the third work in William Shakespeare's tetralogy (or four-play cycle) depicting the WARS OF THE ROSES.

Like the other plays in the series (HENRY VI, PART 1; HENRY VI, PART 2; and RICHARD III), this play is based largely on Edward Hall's chronicle, THE UNION OF THE TWO NOBLE AND ILLUSTRIOUS FAMILIES OF LANCASTER AND YORK. The play begins and ends with the house of YORK triumphant; it runs from the Battle of ST. ALBANS in May 1455, which briefly put Richard PLANTAGENET, duke of York, in power, to the Battle of TEWKESBURY and the murder of HENRY VI in May 1471, which destroyed the direct male line of the house of LANCASTER (see FIRST PROTECTORATE; HENRY VI, MURDER OF).

The main themes of the play—the dissolution of the state and the degradation of its political leadership—tie into the main theme of the tetralogy, which is that the accession of the house of TUDOR in 1485 rescued England from the suffering and chaos that arose from the various usurpations of the throne carried out by ambitious Lancastrians and Yorkists between 1399 and 1483. To serve these themes, Shakespeare compresses what were actually brief periods of active warfare separated by long periods of relative peace into a few weeks of horrific fighting that split both state and society (see MILITARY CAMPAIGNS, DURATION OF).

In the play, the disruption of families, both royal and common, illustrates the general dissolution of the realm. Under pressure from York, Henry VI disinherits his son, Prince EDWARD OF LANCASTER, an act that drives Queen MARGARET OF ANJOU to declare herself divorced from Henry. On the Yorkist side, George PLANTAGENET, duke of Clarence, abandons his brother EDWARD IV, while Edward's own lust and indolence alienate his kinsman Richard NEVILLE, earl of Warwick, who allies with Margaret and reopens the wars. In a foreshadowing of the crimes he will commit in *Richard III,* Richard, duke of Gloucester (see RICHARD III), plots against both his brothers and against anyone else who stands between him and the Crown.

Meanwhile, in act 2, Henry VI, seeking to escape the carnage at the Battle of TOWTON, witnesses the unspeakable grief of two characters known simply as the "son that hath killed his father" and the "father that hath killed his son." Each carries the body of a slain enemy from the field for purposes of plunder, only to discover that his victim is his son/father. Until modern historical research showed that Wars of the Roses campaigns were brief and had relatively little effect on the vast majority of English people below the PEERAGE and GENTRY, this Shakespearean image of widespread political, social, and economic devastation largely shaped popular views of the conflict.

See also Shakespeare and the Wars of the Roses
Further Reading: Norwich, John Julius, *Shakespeare's Kings* (New York: Scribner, 1999); Saccio, Peter, *Shakespeare's English Kings,* 2d ed. (Oxford: Oxford University Press, 2000); the text of *Henry VI, Part 3* can be found at <http://shakespeare.about.com/arts/shakespeare/library/bl3kh6scenes.htm>.

Henry VII, King of England (1457–1509)

First king of the house of TUDOR, Henry VII, the surviving heir of the house of LANCASTER, won the Crown from RICHARD III and the house of YORK at the Battle of BOSWORTH FIELD in August 1485.

The son of Edmund TUDOR, earl of Richmond, a maternal half brother of HENRY VI, and Margaret BEAUFORT, a cousin of Henry VI, Henry Tudor, earl of Richmond, was born three months after his father's death and a few months short of his

Henry VII, first king of the house of Tudor, overthrew Richard III and the house of York at the Battle of Bosworth Field in August 1485. (National Portrait Gallery: NPG 416)

mother's fourteenth birthday. Richmond spent his early years in WALES under the protection of his paternal uncle, Jasper TUDOR, earl of Pembroke. In September 1461, as Yorkist forces secured Wales for EDWARD IV, Pembroke fled, and four-year-old Richmond fell into the hands of William HERBERT, Edward's chief lieutenant in Wales. Herbert kept the boy at Raglan Castle, where he was raised and educated with Herbert's children. After paying the king £1,000 for Richmond's wardship and marriage, Herbert planned to wed the earl to one of his daughters. This scheme miscarried in 1469, when Herbert was executed by Richard NEVILLE, earl of Warwick, after the Battle of EDGECOTE. When Warwick restored Henry VI to the throne in the autumn of 1470, Pembroke, who had returned to England with Warwick, again took charge of his nephew (see EDWARD IV, OVERTHROW OF).

Also briefly reunited with his mother, whom he had seen occasionally during the 1460s, Richmond returned to Wales with his uncle, who secured the country for the READEPTION government. Pembroke then took his nephew to LONDON for an audience with Henry VI, who, upon seeing the fourteen-year-old boy, supposedly exclaimed: "[T]ruly, this is he unto whom we and our adversaries must yield and give over the dominion" (Griffiths and Thomas, p. 71). Because Henry's own son, Prince EDWARD OF LANCASTER, was then alive, as were Richmond's cousin Edmund BEAUFORT, duke of Somerset, and other Lancastrian heirs, such a declaration is most unlikely, although some acknowledgment of kinship by the king is possible. In any event, Richmond made good PROPAGANDA use of the story after he won the Crown.

Because Edward IV's restoration in 1471 resulted in the deaths of Somerset, Prince Edward, and Henry VI himself (see HENRY VI, MURDER OF), the direct male line of Lancaster was extinguished, and the dynasty's claim to the Crown passed to the BEAUFORT FAMILY, a branch of the house of Lancaster. As the son of Margaret Beaufort, and with all his other male Beaufort cousins slain in the wars, Richmond was now the leading Lancastrian claimant. To escape imprisonment or death, Pembroke and his nephew fled from Wales in September 1471. Intending to go to FRANCE, the Tudors were driven by storms to BRITTANY, where Duke FRANCIS welcomed them. Seeking to maintain Brittany's independence from France, and anxious for English assistance, Francis used the Tudors as pawns in negotiations with both countries. In 1472, when Edward IV sent a force under Anthony WOODVILLE, Earl Rivers, to aid the Bretons, Francis agreed to restrict the Tudors' movements and to keep them under close surveillance. In 1476, an English embassy under Bishop Robert STILLINGTON convinced Francis to surrender Richmond. Carried to St. Malo, where a ship awaited, Richmond suffered or pretended illness; the delay allowed a change of heart by Francis, who sent his treasurer, Pierre LANDAIS, to retrieve the earl. Slipping away to SANCTUARY in a local church, Richmond eventually returned safely to the Breton COURT. Although Edward IV and LOUIS XI continued their efforts to obtain Richmond, both failed, and the earl remained in honorable confinement in Brittany until Edward's death in 1483.

By late summer 1483, Richard III's usurpation of the English Crown and the growing belief that he had murdered his nephews made Richmond a more attractive candidate for the throne (see USURPATION OF 1483). While Richmond's mother plotted with Queen Elizabeth WOODVILLE to put the earl on the throne and marry him to ELIZABETH OF YORK, daughter of Edward IV, Henry STAFFORD, duke of Buckingham, deserted Richard and hatched his own plot. In the autumn, the two conspiracies merged into BUCKINGHAM'S REBELLION, an unsuccessful uprising that Richmond himself supported with an abortive descent on the English coast. Although Richard's soldiers tried to draw the earl ashore by posing as friends, Richmond learned of Buckingham's failure and returned safely to Brittany. In 1484, as a growing body of English exiles collected around him, Richmond fled into France, foiling a plot by Pierre Landais to turn him over to Richard's agents.

With French assistance, Richmond and his uncle landed in Wales in August 1485. Leading a force of over 2,000 French and Scottish mercenaries and some 600 English supporters, Richmond crossed Wales and entered England, collecting support along the way from both old Lancastrians and disaffected Yorkists. However, his army was still smaller than the king's when he met Richard in battle near the village of Market Bosworth on 22 August. Defeated by disloyalty in his ranks and by the intervention on Richmond's side of Sir William STANLEY, brother of Thomas STANLEY, Lord Stanley (Richmond's stepfather), Richard was killed on the field, and Richmond was proclaimed king as Henry VII.

As heir of Lancaster, Henry sought to symbolically end the WARS OF THE ROSES by marrying Elizabeth, the heiress of York, in January 1486. Nonetheless, Henry spent much of his reign combating Yorkist attempts to regain the throne. In June 1487, he defeated the partisans of Lambert SIMNEL at the Battle of STOKE. Simnel claimed to be Edward PLANTAGENET, earl of Warwick, the nephew of Edward IV and the last Yorkist claimant in the direct male line. A prisoner in the TOWER OF LONDON since 1485, Warwick was executed in 1499 after being implicated in an escape plot with Perkin WARBECK, another Yorkist pretender who had troubled Henry throughout the 1490s by claiming to be Richard PLANTAGENET, duke of York, the younger son of Edward IV, who had probably died in the Tower with his brother EDWARD V in 1483. Despite these and other Yorkist threats to his dynasty, Henry VII, at his death on 21 April 1509, peacefully passed a stable and strengthened Crown to his son Henry VIII.

See also Princes in the Tower; Yorkist Heirs (after 1485)

Further Reading: Chrimes, S. B., *Henry VII* (New Haven, CT: Yale University Press, 1999); Griffiths, Ralph A., and Roger S. Thomas, *The Making of the Tudor Dynasty* (New York: St. Martin's Press, 1985).

Herbert, William, Earl of Pembroke (d. 1469)

Entrusted with the government of WALES by EDWARD IV, William Herbert, earl of Pembroke, was one of the few fifteenth-century Welshmen to achieve an English PEERAGE and success in English politics.

Born into a GENTRY family that had held land in Wales since the twelfth century, Herbert was knighted by HENRY VI in 1449 and served in FRANCE in the 1450s. An early adherent of Richard PLANTAGENET, duke of York, Herbert, along with his father-in-law, Walter DEVEREUX, Lord Ferrers of Chartley, seized Carmarthen and Aberystwyth castles for the duke in 1456. Although they also imprisoned the king's half brother, Edmund TUDOR, earl of Richmond, the Lancastrian regime treated Herbert leniently, seeking unsuccessfully to win his support.

Herbert fought with Edward, earl of March (the future Edward IV) at the Battle of MOR-

William Herbert, earl of Pembroke, and his wife kneel before the enthroned Edward IV. (Royal MS 18 D f. 6, British Library)

TIMER'S CROSS in February 1461; defeated Jasper TUDOR, earl of Pembroke, at the Battle of TWT HILL in October; forced Tudor out of Wales in 1462; and captured the Lancastrians' last Welsh stronghold at HARLECH CASTLE in 1468. In return for this loyal service, Edward IV raised Herbert to the peerage as Lord Herbert in 1461 and gave him the attainted Jasper Tudor's earldom of Pembroke in 1468. Edward also gave Herbert custody of Pembroke's nephew, Henry Tudor, earl of Richmond, the future HENRY VII. Herbert eventually became a royal councilor, chief justice of North and South Wales, constable of most Welsh royal castles, and the holder of numerous other Welsh offices. He also vastly improved his financial position by securing significant grants of Welsh lands and lordships. By 1468, Herbert was virtually viceroy of Wales.

Herbert's ambition and success brought him into conflict with Richard NEVILLE, earl of Warwick, who envied Herbert's unprecedented position in Wales and who coveted for himself some of Herbert's Welsh lands and offices. After 1466, Herbert sought to make further gains at Warwick's expense by working to widen the growing breach between the earl and the king. When Warwick fomented the ROBIN OF REDESDALE REBELLION in the north in 1469, Pembroke led a Welsh force into the field against the rebels. At the Battle of EDGECOTE on 26 July 1469, the rebels overwhelmed Pembroke's force, taking the earl and his brother, Sir Richard Herbert, prisoners. Two days later both brothers were beheaded without trial at Northampton, by Warwick's orders and in Warwick's presence.

Further Reading: Evans, H. T., *Wales and the Wars of the Roses* (Stroud, Gloucestershire, UK: Alan Sutton Publishing, 1995); Ross, Charles, *Edward IV* (New Haven, CT: Yale University Press, 1998); "William Herbert," in Michael Hicks, *Who's Who in Late Medieval England* (London: Shepheard-Walwyn, 1991), pp. 317–318; Williams, Glanmor, *Renewal and Reformation: Wales, c. 1415–1642* (Oxford: Oxford University Press, 1993).

Heworth, Battle of (1453)

The skirmish at Heworth on 24 August 1453 aggravated the NEVILLE-PERCY FEUD and helped create the political alignments that made possible the war between the houses of LANCASTER and YORK.

After the marriage of his son Sir Thomas NEVILLE to Maud Stanhope, Lady Willoughby, the niece of Ralph Cromwell, Lord Cromwell, Richard NEVILLE, earl of Salisbury, led a wedding party across Heworth

Moor toward his castle at Sheriff Hutton. Besides the bride and groom and a substantial number of RETAINERS, the party included Salisbury's wife and his son John NEVILLE. On the northeast edge of York, Thomas PERCY, Lord Egremont, son of Henry PERCY, second earl of Northumberland, intercepted the Nevilles while leading a force that may have numbered almost 5,000. Egremont's party included his brother, Richard Percy, and John CLIFFORD, the future Lord Clifford.

What occurred next is uncertain. Both sides threatened violence, but neither offered much. Although some participants were injured, no blood was shed. The Nevilles came safely to their destination, but Egremont continued to harass his rivals' lands and tenants. Egremont's actions may have been precipitated by his anger over the possibility that former Percy lands held by Cromwell might, through the marriage, pass eventually to the Nevilles. More likely, Egremont was simply seeking to escalate the quarrel he had already begun with John Neville, and the wedding party, including both John and his father, admirably served his purpose. Because the Neville-Percy feud eventually arrayed the two powerful northern families on opposite sides in the growing political struggle between Richard PLANTAGENET, duke of York, and Edmund BEAUFORT, duke of Somerset, the incident at Heworth was seen by a later chronicler as "the beginning of the greatest sorrow in England" (Hicks, p. 87).

See also Neville Family; North of England and the Wars of the Roses
Further Reading: Griffiths, Ralph A., "Local Rivalries and National Politics: The Percies, the Nevilles and the Duke of Exeter, 1452–1455," in Ralph A. Griffiths, ed., *King and Country: England and Wales in the Fifteenth Century* (London: Hambledon Press, 1991), pp. 321–364; Griffiths, Ralph A., *The Reign of King Henry VI* (Berkeley: University of California Press, 1981); Hicks, Michael, *Warwick the Kingmaker* (Oxford: Blackwell Publishers, 1998); Storey, R. L., *The End of the House of Lancaster*, 2d ed. (Stroud, Gloucestershire, UK: Sutton Publishing, 1999).

Hexham, Battle of (1464)

Fought on 15 May 1464, only three weeks after the Yorkist victory at the Battle of HEDGELEY MOOR, the Battle of Hexham ended the Lancastrian resurgence in Northumbria and ushered in five years of relatively stable Yorkist government.

After regrouping at ALNWICK CASTLE, Henry BEAUFORT, duke of Somerset, and the other Lancastrian survivors of Hedgeley Moor, learned that EDWARD IV was collecting a large army at Leicester with the intention of coming north to destroy Lancastrian insurgency in the region once and for all. Fearing that the Anglo-Scottish talks then under way in York would close SCOTLAND to them, and desperate to boost morale with a quick victory before the arrival of Edward's army, Somerset placed HENRY VI at the head of his force and marched south into the Tyne Valley. Hearing of Somerset's advance, John NEVILLE, Lord Montagu, the victor of Hedgeley Moor, left Newcastle and marched west to intercept the Lancastrians. On the evening of 14 May, Somerset encamped in a meadow along the Tyne two miles south of the town of Hexham and near Bywell Castle, where the duke installed Henry VI. Early the next morning, Montagu passed the castle as he fell unexpectedly on Somerset's camp.

With no time to maneuver for position, Somerset formed his men on low ground with their backs to the river. Montagu charged downhill and smashed into the Lancastrian line, driving the center back toward the water, where many men drowned in their ARMOR or were slain as they tried to cling to the bank. Somerset tried to rally his flanks, but his men were panicked and overmatched, and the Lancastrian line shattered, leaving Somerset a prisoner. The duke was beheaded next day, while Thomas ROOS, Lord Roos, and Robert HUNGERFORD, Lord Hungerford, the other Lancastrian commanders, were captured and executed two days later at Newcastle. By July, Montagu and his brother, Richard NEVILLE, earl of Warwick, had completed the pacification of the northeast by capturing the Lancastrian castles at Alnwick, DUNSTANBURGH, and BAMBURGH. With the capture of Henry VI in Lancashire in 1465, the Lancastrian north gave up rebellion and accepted the rule of Edward IV.

> **See also** North of England and the Wars of the Roses
> **Further Reading:** Haigh, Philip A., *The Military Campaigns of the Wars of the Roses* (Stroud, Gloucestershire, UK: Sutton Publishing, 1995).

The History of King Richard III (More)

As the basis for most sixteenth-century chronicle accounts of RICHARD III, and, through them, the source for William Shakespeare's powerful depiction of the king, Sir Thomas More's *History of King Richard III* has become the most influential and controversial source for the deeds and personality of the last Yorkist monarch.

Sir Thomas More, the famous Tudor statesman who was executed in 1535 for his opposition to the religious proceedings of Henry VIII, wrote the *History* in about 1513, almost thirty years after Richard III's death. More wrote two separate versions of the *History,* one in English and the other (the *Historia Richardi Tertius*) in Latin for a learned international audience. Neither version was completed, and neither was published in More's lifetime. Although manuscript copies of the work were in circulation in the 1530s, it did not appear in print until its incorporation into the 1543 edition of Richard Grafton's *The Chronicle of John Harding* (see HARDYNG'S CHRONICLE). However, Grafton's version and the versions that appeared in other chronicles in the 1540s and 1550s were severely garbled in many details. In 1557, More's nephew, William Rastell, corrected these errors by publishing an English version drawn from one of More's manuscripts. Rastell's text became the basis for most Elizabethan printings of the *History,* including the version published in Raphael Holinshed's *Chronicles of England, Scotland, and Ireland*, the source most likely used by William Shakespeare to write his play *RICHARD III.*

Although less dramatically presented, all the deceit, ambition, and crimes, as well as the physical deformity, imputed to Richard by Shakespeare are found in More's *History*. The *History* also contains a detailed account of the murder of EDWARD V and his brother Richard PLANTAGENET, duke of York, the most damning crime attributed to Richard. Modern historians have thrown doubt on Richard's commission of many of the crimes ascribed to him by More, such as the murder of HENRY VI, and on the severity or even existence of the physical defects alleged by More, but no historian believes that More simply invented these tales. Most of these stories were current in the COURT of HENRY VII and came to More from men who had lived through Richard's reign. Cardinal John MORTON, who witnessed many key events and in whose household the young More served, is the most likely source for many of More's details.

More's reasons for writing the *History* and for leaving it unfinished have been much debated. It has been suggested that the *History* is a satire, and not meant to be an accurate account of events. The work certainly has a moral purpose, intending to illustrate the evil that could befall a kingdom when wise government was replaced by tyranny. Nonetheless, the work is not a piece of anti-Yorkist PROPAGANDA designed to reinforce the legitimacy of the house of TUDOR. Richard is not condemned for being a Yorkist but for being a tyrant. As his later opposition to Henry VIII made clear, More did not believe that tyranny was solely confined to the house of YORK. Rather than allow the *History* to be read as a pro-Tudor propaganda tract, More may have chosen to abandon it, or, and probably more likely, More may simply have lost interest in the work (he left many projects unfinished) or may have grown too busy with government service and other writings to complete such a closely detailed account of a two-year period. In any event, the conventional view of Richard III as it came down to the twentieth century was largely More's creation.

See also Princes in the Tower; Shakespeare and the Wars of the Roses; Usurpation of 1483
Further Reading: Hanham, Alison, *Richard III and His Early Historians 1483–1555* (Oxford: Clarendon Press, 1975); More, Sir Thomas, *The History of King Richard III,* edited by Richard S. Sylvester (New Haven, CT: Yale University Press, 1976); the text of More's *History of King Richard III* is also available on the Richard III Society Web site at <http://www.r3.org/bookcase/more/moretext.html>.

History of the Arrival of Edward IV

The anonymous work entitled, in full, *History of the Arrival of Edward IV in England and the Final Recovery of His Kingdoms from Henry VI* is the most important narrative source for the events that occurred during EDWARD IV's campaign to regain the English Crown in the spring of 1471 (see EDWARD IV, RESTORATION OF).

The *Arrival* covers a period of roughly three months, extending from 2 March to 26 May 1471, that is, from the time Edward IV sailed from BURGUNDY to a few days after his supporters defeated the attack on LONDON by Thomas NEVILLE, the Bastard of Fauconberg. Completed, shortly after the events it recounts, by an unknown writer who described himself as a servant of Edward IV and a witness of "a great part of his exploits" (*Three Chronicles,* p. 147), the *Arrival* was written for or adopted by Edward IV as an official Yorkist account of his restoration to the throne. A short French version of the *Arrival* was completed by the end of May and was distributed on the continent as a newsletter designed to set Edward's version of events before foreign courts. Although it is therefore clearly a piece of Yorkist PROPAGANDA, expressing a point of view favorable to the house of YORK, the *Arrival*'s immediacy and eyewitness perspective make it a valuable historical source for the end of the second phase of the WARS OF THE ROSES.

Although concerned to record the course of Edward's campaign and to explain the reasons for the king's actions, the narrator, who wrote in a detailed and powerful prose style, was candid about Edward's problems. For instance, the writer recorded that Edward attracted little support on his landing, was refused admission by the town of Hull, and was fortunate in not being vigorously pursued by John NEVILLE, marquis of Montagu, the brother of Edward's chief opponent, Richard NEVILLE, earl of Warwick. The *Arrival* also contains the most detailed extant account of the Battle of BARNET, of the campaign that led to the Battle of TEWKESBURY, and of the Bastard of Fauconberg's assault on London. The writer's Yorkist sympathies are most clearly illustrated by his description of the death in the TOWER OF LONDON of HENRY VI, which is most unconvincingly attributed to "pure displeasure and melancholy" (*Three Chronicles*, p. 184).

See also Edward IV, Overthrow of; Henry VI, Murder of
Further Reading: *Three Chronicles of the Reign of Edward IV,* introduction by Keith Dockray (Stroud, Gloucestershire, UK: Alan Sutton Publishing, 1988); the text of the *History of the Arrival of Edward IV* is also available on the Richard III Society Web site at <http://www.r3.org/bookcase/arrival1.html>.

Holland, Henry, Duke of Exeter (1430–1475)

By his intervention in the NEVILLE-PERCY FEUD in the mid-1450s, Henry Holland (or Holand), fourth duke of Exeter, helped create the political alignments that destabilized royal and local government and brought about the WARS OF THE ROSES.

The son of John Holland, duke of Exeter, and a cousin of HENRY VI, Holland married Anne, daughter of Richard PLANTAGENET, duke of York, in 1447. He became duke of Exeter on his father's death in 1447 but, being a minor, was not put in possession of his father's estates until 1450. In 1453–1454, Exeter, who claimed certain estates that had fallen by marriage to the NEVILLE FAMILY, sided with the Percies in the series of violent encounters that erupted between the two families across northern England. In an effort to reduce this disorder, York, during his FIRST PROTECTORATE in

1454, traveled north to restrain Exeter, who, besides supporting the disruptive activities of Thomas PERCY, Lord Egremont, was also claiming the he, rather than York, should be protector of the realm during Henry VI's illness. In July, after the failure of an attempt to ambush York, Exeter fled to LONDON, where he was arrested and confined in Pontefract Castle.

In March 1455, after his recovery, Henry VI released Exeter and restored him to favor at COURT. However, in June, after his victory at the Battle of ST. ALBANS had initiated his SECOND PROTECTORATE, York again imprisoned Exeter, this time in Wallingford Castle. Released again upon the king's resumption of power, Exeter became a staunch supporter of the house of LANCASTER, swearing an oath of allegiance to Henry VI at the COVENTRY PARLIAMENT of November 1459. He fought for Lancaster at the Battle of BLORE HEATH in 1459, the Battle of NORTHAMPTON in 1460, and the Battles of ST. ALBANS and TOWTON in 1461. After Towton, the duke fled into SCOTLAND with the Lancastrian royal family but by October was in WALES, where he fought alongside Jasper TUDOR, earl of Pembroke, at the Battle of TWT HILL. Forced to flee the country after that defeat, Exeter was attainted in November 1461 by EDWARD IV's first PARLIAMENT, which placed the duke's lands in the custody of his wife, Edward IV's sister.

In February 1471, after spending most of the 1460s in exile in BURGUNDY, Exeter returned to England to support the READEPTION government of Henry VI. Severely wounded and left for dead on the field at the Battle of BARNET, Exeter was carried to London and imprisoned until May 1475, when he was released to accompany Edward IV on his French expedition. The duke was drowned in September while returning to England from CALAIS.

See also Henry VI, Illness of; North of England and the Wars of the Roses
Further Reading: Griffiths, Ralph A., *The Reign of King Henry VI* (Berkeley: University of California Press, 1981); Storey, R. L., *The End of the House of Lancaster,* 2d ed. (Stroud, Gloucestershire, UK: Sutton Publishing, 1999).

Howard, John, Duke of Norfolk (d. 1485)

A staunch Yorkist, John Howard was one of the few servants of EDWARD IV to remain loyal to the house of YORK in the 1480s after the usurpation of RICHARD III dethroned Edward's son and reopened the civil wars.

Born into a Suffolk GENTRY family, Howard was a maternal cousin of the Mowbray dukes of Norfolk. He served in FRANCE in the early 1450s, and was knighted by Edward IV after the Battle of TOWTON in 1461. Howard became the first Yorkist sheriff of Norfolk in 1461, served in the northern campaigns of the early 1460s, and was treasurer of the royal household from 1467. In 1470, Howard commanded a fleet against Richard NEVILLE, the rebel earl of Warwick, and was raised to the PEERAGE as Lord Howard.

Remaining quiet during the READEPTION of HENRY VI in 1470–1471, Howard proclaimed for Edward IV in Suffolk immediately upon Edward's landing in England in March 1471. He joined Edward in LONDON in April and fought for the Yorkists at the Battles of BARNET and TEWKESBURY. In the early 1470s, he was deputy at CALAIS for William HASTINGS, Lord Hastings, and in 1475 was one of the chief English negotiators with LOUIS XI during Edward IV's French campaign. He remained briefly in France as a hostage to secure the settlement and took part in several later diplomatic embassies to the French COURT. In 1482, he participated in the campaign against SCOTLAND, commanding a fleet that ravaged the Firth of Forth.

In 1481, on the death of his nine-year-old daughter-in-law, Anne Mowbray, daughter of John MOWBRAY, late duke of Norfolk, Edward IV, being unwilling to allow the extensive Mowbray inheritance to leave the royal family, denied Howard his rightful share of the Norfolk estates. On the king's initiative, PARLIAMENT passed a statute vesting the Norfolk lands in eight-year-old Richard PLANTAGENET, duke of York, the king's second son and Anne Mowbray's husband.

On Edward's death in 1483, Howard supported the duke of Gloucester's usurpation of the throne, being rewarded with elevation to the dukedom of Norfolk and appointment as marshal of England in June, even before Gloucester's coronation as Richard III (see USURPATION OF 1483). Named admiral of England in July 1483, Norfolk was also made steward of the royal Duchy of Lancaster. In the autumn of 1483, Norfolk was active in suppressing BUCKINGHAM'S REBELLION and in 1484 he was part of a diplomatic embassy sent to Scotland to arrange a truce. While acquisition of the Norfolk title was undoubtedly a strong incentive to back Gloucester, the duke seems to have been recognized as one of Richard III's most committed supporters.

On the morning of the Battle of BOSWORTH FIELD in August 1485, a placard appeared on Norfolk's tent that read: "Jock of Norfolk be not too bold / For Dickon thy master is bought and sold." Killed only hours later while leading the van of the royal army, Norfolk was attainted by the first Parliament of HENRY VII. The duke's son, Thomas HOWARD, earl of Surrey, who was imprisoned after Bosworth Field, was eventually able to reverse the ATTAINDER and regain his father's lands and titles through loyal service to the house of TUDOR.

See also all entries under Mowbray
Further Reading: Crawford, Anne, "The Private Life of John Howard: A Study of a Yorkist Lord, His Family and Household," in P. W. Hammond, ed., *Richard III: Loyalty, Lordship and Law* (London: Richard III and Yorkist History Trust, 1986); "John Howard," in Michael Hicks, *Who's Who in Late Medieval England* (London: Shepheard-Walwyn, 1991), pp. 337–339; Ross, Charles, *Richard III* (Berkeley: University of California Press, 1981).

Howard, Thomas, Earl of Surrey and Duke of Norfolk (1443–1524)

A prominent supporter of RICHARD III, Thomas Howard, earl of Surrey, later revived the Howard family fortunes through loyal service to the house of TUDOR.

Like his father, John HOWARD, Thomas was a loyal adherent of the house of YORK. In 1466, Howard became a henchman (i.e., a squire or page) to EDWARD IV, and fought for Edward at the Battles of BARNET and TEWKESBURY in 1471. He accompanied the king on the expedition to FRANCE in 1475 and was knighted in January 1478. In 1483, Howard and his father supported Richard III's usurpation of his nephew's throne (see EDWARD V; USURPATION OF 1483). At the COUNCIL meeting held in the TOWER OF LONDON on 13 June, it was Thomas Howard who, upon Richard's signal, burst into the chamber with armed men to arrest William HASTINGS, Lord Hastings (see COUNCIL MEETING OF 13 JUNE 1483). To reward the Howards' loyalty, Richard created John Howard duke of Norfolk and Thomas Howard earl of Surrey. At Richard's coronation in July, Surrey carried the sword of state before the king, and was soon after appointed steward of the royal household and a member of the royal council. In the autumn, during BUCKINGHAM'S REBELLION, Surrey led the royal forces that recaptured Bodiam Castle from the rebels.

In August 1485, Surrey fought for Richard at the Battle of BOSWORTH FIELD, where both the king and Norfolk were slain. Imprisoned in the Tower by HENRY VII, Surrey was stripped of his lands and title by a bill of ATTAINDER passed in the first PARLIAMENT of the new reign. Although pardoned in March 1486, Surrey remained in confinement until January 1489, when the king restored his title. The earl did not, however, recover his estates until 1501, having by then earned them through loyal service against rebels in Yorkshire and against the Yorkist pretender Perkin WARBECK. After helping to negotiate the marriage of Prince Arthur to Catherine of Aragon in 1501, and the marriage of Princess Margaret to JAMES IV of SCOTLAND in 1502, Surrey finally regained his father's dukedom in 1513 by defeating the Scots and slaying King James at the Battle of Flodden. By his death in 1524, Thomas Howard, the second Howard duke of Norfolk, had effectively erased his Yorkist past and firmly tied his family's future to the house of Tudor.

Further Reading: Head, David, *The Ebbs and Flows of Fortune: The Life of Thomas Howard, Third Duke of Norfolk* (Athens: University of Georgia Press, 1995); Tucker, Melvin J., *The Life of Thomas Howard, Earl of Surrey and Second Duke of Norfolk, 1443–1524* (The Hague, Netherlands: Mouton, 1964).

Hundred Years War (1337–1453)

The "Hundred Years War" is a nineteenth-century term conventionally applied to an intermittent series of Anglo-French wars fought between 1337 and 1453. Spanning the reigns of five monarchs in each country, the Hundred Years War evolved from a conflict over the status of the English Crown's possessions in FRANCE to a struggle for possession of the French Crown itself. By undermining the popularity and credibility of HENRY VI's government, and by initiating the rivalry of the dukes of York and Somerset, the last phase of the Hundred Years War, which culminated in 1453 with the final ejection of the English from all their French territories except CALAIS, was an important contributing cause of the WARS OF THE ROSES.

The first phase of the Hundred Years War, stretching from 1337 to 1360, witnessed major English victories at Sluys (1340), Crécy (1346), and Poitiers (1356). In 1340, Edward III, whose mother was a French princess, claimed the French throne as the rightful possession of the English royal house of PLANTAGENET. However, when the Treaty of Brétigny promised him full sovereignty over his French lands, Edward agreed to renounce his claim to the French Crown. Because this promise of sovereignty was never fulfilled, Edward never made his renunciation, and war resumed in 1369.

The second phase of the war, extending from 1369 to the 1420s, saw a French resurgence under Charles V, which culminated in 1396 in the conclusion of a twenty-eight-year truce between England's Richard II and France's Charles VI. In the opening decade of the fifteenth century, Charles VI's insanity plunged France into political turmoil, as the Burgundian and Armagnac factions fought for control of the government. In 1415, Henry V, second king of the house of LAN-CASTER, exploited this internal disorder by invading France and renewing the Plantagenet claim to the French Crown. After his victory at Agincourt in 1415, Henry conquered Normandy, and by 1420 was in a position to dictate the Treaty of Troyes, which made Henry heir to the French Crown and arranged his marriage to Charles VI's daughter, Catherine of Valois. Thus, on the deaths of both Henry and Charles in 1422, the Crowns of both England and France passed to the infant Henry VI.

During the final phase of the war, CHARLES VII, who had been disinherited by the Treaty of Troyes, secured the French Crown and gradually expelled the English from France. Lacking resources and effective leadership, the government of Henry VI negotiated a truce and the king's marriage to the French princess, MARGARET OF ANJOU, in 1444, and in the next year surrendered the province of Maine. In 1450, the French overran Normandy, and in 1453, at the Battle of CASTILLON, they captured the longtime English province of Gascony.

While not a direct cause of the Wars of the Roses, the English collapse at the end of the Hundred Years War weakened public support for Henry VI and his government and initiated the feud between Richard PLANTAGENET, duke of York, and Edmund BEAUFORT, duke of Somerset, a rivalry that became an important factor in the eventual rise of civil war. As king's lieutenant in France when Normandy was lost, Somerset was much blamed for English military failure, especially by York, whom Somerset had replaced in the French command and who lost extensive French estates through what he believed was Somerset's incompetence. In the 1450s, the bad blood created between the two dukes by the outcome of the Hundred Years War was intensified by the royal favor shown to Somerset and denied to York and by the rival claims of each duke to be Henry's heir and the chief minister in his government. Out of this feud arose eventually the contending parties in the civil wars.

Further Reading: Allmand, Christopher, *The Hundred Years War* (Cambridge: Cambridge University Press, 1988); Curry, Anne, *The Hundred Years War* (New York: Macmillan, 1993); Perroy, Edouard, *The Hundred Years War* (New York: Capricorn Books, 1965); Seward, Desmond, *The Hundred Years War* (New York: Atheneum, 1978).

Hungerford, Robert, Lord Hungerford (1431–1464)

A loyal partisan of the house of LANCASTER, Robert Hungerford, third Lord Hungerford, commanded Lancastrian forces during the fighting in Northumberland in the early 1460s.

Hungerford married the daughter of William Moleyns in 1441 and was recognized as Lord Moleyns in right of his wife from 1445. In the early 1450s, Moleyns engaged in a violent quarrel with John Paston over the Norfolk manor of Gresham, which, after an unsuccessful arbitration by William WAINFLEET, bishop of Winchester, Moleyns eventually surrendered to Paston. In 1452, Moleyns accompanied John Talbot, earl of Shrewsbury, to FRANCE and was captured and held for ransom by the French after the Battle of CASTILLON in 1453. His family sold and mortgaged property to effect his release in 1459, the year he succeeded his father as Lord Hungerford.

In 1460, Hungerford was commander, with Thomas SCALES, Lord Scales, of the Lancastrian garrison holding LONDON. In July, Hungerford and Scales withdrew into the TOWER OF LONDON when the city authorities opened the gates to the Yorkist lords newly landed from CALAIS. While Richard NEVILLE, earl of Warwick, and Edward, earl of March (see EDWARD IV), the son of Richard PLANTAGENET, duke of York, marched north to confront HENRY VI, Warwick's father, Richard NEVILLE, earl of Salisbury, besieged the Lancastrians in the Tower. Warwick's victory at the Battle of NORTHAMPTON on 10 July forced Hungerford and Scales to surrender the Tower shortly thereafter to the new Yorkist regime, although both were allowed to depart safely.

Hungerford fought for Lancaster at the Battle of TOWTON in March 1461, and afterward fled into SCOTLAND with the Lancastrian royal family. Attainted by PARLIAMENT in November 1461 (see ATTAINDER, ACT OF), Hungerford traveled to France in 1462 to seek aid for the Lancastrian cause. By the end of that year, he was commander of the Lancastrian garrison in ALNWICK Castle. Besieged by Warwick, he was saved by the arrival in January 1463 of a relieving army out of Scotland jointly commanded by the Lancastrian Pierre de BRÉZÉ and the Scottish earl of Angus. Hungerford retook Alnwick in the spring of 1463 when the Yorkist commander, Sir Ralph Grey, defected and surrendered the fortress to him. In early 1464, Hungerford assisted Henry BEAUFORT, duke of Somerset, in the Lancastrian campaign that captured much of Northumberland. Along with Thomas ROOS, Lord Roos, he commanded a wing of the Lancastrian force at the Battle of HEDGELEY MOOR in April and again at the Battle of HEXHAM in May. Hungerford was captured after Hexham and executed at Newcastle.

See also all entries under Hungerford
Further Reading: Haigh, Philip A., *The Military Campaigns of the Wars of the Roses* (Stroud, Gloucestershire, UK: Sutton Publishing, 1995); Hicks, Michael, "Piety and Lineage in the Wars of the Roses: The Hungerford Experience," in Ralph A. Griffiths and James Sherborne, eds., *Kings and Nobles in the Later Middle Ages* (New York: St. Martin's Press, 1986), pp. 90–108; Ross, Charles, *Edward IV* (New Haven, CT: Yale University Press, 1998).

Hungerford, Sir Thomas (d. 1469)

As the son and heir of Robert HUNGERFORD, Lord Hungerford, an attainted and executed Lancastrian, Sir Thomas Hungerford fell under suspicion of plotting the overthrow of EDWARD IV in 1468.

Although the ATTAINDER passed against his father in the Yorkist PARLIAMENT of November 1461 deprived Hungerford of the family lands, he was pardoned and knighted by Edward IV in 1462 and shortly thereafter restored to a portion of his father's estates. Financial provision was also made for his mother and younger siblings. In November 1468, following the discovery of the CORNELIUS PLOT and other alleged Lancastrian conspiracies, Hungerford was arrested in Wiltshire along with the heir to another Lancastrian family, Henry COURTENAY, de jure seventh earl of Devon. Although several other suspected Lancastrian plotters were also apprehended, including John de VERE, earl of Oxford, only Hungerford and Courtenay were brought to trial.

In January 1469, both men appeared in Salisbury before Richard, duke of Gloucester (see RICHARD III), who sat as head of a special commission of oyer and terminer (i.e., "to hear and determine," a judicial commission especially useful for quick action in cases of treason and rebellion). Hungerford and Courtenay were charged with meeting agents of MARGARET OF ANJOU on 21 May 1468 for the purpose of plotting the "death and final destruction . . . of the Most Christian Prince, Edward IV" (Ross, p. 123). A jury of sixteen convicted them of treason in the presence of the king himself, and the two men were hanged, drawn, and quartered, an execution of unusual severity for persons of their rank.

Whether or not Hungerford had actually committed the treason of which he was accused is now uncertain. Rumor claimed that both men were victims of Humphrey STAFFORD, a royal favorite who sought to become the leading peer in the West Country and who did become earl of Devon shortly after the trial in May 1469. However, Edward's presence at the trial indicates how serious he considered the case to be. In any event, Hungerford's fate illustrates how dangerous life could be during the WARS OF THE ROSES for anyone identified by past family allegiance with the party out of power.

See also Hungerford, Sir Walter
Further Reading: Hicks, Michael, "Piety and Lineage in the Wars of the Roses: The Hungerford Experience," in Ralph A. Griffiths and James Sherborne, eds., *Kings and Nobles in the Later Middle Ages* (New York: St. Martin's Press,

1986), pp. 90–108; Ross, Charles, *Edward IV* (New Haven, CT: Yale University Press, 1998).

Hungerford, Sir Walter (d. 1516)

A member of a Lancastrian family, Walter Hungerford loyally served EDWARD IV in the 1470s but abandoned RICHARD III and the house of YORK after 1483.

The son of Robert HUNGERFORD, Lord Hungerford, who was beheaded by the Yorkists after the Battle of HEXHAM in 1464, and the brother of Sir Thomas HUNGERFORD, who was executed by Edward IV for supposedly plotting with Lancastrian agents in 1469, Walter Hungerford took no sides during the 1469–1471 phase of the WARS OF THE ROSES. In the 1470s, he entered the service of Edward IV, becoming lieutenant of Dover Castle and sheriff of Wiltshire in 1478–1479. He also became one of the king's esquires of the body (i.e., a personal royal servant), accompanied the king on the French expedition of 1475, and recovered a portion of his family's influence in the West Country, serving as M.P. (i.e., Member of PARLIAMENT) for Wiltshire in 1478 and 1483.

However, after Richard III usurped the throne of his nephew, EDWARD V, in 1483 (see USURPATION OF 1483), Hungerford, although courted with gifts by the new king, maintained his allegiance to the sons of Edward IV and joined Lionel WOODVILLE, Giles Daubeney, and others in leading the southwestern phase of BUCKINGHAM'S REBELLION. Hungerford was pardoned after the failure of the uprising, but his West Country estates were granted to some of Richard's loyal northern supporters (see RICHARD III, NORTHERN AFFINITY OF).

In 1485, Hungerford and Sir Thomas Bourchier were summoned to join the royal army at Nottingham, where Richard awaited the invasion of Henry Tudor, earl of Richmond. Suspicious of their loyalty, Richard supposedly ordered Sir Robert BRACKENBURY to escort both men to his camp. Somewhere along the way, Hungerford and Bourchier escaped from Brackenbury and joined Richmond, with whom they fought at the Battle of BOSWORTH FIELD on 22 August. Knighted on the field by HENRY VII, Hungerford was restored to his family estates and admitted to the royal COUNCIL. He served the new king on several diplomatic and military missions and assisted in the defeat of the Yorkist pretender, Perkin WARBECK, in 1497. Hungerford died in 1516, after years of loyal service to the house of TUDOR.

Further Reading: Gill, Louise, *Richard III and Buckingham's Rebellion* (Stroud, Gloucestershire, UK: Sutton Publishing, 1999); Hicks, Michael, "Piety and Lineage in the Wars of the Roses: The Hungerford Experience," in Ralph A. Griffiths and James Sherborne, eds., *Kings and Nobles in the Later Middle Ages* (New York: St. Martin's Press, 1986), pp. 90–108; Ross, Charles, *Richard III* (Berkeley: University of California Press, 1981).

I

Ireland

As a source of ready manpower and a safe but nearby base for launching invasions of England, Ireland played an important role in the WARS OF THE ROSES.

Fifteenth-century Ireland was divided between the English Lordship, which was centered on Dublin and controlled by Anglo-Irish nobles loyal to the English Crown, and the areas controlled by native Irish clan chiefs, who were largely independent of English rule. In the 1450s, the ancient rivalry between the leading Anglo-Irish families of Ireland, the Fitzgeralds and the Butlers, was subsumed into the conflict developing in England between the houses of LANCASTER and YORK. Thomas FITZGERALD, eighth earl of Desmond, and his kinsman, Thomas FITZGERALD, seventh earl of Kildare, were RETAINERS of Richard PLANTAGENET, duke of York, while James BUTLER, fifth earl of Ormond, was a supporter of HENRY VI. Thus, as the English civil wars evolved, both sides, but particularly York, who had extensive Irish lands, used their Irish connections to draw small but steady streams of troops from Ireland, mainly ARCHERS, axmen, or the light-armed native infantry known as kerns.

Although York held appointment as lord lieutenant of Ireland in the late 1450s, he was largely absent pursuing his political interests in England, a situation that left Kildare, as York's deputy, in charge of the Irish government. With Ormond in England at the Lancastrian COURT, the political leadership of Ireland was thus strongly Yorkist, and the duke found safe haven in Dublin when he fled England after the Battle of LUDFORD BRIDGE in October 1459. Although the Lancastrian government sought to undermine Kildare's authority, especially after the death of York at the Battle of WAKEFIELD in December 1460, the Fitzgerald earls remained loyal to York and were richly rewarded with lands and offices after EDWARD IV's victory at the Battle of TOWTON in March 1461. When Ormond was executed shortly after Towton, the Lancastrian position in Ireland was further weakened.

In 1468, the Fitzgerald earls fell briefly out of favor with Edward IV. Acting on the complaints of Anglo-Irish landowners against the financial exactions imposed by the Fitzgeralds for maintenance of their troops, John TIPTOFT, earl of Worcester, the new English lord deputy, attainted both earls and executed Desmond, thus permanently muting the Yorkist sympathies of the Desmond branch of the family. Because the king soon realized that he needed Fitzgerald support to govern Ireland, especially in view of the continuing Lancastrian threat to England, Edward reversed Kildare's ATTAINDER and reappointed him lord deputy in 1470.

After Kildare's death in 1478, his son, Gerald FITZGERALD, eighth earl of Kildare, maintained his family's Yorkist allegiance, governing Ireland as deputy for RICHARD III's son, Prince Edward, and, after Richard's death in 1485, allowing the island to become a base of operations for Yorkist opponents of HENRY VII. In 1487, he welcomed Lambert SIMNEL to Ireland and accepted Simnel's claim to be Edward PLANTAGENET, earl of Warwick, a Yorkist claimant to the throne. Kildare also allowed John de la POLE, earl of Lincoln, another nephew of Edward IV, to land at Dublin with 2,000 troops supplied by his aunt, MARGARET OF YORK, duchess of BURGUNDY. After permitting Simnel's coronation in Dublin as "Edward VI," Kildare governed Ireland in "King Edward's" name, and allowed Lincoln to recruit Irish troops for an invasion of England, which ended in failure at the Battle of STOKE in June 1487. Although pardoned by Henry VII, Kildare again fell out of favor in the 1490s when he was suspected of supporting Perkin WARBECK, another Yorkist pretender. Warbeck invaded Ireland in 1495 and 1497 but failed both times to establish himself in the island. Restored as lord deputy in 1496, Kildare gradually abandoned his Yorkist sympathies, and Ireland gradually accepted TUDOR rule.

Further Reading: Cosgrove, Art, *Late Medieval Ireland, 1370–1541* (Dublin: Helicon, 1981); Lydon, James, *Ireland in the Later Middle Ages* (Dublin: Gill and Macmillan, 1973); Otway-Ruthven, A. J., *A History of Medieval Ireland* (New York: Barnes and Noble Books, 1980).

Jack Cade's Rebellion (1450)

Distressed by high taxes, corrupt local officials, and the recent loss of Normandy, the commons of Kent, led by a man named Jack (or John) Cade, rose in rebellion in the summer of 1450. Because HENRY VI and his advisors suspected that Richard PLANTAGENET, duke of York, had instigated the uprising, and because York later incorporated many of the rebels' complaints into his criticism of the government, Jack Cade's Rebellion is often seen as a prelude to the WARS OF THE ROSES.

In late May 1450, only weeks after the murder of the king's unpopular chief minister, William de la POLE, duke of Suffolk, a large body of men from the towns and villages of Kent gathered at Blackheath, across the Thames from LONDON, to demand redress of various grievances. Composed of rural peasants, artisans, and tradesmen from the towns, and a small group of clergy and landowning GENTRY, the Kentish rebels were, at least initially, well organized and disciplined. Their elected leader was the mysterious Jack Cade, who also went by the names John Mortimer and John Amendalle. Although he was probably seeking only to attract the duke's supporters to his cause, Cade's use of the name Mortimer—the family name of York's mother—led the government to seriously consider the possibility that York was somehow involved in the rebellion. The rebels denied any connection with York, but their demand that the king rid himself of all advisors linked to the late Suffolk and turn instead to princes of the blood like York only heightened the government's suspicions. The idea that York was behind the Cade uprising, although generally rejected today, became a commonplace of Tudor PROPAGANDA and was even suggested by William Shakespeare in his *HENRY VI, PART 2* (see SHAKESPEARE AND THE WARS OF THE ROSES).

Thanks to the obscurity of Cade's background, and perhaps to government attempts to discredit Cade, rumors soon circulated that the rebel leader was an Irishman related to York, that he was a black magician, and that he had once fled the realm after murdering a pregnant woman. Whatever Cade's history, his manner impressed the royal councilors who met him, and the rebel manifesto crafted under his leadership—the "Complaint of the Commons of Kent"—displayed his skill as a propagandist. Comprising fifteen articles, the "Complaint" focused on the corrupt practices of the king's officials in Kent, who were charged with extortion, perversion of justice, and election fraud. The commons also called for an inquiry into the loss of Normandy and into the misappropriation of royal funds by the king's household servants.

In early June, after submitting their "Complaint" to the COUNCIL, the rebels obeyed an order to withdraw from Blackheath. However, when an advance party of the royal army followed them into Kent, the rebels ambushed and destroyed their pursuers. At news of this repulse, a nervous council committed Lord Saye, the hated former sheriff of Kent, and William Cromer, the equally unpopular current sheriff, to the TOWER OF LONDON. The king then withdrew from the capital. On 4 July, the Londoners, who were sympathetic to many of the rebels' grievances, allowed Cade and his followers to enter the city, where they immediately seized and executed Saye and Cromer. On the night of 5 July, as the rebels grew more disorderly, the citizens, assisted by

Some of the leaders of Jack Cade's Rebellion are hanged to frighten their followers into obedience. (British Library)

the Tower garrison under Thomas SCALES, Lord Scales, drove the insurgents from the city and recaptured London Bridge. This action allowed the council to issue a free pardon on 8 July, and most of the rebels returned home. After invalidating his pardon by attempting to seize Queenborough Castle, Cade was killed on 12 July while resisting arrest. Although the rebellion was over, Cade's name continued to spark unrest in Kent for almost a decade, and the rebels' grievances lived on as the basis of York's opposition to a royal government from which he felt himself excluded.

See also Dartford Uprising
Further Reading: Griffiths, Ralph A., *The Reign of King Henry VI* (Berkeley: University of California Press, 1981); Harvey, I. M. W., *Jack Cade's Rebellion of 1450* (Oxford: Clarendon Press, 1991); Wolffe, Bertram, *Henry VI* (London: Eyre Methuen, 1981).

Jacquetta of Luxembourg, Duchess of Bedford (c. 1416–1472)

Jacquetta of Luxembourg, duchess of Bedford, was the mother of Queen Elizabeth WOOD-

VILLE and the matriarch of the WOODVILLE FAMILY.

The daughter of Pierre, Count of St. Pol, a French nobleman who traced his family to Charlemagne, Jacquetta married John, duke of Bedford, the uncle of HENRY VI, in April 1433. After her husband's death in 1435, the duchess shocked her royal nephew by marrying Richard WOODVILLE, a Northamptonshire gentleman whose father had been Bedford's chamberlain. Because Woodville had nothing but looks to recommend him as a husband for the duchess, the government fined the couple £1,000 for their misalliance. Besides social rank and a connection to the house of LANCASTER, Jacquetta brought her husband land and wealth, and bore him at least fourteen children.

On the outbreak of civil war, the duchess accompanied her husband, now Lord Rivers, to Sandwich, where Queen MARGARET OF ANJOU had ordered him to assemble a fleet. In January 1460, Jacquetta, Rivers, and their eldest son, Anthony WOODVILLE, were captured by Yorkist raiders and carried to CALAIS. Although the duchess was shortly released, her husband and son remained in Yorkist custody. A year later, after the Battle of ST. ALBANS, the LONDON authorities sent Jacquetta to Queen Margaret as part of a deputation seeking the queen's assurance that her army would not plunder the city (see MARCH ON LONDON).

In May 1464, after the Woodvilles had made their peace with the house of YORK, Jacquetta witnessed the secret union of EDWARD IV and her eldest daughter Elizabeth, a match that constituted an even greater misalliance than the duchess's own marriage. Edward spent the next three days with the Woodvilles, and each night Jacquetta brought her daughter secretly to the king. By 1468, Jacquetta and her family were influential enough to be accused of ruining Sir Thomas COOK, a wealthy London merchant who owned a rich tapestry supposedly coveted by the duchess. The traditional account is that Cook refused Jacquetta's demand that he sell her the tapestry at far less than its worth, and

that she then accused him of being a Lancastrian sympathizer. Because Cook's name had surfaced during the recent investigation of the CORNELIUS PLOT, Edward allowed Rivers, as constable of England, to proceed against the merchant. Although Cook had refused a Lancastrian request for money, he had not revealed the contact and was convicted of misprision of treason. A fine of £8,000 ruined Cook, and the duchess obtained her tapestry when Woodville servants ransacked the merchant's house. Much of this story has been called into question by modern historians who suggest that the involvement of the duchess and her family in the Cook case was greatly exaggerated by the anticourt propaganda of Richard NEVILLE, earl of Warwick, and that Cook may indeed have been an active Lancastrian.

In August 1469, Warwick, angered, in part, by the rise of the Woodvilles, rebelled and seized temporary control of the king. After executing Rivers, Warwick arrested Jacquetta on charges of witchcraft; although the basis for these charges is uncertain, Warwick may have accused Jacquetta of using black magic to bewitch Edward into contracting marriage with her daughter. The duchess wrote to the mayor of London, who, remembering her efforts to protect the city from the Lancastrian army in 1461, interceded on her behalf with the COUNCIL. Further investigation revealed that the witnesses against her had been bribed, and the case fell apart. Jacquetta was released and formally exonerated by Edward in February 1470, although the charge of witchcraft resurfaced in 1483 when RICHARD III included it in *TITULUS REGIUS* as one of his justifications for taking the throne from Jacquetta's grandson, EDWARD V. The duchess died in April 1472.

Further Reading: Hicks, Michael, "The Changing Role of the Wydevilles in Yorkist Politics to 1483," in Charles Ross, ed., *Patronage, Pedigree and Power in Later Medieval England* (Stroud, Gloucestershire, UK: Alan Sutton, 1979); MacGibbon, David, *Elizabeth Woodville: Her Life and Times* (London: A. Barker, 1938); Weir, Alison, *The Wars of the Roses* (New York: Ballantine Books, 1995).

James II, King of Scotland
(1430–1460)

As king of SCOTLAND during the early stages of political and dynastic conflict in fifteenth-century England, James II tried to take advantage of those internal dissensions to achieve territorial gains for Scotland at England's expense.

James became king in 1437 on the assassination of his father James I. Although his mother was Joan Beaufort, a younger sister of Edmund BEAUFORT, duke of Somerset, the leading rival in the 1450s of Richard PLANTAGENET, duke of York, James showed no marked partiality for the Lancastrian cause, perhaps because his mother died in 1445, four years before the young king assumed control of the Scottish government. James spent the early years of his majority waging war against the Douglases, one of Scotland's most powerful magnate families. HENRY VI strained relations with James by giving the Douglases asylum in England. In 1455, James sought to recover the border town of BERWICK by exploiting the political upheaval surrounding the Battle of ST. ALBANS. He urged CHARLES VII of FRANCE to coordinate a French attack on CALAIS with a Scottish descent on Berwick. Although Charles refused to cooperate, the hostility of the Yorkist regimes in the mid-1450s led James to launch a series of raids into England in 1456. However, the continued unwillingness of Charles VII to provide assistance forced James to postpone his ambitions concerning Berwick and to conclude a two-year truce with England in June 1457.

Although raids continued along the border, the truce was extended until 1463, and James negotiated with both parties in the English civil war, seeking by any means to find an opportunity to regain Berwick and other border strongholds. With the defeat and capture of Henry VI at the Battle of NORTHAMPTON in July 1460, James seized his chance and laid siege to the castle of Roxburgh, intending, perhaps, to move on to Berwick after the fortress fell. Roxburgh, being on Scottish soil, was to the Scots a provocative symbol of English occupation. However, on 3 August 1460,

in the midst of the siege, one of the royal ARTILLERY pieces exploded, with a fragment hitting and killing the king, who stood nearby. Despite this tragedy, the continuing political turmoil in England was too good an opportunity to be missed, and Queen MARY OF GUELDRES is said to have exhorted the army to redouble its efforts. The siege therefore continued, and Roxburgh fell on 8 August, with the nearby border castle of Wark capitulating to the Scots shortly thereafter. The recovery of Berwick remained to be accomplished by the minority government of the new king, JAMES III.

Further Reading: McGladdery, Christine, *James II* (Edinburgh: John Donald Publishers, 1990).

James III, King of Scotland
(1451–1488)

Early in the reign of James III, Scottish policy toward England revolved around exploitation of the political turmoil caused by the WARS OF THE ROSES to recover the border town of BERWICK. Later in the reign, James weakened his hold on the Scottish Crown by pursuing an unusual policy of accommodation toward England.

James succeeded to the throne in August 1460, when his father, JAMES II, was killed by an ARTILLERY explosion while besieging the English-held castle of Roxburgh. Directed by MARY OF GUELDRES, the Queen Mother, and by Bishop James KENNEDY of St. Andrews, the regency government of the nine-year-old king continued his father's policy of exploiting the English civil war to make Scottish territorial gains. Between December 1460, when Queen MARGARET OF ANJOU arrived in SCOTLAND seeking assistance for the Lancastrian cause, and December 1463, when Scottish support for the house of LANCASTER ceased, the minority government of James III balanced the Lancastrian need for military assistance against the Yorkist need for security to extract concessions from both parties. When the Lancastrian royal family fled into Scotland after the Battle of TOWTON in March 1461, Queen Margaret agreed to cede

English border towns in return for Scottish help against EDWARD IV. Although the citizens of Carlisle refused to obey Margaret's order to admit the Scots, Berwick surrendered to James III in April.

With Berwick achieved and Yorkist pressure increasing, notably through the 1462 Treaty of WESTMINSTER-ARDTORNISH, whereby Edward IV threatened an alliance with rebellious Scottish magnates, enthusiasm for the Lancastrian cause waned. By early 1464, Queen Margaret and Prince EDWARD OF LANCASTER had sailed to FRANCE, HENRY VI had been returned to England, and a truce had been concluded with Edward IV. Although James assumed personal control of the government in 1469, he was intent on consolidating his authority in Scotland and did not intervene when the English conflict revived between 1469 and 1471. In the 1470s, James attempted to improve relations with England by proposing a series of marriages between members of his family, including his son, the future JAMES IV, and members of the house of YORK, including Edward's brother, George PLANTAGENET, duke of Clarence, and his sister MARGARET OF YORK, the widowed duchess of BURGUNDY. None of these unions occurred, mainly for lack of English interest.

Anglo-Scottish relations deteriorated in the late 1470s, when Edward sought to retake Berwick by exploiting internal dissension in Scotland. In 1482, Edward concluded the Treaty of Fotheringhay with James's brother, Alexander, duke of Albany. The agreement called for Albany to surrender Berwick to England in return for assistance in overthrowing James. Richard, duke of Gloucester, recaptured Berwick in August 1482, but the attempt to crown Albany failed. In 1484, James, accepting the loss of Berwick, concluded a truce with RICHARD III. Although a Scottish contingent fought for him at the Battle of BOSWORTH FIELD in August 1485, HENRY VII showed no willingness to yield Berwick, and James was defeated and killed by Scottish rebels in 1488, in part for his failure to pursue a more aggressive policy toward England.

Further Reading: Macdougall, Norman, *James III: A Political Study* (Edinburgh: J. Donald, 1982).

James IV, King of Scotland (1473–1513)

By supporting Yorkist attempts to overthrow HENRY VII and the house of TUDOR, James IV contributed to the continuation of English dynastic strife in the 1490s.

James became king in June 1488, when his father, JAMES III, was defeated and killed at Sauchieburn by a coalition of rebel magnates. Although he had associated himself with the opposition, James was shocked by his father's murder. Nonetheless, he was neither willing nor able to pursue the policy of accommodation with England that had in part led to his father's downfall. By 1489, James was already involved in conspiracies to restore the house of YORK. He received English agents sent from BURGUNDY by MARGARET OF YORK, the sister of EDWARD IV, and messengers from IRELAND, where Yorkist plots were common in the late 1480s. In 1491, James allowed his father's truce with England to lapse but renewed a treaty with FRANCE that pledged him to attack England if Henry VII attacked France.

In 1492, the Yorkist pretender Perkin WARBECK, who claimed to be Richard PLANTAGENET, duke of York, the younger son of Edward IV, wrote to James seeking aid. By 1495, Warbeck was in SCOTLAND, where James publicly acknowledged him as duke of York. The king even permitted his kinswoman, Katherine Gordon, to marry Warbeck, an indication that James may actually have believed Warbeck's claims. If true, this belief did not last long, for by 1496 James was negotiating with the English. Unable to obtain satisfactory terms from Henry VII, who likely balked at any demand for the return of BERWICK, James invaded England on Warbeck's behalf in September 1496. But Warbeck, who had agreed to restore Berwick and, if successful, to reimburse James for the cost of the campaign, could generate no support in England, and the Scottish invasion ended in failure.

Disillusioned with Warbeck and now aware of the difficulty of displacing Henry VII, James sent the pretender from Scotland in July 1497. The king then opened a series of negotiations with Henry, which led to a seven-year truce in September 1497 and a formal treaty of peace (the first with England since 1328) in January 1502. The Treaty of Ayton committed James to marry Henry VII's daughter, Princess Margaret, who became queen of Scotland in August 1503. It was as a result of this marriage that James VI of Scotland, the great-grandson of James IV and the great-great-grandson of Henry VII, became king of England in 1603. Although the Treaty of Ayton reduced the likelihood of Scotland again becoming a haven for Yorkist pretenders, it did not erase hundreds of years of Anglo-Scottish enmity. In 1513, James invaded England while his brother-in-law, Henry VIII, was on campaign in France. Brought to battle at Flodden on 9 September, James IV was slain on the field.

Further Reading: Macdougall, Norman, *James IV* (East Lothian: Tuckwell Press, 1997).

Kennedy, James, Bishop of St. Andrews (c. 1406–1465)

In the early 1460s, as a leading member of JAMES III's regency council, James Kennedy, bishop of St. Andrews, was instrumental in securing asylum in SCOTLAND for the Lancastrian royal family.

The youngest son of a Scottish GENTRY family, and a member, through his mother, of the Scottish royal family, Kennedy was sent to the continent to study theology and canon law. Named bishop of Dunkeld in 1437, Kennedy vigorously pursued ecclesiastical reform, even proposing a reform program to the pope while attending the Council of Florence in 1440. A leading figure in the minority government of JAMES II, Kennedy was appointed bishop of St. Andrews in 1440 and served briefly as chancellor in 1444.

On the unexpected death of James II in 1460, Kennedy became a member of the regency COUNCIL chosen to govern during the minority of James III. Headed by Queen MARY OF GUELDRES, the council was soon confronted by a request for military assistance from Queen MARGARET OF ANJOU, who, since the capture of HENRY VI at the Battle of NORTHAMPTON, was an exile in Scotland with her son Prince EDWARD OF LANCASTER. Although victory at the Battle of WAKEFIELD in December 1460 allowed Margaret and the house of LANCASTER to temporarily regain the ascendancy, EDWARD IV's triumph at the Battle of TOWTON in March 1461 forced the entire Lancastrian royal family to flee again into Scotland. Caught between Margaret's pleas for help and Edward IV's demands for the expulsion of her family, the regency council split, with Kennedy leading the pro-Lancastrian faction known as the "Old Lords." Although the "Young Lords," led by Queen Mary, were willing to talk to the Yorkists, Kennedy frustrated all attempts at negotiation, including a personal visit to the Scottish court in 1462 by Richard NEVILLE, earl of Warwick. As a result of Kennedy's influence and Margaret's willingness to surrender BERWICK, Scotland remained a safe haven and a source of military assistance for the Lancastrians until 1463.

In August 1463, after the failure of a Scottish-Lancastrian invasion of northern England, Margaret and her son left for France, while Henry VI remained in Scotland under Kennedy's protection. In October, LOUIS XI of FRANCE abandoned Scotland and the seemingly hopeless cause of Henry VI by concluding a truce with Edward IV; the agreement called upon both signatories to refuse assistance to the other's enemies. In December, with Queen Mary dead, Kennedy suppressed his Lancastrian sympathies and negotiated a ten-month truce with the Yorkists. Edward agreed to cease supporting the rebel earl of Douglas and Kennedy agreed to give no more aid to the Lancastrians and to begin talks in March 1464 for a more permanent settlement. Although Kennedy at first violated the agreement by taking Henry VI deeper into Scotland for safety, in January 1464 he sent the ex-king into England to the Lancastrian-held castle of BAMBURGH. By Kennedy's death in May 1465, Scotland had achieved a stable if uneasy peace with the Yorkist regime.

See also Westminster-Ardtornish, Treaty of
Further Reading: Dunlop, Annie, *The Life and Times of James Kennedy, Bishop of St. Andrews* (Edinburgh: Oliver and Boyd, 1950); Macdougall,

Norman, *James III* (Edinburgh: J. Donald, 1982); McGladdery, Christine, *James II* (Edinburgh: John Donald Publishers, 1990).

Kent, Earl of. *See* Grey, Edmund, Earl of Kent; Neville, William, Lord Fauconberg and Earl of Kent

Kildare, Earl of. *See* entries under Fitzgerald

Kingmaker. *See* Neville, Richard, Earl of Warwick

King's Council. *See* Council, Royal

Lancaster, House of (1399–1461, 1470–1471)

A branch of the royal family of PLANTA-GENET, which had ruled England since 1154, the house of Lancaster and its partisans comprised one of the parties contending for the throne during the WARS OF THE ROSES.

The family of Lancaster descended from John of Gaunt, duke of Lancaster (1340–1399), the third son of Edward III (r. 1327–1377). The Lancastrians became the ruling dynasty in 1399 when Henry of Bolingbroke, Gaunt's son, deposed his childless cousin Richard II (r. 1377–1399) and assumed the Crown as Henry IV (see RICHARD II, DE-POSITION OF). Because Henry's usurpation broke the normal line of succession, he spent much of his reign (1399–1413) quelling uprisings launched on behalf of the legal heirs, the Mortimers, who descended from Gaunt's older brother, Lionel, duke of Clarence (1338–1368). However, Henry IV survived and in 1413 was peacefully succeeded by his son Henry V (r. 1413–1422), who secured the dynasty on the throne by reviving the HUN-DRED YEARS WAR and uniting England against its ancient enemy, FRANCE. Henry's victory at Agincourt in 1415 and his conquest of much of northern France intensified English pride in the king and his dynasty.

On Henry V's death in 1422, the Crown passed to a nine-month-old infant, HENRY VI, whose mother was Catherine of Valois, the daughter of Charles VI of France. By the 1420 Treaty of Troyes, Henry V was recognized as heir to the French Crown. Thus, upon Charles VI's death in October 1422, Henry VI was proclaimed king of both England and France while still less than a year old. While the king's eldest uncle, John, duke of Bedford (1389–1435), governed France and conducted the ongoing war as his nephew's regent, a council of nobles under the nominal leadership of the king's younger uncle, Humphrey, duke of Gloucester (1390–1447), governed England. In the 1450s, Henry VI, who was politically inept and easily led by favorites, fell victim to on-going mental illness and proved himself unfit to rule (see HENRY VI, ILLNESS OF). Royal weakness revived the long dormant claim of the Mortimers, now embodied in Richard PLANTAGENET, duke of York, whose mother had been a Mortimer. York was heir presumptive to the throne until the birth of Henry's son, Prince EDWARD OF LAN-CASTER, in 1453. In the mid-1450s, York, believing himself excluded from the political power that was his right by birth, sought to govern on behalf of the stricken king.

The Wars of the Roses erupted as nobles, seeking either to retain the influence they exercised as royal favorites, or, like York, to force their way into the circle of royal favor, formed factions around the king and the duke. Long-standing local feuds intensified the struggle, as rivals merged their quarrels into the national conflict. In 1460, York claimed the Crown outright, and in 1461, his son, EDWARD IV, overthrew Henry VI and set the house of YORK on the throne. Al-though Henry VI was briefly restored in 1470–1471, the death of his son at the Battle of TEWKESBURY led to the ex-king's murder and the extinction of the direct male line of Lancaster in May 1471.

Nevertheless, the Lancastrian claim to the Crown survived. Although Henry VI had no

Richard II (left) surrenders his crown to Henry of Bolingbroke, who thereby becomes Henry IV, first king of the house of Lancaster in 1399. (Royal MS 18 E II. f. 401, British Library)

full siblings, and his uncles were childless, the dynasty had a collateral branch that figured prominently in the Wars of the Roses. In 1396, John of Gaunt had married his long-time mistress, Katherine Swynford (d. 1403). Richard II had then legitimated Gaunt's children by Swynford under the name of Beaufort, although Henry IV later barred his half siblings from the succession. During Henry VI's minority, the leading member of the BEAUFORT FAMILY was Henry Beaufort, cardinal-bishop of Winchester (c. 1376–1447). During the Wars of the Roses, Edmund Beaufort and his sons Henry and Edmund, all successively dukes of Somerset (see entries for all under BEAUFORT), were leaders of the Lancastrian party. Although all three dukes of Somerset died in the civil wars, ending the male line of Beaufort in

1471, their cousin, Margaret BEAUFORT, survived and eventually transmitted the Lancastrian claim to the throne to the house of TUDOR.

HENRY VII, Margaret Beaufort's son and the first Tudor monarch, was the grandson of an obscure Welshman, Owen TUDOR, who in the late 1420s secretly married Queen Catherine, Henry VI's widowed mother. The children of this union, Edmund TUDOR, earl of Richmond, and Jasper TUDOR, earl of Pembroke, were thus half siblings of Henry VI. The Tudors' claim to the English Crown derived from Richmond's 1455 marriage to Margaret Beaufort, and it was this claim that Margaret's son realized in 1485, when, as the last male descendent of the Lancastrian and Beaufort lines, he defeated RICHARD III and overthrew the house of York. Henry then symbolically ended the Wars of the Roses by marrying ELIZABETH OF YORK, Edward IV's heir; their son, Henry VIII, a descendent of both Lancaster and York, peacefully succeeded to the throne in 1509.

See also Edward IV, Overthrow of; Edward IV, Restoration of; Appendix 1, "Genealogies"
Further Reading: Allmand, Christopher, *Henry V* (Berkeley: University of California Press, 1992); Griffiths, Ralph A., *The Reign of King Henry VI* (Berkeley: University of California Press, 1981); Griffiths, Ralph A., "The Sense of Dynasty in the Reign of Henry VI," in Ralph A. Griffiths, ed., *King and Country: England and Wales in the Fifteenth Century* (London: Hambledon Press, 1991), pp. 83–101; Kirby, John Lavan, *Henry IV of England* (London: Constable, 1970); Storey, R. L., *The End of the House of Lancaster,* 2d ed. (Stroud, Gloucestershire, UK: Sutton Publishing, 1999); Wolffe, Bertram, *Henry VI* (London: Eyre Methuen, 1981).

Landais, Pierre (d. 1485)

Pierre Landais, treasurer of BRITTANY under Duke FRANCIS II, several times played a key role in Yorkist efforts to obtain custody of Henry Tudor, earl of Richmond (see HENRY VII), the surviving Lancastrian heir.

The first episode occurred in November 1476, five years after EDWARD IV's restoration had sent Richmond and his uncle, Jasper TUDOR, earl of Pembroke, into exile in Brittany (see EDWARD IV, RESTORATION OF). The duke surrendered Richmond to a delegation of English envoys, who had convinced Francis that the king intended to treat Richmond honorably and to marry the earl to his eldest daughter, ELIZABETH OF YORK. Escorted to St. Malo, where a ship waited to carry him to England, Richmond became or pretended to be ill, thereby delaying the ship's departure. In the meantime, Francis, remembering his pledge to keep the Tudors safe, and pressured by advisors sympathetic to Richmond, who told him that the earl's reception in England was likely to be much different than represented, dispatched Landais to St. Malo, where he argued with the ambassadors while Richmond slipped into SANCTUARY in a local church. The townsmen, horrified by the English willingness to violate sanctuary, prevented Richmond from being seized and he was soon able to return safely to the Breton COURT with Landais.

In 1483, Landais's assistance made possible Richmond's descent on England in support of BUCKINGHAM'S REBELLION. Landais persuaded Francis to give Richmond ships, men, and money. He also convinced CHARLES VIII OF FRANCE, who was seeking to make a friend of the powerful treasurer, to allow Henry to return safely to Brittany through Normandy after the failure of the enterprise.

In 1484, Francis fell ill, and Landais had virtual charge of the Breton government. Embroiled in a bitter political struggle with a rival faction of the Breton nobility, and faced with a growing French desire to absorb Brittany, Landais believed that his survival and that of the duchy depended on the friendship of England. He therefore concluded an agreement with William CATESBY, RICHARD III's representative, to surrender Richmond in return for an assurance of Richard's protection. The plan miscarried when Bishop John MORTON learned of it from Breton agents in LONDON and dispatched Christopher URSWICK to warn Richmond, who promptly fled into France with his uncle Pembroke and a small band of supporters. Hearing of Richmond's flight, Landais sent men to recapture the earl, who crossed the frontier less than an hour before his pursuers reached it. Landais's actions so angered Duke Francis that he generously allowed the more than 400 English exiles left behind by Richmond to rejoin the earl in France. Because Landais had cost Brittany its most valuable device for ensuring English aid against France, the treasurer lost the support of the duke and fell from power in 1485. Having made many political enemies, Landais was hung from the walls of Nantes on 19 July.

Further Reading: Griffiths, Ralph A., and Roger S. Thomas, *The Making of the Tudor Dynasty* (New York: St. Martin's Press, 1985); Jones, Michael, *The Creation of Brittany: A Late Medieval State* (London: Hambledon, 1988).

Langstrother, Sir John, Prior of the Hospital of St. John of Jerusalem (1416–1471)

Sir John Langstrother, prior of the Hospital of St. John of Jerusalem, strongly supported the restoration of the house of LANCASTER in 1470–1471.

The son of Thomas Langstrother of Crosthwaite, Sir John, like his elder brother William, joined the Knights of the Hospital of St. John of Jerusalem (also known as "the Hospitallers"), a military religious order established in the eleventh century to provide hospital care and military protection to pilgrims in Jerusalem during the Crusades. Ruled by a grand master, who by the fifteenth century was headquartered on the island of Rhodes, the order's various national provinces were headed by grand commanders or priors. In 1467, after spending most of his early years in the eastern Mediterranean serving as castellan of Rhodes and grand commander of Cyprus, Langstrother won election as prior of the order in England, a position that had been held by Robert Botyll, a noted Yorkist. Because Langstrother's Lancastrian sympathies were well known, EDWARD IV, in an unprecedented act, refused to sanction the Knights' selection and suggested that they accept Richard Woodville as prior instead. A brother of Queen ELIZABETH WOODVILLE, Richard was only a youth and not a member of the Hospitallers. The grand master and council of the order rejected this suggestion and the office remained vacant for two years.

When, after the Battle of EDGECOTE in July 1469, Richard NEVILLE, earl of Warwick, won temporary custody of the king and the government, he appointed Langstrother treasurer of England. Upon regaining his freedom in October, Edward dismissed Langstrother from office and committed him briefly to the TOWER OF LONDON but eventually accepted him as prior of the English Hospitallers. However, in March 1470, Langstrother involved himself in Warwick's second coup attempt by meeting secretly in LONDON with Warwick's allies, including George PLANTA-GENET, duke of Clarence. After the failure of the coup, Langstrother probably fled to the continent with Warwick, for he returned to England with the earl in September (see EDWARD IV, OVERTHROW OF). Entering London on 5 October in the company of George NEVILLE, archbishop of York, Langstrother took command of the Tower for the newly established READEPTION government of HENRY VI. Within days, the prior was reappointed treasurer and also named warden of the mint.

In February 1471, Langstrother was a member of a high-ranking diplomatic mission that signed a ten-year truce and a commercial treaty with LOUIS XI. At the end of February, Warwick sent Langstrother to FRANCE to convey MARGARET OF ANJOU and her son Prince EDWARD OF LANCASTER to England. Delayed by weather, the prior and his party did not land until 14 April, the day of Warwick's death at the Battle of BARNET. An experienced soldier, Langstrother accompanied Queen Margaret on her campaign into the West Country, and, with John WENLOCK, Lord Wenlock, led the Lancastrian center, under the nominal command of the prince, at the Battle of TEWKESBURY on 4 May. After the battle, Langstrother; Edmund BEAUFORT, duke of Somerset; and other Lancastrian survivors took refuge in Tewkesbury Abbey. Two days later, they were removed from SANCTUARY on Edward IV's order and condemned to death for treason. Langstrother and his comrades were executed in the marketplace at Tewkesbury.

Further Reading: P. W. Hammond, *The Battles of Barnet and Tewkesbury* (New York: St. Martin's Press, 1990).

Leadership in Battle. *See* Generalship

Lincoln, Bishop of. *See* Russell, John

Lincoln, Earl of. *See* Pole, John de la, Earl of Lincoln

Lincolnshire Rebellion (1470). *See* Welles Uprising (1470)

Livery and Maintenance

Deriving from the French word *livrée*, "delivered," livery referred to the uniform, in distinctive colors, that a nobleman gave to his RETAINERS, often together with his BADGE or emblem, to denote their membership in his AFFINITY of sworn followers. Maintenance referred to the lord's duty to "maintain" or support his retainers, by word or action, in any lawsuit in which they were involved. The two concepts became linked because liveried retainers were both the recipients and the agents of acts of maintenance. Although accepted aspects of the social system known as BASTARD FEUDALISM, both livery and maintenance were seen by contemporaries as abuses of the system and both were the subjects of largely ineffective action by PARLIAMENT.

In a broader sense, livery also described the bestowing of payment, whether in money, clothing, food and drink, or other forms, by a lord on his retainers for their political and military service, an exchange that was at the heart of bastard feudalism. By the fifteenth century, maintenance, although long forbidden by statute, had become one of the recognized benefits of "good lordship" that a retainer could expect from the magnate to whom he had sworn allegiance. During the 1440s and 1450s, as the influence and authority of the Crown declined under the ineffectual leadership of HENRY VI, maintenance, which had for some time been growing more violent in its application, came increasingly to mean the bribing, intimidating, or even kidnapping of judges, jurors, witnesses, or opposing counselors. For instance, in the 1440s, Sir Thomas Tuddenham, a retainer of William de la POLE, duke of Suffolk and chief minister of Henry VI, severely disrupted the dispensing of justice in Norfolk by committing frequent acts of embracery (i.e., the bribing of jurors) and by threatening people with loss of life or property if they did not comply with the duke's wishes in a lawsuit. Tuddenham and his allies also controlled the appointment of sheriffs and court officials and brought fictitious lawsuits against wealthy individuals to extort money.

To correct abuses of this kind and to restore order to the royal judicial system, the Parliaments of both EDWARD IV and HENRY VII passed acts against retaining (see RETAINING, ACTS AGAINST). Although reduced somewhat by these acts and by the strengthening of royal authority after 1471, livery and maintenance continued to exist until bastard feudalism itself disappeared in the late sixteenth and seventeenth centuries.

Further Reading: Hicks, Michael, *Bastard Feudalism* (London: Longman, 1995).

London

Because London was the political and economic heart of the kingdom, the city's friendship and support were vital to both sides during a civil conflict like the WARS OF THE ROSES. Concerned with prosperity, stability, and their own rights and privileges, Londoners generally sought to remain neutral or, failing that, favored the party that seemed most capable of protecting the city's interests, which, after 1460, was usually the house of YORK.

In 1485, London had a population of over 60,000, making it by far the largest city in the realm. Although smaller than Paris, London was more demographically and economically dominant in England than its French counterpart was in FRANCE. The city was the center of English trade, the site of English government (Westminster was one mile from London), and the source of financial resources that were vital to any regime. In the late 1450s, economic recession, aggravated by the government's haphazard commercial policies and by the official favor shown to foreign merchants (see HANSEATIC LEAGUE), caused much civic dissatisfaction with the Lancastrian administration. After 1456, Queen MARGARET OF ANJOU, seeking to isolate the weak-willed king from outside influences, removed HENRY VI and the royal COURT from Westminster to the Midlands, a transferal of patronage and prestige that further damaged

A late-fifteenth-century depiction of London as a group of knights and their ladies parade through the city on their way to a tournament. (Harley MS 4379 f. 99, British Library)

relations between the city and the house of LANCASTER.

Meanwhile, the city's interest in a Yorkist administration was strengthened by the activities of Richard NEVILLE, earl of Warwick, who, as captain of CALAIS since 1456, controlled the continental entrepôt for London's wool trade. Many city merchants invested heavily in the maintenance of Warwick's garrison, while the earl's piratical attacks on foreign shipping, launched in 1459 after the government cut off funding, won the Yorkists much popularity in the city by allowing Warwick to appear more interested in protecting trade than did the distant Lancastrian regime.

On 2 July 1460, the municipal authorities, after some hesitation, allowed Warwick to enter the city. This decision effectively ended London's neutrality; the city could henceforth expect only harsh treatment from the queen.

After serving as capital of the Yorkist regime instituted by Warwick after the Battle of NORTHAMPTON, the city fell into a panic in January 1461 when the queen's victorious army turned south after the Battle of WAKE-FIELD. Marked by the plunder of Yorkist towns and castles, the Lancastrian MARCH ON LONDON, when exaggerated by Yorkist PROPAGANDA, persuaded city leaders to deny Margaret entrance after her defeat of Warwick at the Battle of ST. ALBANS on 17 February. Instead, Londoners admitted Warwick and Edward, earl of March, and enthusiastically endorsed March's elevation to the throne as EDWARD IV. The queen's failure to take London allowed the Yorkists to survive defeat, crown a king, and use the resources of the city to raise an army that defeated the Lancastrians at the Battle of TOWTON on 29 March.

In 1470, with Edward isolated in the north and popular sentiment swinging to Warwick, the city welcomed the earl and provided willing though moderate financial support for the READEPTION government of Henry VI. In April 1471, with Warwick at Coventry and Edward IV approaching rapidly, the London authorities, influenced by Yorkist lords then in the city and by hopes that a restored Edward would repay his many outstanding loans, allowed the Yorkists to enter the capital. In May, while Edward was in the west winning the Battle of TEWKESBURY, London became the only English town to stand siege during the Wars of the Roses. Warwick's kinsman, Thomas NEVILLE, Bastard of Fauconberg, assaulted the city with a large force of Calais troops and Kentish rebels. As his troops attacked London Bridge and the eastern gates, Fauconberg's ships bombarded the city from the Thames. Fear of plunder as much as loyalty to Edward IV inspired Londoners to a fierce resistance that repelled the attack.

For the rest of Edward's reign, stable government, low taxes, and growing trade ensured the city's loyalty. However, after the king's death in 1483, Londoners reluctantly acquiesced in RICHARD III's deposition of his nephew EDWARD V (see USURPATION OF 1483). Because London had little taste for rule by the WOODVILLE FAMILY, the city approved Richard's protectorship, but several sources, including Sir Thomas More in his *HISTORY OF KING RICHARD III,* describe the lack of enthusiasm with which Richard's claim to the throne was greeted in the city (see SHAW'S SERMON). After Richard's coronation, support for the regime declined as rumors spread that Edward IV's sons had been murdered in the TOWER OF LONDON. As a result, HENRY VII was readily welcomed by the city after his victory at the Battle of BOSWORTH FIELD in 1485.

See also Edward IV, Overthrow of; Edward IV, Restoration of; English Economy and the Wars of the Roses; London Chronicles; Towns and the Wars of the Roses
Further Reading: Baker, Timothy, *Medieval London* (New York, Praeger, 1970); Porter, Roy,

London: A Social History (Cambridge, MA: Harvard University Press, 1994); Sheppard, Francis, *London: A History* (Oxford: Oxford University Press, 1998).

London Chronicles

Although of uneven quality and concentrating on events in the capital and of interest to its citizens, the London chronicles, a series of narrative histories produced in the city in the fifteenth century, provide valuable information on the WARS OF THE ROSES, especially in regard to public opinion in LONDON. Most of these chronicles were the part-time projects of London merchants and were thus compiled for a merchant readership. Although portions of more than thirty London chronicles survive for the civil war period, the most useful are *Gregory's Chronicle* and two narratives by Robert Fabyan (or Fabian)—*The Great Chronicle of London* and *The New Chronicles of England and France.*

Robert Fabyan, who died in 1513, was a London cloth merchant and city alderman who wrote during the later years of HENRY VII. Published in 1516, *The New Chronicles* (also known as *Fabyan's Chronicle*) cover events in both FRANCE and England but are less detailed than Fabyan's *Great Chronicle.* Both works make rather uncritical use of a wide variety of sources, including other chronicles and Fabyan's own experiences (e.g., he was an apprentice to Sir Thomas COOK when that merchant was implicated in the CORNELIUS PLOT in 1468). Aside from the Cook episode, the *Great Chronicle* provides detailed accounts of EDWARD IV's secret marriage to Elizabeth WOODVILLE in 1464 and of the great tournament at Smithfield in 1467. The latter, involving the king's brother-in-law, Anthony WOODVILLE, Lord Scales, and Anthony, the natural son of Duke PHILIP of BURGUNDY, was no doubt an event of particular importance to Londoners. Although writing in Henry VII's reign, and thus obliged to write favorably of the house of TUDOR and critically of RICHARD III, Fabyan is reasonably balanced in his portrayal of Edward IV and more than just a purveyor of Tudor PROPA-GANDA concerning Richard. Although the *Great Chronicle*'s coverage of Richard's reign contains numerous errors, Fabyan recorded some valuable firsthand observations of moods and opinions in London during the period.

Gregory's Chronicle takes its name from William Gregory, a London skinner who likely wrote the portion of the narrative covering the 1440s. The rest of the chronicle, relating events between 1450 and 1469, was continued by an anonymous, perhaps clerical author, who probably wrote in the 1470s. Although containing the usual focus on London, with particularly detailed accounts of JACK CADE'S REBELLION in 1450 and the unpopularity in London of Edward IV's 1465 debasement of the coinage, *Gregory's Chronicle* offers rare personal perspectives and a somewhat broader discussion of national events in the 1460s.

Further Reading: Fabyan, Robert, *The Great Chronicle of London,* edited by A. H. Thomas and I. D. Thornley (Stroud, Gloucestershire, UK: Alan Sutton, 1983); Fabyan, Robert, *The New Chronicles of England and France,* edited by Henry Ellis (London: Printed for F. C. and J. Rivington, 1811); *The Historical Collections of a Citizen of London in the Fifteenth Century [Gregory's Chronicle],* edited by James Gairdner (New York: Johnson Reprint Corporation, 1965).

London, March on. *See* March on London

Losecote Field, Battle of (1470)

Fought on 12 March 1470, the Battle of Losecote Field forced Richard NEVILLE, earl of Warwick, to abandon the house of YORK and seek a reconciliation with the house of LANCASTER.

After the failure of their 1469 attempt to control EDWARD IV, Warwick and his ally George PLANTAGENET, duke of Clarence, the king's brother, awaited an opportunity to overthrow Edward and enthrone Clarence. Their chance came in early March 1470, when a feud erupted in Lincolnshire between

Richard Welles, Lord Welles, and Sir Thomas Burgh, Edward's Master of Horse. When Welles, his son Sir Robert, and his brother-in-law Sir Thomas Dymmock attacked Burgh's manor house, driving him and his family from the shire, Edward intervened on his servant's behalf. Summoned to LONDON, Welles and Dymmock were placed in custody, but Sir Robert remained in the field with the secret encouragement of Warwick, his distant kinsman. Clarence, meanwhile, met Edward in London and delayed the king's departure for Lincolnshire by two days, thereby giving Sir Robert time to raise the commons of the shire with rumors that the king planned to execute the Lincolnshire men who had joined the ROBIN OF REDESDALE REBELLION of the previous summer.

At Royston on 8 March, the day Edward learned that Sir Robert had assembled a large force of rebels, he also received letters from Warwick and Clarence stating that they would soon arrive to assist in crushing the WELLES UPRISING. Still unaware of their involvement, Edward issued COMMISSIONS OF ARRAY that included Warwick, thereby allowing the earl to raise troops with royal approval. The king then forced Welles to write to his son telling Sir Robert to submit or his father and Dymmock would die. On 11 March, Edward learned that the rebels and the troops of Warwick and Clarence were both heading for Leicester, news that raised royal suspicions as to the latter's intentions. Welles's letter prevented a conjunction of the two forces by convincing Sir Robert to retreat to Stamford in an effort to save his father's life. Edward followed and caught the rebels next day near Empingham. The battle opened with the executions of Welles and Dymmock in full view of both armies. The rebels then confirmed Edward's suspicions by advancing with cries of "a Warwick" and "a Clarence." After a barrage of ARTILLERY, the more experienced royal army charged the larger rebel force and scattered it, turning the battle into a rout. Rebels wearing the livery of Warwick and Clarence stripped off their jackets and cast them aside in their flight, giving the battle its name—"Losecote Field."

Sir Robert Welles was captured, as was a servant of Clarence's, who possessed letters from the duke proving his and Warwick's involvement in the uprising. Edward ordered them to disband their forces and come to his presence, but they declined without a safe-conduct, which Edward refused to grant. The king executed Sir Robert on 19 March after he confessed that the objective of the revolt was to place Clarence on the throne. Edward then issued a proclamation denouncing Warwick and Clarence as traitors if they did not surrender by 28 March. Fleeing to Clarence's lordship at Dartmouth near Exeter, the earl, the duke, and their families took ship for FRANCE, where Warwick, abandoning his attempts to find a pliant Yorkist king, began negotiations with MARGARET OF ANJOU for the Lancastrian alliance that allowed the earl to overthrow Edward IV in the following autumn.

See also Angers Agreement; Edward IV, Overthrow of; *Chronicle of the Rebellion in Lincolnshire*
Further Reading: Haigh, Philip A., *The Military Campaigns of the Wars of the Roses* (Stroud, Gloucestershire, UK: Sutton Publishing, 1995).

Louis XI, King of France (1423–1483)

King of France during most of the civil war period, Louis XI tried to use the WARS OF THE ROSES to prevent English intervention in FRANCE and to weaken English support for BRITTANY and BURGUNDY, two independent French provinces that Louis sought to reincorporate into the French Crown. Although physically ugly and eccentric in behavior and dress, Louis used war and diplomacy to continue the centralizing policies of his father, reabsorbing much of the Burgundian state into France and passing a greatly strengthened Crown onto his son, CHARLES VIII.

The eldest son of CHARLES VII, Louis had a poor relationship with his father, against whom he rebelled in 1440. Pardoned for his actions, Louis retired to the Dauphiné, the French province usually entrusted to the heir

to the throne. In 1456, Louis fled to Burgundy after another clash with his father. Upon becoming king in July 1461, Louis dismissed his father's ministers but continued Charles's efforts to increase the authority of the French Crown by reducing the power and independence of the great French feudatories, especially the duke of Burgundy. Because the Burgundian alliance with Henry V had helped make possible the extensive English conquests in France early in the century, Louis saw perpetuation of the Wars of the Roses as an excellent means for diverting English attention from further French adventures. Accordingly, in the early 1460s, Louis provided diplomatic, financial, and military assistance to the house of LANCASTER in an effort to focus EDWARD IV's attention on securing his shaky throne. In 1462, Louis concluded the CHINON AGREEMENT with MARGARET OF ANJOU, who secretly agreed to surrender CALAIS in return for French money and men. When Burgundian intervention prevented the French seizure of Calais, and Yorkist successes in northern En-

Louis XI, king of France from 1461 to 1483, intervened frequently in English affairs during the Wars of the Roses. (Brooklyn Museum)

gland forced Queen Margaret and her French commander, Pierre de BRÉZÉ, to leave SCOTLAND for the continent, Louis began negotiations with Richard NEVILLE, earl of Warwick, for a marriage alliance with Edward IV and the house of YORK.

The 1464 announcement of Edward's secret marriage to Elizabeth WOODVILLE ended these talks, and the importance of Anglo-Burgundian trade to both states led in 1467 to a commercial treaty and in 1468 to an alliance sealed by the marriage of Duke CHARLES of Burgundy with MARGARET OF YORK, sister of Edward IV. The pro-Burgundian policies of the house of York inclined Louis to support Warwick, who fled to France after the failure of his second coup in April 1470. In June, Louis arranged an interview for Warwick with Margaret of Anjou; though stormy, the negotiations between the two longtime enemies were skillfully brokered by Louis. As a party to the resulting ANGERS AGREEMENT, Louis promised to provide Warwick with money and ships to restore HENRY VI in return for the earl's agreement to take England into war with Burgundy as France's ally. Having lost the Somme towns of Amiens, Abbeville, and their adjacent territories to Burgundy in the War of the Public Weal in 1465, Louis was anxious to reverse that defeat. Although Warwick overthrew Edward IV in October 1470, the earl's fulfillment of his promise to declare war on Burgundy convinced a reluctant Duke Charles to provide Edward with the ships and men he required to regain the Crown. By May 1471, Warwick was dead and the house of York was again in power; Louis never received the English assistance he had sought.

The seeming end of the Wars of the Roses in 1471 robbed Louis of opportunities to weaken England by supporting one contending party against the other. Both Louis and Charles of Burgundy paid pensions to English courtiers to obtain their good offices with the English king. In 1475, Edward IV launched the long-threatened Yorkist invasion of France. Perhaps disappointed by the lukewarm support of his allies, Charles of Burgundy and

FRANCIS II of Brittany, or perhaps seeking a financial settlement from the start, Edward met Louis at Picquigny and accepted an annual French pension of £10,000 in return for withdrawing his army.

In 1477, the death of Charles of Burgundy turned Louis's attention toward dismantling the Burgundian state, which was now ruled by Charles's daughter Mary. Louis successfully seized the Duchy of Burgundy, the Somme towns, and territory in northern France, although Mary retained the Netherlands. When he died in August 1483, four months after Edward IV, Louis had almost completed the territorial unification of modern France, and had so strengthened the French state as to largely remove the threat of a successful future invasion from England.

See also Edward IV, Overthrow of; Edward IV, Restoration of

Further Reading: Kendall, Paul Murray, *Louis XI* (New York: W. W. Norton, 1971); Tyrrell, Joseph M., *Louis XI* (Boston: Twayne, 1980).

Louis de Gruthuyse. *See* Gruthuyse, Louis de, Seigneur de la Gruthuyse, Earl of Winchester

Love-Day of 1458

The date 24 March 1458 became known as a "love-day" because it witnessed the apparently successful culmination of HENRY VI's personal attempt to prevent civil war and to restore harmony to a bitterly divided English nobility. On that day, in a symbolic act of reconciliation, the sons and heirs of the noblemen who had been killed at the Battle of ST. ALBANS in 1455 walked arm in arm with the men responsible for their fathers' deaths in a solemn procession led by the king to St. Paul's Cathedral in LONDON.

After their fathers were slain at St. Albans by the forces of Richard PLANTAGENET, duke of York, and his allies Richard NEVILLE, earl of Salisbury, and Richard NEVILLE, earl of Warwick, the sons, Henry BEAUFORT, duke of Somerset, Henry PERCY, earl of Northumberland, and John CLIFFORD, Lord Clifford, clamored for revenge against the Yorkist lords. The country and its political system were thrown into disorder as noblemen of both parties recruited large retinues of armed followers to protect themselves and menace their enemies (see AFFINITY; BASTARD FEUDALISM). To end this turmoil, Henry VI summoned the English PEERAGE to London for a great council to be held in January 1458. York arrived with 400 followers and Salisbury and Warwick with 500 and 600, respectively; Somerset came accompanied by 800 men, and Northumberland; his brother, Thomas PERCY, Lord Egremont; and Clifford brought almost 1,500 between them. To prevent an outbreak of hostilities, tense city officials lodged the Yorkists within the city walls and the Lancastrian lords without, while maintaining a constant armed watch. Despite these precautions, Northumberland, Clifford, and Egremont tried unsuccessfully to ambush York and Salisbury as they rode from London to nearby Westminster.

The settlement eventually accepted by all parties, after long and acrimonious discussions mediated by the king, called for York to pay Somerset 5,000 marks, for Warwick to pay Clifford 1,000 marks, and for Salisbury to forgo fines previously levied on Northumberland and Egremont for hostile actions against the Nevilles during the course of the NEVILLE-PERCY FEUD. The Yorkists were also to endow the abbey at St. Albans with £45 per year for masses to be sung in perpetuity for the souls of the battle dead. The only reciprocal undertaking by a Lancastrian was Egremont's acceptance of a 4,000-mark bond to keep peace with the NEVILLE FAMILY for ten years. Announced on 24 March, and sealed later that day with a procession that saw Queen MARGARET OF ANJOU on the arm of York and Salisbury and Somerset walking side-by-side behind the king, the love-day reconciliation proved only a temporary triumph, for it failed to resolve the key political issue of the day—the exclusion of York and the Nevilles from the exercise of royal power, which was being increasingly monopolized by Queen Margaret and her supporters. By the spring of 1459, the love-day had been forgotten, and both sides were preparing for civil war.

Further Reading: Griffiths, Ralph A., *The Reign of King Henry VI* (Berkeley: University of California Press, 1981); Storey, R. L., *The End of the House of Lancaster,* 2d ed. (Stroud, Gloucestershire, UK: Sutton Publishing, 1999).

Lovell, Francis, Viscount Lovell (c. 1456–c. 1487)

A friend and loyal adherent of RICHARD III, Francis Lovell, Viscount Lovell, was a committed opponent of HENRY VII and a leader of Yorkist efforts to continue the dynastic struggle after 1485.

The son of a Yorkshire nobleman who abandoned his Lancastrian allegiance after EDWARD IV's victory in 1461, Lovell became a ward of the NEVILLE FAMILY at his father's death in 1465. Knighted by the duke of Gloucester while on campaign in SCOTLAND in 1480, Lovell was ennobled as Viscount Lovell by Edward IV in January 1483. Within a month of Edward's death in April 1483, Gloucester granted Lovell the estates of executed or exiled Woodville supporters in Oxfordshire and Berkshire, counties where the Lovell family already held lands. Lovell took a prominent part in Gloucester's coronation as Richard III in July 1483, and was soon thereafter appointed lord chamberlain in succession to the late William HASTINGS, Lord Hastings.

An influential figure at Richard's COURT, Lovell was the frequent recipient of gifts from persons anxious to gain access to the king. Richard attempted to create a power base for Lovell around his family estates in the Thames Valley, giving Lovell various regional lands and offices, including the important constableship of Wallingford Castle. The effort was only partially successful. Because of his northern associations, Lovell was still considered an outsider by local landholders in 1485, and the viscount focused his own activities during the reign on the court and his close association with the king (see RICHARD III, NORTHERN

AFFINITY OF). Along with William CATESBY and Sir Richard RATCLIFFE, Lovell became widely known as a member of Richard's inner circle of advisors. A popular satirical couplet of the time declared, "The cat [Catesby], the rat [Ratcliffe], and Lovell our dog [Lovell's emblem] / rule all England under a hog [referring to Richard III's white boar emblem]."

In August 1485, Lovell fought for Richard III at the Battle of BOSWORTH FIELD, escaping to Yorkshire after the king was killed. He remained in hiding until the spring of 1486, when he emerged to lead an unsuccessful attempt to capture Henry VII during a visit to York (see LOVELL-STAFFORD UPRISING). Fleeing to BURGUNDY, Lovell was welcomed by Duchess MARGARET OF YORK, sister of Richard III; the duchess dispatched Lovell to IRELAND to assist in the effort to replace Henry VII with Lambert SIMNEL, who was claiming to be Edward PLANTAGENET, earl of Warwick, Margaret's nephew. Landing in England with Simnel's force in May 1487, Lovell was probably killed at the Battle of STOKE on 16 June 1487. Although his body was not found on the field after the Yorkist defeat, there is no further record of him after the battle.

> **See also** Usurpation of 1483; Woodville Family; Yorkist Heirs (after 1485)
> **Further Reading:** Bennett, Michael J., *Lambert Simnel and the Battle of Stoke* (New York: St. Martin's Press, 1987); Horrox, Rosemary, *Richard III: A Study in Service* (Cambridge: Cambridge University Press, 1991); Ross, Charles, *Richard III* (Berkeley: University of California Press, 1981).

Lovell-Stafford Uprising (1486)

The Lovell-Stafford uprising of 1486 was the first significant Yorkist rebellion against the new regime of HENRY VII and the house of TUDOR.

In April 1486, eight months after the defeat and death of RICHARD III at the Battle of BOSWORTH FIELD, three Yorkist survivors of the battle, Francis LOVELL, Viscount Lovell, and the brothers Sir Thomas and Sir Humphrey Stafford, left SANCTUARY at Colchester Abbey and began inciting rebellion against Richard's supplanter. Lovell focused his efforts on the area of Yorkshire around Middleham Castle, a former stronghold of Richard III, while the Staffords based themselves in Worcestershire. Henry VII received news of the uprisings in Lincoln, while traveling north with a large retinue on the first royal progress of his reign. Fearing that Lovell would inspire a strong response in traditionally Yorkist areas, Henry hurried northward to deal with the Yorkshire phase of the rebellion, reaching the city of York by 23 April. However, the rebels, lacking any member of the house of YORK around whom to rally, had difficulty recruiting supporters. The king sent his uncle, Jasper TUDOR, duke of Bedford, into Yorkshire to offer pardons to everyone but Lovell, an action that effectively ended the northern part of the uprising and forced Lovell into hiding.

In Worcestershire, the Staffords, having no better success than Lovell, tried to keep their adherents together with rumors that Lovell had captured Henry VII. When these tales were replaced with definite news of Lovell's flight and the king's imminent arrival with an armed retinue, the uprising collapsed, and the Staffords fled again to sanctuary at Culham Abbey. Henry had the Staffords dragged from the abbey and tried for treason before the Court of King's Bench, the justices finally concluding that sanctuary was unavailable in cases of treason. Although both brothers were convicted, only Sir Humphrey was executed.

After finding temporary refuge with several Yorkist gentlemen in the north, Lovell fled to BURGUNDY and the court of Duchess MARGARET OF YORK, the sister of EDWARD IV. In the following year, he involved himself in the LAMBERT SIMNEL plot, a larger and better-organized Yorkist attempt to overthrow Henry VII. Inspired by the Lovell-Stafford uprising, several smaller Yorkist rebellions broke out in England in 1486. Although these were all quickly suppressed, many centered on the former lands and followers of the NEVILLE FAMILY and thereby confirmed for Henry the wisdom of his decision to imprison Edward PLANTAGENET, earl of Warwick, the grandson of Richard NEVILLE, the late earl of Warwick, and the last direct male descendent of the house of York.

See also North of England and the Wars of the Roses; Pole, John de la, Earl of Lincoln; Yorkist Heirs (after 1485)

Further Reading: Bennett, Michael J., *Lambert Simnel and the Battle of Stoke* (New York: St. Martin's Press, 1987).

Ludford Bridge, Battle of (1459)

Because it resulted in the Yorkist leaders' decision to abandon their troops and flee the country, the military encounter at Ludford Bridge on 12–13 October 1459 seemed a final and ignominious end to the attempt by Richard PLANTAGENET, duke of York, to control HENRY VI and the royal government.

After his victory over a Lancastrian force at the Battle of BLORE HEATH in September 1459, Richard NEVILLE, earl of Salisbury, evaded two other royal armies and joined forces with York at the duke's lordship of Ludlow in southern Shropshire. Also at Ludlow was Salisbury's son, Richard NEVILLE, earl of Warwick, with a portion of the CALAIS garrison, the only standing military force of any significance in fifteenth-century England. From Ludlow, York and the Nevilles sent the king a letter setting forth their reasons for taking up arms. Henry responded with a promise of pardon for York and all his adherents, if they would lay down their arms and surrender to the royal forces. Excepted from this offer were those responsible for the Battle of Blore Heath

This depiction of the aftermath of the Battle of Ludford Bridge shows Henry VI enthroned in triumph while the Yorkist lords (the Neville Earls of Salisbury and Warwick and the future Edward IV) flee to Calais. (Harleian MS 7353, British Library)

and the death there of the Lancastrian commander, James TOUCHET, Lord Audley. Because this exception certainly covered Salisbury and could probably be stretched to cover York and Warwick as well, the Yorkists declined to respond to the king's message. Thus, on 12 October, a royal army reached Ludford Bridge and made contact with an entrenched Yorkist force that was probably only one-third its size. Beyond the Nevilles, York had attracted little noble support to his cause, while the royal army comprised the followings of a great number of English peers (see PEERAGE). When the soldiers of the Calais garrison, perhaps remembering their sworn oath to the king, accepted the royal pardon and abandoned York, the Lancastrian advantage in numbers became even greater.

With the defection of the Calais garrison, York lost both his best troops and his most experienced commander, Andrew TROLLOPE, who took with him to the royal camp his knowledge of York's plans and dispositions. As evening approached, York ordered an ARTILLERY barrage to cover the withdrawal of himself, his two eldest sons, and Salisbury and Warwick to Ludlow Castle for the night. However, upon reaching the fortress, the Yorkist leaders collected their personal belongings and scattered in flight, York and his son Edmund PLANTAGENET, earl of Rutland, to IRELAND and Warwick, Salisbury, and York's son Edward, earl of March (see EDWARD IV), to Calais. Abandoned by its commanders, the Yorkist army quickly dispersed the following morning, leaving the Lancastrians to plunder the town of Ludlow and Queen MARGARET OF ANJOU and her supporters in uncontested control of the government.

See also Coventry Parliament; Neville Family
Further Reading: Haigh, Philip A., *The Military Campaigns of the Wars of the Roses* (Stroud, Gloucestershire, UK: Sutton Publishing, 1995); Hodges, Geoffrey, *Ludford Bridge and Mortimer's Cross* (Herefordshire: Long Aston Press, 1989).

Maintenance. *See* Livery and Maintenance

Malory, Sir Thomas (c. 1416–1471)

The life and career of Sir Thomas Malory, the author of *Le Morte d'Arthur (The Death of Arthur)*, one of the greatest literary works of medieval England, illustrates how the quarrel between the houses of LANCASTER and YORK forced even politically insignificant members of the English GENTRY to choose sides.

Because little is known about the writer of *Le Morte d'Arthur*, historians have debated which of several fifteenth-century Thomas Malorys was the author. The most likely candidate is Sir Thomas Malory of Newbold Revel, a Warwickshire knight whose sketchily preserved life best fits the few facts definitely known about the Arthurian writer. In the concluding paragraphs of *Le Morte d'Arthur*, the author stated that the book was completed in the ninth year of EDWARD IV by "Sir Thomas Malory, knight," and also requested his readers to pray "that God will send me good deliverance" (Malory, p. 750). The writer was thus an imprisoned knight who finished his work between 4 March 1469 and 3 March 1470.

Sir Thomas Malory of Newbold Revel was knighted about 1441, and served in PARLIAMENT in 1445 and again in 1449. Malory's life in the 1440s was unexceptional, but he spent most of the 1450s in various LONDON jails. His imprisonment was the result of a crime spree that began in January 1450 when Malory reportedly lay in ambush, with armed men, to murder Humphrey STAFFORD, duke

of Buckingham. In May and again in August, Malory was charged with rape and extortion. In June 1451, Malory and a band of accomplices were accused of stealing livestock, and, in July, Malory and his confederates threatened a house of Warwickshire monks, an action that led to the issuance of orders for his arrest. On 20 July, while Buckingham and a party of sixty men searched for him, Malory and his accomplices vandalized the duke's deer park at Caludon.

Because such violent crimes conflict with the chivalric values enunciated in *Le Morte d'Arthur*, the authorship of the Newbold Revel Malory has been disputed. However, the charges against him may have had more to do with local political rivalries than with outright criminality. Malory's transgressions, which probably originated in a private quarrel with Buckingham, soon entangled Malory in the national political struggle. After Malory's capture in July 1451, the Lancastrian government imprisoned him without trial through the mid-1450s. Because the Lancastrians seemed intent on keeping him confined, and because he had shown himself capable of raising and leading large numbers of men, Malory probably attracted the attention of the Yorkists, who in the late 1450s were seeking any possible supporters. In 1457, after being temporarily released on bail through the good offices of the Yorkist lord, William NEVILLE, Lord Fauconberg, Malory likely became an adherent of Richard NEVILLE, earl of Warwick, Fauconberg's nephew and Buckingham's chief rival in Warwickshire. In early 1462, Malory used Edward IV's general pardon to win his release and wipe out all charges against him. In late 1462, Malory participated in Edward's campaign against the Lancastrian-held castles in northern England (see entries for ALNWICK, BAMBURGH, and DUNSTANBURGH Castles).

Although no legal records confirm the statement in *Le Morte d'Arthur* that he wrote while a prisoner, Malory was one of only fifteen people excluded by name from a general pardon issued by Edward IV in July 1468. This exclusion raises the likelihood that Malory was arrested by the Yorkist government some time in 1468 and remained in confinement until the restoration of HENRY VI in October 1470, over six months after the stated completion of *Le Morte d'Arthur*. Although the reasons for Malory's imprisonment are unclear, the probability is that he was somehow involved in a shadowy Lancastrian conspiracy known as the CORNELIUS PLOT, which came to light in June 1468 (see also COOK, SIR THOMAS). Many of the men excluded from the pardon with Malory were Lancastrians implicated in the plot. According to his tombstone in Greyfriars Church in London, Malory died on 14 March 1471, only a month before the restoration of Edward IV would likely have again jeopardized his freedom.

Further Reading: Field, P. J. C., *The Life and Times of Sir Thomas Malory* (Cambridge: D. S. Brewer, 1993); Malory, Sir Thomas, *Le Morte d'Arthur,* edited by R. M. Lumiansky (London: Collier Macmillan Publishers, 1982).

Mancini, Dominic. *See The Usurpation of Richard III* (Mancini)

Manner and Guiding of the Earl of Warwick at Angers (1470)

Written probably at the direction of Richard NEVILLE, earl of Warwick, the *Manner and Guiding of the Earl of Warwick at Angers* was a contemporary newsletter that was intended to give the earl's friends and allies news of his activities in France in July and August 1470.

Designed to show Warwick's actions in the best light, the *Manner and Guiding* describes the negotiation of and reasons for the ANGERS AGREEMENT, a pact brokered by

LOUIS XI OF FRANCE to create an anti-Yorkist alliance between Warwick and Queen MARGARET OF ANJOU, the exiled wife of HENRY VI. The newsletter depicts Warwick as the initiator of the agreement and emphasizes Margaret's reluctance to accept the alliance, thus showing the earl's skill and patience in bringing the unreasonable queen to agreement and portraying him as calm and deliberate, not as a desperate man grasping at his last political option. To reassure his English RETAINERS, whose support was vital to his coming enterprise, Warwick needed to project such an image.

Although obviously a piece of pro-Warwick PROPAGANDA, and contradicting some of the dates and events given in other contemporary accounts, the *Manner and Guiding* is nonetheless an important source of information for the events of the summer of 1470. It was written by someone (or perhaps by several persons) who were eyewitnesses to the discussions at Angers, and it was produced immediately after the conclusion of those discussions, between 4 August 1470, the date given for Warwick's departure from Angers, and 9 September, the date Warwick's invasion fleet sailed for England. The newsletter was probably distributed in England either during the weeks before the invasion, to prepare Warwick's supporters for his landing, or during the invasion itself in mid-September, to reassure the members of Warwick's AFFINITY that the earl was acting with the blessing and support of the French king and the Lancastrian queen. If modern historians must use the *Manner and Guiding* with care, the document seems to have admirably achieved its original purpose, for Warwick received a large and enthusiastic response when he disembarked in the West Country on 13 September.

See also Edward IV, Overthrow of
Further Reading: Hammond, P. W., *The Battles of Barnet and Tewkesbury* (New York: St. Martin's Press, 1990); Hicks, Michael, *Warwick the Kingmaker* (Oxford: Blackwell Publishers, 1998).

March, Earl of. *See* Edward IV

March on London (1461)

By systematically plundering Yorkist towns and properties as it marched south toward LONDON in the winter of 1461, the army of Queen MARGARET OF ANJOU created great fear in the capital and across southern England. This fear, and the unpopularity it won for HENRY VI and the house of LANCASTER, allowed the Yorkist leaders to hold London and, with the city's support, proclaim a rival king of the house of YORK.

By mid-January 1461, the army that weeks earlier had defeated and killed Richard PLANTAGENET, duke of York, at the Battle of WAKEFIELD, was joined at York by Queen Margaret and the troops she had obtained in SCOTLAND. Although a large part of the Lancastrian force consisted of ill-disciplined northerners, Welshmen, and Margaret's French and Scottish MERCENARIES, it also contained the retinues of Henry BEAUFORT, duke of Somerset; Henry PERCY, earl of Northumberland; and John CLIFFORD, Lord Clifford, the sons of men killed by the Yorkists at the Battle of ST. ALBANS in 1455. As the army marched south, the queen and her commanders, believing that they were at last in a position to destroy their enemies, encouraged their troops to pillage any lands or towns belonging or connected to York. As a result, Grantham, Stamford, Peterborough, Huntingdon, Royston, and other Yorkist sites on the army's line of march suffered severely. News of the destruction spread panic across the south, and especially in London, where shops were closed, valuables hidden, and streets deserted. Always fearful of Scots and northerners, whom they considered wild and uncivilized, large numbers of southerners flocked to London unbidden, seeking to join Richard NEVILLE, earl of Warwick, the one Yorkist leader who seemed capable of protecting the south from Lancastrian pillage (see NORTH OF ENGLAND AND THE WARS OF THE ROSES).

On 12 February, Warwick left London accompanied by Henry VI, who had been in Yorkist custody since July. Besides the men recruited by fear of Lancastrian vengeance, the Yorkist army included RETAINERS of the NEVILLE FAMILY; the retinues of John MOWBRAY, duke of Norfolk, and John de la POLE, earl of Suffolk; and even a troop of handgunners sent by Duke PHILIP of BURGUNDY. On 17 February, Queen Margaret's army defeated Warwick at the Battle of ST. ALBANS. To make matters worse for the Yorkists, the Lancastrians secured the person of Henry VI, who was reunited with his wife and his son, Prince EDWARD OF LANCASTER.

Without a king, the Yorkist regime was ended; with Warwick in flight and a Lancastrian army approaching London, the Yorkist cause also seemed at an end. What saved it was the quick action of York's son, Edward, earl of March, who hurried east from WALES to join Warwick, and London's fear of the Lancastrian army, which skillful Yorkist PROPAGANDA exploited by exaggerating the destruction the army had caused on its march south. Demanding supplies, money, and the city's submission, Queen Margaret got the first two but not the last. After sending a deputation of noble ladies to the queen to beg her not to plunder London (see JACQUETTA OF LUXEMBOURG), city authorities agreed to admit a small Lancastrian contingent. But sentiment in the capital was strongly pro-Yorkist, and the citizens shut the gates against even this force.

On 27 February, March and Warwick entered London to a joyous welcome. Young, vigorous, and handsome, March already seemed more regal to the Londoners than Henry VI ever had. Meanwhile, Margaret, unwilling to launch an assault on the city, withdrew her army into the Lancastrian north. On 3 March, the earl of March was proclaimed king as EDWARD IV, and the next day he was hastily crowned at St. Paul's Cathedral. Thanks in part to the terror generated in the south by the Lancastrian march on London, the house of York held the capital and had a king who was ready to fight to secure his throne.

See also Towton, Battle of
Further Reading: Griffiths, Ralph A., *The Reign of King Henry VI* (Berkeley: University of California Press, 1981); Haigh, Philip A., *The Military Campaigns of the Wars of the Roses* (Stroud,

Gloucestershire, UK: Sutton Publishing, 1995); Ross, Charles, *The Wars of the Roses* (New York: Thames and Hudson, 1987).

Margaret of Anjou, Queen of England (1430–1482)

Queen Margaret of Anjou, wife of HENRY VI, was the effective leader of the house of LANCASTER from the mid-1450s to 1471.

The daughter of René, duke of Anjou, a French nobleman with unrealized claims to various European Crowns, Margaret was be-trothed to Henry VI in 1444. Her marriage sealed an Anglo-French truce negotiated with her uncle, CHARLES VII, by Henry's ambassador, William de la POLE, earl of Suffolk. Married to the king on 23 April 1445, Margaret was crowned in Westminster Abbey on 30 May. Intelligent and energetic, the young queen at first took little part in politics, although she soon associated herself with Suffolk and the COURT faction, which held paramount influence with Henry in the late 1440s. She also became a strong advocate for the peace policy that had made her queen, and

The earl of Shrewsbury presents a book of romances to Queen Margaret of Anjou in about 1445. (Royal MS 15 E VI f. 2, British Library)

she helped ensure the implementation of Henry's promise to surrender the county of Maine to the French in 1448.

In 1450, the loss of Normandy swept Suffolk from power. Embarrassed by financial weakness and shackled by a king who was unfit to rule, Suffolk's unpopular government collapsed amid charges of treason leveled by such opponents as Richard PLANTAGENET, duke of York, the childless king's probable heir. As an increasingly bitter rivalry developed between York and Edmund BEAUFORT, duke of Somerset, Suffolk's successor as chief minister, the queen, who viewed York as a threat to the throne, identified herself closely with Somerset. In August 1453, Henry VI fell into an uncommunicative state that rendered him incapable of ruling (see HENRY VI, ILLNESS OF); in October, Margaret gave birth to a son, Prince EDWARD OF LANCASTER, who displaced York as heir. To safeguard the rights of her child, Margaret sought the regency, but her claim was rejected in favor of York, who was named protector by PARLIAMENT in March 1454.

Henry's recovery ended the FIRST PROTECTORATE in 1455, but the continuing efforts of Margaret and Somerset to destroy York led the duke and his new allies, Richard NEVILLE, earl of Salisbury, and his son, Richard NEVILLE, earl of Warwick, to take up arms. At the Battle of ST. ALBANS in May 1455, the Yorkists killed Somerset and seized the still ailing king, thereby instituting the SECOND PROTECTORATE. In 1456, Henry recovered sufficiently to dismiss York as protector but remained too weak-minded to govern effectively. Over the next three years, Margaret assumed leadership of the anti-York faction. Although she participated in Henry's LOVE-DAY reconciliation of 1458, the queen largely withdrew her husband from LONDON and kept him under her influence in the Midlands.

With the outbreak of war in 1459, Margaret outmaneuvered her enemies at the Battle of LUDFORD BRIDGE in October, and York and the Nevilles fled the country. In November, the queen used the COVENTRY PARLIAMENT to strip her opponents of their lands

and offices through the passage of bills of ATTAINDER. However, in the summer of 1460, Warwick captured the king at the Battle of NORTHAMPTON, allowing York to return from IRELAND to lay formal claim to the Crown. When Parliament passed the compromise Act of ACCORD, which left Henry king but made York his heir, Margaret, who was in WALES with her son, rejected the disinheritance of the prince and gathered forces to oppose the Yorkist regime. These armies slew York and Salisbury at the Battle of WAKEFIELD in December 1460 and then defeated Warwick and recovered the king at the Battle of ST. ALBANS in February 1461. Because her unruly northern army had caused much destruction on its march south (see MARCH ON LONDON), London was wary of admitting the queen's men, and Margaret eventually retreated, allowing Edward, earl of March, York's son, to enter the capital and be proclaimed king as EDWARD IV. On 29 March, Edward defeated the Lancastrians at the Battle of TOWTON, forcing Margaret to flee into SCOTLAND with her son, husband, and chief supporters.

The regency government of JAMES III gave the Lancastrians refuge in return for the surrender of BERWICK. In 1462, Margaret traveled to FRANCE and convinced LOUIS XI to give her a small force, with which she invaded Northumberland and captured the castles of BAMBURGH, DUNSTANBURGH, and ALNWICK. In the next year, the three fortresses were lost, recaptured, and lost again; Margaret and her son were reduced to poverty and several times forced to wander lost and alone along the northern coasts. In August 1463, Margaret and the prince crossed to France, where they remained until 1471. Although the queen engaged in continuous plotting against the Yorkist regime, the Lancastrian cause was dead until revived in 1470 by Warwick, who, having lost influence with Edward IV, sought to reclaim his political dominance by restoring Henry VI. Having formerly accused the queen of many vile things, and having questioned the legitimacy of the prince, Warwick was cordially hated by Margaret, who only consented to talk with him after he made humble submission on his knees. Encouraged by Louis XI, Margaret finally accepted Warwick as an ally and agreed to marry her son to his daughter, Anne NEVILLE (see ANGERS AGREEMENT).

In October 1470, Warwick restored Henry VI, who had been a prisoner in the TOWER OF LONDON since 1465. Margaret and her son landed in England on 14 April 1471, the day of Warwick's death at the Battle of BARNET. Persuaded by supporters to continue the fight, Margaret was defeated and her son was killed at the Battle of TEWKESBURY in May. Captured three days later, she was carried to London, where her husband was murdered on 21 May, ending the house of LANCASTER. Margaret remained in captivity until 1475, when Louis XI ransomed her as part of the Treaty of Picquigny. Forced by the treaty to renounce all claims to the English throne, she was required by Louis to surrender all rights to her French possessions in return for a pension. Margaret died in poverty in August 1482.

> **Further Reading:** Dunn, Diana, "Margaret of Anjou, Queen Consort of Henry VI: A Reassessment of Her Role, 1445–53," in Rowena E. Archer, ed., *Crown, Government and People in the Fifteenth Century* (New York: St. Martin's Press, 1995), pp. 107–144; Erlanger, Philippe, *Margaret of Anjou: Queen of England* (London: Elek Books, 1970); Griffiths, Ralph A., *The Reign of King Henry VI* (Berkeley: University of California Press, 1981).

Margaret of York, Duchess of Burgundy (1446–1503)

After 1485, Margaret of York, sister of EDWARD IV and RICHARD III, used her wealth and influence as duchess of BURGUNDY to support plots to overthrow HENRY VII and restore the house of YORK.

The daughter of Richard PLANTAGENET, duke of York, and his wife, Cecily NEVILLE, Margaret was fourteen when her eldest brother assumed the throne as Edward IV. In March 1466, the king commissioned Richard NEVILLE, earl of Warwick, and William HASTINGS, Lord Hastings, to negotiate Margaret's marriage with CHARLES, Count of Charolais, son of Duke PHILIP of Burgundy. Because the marriage was to be part of a political and commercial alliance between England and Burgundy, LOUIS XI of FRANCE stalled the negotiations with counter proposals until after Philip's death in 1467. Charles, now duke, reopened talks and concluded an agreement in September. Announced to PARLIAMENT in May 1468, two months before Margaret's wedding in Burgundy, the Anglo-Burgundian agreement convinced Louis XI to facilitate the reconciliation of Warwick and MARGARET OF ANJOU, an alliance that enabled the earl to overthrow Edward IV and restore HENRY VI in the autumn of 1470 (see ANGERS AGREEMENT; EDWARD IV, OVERTHROW OF). Edward IV immediately fled to his sister and brother-in-law in Burgundy, where Warwick's agreement with Louis to make war on Charles convinced the duke to assist his brother-in-law in regaining the English throne. Margaret was instrumental in detaching George PLANTAGENET, duke of Clarence, her favorite brother, from his alliance with Warwick; when Edward IV returned to England in March 1471, Clarence rejoined his brother with a large body of much needed troops.

As duchess of Burgundy, Margaret was a noted patron of the arts and of the Church. By 1471, the English merchant William CAXTON had entered her service, probably as a financial advisor. Caxton showed the duchess his half finished English translation of Raoul Lefevre's *Recueil des Histoires de Troie,* a retelling of the legends of Troy. Margaret corrected Caxton's English and encouraged him to complete the work. By late 1471, Caxton was on the duchess's service in Cologne, where he learned the use of the new movable-type printing press. The duchess was thus partially responsible for the first book ever printed in English, Caxton's 1476 edition of *The History of Troy.*

After the death of Richard III and the overthrow of the house of York at the Battle of BOSWORTH FIELD in 1485, Margaret, whose husband had died in 1477, became a persistent supporter of efforts to overthrow Henry VII. Her COURT became a haven for Yorkists exiles, many of whom joined Lambert SIMNEL in IRELAND in 1487. Margaret supported Simnel, who claimed to be her nephew Edward PLANTAGENET, earl of Warwick, with men and money. She provided similar support to Perkin WARBECK, who claimed to be Edward IV's son Richard PLANTAGENET, duke of York. In 1492, Margaret met and publicly recognized Warbeck as York, whom she had last seen in 1480, three years before he disappeared in the TOWER OF LONDON (see PRINCES IN THE TOWER). Whether her acceptance of Warbeck rested more on hope than belief is now difficult to gauge; however, she wrote letters to the courts of Europe affirming her belief and helped sustain Warbeck for six years as a significant threat to Henry VII and the house of TUDOR. Although Warbeck's eventual capture and confession of his imposture forced Margaret to ask Henry to pardon her, she remained a partisan of York until her death in November 1503.

Further Reading: Weightman, Christine, *Margaret of York* (Stroud, Gloucestershire, UK: Alan Sutton, 1993).

Mary of Gueldres, Queen of Scotland (d. 1463)

Hoping to make territorial gains at England's expense, Queen Mary of Gueldres involved SCOTLAND in the WARS OF THE ROSES in the early 1460s.

The daughter of the duke of Gueldres and a kinswoman of Duke PHILIP of BURGUNDY, Mary of Gueldres married JAMES II of Scotland in July 1449. She became regent for her eight-year-old-son JAMES III in August 1460, when her husband was killed by the explosion of one of his own ARTILLERY pieces at the siege of Roxburgh Castle, a border fortress that James was attempting to seize while the English were distracted by civil war. Mary successfully completed the siege, and then, in December, welcomed Queen MARGARET OF ANJOU to Scotland. With HENRY VI in Yorkist custody since the Battle

of NORTHAMPTON in July, and Prince EDWARD OF LANCASTER disinherited by the Act of ACCORD in October, Margaret required military assistance, and Mary was eager to turn that need to Scotland's advantage. For several days over the New Year, the Scottish and Lancastrian queens and their sons met at Lincluden Abbey to conclude a treaty whereby Mary agreed to supply Margaret with Scottish troops in return for the surrender of BERWICK. The queens sealed the pact by arranging a future marriage between Prince Edward and one of James III's sisters. Thus, when Margaret departed for England in January 1461, she was accompanied by a large force of Scottish MERCENARIES.

After EDWARD IV's victory at the Battle of TOWTON in March 1461, the Lancastrian royal family fled into Scotland. Although the Yorkists held the throne, the house of LANCASTER retained sufficient authority in the north to effect the surrender of Berwick to the Scots on 25 April. Mary and the regency council allowed the Lancastrians to use the town as a base for raids into England. These incursions compelled Edward IV to send Richard NEVILLE, earl of Warwick, to Scotland to convince Mary to abandon the Lancastrian cause. Pressed to support the Lancastrians by a COUNCIL faction under Bishop James KENNEDY of St. Andrews and pressured to favor the Yorkists by her uncle the duke of Burgundy, Mary gave Warwick an evasive answer but readily agreed to Queen Margaret's request for money to travel to FRANCE.

With Margaret's influence removed, and with Edward IV threatening to stir up trouble in northern Scotland by concluding the Treaty of WESTMINSTER-ARDTORNISH with the rebellious Lord of the Isles, Mary and the council agreed to a three-month truce with the Yorkist government in the summer of 1462. However, Margaret's return to Scotland in the autumn with a body of French mercenaries revived Mary's hopes of using the English conflict to achieve Scottish expansion. In 1463, several Scottish armies invaded England in concert with Lancastrian forces, including one in June that was accompanied by both

Mary and James III. When Warwick routed this army in July, queen and council lost all enthusiasm for the Lancastrian cause. By Mary's death in the following November, Margaret and her son had sailed for France, and a Scottish envoy was preparing for peace talks with Edward IV.

See also North of England and the Wars of the Roses

Further Reading: Macdougall, Norman, *James III* (Edinburgh: J. Donald, 1982); McGladdery, Christine, *James II* (Edinburgh: John Donald Publishers, 1990).

Memoirs (Commines)

Although particularly useful as a source for fifteenth-century French and Burgundian history, the *Memoirs* of Philippe de Commines (or Commynes), a Burgundian nobleman, are also an important source for English politics and Anglo-French relations in the 1470s.

In 1464, Commines (1447–1511) entered the service of CHARLES, Count of Charolais, who, upon becoming duke of BURGUNDY in 1467, made Commines his chamberlain. In 1472, Commines defected to the service of LOUIS XI of FRANCE, becoming one of the king's most trusted advisors. His influence at COURT diminished after 1477 and vanished completely after Louis's death in 1483, when Commines lost the lands and offices he had acquired. He was imprisoned for two years until 1489, when, in an effort to justify his career, he began writing his *Memoirs*. Running eventually to eight books, the *Memoirs* were completed in 1498.

An eyewitness to many important English interactions with both Burgundy and France in the 1460s and 1470s, Commines was personally acquainted with EDWARD IV, whom he met in 1470 and 1475, and with many leading figures at the Yorkist court. While at CALAIS in 1470, he had contact with Richard NEVILLE, earl of Warwick, and he was present in 1475 at the meeting of Edward IV and Louis XI at Picquigny, where he helped negotiate the Anglo-French treaty. Besides the French campaign of 1475 and the general course of contemporary diplomacy in northwestern Europe, Commines is particularly useful for Warwick's activities in France in 1470 and Edward IV's Burgundian exile in 1470–1471 (see EDWARD IV, OVERTHROW OF). Although an eyewitness to many of the events he describes, Commines also wrote with a moral purpose, seeking to present events as lessons on the proper conduct of government. He wanted government to become more rational and diplomacy to supplant military strength as the chief tool of foreign relations.

Because Commines sometimes altered events to suit his moral purpose, modern historians use the *Memoirs* with caution. Such care is particularly warranted for English affairs, about which Commines often had no firsthand knowledge and for which he was forced to rely upon informants' accounts and on rumors circulating in the French court. Commines wrote in an engaging style and had a gift for detail and psychological analysis, but his reliance on secondhand information and on his own memory, often at twenty years' remove from events, significantly diminishes the accuracy of the *Memoirs* at many points. For English history, an example of this problem is Commines's condemnation of RICHARD III, for whose reign he had to rely solely upon English informants encountered at the French court, which meant that most of his information came from exiled followers of Henry Tudor, earl of Richmond (see HENRY VII), and perhaps even from the earl himself.

Further Reading: Commines, Philippe de, *The Memoirs of Philippe de Commynes*, edited by Samuel Kinser, translated by Isabelle Cazeaux. 2 vols. (Columbia: University of South Carolina Press, 1969–1973); the text of Commines's *Memoirs* is also available on the Richard III Society Web site at <http://www.r3.org/bookcase/de_commynes/decom_1.html>.

Men-at-Arms

Expected to practice the use of arms from an early age, male members of the landowning PEERAGE and GENTRY families of England comprised the ranks of the men-at-arms, a general term for those soldiers in civil war armies who had the greatest training, experience, and equipage for war. Most battles during the WARS OF THE ROSES were decided by the outcome of hand-to-hand combat between dismounted men-at-arms.

Men-at-arms and their RETAINERS—the only component of most armies that could be considered professional—were almost always only a small portion of any civil war force, which might also contain ARTILLERY units and troops of ARCHERS, foreign MERCENARIES, town and county militias, and tenants of landed noblemen (see ARMIES, RECRUITMENT OF). Men-at-arms fought in contingents led by the nobleman or knight who had retained them—William HASTINGS, Lord Hastings, recruited forty men-at-arms for EDWARD IV's invasion of FRANCE in 1475—or as part of the corps of knights or household servants of the king. In his grand cavalry charge at the Battle of BOSWORTH FIELD in 1485, RICHARD III was accompanied into combat by his loyal retinue of men-at-arms.

By the Wars of the Roses, English men-at-arms usually fought on foot, both to improve morale by standing with their men and to make themselves smaller targets for archers (see GENERALSHIP). Because they were generally encased in full ARMOR and their horses were tethered far to the rear, men-at-arms were often less able to escape a lost battle than other soldiers. Especially among the wealthier nobility and gentry, many men-at-arms in rich harness, such as Richard NEVILLE, earl of Warwick, at the Battle of BARNET in 1471, were slain and plundered by common soldiers who caught them as they fled the field.

To the extent allowed by their financial means, men-at-arms entered combat wearing plate armor and wielding the heavy maces, battle-axes, and other WEAPONRY designed to crush the newer, stronger type of armor. Often deployed in lines behind ranks of archers, whose volleys usually opened a fight, contingents of men-at-arms, supported by other more lightly armored foot soldiers, engaged in close combat that usually decided the battle (see BATTLES, NATURE OF). Because

men-at-arms formed the seasoned core of most civil war armies, a preponderance of such experienced troops could overcome an overall inferiority of numbers. For instance, Edward IV's victories at the Battle of MORTIMER'S CROSS in 1461 and the Battle of TEWKESBURY in 1471 are in part ascribed to his superiority on both fields in trained men-at-arms.

Further Reading: Boardman, Andrew W., *The Medieval Soldier in the Wars of the Roses* (Stroud, Gloucestershire, UK: Sutton Publishing, 1998); Gillingham, John, *The Wars of the Roses* (Baton Rouge: Louisiana State University Press, 1981); Goodman, Anthony, *The Wars of the Roses* (New York: Dorset Press, 1981); Ross, Charles, *The Wars of the Roses* (London: Thames and Hudson, 1987).

Mercenaries

Most English armies during the WARS OF THE ROSES contained at least a small contingent of paid troops recruited outside England, or a company of soldiers supplied by a foreign ally. Besides offering an alternative source of manpower when armies had to be raised quickly, such mercenary forces also provided commanders with specialists in particular military skills, such as the use of handguns or crossbows, which were more highly developed on the continent than in England.

Foreign mercenaries fought on many English battlefields. The Lancastrian army at the Battle of MORTIMER'S CROSS in 1461 contained Breton, Welsh, and Irish troops. Richard NEVILLE, earl of Warwick, probably had a troop of Burgundian handgunners at the Battle of ST. ALBANS in February 1461, as did EDWARD IV at the Battle of TOWTON a month later. Scottish troops accompanied the army of Queen MARGARET OF ANJOU on its MARCH ON LONDON in early 1461, and fought for the Lancastrian queen, along with French and Welsh mercenaries, at the subsequent Battles of St. Albans and Towton. Between 1461 and 1464, the Lancastrian leadership, then in exile in SCOTLAND, employed Scottish troops on numerous raids into northern England. Through the 1462 CHINON AGREEMENT with LOUIS XI, Queen Margaret obtained the services of Pierre de

BRÉZÉ and a troop of French mercenaries, while Edward IV returned to England in 1471 leading a Burgundian force supplied by Duke CHARLES. The army that Henry Tudor, earl of Richmond (see HENRY VII), led at the Battle of BOSWORTH FIELD in 1485 contained French, Scottish, and Welsh contingents, while the army of Yorkist rebels that Henry faced two years later at the Battle of STOKE included many German and Irish mercenaries (see SIMNEL, LAMBERT).

The use and size of foreign mercenary forces increased as the wars progressed and English enthusiasm for the struggle declined. Also, defeat in England and the subsequent need to survive in and return from a foreign country, a situation faced by the Lancastrians in 1461 and the Yorkists in 1470 and 1485, gave new urgency to the need for raising foreign mercenaries. However, during a civil war, when a king or claimant to the throne required good relations with the people he sought to rule, the use of mercenaries was problematic. Because they were foreigners, thought to be more interested in opportunities for plunder than in the political success of their employers, mercenaries often inspired fear among the populace. The Lancastrian cause suffered from the panic that Queen Margaret's Scottish (and northern English) troops caused in LONDON and southern England in February 1461. Margaret's later willingness to surrender BERWICK and CALAIS for Scottish and French troops proved to be a great PROPAGANDA boon for the Yorkists, almost canceling out the benefits the queen derived from obtaining the mercenaries. In his *MEMOIRS*, Philippe de Commines described the French troops who accompanied Richmond to England in 1485 as "the loosest and most profligate persons . . . that could be found" (Boardman, p. 90), and the earl threatened harsh penalties for any soldier who committed theft or violence. Although important in battle, foreign mercenaries, if unruly or uncontrolled, were a serious detriment on the march.

The employment of foreign mercenaries also turned the Wars of the Roses into extensions of non-English conflicts. In 1471, French

assistance for the house of LANCASTER during the READEPTION of HENRY VI elicited Burgundian aid for the house of YORK from the personally Lancastrian duke of BURGUNDY. The age-old alliance between FRANCE and Scotland, combined with the generally anti-French stance of the Yorkists, meant that Scottish assistance went more often to the Lancastrians, while the generally pro-Yorkist feeling in IRELAND brought many Irish troops into Yorkist armies. However, mercenary forces of many nationalities fought on both sides during the civil wars.

See also Armies, Recruitment of
Further Reading: Boardman, Andrew W., *The Medieval Soldier in the Wars of the Roses* (Stroud, Gloucestershire, UK: Sutton Publishing, 1998); Gillingham, John, *The Wars of the Roses* (Baton Rouge: Louisiana State University Press, 1981); Goodman, Anthony, *The Wars of the Roses* (New York: Dorset Press, 1981); Ross, Charles, *The Wars of the Roses* (London: Thames and Hudson, 1987).

Military Campaigns, Duration of

Although warfare between Englishmen for control of the government or possession of the Crown occurred from the 1450s to the 1490s, fighting was not continuous throughout the period. The military campaigns of the WARS OF THE ROSES were few, intermittent, and brief.

From the first Battle of ST. ALBANS in May 1455 to the Battle of STOKE in June 1487, adherents of the houses of LANCASTER and YORK engaged in thirteen major battles, such as those at TOWTON, BARNET, and BOSWORTH FIELD; several smaller encounters, such as the Battles of TWT HILL and HEXHAM; and numerous raids, rebellions, and assaults on castles. However, most of this fighting across a span of more than thirty years was compressed into a few active phases of two to three years, within which large armed forces were actually in the field for only a matter of weeks. The main periods of active campaigning occurred between the autumn of 1459 and the spring of 1461, the summer of 1469 and the spring of 1471, and in the autumn of 1483 and the summers of 1485 and 1487.

Being an island kingdom, England had not experienced the nearly continuous warfare that the HUNDRED YEARS WAR and other conflicts and rebellions had brought in the previous century to FRANCE, BURGUNDY, and other continental states. As a result, England lacked the standing armies (and the arbitrary taxation that supported them) that had developed in France under CHARLES VII and in Burgundy under Dukes PHILIP and CHARLES. The only ongoing military establishments in fifteenth-century England were a royal bodyguard of 200 archers created in 1468, the 1,000-man CALAIS garrison, and the forces raised at Crown expense by the wardens of the marches to defend the borders with SCOTLAND. The important role that elements of the Calais garrison had in the outcome of several battles, such as LUDFORD BRIDGE in 1459, illustrated how nonmilitarized England was.

This lack of military experience meant that England lagged behind the continent in the use of ARTILLERY and handguns and in the development of military fortification. Whereas an avoidance of pitched battle and a highly developed siegecraft characterized continental warfare, the Wars of the Roses witnessed almost no sieges, no sacks of major towns, little pillage or destruction of the countryside, and a series of brief campaigns and pitched battles, the winner of which usually gained immediate control of the government. In his *MEMOIRS,* the Burgundian chronicler Philippe de Commines observed that the English "were the most inclined to give battle" and that when fighting erupted in England "one or the other of the rivals is master within ten days or less" (Gillingham, p. 28). With sieges largely unnecessary and the problem of supply making it difficult to keep large armies in the field for long periods, active campaigning, as shown in the following table, occupied less than a year and a half of the more than thirty-year period encompassing the Wars of the Roses.

See also Armies, Recruitment of; Armies, Supplying of

Further Reading: Gillingham, John, *The Wars of the Roses* (Baton Rouge: Louisiana State University Press, 1981); Goodman, Anthony, *The Wars of the Roses* (New York: Dorset Press, 1981); Ross, Charles, *The Wars of the Roses* (London: Thames and Hudson, 1987).

Table 2   Duration of Major Campaigns, 1455–1487★

Campaign	Battles	Duration
1455: 18–22 May	St. Albans	5 days
1459: mid-September to mid-October	Blore Heath, Ludford Bridge	30 days
1460: 26 June–19 July; 9–30 December	Northampton, Wakefield	46 days
1461: 2–26 February; 13 March–1 May	Mortimer's Cross, St. Albans, Towton	75 days
1462–1463: 25 October–6 January	Lancastrian seizures and Yorkist recaptures of the Northumbrian castles of Alnwick, Bamburgh, and Dunstanburgh	74 days
1464: 24 April–15 May	Hedgeley Moor, Hexham	22 days
1469: 5–26 July	Edgecote	22 days
1470: 6 March–14 April; 13 September–6 October	Losecote Field; Overthrow of Edward IV	64 days
1471: 14 March–27 May	Barnet, Tewkesbury; repulse of the Bastard of Fauconberg's assault on London	75 days
1483: 18 October–8 November	Buckingham's Rebellion	22 days
1485: 7–22 August	Bosworth Field	16 days
1487: 4–16 June	Stoke	13 days
Total		**464 days or 66.3 weeks**

★Adapted from Anthony Goodman, *The Wars of the Roses,* New York: Dorset Press, 1981, pp. 227–228.

Montagu, Marquis of. *See* Neville, John, Earl of Northumberland and Marquis of Montagu

More, Sir Thomas. *See The History of King Richard III* (More)

Mortimer Claim to the Throne. *See* Richard II, Deposition of

Mortimer's Cross, Battle of (1461)

The Yorkist victory at the Battle of Mortimer's Cross on 2 February 1461 boosted the confidence of Edward, earl of March (see EDWARD IV), then conducting his first independent command, and brightened the future of the Yorkist cause, then reeling from the recent death of Richard PLANTAGENET, duke of York, at the Battle of WAKEFIELD.

In January 1461, while campaigning along the Welsh border, the eighteen-year-old earl of March heard of his father's death. Anxious to return to LONDON and join forces with his chief ally, Richard NEVILLE, earl of Warwick, March was preparing to leave Gloucester when he learned of a Lancastrian army marching out of WALES from the northwest. This force, commanded by Jasper TUDOR, earl of Pembroke, half brother of HENRY VI, and James BUTLER, earl of Wiltshire, consisted of Pembroke's Welsh tenants and a band of French and Irish MERCENARIES. Turning north, March encountered the Lancastrian force about seventeen miles northwest of Hereford near a place called Mortimer's Cross.

After several hours of maneuvering for position, the two armies clashed at midday on 2 February. Wiltshire, leading the experienced mercenaries, overpowered the Yorkist right wing and drove it from the field. Owen TUDOR, Pembroke's father, tried to outflank the Yorkist left under Sir William HERBERT, but Tudor was himself outflanked in the process, and his force disintegrated. In the center, March eventually overcame stiff resistance from Pembroke's men and swept the field of Lancastrians. After re-forming, Wiltshire's mercenaries supposedly sat down, awaiting the outcome of the battle. When Pembroke's line broke, the mercenaries marched off in search of an employer who could pay them.

Pembroke and Wiltshire both escaped the field, but Owen Tudor was taken and executed in the marketplace at Hereford. After the battle, March revealed that at dawn on 2 February he had seen three suns rise, a miraculous sight that he had taken as an omen of victory in the coming battle. March was so affected by this sign that he later adopted the sunburst as his emblem (see SUN IN SPLENDOR/SUNBURST BADGE). Filled with confidence after his victory, March returned to London, where one month later he was acclaimed as King Edward IV.

Further Reading: Haigh, Philip A., *The Military Campaigns of the Wars of the Roses* (Stroud, Gloucestershire, UK: Sutton Publishing, 1995); Hodges, Geoffrey, *Ludford Bridge and Mortimer's Cross* (Herefordshire: Long Aston Press, 1989).

Morton, John, Cardinal Archbishop of Canterbury (c. 1420–1500)

A longtime Lancastrian, John Morton was a leader of the opposition to RICHARD III during the last phase of the WARS OF THE ROSES and a likely source for Sir Thomas More's later history of Richard's reign.

Morton studied law at Oxford and by the late 1440s became a noted ecclesiastical lawyer in the Court of Arches, the chief court of the archdiocese of Canterbury. Through the patronage of Thomas BOURCHIER, archbishop of Canterbury, Morton won appointment to the COUNCIL of HENRY VI and acquired numerous offices in both church and state throughout the 1450s. During the military campaigns of 1461, Morton accompanied the army of Queen MARGARET OF ANJOU, being present at the Battle of ST. ALBANS in February. After EDWARD IV's victory at the Battle of TOWTON in March, Morton fled to SCOTLAND with the Lancastrian royal family and shared the hardships experienced over the next two years by Margaret and her son,

Prince EDWARD OF LANCASTER. In 1463, he accompanied the queen into exile in FRANCE, and in 1470 helped arrange the alliance between Margaret and her former enemy, Richard NEVILLE, earl of Warwick (see ANGERS AGREEMENT).

Returning to England in September 1470, Morton became an important figure in the READEPTION government of Henry VI. After the death of Warwick at the Battle of BARNET in April 1471, Morton rejoined Margaret and her son, who were newly landed from France. When the Lancastrian cause came to ruin with the prince's death at the Battle of TEWKESBURY in May 1471, Morton submitted to Edward IV and was rapidly taken into royal service. He served on various diplomatic missions and helped negotiate the Treaty of Picquigny with LOUIS XI in 1475. By the king's death in 1483, Morton was a royal councilor and bishop of Ely. Because Morton was loyal to EDWARD V and thus an obstacle to the duke of Gloucester's assumption of the throne, Gloucester arrested Morton at the infamous COUNCIL MEETING OF 13 JUNE 1483 (see USURPATION OF 1483).

After his coronation as Richard III, Gloucester placed Morton in the custody of his chief ally, Henry STAFFORD, duke of Buckingham. Morton encouraged Buckingham's growing dissatisfaction with Richard III and helped put the duke in communication with Margaret BEAUFORT and Queen Elizabeth WOODVILLE, the two principals in a developing plot to place their children, Henry Tudor, earl of Richmond, and ELIZABETH OF YORK, on the English throne. With the failure of BUCKINGHAM'S REBELLION in the autumn of 1483, Morton joined Richmond in France.

After the death of Richard III at the Battle of BOSWORTH FIELD in 1485, Richmond became king as HENRY VII, and Morton became one of the new monarch's most trusted councilors. Morton was named archbishop of Canterbury in October 1486 and chancellor in March 1487. In 1493, Pope Alexander VI made Morton a cardinal at the king's request. Morton died in September 1500. Although some historians assigned the writing of More's *HIS-TORY OF KING RICHARD III* to Morton, recent scholarship has clearly established More's authorship. However, Morton, in whose household More served in the late 1490s, is likely to have been at least one of the sources for the anecdotes that comprise More's work.

Further Reading: Chrimes, S. B., *Henry VII* (New Haven, CT: Yale University Press, 1999); Ross, Charles, *Richard III* (Berkeley: University of California Press, 1981); Seward, Desmond, *The Wars of the Roses* (New York: Viking, 1995).

Mountjoy, Lord. *See* Blount, Walter, Lord Mountjoy

Mowbray, John, Duke of Norfolk (1415–1461)

Although intermittent in his adherence to the house of YORK in the 1450s, John Mowbray, third duke of Norfolk, gave vital support to EDWARD IV at the Battle of TOWTON in 1461. The duke is also a prominent figure in the PASTON LETTERS, the famous fifteenth-century collection of correspondence belonging to the Paston family of Norfolk.

Knighted by HENRY VI in 1426, Norfolk, who succeeded his father in the dukedom in 1432, served on various military and diplomatic missions in FRANCE during the 1430s and 1440s. In 1446, Norfolk went on pilgrimage to Rome, returning in 1447 to serve on an English embassy charged with negotiating the surrender of the French county of Maine. In the early 1450s, Norfolk supported Richard PLANTA-GENET, duke of York, in his rivalry with Edmund BEAUFORT, duke of Somerset. Norfolk and York had several familial ties, York being married to Norfolk's aunt, Cecily NEVILLE, and Norfolk being married to the sister of Henry BOURCHIER, York's brother-in-law. However, by 1454, Norfolk's influence with York was overshadowed by that of Richard NEVILLE, earl of Salisbury, and his son Richard NEVILLE, earl of Warwick, and Norfolk held no office during York's FIRST PROTECTORATE.

By the late 1450s, Norfolk appeared to support the house of LANCASTER, having taken the oath to Henry VI administered at the 1459 COVENTRY PARLIAMENT, which attainted both York and the Nevilles (see ATTAINDER, ACT OF). But after Warwick won control of the king and the government at the Battle of NORTHAMPTON in July 1460, Norfolk openly and firmly adhered to the Yorkist cause. After York's death at the Battle of WAKEFIELD in December 1460, Norfolk, who had remained in LONDON, fought with Warwick at the Battle of ST. ALBANS in February 1461 and was one of the lords present at the 3 March meeting in London at which it was decided that York's eldest son should claim the throne as Edward IV. Norfolk immediately set about raising support for the new king. The duke's arrival with these forces at a critical moment during the Battle of Towton on 29 March 1461 helped turn the tide in Edward's favor. The king rewarded Norfolk with several important offices, including constable of Scarborough Castle, but refused to sanction his seizure of Caister Castle, which the duke was forced to restore to John Paston (see CAISTER CASTLE, SIEGE OF). Norfolk died a few months later in November 1461. His title passed to his son, John MOWBRAY, fourth duke of Norfolk.

Further Reading: Boardman, Andrew W., *The Battle of Towton* (Stroud, Gloucestershire, UK: Sutton Publishing, 1996); Griffiths, Ralph A., *The Reign of King Henry VI* (Berkeley: University of California Press, 1981); Johnson, P. A., *Duke Richard of York* (Oxford: Clarendon Press, 1988).

Mowbray, John, Duke of Norfolk (1444–1476)

An important adherent of the house of YORK, John Mowbray, fourth duke of Norfolk, used EDWARD IV's ongoing need for noble support against the partisans of the house of LANCASTER to ignore the law and seize Caister Castle from the Paston family in 1469 (see CAISTER CASTLE, SIEGE OF).

Norfolk succeeded to his father's title and Yorkist allegiance in 1461. In 1464, Edward IV sent Norfolk into WALES to suppress Lancastrian uprisings. In August 1469, only weeks after the king was taken prisoner by Richard

NEVILLE, earl of Warwick, Norfolk used the king's confinement and the political turmoil that ensued to lay siege to Caister Castle, which Edward had forced the duke's father to restore to Sir John Paston in 1461. After a five-week siege, during which Norfolk rejected all attempts at compromise, Caister fell to the duke on 26 September. Unable to act at the time because of his confinement and unwilling to alienate the support of Norfolk thereafter, Edward IV ignored Paston's requests for assistance, and Caister remained in the duke's hands until his death. Denied his rights by Edward IV, Sir John Paston supported the restoration of HENRY VI in 1470 and fought for Warwick at BARNET in 1471.

When Warwick forced Edward to flee in October 1470, the READEPTION government of Henry VI arrested Norfolk, but soon released him and summoned him to PARLIAMENT (see EDWARD IV, OVERTHROW OF). However, the duke's continuing Yorkist sympathies caused his re-arrest in the spring of 1471, when Edward sought to land in East Anglia in hopes of support from Norfolk. After Edward's victory at the Battle of TEWKESBURY in May 1471, Norfolk presided as marshal of England at the trial of Edmund BEAUFORT, duke of Somerset, and the other Lancastrians taken from SANCTUARY after the battle. Norfolk rode with Edward during the king's triumphal reentry into LONDON on 21 May 1471, but he seems otherwise to have received few rewards and to have lacked the king's confidence. He was not prominent at COURT in the 1470s and was never admitted to the royal COUNCIL. Norfolk died in January 1476, leaving a three-year-old daughter, Anne, whom Edward IV married to his son, Richard PLANTAGENET, duke of York, in 1478. Two years after Anne's death in 1481, Edward pushed through Parliament a bill disinheriting John HOWARD, Norfolk's next heir, and vesting the Norfolk dukedom and estates in the royal family.

See also Mowbray, John, Duke of Norfolk (d. 1461); Paston Letters
Further Reading: Ross, Charles, *Edward IV* (New Haven, CT: Yale University Press, 1998).

N

Navy

During the WARS OF THE ROSES, England had no standing fleet, and naval needs were met by indenting (contracting) with merchants and nobles to supply ships and crews to perform a specified service for a specified time. Not meant for voyaging in the open sea, civil war naval forces operated mainly in the Narrow Seas (i.e., the English Channel), where they undertook to intercept invaders, ward off coastal raiders, transport English armies, protect English traders, and maintain communication and supply lines with CALAIS.

After Henry V's death in 1422, the powerful but expensive fleet that he had built to support military operations in FRANCE was disbanded. Because Henry's conquest of the Norman coast denied the French access to Channel ports, the need for a large English navy seemed to disappear, and the minority government of HENRY VI sold off ships and discharged experienced ship's masters. By the late 1450s, with Normandy lost and civil war looming, Henry VI had no fleet and no money to build one. As a result, control of the Channel fell to the house of YORK after 1456, thanks mainly to the piratical activities of Richard NEVILLE, earl of Warwick. As captain of Calais, Warwick appropriated wool revenues to build a fleet that plundered merchant vessels of various nationalities. While Warwick's piracy embroiled the Lancastrian government with outraged foreign powers, it won the earl and the Yorkist cause much popularity, especially in LONDON, where Warwick was seen as a bold commander striking a much needed blow for English national pride. Warwick's naval success was also a PROPAGANDA windfall for the Yorkists, because it

could be profitably contrasted with Lancastrian ineffectiveness, especially in August 1457 when the government failed to prevent a French squadron under Pierre de BRÉZÉ from sacking Sandwich. In 1460, Warwick defeated the royal fleet under Henry HOLLAND, duke of Exeter, and also attacked Sandwich, where he destroyed a squadron then under construction and captured the Lancastrian commander, Richard WOODVILLE, Lord Rivers, in his bed. Unopposed in the Channel, Warwick crossed to England in June; his popularity as a naval commander convinced London authorities to admit the Yorkists and allowed Warwick to gather the army with which he defeated and captured the king at the Battle of NORTHAMPTON in July.

In the spring of 1470, after the failure of his second coup attempt against EDWARD IV, Warwick put to sea in the naval squadron he had maintained during the 1460s. Denied entry to Calais, Warwick resumed indiscriminate piracy in the Channel before landing in France, where he concluded the ANGERS AGREEMENT with Queen MARGARET OF ANJOU. Now acting in the Lancastrian interest, Warwick eluded the small royal fleet and landed in England, where in October he restored the house of LANCASTER and forced Edward IV to flee to BURGUNDY (see EDWARD IV, OVERTHROW OF). However, Edward, thanks in part to anger generated by Warwick's piracy, was by March 1471 able to obtain shipping to England from the HANSEATIC LEAGUE, a German merchant alliance with which his government had previously been at war.

After defeating Warwick and regaining the throne (see EDWARD IV, RESTORATION

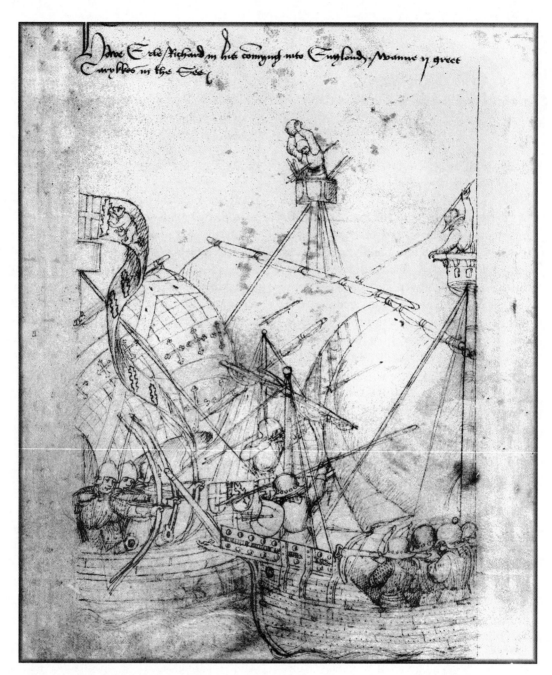

Longbowmen and crossbowmen take aim at one another in this depiction of a fifteenth-century naval battle. (Cotton Jul. E VI Art. 6 f. 18, British Library)

OF), Edward began rebuilding the royal fleet by constructing ships and gathering a new cadre of experienced ship's masters. In the 1460s, he had built the first English royal caravel, the *Edward,* and, after 1471, he constructed fleets to support his invasions of France (1475) and SCOTLAND (early 1480s). Although still meant to carry land troops to fight battles at sea, caravels were smaller, faster vessels than Henry V's high, bulky carracks, and they foreshadowed the quick, agile vessels with which Elizabethan England later defied the might of Spain. Despite these achievements, Edward still desired a small, inexpensive navy, and he maintained his fleet largely to protect trade and intercept invaders, a task that

RICHARD III's flotilla of watching vessels failed to accomplish in August 1485 when Henry Tudor, earl of Richmond, set sail for WALES.

After defeating and killing Richard at the Battle of BOSWORTH FIELD, Richmond, now HENRY VII, continued the naval policy of Edward IV, building new ships and establishing a naval base at Southampton. However, he still indented for vessels when he took an army to defend BRITTANY in 1492, and he, like his predecessor, lacked the naval strength to intercept the invasion forces of such Yorkist pretenders as Lambert SIMNEL and Perkin WARBECK, who both had to be defeated in land battles (see STOKE, BATTLE OF) after their arrival in England.

See also English Economy and the Wars of the Roses
Further Reading: Rodger, N. A. M., *The Safeguard of the Sea: A Naval History of Britain* (New York: W. W. Norton, 1998).

Neville, Anne, Queen of England (c. 1453–1485)

Anne Neville was the younger daughter of Richard NEVILLE, earl of Warwick, and the wife and queen of RICHARD III. In 1470, her father married her to Prince EDWARD OF LANCASTER to seal an alliance with the house of LANCASTER and continue the civil wars; after about 1472, her second husband, Richard, duke of Gloucester, used her name and estates to build a position of political dominance in the north of England.

In July 1470, Anne was with her father in FRANCE, where she was betrothed to Edward, Prince of Wales. The union finalized Warwick's agreement with MARGARET OF ANJOU, the prince's mother, to abandon EDWARD IV and support the restoration to the throne of HENRY VI, the prince's father (see ANGERS AGREEMENT; READEPTION). Warwick left for England in September, but Anne stayed in France with her new husband and mother-in-law until April 1471. After her father's death at the Battle of BARNET on 14 April, and her husband's death three weeks later at the Battle

A drawing depicting Anne Neville, the daughter of Richard Neville, earl of Warwick, and the wife of Richard III. The bear at her feet is the Neville emblem. (British Library)

of TEWKESBURY, Anne came into the custody of her elder sister, Isabel NEVILLE, and her sister's husband, George PLANTAGENET, duke of Clarence, the brother of Edward IV.

By the end of 1471, Anne was at the center of a bitter quarrel between Clarence and his younger brother, Richard, duke of Gloucester. The NEVILLE INHERITANCE DISPUTE involved Gloucester's desire to marry Anne and lay claim to her half of Warwick's vast landholdings as well as to the extensive influence traditionally exercised by the NEVILLE FAMILY in northern England (see NORTH OF ENGLAND AND THE WARS OF THE ROSES).

Unwilling to surrender any of the Neville lands, Clarence supposedly disguised Anne as a LONDON serving girl and hid her in the city. Gloucester discovered her whereabouts and, likely with Anne's connivance, carried her off to SANCTUARY in a London church. Despite the claims of later writers that a long-standing romantic attachment existed between the couple, Gloucester's primary interest in Anne almost certainly involved control of her estates, while Anne's interest in Gloucester probably centered mainly on the protection he could afford her against Clarence. Although the exact date of their marriage is uncertain—some time in 1472 is likely—it was conducted with some haste, since the couple did not even wait for the papal dispensation that was required for cousins to marry (besides the relationship created by their siblings' marriage, Gloucester's mother, Cecily NEVILLE, was Anne's great-aunt).

Anne spent most of the next decade in the north, where Gloucester, thanks in large part to his marriage, became heir to Warwick's lands and political influence (see RICHARD III, NORTHERN AFFINITY OF). Living mainly at Middleham Castle, the Neville stronghold in Yorkshire where her son Edward was born about 1476, Anne took little part in politics until her husband became king as Richard III in 1483. She was crowned with her husband at Westminster on 6 July, but little is known about her life as queen. Deeply affected by the death of her son in April 1484, Anne fell ill herself early in 1485. The likely outcome of her illness must soon have been clear, because rumors of her husband's desire to marry his eldest niece, ELIZABETH OF YORK, began circulating weeks before the queen's death on 16 March 1485. Afterward, rumor claimed that Richard had murdered his wife to make way for his niece, whose intended replacement of Anne was supposedly signaled by the two women wearing identical gowns at the COURT Christmas festivities. Although later Tudor writers proclaimed Richard's murder of his wife as a fact—William Shakespeare certainly implied it in *RICHARD III*—no real evidence exists to support the charge.

See also all other entries under Neville
Further Reading: Hicks, Michael, *Warwick the Kingmaker* (Oxford: Blackwell Publishers, 1998); Ross, Charles, *Richard III* (Berkeley: University of California Press, 1981).

Neville, Cecily, Duchess of York (1415–1495)

Cecily Neville, duchess of York, was the matriarch of the house of YORK and its link with its most important wartime allies, the NEVILLE FAMILY.

Cecily was the last of twenty-three children born to Ralph Neville, earl of Westmorland. Through her mother, the earl's second wife, Cecily was related to the BEAUFORT FAMILY, a junior branch of the house of LANCASTER. In 1429, Cecily married Richard PLANTAGENET, duke of York. Between 1439 and 1455, she bore eleven children, six of whom survived infancy. In the early 1440s, Cecily accompanied her husband to FRANCE, where he served as lord lieutenant for HENRY VI. Her eldest surviving son, Edward (see EDWARD IV), was born in Normandy in 1442, with his brother, Edmund PLANTAGENET, earl of Rutland, following in 1443. When York was appointed lord lieutenant of IRELAND in 1449, Cecily accompanied him to Dublin, where her next son, George PLANTAGENET, duke of Clarence, was born in October. Her last surviving son, Richard (see RICHARD III), was born in England in October 1452.

In the 1450s, York, feeling excluded from the position of leadership that was his due by birth, forged a political alliance with Cecily's eldest full brother, Richard NEVILLE, earl of Salisbury, and with Salisbury's eldest son, Richard NEVILLE, earl of Warwick. Neville support allowed York to challenge the COURT party for power and to eventually vie for the throne. In November 1459, a month after the Battle of LUDFORD BRIDGE forced them to flee the country, York and the Nevilles were attainted by the COVENTRY PARLIAMENT and their estates were confiscated. Left behind, Cecily was placed in the custody of her sister, whose husband,

Humphrey STAFFORD, duke of Buckingham, was charged with supporting the duchess and her children with revenues from the forfeited lands. After York's death at the Battle of WAKEFIELD in December 1460, Cecily sent her youngest sons, George and Richard, to BURGUNDY, from where they were recalled in 1461 by their brother, who was now king as Edward IV.

During her son's reign, Cecily lived mainly at Berkhamstead in Hertfordshire and at Baynard's Castle, her LONDON residence. She took little part in politics, but she was an important figure at family events and, according to Dominic Mancini's USURPATION OF RICHARD III, unsuccessfully opposed her son's marriage to Elizabeth WOODVILLE in 1464. During Edward IV's brief exile in 1470–1471, Cecily helped convince her son Clarence to abandon his alliance with Warwick, who had restored Henry VI, and to reconcile with his brother (see EDWARD IV, OVERTHROW OF; READEPTION). In the 1480s, the duchess became increasingly known for her piety and her devotion to the writings of such female mystics as St. Catherine of Siena and St. Bridget of Sweden. In her later years, Cecily followed a daily routine that included attendance at nine worship services. Although her religious exercises were private and orthodox, they affected public affairs through the influence they exerted on her daughter MARGARET OF YORK, duchess of Burgundy, and her son Richard III, both of whom had the works of the mystics in their personal libraries.

In 1483, as part of his justification for usurping the throne (see USURPATION OF 1483), Richard allowed the spreading of rumors that Edward IV was not York's son but had been fathered on Cecily by another man. This claim, which had been employed by Warwick in 1469 and perhaps raised by Clarence in the 1470s, was, according to Polydore Vergil's ANGLICA HISTORIA, indignantly refuted by the duchess (see also TITULUS REGIUS). After her son's death at the Battle of BOSWORTH FIELD in 1485, Cecily was honorably treated by HENRY VII. Having outlived all her sons, the duchess died in 1495 at age eighty.

See also all other entries under Neville
Further Reading: "Cecily Neville," in Michael Hicks, *Who's Who in Late Medieval England* (London: Shepheard-Walwyn, 1991), pp. 339–341; Johnson, P. A., *Duke Richard of York* (Oxford: Clarendon Press, 1988); Ross, Charles, *Edward IV* (New Haven, CT: Yale University Press, 1998); Ross, Charles, *Richard III* (Berkeley: University of California Press, 1981).

Neville Family

One of the most important magnate families in fifteenth-century England, the Nevilles supplied Richard PLANTAGENET, duke of York, with the political and military resources that allowed him to contend for the English Crown.

The family's preeminent position in the local government and society of northern England was established by Ralph Neville, earl of Westmorland (1354–1425). A series of fortunate family marriages in the fourteenth century brought Neville an extensive landed inheritance, including castles at Raby, Brancepeth, Middleham, and Sheriff Hutton. A RETAINER of John of Gaunt, duke of Lancaster (1340–1399), Neville was created earl of Westmorland in 1397 after marrying Joan Beaufort (d. 1440), Gaunt's legitimated daughter, as his second wife. In 1399, Westmorland tied his family's fortunes to the house of LANCASTER by supporting Joan's half brother, Henry of Bolingbroke, when he assumed the throne as Henry IV (r. 1399–1413) (see RICHARD II, DEPOSITION OF). Westmorland backed Henry throughout all the rebellions of his reign, including those raised by the Percy family, the Nevilles' main rivals for political predominance in northern England.

As a favored councilor of both Henry IV and Henry V (r. 1413–1422), Westmorland established a family claim to the wardenship of the West March (i.e., border) with SCOTLAND. He also acquired a lifetime grant as marshal of England, the wealthy lordship of Richmond, and a series of wardships that allowed him to make prominent and profitable marriages for many of his twenty-three children. Of his thirteen children by Joan Beaufort, the eldest son, Richard NEVILLE, became earl of Salisbury through his marriage, while second son William NEVILLE became Lord Fauconberg through his. Three daughters became duchesses, including the youngest, Cecily NEVILLE, who became duchess of York and mother of two kings of England. By the 1450s, the Nevilles were related to most of the noble families of the kingdom. At his death in 1425, Westmorland left the bulk of his lands to Salisbury, Joan's eldest son, thereby initiating a violent feud between the earls of Westmorland, the descendants of his first marriage, and the sons of his second marriage. This quarrel was later absorbed by the WARS OF THE ROSES, with the Westmorland branch of the family remaining loyal Lancastrians while their cousins became prominent Yorkists.

In the mid-1450s, Salisbury, his brothers, and his sons supported York in his quarrel with Edmund BEAUFORT, duke of Somerset, the favorite of HENRY VI. Although related to both York and Somerset, the Nevilles backed the former because he was in the best position to support them in their escalating feud with the Percy family (see NEVILLE-PERCY FEUD). Thus, even though the Nevilles rose to national prominence through loyalty to the house of Lancaster, Neville support was vital in allowing the house of YORK to seize the throne in 1461.

Although Salisbury was killed with York at the Battle of WAKEFIELD in 1460, the earl's eldest son, Richard NEVILLE, earl of Warwick, became the chief support of York's son EDWARD IV until 1469, when Edward's favoring of the WOODVILLE FAMILY, his wife's relatives, alienated Warwick and caused him to place the extensive Neville AFFINITY in the service of Henry VI. In 1470, Warwick earned his appellation of kingmaker by overthrowing the house of York and restoring the house of Lancaster (see EDWARD IV, OVERTHROW OF). After Warwick's death at the Battle of BARNET in 1471, the Neville estates and affinity were absorbed into the house of York though the marriages of Warwick's daughters to the brothers of Edward IV.

See also North of England and the Wars of the Roses; all entries under Neville and Percy; Appendix 1, "Genealogies"
Further Reading: Hicks, Michael, *Warwick the Kingmaker* (Oxford: Blackwell Publishers, 1998); Kendall, Paul Murray, *Warwick the Kingmaker* (New York: W. W. Norton, 1987); Young, Charles R., *The Making of the Neville Family in England, 1166–1400* (Woodbridge, Suffolk, UK: Boydell and Brewer, 1997).

Neville, George, Archbishop of York (1432–1476)

A younger brother of Richard NEVILLE, earl of Warwick, George Neville, archbishop of York, supported his brother's various attempts to overthrow EDWARD IV.

The fourth son of Richard NEVILLE, earl of Salisbury, George was early marked out for a clerical career. Because he was a member of the powerful NEVILLE FAMILY and a nephew of Richard PLANTAGENET, duke of York, Neville received his first ecclesiastical office in 1446, when he was only about thirteen. He acquired a succession of Church offices in 1454, when his father served as chancellor during York's FIRST PROTECTORATE. In 1455, with the Yorkists again briefly in power during the duke's SECOND PROTECTORATE, Neville received the bishopric of Exeter in fulfillment of a promise that Salisbury had extracted from the Yorkist leaders.

When his father and brother fled the realm in 1459 after the Battle of LUDFORD BRIDGE, Neville submitted to HENRY VI, but he reverted to his Yorkist allegiance in June 1460, when he led an armed force to LONDON to support the return of Salisbury and Warwick from CALAIS. He accompanied Warwick to the Battle of NORTHAMPTON on 10 July, and on 25 July, Henry VI, now in Warwick's custody, appointed Neville chancellor of England. On 4 March 1461, the day of Edward IV's elevation to the throne, Neville preached a public sermon in London at Paul's Cross (i.e., the pulpit in St. Paul's churchyard) defending Edward's right to the Crown. On 10 March, Edward confirmed Neville's appointment as chancellor. During the 1460s, the bishop served on various diplomatic missions and participated in some of Warwick's campaigns against Lancastrian incursions from SCOTLAND. In 1465, Neville followed his installation as archbishop of York with an extravagant feast that was in part a celebration of his family's political preeminence. However, in the late 1460s, the rise of the WOODVILLE FAMILY and of other royal favorites created a rift between the king and Warwick, and the archbishop was stripped of the chancellorship in 1467.

In July 1469, Neville presided in Calais at the unauthorized marriage of Warwick's daughter, Isabel NEVILLE, to George PLANTAGENET, duke of Clarence, the king's brother. The ceremony initiated a coup attempt by Warwick and Clarence, who issued a manifesto, signed by the archbishop, condemning Edward's government. After his brother's victory at the Battle of EDGECOTE in July, the archbishop took Edward IV into custody and brought him to Warwick at Middleham Castle. Compelled by lack of support to release the king, Warwick fled to FRANCE in the spring of 1470 after staging another unsuccessful rebellion. Suspicious of the archbishop, Edward forced him to take a solemn oath of loyalty.

In October 1470, Warwick overthrew Edward and restored the house of LANCASTER (see EDWARD IV, OVERTHROW OF). The archbishop became chancellor in the READEPTION government, but on 11 April 1471, after parading Henry VI through the streets of London in a vain attempt to arouse support, Neville surrendered himself and Henry to Edward. After a brief imprisonment in the TOWER OF LONDON, Neville was pardoned and released. However, in April 1472, he was re-arrested and transported to Calais, where he remained in confinement until 1475. His health broken by his long imprisonment, Archbishop Neville died in June 1476.

See also Edward IV, Restoration of; English Church and the Wars of the Roses; all other entries under Neville
Further Reading: "George Neville," in Michael Hicks, *Who's Who in Late Medieval England* (London: Shepheard-Walwyn, 1991), pp. 315–316; Hicks, Michael, *Warwick the Kingmaker* (Oxford: Blackwell Publishers, 1998); Kendall, Paul Murray, *Warwick the Kingmaker* (New York: W. W. Norton, 1987).

Neville, Sir Humphrey (c. 1439–1469)

A cousin of Richard NEVILLE, earl of Warwick, and a leader of the Lancastrian branch of the NEVILLE FAMILY, Sir Humphrey Neville raised a rebellion in 1469 that forced Warwick to end his own uprising, release EDWARD IV from custody, and return temporarily to his Yorkist allegiance.

Neville was a great-grandson of Ralph Neville, first earl of Westmorland, through Westmorland's first wife, while Warwick was a grandson of Westmorland through Westmorland's second wife, a member of the BEAUFORT FAMILY. Being on bad terms with their half siblings, the descendants of Westmorland's first family were loyal Lancastrians. Three months after Edward IV's victory at the Battle of TOWTON in March 1461, Humphrey Neville and several other Lancastrians raided into Durham from SCOTLAND, where they had followed HENRY VI into exile. Neville was captured, attainted by PARLIAMENT, and imprisoned in the TOWER OF LONDON. In about 1463, he escaped and returned to northern England, where he again agitated for the Lancastrian cause. However, perhaps through the influence of his Yorkist cousins, Neville soon submitted to Edward IV, who granted him pardon and a knighthood.

By April 1464, Neville reverted to his former allegiance, joining the Lancastrian garrison at BAMBURGH CASTLE and setting an unsuccessful ambush for his cousin John NEVILLE, Lord Montagu, Warwick's younger brother. Neville fought with Henry BEAUFORT, duke of Somerset, at the Battle of HEXHAM in May 1464 and, after that defeat, fled into the borderlands between Durham and Northumberland, where he maintained himself against the Yorkist authorities until 1469. Neville probably assisted the northern uprisings of the summer of 1469, whereby Warwick and his new son-in-law, George

PLANTAGENET, duke of Clarence, Edward IV's disaffected brother, were able to capture the king and seize control of the government. Apparently dissatisfied that Warwick was content to rule through Edward IV rather than restore Henry VI, Neville launched an uprising in northern England. Because few nobles would support him against the rebels while he held the king, Warwick was forced to release Edward, from whom he first extracted a pardon for himself and Clarence. Within weeks, Warwick crushed the uprising and captured Neville, who was executed at York in the presence of the king on 29 September.

See also Attainder, Act of; North of England and the Wars of the Roses; Robin of Redesdale Rebellion; all other entries under Neville
Further Reading: Haigh, Philip A., *The Military Campaigns of the Wars of the Roses* (Stroud, Gloucestershire, UK: Sutton Publishing, 1995); Ross, Charles, *Edward IV* (New Haven, CT: Yale University Press, 1998).

Neville Inheritance Dispute (1471–1475)

The Neville inheritance dispute, a quarrel between EDWARD IV's brothers over possession of the vast landholdings and regional influence of the late Richard NEVILLE, earl of Warwick, weakened the house of YORK and contributed to the eventual downfall of George PLANTAGENET, duke of Clarence.

After Edward IV regained the throne in 1471, he rewarded his loyal younger brother, Richard, duke of Gloucester (see RICHARD III), with numerous lands and offices, including many that had belonged to Warwick and the NEVILLE FAMILY. The royal generosity to Gloucester enraged Clarence, the king's other brother, who had supported Warwick and the READEPTION of HENRY VI and was only recently reconciled with Edward IV. As the husband of Isabel NEVILLE, Warwick's eldest daughter, Clarence was further angered by Gloucester's determination to marry Clarence's seventeen-year-old sister-in-law, Anne NEVILLE, a match that would allow Gloucester to claim a portion of the Neville estates. Although some later writers have romanti-

cized the relationship between Gloucester and Anne Neville, the couple probably had more practical reasons for wanting the union. The duke was undoubtedly attracted by the political and economic advantages of marrying a Neville heiress, and Anne, the widow of EDWARD OF LANCASTER, the late Lancastrian Prince of Wales, likely saw Gloucester as the only husband who could enforce her rights against Clarence.

Over the winter of 1471–1472, the two dukes quarreled openly and bitterly, with Clarence even attempting to prevent the marriage by disguising Anne as a kitchen maid and hiding her in LONDON. Gloucester discovered the girl and rushed to marry her. The ceremony, which probably occurred some time in 1472, did not even wait for the necessary papal dispensation allowing a marriage between cousins (besides the relationship created by their siblings' marriage, Gloucester's mother, Cecily NEVILLE, was Anne's great-aunt). After pleading unsuccessfully with Clarence on Gloucester's behalf, Edward IV intervened and imposed a settlement. In return for surrendering a share of the Warwick estates to Gloucester, Clarence was given the Neville earldoms of Warwick and Salisbury and promised recompense from the king should PARLIAMENT take from him or another heir recover from him any of the Neville or other estates granted to him. In addition, Gloucester, who had shown the greater willingness to compromise, resigned to Clarence the office of Great Chamberlain of England.

To implement this family compact, the king and his brothers circumvented the English inheritance laws. Some of Warwick's lands had come to him from his wife; by law, these estates should have passed to the still-living Countess of Warwick. Others of Warwick's estates, having come to him from his father, should by law have passed to his nearest living male relative, George Neville, duke of Bedford, son of his late brother John NEVILLE, Marquis of Montagu. A statute of May 1474 formally vested the Neville lands in Clarence and Gloucester and extinguished the claims of the Countess of Warwick by regarding her as legally dead; an act of February 1475 likewise suppressed Bedford's rights. Ironically, the king had refrained from attainting Warwick in 1471 so that his brothers could acquire the Neville lands by right of inheritance through their wives, thus obtaining for them the protection of the inheritance laws these statutes overruled (see ATTAINDER, ACT OF).

Rather than display the gratitude and cooperation that might be expected of a man recently pardoned for treason, Clarence proved particularly stubborn during the dispute and thus further aroused the king's mistrust. When Clarence continued to involve himself in questionable undertakings, Edward's patience finally ran out, and Clarence was attainted and executed in February 1478, an act by which Edward unwittingly eased Gloucester's path to the throne in 1483 (see CLARENCE, EXECUTION OF).

See also Edward IV, Restoration of; all entries under Neville

Further Reading: Hicks, Michael, *False, Fleeting, Perjur'd Clarence: George, Duke of Clarence, 1449–78* (Bangor, UK: Headstart History, 1992); Ross, Charles, *Edward IV* (New Haven, CT: Yale University Press, 1998); Ross, Charles, *Richard III* (Berkeley: University of California Press, 1981).

A drawing depicting Isabel Neville, duchess of Clarence, wife of George Plantagenet, duke of Clarence. (British Library)

Neville, Isabel, Duchess of Clarence (1451–1476)

When she married George PLANTAGENET, duke of Clarence, brother and heir presumptive of EDWARD IV, Isabel Neville, eldest daughter of Richard NEVILLE, earl of Warwick, sealed an alliance between her father and her husband that reignited the civil wars and temporarily overthrew the house of YORK.

Born at Warwick in September 1451, Isabel was suggested by her father as a possible bride for Clarence in the mid-1460s. Unwilling to allow Warwick to tie the Nevilles to the succession, the king forbade the match. In 1467, Warwick began negotiating secretly at Rome for a papal dispensation to allow the cousins to marry (Clarence's mother, Cecily NEVILLE, was Isabel's great-aunt). Persuaded that the Neville alliance could increase his influence,

and aware that it at least promised him eventual possession of the extensive Neville estates, Clarence supported the scheme, and Isabel married the duke in CALAIS on 11 July 1469.

Immediately after the ceremony, Warwick and Clarence issued a manifesto listing the failings of Edward IV's government and declaring their intention to remedy those evils by force of arms. Although the 1469 rebellion ended in stalemate, a second unsuccessful uprising in April 1470 compelled a pregnant Isabel to take ship at Exeter with her fleeing husband and father. Forced to give birth aboard ship off Calais, Isabel survived, but the child died and was buried at sea. After spending the next nine months in FRANCE with her mother and younger sister, Anne NEVILLE, the duchess returned to England in late 1470 following War-wick's successful restoration of HENRY VI. She was in the West Country in April 1471, when her father died at the Battle of BARNET and her husband reconciled with his brother.

In the early 1470s, Isabel and her sister were at the center of the NEVILLE INHERITANCE DISPUTE, a bitter quarrel between her hus-band and his brother, Richard, duke of Gloucester (see RICHARD III), over posses-sion of the properties the two sisters inherited from their late father. By marrying Anne (probably some time in 1472), Gloucester laid claim to half the Neville estates and to a share of the political influence traditionally exercised by the NEVILLE FAMILY in northern England.

Isabel gave birth to a daughter, Margaret Plantagenet, future Countess of Salisbury, in 1473, and to a son, Edward PLANTAGENET, earl of Warwick, in 1475. Complications aris-ing from the birth of a second son, Richard, in October 1476, led to Isabel's death at age twenty-five on the following 22 December. Deeply affected by the death of his wife, and by the death of her newborn son shortly thereafter, Clarence began his downfall in April 1477 by engineering the seizure, trial, and summary execution of Ankarette Twynho, a servant of Isabel's, whom the duke accused, on slender evidence, of poisoning his wife. Charged with perverting the judicial process, Clarence was arrested in June 1477 and exe-cuted in the following February.

> **See also** Clarence, Execution of; North of England and the Wars of the Roses; all other entries under Neville
> **Further Reading:** Hicks, Michael, *False, Fleeting, Perjur'd Clarence: George, Duke of Clarence, 1449–78* (Bangor, UK: Headstart History, 1992); Hicks, Michael, *Warwick the Kingmaker* (Oxford: Blackwell Publishers, 1998).

Neville, John, Earl of Northumberland and Marquis of Montagu (c. 1430–1471)

John Neville, marquis of Montagu, the younger brother of Richard Neville, earl of Warwick, was a leading political and military figure in northern England during the WARS OF THE ROSES.

The third son of Richard NEVILLE, earl of Salisbury, John took a leading part in the NEVILLE-PERCY FEUD during the 1450s. In 1454, he and his brother Sir Thomas NEVILLE led the Neville forces at the Battle of STAMFORD BRIDGE. He fought along-side his father at the Battle of BLORE HEATH, in September 1459, and so recklessly pursued the fleeing Lancastrians that he was captured. John was released in July 1460 when his brother Warwick won control of HENRY VI and the royal government at the Battle of NORTHAMPTON; the new regime shortly thereafter ennobled John as Lord Montagu. In February 1461, the Lancastrians recaptured Montagu at the Battle of ST. ALBANS, send-ing him into confinement at York. His life preserved the life of Edmund BEAUFORT, the future fourth duke of Somerset, who was Warwick's prisoner. EDWARD IV released Montagu in late March 1461, when the king passed through York after his victory at the Battle of TOWTON.

Montagu spent the early 1460s serving with his brother in the north against repeated Lancastrian incursions from SCOTLAND. He relieved Naworth Castle in July 1462 and as-sisted Warwick in repelling a Scottish invasion in July 1463. In 1464, Montagu was appointed warden of the East March (i.e., Scottish bor-der) and served with his brother on a peace commission to Scotland. He defeated one Lancastrian force at the Battle of HEDGELEY MOOR in April and another at the Battle of HEXHAM in May, and then assisted at the final capture of the castles of ALNWICK, BAM-BURGH, and DUNSTANBURGH, thus ending Lancastrian resistance in Northumberland. His reward for these services was the Percy earl-dom of Northumberland, a grant that made him the chief magnate in the north.

Although less affected by the rise of the WOODVILLE FAMILY than was Warwick, Northumberland lost a chance to marry his son to the wealthy daughter of Henry HOL-LAND, duke of Exeter, when the heiress wed

Thomas GREY, Queen Elizabeth WOOD-VILLE's son, in 1466. How deeply Northumberland was involved in Warwick's coup attempt of 1469 is unclear, for he cooperated in the suppression of the Warwick-inspired ROBIN OF REDESDALE REBELLION. He avoided involvement in his brother's abortive uprising in the spring of 1470, but he also made no effort to assist Edward against Warwick. As a member of the NEVILLE FAMILY, Northumberland aroused the king's suspicions, but as a powerful nobleman whom Edward liked personally, Northumberland still commanded the king's favor. In March 1470, Edward restored the earldom of Northumberland to Henry PERCY, but he sought to maintain John Neville's loyalty by creating him marquis of Montagu and in December 1469 promising his daughter, ELIZABETH OF YORK, as a wife for Montagu's son.

However, when Warwick landed from exile in FRANCE in September 1470, Montagu declared for Henry VI and moved with a large force to intercept Edward at Doncaster. Montagu's defection forced the king to flee the country and left Warwick in charge of the Lancastrian READEPTION government (see EDWARD IV, OVERTHROW OF). When Edward returned in March 1471, Montagu, who had been entrusted with the defense of the north, allowed the Yorkists to land unopposed in Yorkshire. Whatever the reason for this failure to act, it was likely not a betrayal of his brother, for Montagu hurried south to fight and die with Warwick at the Battle of BARNET in April.

> **See also** Edward IV, Restoration of; North of England and the Wars of the Roses; all other entries under Neville
> **Further Reading:** Hicks, Michael, *Warwick the Kingmaker* (Oxford: Blackwell Publishers, 1998); Kendall, Paul Murray, *Warwick the Kingmaker* (New York: W. W. Norton, 1987).

Neville, John, Lord Neville (d. 1461)

A member of the Westmorland branch of the NEVILLE FAMILY and a partisan of the house of LANCASTER, John Neville, Lord Neville, played a prominent part in the Battles of WAKEFIELD and FERRYBRIDGE.

Neville was a son of John Neville, the eldest son of Ralph Neville (1354–1425), first earl of Westmorland, by the earl's first marriage. John Neville was thus a nephew of Richard NEVILLE, earl of Salisbury, Westmorland's eldest son by his second marriage. In the 1440s, when the sons and grandsons of Westmorland's two families fell to squabbling over the old earl's extensive northern estates, John Neville played a prominent part in the struggle. When his uncle Salisbury and his cousin Richard NEVILLE, earl of Warwick, allied themselves with Richard PLANTAGENET, duke of York, in the 1450s, Neville supported HENRY VI, thus merging the family feud into the WARS OF THE ROSES. In 1459, John Neville was raised to the PEERAGE as Lord Neville and attended the COVENTRY PARLIAMENT, which passed bills of ATTAINDER dispossessing his Yorkist cousins.

Neville apparently cooperated with the Yorkist regime established by Warwick in July 1460 when the earl captured the king at the Battle of NORTHAMPTON. On his return from IRELAND in the autumn, York issued a COMMISSION OF ARRAY to Neville, authorizing him to raise troops for the government. When York and Salisbury marched north in December to suppress Lancastrian insurgents, they expected to be reinforced by Neville and his men. However, unbeknownst to the duke, Neville brought the troops he raised under Yorkist authority into the Lancastrian camp. One theory as to why York left the safety of Sandal Castle on 30 December to engage the Lancastrians in open battle is that he mistook a force that appeared behind a body of enemy skirmishers as Neville's promised reinforcements. Mistakenly thinking he had a body of Lancastrians trapped between two Yorkist armies, York sallied forth to his death at the Battle of WAKEFIELD. Salisbury was captured and executed shortly thereafter, apparently without any protest from his Lancastrian nephew.

Although Neville's exact role at Wakefield is unclear and known mostly from Yorkist sources, it was sufficiently pro-Lancastrian for Henry VI to reward him with custody of Salisbury's Yorkshire castles. Neville likely fought with MARGARET OF ANJOU's army at the Battle of ST. ALBANS in February 1461, and he was definitely with the Lancastrian army in the following month, when he was killed at the Battle of FERRYBRIDGE by a body of mounted ARCHERS led by his uncle (and Salisbury's brother), William NEVILLE, Lord Fauconberg.

> **See also** North of England and the Wars of the Roses; all other entries under Neville
> **Further Reading:** Haigh, Philip A., *The Military Campaigns of the Wars of the Roses* (Stroud, Gloucestershire, UK: Sutton Publishing, 1995).

Neville, Lord. *See* Neville, John, Lord Neville

Neville, Richard, Earl of Salisbury (c. 1400–1460)

In the mid-fifteenth century, Richard Neville, earl of Salisbury, was one of the wealthiest and most politically influential nobles in England. By bringing the extensive Neville interest into alliance with Richard PLANTAGENET, duke of York, Salisbury and his eldest son Richard NEVILLE, earl of Warwick, turned York's heretofore ineffective opposition to HENRY VI into a serious threat to the Lancastrian COURT and made possible the eventual seizure of the throne by York's son, EDWARD IV.

The eldest son of Ralph Neville (1354–1425), earl of Westmorland, and the earl's second wife, Joan Beaufort, Neville acquired his father-in-law's wealthy earldom of Salisbury in 1428. After his mother's death in 1440, Salisbury also inherited many of his late father's estates, making him one of the greatest magnates of the north and one of the wealthiest earls in England. During Henry VI's mental illness in the 1450s, the political rivalry between York and Edmund BEAUFORT, duke of Somerset, put Salisbury in a difficult position (see HENRY VI, ILLNESS OF). Related through his Beaufort blood to Somerset, Salisbury was also con-

nected by marriage to York, whose wife was Salisbury's sister Cecily NEVILLE (see BEAUFORT FAMILY). When York, demanding the arrest of Somerset, took up arms against the king in 1452, Salisbury and Warwick worked to reconcile the parties (see DARTFORD UPRISING). Unwilling to see York too severely punished, the Nevilles were also unwilling to forfeit their court connections.

In 1453, several events caused Salisbury and his son to abandon their moderate position and ally with York. In WALES, Somerset and Warwick disputed possession of various estates, while in the north, a variety of disputes with the sons and RETAINERS of Henry PERCY, second earl of Northumberland, led to several violent encounters between the two families and ignited a bitter NEVILLE-PERCY FEUD (see HEWORTH, BATTLE OF; STAMFORD BRIDGE, BATTLE OF). Because these quarrels coincided with the onset of the king's mental illness, the Nevilles expected little help from a court dominated by Somerset and friendly to Northumberland. Because York, himself a substantial northern landowner, was a natural Neville ally against the Percies, Salisbury and his son supported York's appointment as lord protector in March 1454. The duke rewarded Salisbury by naming him lord chancellor.

Henry VI's recovery in January 1455 ended York's protectorship and led to Salisbury's dismissal from office and Northumberland's appointment to the COUNCIL. When the king restored Somerset to favor, York took up arms with the support of Salisbury and Warwick. In May 1455, York and the Nevilles defeated a royal army at the Battle of ST. ALBANS, where they won custody of the king and achieved the deaths of Somerset and Northumberland. In February 1456, when Henry dismissed York again, Salisbury retired to the north. When open warfare erupted between York and the court in 1459, Salisbury led a force of 5,000 to join York at Ludlow in the marches of WALES. On the way, he successfully fought off a Lancastrian force at the Battle of BLORE HEATH on 23 September; however, the arrival of a large royal army at the Battle of LUD-

FORD BRIDGE forced York to flee to IRE-LAND and Salisbury, Warwick, and York's son Edward, earl of March, to sail to CALAIS.

Salisbury, Warwick, and March returned to England in June 1460, entering LONDON unopposed. In July, Warwick's victory at NORTHAMPTON—while Salisbury laid siege to the TOWER OF LONDON—put king and government in Warwick's hands; Salisbury was made great chamberlain, but otherwise left the direction of affairs to his son. In October 1460, Salisbury was reluctant to endorse York's claim to the Crown and supported the Act of ACCORD, which kept Henry VI on the throne but made York his heir in place of ED-WARD OF LANCASTER, Prince of Wales. On 9 December, when York led a force northward against the growing Lancastrian resistance to the settlement, Salisbury accompanied him. York fell at the Battle of WAKEFIELD in Yorkshire on 30 December 1460; Salisbury escaped the battle, but he was captured and executed next day. His head was placed beside the duke's on the Micklegate at York.

See also First Protectorate; Neville Family; North of England and the Wars of the Roses; Second Protectorate; all other entries under Neville
Further Reading: Griffiths, Ralph A, *The Reign of King Henry VI* (Berkeley: University of California Press, 1981); Johnson, P. A., *Duke Richard of York* (Oxford: Clarendon Press, 1988); "Richard Neville," in Michael Hicks, *Who's Who in Late Medieval England* (London: Shepheard-Walwyn, 1991), pp. 289–290.

Neville, Richard, Earl of Warwick (1428–1471)

Known as "the kingmaker," Richard Neville, earl of Warwick, was a central figure in the coming and continuation of the WARS OF THE ROSES. Warwick's support for the house of YORK allowed Richard PLANTAGENET, duke of York, to claim the Crown in 1460 and permitted EDWARD IV, York's son, to win the Crown in 1461. By switching sides in 1470, Warwick also made possible the restoration of HENRY VI and the house of LANCASTER.

The eldest son of Richard NEVILLE, earl of Salisbury, head of a powerful northern family,

The bear badge of Richard Neville, earl of Warwick. (Add. MS 40742 f. 10, British Library)

young Richard married Anne Beauchamp, daughter of the wealthy earl of Warwick, in 1436. In 1449, Anne inherited the bulk of her father's vast estates, and Neville became earl of Warwick by right of his wife. In the early 1450s, Warwick, like his father, took no side in the feud between York and Edmund BEAU-FORT, duke of Somerset. The NEVILLE FAMILY had connections with both dukes, York being married to Warwick's aunt, Cecily NEVILLE, and Somerset being related by blood through Warwick's paternal grandmother. In 1452, when York tried unsuccessfully at DARTFORD to compel the king to arrest Somerset, Warwick and Salisbury sought first to mediate the quarrel and then to limit the punishment inflicted on York. However, by 1453, Warwick's quarrel with his brother-in-law Somerset over division of the Beauchamp inheritance, and the rising influence at court of Salisbury's northern rival, Henry PERCY, earl of Northumberland, drove Warwick and his father into closer alliance with York. When York became protector for the mentally incapacitated Henry VI in 1454 (see HENRY VI, ILLNESS OF), Warwick was admitted to the COUNCIL and associated with his father in the lucrative wardenship of the West March (i.e., western border with SCOTLAND). When Henry's recovery ended York's FIRST PRO-

TECTORATE in early 1455, the return to favor of the Somerset-Northumberland faction absorbed the NEVILLE-PERCY FEUD into the national rivalry between York and Somerset, with Northumberland's standing at court tying the Nevilles more firmly to York.

In May 1455, the Nevilles and York, seeking to remove their opponents from power, resorted to arms; on 22 May, their forces slew Somerset and Northumberland at the Battle of ST. ALBANS, a fight that gave Warwick a not entirely deserved reputation as a successful military leader. The battle and a royal relapse gave York and his allies control of the government until February 1456, when Henry recovered and ended the duke's SECOND PROTECTORATE. An increasing influence in government, Queen MARGARET OF ANJOU was anxious to prevent York's ambition from jeopardizing the future of her son, Prince EDWARD OF LANCASTER; by late 1456, she had largely excluded York and the Nevilles from power. Named captain of CALAIS in 1455, Warwick spent much of the next four years fighting the French and Spanish in the Channel and winning a great reputation as a naval commander. The earl also transformed Calais into a base for Yorkist intrigues. With the outbreak of civil war in 1459, York summoned Warwick and part of the Calais garrison to England, but, after the Yorkist defeat at the Battle of LUDFORD BRIDGE in October, the earl returned to Calais with his father and York's son, Edward, earl of March. After spending the next eight months gathering strength and raiding the English coast, the Yorkist earls entered LONDON in June 1460, and the following month Warwick defeated and captured the king at the Battle of NORTHAMPTON.

With the government now in Warwick's hands, York returned from exile in IRELAND and laid claim to the Crown. Whether or not Warwick initially supported this decision, he backed off when it became apparent that the PEERAGE opposed a change of dynasty. The earl was instrumental in crafting the compromise Act of ACCORD, which left Henry on the throne but disinherited Prince Edward in favor of York and his heirs. The Act of Accord galvanized Lancastrian opposition, and Warwick was left in charge in London when York and Salisbury were killed at the Battle of WAKEFIELD in December 1460. After losing control of the king at the Battle of ST. ALBANS in February 1461, Warwick accepted what he had rejected the previous autumn— the proclamation of a Yorkist monarch. As Edward IV, York's son secured the Crown in March at the Battle of TOWTON, largely with the support of Warwick and the Neville AFFINITY.

Having been vital to Edward's success, Warwick sought, as the new king's chief advisor, to recreate the wide-ranging influence in government that he had enjoyed while holding custody of Henry VI. But Edward, though young, was far more vigorous than his Lancastrian predecessor, and Warwick, though well rewarded, soon found his influence diluted and his interests threatened by other royal favorites, such as William HERBERT, earl of Pembroke. In 1464, the king's secret marriage to Elizabeth WOODVILLE introduced the large and ambitious WOODVILLE FAMILY to COURT and further reduced Warwick's influence. Differences over foreign policy, with Edward leaning toward BURGUNDY and Warwick favoring alliance with FRANCE, also strained relations between the earl and the king, as did Edward's refusal to sanction the marriages of Warwick's two daughters to his brothers. In 1469, Warwick, seeking to again place the king under his tutelage, formed an alliance with George PLANTAGENET, duke of Clarence, Edward's disaffected brother. By instigating the ROBIN OF REDESDALE REBELLION in northern England, and by defeating royal forces at the Battle of EDGECOTE, Warwick won brief custody of the king. However, finding himself unable to govern without Edward's cooperation, Warwick soon released the king. Too strong for Edward to strike down, Warwick launched another coup in early 1470.

With the failure of the 1470 uprising at the Battle of LOSECOTE FIELD, Warwick and Clarence fled to France. Having failed to find a suitable Yorkist monarch through whom to govern, Warwick, with the cooperation of LOUIS XI, negotiated the ANGERS AGREEMENT with his old enemy, Queen Margaret. In return for restoring Henry VI, Warwick won Margaret's acceptance of the marriage of her son to Anne NEVILLE, the earl's younger daughter. In return for Louis's financial assistance, Warwick agreed to bring England into active alliance with France against Burgundy. Returning to England in September 1470, Warwick forced Edward to flee to the continent. Supported by the earl's brothers—John NEVILLE, marquis of Montagu, and George NEVILLE, archbishop of York—by the extensive Neville affinity, and (somewhat lukewarmly) by the Lancastrians, the Warwick-led READEPTION government of Henry VI lasted until April 1471, when Edward IV defeated and killed Warwick at the Battle of BARNET. To secure the north, Edward allowed his brother, Richard, duke of Gloucester (see RICHARD III), to marry Warwick's daughter Anne in about 1472. This union transferred most of Warwick's northern estates and influence to the house of York.

See also Edward IV, Overthrow of; Edward IV, Restoration of; North of England and the Wars of the Roses; Richard III, Northern Affinity of; all other entries under Neville
Further Reading: Hicks, Michael, *Warwick the Kingmaker* (Oxford: Blackwell Publishers, 1998); Kendall, Paul Murray, *Warwick the Kingmaker* (New York: W. W. Norton, 1987).

Neville, Sir Thomas (c. 1429–1460)

Sir Thomas Neville, the second son of Richard NEVILLE, earl of Salisbury, and the younger brother of Richard NEVILLE, earl of Warwick, played a prominent role in the NEVILLE-PERCY FEUD of the 1450s.

HENRY VI knighted Thomas and his younger brother John NEVILLE, the future Lord Montagu, in January 1453. In August, Sir Thomas married Maude Stanhope, the niece of Ralph, Lord Cromwell. Because it enhanced the NEVILLE FAMILY's influence in the north and made possible the future

Neville acquisition of former Percy estates in Cromwell's possession, the marriage aggravated a feud that had broken out earlier in the year between Sir John Neville and Thomas PERCY, Lord Egremont, a younger son of Henry PERCY, earl of Northumberland. Leading a large armed force, Egremont intercepted Sir Thomas Neville's wedding party as it passed northeast of York on 24 August. Besides his new wife, Sir Thomas was accompanied by his parents, his brother John, and a formidable escort of armed RETAINERS. The encounter erupted into the so-called Battle of HEWORTH, a skirmish that resulted in no bloodshed but nonetheless aggravated the feud and drew Sir Thomas into more active participation on his family's behalf. After various incidents and provocations on both sides, Sir Thomas and his brother John defeated and captured Egremont at the Battle of STAMFORD BRIDGE in October 1454.

By 1459, the Neville-Percy feud had merged into the national rivalry between the houses of YORK and LANCASTER, and the Nevilles had become the chief allies of Richard PLANTAGENET, duke of York. In September, Sir Thomas fought with his father at the Battle of BLORE HEATH, where he and his brother John were captured after pursuing the defeated Lancastrians too aggressively. Like his father and brothers, Sir Thomas was included in the bills of ATTAINDER passed against the Yorkist leaders at the COVENTRY PARLIAMENT of November 1459. In July 1460, Sir Thomas and his brother won release from confinement through Warwick's capture of the king at the Battle of NORTHAMPTON. Named to various offices by the new Yorkist government, Sir Thomas became Warwick's lieutenant as warden of the West March (i.e., the Scottish border) and had responsibility for upholding the regime's tenuous authority in the lands of the Crown Duchy of Lancaster. In October, when York laid his claim to the throne before PARLIAMENT, Sir Thomas accompanied Warwick to Westminster to tell the duke that neither the PEERAGE nor the people were willing to accept the deposition of Henry VI. In December, after the compromise

Act of ACCORD provoked Lancastrian resistance across England, Sir Thomas joined the army that his father and York led north from LONDON. He died with them at the Battle of WAKEFIELD on 30 December, and his head was afterwards displayed with those of the duke and Salisbury on the town gates of York.

> **See also** North of England and the Wars of the Roses; all other entries under Neville
> **Further Reading:** Hicks, Michael, *Warwick the Kingmaker* (Oxford: Blackwell Publishers, 1998); Storey, R. L., *The End of the House of Lancaster.* 2d ed. (Stroud, Gloucestershire, UK: Sutton Publishing, 1999).

Neville, Thomas, Bastard of Fauconberg (d. 1471)

Thomas Neville, a cousin and supporter of Richard NEVILLE, earl of Warwick, led the last serious act of resistance against EDWARD IV in 1471.

Known as the Bastard of Fauconberg, Thomas Neville was an illegitimate son of William NEVILLE, Lord Fauconberg and earl of Kent. In April 1470, Neville commanded a squadron in the royal NAVY, but he defected with it to Warwick when his cousin fled England after an unsuccessful rebellion against Edward IV. When Warwick returned and forced Edward to flee the country in October 1470, the earl placed Neville in command of the fleet (see EDWARD IV, OVERTHROW OF). Although he spent weeks patrolling the English Channel in early 1471, Neville was distracted by Breton and Burgundian naval activity and failed to intercept Edward when he crossed to England in March (see EDWARD IV, RESTORATION OF).

In early May, Neville was reinforced by 300 men from the CALAIS garrison. Unaware of the defeat and death of Warwick at the Battle of BARNET on 14 April, Neville landed in Kent and recruited a large army of Lancastrians, economic and social malcontents, and troublemakers interested more in looting than in politics. On 12 May, with his fleet at anchor in the Thames and his army at the gates, Neville demanded entry into LONDON. Ed-

ward was on campaign in the west, but the city authorities refused Neville's demand and beat off an attack across London Bridge. The next day, the citizens also frustrated Neville's attempt to cross the river farther west to attack Westminster. On 14 May, Neville bombarded London from his ships and launched further unsuccessful assaults on London Bridge and the city's eastern approaches. Anthony WOODVILLE, Earl Rivers, one of the Yorkist lords in the city, then scattered Neville's force with a sudden attack out of the TOWER OF LONDON.

Neville withdrew to Blackheath, but he did not abandon his enterprise until advance elements of the royal army, fresh from their victory at the Battle of TEWKESBURY, entered London with news of the king's imminent arrival. When Edward entered the city in triumph on 21 May, Neville was in Sandwich, where he dismissed his Calais troops. On 27 May, finally aware that Lancastrian resistance had collapsed across the country, Neville surrendered himself and his fleet to Richard, duke of Gloucester (see RICHARD III). Pardoned by the king, Neville went into the north to serve under Gloucester, but he was executed, for uncertain reasons, at Middleham Castle in September, his head being set on London Bridge facing Kent.

> **See also** all other entries under Neville
> **Further Reading:** Haigh, Philip A. *The Military Campaigns of the Wars of the Roses* (Stroud, Gloucestershire, UK: Sutton Publishing, 1995); Ross, Charles, *Edward IV* (New Haven, CT: Yale University Press, 1998).

Neville, William, Lord Fauconberg and Earl of Kent (d. 1463)

Brother of Richard NEVILLE, earl of Salisbury, and uncle of Richard NEVILLE, earl of Warwick, William Neville, Lord Fauconberg, was a key Yorkist leader during the first phase of the WARS OF THE ROSES.

Knighted by HENRY VI in 1426, Neville had become Lord Fauconberg two years earlier by right of his wife. From 1436, Fauconberg served on various military and diplomatic

Shown here is the assault on London launched by Thomas Neville, the Bastard of Fauconberg, in May 1471. This was the only attack made on a walled town during the Wars of the Roses. (MS 236, University of Ghent)

missions in FRANCE, including the 1439 siege of Meaux and the 1442 peace negotiations conducted by Richard PLANTAGENET, duke of York. In 1449, Fauconberg was taken prisoner by the French and not released until the following year, when he served on an embassy to CHARLES VII.

His association with York began during the duke's FIRST PROTECTORATE in 1454, when Fauconberg was a member of the COUNCIL. He was with the royal army at the Battle of ST. ALBANS in May 1455, staying with Henry VI in the town square. He seems to have taken a minor role in the battle and to have quietly walked away after the Yorkist leaders, including his brother and nephew, had taken custody of the king. After 1457, Fauconberg served as Warwick's deputy at CALAIS, holding the town in 1459 when the earl returned to England with part of the garrison to support the Yorkist uprising. When the Yorkist cause collapsed at the Battle of LUDFORD BRIDGE in October, Warwick, Salisbury, and Edward, earl of March (see EDWARD IV), were able to retreat to Calais, where Fauconberg readily admitted them.

In June 1460, Fauconberg, accompanied by John DINHAM and John WENLOCK, seized Sandwich, giving the Yorkists a landing place for their invasion of England; in July, he fought with Warwick at NORTHAMPTON, where Henry VI fell again into Yorkist hands. On 28 March 1461, Fauconberg was instrumental in seizing the river crossing at the Battle of FERRYBRIDGE, and next day his expert handling of the Yorkist ARCHERS helped draw the Lancastrians out of their advantageous position at the start of the Battle of TOWTON. Fauconberg remained in the north after the battle, assisting Warwick in suppressing all remaining Lancastrian resistance. Fauconberg was soon after rewarded by elevation to the earldom of Kent. He was appointed admiral of England in 1462 and raided the French coast in an effort to disrupt Lancastrian invasion plans. Kent died in January 1463.

See also Neville Family; all other entries under Neville
Further Reading: Boardman, Andrew W., *The Battle of Towton* (Stroud, Gloucestershire, UK: Sutton Publishing, 1996); Griffiths, Ralph A., *The Reign of King Henry VI* (Berkeley: University of California Press, 1981); Johnson P. A., *Duke Richard of York* (Oxford: Clarendon Press, 1988); Ross, Charles, *Edward IV* (New Haven, CT: Yale University Press, 1998).

Neville-Percy Feud (1450s)

In the mid-1450s, a violent feud erupted between the sons and RETAINERS of Richard NEVILLE, earl of Salisbury, and Henry PERCY, second earl of Northumberland, leaders of the two most powerful noble families in northern England. This quarrel not only threw the north into turmoil and contributed to the disorder plaguing the reign of HENRY VI, it also forged the political alignments that gave the houses of LANCASTER and YORK the political and military strength they needed to fight the WARS OF THE ROSES.

The Percy family had long dominated northeastern England, while the NEVILLE FAMILY had in the last century acquired similar influence in the northwest. Each family held one of the wardenships of the Scottish marches, highly salaried royal offices that made their holders military guardians of the border with SCOTLAND and influential political figures. The Percies had traditionally held the wardenship of the East March, while the Nevilles had usually held the wardenship of the West March after Henry V granted the office to Salisbury in 1420. The two families first fell at odds in the late 1440s, when their joint efforts at repelling Scottish incursions left hard feelings among the restless younger sons of both earls. In the early 1450s, Northumberland's second son, Thomas PERCY, Lord Egremont, began recruiting armed retainers in areas of Neville influence. Whether motivated by lingering resentments over the Scottish war, by disputes over land, or by his own quarrelsome nature, Egremont began harassing Neville tenants and damaging Neville property, and his provocations soon led John NEVILLE, one of Salisbury's younger sons, to reply in kind.

The feud escalated in August 1453, when Egremont and his brother Richard Percy, leading a large band of armed retainers, intercepted the wedding party of Thomas NEVILLE, Salisbury's second son, as it passed near York. Although this encounter, known as the Battle of HEWORTH, ended with little more than harsh words, it extended the feud to other northern families, for the Percies were accompanied by John CLIFFORD, eldest son of Thomas CLIFFORD, Lord Clifford. During the two months following the Heworth incident, most of the principal members of both families were drawn into the quarrel, while partisans of each side attacked the property and tenants of the other. John Neville vandalized Northumberland's house at Catton, Richard Percy terrorized Neville tenants at Gargrave, and the mayor of York met with Salisbury, Egremont, and Lord Poynings, Northumberland's eldest son, in an effort to mediate the dispute. By October 1453, the two families, despite having been ordered to keep the peace by the royal COUNCIL, had assembled large bodies of armed retainers. For three days, the Neville and Percy forces lay within dangerous proximity of one another. Although both earls finally disbanded their armies without a fight, no reconciliation was effected, and tensions remained high.

In 1454, the feud began to merge into national politics. When Salisbury's eldest son, Richard NEVILLE, earl of Warwick, quarreled with Edmund BEAUFORT, duke of Somerset, a royal favorite and chief rival of Richard PLANTAGENET, duke of York, the Nevilles drew closer to York, forming an association that gave them a political advantage over the Percies when York became lord protector for the incapacitated Henry VI (see HENRY VI, ILLNESS OF). Northumberland countered by aligning more closely with Somerset and with Queen MARGARET OF ANJOU, who was becoming leader of the opposition to York. During the summer of 1454, renewed Neville-Percy violence in the north hardened these alliances. Egremont joined Henry HOLLAND, duke of Exeter, in an uprising intended to disrupt York's FIRST PROTECTORATE. Although York's intervention led to Exeter's capture, Egremont continued to attack Neville supporters. In late October, Thomas and John Neville defeated and captured Egremont and his brother Richard Percy at the Battle of STAMFORD BRIDGE in Yorkshire. By obtaining a huge monetary judgment against Egremont from a royal commission, the Nevilles were able to imprison him for debt in LONDON, where he stayed until his escape in 1456.

Meanwhile, the national political struggle turned violent in May 1455, when the forces of York and the Nevilles slew Somerset, Northumberland, and Clifford at the Battle of ST. ALBANS. Northumberland's sons, considering their father's death to be murder perpetrated by the Nevilles, became staunch adherents of the house of Lancaster, while the battle irrevocably committed Salisbury and Warwick to the house of York. Although Henry VI tried to reconcile the Nevilles and Percies as part of his LOVE-DAY peace initiative in 1458, violence continued in the north, and the two families quickly mobilized for battle on the outbreak of civil war in 1459. In July 1460, a Yorkist army led by Warwick slew Egremont at the Battle of NORTHAMPTON, while Henry PERCY, third earl of Northumberland (the former Poynings), was a leader of the Lancastrian force that slew Salisbury, York, and Thomas Neville at the Battle of WAKEFIELD five months later. In March 1461, Northumberland was himself killed fighting York's son, EDWARD IV, at the Battle of TOWTON. By driving each family to opposite sides in the national struggle, the Neville-Percy feud played a key role in the coming of the civil wars.

See also North of England and the Wars of the Roses; all entries under Neville and Percy
Further Reading: Griffiths, Ralph A., "Local Rivalries and National Politics: The Percies, the Nevilles and the Duke of Exeter, 1452–1455," in Ralph A. Griffiths, ed., *King and Country: England and Wales in the Fifteenth Century* (London: Hambledon Press, 1991), pp. 321–364; Storey, R. L., *The End of the House of Lancaster,* 2d ed. (Stroud, Gloucestershire, UK: Sutton Publishing, 1999).

The New Chronicles of England and France. See London Chronicles

Nibley Green, Battle of (1470)

Fought on 20 March 1470 near the Gloucestershire village of the same name, the Battle of Nibley Green was the culmination of an inheritance dispute between Thomas Talbot, Viscount Lisle (1451–1470), and William Berkeley, Lord Berkeley (1426–1492). Occurring while EDWARD IV was on campaign in the north against the rebel forces of Richard

NEVILLE, earl of Warwick, and George PLANTAGENET, duke of Clarence, the battle is a prime example of the local disorder that was common in mid-fifteenth-century England during periods of weak or distracted royal government.

William Berkeley was the son and heir of James, Lord Berkeley, but his possession of the Berkeley title and estates was disputed by Margaret, countess of Shrewsbury. The countess was the granddaughter and coheiress of Thomas, Lord Berkeley, whose estates had passed, not without challenge, to his nephew James, and then, on James's death in 1463, to William, who was thus Lord Thomas's great-nephew. In pursuit of her claims, the countess had arrested and imprisoned Lord William's mother, Isabel Berkeley, when she had attempted to appeal on her husband's behalf to the COUNCIL of HENRY VI in 1452. Lady Berkeley died while still in confinement in Gloucester in September 1452.

On the death of Countess Margaret in June 1468, her claim was taken up by her eighteen-year-old grandson, Lord Lisle. When Warwick's attempts to control the Crown revived political instability in 1469–1470, the Berkeley-Talbot feud, like such other long-running disputes as the Harrington-Stanley feud in Lancashire and the Harcourt-Stafford feud in the Midlands, turned violent during the ensuing period of royal weakness. As in the worst days of Henry VI, aggrieved nobles took up arms to settle their differences. The encounter at Nibley Green arose from a challenge, apparently issued by Berkeley, to settle the matter by combat. With the time and place arranged by the Berkeley and Talbot heralds (i.e., each magnate's official messenger and officer of arms), the battle occurred only eight days after Edward IV defeated Warwick's rebels at the Battle of LOSECOTE FIELD. A bloody fight that was remembered in Gloucestershire well into the seventeenth century, the Battle of Nibley Green resulted in the deaths of Lisle and some 150 others (probably more than died at the Battle of ST. ALBANS in 1455), and in the sack of Lisle's manor at Wotton.

Because his support was deemed vital for the house of YORK, Berkeley apparently suffered little or no punishment for his involvement in the fray. He was made a viscount by Edward IV in 1481 and created earl of Nottingham by RICHARD III in 1483. Berkeley was also favored by the house of TUDOR; HENRY VII named him Earl Marshal of England in 1486 and created him marquis of Berkeley in 1489. He died at Westminster in February 1492.

Further Reading: Goodman, Anthony, *The Wars of the Roses* (New York: Dorset Press, 1981); Ross, Charles, *Edward IV* (New Haven, CT: Yale University Press, 1998).

Nobility. *See* Peerage

Norfolk, Duke of. *See* entries under Howard and Mowbray

Normandy, Seneschal of. *See* Brézé, Pierre de, Seneschal of Normandy

North of England and the Wars of the Roses

Although far from LONDON and subject to the raids and disorders that were endemic on the Scottish border, the northern counties of England played a larger role in the WARS OF THE ROSES than the region's relative lack of wealth and population seemed to warrant. During the conflict, the region witnessed four battles, including various Lancastrian and Scottish incursions in the early 1460s; supported several important uprisings, such as the ROBIN OF REDESDALE REBELLION in 1469; and provided numerous recruits to armies of both sides, but especially to the forces of the house of LANCASTER. The north was also the scene of the NEVILLE-PERCY FEUD, a violent quarrel between the region's two most influential families, which created the political alignments that provided the houses of Lancaster and YORK with vital military resources.

Although occupying a quarter of the total land area of fifteenth-century England, the six northern counties of Cumberland, Durham, Lancashire, Northumberland, Westmorland, and Yorkshire held only about 15 percent of the country's population, with about two-thirds of that number resident in Yorkshire. Since the start of the century, political and social dominance in the region had been shared by two noble families—the Nevilles and the Percies. Both families were charged by the Crown with the defense of the northern border, with the Nevilles usually holding the wardenship of the West March and the Percies the wardenship of the East March. In the early 1450s, the NEVILLE FAMILY was headed by Richard NEVILLE, earl of Salisbury, and his eldest son, Richard NEVILLE, earl of Warwick, while the Percies were headed by Henry PERCY, second earl of Northumberland. The outbreak of a feud between the RETAINERS and younger sons and brothers of these men threw the region into disorder, as each side harassed the tenants and vandalized the property of the other. A dangerous encounter at HEWORTH in 1453 and a pitched battle at STAMFORD BRIDGE in 1454 caused the two families to arrange themselves on opposite sides in the national political rivalry then developing between Richard PLANTAGENET, duke of York, and Edmund BEAUFORT, duke of Somerset. When the forces of York and the Nevilles slew Somerset and Northumberland at the Battle of ST. ALBANS in 1455, the Percies became firm adherents of the house of Lancaster, while the Nevilles committed themselves to the house of York.

Besides the Percy influence, support for Lancaster was strong in the region because the Duchy of Lancaster lands, which had belonged to the dynasty before it took the throne, were centered in Lancashire. Even the senior branch of the Neville family, headed by Ralph Neville, earl of Westmorland, was strongly Lancastrian. Upon publication of the Act of ACCORD in 1460, most of the northern PEERAGE declared for HENRY VI. This northern discontent drew York and Salisbury into the region, where a northern army jointly commanded by Henry PERCY, third earl of Northumberland, slew them at the Battle of WAKEFIELD in December. Returning from SCOTLAND, Queen MARGARET OF ANJOU joined this force and led it toward London, where traditional southern fears of wild and uncouth northerners combined with Yorkist PROPAGANDA to exaggerate tales of plunder by northern soldiers and assist York's son, EDWARD IV, in securing the capital in March 1461 (see MARCH ON LONDON). Besides Northumberland, so many northern Lancastrians were slain in Yorkshire at the subsequent Battle of TOWTON that ten years later Edward IV could still raise little support in the region.

Between 1461 and 1464, the northeastern counties of Durham and Northumberland remained an ongoing war zone. During the period, the Yorkist government mounted several campaigns into the region—to resist Lancastrian incursions from Scotland; to meet French MERCENARIES hired by Margaret of Anjou; to besiege Lancastrian garrisons holding the castles of ALNWICK, BAMBURGH, and DUNSTANBURGH; and to stem a Scottish invasion. In early 1464, after a Lancastrian campaign had overrun most of Northumberland, John NEVILLE, Lord Montagu, defeated the forces of Henry BEAUFORT, duke of Somerset, at the Battles of HEDGELEY MOOR and HEXHAM, thereby ending the war in the north and bringing the region under Yorkist control. In the mid-1460s, Henry VI, having been expelled from Scotland, wandered the region under the protection of Lancastrian GENTRY until his capture in 1465.

In 1469, Warwick used his family's regional influence to stir up several northern rebellions against Edward IV. In 1470, Warwick combined the extensive Neville AFFINTY with lingering regional allegiance to the house of Lancaster to unite the north behind the overthrow of Edward IV and the READEPTION of Henry VI (see EDWARD IV, OVERTHROW OF). However, Warwick's death at the Battle of BARNET in 1471 created a power vacuum in the north. After the Yorkist restoration (see

EDWARD IV, RESTORATION OF), Edward IV filled that vacuum by handing oversight of the region to his brother, Richard, duke of Gloucester, the husband of Warwick's daughter, Anne NEVILLE. As Warwick's heir, Gloucester tried to win the loyalty of traditional Neville retainers for the house of York. Governing from Middleham Castle in Yorkshire, Gloucester gradually built up his own northern affinity, which in 1483 provided many of the chief supporters for his usurpation of the throne as RICHARD III. The COUNCIL that had helped Gloucester govern the north was, after his accession, reconstituted as a formal organ of northern government known as the Council of the North. This body was later adopted and modified by HENRY VII, who used it and his Lancastrian blood to win the allegiance of the north to the house of TUDOR.

> See also Richard III, Northern Affinity of; Usurpation of 1483
> Further Reading: Dockray, Keith, "The Political Legacy of Richard III in Northern England," in Ralph A. Griffiths and James Sherborne, eds., *Kings and Nobles in the Later Middle Ages* (New York: St. Martin's Press, 1986), pp. 205–227; Pollard, A. J., ed., *The North of England in the Reign of Richard III* (New York: St. Martin's Press, 1995); Storey, R. L., "The North of England," in S. B. Chrimes, C. D. Ross, and Ralph A. Griffiths, eds., *Fifteenth Century England, 1399–1509* (Stroud, Gloucestershire, UK: Alan Sutton Publishing, 1995), pp. 129–144.

Northampton, Battle of (1460)

Resulting in the capture of HENRY VI by the Yorkists, and in the deaths of several key Lancastrian noblemen, the Battle of Northampton, fought outside the town of Northampton on 10 July 1460, was a major turning point in the Wars of the Roses. The battle between the royal army and a Yorkist force under Richard NEVILLE, earl of Warwick, the most important ally of Richard PLANTAGENET, duke of York, transformed the duke's cause, which had languished since his flight to IRELAND in the previous autumn. The victory at Northampton allowed the duke to return to England and

lay formal claim to the Crown, and briefly handed effective control of the government to Warwick.

In October 1459, the Yorkist leaders, facing a superior Lancastrian force at the Battle of LUDFORD BRIDGE, abandoned their army and fled the country. York and his second son Edmund PLANTAGENET, earl of Rutland, took ship for Ireland; Warwick; his father, Richard NEVILLE, earl of Salisbury; and Edward, earl of March, York's eldest son (see EDWARD IV), sailed for CALAIS. During the early months of 1460, Warwick maintained himself in Calais against attacks by Henry BEAUFORT, the Lancastrian duke of Somerset. Warwick twice surprised and destroyed Lancastrian fleets under construction at Sandwich, and spent most of April and May in Ireland conferring with York.

In late June, Warwick, Salisbury, and March sailed for England. The Yorkist lords spent several days collecting support from the counties of Kent, Sussex, and Surrey, and arrived before LONDON on 2 July with a sizable force. Because Henry VI and Queen MARGARET OF ANJOU were northwest of London at Coventry with the bulk of their army, the capital contained only a small Lancastrian force under Thomas SCALES, Lord Scales, who withdrew to the TOWER OF LONDON when he realized that the municipal authorities did not intend to resist Warwick's entry into the city. Intending to intercept the royal army as it marched southeast from Coventry, Warwick and March left London by 5 July; Salisbury remained behind to lay siege to the Tower and confine Scales.

Upon reaching Northampton, the royal army took up a defensive position outside the city walls with its back to the River Nene and its front protected by a water-filled ditch and sharpened stakes. As he approached the Lancastrian position on the rainy morning of 10 July, Warwick dispatched several delegations to negotiate with the king. Each delegation was refused access to Henry by Humphrey STAFFORD, duke of Buckingham, the commander of the Lancastrian army. At midafternoon, Warwick ordered an assault on the Lan-

Henry VI is taken prisoner after the Battle of Northampton; behind the king are piled the dead bodies of those slain in his defense. (Harley MS, 7353 f. 8, British Library)

castrian position. The continuing rain put the Lancastrian ARTILLERY out of action, but it also slowed the Yorkist advance, which stalled under a hail of arrows (see ARCHERS). Warwick and March now concentrated their attack on the Lancastrian right flank, which was commanded by Edmund GREY, Lord Grey of Ruthyn. Grey ordered his men to lay down their arms and allow the Yorkists to enter the camp. This defection, which was apparently preplanned, for Warwick's men had been told to spare the life of anyone wearing Grey's livery (see LIVERY AND MAINTENANCE), gave the day to the Yorkists, who quickly rolled up the Lancastrian line.

Northampton was a disaster for the Lancastrians. The king fell into Yorkist hands, and such prominent Lancastrian lords as Bucking-ham; John Talbot, earl of Shrewsbury; and Thomas PERCY, Lord Egremont, were slain defending the royal person. The brief encounter resulted in relatively few other CASUALTIES, but it completely transformed the Yorkist position, which had seemed so bleak after the Battle of Ludford Bridge. Although Queen Margaret and her son Prince EDWARD OF LANCASTER were still at large in WALES, Warwick now controlled both the king and the kingdom, and York was able to return from Ireland in September to claim the throne.

Further Reading: Haigh, Philip A., *The Military Campaigns of the Wars of the Roses* (Stroud, Gloucestershire, UK: Sutton Publishing, 1995); Ross, Charles, *The Wars of the Roses* (New York: Thames and Hudson, 1987).

Northern Affinity of Richard III. *See* Richard III, Northern Affinity of

Northumberland Campaigns, 1461–1464. *See* Alnwick Castle; Bamburgh Castle; Dunstanburgh Castle; Hedgeley Moor, Battle of; Hexham, Battle of

Northumberland, Earl of. *See* Neville, John, Earl of Northumberland and Marquis of Montagu; entries under Percy

Ormond, Earl of. *See* Butler, James, Earl of Wiltshire and Ormond

Oxford Conspiracy (1462)

Uncovered in February 1462, the Oxford Conspiracy was a vague Lancastrian plot that centered on John de Vere, twelfth earl of Oxford (c. 1408–1462), and his eldest son, Sir Aubrey de Vere. Because the failed plot led to the executions of both de Veres, the Oxford Conspiracy not only contributed to the political instability that marked the early 1460s, it also transformed the earl's surviving son, John de VERE, thirteenth earl of Oxford, into an implacable foe of the house of YORK.

During the winter of 1461–1462, rumors of Lancastrian intrigues swept England. Jasper TUDOR, earl of Pembroke, was said to be planning a descent on WALES; Henry BEAUFORT, duke of Somerset, was thought to be preparing an invasion of East Anglia; and a large army of Spaniards and Frenchmen was believed to be poised for a landing in Kent. Another persistent rumor claimed that the earl of Oxford, a powerful Essex magnate and a staunch supporter of HENRY VI and the house of LANCASTER, was behind a series of attacks launched against English coasts by Lancastrian raiders operating out of FRANCE. Thus, when Yorkist agents intercepted letters passing between Oxford and Queen MARGARET OF ANJOU, the discovery only confirmed Yorkist suspicions about the earl's activities.

Arrested on 12 February 1462, Oxford and his son Aubrey were confined to the TOWER OF LONDON. The Yorkist regime, fearful of both internal rebellion and external invasion, dealt quickly and harshly with the de Veres. Tried for treason before John TIPTOFT, earl of Worcester and constable of England, both men were condemned, along with several accomplices who were likely members of Oxford's AFFINITY. The exact nature of Oxford's plotting is unclear. He appears to have been charged with organizing some type of Lancastrian invasion and also possibly with conspiring to lead a party of armed RETAINERS, ostensibly raised on the king's behalf, to intercept and kill EDWARD IV as he rode north to meet Lancastrian incursions from SCOTLAND. One source claims that Aubrey de Vere informed on his father, accusing the earl of planning a Lancastrian landing on the Essex coast. However, such a betrayal, given Sir Aubrey's own condemnation and what is known of his character, seems unlikely.

Sir Aubrey died first, suffering the full horror of execution for treason—hanging, drawing, and quartering—at Westminster on 20 February. Being a member of the PEERAGE, Oxford had his sentence commuted to beheading, which he suffered on 26 February. Because no ATTAINDER was passed against his father, John de Vere, the second son, was allowed to assume his father's title and estates until he was himself arrested for Lancastrian plotting in 1468. Although soon released, the thirteenth earl of Oxford was thereafter a constant opponent of every Yorkist regime.

Further Reading: Seward, Desmond, *The Wars of the Roses* (New York: Viking, 1995).

Oxford, Earl of. *See* Vere, John de, Earl of Oxford

Parliament

As the highest court of the realm, and the national forum for discussion of important public issues, Parliament became during the WARS OF THE ROSES the instrument whereby major political changes were legitimized and new royal regimes recognized.

Fifteenth-century Parliaments consisted of an upper chamber (the Lords) and a lower chamber (the Commons). The membership of the Lords included both laymen—titled nobles summoned by individual writ (see PEERAGE)—and churchmen—twenty-one bishops and some abbots of large monasteries. The Commons, whose membership by 1485 totaled 296, included two knights from each shire and burgesses who represented LONDON and other incorporated towns. The shire representatives—by law county landholders who were knights or who possessed sufficient land to support a knight's estate—were elected by male residents of the county who held lands worth at least forty shillings per year. Voting for burgesses was more idiosyncratic, the electorate being defined by a town's charter, which, in some cases, restricted voting to a small group (see TOWNS AND THE WARS OF THE ROSES).

Fifteenth-century Parliaments were royal instruments of government, summoned and dismissed by the king. The speaker of the Commons, the officer who directed debate and managed business, was almost always a royal councilor and was paid by the Crown after 1461. During the Wars of the Roses, royal governments used their control to ensure that Parliaments confirmed royal titles, such as occurred in 1461 to legitimize the house of YORK, in 1483 to approve RICHARD III's usurpation (see USURPATION OF 1483), and

in 1485 to confirm the right of the house of TUDOR. Victorious regimes also used Parliament to pass bills of ATTAINDER against defeated opponents and to reverse attainders previously passed against supporters. Thus, although the Lancastrians attainted leading Yorkists at the COVENTRY PARLIAMENT in 1459, the first Parliament of EDWARD IV in 1461 reversed many of these attainders and passed new bills against prominent Lancastrians. With each change of political fortune came a new series of attainders and reversals.

To obtain a cooperative Parliament, royal administrations often manipulated borough (i.e., town) elections. Because borough seats comprised almost two-thirds of the Commons, and because town electorates were often small and easily influenced, kings could readily secure the election of royal servants and household officials, even though by law burgesses were to be citizens of the town they represented. For example, in 1478, Edward IV obtained a Parliament that was willing to condemn his brother, George PLANTAGENET, duke of Clarence. Besides some loss of independence, the Wars of the Roses also caused the Commons to lose some legislative initiative. Prior to the 1450s, most bills were initiated by petitions from the Commons, whose main functions were the granting of taxation and the consideration of petitions. Civil war Parliaments saw more bills drafted by the king and his COUNCIL, more attention to royal interests, and greater royal management of business. In general, the wars led to an increase of royal control over Parliament.

Further Reading: Butt, Ronald, *A History of Parliament: The Middle Ages* (London: Constable, 1989).

Parliament of Devils. *See* Coventry
Parliament

Paston Letters

The letters and papers of the Pastons, a politically active East Anglian GENTRY family, comprise the largest and best known archive of private correspondence to survive from the fifteenth century. Because the family's landholdings were constantly threatened by powerful local magnates, the Pastons' political attitudes were shaped by their ongoing need for royal favor and for powerful patrons at COURT who could help secure such favor. Thus, for the earlier phases of the WARS OF THE ROSES, the Paston letters offer valuable insights into the interaction of local and national politics and the nature of political allegiance.

The Paston archive contains over one thousand documents—mainly letters to and from the family—that cover the period from 1418 to 1506, although the most numerous and interesting items relating to national politics date between the late 1450s and 1471. In 1459,

John Paston I (1421–1466) inherited the extensive Norfolk and Suffolk estates of Sir John Fastolf, with whom Paston had formed a close connection over the previous decade. Because both John MOWBRAY, third duke of Norfolk, and John de la POLE, duke of Suffolk, disputed Paston's claim to the Fastolf lands, and especially to the magnificent new manor house at Caister, Paston spent the rest of his life defending his inheritance against lawsuits and attempts at forcible seizure. Much of the Paston correspondence in the 1460s concerns the family's attempts to win the favor of EDWARD IV and of influential members of his family and court. Paston's eldest son, John Paston II (1442–1479), became a member of the royal household, and his younger son, John Paston III (1444–1504), was attached to the household of John MOWBRAY, fourth duke of Norfolk. Despite these connections, and approaches to Richard NEVILLE, earl of Warwick, members of the WOODVILLE FAMILY, and other prominent courtiers, the Pastons' hold on the Fastolf estates continued to be tenuous.

In August 1469, after Warwick rebelled and took the king into custody, Norfolk used the

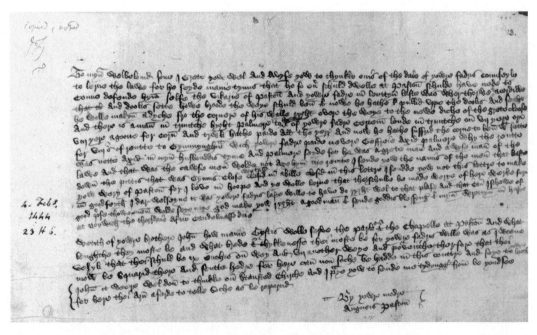

One of the Paston Letters, the richest and best-known surviving collection of letters from fifteenth-century England. (British Library)

temporary eclipse of the Crown to attack Caister, which fell to the duke after a five-week siege (see CAISTER CASTLE, SIEGE OF). Even after Edward regained his freedom, continuing tension with Warwick made Norfolk's support vital to the king and denied the Pastons any hope of royal support. Accordingly, in 1470, the family welcomed the READEPTION of HENRY VI and the house of LANCASTER. The new regime restored Caister to the Pastons, who in April 1471 fought with Warwick against the house of YORK at the Battle of BARNET. However, the subsequent Yorkist restoration (see EDWARD IV, RESTORATION OF) allowed Norfolk to repossess the manor house and forced the Pastons to seek pardon from Edward IV. Norfolk held Caister until his death (without male heirs) in 1476, when the Pastons finally recovered the house, perhaps through the good offices of Anthony WOODVILLE, Earl Rivers, and William HASTINGS, Lord Hastings, influential Yorkist courtiers whom the Pastons had carefully cultivated during the 1470s.

Because the volume and political content of the family's correspondence declines sharply after the death of John Paston II in 1479, the letters are much less useful for the reign of RICHARD III and the final stage of the Wars of the Roses. Although the Pastons' inheritance problems and the intense political activity they generated may have been atypical for a gentry family of the period, the Paston letters, like the correspondence preserved in the contemporary CELY, PLUMPTON, and STONOR archives, are also valuable sources for the social history of the fifteenth century.

Further Reading: Bennett, H. S., *The Pastons and Their England: Studies in an Age of Transition,* 2d ed. (Cambridge: Cambridge University Press, 1990); Davis, Norman, ed., *The Paston Letters: A Selection in Modern Spelling* (Oxford: Oxford University Press, 1999); Davis, Norman, ed. *Paston Letters and Papers of the Fifteenth Century,* 2 vols. (Oxford University Press, 1971, 1976); Gies, Frances, and Joseph Gies, *A Medieval Family: The Pastons of Fifteenth-Century England* (New York: HarperCollins, 1998); Richmond, Colin, *The Paston Family in the Fifteenth Century: The First Phase* (Cambridge: Cambridge University Press, 1990); Richmond, Colin, *The Paston Family in the Fifteenth Century: Fastolf's Will* (Cambridge: Cambridge University Press, 1996); Virgoe, Roger, ed., *Private Life in the Fifteenth Century: Illustrated Letters of the Paston Family* (New York: Weidenfeld and Nicolson, 1989).

Peerage

The peerage or titled nobility of England was more heavily involved in the WARS OF THE ROSES than any other contemporary social group.

The lay peers of England and WALES were landholders characterized by their hereditary titles of nobility and their hereditary right to be summoned personally to PARLIAMENT by the monarch. With the bishops and the abbots of important monastic houses, the peers comprised the House of Lords. In descending order of rank, the five titles of nobility were duke, marquis, earl, viscount, and baron. At the start of the civil war in 1459, England had about sixty-eight titled nobles; by 1500, that number declined to about fifty, but only partially as a result of wartime CASUALTIES. Before the Battle of ST. ALBANS in 1455, the higher peerage consisted of six dukes and twelve earls. Although most of these peers were loyal to HENRY VI before 1461, many submitted afterward to EDWARD IV, who, unlike his Tudor successor HENRY VII, created a large number of new peers. After the Battle of BOSWORTH FIELD in 1485, the higher peerage, thanks to the Yorkist creations, comprised three dukes, one marquis, and sixteen earls, although only two families—the Fitzalan earls of Arundel and the Neville earls of Westmorland—had taken little part in the conflict and had consequently suffered no deaths or loss of property because of the Wars of the Roses.

Because of their political leadership and social dominance, the peerage could not remain neutral in any struggle for control of the government or the Crown. Because the noble families of England controlled the military resources of the realm (see BASTARD FEUDALISM), almost every magnate family was compelled to commit itself to one side or the other at some time during the conflict. The rewards of being on the winning side could be substantial—lands, offices, and local and national influence; however, the penalties for losing could be equally harsh—execution for the head of the family and disinheritance through ATTAINDER for heirs. Some families suffered severely. No less than three Courtenay earls of Devon, three Beaufort dukes of Somerset, and two Percy earls of Northumberland were executed or slain in battle during the Wars of the Roses. The war also extinguished the male lines of the houses of LANCASTER and YORK, the male line of the BEAUFORT FAMILY, and most of the male descendants of the NEVILLE FAMILY, thereby transmitting the wealth and influence of all four to Henry VII, an inheritance that greatly strengthened the position of the house of TUDOR.

Nonetheless, as modern research has shown, the rate of extinction of noble families during the civil war generations was no higher than it had been through the natural failure of heirs in previous generations. This outcome was in part because many nobles submitted to Edward IV after the Battle of TOWTON in 1461 and especially after the Battles of BARNET and TEWKESBURY in 1471; the wastage of war was relatively brief and contained. Edward often extended favor to even his most ardent opponents, and many Lancastrians of the 1460s became loyal Yorkists in the 1470s. Almost two-thirds of the 397 acts of attainder passed in the last half of the fifteenth century were eventually reversed. Also, some peers, such as Thomas STANLEY, Lord Stanley, exercised a vital regional influence that allowed them to never become more than marginally committed to either side.

During the war, peers participated in the fighting for various reasons. Bitter local feuds, such as the NEVILLE-PERCY FEUD in the north, drove rival families to join opposite sides in the civil war. For instance, the Percy family's association with the court of Henry VI disposed the Nevilles to align with Richard PLANTAGENET, duke of York. Once the fighting began, vengeance also became a strong motivator; all the sons of the noblemen killed by the Yorkists at the Battle of St. Albans in 1455, such as John CLIFFORD, Lord Clifford, became unshakable Lancastrians. Many families were drawn into war by ties of kinship and marriage, joining the Yorkists, for example, because they were relatives or longtime allies of the Nevilles, or the Lancastrians because they were closely tied to the Beauforts. In the early stages of the war, many peers participated out of personal loyalty to Henry VI or to York; almost 80 percent of the peerage participated in the Towton campaign in 1461. No later battle was as large or as bloody. By 1485, peerage participation dropped sharply. Thirty years of intermittent strife, during which almost every family had suffered some loss, encouraged most peers to adopt a wait-and-see attitude toward RICHARD III and Henry Tudor, earl of Richmond.

> **See also** Commons (Common People) and the Wars of the Roses; Gentry; entries under Beaufort, Courtenay, and Percy; Appendix 3, "Table of Dynastic Affiliations"; Appendix 4, "Involvement of the Higher Peerage in the Wars of the Roses"
> **Further Reading:** McFarlane, K. B., *The Nobility of Later Medieval England* (Oxford: Clarendon Press, 1973); Pugh, T. B., "The Magnates, Knights and Gentry," in S. B. Chrimes, C. D. Ross, and Ralph A. Griffiths, eds., *Fifteenth-Century England 1399–1509,* 2d ed. (Stroud, Gloucestershire, UK: Alan Sutton, 1995), pp. 86–128; Ross, Charles, *The Wars of the Roses* (London: Thames and Hudson, 1987); Woolgar, C. M., *The Great Household in Late Medieval England* (New Haven, CT: Yale University Press, 1999).

Pembroke, Earl of. *See* Herbert, William, Earl of Pembroke; Tudor, Jasper, Earl of Pembroke and Duke of Bedford

Percy, Henry, Earl of Northumberland (1394–1455)

Through his feud with the NEVILLE FAMILY for dominance in northern England, Henry Percy, second earl of Northumberland, helped cement a series of alliances that allowed Richard PLANTAGENET, duke of York, to seriously contend for control of the royal government and so bring on the Wars of the Roses.

Percy spent his youth seeking to regain the lands and offices lost by his father and grandfather through their rebellion against Henry IV. After his father, Sir Henry Percy (known as Hotspur), died in battle at Shrewsbury in 1403, Percy fled to SCOTLAND with his grandfather, the first earl, who died in rebellion against the king at Bramham Moor in 1408. Held prisoner in Scotland until 1415, Percy was restored to his earldom and to most of his family's lands in March 1416. The new earl saw some service in FRANCE, but spent most of Henry V's reign defending the Scottish border, where the king had appointed him warden of the East March and captain of BERWICK.

Named to HENRY VI's regency COUNCIL in 1422, Northumberland also served on various diplomatic missions, especially to Scotland. In 1436, he received a grant of £100 for life for successfully repelling a Scottish invasion, and in 1437 he was reappointed to the royal council when Henry attained his majority. However, by the 1450s, with the earl no longer active in the council, Northumberland and his sons found themselves unable to compete for royal favor with the Nevilles, the other great magnate family of the north. Rivals for lands and offices, the Percies and Nevilles came to the brink of open war in 1453. In August, Northumberland's second son, Thomas PERCY, Lord Egremont, menaced a Neville wedding party at the Battle of HEWORTH outside York. In October, Northumberland and his sons gathered a large following that for three tense days faced a similar force collected by Richard NEVILLE, earl of Salisbury, leader of the Neville family, and by his son, Richard NEVILLE, earl of Warwick. Although on this occasion the parties declined to fight and disbanded their armies, continued provocations and acts of violence by members of both families kept the north in turmoil throughout 1454.

By 1455, the NEVILLE-PERCY FEUD began to shape national politics, as Northumberland aligned himself and his family with Edmund BEAUFORT, duke of Somerset, a favorite of Henry VI and York's chief rival for control of the king and government. Because a land dispute between Warwick and Somerset had caused the Nevilles to ally with York, Northumberland associated himself with Somerset to nullify the advantage his rivals drew from their association with York (see FIRST PROTECTORATE). While strengthening Somerset's resolve to oppose York, Northumberland's decision also strengthened the Nevilles' determination to support York. These political arrangements created the tensions that exploded in violence at the Battle of ST. ALBANS in May 1455, where York and the Nevilles seized the king and killed both Northumberland and Somerset. Because his sons considered it murder, Northumberland's death merged the Neville-Percy feud into the coming war between the houses of LANCASTER and YORK, and transformed the Percies into staunch Lancastrians.

See also North of England and the Wars of the Roses; all entries under Percy
Further Reading: Griffiths, Ralph A., "Local Rivalries and National Politics: The Percies, the Nevilles and the Duke of Exeter, 1452–1455," in Ralph A. Griffiths, ed., *King and Country: England and Wales in the Fifteenth Century* (London: Hambledon Press, 1991), pp. 321–364; Griffiths, Ralph A., *The Reign of King Henry VI* (Berkeley: University of California Press, 1981); Storey, R. L., *The End of the House of Lancaster*, 2d ed. (Stroud, Gloucestershire, UK: Sutton Publishing, 1999).

Percy, Henry, Earl of Northumberland (1421–1461)

By maintaining his family's feud with the NEVILLE FAMILY, Henry Percy, third earl of Northumberland, contributed to the local disorder and political instability that made possible the WARS OF THE ROSES.

The eldest son of Henry PERCY, second earl of Northumberland, Percy acquired his family's traditional Scottish border offices of warden of the East March and captain of BERWICK. In 1446, he became Lord Poynings after his marriage to the daughter of the last holder of the title. Several times in the late 1440s and 1450s, he led raids into and repelled invasions out of SCOTLAND. In 1448, Poynings was captured and briefly imprisoned by the Scots; in 1451, HENRY VI appointed Poynings to a commission for negotiating a truce with the representatives of JAMES II. Occupied by his duties on the border, Poynings had only a limited involvement in the NEVILLE-PERCY FEUD of the 1450s, which his family conducted mainly under the leadership of his younger brother, Thomas PERCY, Lord Egremont.

After the death of his father at the Battle of ST. ALBANS in May 1455, Poynings succeeded to the earldom of Northumberland and continued his family's rivalry with the Nevilles, whom the earl considered responsible for his father's murder. In early 1458, Northumberland led a large force to LONDON to attend a great COUNCIL summoned by the king to compose the differences between leading nobles. Joined by Henry BEAUFORT, duke of Somerset, and the sons of other peers killed at St. Albans, Northumberland demanded recompense for those deaths from Richard PLANTAGENET, duke of York, and his allies, Richard NEVILLE, earl of Salisbury, and Richard NEVILLE, earl of Warwick. He participated in the LOVE-DAY reconciliation mediated by Henry VI in March 1458, but in November 1459 he supported the ATTAINDER of York and the Nevilles in the COVENTRY PARLIAMENT, and in December 1460 he was a leader of the Lancastrian army that defeated and killed York and Salisbury at the Battle of WAKEFIELD. He marched south with Queen MARGARET OF ANJOU in early 1461 and fought at the Battle of ST. ALBANS on 17 February (see MARCH ON LONDON). He was killed commanding the van of the Lancastrian army at the Battle of TOWTON in late March. The earl was posthumously attainted by the first PARLIAMENT of EDWARD IV, who confined Northumberland's son, Henry PERCY, future fourth earl of Northumberland, for most of the 1460s.

See also North of England and the Wars of the Roses; all entries under Percy

Further Reading: Griffiths, Ralph A., "Local Rivalries and National Politics: The Percies, the Nevilles and the Duke of Exeter, 1452–1455," in Ralph A. Griffiths, ed., *King and Country: England and Wales in the Fifteenth Century* (London: Hambledon Press, 1991), pp. 321–364; Griffiths, Ralph A., *The Reign of King Henry VI* (Berkeley: University of California Press, 1981); Storey, R. L., *The End of the House of Lancaster,* 2d ed. (Stroud, Gloucestershire, UK: Sutton Publishing, 1999).

Percy, Henry, Earl of Northumberland (1446–1489)

By refraining from opposing EDWARD IV in 1471 and from supporting RICHARD III in 1485, Henry Percy, fourth earl of Northumberland, twice affected the course of the WARS OF THE ROSES.

The only son of Henry PERCY, third earl of Northumberland, who died fighting for HENRY VI at the Battle of TOWTON in March 1461, Percy was confined after his father's estates were forfeited to the Crown by act of ATTAINDER. In 1464, Edward IV granted the earldom of Northumberland to John NEVILLE, Lord Montagu, as a reward for Montagu's victories over Lancastrian rebels at the Battles of HEDGELEY MOOR and HEXHAM. However, in October 1469, after freeing himself from the control of Montagu's elder brother, Richard NEVILLE, earl of Warwick, Edward IV released Percy from confinement. In March 1470, after driving Warwick from England, the king stripped Montagu of the earldom of Northumberland and conferred the title on Percy, who also resumed his family's traditional office of warden of the East March (i.e., the eastern border with SCOTLAND). After Edward IV was overthrown in October 1470 (see EDWARD IV, OVERTHROW OF), Northumberland ignored his family's Lancastrian past and did not actively support the READEPTION government of Henry VI, which was controlled by the Percies' ancient rivals, the NEVILLE FAMILY.

When Edward IV landed in northern England in March 1471, Northumberland remained quiet, a neutrality that allowed the Yorkist king time to build support (see ED-

WARD IV, RESTORATION OF). Edward rewarded Northumberland by restoring him to the Scottish wardenship, which Warwick had withdrawn, and by naming him to several additional offices, including the constableship of BAMBURGH CASTLE. Northumberland was appointed chief commissioner to Scotland in 1472 and accompanied the king on the French expedition of 1475. In 1482, the earl participated in the duke of Gloucester's Scottish campaign, and was named captain of the newly recovered town of BERWICK. Gloucester, after taking the throne as Richard III in June 1483, was careful to cultivate Northumberland's support. The earl was confirmed in all his offices and was named great chamberlain of England after Henry STAFFORD, duke of Buckingham, forfeited the office for his involvement in BUCKINGHAM'S REBELLION in the autumn of 1483. Richard also granted Northumberland some of Buckingham's estates, and in 1484 PARLIAMENT returned to him all the Percy lands that had been lost to the family since their rebellion against Henry IV in 1403.

Despite these many rewards, Northumberland's support for Richard III was only lukewarm. In August 1485, when Henry Tudor, earl of Richmond, invaded England, Northumberland obeyed Richard's summons and was present in the royal army at the Battle of BOSWORTH FIELD. Nonetheless, he took no part in the battle, and later writers claimed that he would have defected to Richmond had not a suspicious Richard III kept him under close watch. It is also possible that the fighting drew so rapidly to its conclusion that the earl never had an opportunity to engage; after the battle, Richmond, now HENRY VII, thought Northumberland sufficiently associated with the late king to order the earl's imprisonment. He was, however, soon released, admitted to favor, and restored to all his offices. Northumberland was killed in April 1489 by Yorkshire rebels protesting a recent tax assessment.

See also North of England and the Wars of the Roses; all entries under Percy
Further Reading: "Henry Percy," in Michael Hicks, *Who's Who in Late Medieval England*

(London: Shepheard-Walwyn, 1991), pp. 343–344; Hicks, Michael, "Dynastic Change and Northern Society: The Career of the Fourth Earl of Northumberland, 1470–89," in *Richard III and His Rivals: Magnates and Their Motives in the Wars of the Roses* (London: Hambledon Press, 1991); Ross, Charles, *Edward IV* (New Haven, CT: Yale University Press, 1998); Ross, Charles, *Richard III* (Berkeley: University of California Press, 1981).

Percy, Thomas, Lord Egremont (1422–1460)

By his ruthless pursuit of the NEVILLE-PERCY FEUD in the mid-1450s, Thomas Percy, Lord Egremont, contributed significantly to the creation of the political factions that fueled the WARS OF THE ROSES.

The second son of Henry PERCY, second earl of Northumberland, Percy showed an early aptitude for troublemaking; in 1447, he and a band of confederates were thrown into York jail for disorderly conduct. The next year, during the war with SCOTLAND, Percy defended the family's estates in Cumberland. In 1449, after being created Lord Egremont, Percy began raising a band of armed RETAINERS in Yorkshire and northwestern England, areas dominated by the NEVILLE FAMILY. Motivated perhaps by a dispute over the conduct of the Scottish war, or by a dispute over land, Egremont began to threaten Neville tenants and property. In June 1453, HENRY VI summoned Egremont to COURT, intending to commission him for service in FRANCE, a proposal probably initiated by Richard NEVILLE, earl of Salisbury, as a way to remove Egremont from northern England. When Egremont ignored the royal command, John NEVILLE, one of Salisbury's younger sons, set out in pursuit of Egremont, an action that instigated a series of violent clashes across northern England between the sons and followers of Salisbury and Northumberland.

In August 1453, at the so-called Battle of HEWORTH, Egremont and a large following attacked a Neville wedding party led by Salisbury himself. In 1454, during the FIRST PROTECTORATE of Richard PLANTAGENET, duke of York, Egremont, working in concert with Henry HOLLAND, duke of Exeter, caused great disorder in Yorkshire, forcing York to intervene. Exeter was captured and imprisoned in July, but Egremont remained free until October, when he was defeated and captured by Salisbury's sons at the Battle of STAMFORD BRIDGE. During Egremont's subsequent two-year imprisonment in LONDON, his father was slain by York and the Nevilles at the Battle of ST. ALBANS and his elder brother, Henry PERCY, now third earl of Northumberland, closely allied the Percies with the house of LANCASTER.

Upon his escape from prison in November 1456, Egremont resumed his harassment of the Nevilles. In March 1458, he became part of the king's LOVE-DAY reconciliation, being required by the settlement to give bonds to keep the peace for ten years. However, on the outbreak of civil war in 1459, Egremont took up arms for Henry VI and died defending the king at the Battle of NORTHAMPTON in July 1460. Because he was one of an unusually high number of Lancastrian lords to be slain at Northampton, it is probable that, like his father at St. Albans, he was specifically targeted for death by the Yorkist leaders.

> **See also** North of England and the Wars of the Roses; all entries under Percy
> **Further Reading:** Griffiths, Ralph A., "Local Rivalries and National Politics: The Percies, the Nevilles and the Duke of Exeter, 1452–1455," in Ralph A. Griffiths, ed., *King and Country: England and Wales in the Fifteenth Century* (London: Hambledon Press, 1991), pp. 321–364; Griffiths, Ralph A., *The Reign of King Henry VI* (Berkeley: University of California Press, 1981); Storey, R. L., *The End of the House of Lancaster*, 2d ed. (Stroud, Gloucestershire, UK: Sutton Publishing, 1999).

Percy-Neville Feud. *See* Neville-Percy Feud

Philip, Duke of Burgundy (1396–1467)

As ruler of one of the wealthiest states in fifteenth-century Europe, and as the chief rival of the kings of FRANCE, Philip "the Good,"
duke of BURGUNDY, was an important potential source of foreign support for both English factions during the WARS OF THE ROSES.

Philip became duke in 1419 upon the assassination of his father, Duke John the Fearless, who was killed by followers of the Dauphin Charles, the son and heir of Charles VI of France. To avenge his father's murder, Philip recognized Henry V of England as heir to the French Crown, thereby creating an Anglo-Burgundian alliance that allowed Henry to overrun much of northern France. Upon the deaths of both Henry V and Charles VI in 1422, Philip accepted HENRY VI as king of France, while the Dauphin, now CHARLES VII, strove to secure the French Crown for himself. In 1429, disputes with the English led Philip to negotiate with Charles, but the duke returned to his English alliance when Henry's government ceded to him the French county of Champagne. However, in 1435, Philip abandoned Henry VI and concluded the Treaty of Arras with Charles VII, who purchased the duke's alliance by ceding to him a series of strategic towns along the Franco-Burgundian border. Left to fight alone, the English were finally driven out of France in 1453 (see HUNDRED YEARS WAR).

By the late 1450s, the expulsion of the English allowed the French Crown to focus on reducing the power of Burgundy; Charles VII sought to eventually reabsorb French Burgundy into the French state. This policy and Charles's support for the house of LANCASTER—Queen MARGARET OF ANJOU was his niece and the Yorkists advocated reestablishing the French empire lost by Henry VI—led Philip to cautiously favor the house of YORK. Although angered by the piracy of Richard NEVILLE, earl of Warwick, who held CALAIS for the Yorkists, Philip in 1460 advised his kinswoman, MARY OF GUELDRES, queen-regent of SCOTLAND, to deny aid to Queen Margaret. In 1461, the duke supplied a troop of handgunners to fight for EDWARD IV at the Battle of TOWTON, and in 1462, Philip largely nullified the CHINON AGREEMENT between LOUIS XI and

Queen Margaret by refusing to allow French troops to cross Burgundian soil to attack Calais. Philip also continued to provide the Yorkist government with diplomatic assistance in Scotland and elsewhere.

Although Philip declined a marriage connection with the still insecure house of York in 1461, and Anglo-Burgundian relations were strained by a commercial dispute in 1464, mutual suspicion of France and the ties of a lucrative and long-standing trade relationship brought the two states closer together after 1465. By Philip's death in 1467, Burgundy and Yorkist England were on the verge of a formal alliance, which was concluded in 1468 by Philip's son and heir, Duke CHARLES.

Further Reading: Vaughan, Richard, *Philip the Good: The Apogee of Burgundy* (New York: Barnes and Noble, 1970).

Plantagenet, Cecily, Duchess of York. *See* Neville, Cecily, Duchess of York

Plantagenet, Edmund, Earl of Rutland (1443–1460)

Edmund Plantagenet, earl of Rutland, the second son of Richard PLANTAGENET, duke of York, was slain with his father at the Battle of WAKEFIELD in 1460. The manner of his death further embittered relations between the contending families in the WARS OF THE ROSES.

Born in Normandy in May 1443 while his father was serving in FRANCE as lord lieutenant, Rutland was named heir to York's various Norman lands, an attempt by the duke to preserve his vast English inheritance intact for his eldest son, Edward, earl of March (see EDWARD IV). The loss of Normandy to the French in 1450 put an end to this scheme, and no further provision was made for Rutland (see HUNDRED YEARS WAR). In October 1459, the sixteen-year-old earl was present with his father and elder brother at the Battle of LUDFORD BRIDGE. When the defection of his troops forced the duke to flee

the field, Rutland accompanied York to IRELAND, while March withdrew to CALAIS with his father's allies, Richard NEVILLE, earl of Salisbury, and Richard NEVILLE, earl of Warwick.

Rutland returned to England with his father in September 1460, two months after Warwick's victory at the Battle of NORTHAMPTON put HENRY VI and the royal government under Yorkist control. The Act of ACCORD of October 1460 placed Rutland in the succession to the Crown behind his father and elder brother, and the accompanying financial settlement gave Rutland 1,000 marks per year out of the former revenues of the disinherited Lancastrian heir, EDWARD OF LANCASTER, Prince of Wales. On 2 December, Rutland was part of the armed force that his father and Salisbury led out of LONDON to quell Lancastrian unrest in the north (see NORTH OF ENGLAND AND THE WARS OF THE ROSES).

Only seventeen, Rutland died on 30 December at the Battle of Wakefield, where he was killed on or near Wakefield Bridge by John CLIFFORD, Lord Clifford, whose father, Thomas CLIFFORD, Lord Clifford, had been slain by York's forces at the Battle of ST. ALBANS in 1455. Although the slaying of Rutland at such a young age was later much romanticized, especially by the Tudor chronicler Edward Hall, who had Clifford refuse Rutland's plea for mercy with the words, "By God's blood, thy father slew mine, and so I will do thee and all thy kin" (Haigh, p. 75), the exact circumstances of Rutland's death are uncertain. After the battle, the earl's head was placed next to his father's on the walls of York. Rutland was hastily interred with the duke at St. Richard's Priory in Pontefract, where both remained until 1476, when Edward IV removed his brother and father to a splendid tomb at the house of YORK's family home at Fotheringhay.

See also *The Union of the Two Noble and Illustrious Families of Lancaster and York* (Hall); other entries under Plantagenet
Further Reading: Haigh, Philip A., *The Battle of Wakefield 1460* (Stroud, Gloucestershire, UK:

Sutton Publishing, 1996); Johnson, P. A., *Duke Richard of York* (Oxford: Clarendon Press, 1988).

Plantagenet, Edward, Earl of Warwick (1475–1499)

After the death of RICHARD III in 1485, Edward Plantagenet, Earl of Warwick, the son of George PLANTAGENET, duke of Clarence, and thus a nephew of EDWARD IV and a grandson of Richard NEVILLE, earl of Warwick, became the last Yorkist claimant to the throne in the direct male line and a natural focus for conspiracies against the house of TUDOR.

Born in February 1475, Warwick lost his mother, Isabel NEVILLE, when he was not yet two, and his father when he was three (see CLARENCE, EXECUTION OF). Little is known of his upbringing, though he seems to have come for a time under the care of his aunt, Anne NEVILLE, Richard III's queen. In 1483, Richard III, seeking to remove all the children of his older brothers from his path to the throne, declared Warwick barred from the succession because of his father's ATTAINDER for treason in 1478. Although he knighted Warwick later in the year and briefly considered naming the earl his heir on his own son's death in 1484, Richard confined Warwick in the northern castle of Sheriff Hutton.

In August 1485, only days after he won the Crown at the Battle of BOSWORTH FIELD, HENRY VII had the ten-year-old Warwick conveyed from Sheriff Hutton to the TOWER OF LONDON. Almost immediately, rumors began to surface that Warwick had escaped, and the earl, although still confined, became a key component in various plots to restore the house of YORK to the throne. In February 1487, Warwick was paraded through the streets of LONDON in an effort to discredit Lambert SIMNEL, whose impersonation of Warwick instigated a Yorkist invasion that Henry defeated at the Battle of STOKE in the following June. In 1489, several men were hanged for participation in a conspiracy to free Warwick, and in 1499, Ralph Wilford, yet another Warwick impersonator, was executed.

By the end of the 1490s, continual Yorkist plotting and the urgings of Ferdinand and Isabella of Spain to secure the succession before they married their daughter into the house of Tudor convinced Henry VII to eliminate Warwick. The earl, who had been left ill-educated and naive by the circumstances of his life, was induced by a fellow prisoner, Perkin WARBECK, who had himself impersonated one of the sons of Edward IV, to agree to a plan of escape (see PLANTAGENET, RICHARD, DUKE OF YORK [c. 1483]). The scheme, which may have been laid by royal agents to trap Warbeck and Warwick, came to light, and both men were condemned and executed in November 1499. Several weeks later, in January 1500, the Spanish ambassador informed Ferdinand and Isabella that "not a doubtful drop of royal blood remains in this kingdom" (Chrimes, p. 284, n. 8).

See also other entries under Plantagenet
Further Reading: Arthurson, Ian, *The Perkin Warbeck Conspiracy, 1491–1499* (Stroud, Gloucestershire, UK: Sutton Publishing, 1997); Chrimes, S. B., *Henry VII* (New Haven, CT: Yale University Press, 1999); Ross, Charles, *Richard III* (Berkeley: University of California Press, 1981).

Plantagenet, Elizabeth, Queen of England. *See* Elizabeth of York, Queen of England

Plantagenet, George, Duke of Clarence (1449–1478)

By his alliance with Richard NEVILLE, earl of Warwick, George Plantagenet, duke of Clarence, younger brother of EDWARD IV, divided the house of YORK and helped revive the WARS OF THE ROSES in 1469.

Born in IRELAND during the governorship of his father, Richard PLANTAGENET, duke of York, George and his younger brother Richard were taken for safety to BURGUNDY after their father's death at the Battle of WAKEFIELD in December 1460. After the accession of their elder brother as Edward IV in March 1461, the boys returned to England, where George was created duke of Clarence. As heir to the throne, Clarence was given numerous lands and offices, including the lord lieutenancy of Ireland in 1462. Edward IV's secret marriage to Elizabeth WOODVILLE in 1464 introduced the queen's large and ambitious family to COURT and threatened the political positions and economic prospects of both Warwick and Clarence (see WOODVILLE FAMILY). In July 1469, Clarence defied his brother and married Warwick's daughter, Isabel NEVILLE, at CALAIS. After the ceremony, Clarence and Warwick issued a manifesto calling upon true Englishmen to take arms with them against the king's corrupt administration. Although Edward briefly became their prisoner after the Battle of EDGECOTE (see ROBIN OF REDESDALE REBELLION), Clarence and Warwick, while strong enough to force the king to pardon them, were unable to generate the political support necessary to rule the kingdom in his name.

In the spring of 1470, while Clarence sought to assure Edward of their loyalty, Warwick instigated a second series of rebellions in northern England (see WELLES UPRISING). Only when he heard the rebels at LOSECOTE FIELD advance into battle with cries of "a Clarence" did Edward know that his brother had again betrayed him. Compelled to flee to FRANCE with Warwick, Clarence returned in September when Warwick overthrew Edward IV and restored HENRY VI to the throne (see EDWARD IV, OVERTHROW OF). The Lancastrian restoration left Clarence in an uncomfortable position, with little role in the READEPTION government and less chance of the Crown. Although Warwick tried to buy Clarence's support by giving him his father's entire estate, the duke heeded the urgings of his mother, Cecily NEVILLE, and his sisters and reconciled with Edward IV when his brother returned to England in the spring of 1471. After fighting with Edward at the Battles of BARNET and TEWKESBURY, Clarence was restored to most of his lands and offices (see EDWARD IV, RESTORATION OF).

In the early 1470s, Clarence became involved in the bitter NEVILLE INHERITANCE

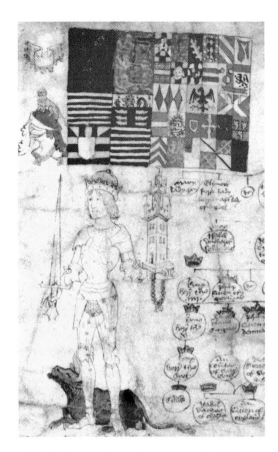

A drawing depicting George Plantagenet, duke of Clarence, brother of Edward IV. (British Library)

DISPUTE with his younger brother, Richard, duke of Gloucester (see RICHARD III). To avoid sharing his wife's vast inheritance, Clarence sought first to thwart Gloucester's marriage to his sister-in-law, Anne NEVILLE, and then, after the marriage occurred in about 1472, to prevent Gloucester from enforcing his new wife's right to a portion of the Neville properties. The king finally intervened and, through PARLIAMENT, imposed a settlement that met many of Clarence's demands but gave the bulk of Warwick's northern estates to Gloucester. Although Clarence accompanied his brothers on the French expedition of 1475, the death of Duchess Isabel in December 1476 again strained relations with the king, who refused to countenance several proposed marriages for Clarence, including a match with Mary, only child of CHARLES, duke of Burgundy. Two trials in 1477 further estranged

Clarence from his brother. In the trial of Thomas Burdett, a gentleman with close ties to Clarence was convicted and condemned, with his associates, for plotting the death of the king and his sons through sorcery, a scheme that, if successful, would have brought Clarence to the throne. In the trial of Ankarette Twynho, Clarence had a former household servant, whom he accused of poisoning his wife, seized, tried, and executed in a single day.

The first trial may have aroused Edward's suspicion of his brother's intentions. The second, because it involved several former servants, may have been Clarence's way of taking revenge on people whom he suspected were supplying the queen's family with information they used to undermine his relationship with the king. Because of Clarence's past record and the evidence of the Burdett trial, the queen likely considered him a threat to her son's accession. Edward IV arrested his brother in June 1477 and in the following January personally charged Clarence in Parliament with actions tending to treason. The duke was condemned by act of ATTAINDER and executed privately in the TOWER OF LONDON in February 1478. Although later rumor claimed the duke was drowned in a butt of malmsey wine, the exact method of his execution is uncertain. In 1483, Clarence's execution, which his brother Gloucester was said to have opposed, eased Gloucester's usurpation of EDWARD V's throne, for it both removed the duke from the succession and provided an excuse to also bar his son, Edward PLANTAGENET, earl of Warwick (see USURPATION OF 1483).

See also other entries under Plantagenet
Further Reading: "George, Duke of Clarence," in Michael Hicks, *Who's Who in Late Medieval England* (London: Shepheard-Walwyn, 1991), pp. 331–333; Hicks, Michael, *False, Fleeting, Perjur'd Clarence: George, Duke of Clarence, 1449–78* (Bangor, UK: Headstart History, 1992).

Plantagenet, George, Duke of Clarence, Execution of. *See* Clarence, Execution of

Plantagenet, House of (1154–1485)

The name "Plantagenet" has been used by historians since the seventeenth century to refer to the English royal family that descended from Henry II (r. 1154–1189) and that in the fifteenth century split into the contending royal houses of LANCASTER and YORK.

The word originated as a nickname for Henry II's father, Geoffrey le Bel, Count of Anjou. Although the exact meaning of the name is unknown, it was suggested in the nineteenth century that it derived from Geoffrey's habit of wearing a sprig of broom (*Planta genista*) in his helm or cap. Other less widely accepted explanations claim that Geoffrey had a fondness for hunting among the broom or that Geoffrey planted broom as cover to improve his hunting. The name Plantagenet was never used by Henry II or his successors or applied to them by contemporaries; it was first adopted as a surname in the late 1440s by Richard PLANTAGENET, duke of York, head of the Yorkist branch of the royal family. Then heir presumptive to a childless HENRY VI, third king of the Lancastrian branch of the family, York probably assumed the name to emphasize his direct descent from Henry II and so illustrate the superiority of his claim to the Crown over that of his political rival, Edmund BEAUFORT, duke of Somerset. The duke was head of the BEAUFORT FAMILY, a junior branch of the Lancastrian line.

From 1189, succession in the line of Henry II had occurred with little difficulty, the Crown passing smoothly from father to son or brother to brother. However, in 1399, the deposition of Richard II (r. 1377–1399) and his replacement by his cousin Henry IV (r. 1399–1413), formerly duke of Lancaster, bypassed the legal line of succession. The Lancastrian usurpation disinherited Richard II's heir, Edmund Mortimer, the eight-year-old earl of March (1391–1425), the great-grandson of Richard's eldest uncle, Lionel, duke of Clarence (1338–1368). Henry IV was the son of a younger uncle, John of Gaunt, duke of Lancaster (1340–1399). In the 1440s, York could claim descent from two uncles of

Richard II—through his Mortimer mother from Clarence and through his (Plantagenet) father from Edmund, duke of York (1341–1402). While York's direct descent in the paternal line was clearly inferior to the Lancastrian claim because it derived from a younger uncle, the superiority of his Mortimer claim from an elder uncle was open to question because it descended to him through a woman. In 1460, when the dangerous possibilities of civil war persuaded York to press his claim, he used his Mortimer ancestry to petition for the Crown by right of succession. With this act, he transformed the political struggles of the 1450s into the WARS OF THE ROSES, a dynastic civil war between two branches of the house of Plantagenet.

See also Richard II, Deposition of; other entries under Plantagenet
Further Reading: Griffiths, Ralph A., "The Crown and the Royal Family in Later Medieval England," in Ralph A. Griffiths and James Sherborne, eds., *Kings and Nobles in the Later Middle Ages* (New York: St. Martin's Press, 1986), pp. 15–26; Harvey, John, *The Plantagenets,* 3d ed. (London: Severn House, 1976); Weir, Alison, *The Wars of the Roses* (New York: Ballantine Books, 1995).

Plantagenet, Margaret, Duchess of Burgundy. *See* Margaret of York, Duchess of Burgundy

Plantagenet, Richard, Duke of Gloucester. *See* Richard III

Plantagenet, Richard, Duke of York (1411–1460)

By laying claim to the Crown of England, Richard Plantagenet, duke of York, transformed a factional struggle for control of the royal government into a dynastic civil war, pitting his family, the house of YORK, against the reigning royal house of LANCASTER.

The son of Richard, earl of Cambridge (c. 1375–1415), and Anne Mortimer (1390–1411), York was descended from Edward III (r.

1327–1377) through both parents. Although his paternal grandfather, Edmund, duke of York (1341–1402), was Edward's fourth son, York's claim to the Crown rested on his descent from his maternal great-great grandfather, Lionel, duke of Clarence (1338–1368), Edward's second son. Despite deriving from the maternal line, York's claim through Clarence rivaled that of his kinsman, HENRY VI, because the king was a great-grandson of Edward III's third son, John, duke of Lancaster (1340–1399).

In 1425, upon the death of his uncle, Edmund Mortimer, earl of March, York inherited both the Mortimer claim to the throne and the family's vast estates, which, with his paternal inheritance, made York the wealthiest member of the English PEERAGE. Knighted by Henry VI in 1426, York accompanied the king to FRANCE in 1430. In 1429, York married Cecily NEVILLE, daughter of Ralph Neville, earl of Westmorland (c. 1364–1425). Appointed king's lieutenant in France in 1436, and reappointed in 1440, York was given generous French land grants. In 1445, the government recalled York, who became heir apparent to the childless Henry VI in 1447. Although he held extensive estates in WALES and IRELAND, York considered his 1447 appointment as king's lieutenant in Ireland to be banishment and did not travel to Dublin until 1449.

This eagle badge was one of the devices used by Richard Plantagenet, duke of York. (Add MS 40742 f. 5, British Library)

Angered by the government's failure to repay debts incurred while in the royal service abroad, as well as by what he viewed as his exclusion from the political position that was due him by birth, York returned to England in 1450, only months after dissatisfaction with Henry VI's government led to the outbreak of JACK CADE'S REBELLION. Suspected by the COURT of fomenting the uprising, York quarreled with Edmund BEAUFORT, duke of Somerset, whom York (and others) held responsible for the recent loss of Normandy. However, Somerset remained in high favor at court, and York, fearing that the duke was endeavoring to destroy him, took up arms in 1452 to compel the king to arrest Somerset. Although Henry initially agreed to York's demands, the duke's uprising collapsed at DARTFORD when few nobles supported him, and the king reneged on his promise to abandon Somerset. Although forced only to swear loyalty to Henry, York was politically isolated and excluded from government.

This situation was transformed in 1453 by the onset of the king's mental illness and by the birth of the king's son, Prince EDWARD OF LANCASTER (see HENRY VI, ILLNESS OF). The first event led to Somerset's arrest and York's appointment as protector of the realm in March 1454, and the second made an implacable opponent of Queen MARGARET OF ANJOU, who was concerned for her son's future and suspicious of York's ambition. In February 1455, Henry's recovery ended York's FIRST PROTECTORATE. However, the king, now increasingly under the queen's influence, restored Somerset to favor, and the renewed quarrel between the two dukes soon absorbed various local feuds, including the NEVILLE-PERCY FEUD in northern England. As Henry PERCY, earl of Northumberland, drew closer to the court, York formed an alliance with the earl's rivals, Richard NEVILLE, earl of Salisbury, who was the duke's brother-in-law, and Salisbury's son, Richard NEVILLE, earl of Warwick. Backed by the extensive political and military resources of the NEVILLE FAMILY, York again sought to force the king to abandon Somerset. At the Battle of ST. ALBANS in May 1455, York and the Nevilles slew Somerset and Northumberland and took control of Henry and the royal government.

In November, after Henry suffered a relapse, PARLIAMENT reappointed York as protector, but the SECOND PROTECTORATE ended with the king's recovery in February 1456. Despite Henry's abortive LOVE-DAY, an attempt in 1458 to reconcile York and the Nevilles with the queen and the heirs of the nobles who had been slain at St. Albans, factions formed around both parties after 1456, and civil war erupted in 1459. After the Battle of LUDFORD BRIDGE in October, York fled to Ireland, where he was popular, and the Nevilles withdrew to CALAIS, where Warwick was captain. In June 1460, the Nevilles, accompanied by York's son, Edward, returned to LONDON; in July, Warwick captured the king at the Battle of NORTHAMPTON, thereby allowing York to return from Ireland in September. On 16 October, the duke made formal claim to the Crown by right of inheritance, but Parliament received the petition with little enthusiasm. By the end of the month, Parliament, with the acquiescence of both the king and the duke, passed the Act of ACCORD, a settlement that left Henry on the throne but disinherited Prince Edward in favor of York and his heirs.

Immediately rejected by the queen and her supporters, the Act of Accord drove Lancastrians across England to rise against the Yorkist regime. With northern England in rebellion, York and Salisbury marched out of London in early December (see NORTH OF ENGLAND AND THE WARS OF THE ROSES). After some difficulty, the duke reached his Yorkshire castle of Sandal just before Christmas. On 30 December, York left Sandal to attack the Lancastrian forces converging on the castle. Commanded by Henry BEAUFORT, duke of Somerset, John CLIFFORD, Lord Clifford, and other sons of nobles slain at St. Albans, the Lancastrian army surrounded and killed the duke at the Battle of WAKEFIELD. York's death passed his claim to the throne to his son, who, within weeks, fulfilled his father's thwarted ambition by being proclaimed king as EDWARD IV. After Wakefield, the victorious Lancastrians adorned York's head with a paper crown and set it, along with those of Salisbury and the duke's son, Edmund PLANTAGENET, earl of Rutland, on the gates of York.

See also other entries under Plantagenet
Further Reading: Johnson, P. A., *Duke Richard of York* (Oxford: Clarendon Press, 1988); Pugh, T. B., "Richard Plantagenet (1411–60), Duke of York, as the King's Lieutenant in France and Ireland," in J. G. Rowe, ed., *Aspects of Late Medieval Government and Society* (Toronto: University of Toronto Press, 1986).

Plantagenet, Richard, Duke of York (1473–c. 1483)

The second son of EDWARD IV, Richard Plantagenet, duke of York, disappeared in the TOWER OF LONDON in 1483, thus casting suspicion for his murder and that of his brother on his uncle RICHARD III and serving as motivation for further political unrest throughout the 1480s and 1490s.

Born in August 1473, Richard was given his grandfather's title, duke of York, in May 1474. Soon after the death of John MOWBRAY, duke of Norfolk, in January 1476, Edward IV, in an effort to bring the extensive Mowbray estates into the royal family, betrothed York to Norfolk's heir, four-year-old Anne Mowbray. York received the Mowbray titles of earl of Nottingham and duke of Norfolk by February 1477, but did not marry the Mowbray heiress until January 1478, when he was four and she was five. Upon his daughter-in-law's death in 1481, the king had PARLIAMENT vest York with his wife's estates, an act that disinherited John HOWARD, Lord Howard, a royal RETAINER who was next heir at law to the Mowbray lands.

When his father died in April 1483, York was in LONDON with his mother, Queen Elizabeth WOODVILLE. York's elder brother, EDWARD V, was at Ludlow in the keeping of his maternal uncle Anthony WOODVILLE, Earl Rivers. Three weeks later, when word reached London that Richard, duke of Gloucester, the king's paternal uncle, had arrested Woodville and taken custody of Edward V, the queen fled to SANCTUARY at Westminster with York and his sisters. On 16 June, Gloucester, arguing that Edward V could not be crowned in the absence of his brother and heir, surrounded Westminster with troops and threatened to forcibly remove the duke from sanctuary. Thomas BOURCHIER, archbishop of Canterbury, apparently acting in good faith, convinced the queen to surrender her son, promising that York would be returned to her after the coronation. The duke was immediately lodged in the Tower with his brother, whose personal servants were shortly thereafter withdrawn. Declared illegitimate and barred from the succession, the princes were then moved to the inner apartments of the fortress (see BUTLER PRECONTRACT; *TITULUS REGIUS*). Although York and his brother were seen occasionally in the Tower garden after Gloucester's 6 July coronation as Richard III, by late summer, they were seen no more (see USURPATION OF 1483). Rumors in England and abroad whispered that the princes were dead by the king's order, an unproven claim that is still hotly debated.

The unexplained disappearance of York and his brother undermined support for Richard III and revived dynastic warfare; in the autumn of 1483, former Yorkists joined BUCKINGHAM'S REBELLION, an uprising led by Henry STAFFORD, duke of Buckingham, to replace Richard III with the remaining Lancastrian claimant, Henry Tudor, earl of Richmond. After Richmond won the throne as HENRY VII in 1485, York remained the focus of civil unrest; rumors that he was alive fueled Yorkist attempts to overthrow the house of TUDOR. In the 1490s, as part of an ultimately unsuccessful effort to dethrone Henry VII, a young Fleming named PERKIN WARBECK mobilized widespread support for his cause by claiming to be Richard, duke of York.

See also Princes in the Tower; other entries under Plantagenet
Further Reading: Fields, Bertram, *Royal Blood: Richard III and the Mystery of the Princes* (New York: Regan Books, 1998); Jenkins, Elizabeth, *The Princes*

in the Tower (New York: Coward, McCann and Geoghegan, 1978); More, Sir Thomas, *The History of King Richard III,* edited by Richard S. Sylvester (New Haven, CT: Yale University Press, 1976); Pollard, A. J., *Richard III and the Princes in the Tower* (New York: St. Martin's Press, 1991); Ross, Charles, *Richard III* (Berkeley: University of California Press, 1981); Weir, Alison, *The Princes in the Tower* (New York: Ballantine Books, 1992); Williamson, Audrey, *The Mystery of the Princes* (Chicago: Academy Chicago Publishers, 1986); the text of More's *History of King Richard III* is also available on the Richard III Society Web site at <http://www.r3.org/bookcase/more/moretext.html>.

Plumpton Letters and Papers

The surviving letters and papers of the Plumptons of Yorkshire are a valuable source of information on the lives and concerns of a northern GENTRY family during the WARS OF THE ROSES.

The Plumpton archive contains about 250 letters and almost 1,000 estate and other family documents. The correspondence dates from 1461 to the mid-sixteenth century, with most of the letters written during the reigns of HENRY VII and Henry VIII, when the family was headed by Sir Robert Plumpton (1453–1525) and his son William Plumpton (d. 1547). For the civil wars, the most relevant letters are the earlier ones relating to ED-WARD IV's reign; this correspondence concerns Sir Robert's father, Sir William Plumpton (1404–1480), who was a long-standing RETAINER of the Percy earls of Northumberland. As rivals of the NEVILLE FAMILY (see NEVILLE-PERCY FEUD), the Percies were partisans of the house of LANCASTER, and Sir William followed his lord, Henry PERCY, third earl of Northumberland, into the service of HENRY VI. Sir William fought at the Battle of TOWTON in 1461 and spent some months following the battle in confinement in the TOWER OF LONDON, but he somehow escaped ATTAINDER by the Yorkist PARLIA-MENT.

In the 1460s, Sir William lived uneasily under the northern dominance of Richard NEVILLE, earl of Warwick, but won greater favor with the house of YORK after 1470,

when Edward IV released the Percy heir from confinement and recognized him as Henry PERCY, fourth earl of Northumberland. Through the patronage of the new earl, Sir William held a number of local offices, as did his son Sir Robert, who fought under Northumberland in the duke of Gloucester's campaigns in SCOTLAND in the early 1480s. Although the letters for RICHARD III's reign are few, those from the previous decade shed light on Richard's exercise of power in the north as duke of Gloucester.

The letters for the reign of Henry VII are fuller and more numerous, describing such events as the coronation of Henry's queen, ELIZABETH OF YORK; the suppression of the northern rebellion of 1489, which began with the murder of Northumberland; and the trials in 1499 of Perkin WARBECK, the Yorkist pretender, and Edward PLANTAGENET, earl of Warwick, the remaining male heir of the house of York. Besides illuminating key events in the north, the letters from the years before 1500 provide a limited but useful view of the political activities of a gentry family during the Yorkist and early Tudor periods.

See also North of England and the Wars of the Roses

Further Reading: Kirby, Joan, ed., *The Plumpton Letters and Papers* (Cambridge: Cambridge University Press, 1996); Stapleton, Thomas, ed., *The Plumpton Correspondence* (London: Camden Society, 1839; reprint, Stroud, Gloucestershire, UK: Alan Sutton, 1990).

Pole, John de la, Duke of Suffolk (1442–1491)

Because of the influence he exercised in East Anglia, John de la Pole, second duke of Suffolk, was courted by all sides in the civil wars, even though he seems to have been a man of little political ability.

His father, William de la POLE, first duke of Suffolk, was chief minister to HENRY VI until the duke was driven from power and murdered during the political upheavals of 1450. Henry VI confirmed de la Pole in his father's title in 1455, but, by 1458, Suffolk had married Elizabeth, daughter of Richard

PLANTAGENET, duke of York, a connection that cost the duke demotion to earl of Suffolk when Queen MARGARET OF ANJOU held power in 1459. Suffolk thereafter aligned himself with the house of YORK, fighting with Richard NEVILLE, earl of Warwick, at the Battle of ST. ALBANS in February 1461. After EDWARD IV won the throne at the Battle of TOWTON in March 1461, Suffolk received surprisingly few rewards from his brother-in-law; he was not even re-created duke of Suffolk until 1463.

This lack of favor may have stemmed from personal dislike, or from the king's low opinion of Suffolk's abilities; it did not, however, blind Edward to his need for the duke's support in the conflict with the house of LANCASTER, as the Paston family discovered in 1469 when the king refused to help them against the duke, even when he was shown the ruins of a Paston manor destroyed by Suffolk's men (see Paston Letters). This stance paid off for Edward when Suffolk sided with him against the Warwick-inspired uprisings of 1469–1470. When Warwick drove Edward from England in October 1470, the duke quietly withdrew to his estates, emerging again in the spring to support Edward's restoration to the throne (see EDWARD IV, RESTORATION OF). Suffolk was thereafter more consistently favored than he had been in the 1460s, but he never achieved a position of trust or influence with the king. He accompanied Edward on the French expedition of 1475 and was appointed lord lieutenant of IRELAND in 1478, although he never assumed the office.

Upon Edward IV's death in 1483, Suffolk acquiesced in the usurpation of RICHARD III. Although Suffolk's eldest son, John de la POLE, earl of Lincoln, was looked upon as Richard's heir after the death of the king's son in 1484, the duke himself no more enjoyed the confidence of Richard III than he had that of Richard's brother. After Richard's death at the Battle of BOSWORTH FIELD in August 1485, Suffolk readily submitted to HENRY VII, receiving as reward the constableship of Wallingford Castle. The duke thereafter retained Henry's trust, even after Lincoln died

fighting for the Yorkist pretender Lambert SIMNEL at the Battle of STOKE in June 1487. Suffolk died in 1491.

Further Reading: Ross, Charles, *Edward IV* (New Haven, CT: Yale University Press, 1998); Ross, Charles, *Richard III* (Berkeley: University of California Press, 1981).

Pole, John de la, Earl of Lincoln (c. 1464–1487)

A nephew of EDWARD IV and RICHARD III, John de la Pole, earl of Lincoln, was a leader of Lambert SIMNEL's 1487 attempt to reopen the civil wars and restore the house of YORK to the throne.

The eldest son of John de la POLE, second duke of Suffolk, and Elizabeth Plantagenet, sister of Edward IV, de la Pole was created earl of Lincoln by his uncle in 1467. Upon Edward IV's death in 1483, Lincoln became a firm adherent of Richard III, who appointed the earl president of the Council of the North, an administrative body established to maintain order on the distant Scottish border. When Prince Edward, the king's son, died in April 1484, Richard appointed Lincoln lord lieutenant of IRELAND in his son's place, although the actual government of Ireland remained in the hands of a deputy, Gerald FITZGERALD, earl of Kildare.

Although never publicly proclaimed heir to the throne, Lincoln was, following the death of the prince, the nearest adult after the king in the Yorkist line of succession. Lincoln's cousin, Edward PLANTAGENET, earl of Warwick, the son of Richard III's late brother, George PLANTAGENET, duke of Clarence, had a superior claim to the throne because it descended from the direct male line, but the earl was only nine in 1484 and was barred from the succession, according to the statute *TITULUS REGIUS,* by his father's ATTAINDER. Richard therefore signaled his acceptance of Lincoln as heir by granting the earl lands worth over £300 per year and a pension of £176 per year drawn from the Duchy of Cornwall, which was usually given to the heir to the throne.

Lincoln was present when Richard was defeated and killed at the Battle of BOSWORTH FIELD in August 1485. Hoping to win the support of the earl and his family, HENRY VII only required Lincoln to swear an oath of loyalty. But the earl was apparently unwilling to renounce his own claim to the Crown, and in early 1487 he fled to BURGUNDY, where his aunt, MARGARET OF YORK, duchess of Burgundy, gave him troops with which to support Lambert Simnel, a Yorkist pretender who was gathering an army in Ireland by impersonating Warwick. Upon his arrival in Dublin, Lincoln openly accepted Simnel's claim, though, in private, he probably saw his own accession as the ultimate goal of the enterprise. Crossing to England with Simnel's army, Lincoln was killed at the Battle of STOKE in June 1487. His younger brothers, Edmund and Richard de la Pole, continued to oppose the TUDOR regime.

See also Yorkist Heirs (after 1485)
Further Reading: Bennett, Michael, *Lambert Simnel and the Battle of Stoke* (New York: St. Martin's Press, 1987); Chrimes, S. B., *Henry VII* (New Haven, CT: Yale University Press, 1999); Ross, Charles, *Richard III* (Berkeley: University of California Press, 1981).

Pole, William de la, Duke of Suffolk (1396–1450)

As first minister of HENRY VI, William de la Pole, duke of Suffolk, so monopolized royal favor that Richard PLANTAGENET, duke of York, believed himself unjustly excluded from his rightful place in government and undertook efforts to force the king to take him into office.

After becoming earl on his brother's death at the Battle of Agincourt in 1415, Suffolk served in FRANCE throughout the 1420s (see HUNDRED YEARS WAR). He was in command at the siege of Orleans when the city was relieved by Joan of Arc in May 1429. In June, he surrendered to the French at Jargeau, and he purchased his freedom only by selling his lands in Normandy. Suffolk was admitted to the royal COUNCIL in 1431, and thereafter

he gradually associated himself with the political faction led by Cardinal Henry Beaufort (c. 1376–1447) and with the peace policy Beaufort advocated. This association threw Suffolk into increasing rivalry with the king's uncle, Humphrey, duke of Gloucester (1390–1447), who favored more vigorous prosecution of the war.

By the early 1440s, Suffolk was a personal favorite of Henry VI, who also supported peace with France and who granted the earl a succession of important and lucrative offices. In 1444, Suffolk negotiated the king's marriage to MARGARET OF ANJOU, a kinswoman of CHARLES VII of France. Although Henry hoped the marriage would be part of a general peace agreement, Suffolk was forced to settle for a two-year truce. The earl stood proxy for Henry during the formal betrothal ceremony in France, but then he was not allowed to escort the bride to England until Henry VI had agreed to surrender the county of Maine. Although belonging to the king, responsibility for this unpopular decision, which was implemented in 1448, was later imputed to Suffolk by the people. Trusted by both the king and the queen, Suffolk became the effective head of government in 1447 after the deaths of Gloucester and Beaufort. Secure in royal favor, Suffolk removed York, who was heir to the throne, from command in France and sent him into practical exile as king's lieutenant in IRELAND. York's replacement in France was Edmund BEAUFORT, duke of Somerset, a supporter of Suffolk's who also had a claim to the Crown. These actions intensified York's alienation from the court and sharpened his rivalry with Somerset.

Raised to a dukedom in 1448 and granted various other rewards and offices, Suffolk used his position to enrich himself and his supporters. Although the king's grants were freely given and most of Suffolk's actions were common practice, the extreme poverty of Henry's government made Suffolk's monopoly of royal patronage highly unpopular, both with unfavored nobles like York and with the commons (see COMMONS [COMMON PEOPLE] AND

THE WARS OF THE ROSES). When the French overran Normandy in 1449, in part through the incompetence of Somerset, popular hatred of Suffolk, already fueled by the surrender of Maine, exploded. The duke was arrested in January 1450, when PARLIAMENT charged him with various offenses, including corruption and mishandling the French war. Although the king was loath to proceed against his minister, the House of Commons was adamant, and Henry compromised by banishing Suffolk from England for five years. On 2 May, the ship bearing Suffolk to the continent was intercepted by a royal vessel, the crew of which seized and murdered the duke. Although nothing can now be proven, the mysterious circumstances surrounding Suffolk's death suggest the involvement of York or another of the duke's noble opponents.

Further Reading: Griffiths, Ralph, *The Reign of King Henry VI* (Berkeley: University of California Press, 1981); "William de la Pole," in Michael Hicks, *Who's Who in Late Medieval England* (London: Shepheard-Walwyn, 1991), pp. 272–274; Wolffe, Bertram, *Henry VI* (London: Eyre Methuen, 1981).

Precontract. *See* Butler Precontract

Prerogative

The royal prerogative comprised all the powers and privileges that English law reserved for the Crown to enable it to effectively govern the realm. Although its full extent was vaguely defined and depended in part on the personality of the monarch, the prerogative included such rights and duties as summoning and dismissing PARLIAMENT, issuing proclamations, appointing and dismissing ministers and judges, conducting foreign policy, and ensuring the maintenance of public order and the administration of impartial justice. The WARS OF THE ROSES, because they both arose from and contributed to a breakdown of law, order, and good government, led to a general increase in the prerogative and personal power of the monarch.

Even before the onset of his mental illness in 1453, HENRY VI had shown himself incapable of exercising royal authority in a vigorous and evenhanded manner (see HENRY VI, ILLNESS OF). During his personal rule, the Crown ceased to be an arbiter of noble feuds, a guarantor of justice and order, or a promoter of prosperity. To regain the political and economic benefits of peace and the rule of law, most citizens of late fifteenth-century England were willing to countenance the strengthening of the royal prerogative, even if such an increase in royal power meant more arbitrary government. The destruction of the house of LANCASTER in 1471 allowed EDWARD IV to rule thereafter with greater authority and firmness. Although he occasionally bent or overrode law or custom to secure his throne or benefit the house of YORK, and although redress at law was difficult to obtain against any of the great nobles upon whom he relied for military support (see PEERAGE), Edward IV won much popularity by reducing the level of violence and improving the quality of justice throughout the kingdom.

Edward won further praise, especially in LONDON, for avoiding foreign wars and for encouraging English trade (see ENGLISH ECONOMY AND THE WARS OF THE ROSES). Because Parliament was associated with the granting of taxation rather than with oversight of the Crown, the infrequency of sessions after 1471 only enhanced Edward's standing with the people, who became more willing to accept an expanded prerogative in return for domestic peace and low taxes. Although HENRY VII never enjoyed the personal popularity of Edward IV, he achieved the same level of popular acceptance for his increasingly repressive rule by following many of Edward's policies. The house of TUDOR benefited from the deep respect for authority engrained in the English people by their memory of the disorder and dissension caused by the Wars of the Roses.

See also Bastard Feudalism; Courtenay-Bonville Feud; Neville-Percy Feud
Further Reading: Carpenter, Christine, *The Wars of the Roses* (Cambridge: Cambridge University

Press, 1997); Ross, Charles, *The Wars of the Roses* (London: Thames and Hudson, 1987).

Princes in the Tower

The term "Princes in the Tower" refers to the sons of EDWARD IV and their mysterious disappearance while lodged in the TOWER OF LONDON in 1483. Because their guardian at the time, their uncle RICHARD III, seized the throne of his eldest nephew, five centuries of debate have swirled around the question of whether or not Richard was responsible for the boys' presumed murder. The princes' disappearance, by creating an alliance of dissident Yorkists and former Lancastrians to support the claim to the throne of Henry Tudor, earl of Richmond (see HENRY VII), initiated the destruction of the house of YORK and the last phase of the WARS OF THE ROSES.

The only detailed written account of the murders of EDWARD V and his younger brother Richard PLANTAGENET, duke of York, is contained in Sir Thomas More's *HISTORY OF KING RICHARD III,* which was written about 1513. More claimed that his information was based on a confession to the crime given in 1502 by Sir James TYRELL, a former servant of Richard III then facing execution for treason. Because this confession has never been found, it has been dismissed by some writers as an invention of More's. According to More, Richard, after his coronation on 6 July, sent a trusted servant named John Green to Sir Robert BRACKENBURY, constable of the Tower, with a written order to put the princes to death in any manner Brackenbury chose to employ. Brackenbury refused, saying that he would never do such a thing even if he died for his disobedience. Dejected, Richard wondered aloud to an unnamed servant whether he could trust anyone to carry out his wishes. The servant replied that there was one who waited without the chamber for whom "the thing were right hard that he would refuse" the king (More, p. 86). This ambitious servant was Tyrell, whom Richard then ordered to arrange the princes' deaths. To assist Tyrell, Richard withdrew all the princes' fa-miliar servants from the Tower and had the boys placed in the keeping of a man "called Black Will or Will Slaughter" (p. 87).

To carry out the actual murder, Tyrell recruited Miles Forest, "a fellow fleshed in murder before time" and one of the four persons then responsible (presumably with Slaughter) for the boys' keeping in the Tower, and John Dighton, "a big, broad, square, strong knave" who was Tyrell's horsekeeper (p. 88). About midnight, while the princes were sleeping, Forest and Dighton stole into their chamber, "bewrapped . . . and entangled them" in their bedclothes, and so smothered them to death. The murderers then laid the bodies naked on the bed and fetched Tyrell to view them before burying the princes at the foot of a Tower stair "under a great heap of stones" (p. 88). Richard, upon being informed of the murders by Tyrell, was well pleased, but ordered that the bodies be reinterred in a more fitting manner, whereupon a priest of Brackenbury's secretly reburied them in a location unknown to More.

Whether a literary creation of More's based on tales current during his youth or an accurate account of the murder of the princes, More's story became the inspiration for William Shakespeare's *RICHARD III* and was probably also known to More's contemporary Polydore Vergil, whose *ANGLICA HISTORIA* ascribes the murders to an unwilling Tyrell, but otherwise gives no details. Over the centuries, four main theories (among many other lesser ones) have been devised to explain the disappearance of the princes. The most likely and most accepted is that Richard III, whether in the manner described by More or otherwise, was responsible for the boys' deaths. However, Richard's many defenders, who have grown steadily in number since the seventeenth century, have made plausible cases that the princes were killed by Henry STAFFORD, duke of Buckingham, who as Richard's chief ally had access to the Tower in 1483; by Henry VII, whose ability to hold the Crown would have been considerably weakened had he found the boys alive when he took power in 1485; or by disease, the plague or something else the princes may have contracted in the Tower during their confinement. Because none of these theories can now be definitively proved or eliminated, the debate over the fate of the princes and the guilt or innocence of Richard III remains the most passionately argued in English history.

See also Bones of 1674
Further Reading: Fields, Bertram, *Royal Blood: Richard III and the Mystery of the Princes* (New York: Regan Books, 1998); Jenkins, Elizabeth, *The Princes in the Tower* (New York: Coward, McCann and Geoghegan, 1978); More, Sir Thomas, *The History of King Richard III,* edited by Richard S. Sylvester (New Haven, CT: Yale University Press, 1976); Pollard, A. J., *Richard III and the Princes in the Tower* (New York: St. Martin's Press, 1991); Weir, Alison, *The Princes in the Tower* (New York: Ballantine Books, 1992); Williamson, Audrey, *The Mystery of the Princes* (Chicago: Academy Chicago Publishers, 1986); the text of More's *History of King Richard III* is also available on the Richard III Society Web site at <http://www.r3.org/bookcase/more/moretext.html>.

Prior of the Hospital of St. John of Jerusalem. *See* Langstrother, Sir John, Prior of the Hospital of St. John of Jerusalem

Propaganda

Throughout the WARS OF THE ROSES, the contending factions issued newsletters, manifestos, and other declarations to justify themselves and vilify their opponents—propaganda efforts aimed at winning support both in England and overseas.

From the start of the political struggle in the 1450s, the Yorkists strove to present their cause to the public in the best possible light. To deflect charges of rebellion, the Yorkists issued proclamations stressing their loyalty to HENRY VI and explaining their actions as merely a desire to petition the king for redress of grievances. They justified their rather unorthodox method of petitioning under arms by claiming that it was a regrettable necessity. They maintained that the royal councilors responsible for their grievances were seeking to deny them a fair hearing and even to destroy them. After the Battle of ST. ALBANS in May 1455, the Yorkists worked to eradicate the treasonable impression left by their violence. They treated the king with great deference, escorted him to LONDON with full royal honors, swore loyalty to him at an impressive crown-wearing ceremony, and obtained pardons from him that were duly ratified in PARLIAMENT. The pardons blamed the battle on Edmund BEAUFORT, the slain duke of Somerset, and on several other obscure royal officials, and new proclamations emphasized how these culprits had foiled exhaustive Yorkist attempts to avoid combat through negotiation.

After 1461, EDWARD IV continued the Yorkist use of propaganda. By exaggerating the horrors perpetrated by Queen MARGARET OF ANJOU's army as it plundered Yorkist lands and towns during its MARCH ON LONDON in 1461, the Yorkists heightened fears of Lancastrian pillage in the capital and disposed London to admit Edward IV and accept him as king. In 1471, Edward commissioned the HISTORY OF THE ARRIVAL OF EDWARD IV, a newsletter that quickly disseminated Edward's version of his restoration among foreign courts (see EDWARD IV, RESTORATION OF). Perhaps because they considered the house of LANCASTER the legitimate holder of the Crown, Lancastrian leaders were less inclined to use propaganda and more interested in obtaining foreign assistance. These latter efforts provided Edward with excellent propaganda opportunities; for instance, he made great use of Margaret's surrender of BERWICK to SCOTLAND in 1461. To avoid similar damaging attacks in 1462 when she concluded the CHINON AGREEMENT with LOUIS XI of FRANCE, Margaret insisted that her willingness to surrender CALAIS remain secret.

Richard NEVILLE, earl of Warwick, proved particularly adept at the use of propaganda. His landing in England in June 1460 was accompanied by the issuance of a manifesto detailing the oppressions perpetrated by Henry VI's evil councilors and justifying Warwick's actions as an attempt to right those wrongs.

In this Yorkist propaganda piece from 1461, Edward IV is shown at the top of the wheel of fortune; Edward's brothers, the dukes of Clarence and Gloucester, are shown on the rise, while Henry VI falls and is crushed. (Harley MS 7353 f. 2, British Library)

Warwick used the same technique against Edward IV in 1469, when the earl and George PLANTAGENET, duke of Clarence, issued a manifesto from Calais that denounced the failings of Edward's government and declared the correction of those evils their reason for taking arms against the king. In 1470, when he returned to England to overthrow Edward IV, Warwick distributed a propaganda tract entitled the *MANNER AND GUIDING OF THE EARL OF WARWICK AT ANGERS,* which described and justified the earl's conclusion of the ANGERS AGREEMENT with Margaret of Anjou, thereby reassuring both Warwick's supporters and longtime Lancastrians (see EDWARD IV, OVERTHROW OF).

RICHARD III carefully staged the USURPATION OF 1483, using the BUTLER PRE-CONTRACT and Dr. SHAW'S SERMON to justify to the people his seizure of EDWARD V's throne. In 1485, he issued proclamations claiming that Henry Tudor, earl of Richmond, was plotting to allow foreigners to invade and despoil the realm. After 1485, when Yorkists like John de la POLE, earl of Lincoln, led foreign MERCENARIES against HENRY VII, they had to justify their actions against Henry's own antiforeign propaganda. Henry highlighted the blessings of Tudor rule by using various agents and media to blacken the reputation of Richard III, a propaganda effort that continues to affect Richard's image to this day. Henry also fostered the ubiquitous roses motif, that is, the blending of the red and white roses, as a symbol of the peace and unity conferred on England by the house of TUDOR, an image that eventually lent itself to the naming of the fifteenth-century civil wars.

Further Reading: Allan, Alison, "Yorkist Propaganda: Pedigree, Prophecy and the 'British History' in the Reign of Edward IV," in Charles Ross, ed., *Patronage, Pedigree and Power n Later Medieval England* (Stroud, Gloucestershire, UK: Alan Sutton, 1979), pp. 171–192; Ross, Charles, "Rumour, Propaganda and Popular Opinion during the Wars of the Roses," in Ralph A. Griffiths, ed., *Patronage, the Crown and the Provinces in Later Medieval England* (Atlantic Highlands, NJ: Humanities Press, 1981), pp. 15–32.

Protectorates of the Duke of York.

See First Protectorate; Second Protectorate

Radford, Nicholas (d. 1455)

The murder of Nicholas Radford, a respected Devonshire attorney, was the most notorious episode in the violent COURTENAY-BON-VILLE FEUD, which convulsed the West Country in the 1450s and helped create the political alliances that initiated the WARS OF THE ROSES.

Although a councilor of William BON-VILLE, Lord Bonville, the chief West Country rival of Thomas COURTENAY, fifth earl of Devon, Radford also had a long and apparently harmonious association with the Courtenay family. In 1423, when Devon was a minor, Radford was appointed surveyor and steward of the earl's lands. His oversight of the earldom must have been satisfactory, for Radford stood as godfather to Devon's son Henry COURTENAY in about 1440, and served as a feoffee (i.e., trustee) with Devon for the lands of various Devonshire gentlemen, including several Courtenay relatives.

In October 1455, Devon and his sons launched a series of attacks across the West Country against the supporters and properties of Bonville. Around midnight on 23 October, Thomas COURTENAY, the earl's heir, led a large body of men to Radford's house. Setting Radford's gate afire, the men called upon the attorney to come down. Learning that the intruders were led by a Courtenay, from whom he expected no harm, the elderly Radford admitted the men, who then proceeded to ransack the house while Courtney engaged Radford in conversation. So thorough was the sacking that Courtenay's men did not neglect the sheets upon the bed, which were obtained by dumping Radford's invalid wife onto the floor. Courtenay then demanded that Radford accompany him to his father at Tiverton, about six miles away. Radford agreed to come, but he was told he must walk the entire distance, for Courtenay's men had already driven off his horses. When the party had gone only a short distance from the house, Courtenay departed, and six of his men set upon Radford, stabbing him and cutting his throat.

Days later, as Radford's body was being prepared for burial, a party led by Henry Courtenay, Radford's godson, broke into the chamber and held a mock inquest over the corpse, finding that the unfortunate Radford had died a suicide. They then dumped the naked body into the grave and pelted it with stones until it was unrecognizable and therefore useless for a proper inquest. The reasons for the Courtenays' murderous hatred of Radford are unclear, but they may have been related to Radford's recent successful representation of Bonville in a lawsuit against Devon. The obviously premeditated murder and its outrageous aftermath shocked contemporaries and won the Courtenays an evil reputation. In 1461, when Thomas Courtenay, the sixth earl and leader of the Radford murder party, was executed after the Battle of TOWTON, a correspondent of John Paston wrote: "The Earl of Devonshire is dead justly" (Davis, 2, p. 230).

Further Reading: Cherry, Martin, "The Struggle for Power in Mid-Fifteenth-Century Devonshire" in Ralph A. Griffiths, ed., *Patronage, the Crown and the Provinces in Later Medieval England* (Atlantic Highlands, NJ: Humanities Press, 1981), pp. 123–144; Davis, Norman, ed., *The Paston Letters and Papers of the Fifteenth Century,* 2 vols. (Oxford: Oxford University Press, 1971, 1976); Storey, R. L., *The End of the House of Lancaster,* 2d ed. (Stroud, Gloucestershire, UK: Sutton Publishing, 1999); for a contemporary description of Radford's death, see Warrington, John, ed., *The Paston Letters,* vol. 1 (New York: E. P. Dutton, 1956), pp. 110–111.

Ratcliffe, Sir Richard (d. 1485)

In 1483, when RICHARD III usurped his nephew's throne and thereby reopened the civil wars, Sir Richard Ratcliffe (or Radcliffe) became one of the new king's most trusted advisors.

Born into a Lancashire GENTRY family of Yorkist allegiance, Ratcliffe fought at the Battle of TEWKESBURY in 1471 and was knighted on the field by EDWARD IV. Some time during the 1470s, Ratcliffe entered the service of the king's brother, Richard, duke of Gloucester, whom he accompanied on the Scottish campaign of 1482. In June 1483, Gloucester sent Ratcliffe into the north to raise forces to support the duke's forthcoming seizure of EDWARD V's Crown. Having collected almost 5,000 men from Gloucester's loyal northern following, Ratcliffe stopped at Pontefract Castle, where, on about 25 June, he carried out the duke's orders to execute Anthony WOODVILLE, Earl Rivers, and Sir Richard Grey, the brother and son, respectively, of Queen Elizabeth WOODVILLE. For this service, Gloucester, now king as Richard III, made Ratcliffe a Knight of the Garter (a prestigious order of chivalry), a knight of the body (a close personal servant), and sheriff of Westmorland for life. Ratcliffe also received several other lucrative offices and lands worth £650 a year, a sum exceeded only by the land grants made to John HOWARD, duke of Norfolk; Henry PERCY, fourth earl of Northumberland; and Thomas STANLEY, Lord Stanley, all noblemen whose support was vital to the new regime.

Along with William CATESBY and Francis LOVELL, Lord Lovell, Ratcliffe became widely known as a member of Richard's inner circle of advisors. A popular satirical couplet of the time declared that "The cat [Catesby], the rat [Ratcliffe], and Lovell our dog [Lovell's emblem], / Rule all England under a hog [referring to Richard III's white boar emblem]." In March 1485, after the death of Queen Anne NEVILLE, Ratcliffe and Catesby told the king that he must publicly disavow any intention of marrying ELIZABETH OF YORK, Edward IV's eldest daughter. They argued that the marriage would alienate even the king's loyal northerners and would give substance to the rumor that he had murdered his wife to have his niece. Ratcliffe died the following August fighting for Richard III at the Battle of BOSWORTH FIELD. Ratcliffe's lands were confiscated by HENRY VII, although the act of ATTAINDER passed against him in the first PARLIAMENT of the new reign was reversed in 1495 at his son's request.

See also North of England and the Wars of the Roses; Richard III, Northern Affinity of; Usurpation of 1483
Further Reading: Ross, Charles, *Richard III* (Berkeley: University of California Press, 1981).

Readeption (1470–1471)

Upon HENRY VI's restoration to the throne, all letters, writs, and official records began styling the king's regnal year as "the 49th year of the reign of Henry VI and the first of his readeption to royal power" (Weir, p. 177). Because of this formula, historians refer simply to "the Readeption" when describing the period of restored Lancastrian government between October 1470 and April 1471.

In August 1470, the conclusion of the ANGERS AGREEMENT between Queen MARGARET OF ANJOU and Richard NEVILLE, earl of Warwick, created an alliance between the house of LANCASTER and supporters of the NEVILLE FAMILY that drove EDWARD IV and the house of YORK from the throne in October (see EDWARD IV, OVERTHROW OF). Upon entering LONDON, Warwick and his ally, Edward IV's brother, George PLANTAGENET, duke of Clarence, removed Henry VI from captivity in the TOWER OF LONDON and installed him with great ceremony in the bishop's palace, where he remained for the next six months as the inert figurehead of a government controlled by Warwick. Taking the offices of king's lieutenant, chamberlain of England, and captain of CALAIS, Warwick appointed or reappointed all royal officials in Henry's name and issued summonses for a PARLIAMENT, which met in November.

The composition and acts of the Readeption Parliament are largely unknown because its records were destroyed by the Yorkists upon their return to power. However, the assembly attainted Edward IV and his brother, Richard, duke of Gloucester (see RICHARD III), and reversed ATTAINDERS of Lancastrians passed under Edward. Parliament also authorized the negotiation of peace with FRANCE, and Warwick, in accordance with his compact with LOUIS XI, raised forces to support Louis against Duke CHARLES of BURGUNDY, actions that convinced the duke to support Edward, who had fled to Burgundy in October 1470.

Distrusted by many Lancastrians, Warwick was hampered by the failure of Queen Margaret and her son to leave France. Young and vigorous, Prince EDWARD OF LANCASTER might have given the Lancastrian cause greater energy and purpose. The Readeption government was also weakened by the anomalous position of Clarence. Although the duke was appointed lord lieutenant of IRELAND, Clarence's loyalty to Warwick was effectively undermined by his mother, Cecily NEVILLE, duchess of York, and his sisters. When Edward returned in March, Clarence abandoned the earl.

The Readeption collapsed when Edward IV defeated and killed Warwick at the Battle of BARNET on 14 April 1471, the very day Queen Margaret and the prince landed in England. Raising an army in the West Country, Margaret was defeated and her son was slain at the Battle of TEWKESBURY on 4 May (see EDWARD IV, RESTORATION OF). With the prince dead, Edward had Henry VI quietly murdered in the Tower on 21 May, thus extinguishing the male line of Lancaster (see HENRY VI, MURDER OF). Queen Margaret remained a prisoner until 1475, when she was ransomed and returned to France by Louis XI.

Further Reading: Gillingham, John, *The Wars of the Roses* (Baton Rouge: Louisiana State University Press, 1981); Goodman, Anthony, *The Wars of the Roses* (New York: Dorset Press, 1981); Griffiths, Ralph A., *The Reign of King Henry VI* (Berkeley: University of California Press, 1981); Hicks, Michael, *Warwick the Kingmaker* (Oxford: Blackwell Publishers, 1998); Ross, Charles, *Edward IV* (New Haven, CT: Yale University Press, 1998); Weir, Alison, *The Wars of the Roses* (New York: Ballantine Books, 1995); Wolffe, Bertram, *Henry VI* (London: Eyre Methuen, 1981).

Rebellion of 1483. *See* Buckingham's Rebellion

Recruitment of Armies. *See* Armies, Recruitment of

Recueil des Croniques et Anchiennes Istories de la Grant Bretaigne, a present nomme Engleterre (Waurin)

Jean de Waurin's *Recueil des Croniques et Anchiennes Istories de la Grant Bretaigne, a present nomme Engleterre* (*A Collection of the Chronicles and Ancient Histories of Great Britain, Now Called England*) is a useful, if difficult, source for the early stages of the WARS OF THE ROSES and the first reign of EDWARD IV.

Jean de Waurin (or Wavrin) (1395–1475) was the natural son of a Burgundian nobleman, who, after being officially legitimized in 1437, entered the service of both Dukes PHILIP and CHARLES of BURGUNDY. Pro-English in his outlook, he visited England in 1467 to attend the royal tournament fought at Smithfield by Anthony, Bastard of Burgundy (the natural son of Duke Philip), and Edward IV's brother-in-law, Anthony WOODVILLE, Lord Scales, He was also in CALAIS with Duke Charles in 1469 for a meeting with Richard NEVILLE, earl of Warwick. Because Waurin's chronicle of England, Burgundy, and northwestern FRANCE in the period 1461–1471 was likely written between 1465 and Waurin's death in 1475, the *Recueil* is a nearly contemporary account of the events it describes.

However, modern historians have seriously questioned Waurin's reliability. Although the

Jean de Waurin presents a copy of his chronicles to Edward IV. The man wearing the garter in the right foreground is thought to be the king's brother, Richard, duke of Gloucester (later Richard III). (Royal MS 15 E IV f. 14, British Library)

Recueil contains some unique information about English affairs, Waurin is often unclear as to the sources of his information. Like other continental writers about events in England, Waurin seems to have had access to some of the newsletters and other PROPAGANDA pieces issued by the two sides in the English civil war, such as Warwick's *MANNER AND GUIDING OF THE EARL OF WARWICK AT ANGERS,* which described and justified the earl's conclusion of the ANGERS AGREE-MENT with Queen MARGARET OF ANJOU in 1470, and the Yorkist *HISTORY OF THE ARRIVAL OF EDWARD IV,* which offered Edward's version of his successful campaign to regain the throne in 1471 (see EDWARD IV, RESTORATION OF). Waurin's uncritical reliance on such obviously partisan sources, as well as his often confused chronology, his tendency to create fictional speeches for his characters, and his imaginative reconstructions of events based on what he felt must have occurred, have led some scholars to dismiss the *Recueil* as worthless. However, other historians maintain that, when used with care, the *Recueil* is a useful source for many events in the 1460s.

Further Reading: Ross, Charles, *Edward IV* (New Haven, CT: Yale University Press, 1998); Waurin, Jean, *Recueil des Croniques et Anchiennes Istories de la Grant Bretaigne, a present nomme Engleterre,* 5 vols., edited and translated by Sir William Hardy (London: Longman, Green, and Roberts, 1864–1891).

Retainers

In the social system known as BASTARD FEUDALISM, members of the PEERAGE and GENTRY recruited sworn followers known as retainers to provide a particular type of service in return for monetary fees or the exercise of the lord's influence on their behalf.

Retainers often bound themselves to a lord by a written contact known as an indenture of retainer, which normally specified the type of service to be provided and the amount of the fees or wages to be paid. The indenture was so named because it was cut along an indented line to allow a matching portion to be given to each party to the contract. Although retainers summoned to arms as part of a great magnate's AFFINITY formed the core of many civil war armies, most retainers supplied nonmilitary service, functioning as domestic servants, household officers, legal advisors, and estate agents. Although most retainers were liable for military service in times of need, as occurred frequently during the WARS OF THE ROSES, large numbers of exclusively military retainers were often hastily recruited when a campaign or battle was imminent (see ARMIES, RECRUITMENT OF). For such emergencies, a magnate also usually had a number of "well-willers," men not under formal indenture but who had enjoyed the lord's favor and influence and who could be approached for military service. To clearly proclaim a retainer's allegiance, especially in battle, a nobleman often supplied his retainers with a special livery (i.e., uniform) or with his personal or family BADGE. For instance, in the poem, *THE SONG OF LADY BESSY,* the retainers of Sir William STANLEY are described as wearing coats "as red as any blood" on which they displayed Stanley's hart's head badge (Boardman, p. 66).

The king also retained men for various types of service; Sir Thomas Montgomery was given a livery of crimson cloth of gold to distinguish him as one of EDWARD IV's knights of the body (a royal bodyguard). Wearing the king's white boar badge, RICHARD III's retinue of household knights charged with him into the heart of the enemy force at the Battle of BOSWORTH FIELD. All indentures contained a provision that declared the retainer's allegiance to the king superior to his allegiance to the contracting lord. However, the Wars of the Roses, being a civil conflict, forced many retainers to make difficult choices between serving their lord, whose family may have long held the allegiance of the retainer's family, and serving the king the lord opposed—a dilemma that faced many retainers of Richard PLANTAGENET, duke of York, when the duke openly challenged HENRY VI in 1460. A man could also be retained by two lords, a circumstance that created further difficulties when one lord supported the house of LANCASTER and the other the house of YORK.

Throughout the fifteenth century, PARLIAMENT enacted numerous anti-retaining statutes in an effort to curb the abusive use of armed retainers to conduct local feuds, attack political rivals, intimidate judges and juries (a practice known as embracery), and generally cause disorder and mayhem. Edward IV's statute of 1468 tried to define who could be retained and for what purposes, and HENRY VII's law of 1504 prohibited retaining without royal license. Neither statute was entirely successful because kings continued to rely on their own and their nobles' retainers to form the armies they required to fight foreign wars and suppress internal rebellions. As a result, the practice of retaining remained in use well into the sixteenth century.

See also Livery and Maintenance; Retaining, Acts Against

Further Reading: Boardman, Andrew W., *The Medieval Soldier in the Wars of the Roses* (Stroud, Gloucestershire, UK: Sutton Publishing, 1998); Hicks, Michael, *Bastard Feudalism* (London: Longman, 1995); Hicks, Michael, "Lord Hastings' Indentured Retainers?" in *Richard III and His Rivals: Magnates and Their Motives in the Wars of the Roses* (London: Hambledon Press, 1991); Rowney, I., "Resources and Retaining in Yorkist England: William, Lord Hastings, and the Honour of Tutbury," in A. J. Pollard, ed., *Property and Politics: Essays in Later Medieval English History* (Stroud, Gloucestershire, UK: Alan Sutton, 1984).

Retaining, Acts against

The heart of the social system known as BASTARD FEUDALISM was the creation by members of the PEERAGE and GENTRY of an AFFINITY of sworn RETAINERS who indented (contracted) for life to support their lord in war and peace in return for money and the exercise of the lord's influence in their behalf. This system not only enabled powerful magnates to summon bands of armed supporters for WARS OF THE ROSES armies, it also allowed them to feud with their rivals and to disrupt the order and administration of their localities. Concerned by what they perceived to be a high level of violence and disorder arising from the unchecked recruitment of retainers, fifteenth-century kings and PARLIAMENTS enacted various statutes to control the practice.

Because they relied on the system to raise large portions of their own military forces, neither EDWARD IV nor HENRY VII wanted to abolish retaining. They sought only to secure the benefits of the system to themselves, while repressing their subjects' ability to use the system for private purposes that disrupted public order and corrupted royal justice. Because kings sought both to continue retaining themselves and to curb retaining by their nobles, anti-retaining statutes tended to be vague and difficult to enforce, leaving the manner of their application to the discretion of the monarch and the circumstances of particular cases.

Attempts to limit retaining had been undertaken long before the outbreak of the Wars of the Roses. A statute passed in 1390 during the reign of Richard II prohibited retaining by anyone other than a nobleman, although enforcement of the act was virtually nonexistent by the mid-fifteenth century. In 1467, the House of Commons asked Edward IV to take strong action to combat the rise in murders, riots, and other disorders that seemed to be occurring throughout the kingdom. The resulting statute, enacted by Parliament in 1468, limited retainers to menial servants, household officers, and legal advisors. However, the act's definitions of what constituted legal retaining were vague, and continuing outrages moved the Parliament of 1472 to request the king to tighten enforcement of the statute and issue a proclamation reiterating the penalties prescribed under it for illegal retaining and abuses of LIVERY AND MAINTENANCE. In the last session of Edward's reign in 1483, Parliament again asked for more vigorous enforcement of the 1468 act.

In 1486, after the Crown passed from the house of YORK to the house of TUDOR, the new monarch, Henry VII, persuaded the lords and commons in Parliament to take an oath to refrain from illegally retaining or being retained. Henry also used acts of ATTAINDER and an unprecedentedly extensive system of bonds and recognizances to bring magnates under royal control. (Recognizances were sums of money pledged as security for loyal service or for performance of a certain act; disloyalty or failure to perform brought the sum due and left the nobleman indebted to the Crown.) *De Retentionibus Illicitis* (1504), the major anti-retaining statute enacted under Henry VII, prohibited retaining without a royal license, but it lapsed at the king's death in 1509. Under Henry VIII, the regulation of retaining again followed the provisions of the 1468 act, with the Crown forbidding or licensing retaining on a case-by-case basis.

Further Reading: Chrimes, S. B., *Henry VII* (New Haven, CT: Yale University Press, 1999); Hicks, Michael, *Bastard Feudalism* (London: Longman, 1995); Ross, Charles, *Edward IV* (New Haven, CT: Yale University Press, 1998).

Rhys ap Thomas (1449–1525)

The leader of an influential Welsh family, Rhys ap Thomas provided vital support to Henry Tudor, earl of Richmond (see HENRY VII), during his campaign to overthrow RICHARD III in 1485.

The son of THOMAS AP GRUFFYDD, a loyal adherent of the house of LANCASTER, Rhys spent the late 1460s in exile in BURGUNDY with his father. After the deaths of his father and elder brothers in the early 1470s, Rhys became head of his family. Although shorn of the influence his grandfather had once exercised across southwestern WALES, Rhys made peace with EDWARD IV and remained an important figure in Welsh affairs throughout the 1470s. After Edward's death in 1483, Richard III placed the government of Wales in the hands of his ally, Henry STAFFORD, duke of Buckingham, an important landowner in Wales and the marches (i.e., the Welsh borderlands). When Buckingham betrayed Richard that autumn, Rhys declined to join BUCKINGHAM'S REBELLION, probably because he saw the duke's unprecedented authority as a threat to his family's position.

Because Richmond, the remaining Lancastrian heir, was of Welsh blood, Richard began cultivating support in Wales in 1484. Unable to find many loyal Yorkists in southwestern Wales, Richard courted former Lancastrians, such as Rhys, who received an annuity from the king in February 1484. The grant was the first important mark of favor bestowed on Rhys's family by the house of YORK in over two decades. To ensure Rhys's loyalty, Richard demanded that he swear an oath of fidelity and hand over his only son as a hostage. Rhys declared himself willing to take the oath, but he begged the king to reconsider the hostage demand. The boy seems never to have been surrendered, but the threat to his heir probably weakened Rhys's attachment to Richard. By 1485, Rhys was being recruited by Richmond's agents. Although Rhys replied favorably to Richmond's request, he did not join the earl when he landed in Wales in August, and rumors swept Richmond's army that Rhys was hostile. In fact, Rhys did nothing,

shadowing Richmond's force but neither helping nor hindering his march across Wales. Although Rhys's apparent indecision caused Richmond some anxious moments, it was probably a scheme to convince the king that Rhys intended to attack the invaders before they reached England. If this was his plan, it worked, for Richard, hearing of the landing on 11 August, did not march until 15 August, when he fell into a rage upon learning that Richmond had crossed Wales unopposed.

About 13 August, Rhys openly joined Richmond, who promised to appoint Rhys lieutenant in Wales. According to THE SONG OF LADY BESSY, Rhys brought "eight thousand spears" into Richmond's camp, while THE ROSE OF ENGLAND says that Rhys drew "Wales with him" (Evans, p. 132). Although both claims are likely exaggerated, Rhys clearly brought a welcome and considerable addition to Richmond's strength. Rhys distinguished himself in Richmond's service at the Battle of BOSWORTH FIELD on 22 August and is one of several men who were later said to have struck the blow that killed the king. Although this claim cannot be substantiated, a Welsh poem states that Rhys "killed the boar [Richard's badge], destroyed his head," and the Burgundian writer Jean Molinet declared that a Welshman struck the fatal blow (Griffiths, p. 43).

Knighted three days after Bosworth, Sir Rhys was well rewarded for his service. Under the king's uncle, Jasper TUDOR, duke of Bedford, Sir Rhys served as king's deputy in South Wales, and became justiciar of the region after Bedford's death in 1495. He helped suppress the Yorkist uprisings in 1486 and fought against the Lambert SIMNEL rebels at the Battle of STOKE in 1487 (see LOVELL-STAFFORD UPRISING). A royal councilor and a member of the king's household, Sir Rhys fought against the Cornish rebels at Blackheath in 1497 and later that year against Perkin WARBECK in the West Country. A personal friend of the king's, Sir Rhys was entrusted with building a new tomb in Wales for Henry's father, Edmund TUDOR, earl of Richmond. In 1505, Sir Rhys was elected a

Knight of the Garter. After Henry's death in 1509, Sir Rhys continued to serve the house of TUDOR until his death in 1525.

> **Further Reading:** Evans, H. T., *Wales and the Wars of the Roses* (Stroud, Gloucestershire, UK: Alan Sutton Publishing, 1995); Griffiths, Ralph A., *Sir Rhys ap Thomas and His Family* (Cardiff, UK: University of Wales Press, 1993).

Richard, Duke of York. *See*

Plantagenet, Richard, Duke of York (1411–1460); Plantagenet, Richard, Duke of York (1473–c. 1483)

Richard II, Deposition of (1399)

In the sixteenth century, William SHAKESPEARE and his contemporaries, concerned with the uncertain succession of the house of TUDOR, viewed the deposition of Richard II in 1399 as the cause and starting point of the WARS OF THE ROSES.

In late June 1399, Henry of Bolingbroke, duke of Lancaster, returned to England from continental exile to claim his late father's extensive estates, an inheritance of which he had been deprived by his cousin Richard II (r. 1377–1399). Nervous about the king's willingness to abrogate the property rights of a subject, and angered by a series of high-handed and arbitrary royal actions, the English ruling classes quickly abandoned the childless king in favor of his Lancastrian kinsman. On 29 September, Richard II, a prisoner in the TOWER OF LONDON, reluctantly bowed to pressure and resigned his Crown to his cousin. When this action was confirmed next day by PARLIAMENT, Richard ceased to be king, and the throne passed to Henry IV (r. 1399–1413), first king of the house of LANCASTER.

The Lancastrian usurpation, although approved at the time by the political elite of the realm, bypassed the line of legal succession. In 1399, Richard II's heir was Edmund Mortimer, the eight-year-old earl of March (1391–1425), the grandson of his cousin Philippa (1355–1381), only child of Lionel, duke of Clarence (1338–1368), second son of Edward III (r. 1327–1377). Henry IV, the new king, was the eldest son of John of Gaunt, duke of Lancaster (1340–1399), third son of Edward III. Within months of Henry's accession, disgruntled former supporters were disputing his right to the throne. Chief among these opponents were Sir Henry Percy (known as Hotspur, 1361–1403), who was married to March's aunt, and Sir Edmund Mortimer (1376–1409), March's uncle. Henry IV survived a series of pro-Mortimer uprisings in the early years of his reign and successfully passed his Crown to his son, Henry V (r. 1413–1422). The second Lancastrian king secured the dynasty by reopening the HUNDRED YEARS WAR, crushing the French at the Battle of Agincourt in 1415, and conquering much of northern FRANCE, actions that made the king and his family a focus of national pride. When March died childless in 1425, his family's claim to the throne, which passed to his sister's fourteen-year-old son, Richard PLANTAGENET, duke of York, was virtually forgotten.

It only revived in 1460, when York, after striving unsuccessfully for years to control the government of the incompetent HENRY VI, the third Lancastrian monarch, laid the house of YORK's claim to the Crown before Parliament. York's action, which led in 1461 to his son's coronation as EDWARD IV, turned the political rivalries of the 1450s into the intermittent dynastic wars of the following three decades. When HENRY VII established the Tudor dynasty on the throne in 1485, his propagandists stressed the horrors of the dynastic warfare from which the new king had rescued England (see PROPAGANDA). Sixteenth-century Englishmen, most notably represented by Shakespeare in his history plays, traced the root of these horrors to the 1399 disruption in the natural line of succession. Although most modern historians reject this view, finding the origins of the wars in Henry VI's inability to function effectively as king and in the local feuds and national ambitions of wealthy and militarily powerful noblemen, the deposition of Richard II is still sometimes taken as the start of the Wars of the Roses.

Prior to his formal deposition, Richard II is confined in the Tower of London by his cousin Henry of Bolingbroke, the future Henry IV. (Harley MS 4380 f. 181, British Library)

Further Reading: Bennett, Michael, *Richard II and the Revolution of 1399* (Stroud, Gloucestershire, UK: Sutton Publishing, 1999); Saul, Nigel, *Richard II* (New Haven, CT: Yale University Press, 1997); Strohm, Paul, *England's Empty Throne: Usurpation and the Language of Legitimation, 1399–1422* (New Haven, CT: Yale University Press, 1998); the text of William Shakespeare's play *Richard II* can be found online at <http://shakespeare.about.com/arts/shakespeare/library/blrichardiiscenes.htm>.

Richard III, King of England (1452–1485)

Richard III, the last king of the houses of YORK and PLANTAGENET, is the most controversial monarch in English history. By deposing and then perhaps murdering his nephew, Richard revived the WARS OF THE ROSES, thereby destroying himself and his dynasty and making possible the rule of the house of TUDOR.

Born on 2 October 1452, Richard was the youngest son of Richard PLANTAGENET, duke of York, and his wife, Cecily NEVILLE. In October 1459, following his father's flight from the field of LUDFORD BRIDGE, seven-year-old Richard, along with his mother and elder brother, George PLANTAGENET, fell into the custody of HENRY VI, who entrusted them to the duchess's sister. They regained their freedom in July 1460 after the king was captured by the Yorkists at the Battle of NORTHAMPTON. In September, the duchess brought the boys to LONDON, where PARLIAMENT answered York's demand for the Crown by enacting the compromise Act of ACCORD, which made the duke heir to Henry VI. Following York's death at the Battle of WAKEFIELD in December and the Yorkist defeat at the Battle of ST. ALBANS in February 1461, Cecily sent Richard and George to safety in BURGUNDY. However, both were recalled to England in April, only weeks after their eldest brother won the Battle of TOWTON and thereby secured the throne as EDWARD IV.

At Edward's coronation in June 1461, Richard was created duke of Gloucester and his brother George duke of Clarence. Although only nine, Gloucester was given liberal grants of land and office, including appointment as lord admiral. In 1469, when Richard NEVILLE, earl of Warwick, convinced Clarence to join a coup against Edward, Gloucester remained loyal to his brother and was rewarded with a lifetime appointment as constable of England. In August 1470, after the failure of a second rebellion drove Warwick and Clarence from the realm, Gloucester's continued loyalty earned him further rewards, including offices traditionally held by the NEVILLE FAMILY. When the rebel magnates returned in October and forced the king to flee, Gloucester was one of a handful of supporters who accompanied Edward to exile in Burgundy (see EDWARD IV, OVERTHROW OF). Returning to England with Edward in March 1471, Gloucester, now eighteen, commanded the van of the Yorkist army at the Battle of BARNET, where Warwick was slain, and at the Battle of TEWKESBURY, where Prince EDWARD OF LANCASTER died (see EDWARD IV, RESTORATION OF). Although various reports claimed that Gloucester helped kill the prince and later murdered Henry VI in the TOWER OF LONDON, the former seems to have fallen during the fighting, and the latter was almost certainly slain on the orders of Edward IV (see HENRY VI, MURDER OF). Gloucester's direct involvement in either death, though possible, cannot now be proven.

In the 1470s, Gloucester continued to render loyal service to his brother, who continued to reward the duke with lands and offices, especially in the north. Marriage to Anne NEVILLE, Warwick's younger daughter, entangled Gloucester in a bitter dispute with Clarence, who was married to Isabel NEVILLE, the elder sister, over division of the late earl's lands (see NEVILLE INHERITANCE DISPUTE). Settlement of the quarrel required royal intervention, but it left Gloucester heir to the Neville influence in the north, where the duke resided after 1475 (see NORTH OF ENGLAND AND THE WARS OF THE ROSES). By 1480, thanks to his Neville connections, his brother's support, and his own

Richard III, brother of Edward IV, deposed his nephew Edward V in June 1483. (National Portrait Gallery: NPG 148)

abilities, Gloucester had constructed a loyal and extensive AFFINITY in the north, which he governed on Edward's behalf. This network of northern RETAINERS proved both a blessing and curse after Gloucester became king in 1483 (see RICHARD III, NORTHERN AFFINITY OF).

In 1475, Gloucester participated in Edward's invasion of FRANCE. Disapproving of his brother's decision to eschew military glory in favor of a French pension, Gloucester absented himself from the signing of the Treaty of Picquigny. In the early 1480s, Gloucester implemented Edward's militant policy toward SCOTLAND. The duke's several campaigns against the Scots recovered BERWICK, but otherwise they achieved little and cost much, and have led later writers to question his ability as a military commander. He was also suspected of encouraging the king to eliminate the troublesome Clarence, although no evidence exists to link Gloucester directly to the duke's ATTAINDER and execution in 1478.

The king was likely the driving force behind Clarence's destruction, and Gloucester's acquiescence—whether eager or reluctant—came only at Edward's bidding (see CLARENCE, EXECUTION OF).

When Edward IV died on 9 April 1483, Gloucester was in the north. Although he immediately swore allegiance to his nephew, EDWARD V, the duke was suspicious of his sister-in-law, Queen Elizabeth WOODVILLE, and of the ambitious WOODVILLE FAMILY, around whom an extensive political interest had formed in the 1470s. Supported by William HASTINGS, Lord Hastings, and other royal servants who feared that the Woodvilles meant to use their influence with Edward to control the government, Gloucester seized the king, arrested Anthony WOODVILLE, Earl Rivers, and frightened the queen into taking SANCTUARY at Westminster. In June, when Hastings and others began to mistrust Gloucester's intentions, the duke, who had been named lord protector, executed Hastings and secured custody of the king's brother, Richard PLANTAGENET, duke of York (see COUNCIL MEETING OF 13 JUNE 1483). Having at some point concluded that his best interests required him to take the throne, Gloucester, assisted by Henry STAFFORD, duke of Buckingham, launched a PROPAGANDA campaign to discredit his nephews' right to the Crown and to advance his own claim (see BUTLER PRECONTRACT; SHAW'S SERMON; *TITULUS REGIUS;* USURPATION OF 1483). Although Gloucester won enough support in London to have himself crowned king as Richard III on 6 July, the usurpation, which was almost immediately followed by rumors that Edward V and York had been murdered in the Tower, drove many Yorkists to join former Lancastrians in seeking to overthrow Richard in favor of Henry Tudor, earl of Richmond (see HENRY VII), the last heir of the house of LANCASTER.

Never able to overcome the opposition generated by the usurpation, Richard's regime was always narrowly based and threatened by betrayal and indifference among the PEERAGE and GENTRY. After the failure of BUCKING-

HAM'S REBELLION—so-called because of the involvement in it of Richard's former ally Buckingham—many southern gentlemen either fled to Richmond in BRITTANY or became too untrustworthy for further employment. Forced to intrude his northern supporters into the leadership of southern counties, Richard reaped further ill will, which only intensified the condemnation and mistrust arising from his silence regarding the disappearance of the PRINCES IN THE TOWER. The death of his son in 1484 and of his queen in 1485 further weakened the king's position and led to damaging rumors, which Richard had to personally disavow, that he intended to marry his niece, ELIZABETH OF YORK. Accused of tyranny and suspected of murder, the king confronted Richmond at BOSWORTH FIELD on 22 August 1485. Although Richard commanded the larger force, the defection of Thomas STANLEY, Lord Stanley, and his brother Sir William STANLEY, combined with the lukewarm adherence of other lords, such as Henry PERCY, earl of Northumberland, led to the king's defeat and death.

After Bosworth, the continuing mystery surrounding the fate of the princes, as well as the new dynasty's need to justify itself through the misdeeds of its predecessors, fostered the writing of a series of works that progressively blackened the reputation of Richard III (see ANGLICA HISTORIA; HISTORY OF KING RICHARD III; UNION OF THE TWO NOBLE AND ILLUSTRIOUS FAMILIES OF LANCASTER AND YORK). Culminating in William Shakespeare's brilliant play, RICHARD III, and answered later by many passionate defenses of Richard and his actions, these writings created a controversy that continues unabated to this day.

See also: Richard III, Historical Views of
Further Reading: Hicks, Michael, *Richard III: The Man behind the Myth* (London: Collins and Brown, 1991); Horrox, Rosemary, *Richard III: A Study in Service* (Cambridge: Cambridge University Press, 1991); Kendall, Paul Murray, *Richard the Third* (New York: W. W. Norton, 1956); Potter, Jeremy, *Good King Richard? An Account of Richard III and His Reputation* (London: Constable, 1994); Ross, Charles, *Richard III* (Berkeley: University of California Press, 1981); see also the Richard III Society Web site at <http://www.r3.org> for a variety of sources and materials relating to Richard III and his reign.

Richard III, Historical Views of

RICHARD III is the most controversial ruler in English history. In the five centuries since his death, he has been condemned as a tyrant and murderer and praised as a good and strong king. Few of the many studies of Richard that have appeared since 1485 take a moderate position on his character and actions. For more than a century after the Battle of BOSWORTH FIELD, the last king of the house of PLANTAGENET was vilified by historians and chroniclers writing under the rule of HENRY VII and his descendants. In the 1590s, this vilification was given its most memorable form by William Shakespeare, whose play RICHARD III turned the king into one of the great villains of English literature. However, after the end of the house of TUDOR in 1603, a series of increasingly vigorous defenses of Richard were published, and in the twentieth century, growing numbers of defenders and detractors presented their views of Richard in a variety of print and nonprint formats.

The only strictly contemporary account of Richard is Dominic Mancini's USURPATION OF RICHARD III, a critical description of the USURPATION OF 1483 written before the end of that year by an Italian visitor to England. A near-contemporary account of Richard's entire reign is the so-called second continuation of the CROYLAND CHRONICLE, which was probably completed in 1486. Although generally hostile to Richard, whom he viewed as a deceitful tyrant, the anonymous chronicler was particularly outraged by Richard's intrusion of northern men into the administration of southern counties (see RICHARD III, NORTHERN AFFINITY OF).

The raw material for the classic Shakespearean portrait of a physically deformed king who murdered his way to the throne was developed in the sixteenth century by a series of writers and chroniclers. Although neither

Henry VII nor Henry VIII formally encouraged the writing of anti-Richard PROPAGANDA, both fostered the view that the accession of the house of Tudor rescued England from the disorder of the WARS OF THE ROSES and the tyranny of Richard III. Accepting this official view of the recent past, and drawing upon the memories of old opponents of Richard at the Tudor COURT, writers like Polydore Vergil in his *ANGLICA HISTORIA* and Sir Thomas More in his *HISTORY OF KING RICHARD III* proclaimed Richard's ambition and ruthlessness, described his physical deformities, and listed his many victims. The antiquary John ROUS, writing in the 1490s, contributed some of the coarser elements of the portrait, claiming that Richard was two years in his mother's womb and emerged at birth with teeth and shoulder-length hair. In his *UNION OF THE TWO NOBLE AND ILLUSTRIOUS FAMILIES OF LANCASTER AND YORK,* the chronicler Edward Hall based his depiction of Richard on Vergil and More, but he so blackened their portrayals as to create a king who foreshadowed Shakespeare's evil monster.

When the later Tudor chroniclers Richard Grafton and Raphael Holinshed incorporated Hall's Richard into their works, they transmitted the accounts of Vergil and More to Shakespeare, who used their chronicles as sources for his enormously influential play, *Richard III* (see SHAKESPEARE AND THE WARS OF THE ROSES). However, even in the Elizabethan period, historians like William Camden and John Stow quietly suggested that Richard's role in the deaths of EDWARD V and Richard PLANTAGENET, duke of York, was uncertain. The first full-scale defense of Richard was written in 1619 by Sir George Buck, Master of Revels to James I. In his *History of King Richard the Third,* Buck praised the king for his courage and justice, declared all charges against him to be unproven, and condemned the Tudor historical tradition for maligning an innocent man. Although the seventeenth and eighteenth centuries saw other writers take up Richard's cause, the Tudor/Shakespearean image of the king continued to dominate. In

1768, however, Horace Walpole published his *Historic Doubts on the Life and Reign of Richard III,* in which he convincingly exposed many of the weaknesses and inconsistencies of the traditional depiction, argued that many of Richard's supposed crimes were contrary to his own best interests, and attempted (rather less convincingly) to shift blame to Henry VII.

The nineteenth century witnessed romantic portrayals of Richard, such as Caroline Halsted's *Richard III as Duke of Gloucester and King of England,* which absolves the king of virtually all crimes and borders on hagiography, and the scholarship of prominent Victorian historians such as John Richard Green, William Stubbs, and James Gairdner, who largely accepted the Tudor portrait. In the twentieth century, the debate assumed a variety of new forms. In the 1920s (Britain) and 1930s (United States), the forerunners of the Richard III Society, organizations dedicated to researching and reassessing Richard's role in English history, were organized. In 1984, London Weekend Television staged a mock trial in which a jury found Richard not guilty of murdering his nephews. Since the 1960s, many fictional works sympathetic to Richard, such as Sharon Kay Penman's *The Sunne in Splendour* (1982), have been published. On the other side, historian A. L. Rowse in his *Bosworth Field* (1966) compared Richard to Adolf Hitler, while Desmond Seward in his *Richard III: England's Black Legend* (1984) proclaimed the Tudor view of the villainous king to be entirely credible. Although many of the more spectacular elements of the Tudor tradition have been largely refuted, and the pro-Richard position has won much popular sympathy, many historians still find Richard responsible for the deaths of the PRINCES IN THE TOWER.

Further Reading: Buck, Sir George, *The History of King Richard III,* edited by A. N. Kincaid (Stroud, Gloucestershire, UK: Sutton Publishing, 1982); Dockray, Keith, *Richard III: A Source Book* (Stroud, Gloucestershire, UK: Sutton Publishing, 1997); Gairdner, James, *History of the Life and Reign of Richard the Third,* 2d ed. (Cambridge: Cambridge University Press, 1898); Green, J. R., *A Short History of the English People* (London, 1874); Halsted,

Caroline A., *Richard III as Duke of Gloucester and King of England*, 2 vols. (London, 1844; reprinted Stroud, Gloucestershire, UK: Sutton Publishing, 1977); Ross, Charles, *Richard III* (Berkeley: University of California Press, 1981); Rowse, A. L., *Bosworth Field: From Medieval to Tudor England* (Garden City, NY: Doubleday, 1966); Seward, Desmond, *Richard III: England's Black Legend* (New York: Franklin Watts, 1984); Stubbs, William, *The Constitutional History of England*, 3 vols. (Oxford: Oxford University Press, 1878); Walpole, Horace, *Historic Doubts on the Life and Reign of Richard III*, edited by P.W. Hammond (Stroud, Gloucestershire, UK: Sutton Publishing, 1987); see also the Richard III Society Web site at <http://www.r3.org/bookcase/texts> for excerpts of many of the publications mentioned in this entry.

Richard III, Northern Affinity of

In the autumn of 1483, many gentlemen of the southern and western shires joined BUCKINGHAM'S REBELLION, an ultimately unsuccessful effort to overthrow RICHARD III in favor of Henry Tudor, earl of Richmond (see HENRY VII). Because most of these rebels either joined Richmond in exile in BRITTANY or were henceforth denied public employment by Richard, the king had few politically reliable men to whom he could entrust important military and administrative posts in southern and southwestern England. This lack of southern support left Richard heavily dependent on his northern RETAINERS and servants, men who had helped him govern the north in the 1470s when he was duke of Gloucester. By intruding members of his northern AFFINITY into positions of power and influence in the south, Richard may have further alienated the southern GENTRY and thereby increased the political instability that fostered renewal of the WARS OF THE ROSES.

The PARLIAMENT of January 1484 passed bills of ATTAINDER against 104 persons who had been implicated in the recent uprising. Although one-third of these men were eventually pardoned and restored to their estates, the continuing threat of an invasion by Richmond meant most of them could no longer be trusted to hold official positions in their coun-

ties. Within weeks of the end of the rebellion, northerners entered the southern counties as commissioners charged with arresting rebels and seizing their lands and property. Before the end of November, Richard signaled his unwillingness to trust the southern gentry by appointing numerous northerners to offices in the southern shires, such as Edward Redman of Yorkshire, who became sheriff of Somerset and Devon; John Musgrave of Cumberland, who became sheriff of Wiltshire; and Robert BRACKENBURY of Durham, who became sheriff of Kent. When the redistribution of forfeited lands began after the parliamentary session, northerners reaped rich rewards, especially in the southwestern counties. Sir Richard RATCLIFFE, one of the king's most loyal northern supporters, as well as two prominent members of the northern PEERAGE, Thomas STANLEY, Lord Stanley, and Henry PERCY, fourth earl of Northumberland, received extensive estates in Somerset, Wiltshire, Devon, and Cornwall. Other northern men were named to southern commissions of the peace and to other local offices, thus giving them administrative control of areas in which they and their families were otherwise unknown.

These appointments intruded outsiders into tight-knit shire communities that consisted of long-established gentry families who were linked by blood, marriage, history, and a set of shared interests. Strongly parochial and resentful of outside interference, southern and southwestern gentry families looked upon the northerners suddenly thrust into authority over them almost as foreign occupiers who had seized the offices and influence that they believed were theirs by right. As the writer of the CROYLAND CHRONICLE lamented, Richard III distributed southern lands and offices "among his northern adherents, whom he planted ... throughout his dominions, to the disgrace and loudly expressed sorrow of all the people of the south, who daily longed ... for the ... return of their ancient rulers, rather than the present tyranny of these people" (Ross, p. 123). Although the Croyland chronicler was notoriously distrustful of northerners and may therefore have exaggerated the extent of northern intrusion into the south, the appointments clearly hurt Richard's standing in southern England, especially when combined with the growing rumors that he had ordered the deaths of his nephews, EDWARD V and Richard PLANTAGENET, duke of York. At the Battle of BOSWORTH FIELD in 1485, many leaders of the southern gentry fought for Richmond, and almost none for Richard III.

See also North of England and the Wars of the Roses

Further Reading: Dockray, Keith, "The Political Legacy of Richard III in Northern England," in Ralph A. Griffiths and James Sherborne, eds., *Kings and Nobles in the Later Middle Ages* (New York: St. Martin's Press, 1986), pp. 205–227; Horrox, Rosemary, *Richard III: A Study in Service* (Cambridge: Cambridge University Press, 1991); Ross, Charles, *Richard III* (Berkeley: University of California Press, 1981).

Richard III (Shakespeare)

Written probably in late 1591, *Richard III* is the final component in William Shakespeare's tetralogy (i.e., four-play cycle) depicting the WARS OF THE ROSES. Because of its powerfully drawn central character, *Richard III* is among the most popular of Shakespeare's plays, and this popularity has allowed the playwright's striking depiction of the villainous king to become the dominant popular image of the historical RICHARD III.

Based largely upon Edward Hall's chronicle, *THE UNION OF THE TWO NOBLE AND ILLUSTRIOUS FAMILIES OF LANCASTER AND YORK*, the play ultimately relies upon Hall's chief source, Sir Thomas More's *HISTORY OF KING RICHARD III*, for much of its portrayal of the last king of the houses of YORK and PLANTAGENET. Concluding with Richard's defeat and death at the Battle of BOSWORTH FIELD, the play completes the main theme of the tetralogy, which is that the suffering and civil war brought upon England by the house of LANCASTER's usurpation of the throne in 1399 and intensified by Richard III's murderous seizure of the Crown in 1483 were happily ended by the accession of the house of TUDOR (see RICHARD II, DEPOSITION OF). By magnifying Richard's capacity for evil, and by giving the king a witty enthusiasm for the commission of crime, Shakespeare makes Richard the perfect contrast to his virtuous Tudor successor, HENRY VII. Although his wicked king is based on an image of Richard III created a century earlier by Tudor PROPAGANDA, Shakespeare sharpens the villainy he found in More and other sources to serve the dramatic purposes of his work.

To illustrate the king's evil nature, Shakespeare gives Richard a hunched back, a detail taken from More. Shakespeare also makes Richard responsible for a host of deaths, including, in the earlier plays of the cycle, those of Edmund BEAUFORT, duke of Somerset; HENRY VI; and (with his brothers) EDWARD OF LANCASTER, Prince of Wales. In *Richard III*, Shakespeare has Richard arrange the murders of his brother, George PLANTAGENET, duke of Clarence; his wife, Anne NEVILLE (whose killing by Richard is implied); and his nephews, EDWARD V and Richard PLANTAGENET, duke of York. Clearly innocent of Somerset's death, which occurred in 1455 at the Battle of ST. ALBANS when Richard was only two, the king has also been absolved of each of the other deaths by at least some modern scholars, and his physical deformity has been rejected by many. While most historians now accept that Richard ordered the murders of his nephews, the fate of EDWARD IV's sons remains highly controversial, and many other possible culprits have been suggested. However, wherever they stand on the question of the PRINCES IN THE TOWER, almost all modern writers accept that Shakespeare's *Richard III* is a highly distorted and inaccurate view of the historical monarch.

See also *Henry VI, Part 1; Henry VI, Part 2; Henry VI, Part 3; Richard III*, Historical Views of; Shakespeare and the Wars of the Roses

Further Reading: Norwich, John Julius, *Shakespeare's Kings* (New York: Scribner, 1999); Saccio, Peter, *Shakespeare's English Kings*, 2d ed. (Oxford: Oxford University Press, 2000); the text of *Richard III* can be found online at <http://shakespeare.about.com/arts/shakespeare/library/blrichardiiiscenes.htm>.

Richmond, Countess of. *See* Beaufort, Margaret, Countess of Richmond and Derby

Richmond, Earl of. *See* Henry VII; Tudor, Edmund, Earl of Richmond

Rivers, Earl. *See* entries under Woodville

Robin of Holderness Rebellion (1469)

Occurring in Yorkshire in May 1569, in the same county and at about the same time as the ROBIN OF REDESDALE REBELLION, the Robin of Holderness uprising contributed to the disorder that allowed Richard NEVILLE, earl of Warwick, to launch his first coup against EDWARD IV.

According to Polydore Vergil's *ANGLICA HISTORIA,* the Robin of Holderness Rebellion was an armed protest against a tax levied on the landholders of northern England by the Hospital of St. Leonard in York. The hospital claimed a thrave (i.e., twenty-four sheaves of grain) each year. By 1469, the tax was nearly a century old, and it had been causing discontent among the taxpayers for almost as long. Following the lead of Sir William Conyers, who had just raised a rebellion under the name of Robin of Redesdale, and perhaps timing his uprising to coincide with the Redesdale movement, Robert Hillyard, a tenant of the Lancastrian Percy family, took the name Robin of Holderness and led the tax protesters toward York. Before reaching their destination, the Holderness rebels were dispersed by John NEVILLE, earl of Northumberland, who seized Robin and executed him before the gates of York. Thus, although some Holderness rebels may have later joined the Redesdale rebellion, the former was apparently unrelated to the latter and not, like the Redesdale rebellion, part of Warwick's plan to seize control of the government.

The only contemporary account of the Holderness uprising does not mention the tax but claims instead that the rebels sought to restore Henry PERCY, then in the TOWER OF LONDON, to his family's earldom of Northumberland This goal explains why John Neville, who currently held the Percy earldom, so effectively suppressed the rebellion. What is confusing about the episode is the appearance of a living Robert Hillyard in documents dating to the decade after his apparent execution in 1469. Although there may have been two Hillyards, a modern historian (see Haigh, p. 192) suggests a more likely explanation. The entire Robin of Holderness Rebellion was fabricated by Warwick or his brother Northumberland to convince Edward IV that the latter was a loyal subject even while the former was engaged in treason. Robert Hillyard is recorded as submitting himself to the king at York in March 1470 after the failure of Warwick's second rebellion. Four days later, Edward granted Percy the earldom of Northumberland and created John Neville marquis of Montagu, a technically higher title that carried far less land. Hillyard's appearance at York in 1470 may have revealed the truth about the Holderness uprising of the previous year, and the consequences of those revelations may have led in part to Montagu's abandonment of Edward IV in the autumn of 1470, when Warwick finally succeeded in overthrowing the house of YORK.

Further Reading: Haigh, Philip A., *The Military Campaigns of the Wars of the Roses* (Stroud, Gloucestershire, UK: Sutton Publishing, 1995); Ross, Charles, *Edward IV* (New Haven, CT: Yale University Press, 1998).

Robin of Redesdale Rebellion (1469)

The Robin of Redesdale Rebellion, an uprising in Yorkshire in the spring of 1469, was secretly directed by Richard NEVILLE, earl of Warwick, as part of his plan to wrest control of the kingdom from EDWARD IV.

Although the Redesdale rebellion, along with several other nearly simultaneous uprisings, such as the ROBIN OF HOLDERNESS REBELLION, opened the second phase of the

WARS OF THE ROSES, in which Edward IV was eventually to lose and regain his throne, little is known for certain about the nature and course of these movements. The contemporary evidence for the northern disorders of 1469 is slight and contradictory, and modern historians have proposed several accounts of events. In late April 1469, a large body of troublemakers under a mysterious captain calling himself Robin of Redesdale (or Robin Mend-All) was scattered by John NEVILLE, earl of Northumberland, Warwick's brother. Whether these first disorders were unrelated to Warwick, or whether Robin had simply taken the field before the earl was ready to support him, is unclear. Northumberland's role is also uncertain; the earl may have been unaware of his brother's plans, or he may have acted only to make the king think so. In any event, Northumberland moved with sufficient slowness to allow Robin to escape.

In late May or early June, Robin of Redesdale, who was possibly Sir William Conyers, a kinsman of Warwick's, incited a new uprising and issued a manifesto denouncing Edward's government. The rebels demanded that Edward remove his wicked advisors, namely the WOODVILLE FAMILY and such other rivals of Warwick as William HERBERT, earl of Pembroke. Although Robin called his pronouncement a "popular petition" (Haigh, p. 99), it was probably drafted by Warwick, for it ominously compared Edward's regime to those of Edward II, Richard II, and HENRY VI, all monarchs who had been deposed. As the king moved north to suppress the rebellion, Warwick cemented his alliance with Edward's brother, George PLANTAGENET, duke of Clarence, by arranging the duke's marriage to his eldest daughter, Isabel NEVILLE. By mid-July, Warwick and Clarence had openly declared their support for the aims of the Redesdale manifesto, while the rebel leader had raised sufficient support to outnumber the king's forces and threaten Edward's position at Nottingham. On 26 July, Robin, who was marching south to join Warwick and to cut the road to LONDON, clashed with a royalist army under Pembroke at the Battle of EDGE-

COTE. Pembroke was defeated, captured, and executed, but Robin of Redesdale and many of his rebels also died in the battle. Hemmed in by superior forces, Edward surrendered himself to Warwick's custody on 29 July.

Finding themselves unable to govern effectively without Edward's cooperation, Warwick and Clarence extracted a pardon from the king and released him before the end of the year. With the failure of their 1469 coup attempt, Warwick and Clarence raised another rebellion in the following spring. Robin of Redesdale resurfaced in March 1470, apparently in the person of Sir John Conyers, Sir William's brother, who assumed the guise of Robin to briefly involve himself in the new uprising. He submitted to the king at York in late March, having done little to support Warwick but much to confuse later historians as to the identity of the original Robin of Redesdale.

See also North of England and the Wars of the Roses

Further Reading: Haigh, Philip A., *The Military Campaigns of the Wars of the Roses* (Stroud, Gloucestershire, UK: Sutton Publishing, 1995); Ross, Charles, *Edward IV* (New Haven, CT: Yale University Press, 1998).

Roos, Thomas, Lord Roos (1427–1464)

A loyal partisan of the house of LANCASTER, Thomas Roos, Lord Roos, played a large role in the Lancastrian victory at the Battle of WAKEFIELD in 1460 and in the Lancastrian campaigns in Northumberland in 1464.

Succeeding to the important northern lordship of Roos in 1446, Roos fought in Normandy in 1449–1450, being one of the hostages given to the French on the surrender of Rouen. In 1452, he was given ships and charged with guarding the eastern coasts from French invasion. In 1453, at the height of the NEVILLE-PERCY FEUD, Roos was an active ally of the Percy family. He fought for HENRY VI at the Battle of ST. ALBANS in May 1455 and served on various Lancastrian commissions in the north between 1457 and 1460, receiving an annuity in the latter year for his services against Yorkist rebels. He was at CALAIS with Henry BEAUFORT, duke of Somerset, in 1460, when the duke tried unsuccessfully to wrest the town from Yorkist control. In the autumn of 1460, Roos helped rouse the north against the Act of ACCORD, which disinherited Prince EDWARD OF LANCASTER; he was also a leader of the Lancastrian army at the Battle of Wakefield in December, being the first to attack the forces of Richard PLANTAGENET, duke of York, when the duke issued forth from Sandal Castle.

After marching south from Wakefield with Queen MARGARET OF ANJOU's army, Roos fought for Lancaster at the Battle of ST. ALBANS in February 1461 and again at the Battle of TOWTON in March. After that defeat, he fled into SCOTLAND with the Lancastrian royal family. He resumed his opposition to the house of YORK in the following June, when he carried Henry VI with him on a raid into Durham. Roos raised the king's banner at Brancepeth Castle, but little support materialized, and Roos and his men quickly withdrew to Scotland before the local levies could be mobilized against them. Roos was included in the ATTAINDERS passed in EDWARD IV's first PARLIAMENT in November 1461, and most of Roos's property was granted to Edward's ally William HASTINGS, Lord Hastings, in 1462. Roos was part of the Lancastrian garrison that surrendered BAMBURGH CASTLE in December 1462 and was actively involved in Somerset's campaign in Northumberland in early 1464. Along with Robert HUNGERFORD, Lord Hungerford, Roos commanded a wing of the Lancastrian force at the Battle of HEDGELEY MOOR in April 1464 and again at the Battle of HEXHAM in May. He was captured after Hexham and executed two days later at Newcastle.

See also North of England and the Wars of the Roses
Further Reading: Haigh, Philip A., *The Military Campaigns of the Wars of the Roses* (Stroud, Gloucestershire, UK: Sutton Publishing, 1995); Ross, Charles, *Edward IV* (New Haven, CT: Yale University Press, 1998).

The Rose of England

Describing one of the last campaigns of the Wars of the Roses, *The Rose of England* is the earliest of the ballads inspired by the Battle of BOSWORTH FIELD.

Although the ballad was likely written in late 1485 only months after the battle, the earliest extant copy dates from the mid-seventeenth century. The prominence in the story of Thomas STANLEY, Lord Stanley, and his brother Sir William STANLEY, indicates that *The Rose of England,* like another later Bosworth ballad, THE SONG OF LADY BESSY, was composed by someone in the Stanley family circle.

The poem is an extended allegory, casting England as a garden wherein grew a rose bush (the house of LANCASTER) that was destroyed by a White Boar (RICHARD III). Driven into exile, the last sprig of rose (Henry Tudor, earl of Richmond, the future HENRY VII) returns to England with the Blue Boar (John de VERE, earl of Oxford) and summons to his assistance the Old Eagle (Lord Stanley). Winning the support of Rhys ap THOMAS and other Welshmen (see WALES), Richmond marches to Shrewsbury, where he is denied admittance until Sir William Stanley instructs the town bailiff to open the gates. This possibly authentic detail is the only indication we have that it was the Stanleys who delivered the town to Richmond. When Richmond meets the Stanleys at Atherstone, the ballad adds another possibly authentic detail to its description of the earl's greeting: "How earl Richmond took his hat in hand / And said, 'Cheshire and Lancashire, welcome to me!'" (Rowse, p. 252).

The battle description consists mainly of praise for the skill and valor displayed by Richmond's chief captains, Oxford ("He was both wary and wise of wit") and the Stanleys ("How they laid about them lustily"). Like *The Song of Lady Bessy,* this ballad recounts the near beheading of Stanley's son, Lord Strange, who was preserved to "come to his nest again" when the start of the battle caused Richard to delay Strange's execution (Bennett, p. 170). The defiant bravery of the king, depicted in both *THE BALLAD OF BOSWORTH FIELD* and *The Song of Lady Bessy,* is here passed over for a simple declaration of Richard's death.

> But now is the fierce field foughten and
> ended,
> And the White Boar there lieth slain.
> (Bennett, p. 170)

The poem ends with a joyous exclamation that the red rose (Henry VII) flourishes again and with a prayer that God may confound the king's foes and love him "night and day." Thus, except for some small details of the Stanleys and their forces (e.g., they wore coats of "white and red"), the ballad is of slight use as a source for the battle itself, and may be, as some modern historians have suggested of all the Bosworth ballads, purely fiction.

Further Reading: Bennett, Michael, *The Battle of Bosworth* (New York: St. Martin's Press, 1985); Rowse, A. L., *Bosworth Field: From Medieval to Tudor England* (Garden City, NY: Doubleday, 1966).

Rotherham, Thomas, Archbishop of York (1423–1500)

Chancellor of England under EDWARD IV, and a political client of Queen Elizabeth WOODVILLE, Thomas Rotherham, archbishop of York, supported the house of YORK until he fell into disfavor with RICHARD III in 1483.

Born into a Yorkshire gentry family and educated at a local grammar school, Rotherham was elected a fellow of King's College, Cambridge, in 1444. He held various ecclesiastical livings in the 1450s and 1460s and took a degree at Oxford in 1463. In the late 1450s, he became chaplain to John de VERE, the future Lancastrian earl of Oxford, who may have introduced Rotherham to the COURT of HENRY VI. Here he may have met Elizabeth Woodville, then the wife of Sir John Grey and a lady-in-waiting to Queen MARGARET OF ANJOU. After her marriage to Edward IV in 1464, Elizabeth became Rotherham's patron, and she was likely responsible for his appointment as keeper of the royal privy seal in 1467.

Rapidly gaining the king's confidence, Rotherham was named to diplomatic missions to FRANCE and BURGUNDY and became bishop of Rochester in 1468. He did not support the READEPTION government of Henry VI, and in the spring of 1471 warned Edward IV, who was then returning from exile to reclaim his Crown, not to attempt a landing on the closely watched coast of East Anglia (see EDWARD IV, RESTORATION OF).

In March 1472, Edward promoted Rotherham to the bishopric of Lincoln, and in 1474 the king appointed him chancellor of England. Like many of Edward IV's bishops, Rotherham was a man of humble origins who was promoted to high church office because of his loyalty to the king and his usefulness in secular government. Rotherham accompanied Edward on the French expedition of 1475 and was one of the English lords who received a large pension from LOUIS XI of France. Said to be skilled in managing PARLIAMENT, Rotherham opened the tense 1478 session that condemned the king's brother, George PLANTAGENET, duke of Clarence. In 1480, Rotherham became archbishop of York.

On Edward's death in April 1483, Rotherham's connections with the queen made him suspect in the eyes of Richard, duke of Gloucester, the late king's only surviving brother, who believed the WOODVILLE FAMILY was seeking to deprive him of the regency. Rotherham intensified the duke's mistrust by surrendering the Great Seal of England, the seal entrusted to the chancellor for the authentication of official documents, to the queen after fear of Gloucester drove her to SANCATUARY at Westminster in early May 1483. Thinking better of this act, Rotherham quickly recovered the Great Seal, but on 10 May Gloucester, now acting as protector for EDWARD V, replaced the archbishop as chancellor with Bishop John RUSSELL. On 13 June, Gloucester arrested Rotherham, along with William HASTINGS, Lord Hastings, and other likely opponents, at a COUNCIL meeting held in the TOWER OF LONDON (see COUNCIL MEETING OF 13 JUNE 1483). Although released shortly thereafter through an appeal from Cambridge University, which he served as chancellor, Rotherham took little further part in government, either during Richard III's reign or during the reign of HENRY VII. Noted in later life as a prominent benefactor of the English universities, Rotherham died in 1500.

See also Usurpation of 1483
Further Reading: Ross Charles, *Edward IV* (New Haven, CT: Yale University Press, 1998); Ross, Charles, *Richard III* (Berkeley: University of California Press, 1981).

Rous, John (c. 1411–1491)

Although the accuracy and value of his historical writings and judgments have been questioned, John Rous of Warwickshire, a chantry priest with antiquarian interests, is recognized as an important source for contemporary perceptions and attitudes during the WARS OF THE ROSES.

Born at Warwick and educated at Oxford, Rous was in 1445 appointed a chaplain of the chantry chapel at Guy's Cliff in Warwickshire. His office, which he retained for the rest of his life, required him to celebrate daily Mass for the chantry's late founder, Richard Beauchamp, earl of Warwick. His duties allowed him time to indulge his interest in antiquarian studies, that is, to collect manuscripts and artifacts relating to the history of his locality, to conduct historical research, and to write up his findings. He undertook periodic trips—once to WALES and once to LONDON—to study local historical records and to borrow or buy research materials. In 1459, he attended the COVENTRY PARLIAMENT, where the Lancastrian government, busy passing ATTAINDERS against leading Yorkists, ignored his petition asking that the PEERAGE be prevented from oppressing country towns (see TOWNS AND THE WARS OF THE ROSES).

Rous's most important writings are the two versions of the *Rous Rolls,* elaborately illustrated histories of the earls of Warwick written on rolls of parchment, and the "Historia Regum Angliae" ("History of the Kings of England"), which, in its national scope, departs from Rous's usual interest in local history. The earlier English version of the *Rous Rolls,* written before 1485, is highly favorable to the house of YORK and flattering to RICHARD III. The later Latin version, containing fulsome praise for the houses of LANCASTER and TUDOR, was clearly intended to curry favor with HENRY VII. The "Historia," which carried the history of England to the birth of Prince Arthur in 1486, roundly condemns Richard III as ruling "in the way Antichrist is to reign," and includes some of the more shocking elements of the anti-Ricardian PROPAGANDA that developed after 1485. For instance, Rous claimed that Richard was two years in his mother's womb, finally emerging "with teeth and hair to his shoulders." Nonetheless, even Rous admitted that Richard "bore himself like a gallant knight [and] honourably defended himself to his last breath" at the Battle of BOSWORTH FIELD in 1485 (all quotes Dockray, p. xxi).

As an old man whose clerical living depended on royal favor, Rous's bias toward the party in power is understandable; no one could praise Richard III under the Tudors any more that one could praise HENRY VI under the Yorkists. Rous also did much for the study of local history, and his writings are useful as a reflection of the opinions and interests of educated country people during the late fifteenth century. However, his indiscriminate handling of sources, his ready acceptance of myths and miraculous tales, and his factual inaccuracies have led modern historians to make only limited and cautious use of Rous as a source for the civil wars.

Further Reading: Dockray, Keith. *Richard III: A Source Book* (Stroud, Gloucestershire, UK: Sutton Publishing, 1997); "John Rous," in Michael Hicks, *Who's Who in Late Medieval England* (London: Shepheard-Walwyn, 1991), pp. 345–349; Rous, John, "The History of the Kings of England," in Alison Hanham, *Richard III and His Early Historians, 1483–1535* (Oxford: Clarendon Press, 1975), pp. 118–124; Rous, John. *The Rous Roll,* reprint ed. (Stroud, Gloucestershire, UK: Alan Sutton, 1980).

Royal Council. *See* Council, Royal

Royal Court. *See* Court, Royal

Russell, John, Bishop of Lincoln (d. 1494)

Bishop John Russell of Lincoln was an important clerical servant of EDWARD IV and chancellor of England under RICHARD III.

Born in Winchester, Russell was educated at Oxford, where he taught until about 1462. In the mid-1460s, he entered the service of Edward IV, who employed Russell on various diplomatic missions, including the negotiations surrounding the marriage of the king's sister, MARGARET OF YORK, to Duke CHARLES of BURGUNDY in 1468. In February 1471, Russell also acted as a diplomat for the READEPTION government of HENRY VI, but he was readily taken back into Yorkist service after Edward IV's restoration in April. In 1472, Edward again sent Russell to Burgundy, and in 1474, the king appointed him keeper of the privy seal and dispatched him to SCOTLAND to negotiate a marriage between Edward's daughter Cecily and the son of JAMES III. Russell became bishop of Rochester in 1476 and bishop of Lincoln in 1480. One of the executors of Edward IV's will, Russell helped officiate at the king's funeral in April 1483.

On 10 May 1483, Richard, duke of Gloucester, having assumed the protectorship of his nephew EDWARD V, dismissed Archbishop Thomas ROTHERHAM of York from the chancellorship, replacing him with Russell. According to some sources, the bishop, who was experienced and learned and a natural choice for the post, accepted office with reluctance. Although Russell served Gloucester loyally when he became king as Richard III, there seems to have been no close bond between Richard and his chancellor, who may have felt betrayed when Richard took his nephew's crown in June 1483 (see USURPATION OF 1483). In any event, as chancellor, Russell handled negotiations with both Scotland and BRITTANY, and he may have assisted Archbishop Thomas BOURCHIER in persuading Queen Elizabeth WOODVILLE to release her younger son, Richard PLANTAGENET, duke of York, into Gloucester's custody. Having perhaps grown uncertain of his chancellor's loyalty, Richard dismissed Russell from office on 29 July 1485, less than a month before the Battle of BOSWORTH FIELD. After Richard's death, Russell was taken readily into favor by HENRY VII, who, like his Yorkist predecessors, employed the bishop as a diplomat. After spending his last years mainly in his diocese, Russell died in December 1494.

Because Russell closely fit the author profile that emerges from the work itself—an educated cleric who was familiar with the workings of Richard's government and who was an eyewitness to at least some of the events being described—some modern historians identified Russell as the author of the *CROYLAND CHRONICLE,* a useful source for the last decade of Edward IV and for the reign of Richard III. However, most scholars today dismiss that claim, arguing that the *Chronicle* is much different in style from any of Russell's known writings.

Further Reading: Ross, Charles, *Richard III* (Berkeley: University of California Press, 1981).

Rutland, Earl of. *See* Plantagenet, Edmund, Earl of Rutland

St. Albans, Abbot of. *See*
Whethamstede, John, Abbot of St. Albans

St. Albans, Battle of (1455)

As the first armed encounter between the military forces of HENRY VI and those of Richard PLANTAGENET, duke of York, the battle fought at St. Albans in the southeastern county of Hertfordshire on 22 May 1455 is often considered the starting point of the Wars of the Roses.

When Henry VI recovered his health in January 1455, York's FIRST PROTECTORATE ceased, and the king released York's rival, Edmund BEAUFORT, duke of Somerset, from the TOWER OF LONDON. York's allies, Richard NEVILLE, earl of Salisbury, and his son, Richard NEVILLE, earl of Warwick, also found their chief enemies, Henry PERCY, earl of Northumberland, and his sons, back in royal favor. Without taking leave of the king, York and the Nevilles left LONDON for their estates in the north. In April, the king and his advisors summoned the three peers to a great council to be held at Leicester on 21 May. Believing the council was an attempt to force them into an oath of submission, if not something worse, the disaffected lords gathered forces to intercept Henry on his way to the council, seeking thereby to restore their control of the royal government by seizing control of the royal person.

Hearing of York's southward march, Henry sent the duke a letter ordering him to disarm or be branded a traitor. York's reply, that only the arrest of Somerset would appease him, reached Henry on 21 May shortly after he had left London, accompanied by Somerset,

Northumberland, and various other peers. The royal army, command of which Henry had only hours before transferred from Somerset to Humphrey STAFFORD, duke of Buckingham, reached St. Albans at about 9 A.M. on 22 May. The king set up his standard in the town square, while York and the Nevilles deployed on a ridge east of town. After an hour of fruitless negotiation, hostilities commenced around 10 A.M., with the Yorkists storming the town gates. Fighting in such close quarters nullified the Yorkist advantage in numbers, and the Lancastrians stood firm until Warwick led a small force through the gardens and lanes of the town, bursting into the square to cut the royal army in two.

Warwick's attack, which won him a mighty reputation, caused many of the royal troops to flee and allowed the entire Yorkist army to flood the square and overwhelm the remnant of men guarding the king. Henry and Buckingham were both wounded by arrows during the fighting in the square. Within minutes, Yorkist troops killed Somerset, Northumberland, and Thomas CLIFFORD, Lord Clifford. Under cover of battle, York and the Nevilles had eliminated their chief rivals at one stroke. Now under York's "protection," Henry made peace with the victors, who had him removed to the safety of the abbey. Next day, the king, riding between York and Salisbury, returned to London, where York formally began his parliament-sanctioned SECOND PROTECTORATE in November 1455. Besides placing the king and the government in York's hands, the Battle of St. Albans turned the sons of the slain peers into bitter enemies of York and ensured that his period of power would be troubled and brief and that civil strife would continue.

See also Council, Royal; Love-Day of 1458
Further Reading: Haigh, Philip A., *The Military Campaigns of the Wars of the Roses* (Stroud, Gloucestershire, UK: Sutton Publishing, 1995); Ross, Charles, *The Wars of the Roses* (New York: Thames and Hudson, 1987).

St. Albans, Battle of (1461)

Fought on 17 February 1461, the second Battle of St. Albans was a Lancastrian victory that reunited HENRY VI with his family and threatened the destruction of the Yorkist cause.

After the death of Richard PLANTA-GENET, duke of York, at the Battle of WAKEFIELD in December 1460, the Lancastrian forces that had defeated him joined at York with Queen MARGARET OF ANJOU and the Scots and French MERCENARIES that she had gathered in SCOTLAND. Plundering Yorkist towns as it marched south, the queen's army panicked LONDON, where Richard NEVILLE, earl of Warwick, the custodian of Henry VI, was seen as the only man able to defend southern England from Margaret's horde of Scots and northerners (see MARCH ON LONDON), a viewpoint encouraged by Warwick's PROPAGANDA efforts. Warwick and the king led a large army out of London on 12 February and reached St. Albans the next day. Unsure of the Lancastrians' whereabouts, Warwick deployed his army on a broad front extending through and north of St. Albans. On the evening of 16 February, Warwick received reports that the Lancastrians were nearby at Dunstable, where they were said to have overwhelmed a small Yorkist outpost. Believing the Lancastrians were much further away, the earl dismissed the report.

However, the Dunstable information was true, and Margaret's army reached St. Albans early the next morning. Andrew TROLLOPE led a Lancastrian force into the town, where they surprised a body of Yorkist ARCHERS. The Yorkists repulsed Trollope's initial assault, but Warwick's brother, John NEVILLE, Lord Montagu, in command of the Yorkist left, had to quickly reposition his troops. Deployed to meet an attack from the west, they now needed to face south to meet the Lancastrians advancing on them from the town. When his scouts informed him of an unguarded lane into St. Albans, Henry BEAUFORT, duke of Somerset, the Lancastrian commander, repeated Warwick's maneuver from the first Battle of ST. ALBANS in 1455 and sent a force streaming into the square to drive out the Yorkists and capture the town. After a brief rest, the Lancastrians renewed their attack around noon, their entire army falling upon the Yorkist left under Montagu. Hindered by the hedgerows and lanes that had so strengthened the initial Yorkist position, Montagu's messengers had difficulty finding Warwick, who commanded the Yorkist center, and Warwick had equal trouble bringing his troops into position to aid Montagu. The defection of part of his force caused Montagu's line to collapse, and Warwick arrived in late afternoon to find Montagu a prisoner and his troops in flight. Panicked by rumors and the sight of fleeing comrades, Warwick's men began to desert; the earl rallied what forces he could and withdrew from the field.

That evening, Lancastrian troops discovered Henry VI sitting under a tree, deserted by all except William BONVILLE, Lord Bonville, and Sir Thomas Kyrill, who had stayed with Henry on his personal assurance that they would not be harmed. Henry was reunited with his wife and son, Prince EDWARD OF LANCASTER, who knighted Trollope and, on his mother's instructions, ordered the executions of Bonville and Kyrill. Because Somerset's brother was a prisoner of Warwick, Montagu was spared and sent to York. Having lost control of Henry VI, the Yorkist regime that had governed England since July 1460 was over. Warwick joined with Edward, earl of March, York's son, on 22 February, and the Yorkists entered London four days later, Margaret's army having moved north after being denied entry to the capital by its terrified inhabitants. Playing on southern fears of the Lancastrian host, the Yorkists proclaimed March king as EDWARD IV on 4 March, and the stage was set for a great battle between rival monarchs.

See also Towton, Battle of
Further Reading: Haigh, Philip A., *The Military Campaigns of the Wars of the Roses* (Stroud, Gloucestershire, UK: Sutton Publishing, 1995).

St. Andrews, Bishop of. *See* Kennedy, James

Salisbury, Bishop of. *See* Woodville, Lionel

Salisbury, Earl of. *See* Neville, Richard, Earl of Salisbury

Sanctuary

Sanctuary was a right of the English Church whereby cathedrals, abbeys, churches, and churchyards could serve as places of refuge for criminals, debtors, victims of abuse, and political refugees.

In theory, a person claiming sanctuary could remain unmolested in the sanctuary precincts for forty days, after which time the person had to either stand trial for his offense or confess and swear to abjure (i.e., leave) the realm. If the latter, the offender was escorted from sanctuary to the nearest port by a local constable. If no ship was immediately available, the person had to daily wade into the sea up to his knees and cry out for passage until a vessel could be found to transport him. During the Middle Ages, certain English liberties (i.e., jurisdictions exempt from royal authority) and certain sanctuaries possessing papal or royal charters were accepted as permanent places of refuge. Although the right of sanctuary was found throughout Christian Europe, it was nowhere so widely used or so highly formalized as in England.

During the WARS OF THE ROSES, the concept of sanctuary for political offenders and political refugees was both widely applied and widely violated. Queen Elizabeth WOODVILLE fled twice into sanctuary at Westminster. From October 1470 to April 1471, during the READEPTION of HENRY VI, the queen remained unmolested at the abbey, even giving birth there to her son, the future EDWARD V. Elizabeth's second period in sanctuary, from May 1483 to March 1484, was occasioned by the death of her husband, EDWARD IV, and the ensuing political coup of her brother-in-law, Richard, duke of Gloucester, who seized custody of Edward V to prevent the establishment of a government dominated by the WOODVILLE FAMILY. In June 1483, Gloucester either pressured or compelled Elizabeth to send her son Richard PLANTAGENET, duke of York, out of sanctuary and into the duke's custody (see USURPATION OF 1483). The queen herself remained at Westminster until finally coaxed from sanctuary by a promise of support for her daughters, who had shared her confinement.

Several times during the wars, victors on the battlefield violated sanctuary to seize and execute losers. Edward IV had Edmund BEAUFORT, duke of Somerset, and other Lancastrian survivors of the Battle of TEWKESBURY forcibly removed from Tewkesbury Abbey. Two days after the battle, Somerset and most of his sanctuary companions were condemned and then beheaded in Tewkesbury marketplace. In April 1486, Francis LOVELL, Lord Lovell, and the brothers Sir Thomas and Sir Humphrey Stafford, adherents of RICHARD III who had been in sanctuary since the Battle of BOSWORTH FIELD in the previous August, emerged from their refuge to incite rebellion against HENRY VII (see LOVELL-STAFFORD UPRISING). When the Staffords returned to sanctuary in May after the rebellion collapsed, Henry ordered them seized and brought out for trial, an action that resulted in the condemnation of both and the execution of Sir Humphrey. The Stafford case led to the first legal limitations on the right of sanctuary; after much debate, the Stafford judges ruled that sanctuary did not apply in cases of treason or for second offenses.

Further Reading: Gillingham, John, *The Wars of the Roses* (Baton Rouge: Louisiana State University Press, 1981); Goodman, Anthony, *The Wars of the Roses* (New York: Dorset Press, 1981);

Kendall, Paul Murray, *The Yorkist Age* (New York: W. W. Norton, 1962); Ross, Charles, *The Wars of the Roses* (New York: Thames and Hudson, 1987).

Scales, Thomas, Lord Scales (1399–1460)

A principal advisor of Queen MARGARET OF ANJOU, Thomas Scales, seventh Lord Scales, held the TOWER OF LONDON against the Yorkists in 1460.

Succeeding his brother in the family PEER-AGE in 1420, Scales led a company of men to FRANCE in 1422. He spent most of the next decade in the service of the king's uncle, John, duke of Bedford (1389–1435), and by 1429 was sufficiently prominent in the English command to be mentioned in a letter by Joan of Arc. During the early 1430s, he was seneschal of Normandy and captain of numerous English-held fortresses. In the 1440s, he fought in Normandy during the lieutenancies of both Richard PLANTAGENET, duke of York, and Edmund BEAUFORT, duke of Somerset, and probably remained militarily active in the province until its fall to the French in 1450.

Upon the eruption of JACK CADE'S RE-BELLION in 1450, Scales held the Tower for the government and commanded the loyal Londoners who defended London Bridge against the rebels on the night of 5–6 July. After the suppression of Cade's uprising, Scales was appointed to a commission charged with looking into abuses committed in his native Norfolk by local followers of the late William de la POLE, duke of Suffolk, the former chief minister of HENRY VI. Himself a Suffolk supporter, Scales protected many of the men under investigation. In 1453, when the king's illness and the birth of her son, Prince ED-WARD OF LANCASTER, drew her into politics, Queen Margaret turned to Scales for political advice (see HENRY VI, ILLNESS OF). On the outbreak of civil war in 1459, Scales became a prominent Lancastrian, suppressing Yorkist activity in Norfolk and sharing responsibility for the defense of Sandwich with Richard WOODVILLE, Lord Rivers, and his son, Anthony WOODVILLE.

To stiffen LONDON's resistance to an invasion from Yorkist-held CALAIS, the Lancastrian government placed Scales and Robert HUNGERFORD, Lord Hungerford, in command of the Tower in 1460, despite the Londoners' protests that they could defend themselves. In July 1460, Scales and his colleagues failed to prevent the entry into London of Yorkist forces under Richard NEVILLE, earl of Salisbury, and his son Richard NEVILLE, earl of Warwick. Forced to withdraw into the Tower, Scales began a bombardment of the city that caused much damage and some deaths among citizens. When, after the Battle of NORTHAMPTON, Warwick returned to the city with the captive king, the Londoners joined with the Yorkists in besieging Scales and Hungerford in the Tower. On 19 July, while in the midst of negotiations to surrender the fortress, Scales was allowed to flee upriver to take SANCTUARY at Westminster; although the Yorkists were willing to spare his life, the citizens of London were less forgiving. Recognized by London boatmen, Scales was pursued and murdered, and his naked body was cast upon the Southwark shore.

Further Reading: Griffiths, Ralph A., *The Reign of King Henry VI* (Berkeley: University of California Press, 1981); Johnson, P. A., *Duke Richard of York* (Oxford: Clarendon Press, 1988).

Scotland

Since Edward I's intervention in Scottish affairs in the late thirteenth century, Scotland had generally acted in alliance with FRANCE against English interests. During the WARS OF THE ROSES, the Scots intervened in England to achieve territorial gains at England's expense. In the early 1460s, Scottish involvement in English affairs prolonged military activity in northern England and prevented the house of YORK from fully securing the English Crown; in the mid-1490s, Scottish intervention similarly threatened the house of TUDOR.

News of the Battle of ST. ALBANS in 1455 led JAMES II of Scotland to propose that CHARLES VII of France assault CALAIS while the Scots besieged BERWICK. When Charles declined, James launched a series of border raids, but in 1457 concluded a two-year truce with England that was eventually extended to 1463. However, the capture of HENRY VI at the Battle of NORTHAMPTON in July 1460 prompted James to besiege the English-held border castle of Roxburgh. Although James was killed in early August by the explosion of one of his own ARTILLERY pieces, Roxburgh and the nearby castle of Wark fell to the Scots shortly thereafter.

Because JAMES III was only nine, a regency COUNCIL headed by Queen MARY OF GUELDRES and influenced by its most experienced member, James KENNEDY, bishop of St. Andrews, assumed the government. In late 1460, the flight into Scotland of Queen MARGARET OF ANJOU and her son Prince EDWARD OF LANCASTER offered the Scots opportunities for further gains. Although pressured by her kinsman, Duke PHILIP of BURGUNDY, to resist Margaret's appeals for assistance, Queen Mary, in early January 1461, concluded an agreement with Margaret that called for the surrender of Berwick and the marriage of Prince Edward to a sister of James III in return for Scottish military aid. Later in the month, when Margaret reentered England to assume command of the Lancastrian army that had slain Richard PLANTAGENET, duke of York, at the Battle of WAKEFIELD on 30 December, Scottish troops accompanied her. During Margaret's subsequent MARCH ON LONDON, the presence of these Scottish MERCENARIES was one cause of the panic that gripped the capital and southern counties at the queen's approach, providing the Yorkists with both a PROPAGANDA boon and an opportunity to enter LONDON and proclaim York's son king as EDWARD IV.

Defeat at the Battle of TOWTON in March 1461 forced the entire Lancastrian royal family to flee into Scotland. Torn between Lancastrian pleas for assistance and Yorkist demands for the return of the exiles, the Scottish regency council split. The so-called Old Lords, led by Kennedy, supported the house of LANCASTER, while the Young Lords, led by Queen Mary, were more willing to accommodate the house of York. However, Queen Mar-

garet's willingness to hand over Berwick, which surrendered to James III in April, tipped the balance toward the Lancastrians, who were thus able to use Scotland as a base for military operations against northern England. With Scottish support, the Lancastrians several times invaded England and seized the castles of ALNWICK, BAMBURGH, and DUNSTANBURGH. Edward IV countered by concluding the Treaty of WESTMINSTER-ARDTORNISH with disaffected magnates in northern Scotland. By 1463, such internal threats, combined with the achievement of Berwick and military defeats in northern England, destroyed Scottish enthusiasm for the Lancastrian cause. Margaret sailed to France in August, and Kennedy, under the terms of the truce, reluctantly sent Henry VI into England in January 1464. By 1465, Scotland and Yorkist England were at peace.

When the Wars of the Roses resumed in 1469, James III was engaged in consolidating his authority in Scotland and did not intervene in the English conflict. In the 1470s, James altered the traditional anti-English tone of Scottish foreign policy by proposing a series of marriages between the houses of York and Stuart (the Scottish royal family). These attempts at improved Anglo-Scottish relations foundered on the English desire to regain Berwick. In 1482, Edward concluded the Treaty of Fotheringhay with Alexander, duke of Albany, James's dissident brother, who agreed to restore the town to the English in return for assistance in overthrowing James. Richard, duke of Gloucester, invaded Scotland and captured Berwick in August, but James remained king and in 1484 concluded a truce with RICHARD III (the former Gloucester), who, having recently displaced his nephew EDWARD V, sat uneasily on his throne and wanted no trouble with Scotland. However, neither Richard, nor his successor, HENRY VII, who had a Scottish contingent in his army when he won the Crown at the Battle of BOSWORTH FIELD in 1485, were willing to surrender Berwick.

In 1488, a coalition of Scottish magnates, angered in part by their king's failure to pursue a more anti-English policy, defeated and slew

James III at the Battle of Sauchieburn. Although horrified by his father's murder, the new king, JAMES IV, had associated himself with the rebels and was determined to be more assertive in his relations with the English.

In 1491, James ended his father's truce with England and renewed the traditional French alliance, agreeing to attack England should Henry VII invade France. Involving himself in Yorkist conspiracies against the house of Tudor, James invited Perkin WARBECK to Scotland. In 1495, the Scottish king publicly acknowledged Warbeck as Richard PLANTAGENET, duke of York, the younger son of Edward IV who had disappeared in the TOWER OF LONDON in 1483. When his support of Warbeck failed to persuade Henry VII to restore Berwick, James invaded England on Warbeck's behalf in 1496, the pretender having agreed to surrender Berwick when he won the Crown. When northern England displayed no enthusiasm for Warbeck, the invasion collapsed. James expelled the pretender from Scotland in 1497 and soon after opened talks that led to a formal peace treaty in 1502. Unlike the other Scottish gains derived from the Wars of the Roses, the Treaty of Ayton had important long-term effects. By arranging the 1503 marriage of James IV and Margaret Tudor, the daughter of Henry VII, the treaty made possible the 1603 union of the Crowns of Scotland and England in the person of James's great-grandson, James VI.

See also North of England and the Wars of the Roses
Further Reading: Macdougall, Norman, *James III: A Political Study* (Edinburgh: J. Donald, 1982); McGladdery, Christine, *James II* (Edinburgh: John Donald Publishers, 1990); Macdougall, Norman, *James IV* (East Lothian, UK: Tuckwell Press, 1997); Nicholson, Ranald, *Scotland: The Later Middle Ages,* vol. 2 of *The Edinburgh History of Scotland* (New York: Barnes and Noble, 1974); Wormald, Jenny, *Court, Kirk, and Community: Scotland, 1470–1625* (Toronto: University of Toronto Press, 1981).

Second Protectorate (1455–1456)

Although officially in existence only from November 1455 to February 1456, the second protectorate of Richard PLANTAGENET, duke of York, actually began in May 1455, when York captured HENRY VI at the Battle of ST. ALBANS. Unlike the FIRST PROTECTORATE of 1454, whereby PARLIAMENT responded to the king's mental incapacity by vesting certain powers of the Crown in York as protector (see HENRY VI, ILLNESS OF), the second protectorate gave formal parliamentary recognition to the dominant political position the duke had won at St. Albans. Because of its openly partisan nature, the second protectorate accelerated the formation of factions around York and Queen MARGARET OF ANJOU and thereby created the political instability that fostered the WARS OF THE ROSES.

Besides giving them custody of the king, St. Albans allowed York and his Neville allies—Richard NEVILLE, earl of Salisbury, and his son Richard NEVILLE, earl of Warwick—to eliminate their three main rivals—Edmund BEAUFORT, duke of Somerset; Henry PERCY, earl of Northumberland; and Thomas CLIFFORD, Lord Clifford. Showing Henry great deference, the victors escorted him to LONDON, where they summoned a Parliament to sanction their control of the government and to legitimize Yorkist PROPAGANDA by affixing blame for the recent violence on Somerset. The late duke's offices were divided among the Yorkist leaders, with York becoming Lord Constable and Warwick obtaining the vitally important captaincy of CALAIS. Parliament also granted anyone in the Yorkist army formal pardon for anything done at St. Albans. York next sought to win popular favor and to weaken the queen and her faction by proposing to limit expenditure in the royal household and administration.

When Parliament reconvened in November, Henry VI was too ill to attend, and York used the king's indisposition and the eruption of various disorders around the country to convince a reluctant assembly to authorize his second term as lord protector. In December, York used his new authority to quell the violent COURTENAY-BONVILLE FEUD by imprisoning Thomas COURTENAY, earl of

Devon, in the TOWER OF LONDON. Although York thereby pacified the West Country, he also ensured the future adherence of the Courtenays to the house of LANCASTER. Despite York's efforts to broaden his support among the PEERAGE, such interventions in local disputes only further divided the nobility into partisans of one side or the other. On 25 February 1456, a seemingly healthy king came to Parliament and formally ended the second protectorate. To promote concord, Henry retained York as his chief minister, while the Nevilles remained influential members of the royal COUNCIL. The queen, however, was determined to prevent a third protectorate; during the next three years, she used her influence over Henry to undermine York's position and to gradually take control of the government, a situation that led to civil war in 1459.

Further Reading: Griffiths, Ralph A., *The Reign of Henry VI* (Berkeley: University of California Press, 1981); Johnson, P. A., *Duke Richard of York* (Oxford: Clarendon Press, 1988).

Shakespeare and the Wars of the Roses

In the early 1590s, the Elizabethan playwright William Shakespeare wrote a series of four plays based on the people and events of the WARS OF THE ROSES. Because Shakespeare is today considered one of the greatest writers in the English language, his four plays, although never intended as objective works of history, have heavily influenced modern perceptions of the course, nature, and personalities of the civil wars.

The plays, *HENRY VI, PART 1, HENRY VI, PART 2, HENRY VI, PART 3,* and *RICHARD III,* cover the period from the funeral of Henry V in 1422 to the death of RICHARD III at the Battle of BOSWORTH FIELD in 1485. For the events of the period, Shakespeare's chief sources were the best-known English histories of his day, the 1587 edition of Raphael Holinshed's *The Chronicles of England, Scotland, and Ireland,* the 1550 edition of Edward Hall's THE UNION OF THE TWO NOBLE AND ILLUSTRIOUS FAMILIES OF LANCASTER AND YORK, and Robert Fabyan's 1516 edition of *The New Chronicles of England and France* (see LONDON CHRONICLES). Shakespeare also consulted the 1587 edition of *A Mirror for Magistrates,* a sixteenth-century series of verse biographies of figures from English history; because the *Mirror* had a moral purpose—warning readers of the evil ends of wicked rulers—it particularly influenced Shakespeare's depiction of villains, especially his Richard III.

Because Shakespeare wrote during the reign of HENRY VII's granddaughter and after a century of rule by the house of TUDOR, the sources he used, while generally accurate as to chronology, were often biased in favor of the ruling dynasty. They portrayed Henry VII's accession as rescuing England from a long, dark period of political chaos and social disorder, and they depicted Henry's predecessors from the house of YORK, especially Richard III, as flawed and selfish men whose political ambitions ruined England. Shakespeare reproduces this bias in his plays, and, being interested in good drama rather than accurate history, exaggerates it for effect.

Throughout the plays, Shakespeare jumbles and compresses the chronology of events, making the conflict appear to be a long, unending series of terrible battles that had a devastating effect on England. This practice basically ignores the long periods of relative peace and stability that marked most of EDWARD IV's reign, drastically overstates the suffering and disruption cased by the conflict, and heavily overemphasizes the benefits brought by the Tudor victory. Although brief and concentrated in the years 1459–1461, 1469–1471, and 1483–1487, the military campaigns of the Wars of the Roses appear in Shakespeare's plays to be extremely bloody, highly destructive, and virtually continuous across a thirty-year period.

Shakespeare also exaggerates the greed and ambition of leading Yorkists. He portrays Richard PLANTAGENET, duke of York (d. 1460), as scheming for years to seize the throne. Although the real York was at the center of the political turmoil of the 1450s,

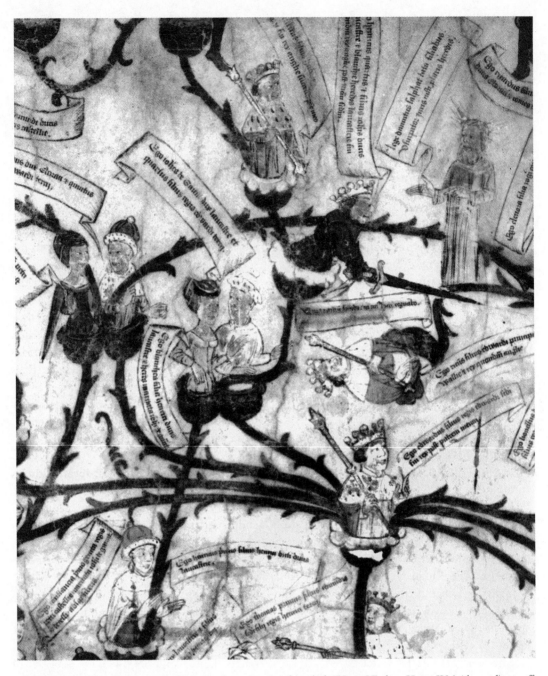

This Yorkist genealogy illustrates one of the main themes running through the Henry VI plays. Henry IV (with sword) cuts off the line of Richard II, while a prophet (to the right) foretells the doom that will descend on the house of Lancaster for this usurpation. (Harley MS 7353 f. 11, British Library)

he sought to control the government as HENRY VI's chief minister. York did not claim the Crown until 1460, when all other political options had been exhausted and taking the throne seemed the only way to save his career and possibly his life. In Shake-speare's portrayal of York's son, Richard III, the selfish ambition the playwright imputed to the duke is spectacularly magnified. Richard is one of the great Shakespearean villains. Although Tudor historians readily condemned Richard, especially for the murder of his nephews, EDWARD V and Richard PLANTAGENET, duke of York (d. c. 1483), Shakespeare moved well beyond his sources to show Richard plotting to seize the Crown at a time when the real Richard was only a child; Shakespeare also made Richard responsible for the deaths of many other major figures of the Wars of the Roses, including Henry VI and Prince EDWARD of Lancaster, and even for the deaths of his own brother and wife, George PLANTAGENET, duke of Clarence, and Anne NEVILLE.

Despite a lack of evidence that the historical Richard had anything to do with these latter deaths, Shakespeare makes his Richard III the horrifying culmination of the grand theme that infuses the entire cycle of history plays (i.e., from *Richard II* through *1 and 2 Henry IV* and *Henry V* to the four plays of the Wars of the Roses series). That theme, which is broadly based on fifteenth-century English history, is that the deposition of Richard II in 1399 overthrew the divine order and plunged England into decades of war and suffering. The ambition of Henry IV, Richard's supplanter and first king of the house of LANCASTER, was punished through the weakness and incapacity of his grandson, Henry VI, which in turn encouraged the ambition of York and his heirs and thereby ushered in the devastating Wars of the Roses. The house of Lancaster was overthrown, and the house of York ruled for a time, but it destroyed itself through the villainy of Richard III, whose overthrow by Henry VII allowed for a return to prosperity and order under the divinely sanctioned house of Tudor. To play out this theme, Shakespeare alters and exaggerates the people and events of the Wars of the Roses, doing so in such magnificent fashion that his fictional depictions often became accepted history.

See also Campaigns, Duration of; *The History of King Richard III* (More); Richard II, Deposition of

Further Reading: Norwich, John Julius, *Shakespeare's Kings* (New York: Scribner, 1999); Saccio, Peter, *Shakespeare's English Kings*, 2d ed. (Oxford: Oxford University Press, 2000).

Shakespeare, William. *See Henry VI, Part 1; Henry VI, Part 2; Henry VI, Part 3; Richard III; Shakespeare and the Wars of the Roses*

Shaw, Dr. Ralph. *See* Shaw's Sermon

Shaw's Sermon (1483)

The sermon delivered by Dr. Ralph Shaw (or Sha) from the open-air pulpit at Paul's Cross in LONDON on Sunday 22 June 1483 was the first public exposition of the duke of Gloucester's claim to the throne. After weeks of uncertainty as to the duke's intentions, Shaw's sermon signaled Gloucester's decision to depose his nephew EDWARD V and take the throne himself as RICHARD III (see USURPATION OF 1483).

Standing near the cross in the churchyard of St. Paul's Cathedral in London, the Paul's Cross pulpit was the recognized forum for official announcements and explanations of government policy. Dr. Ralph Shaw, a Cambridge doctor of divinity and a prominent preacher, was the brother of the mayor of London, Edmund Shaw. Commissioned by Gloucester, or perhaps by Henry STAFFORD, duke of Buckingham, the duke's ally, Shaw preached on the text "bastard slips shall not take deep root." Although the specifics of Shaw's sermon are uncertain, the preacher seems to have announced the existence of the BUTLER PRECONTRACT, EDWARD IV's betrothal to Lady Eleanor Butler, which, if genuine, invalidated the king's later marriage to Elizabeth WOODVILLE and thereby rendered his children illegitimate and clouded their right to inherit the Crown. The existence of this precontract was later said to have been confirmed by Bishop Robert STILLINGTON, before whom Edward and Lady Eleanor had pledged their betrothal.

According to Sir Thomas More's *HISTORY OF KING RICHARD III* and Polydore Vergil's *ANGLICA HISTORIA,* Shaw also questioned the legitimacy of Gloucester's brothers, Edward IV and George PLANTAGENET, duke of

Clarence, an allegation that amounted to an accusation of adultery against Gloucester's mother, Cecily NEVILLE, duchess of York. The preacher supported this assertion by proclaiming Gloucester's resemblance to his father, Richard PLANTAGENET, duke of York, a likeness supposedly shared by neither Clarence nor the late king. In his account, More claimed that Gloucester had planned to appear before Shaw's audience at the very moment that the preacher declared the duke's face to be "the very print of his [father's] visage" (Seward, p. 105), hoping thereby to inspire the crowd to a spontaneous acclamation of kingship. However, Shaw spoke too fast, Gloucester came too late, and the preacher had to awkwardly repeat his earlier remarks to a stunned and silent audience.

Although Buckingham took up Shaw's theme in an eloquent speech two days later at the Guildhall and Gloucester was crowned as planned on 6 July, most sources agree that Shaw's sermon was ill received. In his *USURPATION OF RICHARD III,* Dominic Mancini characterized the speech as contrary "to all decency and religion" (Mancini, p. 95), and various LONDON CHRONICLES claim the sermon destroyed Shaw's reputation and so burdened him with remorse and public odium that he died of shame the following year.

See also *Titulus Regius*
Further Reading: Mancini, Dominic, *The Usurpation of Richard III,* edited and translated by C. A. J. Armstrong (Stroud, Gloucestershire, UK: Alan Sutton, 1989); Ross, Charles, *Richard III* (Berkeley: University of California Press, 1981); Seward, Desmond, *Richard III: England's Black Legend* (New York: Franklin Watts, 1984).

Shore, Elizabeth (Jane) (d. 1527)

Through sexual liaisons with EDWARD IV and several prominent courtiers, Elizabeth Shore, better known as Jane Shore, became entangled in the political intrigues that led to the usurpation of RICHARD III and the revival of civil war in the 1480s.

One of Edward IV's many mistresses, Shore was, according to Sir Thomas More's *HIS-*

TORY OF KING RICHARD III, the king's favorite—less for her beauty than for her engaging personality. "Proper she was and fair. . . . Yet delighted not men so much in her beauty, as in her pleasant behaviour. For a proper wit had she, and could both read well and write, merry of company, ready and quick of answer, neither mute nor full of babble, sometimes taunting without displeasure and not without disport" (Ross, Richard III, p. 137).

The daughter of a LONDON merchant and the wife of William Shore, a London goldsmith, Jane Shore may have become the king's mistress in about 1470. Although Edward never allowed his lovers to become political figures, Shore, again according to More, exercised a benign influence over the king, tending to mollify him when he was angry or displeased with anyone.

Upon Edward's death in April 1483, Shore may have become the lover of Thomas GREY, marquis of Dorset, and then of his rival, William HASTINGS, Lord Hastings. If this second relationship occurred, it may have involved her in politics, for on 13 June 1483, at a council meeting in the TOWER OF LONDON, Richard, duke of Gloucester, charged Shore and Queen Elizabeth WOODVILLE with trying, on Hastings's urging, to destroy him through sorcery (see COUNCIL MEETING OF 13 JUNE 1483). The accusation led to Hastings's summary execution and to Shore's arrest. Forced soon after to do public penance as a harlot by walking through London dressed only in her kirtle (underskirt or gown) and carrying a lighted taper, Shore was afterward imprisoned in Ludgate. Although it is possible that Shore participated, perhaps as a go-between, in anti-Gloucester plots involving either Hastings or Dorset, her active cooperation with her late lover's wife in sorcery is most unlikely. Both contemporary writers, like More and Polydore Vergil in his *ANGLICA HISTORIA,* and many modern historians believe that Gloucester's charges were largely invented to destroy Hastings, who was loyal to EDWARD V and thus a serious obstacle to the duke's plan to take the throne (see USURPATION OF 1483).

While in prison, Shore charmed the king's solicitor, Thomas Lynom, who sought permission to marry her, Shore's husband having presumably died. Richard III (the former duke of Gloucester) told his chancellor, John RUSSELL, bishop of Lincoln, to dissuade Lynom from such a foolish action, but he gave permission for the match should the solicitor be adamant. Whether or not the marriage occurred is unclear, for beside the fact that she was still living in London in poverty in Henry VIII's reign, almost nothing is known of Shore's life after 1484.

Further Reading: Ross, Charles, *Edward IV* (New Haven, CT: Yale University Press, 1998); Ross, Charles, *Richard III* (Berkeley: University of California Press, 1981); Seward, Desmond, *The Wars of the Roses* (New York: Viking, 1995).

Simnel, Lambert (c. 1475–c. 1525)

Lambert Simnel, a boy of obscure origins, impersonated Edward PLANTAGENET, earl of Warwick, as part of the first major effort to overthrow HENRY VII and restore the house of YORK.

Little is known of Simnel, whose very name may have been an invention. The official account of Simnel's background, as given later by Polydore Vergil in his *ANGLICA HISTORIA,* claimed that he was the son of Thomas Simnel of Oxford, who was variously described as a baker, joiner, or shoemaker. About 1486, a priest named Richard (or William) Simonds conceived a plan to pass off Simnel, who was apparently an attractive and intelligent youth, as one of the sons of EDWARD IV, who had disappeared in the TOWER OF LONDON in 1483. However, upon hearing a rumor that Warwick had escaped from captivity, Simonds took Simnel to IRELAND, which was strongly Yorkist, and declared him to be the earl and rightful king of England. Gerald FITZGERALD, earl of Kildare, the Irish lord deputy, allowed himself to be persuaded that Simnel was Warwick, while Yorkists in England and abroad also accepted the imposture. MARGARET OF YORK, duchess of BURGUNDY and sister of Edward IV, formally recognized Simnel as her nephew and dispatched to Ireland a body of German MERCENARIES. Francis LOVELL, Lord Lovell, a former confidant of RICHARD III, traveled to Ireland from Burgundy, and John de la POLE, earl of Lincoln, another nephew of Margaret's and heir apparent to Richard III, slipped across the Irish Sea to Dublin. Because all were probably aware that Simnel was an impostor, the Yorkist leaders likely planned to use the movement that had formed around him to eventually put Lincoln on the throne.

To meet the growing threat, Henry VII had the real Warwick paraded through the streets of LONDON. The king also banished his mother-in-law, ELIZABETH WOODVILLE, wife of Edward IV, to a nunnery, perhaps because he had learned of her involvement in the Simnel enterprise. On 24 May 1487, Simnel was crowned in Dublin as "Edward VI"; the Irish government accepted his authority, and coins and proclamations were issued in his name. On 4 June, Simnel crossed to England accompanied by Simonds, his chief Yorkist supporters, and his force of German and Irish mercenaries. Enlarged by the retinues of various Yorkist gentleman, Simnel's army encountered the king's forces on 16 June. After a stiff three-hour fight, the Battle of STOKE ended in the deaths of Lincoln and Lovell and the captures of Simonds and Simnel. While the former was imprisoned for life, the latter was pardoned. To emphasize Simnel's unimportance and low birth, Henry supposedly sent the boy to serve in the royal kitchens. Little is known of the remainder of Simnel's life; he appears to have been employed for a time as a royal falconer and to have later transferred out of royal service. He probably died about 1525, although some accounts have him living into the early 1530s.

See also Warbeck, Perkin; Yorkist Heirs (after 1485)
Further Reading: Bennett, Michael J., *Lambert Simnel and the Battle of Stoke* (New York: St. Martin's Press, 1987).

Skeletons in the Tower. *See* Bones of 1674

Social Classes. *See* Commons (Common People) and the Wars of the Roses; Gentry; Peerage

Somerset, Duke of. *See* entries under Beaufort

The Song of Lady Bessy

The Song of Lady Bessy is one of several ballads inspired by the Battle of BOSWORTH FIELD.

The poem was written by someone associated with the Stanley family, for Thomas STANLEY, Lord Stanley, and his brother Sir William STANLEY are central characters. A possible author is Humphrey Brereton, who hailed from the Stanley-dominated county of Cheshire and who also figures prominently in the story. Although the earliest extant text of the ballad dates from about 1600, and many of the poem's more romantic touches seem Elizabethan in origin, *The Song of Lady Bessy* was probably written during the reign of HENRY VII (1485–1509), for it ends by praying God to "save and keep our comely Queen," Henry VII's wife ELIZABETH OF YORK, the "Lady Bessy" of the title.

The ballad begins with Elizabeth appealing to Lord Stanley to help her resist the marriage proposal of her uncle RICHARD III. Rather than marry her brothers' murderer, Elizabeth is ready to kill herself. Stanley enlists the aid of his brother, his sons, and other former servants of EDWARD IV, Elizabeth's late father. The conspirators meet secretly in LONDON on 3 May 1485 and agree to support the cause of Henry Tudor, earl of Richmond, who has sworn to marry Elizabeth upon coming to the throne. Elizabeth and the Stanleys dispatch Brereton with money and messages for Richmond, who is found at "Bigeram" abbey. Richmond agrees to come to England by Michaelmas, and Stanley withdraws from London, leaving his son Lord Strange in the king's hands. On Richmond's arrival, Sir William Stanley openly defies the king's summons, and Lord Stanley meets with the earl and promises to help him win the throne and Lady Bessy.

At Bosworth, Richard orders Lord Strange's execution when he sees Stanley's men waiting in the distance. Sir William Harrington pleads for Strange's life, which is spared when the sudden onset of battle distracts the king. The poem next describes the death of John HOWARD, duke of Norfolk, and the flight of other lords in Richard's army during the noise and confusion of combat. When Harrington urges Richard to flee, the king responds:

> Give me my battle-axe in my hand,
> And set my crown on my head so high!
> For by Him that made both sun and moon,
> King of England this day I will die!
> (Bennett, p. 175)

Richard is slain and his mangled body is carried to Leicester, where Lady Bessy rebukes it for the murder of her brothers—"How like you the killing of my brethren dear? Welcome, gentle uncle, home" (Rowse, p. 255). The poem appears to contain several memories of actual events; for instance, the ballad states that "The shots of guns were so fierce" (Rowse, p. 254), a detail confirmed by the later finding on the field of ARTILLERY balls, perhaps from the serpentines Richmond was known to possess. The poem is also the only description we have of the plotting conducted in England against Richard in the months before the Battle of Bosworth Field. Nonetheless, because much of what the poem relates cannot be verified or is demonstrably untrue, it has only limited use as a source for the battle, and it is, like the other Bosworth ballads, considered pure fiction by some modern historians.

See also *The Ballad of Bosworth Field;* Princes in the Tower; *The Rose of England;* Usurpation of 1483

Further Reading: Bennett, Michael, *The Battle of Bosworth* (New York: St. Martin's Press, 1985); Rowse, A. L., *Bosworth Field: From Medieval to Tudor England* (Garden City, NY: Doubleday, 1966).

Stafford, Henry, Duke of Buckingham (c. 1454–1483)

Henry Stafford, duke of Buckingham, was instrumental in ensuring the success of

RICHARD III's usurpation of the throne in 1483, an act that revived the WARS OF THE ROSES.

A grandson of both Humphrey STAFFORD, duke of Buckingham, and Edmund BEAUFORT, duke of Somerset, Stafford became duke of Buckingham in 1460 on his grandfather's death at the Battle of NORTHAMPTON. In 1466, EDWARD IV married the wealthy young duke to his sister-in-law, Katherine Woodville, daughter of Richard WOODVILLE, Earl Rivers. Although willing to tie the duke's estates and following to the growing Woodville interest, Edward otherwise gave Buckingham little employment, and the duke remained a rather obscure figure for someone of his wealth and royal blood.

However, Buckingham came into immediate prominence on Edward's death in April 1483, when he joined forces with Richard, duke of Gloucester, to help him seize custody of EDWARD V from Anthony WOODVILLE, Earl Rivers, the young king's uncle and governor. Aware of his need for Buckingham's support, Gloucester made the duke all-powerful in WALES, appointing him to the most important Welsh offices and giving him the keeping of all royal castles in the principality. In return, Buckingham presided at a 25 June assembly of notables in LONDON that devised a petition asking Gloucester to take the throne, and next day he led a deputation to Baynard's Castle to personally present the petition to Richard. Buckingham was also the most conspicuous peer at Richard III's coronation on 6 July, officiating as high steward and carrying the royal train.

Although rewarded with more offices and estates, Buckingham rose in rebellion in October against the king he had helped crown (see BUCKINGHAM'S REBELLION). The reasons for his surprising action remain uncertain. The traditional reason, used by William Shakespeare in his play RICHARD III, is the king's failure to keep a promise to return to the duke certain lands to which he had a claim, but this theory is dismissed by most modern historians because Richard restored the lands in question in July 1483. The duke may have been disturbed by Richard's murder of Edward V and his brother, although a modern case has been made that Buckingham was himself responsible for their deaths. A descendent of Edward III, he may have sought the Crown for himself, being encouraged in this ambition, as Sir Thomas More claimed in his HISTORY OF KING RICHARD III, by Bishop John MORTON, a prisoner entrusted to Buckingham's keeping by Richard III. He may have feared his fate should a conspiracy rapidly being formed by Queen Elizabeth WOODVILLE and Margaret BEAUFORT, Countess of Richmond, put Margaret's son, Henry Tudor, earl of Richmond (see HENRY VII), on the throne without his help. In any event, Morton put Buckingham in touch with the Tudor conspirators, and the duke rose in concert with them in October.

Declared the "most untrue creature living" by Richard on 11 October (Ross, p. 116), Buckingham was captured by royal forces at the end of the month after severe flooding on the Severn and Wye rivers prevented his force from moving east while royal forces cut off his retreat to the west. Betrayed by a RETAINER for the £1,000 reward placed on his head by the king, Buckingham was carried to Salisbury and executed in the marketplace on 2 November without trial or royal audience.

See also Plantagenet, Richard, Duke of York (1473–c. 1483); Princes in the Tower; Usurpation of 1483; other entries under Stafford

Further Reading: Gill, Louise, *Richard III and Buckingham's Rebellion* (Stroud, Gloucestershire, UK: Sutton Publishing, 1999); "Henry Stafford," in Michael Hicks, *Who's Who in Late Medieval England* (London: Shepheard-Walwyn, 1991), pp. 363–364; Rawcliffe, Carole, *The Staffords: Earls of Stafford and Dukes of Buckingham, 1394–1521* (Cambridge: Cambridge University Press, 1978); Ross, Charles, *Richard III* (Berkeley: University of California Press, 1981).

Stafford, Humphrey, Duke of Buckingham (1402–1460)

Humphrey Stafford, duke of Buckingham, was one of the wealthiest magnates and largest landowners in fifteenth-century England, as well as a force for political moderation in the early stages of the WARS OF THE ROSES.

Stafford was only a year old when his father's death at the Battle of Shrewsbury made him earl of Stafford. From his mother, a granddaughter of Edward III, Stafford inherited royal blood and extensive estates. In 1421, Henry V knighted Stafford for his military service in FRANCE, and, by 1424, the young earl was a prominent member of HENRY VI's regency COUNCIL. Traveling abroad with the king in 1430, Stafford was appointed constable of France and governor of Paris. He participated in several French campaigns in the 1430s and was named captain of CALAIS in 1442. Created duke of Buckingham in 1444, he took a lead role over the next two years in the peace negotiations with France.

Although related to both Richard PLANTAGENET, duke of York, and Edmund BEAUFORT, duke of Somerset, and married to a sister of Richard NEVILLE, earl of Salisbury, Buckingham associated himself with neither the Lancastrian nor the Yorkist faction in the 1450s. He disliked York's ambition but opposed the imposition of a severe punishment on York after his submission following the DARTFORD UPRISING in 1452, and he cooperated with the duke during his FIRST PROTECTORATE in 1454. In 1455, Buckingham commanded the royal army at the Battle of ST. ALBANS, where he refused to surrender Somerset to York and negotiated unsuccessfully for a peaceful settlement. He stayed with the king during the ensuing battle and was wounded in the face by an arrow.

Buckingham again worked with York in the years after St. Albans, but his fundamental loyalty was to Henry VI, and he stood with the king when hostilities broke out in 1459. Buckingham was with the royal army at the Battle of LUDFORD BRIDGE and attended the COVENTRY PARLIAMENT at which York and his Neville allies were attainted of treason (see ATTAINDER, ACT OF). In July 1460, the duke commanded the royal army at NORTHAMPTON, and repeatedly turned away messengers from Richard NEVILLE, earl of Warwick, who were seeking to arrange an audience for Warwick with the king. When the Yorkists overwhelmed the Lancastrian line, Buckingham was one of the peers who were slain defending the royal person. He had probably been marked for destruction by the Yorkists, as Somerset had been at the Battle of St. Albans; by 1460, the worsening civil conflict had moved beyond the policy of moderation and reconciliation that Buckingham represented.

See also other entries under Stafford
Further Reading: Griffiths, Ralph A., *The Reign of King Henry VI* (Berkeley: University of California Press, 1981); "Humphrey Stafford," in Michael Hicks, *Who's Who in Late Medieval England* (London: Shepheard-Walwyn, 1991), pp. 287–289; Rawcliffe, Carole, *The Staffords: Earls of Stafford and Dukes of Buckingham, 1394–1521* (Cambridge: Cambridge University Press, 1978).

Stafford, Humphrey, Earl of Devon (1439–1469)

A loyal Yorkist, Humphrey Stafford was one of the men EDWARD IV raised to local political prominence in the 1460s, in an effort to build support for the Yorkist regime and to defend against Lancastrian insurgency.

A member of a southwestern GENTRY family distantly related to the dukes of Buckingham, Stafford was an early adherent to the Yorkist cause. He fought at the Battle of MORTIMER'S CROSS in February 1461, was knighted by Edward IV after the Battle of TOWTON in late March, and was raised to the PEERAGE as Lord Stafford of Southwick in July. By 1463, Edward began positioning Stafford as the chief royal agent in the southwest, a region notoriously Lancastrian in its sympathies. The king appointed him to numerous local offices, granted him many forfeited southwestern estates, and gave him many local wardships. Stafford also served on various political and administrative commissions across the region.

In 1469, Stafford was admitted to the royal COUNCIL and served on the commission that tried Henry COURTENAY, earl of Devon, for plotting treason with agents of Queen MARGARET OF ANJOU. Perhaps because Stafford was given Devon's lands and title in May 1469, he was later accused of having engineered Devon's trial and execution. Although Stafford was ambitious, the keen personal interest that the king took in the trial indicates how seriously he took the charges and makes it more likely that Stafford was merely the beneficiary rather than the instigator of Devon's downfall.

Within weeks of his promotion, the new earl was identified in a rebel manifesto inspired by Richard NEVILLE, earl of Warwick, as one of a crowd of grasping courtiers who were impoverishing the kingdom for their own gain. Blaming the shrinking of his political influence on the rise of royal favorites like Devon and the WOODVILLE FAMILY, Warwick tried to overawe the king by instigating the ROBIN OF REDESDALE REBELLION in the summer of 1469. Ordered to raise troops to quell the uprising, Devon joined forces with William HERBERT, earl of Pembroke. Near Banbury on 25 July, the two earls quarreled over billeting arrangements and wound up in separate encampments, Devon taking most of the ARCHERS with him. When Pembroke was attacked by the rebels next morning at EDGECOTE, the lack of archers contributed to his defeat. Devon marched to the field of battle, but either came too late to affect the outcome or was unable to engage his forces. The earl fled into the West Country, but was seized and executed on 17 August by the common people of Bridgwater, who may have been acting either in Warwick's or the Courtenays' interest.

See also other entries under Stafford
Further Reading: Ross, Charles, *Edward IV* (New Haven, CT: Yale University Press, 1998).

Stamford Bridge, Battle of (1454)

Fought on or about 31 October 1454, the Battle of Stamford Bridge was one of the most violent episodes of the NEVILLE-PERCY FEUD and an important factor in cementing the political alignments that led to civil war.

In June 1454, after more than a year of harassing and destroying the partisans and property of the rival NEVILLE FAMILY, Thomas PERCY, Lord Egremont, second son of Henry PERCY, second earl of Northumberland, joined with Henry HOLLAND, duke of Exeter, in an uprising aimed at disrupting the FIRST PROTECTORATE of Richard PLANTAGENET, duke of York. Exeter claimed that he had more right to be protector of the realm during HENRY VI's illness than had York, and Egremont saw the duke's rebellion as an opportunity to escalate his attacks on York's allies, the Nevilles, with whom Egremont's family was vying for political dominance in northern England. When York marched north to quell the uprising, Exeter fled to LONDON, where he was hauled from SANCTUARY and imprisoned in July. Egremont remained at large, recruiting followers from among the Percy tenantry.

In late October, while leading a band of more than 200 Percy RETAINERS, Egremont and his younger brother Richard Percy encountered a force led by Thomas and John NEVILLE, younger sons of Richard NEVILLE, earl of Salisbury. The two forces collided east of York on the Neville manor of Stamford Bridge, near the site of the like-named battle where King Harold defeated Scandinavian invaders in 1066. Because most of their men seem to have fled before battle was fully engaged, Egremont and his brother fell into the hands of the Nevilles, who carried them to Middleham Castle. A Neville-convened commission in York found Egremont liable to Salisbury for over £11,000 in damages, a staggering sum well beyond the prisoner's means. The judgment allowed the Nevilles to commit Egremont and his brother to prison in London as debtors, a confinement that lasted until the Percies' escape in November 1456.

In the late 1450s, the mutual hostility that manifested itself at Stamford Bridge drove the Nevilles to ally themselves with York for support against the Percies, while the Percies felt obliged to ally themselves with the COURT faction of Henry VI for support against the Nevilles. Although Henry VI tried to reconcile the parties with his LOVE-DAY of March 1458, a settlement that required Egremont to give bonds to keep the peace and Salisbury to drop the monetary judgment against Egremont, the Neville and Percy alliances endured and gave the houses of LANCASTER and YORK the strength and confidence they needed to proceed to open war with one another in 1459.

See also Henry VI, Illness of; North of England and the Wars of the Roses

Further Reading: Griffiths, Ralph A., "Local Rivalries and National Politics: The Percies, the Nevilles and the Duke of Exeter, 1452–1455" in Ralph A. Griffiths, ed., *King and Country: England and Wales in the Fifteenth Century* (London: Hambledon Press, 1991), pp. 321–364; Griffiths, Ralph A., *The Reign of King Henry VI* (Berkeley: University of California Press, 1981); Storey, R. L., *The End of the House of Lancaster,* 2d ed. (Stroud, Gloucestershire, UK: Sutton Publishing, 1999).

Stanley, Thomas, Earl of Derby (c. 1435–1504)

A powerful nobleman in northwestern England, Thomas Stanley, second Lord Stanley, survived the WARS OF THE ROSES by not adhering strongly to any party and by repeatedly demonstrating a remarkable ability to switch sides at the most favorable moment.

In 1459, Stanley raised a large force on the command of Queen MARGARET OF ANJOU but simultaneously gave a conditional promise of support to her Yorkist opponent Richard NEVILLE, earl of Salisbury, who was Stanley's father-in-law. However, when Salisbury engaged the Lancastrians at the Battle of BLORE HEATH, Stanley, who was only a few miles away, kept his troops out of the fight. Although Stanley was accused of treason by the Lancastrian-controlled COVENTRY PARLIAMENT, the queen chose to overlook his dealings with Salisbury, and Stanley fought for HENRY VI at the Battle of NORTHAMPTON in 1460.

Stanley's Lancastrian allegiance fell away in 1461 when EDWARD IV won the throne and conferred upon him various lands and offices. In the spring of 1470, Stanley refused to assist the ultimately unsuccessful revolt launched by his brother-in-law, Richard NEVILLE, earl of Warwick, but when Warwick returned in Oc-

tober and drove Edward from the kingdom, Stanley supported the READEPTION government of Henry VI (see EDWARD IV, OVERTHROW OF). When Edward returned in March 1471, Stanley remained carefully aloof and was rewarded by the victorious Yorkists with appointments as lord steward and royal councilor (see EDWARD IV, RESTORATION OF). In 1475, Stanley accompanied Edward IV on his French campaign, and in 1482, Stanley held a command in the duke of Gloucester's Scottish campaign.

After the death of Edward IV, Gloucester, fearing that Stanley might oppose his bid for the throne, arrested Stanley at the infamous COUNCIL MEETING OF 13 JUNE 1483. However, by July, Stanley was free and sufficiently in favor to carry the mace at Gloucester's coronation as RICHARD III (see USURPATION OF 1483). Married to MARGARET BEAUFORT since 1472, Stanley carefully distanced himself from her involvement in plots on behalf of her son, Henry Tudor, earl of Richmond, in the autumn of 1483. After the failure of BUCKINGHAM'S REBELLION, Margaret was placed in her husband's keeping and all her lands were transferred to his custody. Stanley retained Richard's favor until the summer of 1485, when Stanley's extended absence from COURT aroused the king's suspicion. Refusing Richard's summons to return, he sent his son Lord Strange, who found himself a prisoner under threat of death when Richmond landed in August in WALES and marched unimpeded through Stanley territory. Although he met with Richmond, and his brother Sir William STANLEY gave the earl active assistance, Stanley remained cautiously neutral at the Battle of BOSWORTH FIELD on 22 August, ignoring both the pleas of Richmond and the orders of Richard. The battle was decided in Richmond's favor by the intervention of Sir William Stanley. Lord Strange survived the battle when Richard's order for his execution went unheeded.

As stepfather to the new king, HENRY VII, Stanley was in high favor, being created earl of Derby in October 1485. He was also confirmed in all his offices and granted the estates of attainted Yorkists. Derby stood as godfather to Prince Arthur in 1486 and survived his brother's execution for treason in 1495 by again remaining carefully neutral. He died in Lancashire in July 1504.

Further Reading: Bagley, John J., *The Earls of Derby, 1485–1985* (London: Sidgwick and Jackson, 1985); Coward, Barry, *The Stanleys, Lords Stanley, and Earls of Derby, 1385–1672* (Manchester: Manchester University Press, 1983).

Stanley, Sir William (d. 1495)

By his timely intervention during the Battle of BOSWORTH FIELD in 1485, Sir William Stanley ensured the overthrow of RICHARD III and the accession to the English throne of HENRY VII and the house of TUDOR.

In September 1459, Stanley eschewed the careful neutrality of his elder brother Thomas STANLEY, Lord Stanley, and declared himself an open partisan of the house of YORK by fighting with Richard NEVILLE, earl of Salisbury, against the Lancastrian forces at the Battle of BLORE HEATH. Although attainted by the COVENTRY PARLIAMENT in late 1459, Stanley survived, perhaps by fleeing abroad, to fight for EDWARD IV at the Battle of TOWTON in March 1461. Well rewarded with lands and offices, especially in the Stanley-dominated counties of Chester and Lancashire, Stanley won further favor after the Battle of HEXHAM in 1464, receiving the lands of the late Lancastrian nobleman, John CLIFFORD, Lord Clifford.

Upon Edward IV's return from exile in the spring of 1471, Stanley was among the first gentlemen to rally to the Yorkist cause, joining Edward at Nottingham with 300 men (see EDWARD IV, RESTORATION OF). In the autumn of 1483, after the suppression of BUCKINGHAM'S REBELLION, Richard III sought to win Stanley's support by granting him numerous lands and offices in WALES, including some formerly held by Henry STAFFORD, the late duke of Buckingham. Despite these rewards, Stanley disappointed the king in August 1485 by failing to contest the entry into England of Henry Tudor, earl of Richmond. On

17 August, Stanley met with Richmond in Stafford, but did not join forces with the earl, even though Stanley had already been proclaimed a traitor by the king on the strength of a confession extracted from Stanley's nephew, Lord Strange. At Bosworth Field, the Stanleys took up a position between the royal and rebel armies, leaving both sides unclear as to their intentions. Perhaps fearing for his life should Richard win, Sir William Stanley led his troops into battle when the king charged unexpectedly into Richmond's lines. By blunting the royal charge and killing Richard, Stanley's attack ensured Richmond's victory.

Now enthroned as Henry VII, Richmond rewarded Stanley with appointment as lord chamberlain and confirmation of Richard III's Welsh land grants. However, in late 1494, Henry arrested Stanley on suspicion of involvement in Perkin WARBECK's attempt to seize the throne by claiming to be one of the sons of Edward IV. Tried and convicted of treason, Stanley was beheaded at the TOWER OF LONDON in February 1495.

Further Reading: Bagley, John J., *The Earls of Derby, 1485–1985* (London: Sidgwick and Jackson, 1985); Coward, Barry, *The Stanleys, Lords Stanley, and Earls of Derby, 1385–1672* (Manchester: Manchester University Press, 1983).

Stillington, Robert, Bishop of Bath and Wells (d. 1491)

In 1483, Robert Stillington, bishop of Bath and Wells, supposedly supplied Richard, duke of Gloucester, with the information the duke used to depose his nephew and thereby reanimate the Wars of the Roses.

Born in Yorkshire, Stillington graduated from Oxford in about 1442 and thereafter rose steadily through the ecclesiastical hierarchy. He attached himself to the Yorkist cause in the late 1450s, and in July 1460 was appointed keeper of the privy seal by Richard NEVILLE, earl of Warwick, who was then, as a consequence of his recent victory at the Battle of NORTHAMPTON, in control of HENRY VI and the royal government. In 1465, Stillington was elected bishop of Bath and Wells, and in

June 1467, EDWARD IV appointed the bishop chancellor of England. He was deprived of the chancellorship by Warwick when the earl overthrew Edward IV in the autumn of 1470, but restored to office by Edward upon his return to the throne in the spring of 1471. Stillington resigned the chancellorship in 1475 and was then employed by Edward IV on an ultimately unsuccessful effort to induce FRANCIS II, duke of BRITTANY, to surrender Henry Tudor, earl of Richmond (see HENRY VII), the surviving Lancastrian claimant to the throne.

At the accession of EDWARD V in 1483, Stillington informed Richard, duke of Gloucester, the king's paternal uncle, that Edward IV had contracted marriage with one Eleanor Butler prior to his marriage to Elizabeth WOODVILLE; Gloucester accepted the BUTLER PRECONTRACT as grounds for deposing Edward V, holding that the Butler betrothal illegitimized the king and his siblings as offspring of an invalid marriage. As incorporated in the 1484 statute TITULUS REGIUS, Stillington's claims became the basis of Gloucester's formal justification for taking the Crown. Many contemporary commentators and most modern historians have dismissed Stillington's supposed revelations as an invention by Gloucester to legitimize his usurpation. They point out that the story was unknown before 1483, and that the timing of its appearance was too convenient for Gloucester's ambition to be credible. The duke's supporters argue that Stillington's mysterious imprisonment in 1478 for uttering words prejudicial to the king was the bishop's punishment for divulging the precontract story to Edward IV's brother, George PLANTAGENET, duke of Clarence. The truth of Stillington's revelations cannot now be determined.

In July 1483, Stillington officiated at Gloucester's coronation as RICHARD III, and thereafter became a favored member of Richard's COUNCIL. Shortly after his victory at the Battle of BOSWORTH FIELD in August 1485, Henry VII, Richard's supplanter, ordered Stillington's arrest, but pardoned the bishop three months later. Henry had his first PARLIAMENT repeal *Titulus Regius,* but took no action against the supposed author of the statute's contents. In 1487, Stillington involved himself in the uprising instigated by Lambert SIMNEL, who claimed to be the Yorkist heir, Edward PLANTAGENET, earl of Warwick. After the collapse of Simnel's enterprise at the Battle of STOKE in June 1487, the king imprisoned Stillington at Windsor, where the bishop died in May 1491.

See also Edward IV, Overthrow of; Edward IV, Restoration of; Shaw's Sermon; Usurpation of 1483

Further Reading: Kendall, Paul Murray, *Richard the Third* (New York: W. W. Norton, 1956); Levine, Mortimer, *Tudor Dynastic Problems, 1460–1571* (London: George Allen and Unwin, 1973); Ross, Charles, *Edward IV* (New Haven, CT: Yale University Press, 1998); Ross, Charles, *Richard III* (Berkeley: University of California Press, 1981).

Stoke, Battle of (1487)

Considered the last major battle of the WARS OF THE ROSES, the Battle of Stoke, fought on 16 June 1487, ended the first significant attempt to overthrow HENRY VII and restore the house of YORK.

The failure of the 1486 LOVELL-STAFFORD UPRISING resulted in large part from the lack of a Yorkist candidate for the throne to rally support. This deficiency was remedied in 1487, when a priest named Richard (or William) Simonds arrived in IRELAND with a boy Simonds claimed was Edward PLANTAGENET, earl of Warwick, the nephew of EDWARD IV. Although the child was in reality Lambert SIMNEL, the son of an Oxford tradesman, he was apparently attractive and intelligent and well coached by Simonds to play the part of a Yorkist prince. Gerald FITZGERALD, earl of Kildare, the Irish lord deputy, immediately accepted Simnel as Warwick, not, probably, out of genuine belief, but in the hope that a Yorkist regime restored with Irish assistance would grant Ireland greater autonomy. Having won a base in Ireland, the Simnel imposture gained further support in BUR-

GUNDY, where Duchess MARGARET OF YORK, the real Warwick's aunt, and such prominent Yorkist exiles as Francis LOVELL, Lord Lovell, and John de la POLE, earl of Lincoln, another nephew of Edward IV, joined the movement. Lincoln and Lovell came to Dublin for the 24 May coronation of Simnel as "Edward VI," bringing with them men and money supplied by Margaret. Although the ultimate intent of the Yorkist leaders was probably to enthrone Lincoln, they were willing to use Simnel as a figurehead to generate support for a Yorkist restoration.

In LONDON, Henry VII took the real Warwick from the TOWER OF LONDON and paraded him through the streets. On 4 June 1487, the Yorkists landed on the Lancashire coast. As the rebels crossed Yorkshire, they gathered significant gentry support and enlarged their numbers to almost 9,000 men, although the city of York denied them entry and such prominent northern lords as Henry PERCY, earl of Northumberland, and Thomas STANLEY, earl of Derby, mobilized for the king. On the morning of 16 June, the Yorkist army, which comprised strong contingents of German and Irish MERCENARIES as well as the English forces picked up on the march, formed a line of battle on a hill southwest of the Nottinghamshire village of East Stoke. The king and his commanders were unaware of how close the rebel forces were, and they advanced in columns, unprepared for battle. John de VERE, earl of Oxford, commander of the royal vanguard, was the first to encounter the Yorkists. To stay in the open awaiting the king and the rest of the army was to invite destruction; to retreat was to risk disintegration through panic and low morale. Oxford therefore decided to attack the larger force, sending messengers to advise Henry to advance with all speed.

At about 9 A.M., Oxford's ARCHERS opened the battle, doing particular execution among the lightly armored Irish, who then charged downhill taking the rest of the Yorkist army with them. Although Oxford's men were experienced fighters, they were hard-pressed by the larger Yorkist force, and only the timely arrival of the rest of the royal army under the king and his uncle, Jasper TUDOR, earl of Bedford, saved Oxford from defeat. Unable to stand against fresh troops, the Yorkist line broke, and many rebels were killed as they fled down a steep ravine. Lincoln died on the field, as did Lovell, although his body was never found. Simnel was captured, pardoned, and set to work in the royal kitchens. Henry VII had survived the first Yorkist attempt on his throne.

See also Warbeck, Perkin; Yorkist Heirs (after 1485)

Further Reading: Bennett, Michael J., *Lambert Simnel and the Battle of Stoke* (New York: St. Martin's Press, 1987).

Stonor Letters and Papers

The letters and papers of the Stonors, members of an established Oxfordshire GENTRY family, are one of the most important surviving family archives from the fifteenth century. The Stonor documents are particularly valuable because they provide a view of gentry life during the WARS OF THE ROSES that is in distinct contrast to the view offered by the PASTON LETTERS, the most famous surviving collection of fifteenth-century correspondence.

Although the Stonor archive contains documents ranging in date from 1290 to 1483, the bulk of the material dates to the late fifteenth century and relates to Thomas Stonor (1424–1474) and to his son Sir William Stonor (1449–1494). Thomas married a natural daughter of HENRY VI's chief minister, William de la POLE, duke of Suffolk, but this connection to the house of LANCASTER did not induce Thomas to support Henry. The elder Stonor avoided serious commitment to either side during the first two phases of the Wars of the Roses. After 1474, William Stonor improved the family's financial position by engaging in the wool trade and by marrying a series of wealthy wives, including the widow of a prosperous LONDON merchant and the daughter of the late John NEVILLE, marquis of

Montagu, the younger brother of Richard NEVILLE, earl of Warwick.

William also advanced through service to the house of YORK. He represented Oxfordshire in the PARLIAMENT of 1478, which acquiesced in EDWARD IV's attainder of his brother George PLANTAGENET, duke of Clarence. Knighted during the 1478 celebrations surrounding the marriage of Edward's younger son, Richard PLANTAGENET, duke of York, Stonor, by 1479, also held appointment as knight of the body, a privileged position of personal service to the monarch. Stonor also attached himself to Thomas GREY, marquis of Dorset, and to the WOODVILLE FAMILY interest. Sir William's loyalty to EDWARD V led him to undertake the family's one serious involvement in the civil wars. In October 1483, he joined BUCKINGHAM'S REBELLION against RICHARD III. Upon the collapse of the uprising, Sir William, who may have fled with Dorset to BRITTANY, lost his estates through ATTAINDER, although all were restored by HENRY VII in 1485.

The Stonor archive, which includes over 300 letters, household accounts, wills, and other documents, owes its preservation either to being confiscated in 1483 (when the collection ends) or to being gathered as evidence for an inheritance dispute case in 1500. The documents shed little light on political or military affairs, but therein lies their importance. Unlike the Paston letters, which are full of the political turmoil that afflicted East Anglia during the period, the Stonor papers show how peaceful life was for the Midlands gentry, many of whom seem to have avoided involvement in the civil conflict. The Stonor documents support what most historians now believe—for many people the Wars of the Roses caused only minimal disruption of their lives.

See also Cely Letters and Papers; Military Campaigns, Duration of; Plumpton Letters and Papers

Further Reading: Carpenter, Christine, ed., *Kingsford's Stonor Letters and Papers, 1290–1483*

(Cambridge: Cambridge University Press, 1996).

Suffolk, Duke of. See entries under Pole

Sun in Splendor/Sunburst Badge

Although history has closely identified the house of YORK with the white rose emblem, the favorite personal badge of EDWARD IV was the Sun in Splendor or the bright golden sunburst.

The badge apparently derived from a meteorological phenomenon that appeared in the sky to Edward, then earl of March, before the Battle of MORTIMER'S CROSS in February 1461. On the morning of the battle, which was fought only a month after the death of his father, Richard PLANTAGENET, duke of York, Edward saw three suns shining "in the firmament . . . full clear" (Ross, p. 53). Taking this sight to be an omen of victory, Edward went on to win the first battle fought under his leadership. Edward's sunburst badge was soon closely associated with the king and his family. It appeared frequently on buildings constructed or refurbished by Edward, such as St. George's Chapel at Windsor and Tewkesbury Abbey near the site of the 1471 Yorkist victory at the Battle of TEWKESBURY. The emblem also found its way into manuscripts written under Yorkist auspices and onto tapestries or apparel created for the Yorkist COURT.

The streaming sunburst badge also played an important role in the Battle of BARNET in April 1471. As the positions of the two struggling armies shifted on the fog-shrouded field, the men of John de VERE, earl of Oxford, one of the Lancastrian commanders, came up unexpectedly behind some of their own men as they tried to reengage after driving part of the Yorkist army from the fight. Because they were wearing Oxford's badge of a star with streams, they were mistaken in the mist for Yorkist troops wearing the well-known sunburst badge, the sun with streams, of Edward IV. When Lancastrian ARCHERS opened fire on them, Oxford's surprised and confused men thought themselves betrayed and fled the field crying "treason!" The incident severely demoralized the Lancastrian line, which soon after broke, allowing Edward's men to surge forward, killing the fleeing Richard NEVILLE, earl of Warwick, and winning the battle.

See also Badges; Bastard Feudalism
Further Reading: Ross, Charles, *The Wars of the Roses* (New York: Thames and Hudson, 1987).

Surrey, Earl of. *See* Howard, Thomas, Earl of Surrey and Duke of Norfolk

Tailboys, Sir William (c. 1416–1464)

Although responsible for numerous crimes in his county and therefore a prime example of the local corruption and disorder that made HENRY VI's government so ineffective and unpopular, Sir William Tailboys (or Talboys) was a staunch partisan of the house of LANCASTER after the outbreak of the WARS OF THE ROSES.

Born into a Lincolnshire GENTRY family that descended from a Norman follower of William the Conqueror, Tailboys entered the king's household in 1441 and married the daughter of a prominent courtier, William BONVILLE, Lord Bonville, in 1446. Possessed of a fierce temper and an aggressive nature, Tailboys deeply involved himself in the magnate feuds that disturbed Lincolnshire in the 1440s. In November 1449, perhaps in pursuit of these local quarrels, Tailboys assaulted Ralph Cromwell, Lord Cromwell, at Westminster, an act that Cromwell and others attributed to Tailboys's political patron, William de la POLE, duke of Suffolk. Tailboys's violence helped precipitate Suffolk's impeachment by PARLIAMENT in early 1450. The duke's protection of Tailboys for the Westminster assault and for earlier disorders was used as evidence of Suffolk's corruption and abuse of power.

After Suffolk's fall, Tailboys was fined and briefly imprisoned, but he continued to conspire against his Lincolnshire enemies, and in 1452 he attempted to falsely implicate Cromwell in the unsuccessful DARTFORD UPRISING undertaken by Richard PLANTAGENET, duke of York. When civil war erupted in 1459, Tailboys was a firm Lancastrian. He fought for Queen MARGARET OF ANJOU at the Battle of ST. ALBANS in February 1461 and was knighted after the battle by Henry VI. After the Battle of TOWTON in March 1461, he fled into SCOTLAND with the Lancastrian royal family. EDWARD IV seized Tailboys's estates in May, and the first Yorkist Parliament included him in a bill of ATTAINDER in November.

In the same month, Tailboys led a force into England and recaptured ALNWICK CASTLE for Henry VI. He then marched to DUNSTANBURGH CASTLE, where Sir Ralph Percy, whom Edward had retained in command when the Yorkists took the fortress, surrendered the castle to him. Tailboys himself surrendered Alnwick in July 1462 to a force under William HASTINGS, Lord Hastings, and Sir John HOWARD, who allowed him to withdraw into Scotland. In April 1464, Tailboys fought under Henry BEAUFORT, duke of Somerset, at the Battle of HEDGELEY MOOR. One month later, he fought again with Somerset at the Battle of HEXHAM. Shortly after the battle, soldiers of John NEVILLE, Lord Montagu, the victor of Hexham, captured Tailboys as he hid in a coal pit. A large sum of money, apparently Lancastrian war funds, was found on his person. Tailboys was then taken to Newcastle and executed.

Further Reading: Haigh, Philip A., *The Military Campaigns of the Wars of the Roses* (Stroud, Gloucestershire, UK: Sutton Publishing, 1995); Ross, Charles, *Edward IV* (New Haven, CT: Yale University Press, 1998).

Tewkesbury, Battle of (1471)

The Battle of Tewkesbury, fought on 4 May 1471, completed EDWARD IV's restoration

Edward IV (crowned at center right) leads his army against the Lancastrians at the Battle of Tewkesbury in May 1471. (MS 236, University of Ghent)

to the throne and destroyed the Lancastrian cause.

On 14 April 1471, the day Richard NEVILLE, earl of Warwick, was defeated and slain at the Battle of BARNET, Queen MAR-GARET OF ANJOU and her son EDWARD OF LANCASTER, Prince of Wales, landed in En-

gland. Met by Edmund BEAUFORT, duke of Somerset, and other loyal Lancastrians, the queen, although grieved to hear of HENRY VI's reimprisonment in the TOWER OF LONDON, was persuaded to continue the war by marching into the West Country, where support for her cause was strong. On 19 April,

Edward IV left LONDON and marched slowly westward through the Thames Valley collecting reinforcements to make good his losses at the Battle of Barnet. His aim was to prevent Margaret, who was gathering substantial forces in the West Country, from turning north and crossing the Severn River into WALES, where she could join with the troops of Jasper TUDOR, earl of Pembroke.

Entering Bristol in late April, the Lancastrians acquired much needed provisions before continuing their march toward the Severn. Drawn southward away from the river by a Lancastrian feint toward Sodbury, Edward made up the lost time with the help of Sir Richard Beauchamp, who held the river crossing at Gloucester against the queen's army and so compelled it to move upriver to the ford at Tewkesbury. After a forced march of over thirty miles, the Yorkist army arrived at Tewkesbury on the evening of 3 May. Although the Lancastrians held a strong position, they had not been able to cross the river.

Early the next morning, before battle commenced, Edward sent a small force of spearmen to reconnoitre a nearby wooded area from which he feared the Lancastrians might launch the kind of surprise flank attack they had employed at the Battle of TOWTON in 1461. Finding the woods unoccupied, the spearmen waited there for the fighting to begin. Meanwhile, Somerset, the Lancastrian commander, used a small hill to his right to hide a flanking move with which he hoped to surprise and roll up the Yorkist line, much as the Yorkists had done to win the Battle of NORTHAMPTON in 1460. After opening barrages by the ARCHERS and ARTILLERY, the armies advanced upon one another. Somerset's flank attack surprised the Yorkist van under Edward's brother, Richard, duke of Gloucester (see RICHARD III), but the expected supporting attack by the rest of the Lancastrian army under John WENLOCK, Lord Wenlock, failed to materialize. Instead of catching the Yorkists between two wings of his army, Somerset now found himself heavily engaged by Gloucester in his front and assailed by the hidden Yorkist spearmen from the rear.

Under this double assault, Somerset's troops broke and fled toward the river, pursued by Gloucester's men.

Edward IV drove the rest of his army forward and quickly overwhelmed the remainder of the Lancastrian force. Enraged at Wenlock's failure to support him, Somerset is supposed to have slain Wenlock with a battle-ax, thus depriving the Lancastrian army of leadership at a crucial moment. Somerset survived the battle, but he was executed at Tewkesbury several days later after being dragged out of SANCTUARY at the local abbey. At some point in the final rout, the Prince of Wales, who was nominally in command of Wenlock's force, was killed on the field. Various unreliable accounts claim that he was slain by Gloucester; died crying out for aid from his brother-in-law, George PLANTAGENET, duke of Clarence; or was captured and slain in the king's presence. In all likelihood, he was killed while fleeing the battle, slain by Yorkist soldiers seeking a rich lord to plunder. Queen Margaret was captured two days later and imprisoned in the Tower, where, on 21 May, Edward IV completed the destruction of the house of LANCASTER by ordering the murder of Henry VI (see HENRY VI, MURDER OF).

Further Reading: Haigh, Philip A., *The Military Campaigns of the Wars of the Roses* (Stroud, Gloucestershire, UK: Sutton Publishing, 1995); Hammond, P. W., *The Battles of Barnet and Tewkesbury* (New York: St. Martin's Press, 1990).

Thomas ap Gruffydd (d. 1473)

During the 1460s, Thomas ap Gruffydd led one of the most influential Lancastrian families in South WALES.

The son of Gruffydd ap Nicholas, Thomas helped his father establish their family's ascendancy throughout southwest Wales in the 1440s and 1450s. This dominance was often achieved by force and in defiance of the law and the will of a weak and distant king. The family's position was threatened after 1455, when the struggle between the English houses of LANCASTER and YORK spilled into

Wales, forcing many Welsh families to choose sides. In 1456, HENRY VI sent his half brother, Edmund TUDOR, earl of Richmond, to Wales to reestablish royal authority. Within months, Richmond was at war with William HERBERT and Walter DEVEREUX, the chief Welsh lieutenants of Richard PLANTAGENET, duke of York. By joining with Richmond, Thomas and his father earned a royal pardon for all past offences in October 1456. Although the earl died in November, the decision was, at least initially, a wise one, for Richmond's brother, Jasper TUDOR, earl of Pembroke, restored Lancastrian control to much of Wales over the next three years.

After his father's death in 1460, Thomas and his brothers maintained their Lancastrian allegiance, fighting alongside Pembroke at the Battle of MORTIMER'S CROSS in February 1461, and holding the castle of Carreg Cennen against a Yorkist siege until May 1462. Compelled at last to surrender the castle, Thomas negotiated an agreement that guaranteed his freedom. Thereafter, Thomas and his brothers led the continuing resistance to Yorkist rule in southern and western Wales. After an unsuccessful uprising in 1464, Thomas and his younger son RHYS AP THOMAS fled to BURGUNDY, where they entered the service of Duke PHILIP and, after his death in 1467, the service of his son Duke CHARLES.

In Wales, Thomas's brothers and older sons so vexed the Yorkist regime that EDWARD IV specifically excluded them from a pardon offered to the Lancastrian defenders of HARLECH CASTLE in July 1468. After Richard NEVILLE, earl of Warwick, restored Henry VI to the throne in October 1470, the Lancastrian READEPTION government offered the family a full pardon, and Pembroke's return to Wales restored the family's local authority (see EDWARD IV, OVERTHROW OF). Thomas and his son returned from the continent in 1471, only to find that Edward IV had regained the throne (see EDWARD IV, RESTORATION OF). Although some of his relatives submitted, Thomas continued at odds with the Herberts, the chief Yorkist family of Wales. He was killed in about 1473 in an encounter with Herbert forces in southern Wales. Although at peace with Edward IV, Thomas's family was superseded in its local influence in the 1470s by the COUNCIL that ruled Wales in the name of Prince Edward (see EDWARD V).

Further Reading: Evans, H. T., *Wales and the Wars of the Roses* (Stroud, Gloucestershire, UK: Alan Sutton Publishing, 1995); Griffiths, Ralph A., *Sir Rhys ap Thomas and His Family* (Cardiff, UK: University of Wales Press, 1993).

Tiptoft, John, Earl of Worcester (c. 1427–1470)

John Tiptoft, earl of Worcester, was noted both for his humanist scholarship and for the cruelty with which he exercised the office of constable of England.

Created earl of Worcester in 1449, he was appointed treasurer in 1452, royal councilor in 1453, and lord deputy of IRELAND in 1456. Sent on embassy to Italy about 1458, he studied Latin at Padua, explored the antiquities of Venice and Florence, and even visited Palestine. While staying at the papal court in Rome, he supposedly impressed Pius II with his Latin, and he is said to have depleted the libraries of Italy with the quantity of his book purchases.

Having missed the political upheavals of 1459–1460, Worcester returned to England in 1461 and was received with immediate favor by the new Yorkist regime. EDWARD IV appointed the earl chief justice of North WALES, constable of the TOWER OF LONDON, and constable of England. In February 1462, he tried and condemned various accused traitors in his constable's court; among those suffering were John de Vere, twelfth earl of Oxford; his son Aubrey; and Sir Thomas Tuddenham (see OXFORD CONSPIRACY). In 1464, he condemned Sir Ralph Grey and numerous other recently captured Lancastrian rebels. In 1467, he was again appointed lord deputy of Ireland, where he added to his growing reputation for cruelty by executing his predecessor in office, Thomas FITZGERALD, earl of Desmond.

The dragon badge of John Tiptoft, earl of Worcester. (Add. MS 40742 f. 10, British Library)

Worcester rode with the king in the spring of 1470 in the campaign against the Lincolnshire rebellion instigated by Richard NEVILLE, earl of Warwick, and by Edward's brother, George PLANTAGENET, duke of Clarence. Reappointed constable, Worcester condemned numerous rebels to be hanged, drawn, and quartered. He won for himself the sobriquet "butcher of England" by impaling, apparently without the king's consent, the heads and bodies of the condemned traitors, an innovation in the traditional mode of execution that many English people found particularly distasteful. When Warwick forced Edward IV to flee the country in October 1470, Worcester went into hiding but was quickly captured (see EDWARD IV, OVERTHROW OF). Accused of indulging his Italian tastes by introducing the tyrannical "law of Padua" into England, Worcester was tried and condemned in a constable's court presided over by John de VERE, thirteenth earl of Oxford, whose father and brother Worcester had condemned in 1462. At his execution on 18 October 1470, Worcester supposedly asked the headsman to strike three blows in honor of the trinity. In 1481, William CAXTON printed several of Worcester's English translations of Latin works.

Further Reading: "John Tiptoft," in Michael Hicks, *Who's Who in Late Medieval England* (London: Shepheard-Walwyn, 1991), pp. 320–321; Mitchell, R. J., *John Tiptoft* (London: Longmans,

Green, 1938); Weiss, Roberto, *Humanism in England during the Fifteenth Century* (Oxford: Blackwell, 1967).

Titulus Regius

Titulus Regius ("royal title") is the document that formally declares RICHARD III's title to the throne. Incorporated into an act of PARLIAMENT in 1484, the document is there described as a "roll of parchment" or petition presented by "the three estates of this realm" to Richard, duke of Gloucester, requesting him to take the Crown. The petition, which was likely compiled at Richard's direction, justifies his accession by explaining why the children of his older brothers were barred from the succession. Because it was presented to Richard before he took the throne, probably at a meeting in LONDON on 26 June 1483, *Titulus Regius* is the first and clearest statement of Richard's reasons for replacing his nephew as king.

The petition, which Richard had widely published after its presentation, invalidates the marriage of EDWARD IV and Elizabeth WOODVILLE by stating, without giving any sources, that Edward was not free to marry Elizabeth because he was already betrothed to Eleanor Butler. The BUTLER PRECONTRACT meant that king and queen were living "together sinfully and damnably in adultery," and that all their children, including EDWARD V and his brother Richard PLANTAGENET, duke of York, were "bastards . . . unable to inherit or to claim anything by inheritance." *Titulus Regius* also condemns the Woodville marriage as having been contrived by witchcraft, worked upon the king by the bride and her mother, JACQUETTA OF LUXEMBOURG, duchess of Bedford, and as having been made in secret, "without reading of banns" and contrary to "the laudable customs of the Church of England." Because George PLANTAGENET, duke of Clarence, Richard's other brother, was "convicted and attainted of high treason" in 1478, his son Edward PLANTAGENET, earl of Warwick, was likewise "disabled . . . of all right and claim . . . to the crown and dignity royal." With all Richard's

The opening of the statute Titulus Regius *showing (halfway down) the text of the petition that was presented to Richard, duke of Gloucester, in June 1483 to urge him to take the throne. (Public Record Office: PRO C 65/114)*

nephews and nieces thus barred from the succession, *Titulus Regius* declares Richard to be the only "person living . . . that by right may claim the said crown and dignity royal by way of inheritance."

The document also argues that Richard III's accession is necessary for the restoration of good government, which suffered under Edward IV due to his acceptance of the "counsel of persons, insolent, vicious, and of inordinate avarice," meaning, the queen's family, the Woodvilles. Edward is characterized as "delighting in adulation and flattery, and led by sensuality and concupiscence," while

Richard is praised for his "great wit, prudence, justice, princely courage, and memorable and laudable acts in diverse battles." The document also hints at the rumored illegitimacy of Edward IV and Clarence, who were born abroad in Rouen and Dublin, respectively, by stating that Richard was "born within this land," whereby the estates might have "more certain knowledge of your birth and filiation." *Titulus Regius* also declares Richard "the undoubted son and heir of Richard, late Duke of York," thereby implying Richard's acceptance of doubts as to his brothers' paternity and as to his mother's fidelity.

Although serving as the justification for Richard III's usurpation, the declarations of *Titulus Regius* were apparently not universally accepted, especially after the disappearance of Edward IV's sons in the TOWER OF LONDON in the late summer of 1483. In 1484, Richard's first and only Parliament gave the petition statutory authority, explaining that such enactment was necessary to settle the "doubts, questions, and ambiguities" that had arisen since 1483 "in the minds of diverse persons." Because *Titulus Regius* questioned the legitimacy of his soon-to-be queen, ELIZABETH OF YORK, HENRY VII had the act repealed by his first Parliament in 1485 and sought to destroy all existing copies of the document.

See also Neville, Cecily, Duchess of York; Plantagenet, Richard, Duke of York (d. 1460); Princes in the Tower; Usurpation of 1483; Woodville Family
Further Reading: Hicks, Michael, *Richard III: The Man behind the Myth* (London: Collins and Brown, 1991); the text of *Titulus Regius* is available on the Richard III Society Web site at <http://www.r3.org/bookcase/texts/tit_reg.html>.

Touchet, James, Lord Audley (c. 1398–1459)

James Touchet (or Tuchet), fifth Lord Audley, was commander of the Lancastrian forces at the Battle of BLORE HEATH in September 1459.

Although over sixty at the time, Audley had military experience, having been coleader of an English army sent to FRANCE in 1431 and one of the nobles who helped suppress JACK CADE'S REBELLION in 1450. Audley also served as justiciar of South WALES from 1423 to 1438, and as chamberlain of that region from 1439 until his death. An important landholder in Staffordshire, Shropshire, and Cheshire, and a strong supporter of HENRY VI, Audley was a natural choice for leadership of the Lancastrian forces ordered by Queen MARGARET OF ANJOU to intercept Richard NEVILLE, earl of Salisbury, as he crossed Staffordshire with his army in the autumn of 1459.

Many of the men in Audley's force were his own tenants, whom he had raised quickly on the queen's summons. Audley's support of the Lancastrian cause may have rested in part on a long-standing grievance involving his wife's fruitless attempt to lay claim, as an illegitimate daughter, to her father's estates, which had passed to Salisbury and to Richard PLANTAGENET, duke of York. At Blore Heath on 23 September, Audley led several assaults against Salisbury's smaller force. In the midst of battle, Sir Roger Kynaston of Hordley, a RETAINER of York's, slew Audley, whose army was eventually defeated and scattered.

Further Reading: Griffiths, Ralph A., *The Reign of King Henry VI* (Berkeley: University of California Press, 1981); Haigh, Philip A., *The Military Campaigns of the Wars of the Roses* (Stroud, Gloucestershire, UK: Sutton Publishing, 1995); Swynnerton, Brian, and William Swinnerton, *The Battle of Blore Heath, 1459* (Nuneaton: Paddy Griffith Associates, 1995).

Tours, Treaty of. *See* Chinon Agreement

Tower of London

Although also a fortress, armory, and royal residence, the Tower of London was the principal English state prison, and as such it was the place of imprisonment and execution for many prominent figures during the WARS OF THE ROSES.

In 1077, William the Conqueror began building a large stone castle along the Thames

A late-fifteenth-century depiction of the Tower of London, much as it appeared when Edward V and his brother were lodged there in 1483. (Royal MS 16 F II f. 73, British Library)

at the southeast corner of the old Roman wall surrounding LONDON. Known as the White Tower because it was originally whitewashed, William's fortress had by the fifteenth century become the center of a large complex of defensive walls and towers constructed by various medieval monarchs. The Tower first became a factor in the civil wars in July 1460.

After the city authorities allowed Richard NEVILLE, earl of Warwick, and the other Yorkist earls from CALAIS to enter London, the city's Lancastrian garrison withdrew to the Tower, where it held out for weeks under the command of Thomas SCALES, Lord Scales. After his capitulation, Scales was released by the Yorkists, but murdered by Londoners enraged at the death and destruction his Tower guns had rained on the city.

After his accession, EDWARD IV enlarged the Tower fortifications and built the first permanent scaffold on Tower Hill. To pacify the city authorities, who had previously enjoyed the financial benefits deriving from the crowds that attended public executions, Edward allowed the city to supervise all Tower Hill executions. The most prominent Tower prisoner during the wars was HENRY VI, who, except for the months of his READEPTION in 1470–1471, was confined in the Wakefield Tower from 1465 to 1471. Although Lancastrian writers complained that Henry was ill-treated during his imprisonment, contemporary Tower accounts indicate that he had a generous allowance for food and clothing, was allowed to hear Mass, and had occasional visitors. Henry was murdered in the Tower on the night of 21 May 1471, shortly before his wife, Queen MARGARET OF ANJOU, was also confined there. Another mysterious death occurred in the Tower in February 1478, when George PLANTAGENET, duke of Clarence, Edward IV's brother, was executed privately in the fortress by unknown means, although legend claims the duke was drowned in a butt of malmsey wine.

The Tower was the site of several momentous events in 1483, including the dramatic COUNCIL MEETING OF 13 JUNE, during which William HASTINGS, Lord Hastings, was arrested and summarily executed on Tower Hill, ostensibly for plotting against Richard, duke of Gloucester. During the following months, after Gloucester had seized the throne as RICHARD III, his deposed nephew EDWARD V and Edward's brother, Richard PLANTAGENET, duke of York, disappeared in the Tower, where they were probably murdered on Richard's order. Later accounts of the princes' deaths claimed they were buried secretly in the Tower, a claim that gained credence in 1674 when two sets of bones belonging to boys their age were uncovered during Tower renovations.

See also Bones of 1674; Clarence, Executions of; Princes in the Tower

Further Reading: Mears, Kenneth J., *The Tower of London: 900 Years of English History* (Oxford: Phaidon, 1988); Wilson, Derek A., *The Tower of London: A Thousand Years* (London: Allison and Busby, 1998).

Towns and the Wars of the Roses

Because the English had little experience or expertise in siege warfare, the WARS OF THE ROSES witnessed only one assault on a walled city (LONDON in 1471) and saw little battle damage inflicted on English towns. Because most towns sought to avoid the political penalties and financial burdens of taking sides, few made strong commitments to either party.

Although most towns contained partisans of both the house of LANCASTER and the house of YORK, municipal governments tried to avoid all but the most token involvement in the civil wars. Small boroughs located in an area dominated by a powerful magnate often had little option but to follow his political lead; however, larger towns, being independent corporations, sought to remain neutral or to avoid association with the losing side. But neutrality was often difficult to achieve. For instance, in 1470, the town of Salisbury received both a demand for men from Richard NEVILLE, earl of Warwick, and an order from EDWARD IV to deny the earl troops. When Warwick's representative refused an offer of money instead of men, the town sent the requested troops, largely because Warwick was nearby while the king was far away in the north. In 1471, Salisbury first promised men to the READEPTION government of HENRY VI, then offered the troops to Edward IV after his victory at the Battle of BARNET, and finally reneged on that promise when MARGARET OF ANJOU landed nearby. In the end, only fourteen men from Salisbury fought at the Battle of TEWKESBURY, having joined the Yorkist army as Edward IV passed near the town on his westward march.

Although London denied Queen Margaret entry in 1461 and repelled the attack of Thomas NEVILLE, the Bastard of Fauconberg, in 1471, both decisions were based largely on the fear of being plundered; in most cases, a town willingly opened its gates to a victorious army operating in its neighborhood. However, such decisions could have serious consequences should the fortunes of war change. Bristol paid heavy fines for admitting the Lancastrian army during the Tewkesbury campaign of 1471, and Canterbury suffered fines and loss of privileges for too ardently supporting Fauconberg's enterprise. The desire to avoid disfavor, combined with an equally strong desire to avoid the expense of equipping troops, explains why towns supplied relatively few men to civil war armies. For example, the large city of Norwich tardily raised only 120 men for the Battle of TOWTON in 1461, but four years earlier had easily raised over 600 to defend the town itself from a threatened French attack. In 1485, the city of York, which claimed a special relationship with RICHARD III, provided only eighty men to fight for the king at the Battle of BOSWORTH FIELD. In general, the high political and financial costs of commitment kept most towns from active involvement in the Wars of the Roses.

See also English Economy and the Wars of the Roses; March on London

Further Reading: Gillingham, John, *The Wars of the Roses* (Baton Rouge: Louisiana State University Press, 1981); Goodman, Anthony, *The Wars of the Roses* (New York: Dorset Press, 1981); Ross, Charles, *The Wars of the Roses* (London: Thames and Hudson, 1987).

Towton, Battle of (1461)

Fought on 29 March 1461, Towton was the largest and bloodiest battle of the Wars of the Roses. Although the Yorkist victory left EDWARD IV in possession of the Crown, HENRY VI and his family fled to SCOTLAND after the battle, leaving England with two living, anointed monarchs and ensuring that dynastic conflict and political turmoil would continue for the next decade.

After the death of Richard PLANTAGENET, duke of York, at the Battle of WAKEFIELD in December 1460, Edward, earl of March, the duke's eldest son, assumed leadership of the Yorkist cause. March joined forces with Richard NEVILLE, earl of Warwick, on 22 February 1461, five days after Queen MARGARET OF ANJOU had defeated Warwick at the Battle of ST. ALBANS and reunited herself and her son with Henry VI. While the queen's army withdrew into the north, March entered LONDON, where he was crowned as Edward IV on 4 March. Leaving the capital on 13 March, Edward moved slowly northward to give his principal lieutenants time to raise troops. He united with two of them, Warwick and William NEVILLE, Lord Fauconberg, on the road to York, but the third, John MOWBRAY, duke of Norfolk, had not yet arrived when the Yorkist army reached Pontefract on 27 March. Receiving a message that Norfolk was close, Edward advanced against the Lancastrian army, which had taken up a position about fifteen miles southwest of York, near the village of Towton.

After two engagements at FERRYBRIDGE on 27 and 28 March, the armies met next day, a cold and snowy Palm Sunday. Henry BEAUFORT, duke of Somerset (Henry VI stayed in York with his family), led a Lancastrian army—probably the largest of the war—that contained most of the nobility of England. Commanded personally by Edward, the smaller Yorkist force included few nobles. For hours, the two armies struggled in the bitter weather. When a concealed Lancastrian force fell on the Yorkist left in the early afternoon, Edward's line, which had been slowly giving ground, almost collapsed, but the young king's presence helped to steady the men (see GENERALSHIP). In midafternoon, Norfolk arrived and attacked the Lancastrian left. Confronted by these fresh troops, the Lancastrian line broke, turning the battle into a rout and leaving several important Lancastrians dead on the field, including Henry PERCY, earl of Northumberland, and Sir Andrew TROLLOPE. Somerset escaped with Henry VI and his family, and several other prominent Lancastrians were captured and executed afterwards. Although likely exaggerated, the contemporary estimates of 28,000 dead on the field suggest that Towton was the largest, longest, and bloodiest battle of the war.

See also Battles, Nature of; Casualties; Edward of Lancaster, Prince of Wales

Further Reading: Boardman, Andrew W., *The Battle of Towton* (Stroud, Gloucestershire, UK: Sutton Publishing, 1996); Haigh, Philip A., *The Military Campaigns of the Wars of the Roses* (Stroud, Gloucestershire, UK: Sutton Publishing, 1995).

Trollope, Sir Andrew (d. 1461)

Having acquired a reputation for courage and skill in the French wars, Sir Andrew Trollope was perhaps the most famous professional soldier in England at the start of the WARS OF THE ROSES.

Although Jean de Waurin claimed Trollope was of lower class origins, little is known of his early life. Trollope fought with distinction in Normandy in the 1440s, returning to England in 1450 after the surrender of Falaise. By 1453, he was in CALAIS, holding an appointment as sergeant-porter of the garrison. When Richard NEVILLE, earl of Warwick, who had been captain of Calais since 1456, brought part of the garrison to England to support Richard PLANTAGENET, duke of York, in 1459, Trollope came with him.

On the night of 12 October 1459 at the Battle of LUDFORD BRIDGE, Trollope accepted HENRY VI's offer of pardon and switched sides, bringing the Calais garrison with him into the Lancastrian camp. Because Trollope was privy to all York's plans, the duke's position became untenable, and the Yorkist leaders fled the field during the night. In November, Trollope accompanied Henry BEAUFORT, duke of Somerset, to Calais, where the duke tried unsuccessfully to wrest the town from Warwick. After receiving news of Warwick's capture of Henry VI at the Battle of NORTHAMPTON in July 1460, Somerset and Trollope surrendered their stronghold at Guisnes and withdrew into FRANCE. Trollope was in northern England by December, when he and Somerset led the Lancastrian force that defeated and killed York at the Battle of WAKEFIELD.

Trollope was also one of the leaders of the unruly Lancastrian force that surged south from Wakefield to defeat Warwick at the Battle of ST. ALBANS on 17 February 1461 (see MARCH ON LONDON). After the battle, which reunited Henry VI with his family, the king knighted his son Prince EDWARD OF LANCASTER, who in turn knighted Trollope. Sir Andrew supposedly joked that he did not deserve the honor, having killed only fifteen men due to a foot injury inflicted by a caltrop (i.e., a pointed, metal, anticavalry device). After the Battle of St. Albans, Trollope withdrew with the Lancastrian army into Yorkshire, where he died six weeks later at the Battle of TOWTON.

See also *Recueil des Croniques et Anchiennes Istories de la Grant Bretaigne, a present nomme Engleterre* (Waurin)
Further Reading: Boardman, Andrew W., *The Battle of Towton* (Stroud, Gloucestershire, UK: Sutton Publishing, 1996); Haigh, Philip A., *The Military Campaigns of the Wars of the Roses* (Stroud, Gloucestershire, UK: Sutton Publishing, 1995).

Tuchet, James, Lord Audley. *See* Touchet, James, Lord Audley

Tudor, Edmund, Earl of Richmond (c. 1430–1456)

As a half brother of HENRY VI and a member of an ancient Welsh family, Edmund Tudor, earl of Richmond, was charged with securing WALES for the house of LANCASTER in the mid-1450s. Through his marriage to Margaret BEAUFORT, a kinswoman of Henry VI, Tudor secured a place in the succession for his posthumous son, Henry Tudor, who, as the last heir of Lancaster, established the Welsh house of TUDOR on the English throne in 1485.

Edmund Tudor was the eldest son of a secret marriage between Catherine of Valois, the widowed mother of Henry VI, and one of her household servants, a Welshman named Owen TUDOR. After his mother's death in 1437, Edmund and his younger brother, Jasper TUDOR, were put in the custody of the abbess of Barking until 1440, when Henry VI made provision for their education as English gentlemen. Although the Tudors lacked English royal blood and had no claim to the throne, the king acknowledged them as half brothers and knighted Edmund in December 1449. In 1452, Henry VI, who had no full siblings nor (at the time) children, sought to expand the royal family by raising the Tudors to the PEERAGE—Edmund as earl of Richmond and Jasper as earl of Pembroke. To support the dignity of these new titles, the king granted both brothers extensive estates.

In 1454, when Richard PLANTAGENET, duke of York, became protector for the mentally incapacitated king (see HENRY VI, ILLNESS OF), Richmond and Pembroke maintained good relations with the duke. Although loyal to Henry, neither Tudor was closely identified with York's rivals, and both supported reforms to the royal COURT and household proposed by York. In 1455, a recovered Henry VI arranged Richmond's marriage to twelve-year-old Margaret Beaufort, a wealthy heiress and royal cousin. This marriage tied Richmond more firmly to the Lancastrian dynasty and promised his children a distant place in the succession.

Because of his Welsh name and blood, Richmond was sent to Wales in 1455 as the king's representative. The appointment may have been made by York, who was a large Welsh landowner and again in charge of the government following the Battle of ST. ALBANS in May 1455. In Wales, where local rivalries were already aligning with the houses of Lancaster or YORK, Richmond worked to reduce disorder, a task that required him to take arms against Welsh rebels. By August 1456, he had greatly restored royal authority, an achievement that threatened York, who was no longer in control of the royal government. To recover York's position in Wales, the duke's chief Welsh lieutenants, Sir William HERBERT and Sir Walter DEVEREUX, captured and imprisoned Richmond. Although shortly released from confinement, Richmond died at Carmarthen on 1 November 1456 at the age of twenty-six. His death was probably due to illness, but foul play is possible, given his age and the increasing political turmoil in which he was embroiled. Almost three months after Richmond's death, on 28 January 1457, the earl's widow gave birth to a son who in 1485 became king as HENRY VII.

> **See also** all other entries under Tudor
> **Further Reading:** Evans, H. T., *Wales and the Wars of the Roses* (Stroud, Gloucestershire, UK: Alan Sutton Publishing, 1995); Griffiths, Ralph A., *The Reign of King Henry VI* (Berkeley: University of California Press, 1981); Griffiths, Ralph A., and Roger S. Thomas, *The Making of the Tudor Dynasty* (New York: St. Martin's Press, 1985).

Tudor, House of (1485–1603)

As a result of the WARS OF THE ROSES, the Welsh house of Tudor succeeded to the English throne in 1485.

The family originated in northwest Wales, where it had held property since at least the thirteenth century. The Tudors traced their ancestry to Ednyfed Fychan (d. 1246), steward to the Welsh prince Llywelyn the Great. About 1420, Owain ap Maredudd (Owain son of Maredudd), a descendent of Ednyfed Fychan, came to England and anglicized his name to Owen TUDOR (from Tudur, his grandfather's name), perhaps to avoid the civil disabilities placed on Welshmen by English law. He obtained a position in the household of Catherine of Valois, the widowed queen of Henry V (r. 1413–1422), and mother of HENRY VI. Catherine soon fell in love with her servant, and the two were married secretly because the COUNCIL that governed for the young king would never have sanctioned a marriage between the Queen Mother and an obscure Welshman. The union produced several children, who remained in their mother's care until her death in 1437.

Although half siblings of Henry VI, the Tudor children had no English royal blood and no place in the English succession. In 1452, Henry VI, who had no full siblings and was then childless, brought his half brothers Edmund and Jasper (see entries for both under TUDOR) to court, endowed them with property, and raised them to the English PEERAGE as earl of Richmond (Edmund) and earl of Pembroke (Jasper). To tie the Tudors more closely to the royal family, Henry married his cousin Margaret BEAUFORT to Richmond in 1455. Besides having a distant claim to the throne through the BEAUFORT FAMILY's connection with the house of LANCASTER, Margaret was also a wealthy heiress. In January 1457, three months after Richmond's death, Margaret gave birth to a son, who was named Henry in honor of the king. In 1471, Prince EDWARD OF LANCASTER and Edmund BEAUFORT, fourth duke of Somerset, died at the Battle of TEWKESBURY, and Henry VI, his life no longer protected by his son's, was murdered in the TOWER OF LONDON (see HENRY VI, MURDER OF). These deaths ended the direct male lines of Lancaster and Beaufort and made Henry Tudor, earl of Richmond, the surviving male heir of both families.

From 1471 to 1483, Richmond, accompanied by his uncle Pembroke, lived in exile in BRITTANY; with the house of YORK firmly established on the throne, his prospects of becoming king were slight. However, RICHARD III's usurpation of the Crown, followed by his probable murder of EDWARD V and his brother, forged an alliance of Lancastrians and disaffected Yorkists that plotted to enthrone Richmond (see PRINCES IN THE TOWER; USURPATION OF 1483). Despite the failure of the autumn 1483 uprising known as BUCKINGHAM'S REBELLION, a growing number of English exiles joined Richmond in FRANCE, from where he launched a new invasion in 1485. On 22 August, Richmond won the Crown at the Battle of BOSWORTH FIELD, becoming HENRY VII, first king of the house of Tudor. By marrying ELIZABETH OF YORK, daughter of EDWARD IV, Henry ensured that his children would be descendants of both Lancaster and York. The Tudor dynasty ruled England for 118 years, until 1603. Henry VII was succeeded by his son, Henry VIII (r. 1509–1547), and by three grandchildren—Edward VI (r. 1547–1553), Mary I (r. 1553–1558), and Elizabeth I (r. 1558–1603).

The standard of Henry VII, first king of the house of Tudor, along with various Tudor emblems and devices, including a thorn bush, various roses, and the Beaufort family portcullis (the drawbridge with chains). (Harley MS 4632 f. 237, British Library)

See also: Appendix 1, "Genealogies"
Further Reading: Chrimes, S. B., *Henry VII* (New Haven, CT: Yale University Press, 1999); Griffiths, Ralph A., and Roger S. Thomas, *The Making of the Tudor Dynasty* (New York: St. Martin's Press, 1985).

Tudor, Jasper, Earl of Pembroke and Duke of Bedford (c. 1431–1495)

As a half brother of HENRY VI and a member of an ancient Welsh family, Jasper Tudor, earl of Pembroke, rallied WALES for the house of LANCASTER during the WARS OF THE ROSES. As uncle of Henry Tudor, earl of Richmond, the future HENRY VII, Pembroke protected his nephew from Yorkist intrigues, shared his long Breton exile, and served as his most trusted advisor.

Jasper Tudor was the second son of the clandestine marriage between Catherine of Valois, daughter of Charles VI of France and widow of Henry V of England, and Owen TUDOR, a Welsh gentleman of Catherine's household. In 1452, Henry VI formally recognized the Tudors as his uterine brothers, ennobling Jasper as earl of Pembroke and Edmund as earl of Richmond. Having no English royal blood, the brothers had no claim to the throne, but their new positions expanded the family of a king who lacked both siblings and (at the time) children. Pembroke was present with the king at the Battle of ST. ALBANS in May 1455. After Richmond's death in November 1456, Pembroke succeeded his brother as Henry VI's chief lieutenant in Wales. Pembroke also sheltered his thirteen-year-old sister-in-law, Margaret BEAUFORT, countess of Richmond, who gave birth to a son, Henry Tudor, in January 1457.

After the eruption of open warfare in 1459, Pembroke led the Lancastrian cause in Wales, capturing Denbigh Castle from the Yorkists in May 1460, and giving refuge to MARGARET OF ANJOU and her son EDWARD OF LANCASTER, Prince of Wales, after the disastrous Battle of NORTHAMPTON in July. In February 1461, Edward, earl of March, the future EDWARD IV, defeated Pembroke at MOR-

TIMER'S CROSS in Wales. After the Lancastrian defeat at the Battle of TOWTON in March, Pembroke held Wales for Henry VI until October, when Edward IV's lieutenant in Wales, William HERBERT, Lord Herbert, defeated Pembroke at the Battle of TWT HILL, forcing him to sail for BRITTANY. In 1462, Pembroke briefly held BAMBURGH CASTLE for Henry VI, but fled to SCOTLAND when Edward IV refused him suitable terms of surrender. After spending most of the 1460s shuttling among Scotland, England, and FRANCE on diplomatic missions for Queen Margaret, Pembroke landed in Wales in 1468; he burned Denbigh and harassed Welsh Yorkists until forced by Herbert to return to Brittany.

In 1470, Pembroke accompanied Richard NEVILLE, earl of Warwick, to England, when Warwick launched his attempt to restore Henry VI (see EDWARD IV, OVERTHROW OF). Pembroke took charge of securing Wales for Lancaster. The death of Prince Edward at TEWKESBURY in May 1471 and the subsequent murder of Henry VI in the TOWER OF LONDON left Henry Tudor as the remaining Lancastrian claimant to the throne (see HENRY VI, MURDER OF). To protect his nephew, Pembroke fled with the boy for France in September 1471. Blown off course to Brittany, uncle and nephew spent the next twelve years in the increasingly rigorous custody of FRANCIS, duke of Brittany, who used them to extract diplomatic advantage from both England and France.

The usurpation of RICHARD III in 1483 greatly enhanced Henry Tudor's political position, and in the autumn the Tudors became part of an unsuccessful uprising that included Henry STAFFORD, duke of Buckingham, heretofore one of Richard's closest supporters (see BUCKINGHAM'S REBELLION). In November, news of Buckingham's defeat and execution caused the Tudors to abort a planned landing in England. Returning to Brittany, Pembroke became leader of the exiles who gathered around his nephew. In August 1485, in an attempt to win the throne, the Tudors landed in Wales, hoping to exploit Pembroke's influence in the region. Pembroke was present at BOSWORTH FIELD on 22 August 1485, when his nephew won the Crown.

One of the new king's most trusted supporters, Pembroke became duke of Bedford and a privy councilor in 1485. He was also appointed lieutenant of CALAIS, lord lieutenant of IRELAND, and marshal of England. Bedford also took an active role in suppressing the Lambert SIMNEL uprising, fighting for the king at the Battle of STOKE in 1487. Although married to the widow of Buckingham in 1485, Bedford died without issue in December 1495.

See also Tudor, Edmund, Earl of Richmond; Usurpation of 1483; other entries under Tudor
Further Reading: Evans, H. T., *Wales and the Wars of the Roses* (Stroud, Gloucestershire, UK: Alan Sutton Publishing, 1995); Griffiths, Ralph A., and Roger S. Thomas, *The Making of the Tudor Dynasty* (New York: St. Martin's Press, 1985); "Jasper Tudor," in Michael Hicks, *Who's Who in Late Medieval England* (London: Shepheard-Walwyn, 1991), pp. 305–307.

Tudor, Owen (d. 1461)

Through his marriage to the widow of HENRY V, Owen Tudor, the grandfather of HENRY VII, established the Welsh house of TUDOR as part of the English nobility.

Owain ap Maredudd (Owain son of Maredudd), son of an ancient Welsh landholding family, came to England around 1420. Anglicizing his name to Owen Tudor (from Tudur, his grandfather's name), he obtained a position in the household of Catherine of Valois, the wife of Henry V. He began a sexual relationship with the widowed queen some time in the late 1420s. Because a statute of 1428 had made it unlawful to marry the dowager queen without the king's consent, something the regency COUNCIL then ruling for HENRY VI was unlikely to give to an obscure Welshman, the couple's marriage, which occurred about 1430, was kept secret. The truth came out when Catherine became pregnant, giving birth to at least four children in the 1430s.

As long as Catherine lived, the couple was not molested, and Tudor was granted the

rights of an Englishman by PARLIAMENT in 1432. On the queen's death in 1437, the Tudor children were placed in the care of the abbess of Barking, and Owen Tudor was summoned to the king's presence. Fearful of prosecution under the statute of 1428, Tudor demanded a safe-conduct and immediately took SANCTUARY at Westminster upon arriving in LONDON. Finally persuaded by friends to appear before the council, he acquitted himself of any changes related to the marriage and was released. However, on his way to WALES, he was arrested and committed to Newgate prison, and all his possessions were confiscated. He remained in confinement until July 1439. In November, the king pardoned Tudor for all offenses and graciously took him into the royal household.

Henry VI also treated his Tudor half brothers with kindness, paying for their education and raising the two eldest to the English PEERAGE in 1452—Edmund TUDOR as earl of Richmond and Jasper TUDOR as earl of Pembroke. After 1439, Owen Tudor lived quietly as an English gentleman, having received a pension and several minor offices from Henry VI. When civil war erupted in 1459, Tudor, as a loyal Lancastrian, acquired some of the estates stripped from the exiled Yorkist leaders by the COVENTRY PARLIAMENT. A member of the Lancastrian force that fought under his son Pembroke at the Battle of MORTIMER'S CROSS in February 1461, Tudor was captured and executed by order of Edward, earl of March (see EDWARD IV).

See also all other entries under Tudor
Further Reading: Griffiths, Ralph A., and Roger S. Thomas, *The Making of the Tudor Dynasty* (New York: St. Martin's Press, 1985).

Tunstall, Sir Richard (d. 1492)

Sir Richard Tunstall is an example of the many committed Lancastrians who submitted to EDWARD IV after the final defeat of the house of LANCASTER at the Battle of TEWKESBURY in 1471.

Born into a Lancashire GENTRY family, Tunstall was knighted by HENRY VI in about

1452. A member of the royal household, Tunstall was a staunch Lancastrian, who fought for Henry VI at the Battle of WAKEFIELD in 1460 and the Battles of ST. ALBANS and TOWTON in 1461. After the latter defeat, Tunstall fled into SCOTLAND with the Lancastrian royal family. Attainted by the first Yorkist PARLIAMENT in 1461, Tunstall was soon deeply involved in the Lancastrian campaigns in Northumberland, being captured with the garrison at the fall of BAMBURGH CASTLE in July 1462 but escaping to serve with Queen MARGARET OF ANJOU's garrisons in both DUNSTANBURGH and ALNWICK Castles. In 1463, Tunstall appeared in WALES as a member of the Lancastrian garrison holding HARLECH CASTLE. By early 1464, he was back in Northumberland, where he fought with Henry BEAUFORT, duke of Somerset, at the Battles of HEDGELEY MOOR and HEXHAM. After the collapse of Lancastrian resistance in Northumberland, Tunstall escorted Henry VI into Lancashire, where the king was hidden by friendly gentlemen for over a year. Tunstall returned to Harlech, and he finally fell into Yorkist hands when the castle fell in August 1468.

Conveyed to the TOWER OF LONDON with other Englishmen in the Harlech garrison, Tunstall was pardoned by Edward IV in December but reverted to his Lancastrian allegiance in the autumn of 1470, when Richard NEVILLE, earl of Warwick, restored Henry VI to the throne (see EDWARD IV, OVERTHROW OF). Tunstall joined the READEPTION government as Henry VI's chamberlain, but he was once again attainted after the death of Warwick and the collapse of the regime in 1471 (see EDWARD IV, RESTORATION OF). By 1473, Tunstall had submitted to Edward IV and achieved reversal of his ATTAINDER. He was thereafter highly favored by both Edward IV and RICHARD III, each of whom employed him as a diplomat. Although Richard rewarded him for his services to the house of YORK with membership in the Order of the Garter (a prestigious English order of chivalry), Tunstall may have turned against the king in 1485. According to the *BALLAD OF BOSWORTH FIELD*,

Tunstall was one of four knights who joined the army of Henry Tudor, earl of Richmond, when the earl invaded England in August to claim the Crown. Tunstall's abandonment of Richard and his presence at the Battle of BOSWORTH FIELD are uncertain; in August 1485, he may have been in CALAIS, where he held a diplomatic post. In any event, Tunstall prospered in the reign of HENRY VII, receiving numerous rewards and being admitted to the royal COUNCIL. He died a loyal servant of the house of TUDOR in 1492.

Further Reading: Boardman, Andrew W., *The Medieval Soldier in the Wars of the Roses* (Stroud, Gloucestershire, UK: Sutton Publishing, 1998).

Tuthill, Battle of. *See* Twt Hill, Battle of

Twt Hill, Battle of (1461)

Although a relatively small skirmish, the Battle of Twt Hill (or Tuthill), fought on 16 October 1461, ended open warfare in WALES, and brought all Wales, except HARLECH CASTLE, under the new regime of EDWARD IV.

After the Yorkist victory at the Battle of TOWTON in March 1461, Jasper TUDOR, earl of Pembroke, continued to hold the Welsh fortresses of Pembroke, Denbigh, and Harlech for his half brother, HENRY VI. To quell Lancastrian resistance in Wales, Edward accompanied his army to Hereford in September, but left the actual campaigning to his chief Welsh lieutenants, Sir William HERBERT; Henry BOURCHIER, earl of Essex; and Walter DEVEREUX, Lord Ferrers. After a short stay at Ludlow, the king returned to LONDON for the opening of his first PARLIAMENT on 4 November.

Meanwhile, the Yorkist commanders captured Pembroke Castle on 30 September, after which Herbert led the bulk of the royal army into North Wales to pursue the earl of Pembroke, who was thought to be hiding in the mountain fastnesses of Snowdon with Henry HOLLAND, duke of Exeter. The duke, who had fought at the Battle of Towton, may have brought reinforcements to Pembroke by sea, for the Lancastrian leaders were able to put a force in the field and meet Herbert in battle at Twt Hill outside the walls of Carnarvon in northwest Wales.

Although almost nothing is known of the course of the battle, the result was a complete victory for Herbert, who destroyed the last Lancastrian field force in Wales. Exeter and Pembroke escaped the battle and fled the country, with Pembroke sailing for IRELAND. The defeat isolated the remaining Lancastrian castles; Denbigh surrendered in January 1462, and the western fortress of Carreg Cennen capitulated in May. Although most Welsh Lancastrians had ended active resistance by mid-1462, Harlech Castle, which could be resupplied by sea and thus required a costly and difficult effort to reduce, continued in Lancastrian hands until 1468, while all Wales remained vulnerable to seaborne invasion and to the ongoing intrigues of Pembroke.

Further Reading: Evans, H. T., *Wales and the Wars of the Roses* (Stroud, Gloucestershire, UK: Alan Sutton Publishing, 1995); Haigh, Philip A., *The Military Campaigns of the Wars of the Roses* (Stroud, Gloucestershire, UK: Sutton Publishing, 1995).

Tyrell, Sir James (1445–1502)

Sir James Tyrell (or Tyrrell) was reputed to be RICHARD III's agent in carrying out the murders of EDWARD V and his younger brother, Richard PLANTAGENET, duke of York.

The eldest son of a Suffolk GENTRY family, Tyrell fought for EDWARD IV at the Battle of TEWKESBURY in May 1471 and was knighted after the battle. By 1472, Tyrell was a trusted RETAINER of Richard, duke of Gloucester, the king's brother. The duke made Tyrell his chief agent in WALES by appointing him sheriff of Glamorgan and constable of Cardiff. In 1482, Tyrell served in Gloucester's Scottish campaign, being made a knight-banneret by the duke.

Tyrell greatly benefited from Gloucester's usurpation of the throne in July 1483 (see USURPATION OF 1483). The new king

showed his confidence in Tyrell's loyalty and abilities by strengthening Tyrell's control of the royal lands in Wales through the grant of various additional stewardships and castle constableships. Tyrell's appointments as a knight of the body (i.e., one of the king's closest personal servants), as Master of Horse, and as chamberlain of the Exchequer all indicated the position of trust he held with Richard III. In 1485, although retaining Tyrell in his Welsh commands, Richard III sent him to CALAIS to take charge of the key fortress of Guisnes after the previous commander's defection to Henry Tudor, earl of Richmond. Because of his posting to Guisnes, Tyrell was not in England in August 1485 and was thus unable to oppose Richmond's landing in Wales or to fight for the king at the Battle of BOSWORTH FIELD.

After Richard's defeat and death, Tyrell was one of the few supporters of the late king to also become a trusted servant of HENRY VII. Although he lost some offices and lands, Tyrell remained a knight of the body and sheriff of Glamorgan. He also took a prominent part in the ceremonies surrounding the signing of the Treaty of Etaples in 1492, the creation of Prince Henry as duke of York in 1494, and the reception of Catherine of Aragon in 1501. In August 1501, Tyrell was implicated in a plot led by Edmund de la Pole, earl of Suffolk, the Yorkist claimant to the throne (see YORKIST HEIRS [AFTER 1485]). The conspiracy involved the surrender of Guisnes, then in Tyrell's charge, and it led to Tyrell's arrest and eventual execution for treason in May 1502.

According to the later accounts of Sir Thomas More and Polydore Vergil, neither of whom were eyewitnesses, Tyrell, while lying under sentence of death in the TOWER OF LONDON, confessed to having murdered the sons of Edward IV there at the direction of Richard III in the summer of 1483. This alleged confession, the text of which has not survived, forms the basis of the murder story as we know it today. Although likely enough, the story as supposedly related by Tyrell cannot be conclusively proven and must remain only one possible explanation of the fate of the princes.

See also *Anglica Historia* (Vergil); *The History of King Richard III* (More); Princes in the Tower
Further Reading: Horrox, Rosemary, *Richard III: A Study in Service* (Cambridge: Cambridge University Press, 1991); "James Tyrell," in Michael Hicks, *Who's Who in Late Medieval England* (London: Shepheard-Walwyn, 1991), pp. 364–366; More, Sir Thomas, *History of King Richard III,* in Paul Murray Kendall, ed., *Richard III: The Great Debate* (New York: W. W. Norton, 1992), pp. 31–143; Ross, Charles, *Richard III* (Berkeley: University of California Press, 1981).

The Union of the Two Noble and Illustrious Families of Lancaster and York (Hall)

The Union of the Two Noble and Illustrious Families of Lancaster and York, a chronicle written by the Tudor historian Edward Hall (1498–1547), was a major source for William Shakespeare's four-play cycle depicting the WARS OF THE ROSES. As its title indicates, Hall's chronicle was also one of the earliest and fullest expositions of the influential historical tradition that viewed the house of TUDOR as rescuing England from the political chaos and economic destruction caused by the fifteenth-century civil wars.

Reformist in religion, Edward Hall was a Cambridge-educated lawyer and a frequent M.P. (member of PARLIAMENT). His chronicle, which was published in 1548, covers the period from the deposition of Richard II in 1399 to the death of Henry VIII in 1547. Hall himself carried the narrative to 1532, with fellow chronicler Richard Grafton using Hall's notes to complete the work. Like most Tudor historians, Hall saw history as an instrument for teaching moral lessons, for presenting both edifying and cautionary examples of the past behavior of princes. Beset by religious strife and dynastic uncertainty, sixteenth-century England tended to project its fears onto the history of the fifteenth century, which, as Hall's writing illustrates, was seen as a horrible time of civil strife: "What misery, what murder and what execrable plagues this famous region hath suffered by the division and dissension of the renowned houses of Lancaster and York, my wit cannot comprehend nor my tongue declare, neither yet my pen fully set forth" (Ross, p. 7).

Drawing upon Sir Thomas More's *HISTORY OF KING RICHARD III* and Polydore Vergil's *ANGLICA HISTORIA,* Hall fully developed the idea that the Lancastrian usurpation of 1399 was the root cause of civil strife in the fifteenth century. God punished the house of LANCASTER for its usurpation by rendering HENRY VI incapable of ruling and by allowing the usurpation of the house of YORK, which was itself punished for its ambition and for the dreadful tyranny of RICHARD III by the ultimate victory of HENRY VII and the house of Tudor. In the 1460s, Yorkist PROPAGANDA had initiated the idea that EDWARD IV's accession set right the disruption in the divine order caused by the Lancastrians in 1399. Hall, writing under the Tudors when stories of Richard III's crimes were current, extended this notion by blackening the already negative portrayal of Richard that he had received from More and Vergil and by bequeathing it to Raphael Holinshed and later Tudor chroniclers, who, in turn, became sources for Shakespeare's shocking villain in the play *RICHARD III.* In this way, Hall's *Union* shaped later popular views of both Richard and the Wars of the Roses.

See also Richard II, Deposition of; Shakespeare and the Wars of the Roses
Further Reading: Ellis, Henry, ed., *Hall's Chronicle* (reprint ed., New York: AMS Press, 1965); Ross, Charles, *The Wars of the Roses* (London: Thames and Hudson, 1987).

Urswick, Christopher (1448–1521)

Between 1483 and 1485, during the last phase of the WARS OF THE ROSES, the priest Christopher Urswick served both Margaret

BEAUFORT and her son Henry Tudor, earl of Richmond, as a trusted agent in their efforts to wrest the Crown from RICHARD III and the house of YORK.

Urswick, who may have belonged to a Lancashire GENTRY family long associated with the Stanleys, was brought to the attention of Margaret Beaufort, then wife of Thomas STANLEY, Lord Stanley, by Margaret's trusted Welsh physician, Lewis Caerleon. Because she sought to overthrow Richard III in favor of her exiled son, Margaret needed able and discreet servants; accordingly, she took Urswick into her household as her confessor. In 1483, Dr. Caerleon, who was also personal physician to Queen Elizabeth WOODVILLE, then in SANCTUARY at Westminster, acted as go-between for Margaret and the former queen, who concocted between them a plan whereby Richmond agreed to marry ELIZABETH OF YORK, EDWARD IV's daughter, in return for the support of the WOODVILLE FAMILY and other dissident Yorkists. Margaret proposed sending Urswick to BRITTANY to inform Richmond of the queen's involvement and the marriage plan, but news that Henry STAFFORD, duke of Buckingham, was willing to abandon Richard and join the conspiracy caused Margaret to cancel Urswick's mission and send another deputation instead.

After the failure of BUCKINGHAM'S REBELLION in the autumn of 1483, Urswick fled to BURGUNDY with Bishop John MORTON. In 1484, when Morton discovered that Richard III was secretly negotiating with the Breton treasurer, Pierre LANDAIS, to have Richmond surrendered into English custody, the bishop dispatched Urswick to Brittany to warn Richmond, who, in turn, sent Urswick to CHARLES VIII to request asylum in FRANCE. After obtaining the king's approval, Urswick returned to Richmond, who shortly thereafter fled to the French COURT. Having helped save the earl's life, Urswick became Richmond's confessor, advisor, and confidential agent. In 1485, fearing that Richard III might marry Elizabeth of York to someone else, Richmond considered sending Urswick

into northern England to persuade Henry PERCY, earl of Northumberland, to arrange a marriage for Richmond with one of Northumberland's sisters-in-law, the daughters of the late Welsh Yorkist, William HERBERT, earl of Pembroke. Although he probably never reached Northumberland, the importance of the mission indicated Urswick's standing with Richmond.

Urswick accompanied Richmond's army to WALES in August 1485 and was likely present at the Battle of BOSWORTH FIELD, although, as a cleric, he did not fight. Richmond, now HENRY VII, rewarded Urswick with numerous appointments—king's almoner, dean of York, and, in 1495, dean of Windsor. A loyal supporter of the house of TUDOR until his death in 1521, Urswick was also a friend of the historian Polydore Vergil and thus a likely source for Vergil's ANGLICA HISTORIA, which is particularly reliable for Richmond's activities between 1483 and 1485.

Further Reading: Griffiths, Ralph S., and Roger S. Thomas. *The Making of the Tudor Dynasty* (New York: St. Martin's Press, 1985).

Usurpation of 1483

In June 1483, when Richard, duke of Gloucester (see RICHARD III), usurped his nephew's throne, he alienated many loyal followers of the house of YORK, revived the claim of the surviving heir of the house of LANCASTER, and reopened the WARS OF THE ROSES.

On 9 April 1483, EDWARD IV died at Westminster at age forty, leaving his Crown to his twelve-year-old son. Prince Edward, now EDWARD V, was at Ludlow on the Welsh border, under the supervision of his maternal uncle, Anthony WOODVILLE, Earl Rivers. Gloucester, Edward's only surviving paternal uncle, was in the north. Although word of the king's death reached neither of them until about 14 April, the royal COUNCIL in LONDON, following precedents established during previous royal minorities, assumed control of the government and set the new king's coronation for 4 May. Having been named protector by Edward IV, Gloucester started south on 23 April, one day before his nephew left Ludlow. Although Gloucester was the logical choice for protector, the WOODVILLE FAMILY, Edward V's maternal relatives, were in a good position to dominate the regency government. Rivers had custody of and influence over the king; Queen Elizabeth WOODVILLE and her son Thomas GREY, marquis of Dorset, controlled the TOWER OF LONDON and the royal treasury; and the queen's brother, Sir Edward Woodville, controlled the fleet.

The prospect of a Woodville ascendancy dismayed many, including William HASTINGS, Lord Hastings, a friend of Edward IV and a rival of both Rivers and Dorset. Fearful that Rivers would bring an army to London to impose Woodville rule, Hastings convinced the council to limit the royal escort to 2,000 men. On 29 April, Gloucester, accompanied by Henry STAFFORD, duke of Buckingham, met Rivers at Northampton, where the three men apparently spent a convivial evening. However, at dawn the next morning, Rivers; the king's half brother, Richard Grey; and the king's chamberlain, Thomas VAUGHAN, were denounced as traitors and arrested. Hustled off to Gloucester's northern strongholds, all three were executed in late June. Gloucester and Buckingham rode to Stony Stratford and took custody of Edward, who vigorously but unsuccessfully protested Rivers's detention. Fearing for his political future, and perhaps even for his life, Gloucester had decided to strike the Woodvilles before they struck at him.

About 1 May, when word of Rivers's arrest reached London, the queen took SANCTUARY at Westminster with her daughters and her younger son, Richard PLANTAGENET, duke of York. Hastings, meanwhile, persuaded a nervous council that Gloucester's actions were justified. Entering the capital on 4 May, the king was briefly housed in the bishop of London's palace, before being transferred to the Tower. On 8 May, the council formally appointed Gloucester protector, summoned PARLIAMENT for late June, and rescheduled Edward's coronation for 22 June.

Matters stood thus until 13 June, when Gloucester launched a second series of unexpected arrests, seizing Hastings, Archbishop Thomas ROTHERHAM, Bishop John MORTON, and Thomas STANLEY, Lord Stanley, during a council meeting in the Tower (see COUNCIL MEETING OF 13 JUNE 1483). Accused of plotting against the protector, Hastings was summarily executed. Although his support had helped Gloucester forestall a Woodville coup, Hastings, who was firmly committed to Edward V, had apparently grown suspicious of the duke's intentions, and he may even have plotted against Gloucester with the Woodvilles. Three days later, Cardinal Thomas BOURCHIER, speaking on Gloucester's behalf, persuaded the queen to surrender York, who joined his brother in the Tower. On 17 June, both Parliament and the coronation were delayed until November. Apparently, at some point in late May or early June Gloucester had decided that his best interests required him to seize the throne for himself

On 22 June, the popular preacher Ralph Shaw, speaking at Paul's Cross in London, proclaimed the bastardy of Edward IV's children and declared Gloucester the true heir of York. To support his claims, Shaw alleged the existence, recently revealed by Bishop Robert STILLINGTON, of the BUTLER PRECONTRACT, a marriage agreement entered into by Edward IV before his union with Queen Elizabeth (see SHAW'S SERMON). If genuine, this precontract invalidated the Woodville marriage and made the princes illegitimate and thus unable to inherit the throne. On 24 June, Buckingham addressed the London authorities at the Guildhall, where he again set forth Gloucester's right to the Crown and urged the citizens to call upon the duke to take the throne. He repeated this call next day at a meeting of the lords assembled in London, who drafted a petition requesting Gloucester to assume the Crown (see TITULUS REGIUS).

On 26 June, Buckingham led this assembly and a deputation of London citizens to Baynard's Castle, where they prevailed upon the briefly reluctant duke to accede to their request. Gloucester then rode to Westminster, seated himself upon the throne, and set his coronation for 6 July. The usurpation was complete—the reign of Edward V had ended and that of Richard III had begun. Opposition to the usurpation, along with revulsion arising from the belief that the princes were subsequently murdered by Richard, created a coalition of dissident Yorkists and former Lancastrians that revived the civil wars by supporting the efforts of Henry Tudor, earl of Richmond (see HENRY VII), the Lancastrian heir, to overthrow Richard.

See also Bosworth Field, Battle of
Further Reading: Kendall, Paul Murray, *Richard the Third* (New York: W. W. Norton, 1956); Mancini, Dominic, *The Usurpation of Richard III*, edited and translated by C. A. J. Armstrong (Stroud, Gloucestershire, UK: Alan Sutton, 1989); Ross, Charles, *Richard III* (Berkeley: University of California Press, 1981); see also the Richard III Society Web site at <http://www.r3.org> for various materials relating to the usurpation of 1483.

The Usurpation of Richard III (Mancini)

Dominic Mancini's Latin work *De Occupatione Regni Anglie per Riccardum Tercium* (usually translated as *The Usurpation of Richard III*) is the only contemporary account of the events surrounding RICHARD III's seizure of the English throne in 1483 (see USURPATION OF 1483).

At the behest of his patron, Angelo Cato, archbishop of Vienne, the Italian cleric Dominic Mancini (c. 1434–c. 1514) came to England in 1482 as part of a French diplomatic mission. Recalled to FRANCE by Cato in July 1483, Mancini thus spent the critical months of April to July 1483, the period from EDWARD IV's death to Richard III's coronation, in LONDON. Upon Mancini's return, Cato asked him to write an account of Richard's seizure of the throne of his nephew EDWARD V; the result was the *Usurpation,* which, according to Mancini, was completed on 1 December 1483, about six months after the events it describes. Mancini's manuscript then disappeared until 1934, when it was discovered in the municipal library at Lille, France. Written before the accession of HENRY VII and

thus unaffected by the anti-Richard PROPAGANDA emanating from the Tudor COURT after the Battle of BOSWORTH FIELD in 1485, the *Usurpation* was immediately recognized as an extremely valuable source for a controversial period of English history.

Mancini was highly critical of Richard III, portraying him as deceitful, ambitious, and ruthless, motivated by an "insane lust for power" (Dockray, p. xvii) that drove him to eliminate anyone who stood between himself and the Crown. Coming from someone who appeared to be an independent observer and an eyewitness to at least some of the events described, this was a powerful indictment of the king. However, modern scholars have questioned the accuracy of the *Usurpation*. Unfamiliar with England and its politics, Mancini probably spoke little English, never left London, and may have been influenced by a desire to write a dramatic story for his patron. Although vague about his sources, Mancini probably got much of his information from fellow Italians resident in London, who interpreted for him current rumors and Richard's own propaganda declarations. In the *Usurpation,* Mancini himself warned Cato not to expect "the names of individual men and places or that this account shall be complete in all details" (Dockray, p. xvi).

Mancini gets wrong the date of Edward IV's death and incorrectly places the surrender of Richard PLANTAGENET, duke of York, before the execution of William HASTINGS, Lord Hastings. The only informant named by Mancini is Dr. John Argentine, personal physician to Edward V and one of the last persons to see him and his brother alive in the TOWER OF LONDON. Mention of Argentine may indicate that much of Mancini's information ultimately derived from supporters of Edward V, a fact that would explain the *Usurpation*'s hostile depiction of Richard III.

See also Princes in the Tower
Further Reading: Dockray, Keith, *Richard III: A Source Book* (Stroud, Gloucestershire, UK: Sutton Publishing, 1997); Mancini, Dominic, *The Usurpation of Richard III,* edited and translated by C. A. J. Armstrong (Stroud, Gloucestershire, UK: Alan Sutton, 1989).

Vaughan, Sir Thomas (d. 1483)

Sir Thomas Vaughan was one of the chief Welsh adherents of the house of YORK.

A supporter of Richard PLANTAGENET, duke of York, Vaughan was included among the acts of ATTAINDER passed against leading Yorkists in the COVENTRY PARLIAMENT of 1459. He probably fought for the Yorkists at the Battle of MORTIMER'S CROSS in February 1461 and at the Battle of TOWTON a month later. EDWARD IV rewarded him with numerous offices, including the treasurership of the royal chamber, which Vaughan acquired in 1465. In 1470, Vaughan was one of the commissioners sent to BURGUNDY to confer the Garter (symbol of a prestigious order of chivalry) on Duke CHARLES. A political ally of the WOODVILLE FAMILY, Vaughan was also a member of Edward IV's inner circle of household servants. In 1473, while retaining his position in the royal chamber, Vaughan was also appointed treasurer of Prince Edward's chamber, an office of great trust that made Vaughan an influential member of the prince's COUNCIL in WALES. The king knighted Vaughan in 1475.

On Edward IV's death in April 1483, Vaughan was with the prince (now EDWARD V) at Ludlow on the Welsh marches (i.e., border). Along with Anthony WOODVILLE, Earl Rivers, the new king's uncle and the governor of his household, Vaughan set out with the royal party for LONDON. On 29 April, Vaughan remained with Edward at Stony Stratford while Rivers returned to Northampton to meet the king's paternal uncle, Richard, duke of Gloucester (see RICHARD III), who was riding south with Henry STAFFORD, duke of Buckingham. Next day, upon their ar-

rival in Stony Stratford, Gloucester and Buckingham arrested Vaughan and the king's half brother Richard Grey and sent them north to join Rivers in confinement in one of Gloucester's Yorkshire strongholds.

Told that Vaughan and the others had hastened Edward IV's death by encouraging his involvement in their debaucheries and that they had plotted to deprive Gloucester of his rightful office as regent, Edward V vigorously if vainly protested their innocence. Because of Vaughan's connections with the Woodvilles and his well-known loyalty to Edward IV, Gloucester probably considered him a likely opponent of any attempt to seize Edward V's throne. Acting on Gloucester's orders, and probably without granting any form of trial, Sir Richard RATCLIFFE oversaw the execution of Vaughan, Rivers, and Grey at Pontefract on 25 June 1483.

See also Usurpation of 1483
Further Reading: Evans, H. T., *Wales and the Wars of the Roses* (Stroud, Gloucestershire, UK: Alan Sutton Publishing, 1995); Ross, Charles, *Richard III* (Berkeley: University of California Press, 1981).

Vere, John de, Earl of Oxford (1443–1513)

A staunch partisan of the house of LANCASTER, John de Vere, thirteenth earl of Oxford, helped overthrow the house of YORK in both 1470 and 1485.

The second son of the twelfth earl, Oxford succeeded to the family title in 1462, when EDWARD IV executed his father and elder brother for allegedly plotting a Lancastrian invasion (see OXFORD CONSPIRACY). In 1468,

Oxford also fell under suspicion of Lancastrian dealings and spent some months in the TOWER OF LONDON. In the spring of 1470, he fled England for the continent with his brother-in-law, Richard NEVILLE, earl of Warwick, who was then in rebellion against Edward IV. When Warwick restored HENRY VI in the following autumn, Oxford became constable of England and used his position to pronounce sentence of death on John TIPTOFT, earl of Worcester, the Yorkist constable who had condemned his father and brother (see EDWARD IV, OVERTHROW OF). Oxford commanded the Lancastrian van at the Battle of BARNET in April 1471 and fled to FRANCE after Edward IV's restoration (see EDWARD IV, RESTORATION OF). In September 1473, the earl landed in Cornwall and seized St. Michael's Mount, which he held for two months until forced by siege to surrender. PARLIAMENT attainted Oxford in 1475, and Edward IV imprisoned him at the CALAIS fortress of Hammes, from which he escaped with the help of the governor, Sir James Blount, in 1484.

Upon gaining his freedom, the earl, like Blount, joined Henry Tudor, earl of Richmond, in France. Oxford returned to Hammes later in the year and obtained leave for the fortress's pro-Richmond garrison to depart unmolested. Landing in England with Richmond in 1485, Oxford served as captain-general of the earl's army and commanded its right wing at the Battle of BOSWORTH FIELD on 22 August. The success of Oxford's initial assault upon the royal army likely convinced RICHARD III to launch his charge against Richmond's position, which in turn caused Sir William STANLEY to abandon his neutrality and intervene decisively on Richmond's behalf.

Now king as HENRY VII, Richmond rewarded Oxford with numerous offices, including chamberlain of England, constable of the Tower, and lord admiral. The earl commanded the van of the royal army against Yorkist rebels at the Battle of STOKE in 1487 and helped crush the Cornish uprising of 1497 (see SIMNEL, LAMBERT). In 1499, as steward of England, he condemned to death Edward PLANTAGENET, earl of Warwick, the last direct male heir of the house of York. Oxford outlived Henry VII by four years, dying in March 1513.

Further Reading: "John Vere," in Michael Hicks, *Who's Who in Late Medieval England* (London: Shepheard-Walwyn, 1991), pp. 335–337; Ross, Charles, *Edward IV* (New Haven, CT: Yale University Press, 1998); Ross, Charles, *Richard III* (Berkeley: University of California Press, 1981); Seward, Desmond, *The Wars of the Roses* (New York: Viking, 1995).

Vergil, Polydore. *See Anglica Historia*

Wainfleet, William, Bishop of Winchester (c. 1395–1486)

William Wainfleet (or Waynfleet) was chancellor under HENRY VI in the late 1450s and bishop of Winchester throughout the WARS OF THE ROSES.

The son of a Lincolnshire gentleman, Wainfleet was ordained in 1426. Through the patronage of Henry Beaufort, bishop of Winchester (see BEAUFORT FAMILY), Wainfleet acquired various Church offices and was presented at court in 1440. In 1447, Henry VI nominated Wainfleet to be Beaufort's successor in the wealthy bishopric of Winchester. As the king came to rely increasingly on his advice, Wainfleet negotiated for the government with Jack Cade (see JACK CADE'S REBELLION) in 1450 and with Richard PLANTAGENET, duke of York, during the duke's DARTFORD UPRISING in 1452. In March 1454, the bishop led a parliamentary delegation to Windsor that tried unsuccessfully to communicate with the stricken king (see HENRY VI, ILLNESS OF). During York's FIRST PROTECTORATE in 1454, Wainfleet frequently attended the COUNCIL to safeguard the interests of the king against York and his colleagues. After his recovery in early 1455, Henry dismissed York, but the duke and his allies, Richard NEVILLE, earl of Salisbury, and his son Richard NEVILLE, earl of Warwick, took up arms and regained power at the Battle of ST. ALBANS in May. Wainfleet thereafter was a moderate Lancastrian, supporting the king but showing a willingness to work with York.

In October 1456, after the end of York's SECOND PROTECTORATE, Henry appointed Wainfleet chancellor. In 1457, the bishop became one of Prince EDWARD OF LANCASTER's tutors and obtained license to found a new college at Oxford named Magdalen. With the start of civil war in 1459, Wainfleet became a staunch Lancastrian, presiding over the COVENTRY PARLIAMENT and the passage there of bills of ATTAINDER against York and the Nevilles. After EDWARD IV won the throne in 1461, Wainfleet went briefly into hiding, but submitted to the new king by the end of the year. When Warwick restored Henry VI in 1470, Wainfleet reverted to his Lancastrian allegiance and personally escorted the king from the TOWER OF LONDON (see EDWARD IV, OVERTHROW OF).

Edward IV's restoration in 1471, which was accompanied by the death of Prince Edward in battle and the murder of Henry VI in the Tower, forced the bishop to again seek pardon from the Yorkist monarch (see HENRY VI, MURDER OF). Wainfleet spent the 1470s serving at COURT and completing the construction of Magdalen College and Henry VI's foundation at Eton. The aging bishop acquiesced in RICHARD III's usurpation in 1483 and in July 1485 even gave the king a loan (probably under compulsion) to help repel the expected invasion of Henry Tudor, earl of Richmond, the inheritor of the Lancastrian claim (see USURPATION OF 1483). Wainfleet died, near age ninety, in April 1486, eight months after Richmond won the throne as HENRY VII.

See also Edward IV, Restoration of; English Church and the Wars of the Roses; Readeption
Further Reading: Davis, V., "William Waynflete and the Educational Revolution of the Fifteenth Century," in J. T. Rosenthal and C. F. Richmond, eds., *People, Politics and Community in the Later*

Middle Ages (Stroud, Gloucestershire, UK: Alan Sutton, 1987), pp. 40–59; Griffiths, Ralph A., *The Reign of King Henry VI* (Berkeley: University of California Press, 1981); "William Waynflete," in Michael Hicks, *Who's Who in Late Medieval England* (London: Shepheard-Walwyn, 1991), pp. 274–276; Wolffe, Bertram, *Henry VI* (London: Eyre Methuen, 1981).

Wakefield, Battle of (1460)

The chief consequence of the Lancastrian victory at the Battle of Wakefield on 30 December 1460 was the death in battle of Richard PLANTAGENET, duke of York, and the transferal thereby of the duke's claim to the throne to his son Edward, earl of March, the future EDWARD IV. The battle revived Lancastrian fortunes, which had seemed so bleak after HENRY VI's defeat and capture at the Battle of NORTHAMPTON the previous July, and also led to the deaths of York's ally Richard NEVILLE, earl of Salisbury, and York's second son Edmund PLANTAGENET, earl of Rutland.

In September 1460, two months after the Battle of Northampton, York returned to England from exile in IRELAND. In October, York laid his claim to the throne before PARLIAMENT. The assembled lords forced the duke to accept the Act of ACCORD, which allowed Henry to remain king but settled the succession on York and his heirs. In WALES, Queen MARGARET OF ANJOU refused to accept the disinheritance of her son EDWARD OF LANCASTER, Prince of Wales, and Lancastrian nobles throughout England took up arms against the Yorkist regime. In the north, Henry BEAUFORT, duke of Somerset, joined forces with John CLIFFORD, Lord Clifford, Henry PERCY, earl of Northumberland, and other lords to create a sizable Lancastrian army.

Forced to respond to this threat, York and Salisbury left LONDON on 9 December with a force of about 6,000. They hoped to rendezvous with John NEVILLE, Lord Neville, Salisbury's kinsman, and bring the Lancastrians to battle. Although attacked en route by Somerset's men, York safely reached Sandal Castle south of Wakefield in Yorkshire on 21 December 1460. York found the castle poorly prepared to receive his army, and the presence in the vicinity of Lancastrian forces prevented collection of sufficient provisions for the duke's men. Assuming various positions around the castle, the Lancastrian lords, who had no siege ARTILLERY, sought to draw York outside by sending insulting messages and cutting off his foraging parties.

This drawing depicts Sandal Castle, from which Richard Plantagenet, duke of York, rode to his death at the Battle of Wakefield in December 1460. (Public Record Office: PRO MPC 97)

On 30 December, Yorkist foragers came under attack north of the castle within sight of the walls. For reasons that are now unclear, York chose to leave the safety of the castle and sallied forth with the bulk of his force. Surrounded by enemies and unable to flee, York was slain in the field. Rutland was killed by Clifford as the earl attempted to flee after the battle, and Salisbury was captured and executed the next day. All three had their heads stuck on Micklegate Bar in York, the duke's topped with a mocking paper crown.

See also North of England and the Wars of the Roses

Further Reading: Haigh, Philip A., *The Battle of Wakefield 1460* (Stroud, Gloucestershire, UK: Sutton Publishing, 1996); Johnson, P. A., *Duke Richard of York* (Oxford: Clarendon Press, 1988).

Wales

Because many key civil war figures inherited Welsh blood, owned Welsh estates, and recruited Welsh RETAINERS, Wales played a central role in the WARS OF THE ROSES.

Wales in the fifteenth century was divided into two distinct administrative entities: the Principality of Wales, governed by the monarch or by the heir to the throne as Prince of Wales, and the lordships of the marches, governed independently by various noblemen. The principality was divided into shires centered on the towns of Carmarthen in the south and Carnarvon in the north. Each group of shires was governed by a justiciar and a chamberlain appointed by the Crown. Within the marcher lordships, neither royal writs nor royal officials had any authority. Each lord had complete responsibility for government within his own lordship; he could impose his own taxes, appoint his own officials, and operate his own law courts.

The house of LANCASTER enjoyed a blood connection to Wales through HENRY VI's Welsh half brothers, Edmund TUDOR, earl of Richmond, and Jasper TUDOR, earl of Pembroke. The house of YORK inherited Welsh blood from the Mortimers, the maternal relatives of Richard PLANTAGENET, duke of York, and members of the most powerful marcher family of the fourteenth century. Because he was heir to the Mortimer earldom of March, EDWARD IV incorporated over half the Welsh marcher lordships into the Crown when he became king in 1461. These lordships and that of Glamorgan, which was held by Richard NEVILLE, earl of Warwick, were the Welsh centers of Yorkist support before 1470, while Lancastrian sentiment was strongest in the principality and in Jasper Tudor's lordship of Pembroke.

During the 1450s, local Welsh feuds, like similar English feuds, were subsumed in the struggle between Lancaster and York. In 1455, after his victory at the Battle of ST. ALBANS, York had PARLIAMENT appoint a committee of marcher lords and royal officials to devise effective government for Wales. However, within a year, Edmund Tudor, Henry VI's lieutenant in Wales, was at war with leading Welsh Yorkists; after Tudor's death in 1456, his brother, Jasper, consolidated Welsh support for the king. In 1461, two battles—MORTIMER'S CROSS in February and TWT HILL in October—broke Pembroke's hold on Wales and initiated a period of Yorkist government under William HERBERT (later earl of Pembroke). By 1468, Herbert was lord, custodian, or chief official of almost all Welsh shires and lordships, a dominance that clashed with Warwick's Welsh ambitions. In 1469, when his rebels captured Herbert at the Battle of EDGECOTE, Warwick ordered Herbert's execution, thereby depriving Edward IV of a valuable servant.

In the 1470s, Edward filled this vacuum by creating his son (see EDWARD V) Prince of Wales and by appointing a COUNCIL to govern Wales in his name. Operating from Ludlow in the marches, the council, which was headed by Anthony WOODVILLE, Earl Rivers, eventually exercised full authority in the principality and royal lordships and supervisory jurisdiction in the private lordships and adjoining English shires. This conciliar arrangement collapsed in May 1483, when Richard, duke of Gloucester (see RICHARD III), now lord protector for his nephew Edward V, arrested Rivers and vested the government of all royal lands in Wales in his ally,

Henry STAFFORD, duke of Buckingham, who already was a marcher lord. Although his grant was for life, the duke did not hold it long; he was executed for treason in November after the failure of BUCKINGHAM'S REBELLION. The subsequent weakness of Richard III in Wales, combined with the lingering influence there of Jasper Tudor, allowed the latter's nephew, Henry Tudor, earl of Richmond, to successfully land in and march through Wales in August 1485.

After winning the Crown at the Battle of BOSWORTH FIELD, Richmond, now HENRY VII, used the house of TUDOR's Welsh ancestry to win Welsh support for the new dynasty. First, Jasper Tudor was created duke of Bedford and given extensive authority in the principality; next, following the example of Edward IV, a council nominally under the direction of Prince Arthur (whose very name was an appeal to the Welsh) was granted oversight of royal lordships. Thereafter, Wales fell increasingly under royal control until Henry VIII, through statutes passed in 1536 and 1543, achieved Welsh union with England by abolishing the marcher lordships and dividing Wales into shires governed in the same manner as English counties.

See also Rhys ap Thomas; Thomas ap Gruffydd
Further Reading: Davies, John, *A History of Wales* (London: The Penguin Group, 1993); Evans, H. T., *Wales and the Wars of the Roses* (Stroud, Gloucestershire, UK: Alan Sutton Publishing, 1995); Griffiths, Ralph A., "Wales and the Marches," in S. B. Chrimes, C. D. Ross, and Ralph A. Griffiths, *Fifteenth-Century England, 1399–1509*, 2d ed. (Stroud, Gloucestershire, UK: Alan Sutton, 1995); Williams, Glanmor, *Renewal and Reformation: Wales, c. 1415–1642* (Oxford: Oxford University Press, 1993).

War in the North. *See* Alnwick Castle; Bamburgh Castle; Dunstanburgh Castle; Hedgeley Moor, Battle of; Hexham, Battle of

Warbeck, Perkin (1475–1499)

By impersonating a son of EDWARD IV, Perkin Warbeck became the center of a York-ist conspiracy to overthrow HENRY VII and the house of TUDOR.

Born in the Netherlands, Warbeck took service with a Breton cloth merchant, who used the handsome youth to model his finery. In 1491, the young man accompanied his master to IRELAND, where Warbeck's aristocratic manner attracted the attention of Yorkist sympathizers who encouraged the belief that Warbeck was of royal blood. In November, Warbeck paraded through Dublin claiming to be Edward IV's younger son, Richard PLANTAGENET, duke of York, who had disappeared in the TOWER OF LONDON in 1483. Warbeck also began calling himself "Richard IV," the rightful king of England. By December, Henry VII feared that Warbeck would win control of Ireland, just as LAMBERT SIMNEL, an earlier Yorkist pretender, had done in 1487. The king dispatched an army to Ireland that dispersed Warbeck's supporters and forced the pretender to accept an invitation from CHARLES VIII to come to FRANCE.

Claiming to be Richard, duke of York, the younger son of Edward IV, Perkin Warbeck spent much of the 1490s seeking to overthrow Henry VII and the house of Tudor. (Bibliotheque Municipale d'Arras)

Anxious to make trouble for Henry, who was opposing French attempts to absorb BRITTANY, Charles treated Warbeck as an honored guest until November 1492, when the conclusion of the Treaty of Etaples with England forced Charles to expel Warbeck. The pretender then withdrew to the Netherlands, where he was welcomed by MARGARET OF YORK, the dowager duchess of BURGUNDY; the sister of Edward IV and RICHARD III and a longtime foe of Henry VII, Margaret formally recognized Warbeck as her nephew. Backed by the duchess and by Duke Philip of Burgundy, Warbeck invaded England with fourteen ships in June 1495. However, when a rebel landing party was quickly overwhelmed in Kent, Warbeck decided to return to Ireland. When an Irish landing was also repulsed, Warbeck sailed for SCOTLAND, where JAMES IV, hoping to reacquire BERWICK, was also eager to make difficulties for Henry. James recognized Warbeck as "Richard IV" and allowed him to marry a royal kinswoman, Lady Katherine Gordon. In September 1496, James invaded northern England, ostensibly on Warbeck's behalf (see NORTH OF ENGLAND AND THE WARS OF THE ROSES). The enterprise aroused no support for a Yorkist restoration, and the Scottish army soon withdrew. By the spring of 1497, James was listening to offers of alliance from LONDON, and Warbeck once again found himself forced to depart.

After another abortive attempt on Ireland, Warbeck and a small band of supporters landed in Cornwall in September 1497. Hoping to revive a recently quelled Cornish uprising, Warbeck attracted thousands of recruits, but was unable to capture Exeter and was soon forced to surrender. After making a full confession of his imposture to the king, Warbeck was confined at Westminster, and his wife was allowed to become lady-in-waiting to Queen ELIZABETH OF YORK. In June 1498, Warbeck fled, but he was recaptured and imprisoned in the Tower. When Ferdinand and Isabella of Spain expressed reservations about marrying their daughter to Henry's son so long as any royal pretender remained in En-

gland, the king had Warbeck tried for treason along with his fellow prisoner, Edward PLANTAGENET, earl of Warwick, the last direct male descendent of the house of YORK. Warbeck and Warwick were convicted and executed in November 1499.

See also Yorkist Heirs (after 1485)
Further Reading: Arthurson, Ian, *The Perkin Warbeck Conspiracy, 1491–1499* (Stroud, Gloucestershire, UK: Sutton Publishing, 1997).

Warkworth's Chronicle

A Chronicle of the First Thirteen Years of the Reign of King Edward the Fourth, popularly known as *Warkworth's Chronicle,* after its probable author John Warkworth, is an important source of information for events in England between 1461 and 1474, and especially for the second phase of the WARS OF THE ROSES between 1469 and 1471.

John Warkworth is a rather obscure figure. Believed to be a northerner, born perhaps near the village of Warkworth in Northumberland, he studied at Oxford and became chaplain to Bishop William Grey of Ely in the 1450s. In 1473, he became master of St. Peter's College, Cambridge, a position he held until his death in 1500. In 1483, Warkworth presented his college with a handwritten copy of the *Brut* chronicle to which was appended, as a continuation, the only surviving copy of what became known as *Warkworth's Chronicle.* Whether Warkworth actually wrote the chronicle, or simply caused it to be written for his use, is uncertain.

Although covering the reign of EDWARD IV, *Warkworth's Chronicle* has a distinct Lancastrian bias. The chronicle is sympathetic to HENRY VI, whose restoration in 1470 is described as giving great joy to "the more part of the people" (*Three Chronicles,* p. 33), and it is critical of Edward IV, who is particularly condemned for his financial exactions. The chronicle also mentions the dissatisfaction of Richard NEVILLE, earl of Warwick, with Edward's 1464 marriage to Elizabeth WOODVILLE and roundly condemns John TIPTOFT, the Yorkist earl of Worcester, who for his execution of Lancastrian sympathizers is said to have been "greatly behated among the people" (*Three Chronicles,* p. 31). The chronicler also hinted that Richard, duke of Gloucester (see RICHARD III), Edward's brother, had some responsibility for Henry VI's death in the TOWER OF LONDON in 1471 (see HENRY VI, MURDER OF).

Warkworth's Chronicle also displays an unusual and therefore valuable northern perspective. It provides information on the Lancastrian resistance that centered on the northern castles of ALNWICK, BAMBURGH, and DUNSTANBURGH between 1461 and 1464, and it is a major source for northern rebellions, such as the ROBIN OF REDESDALE REBELLION in 1469 and the WELLES UPRISING in Lincolnshire in 1470. The chronicle also describes the Battles of BARNET and TEWKESBURY; the 1471 assault on LONDON by Thomas NEVILLE, the Bastard of Fauconberg; and the 1473 seizure of St. Michael's Mount in Cornwall by John de VERE, the die-hard Lancastrian earl of Oxford. Although frequently confusing and often incorrect in details, *Warkworth's Chronicle* is a useful source for the earlier years of Edward IV's reign.

> **See also** North of England and the Wars of the Roses
> **Further Reading:** *Three Chronicles of the Reign of Edward IV,* Introduction by Keith Dockray (Stroud, Gloucestershire, UK: Alan Sutton Publishing, 1988); the text of *Warkworth's Chronicle* is also available on the Richard III Society Web site at <http://www.r3.org/bookcase/warkwort/worthi.html>.

Wars of the Roses, Causes of

Civil war erupted in fifteenth-century England for many interrelated reasons. While Tudor and Elizabethan commentators found the chief cause of the conflict in the 1399 deposition of Richard II and its attendant break in the legal line of succession, historians working in the twentieth century proposed numerous other causes, including BASTARD FEUDALISM, economic weakness, royal incompetence, and military defeat in FRANCE.

Although all these ideas have been closely examined and many have been discredited or modified, debate continues, both on questions of how and why the WARS OF THE ROSES began and on questions of how best to relate and evaluate the various causation theories being proposed.

The oldest theory of causation is the dynastic, which states that the wars were disputes over title to the throne. The Lancastrian usurpation of 1399 led to civil strife because it vested the Crown in a branch of the royal family whose right to it was inferior to that of other members of the family. As originally enunciated by Tudor writers, and especially by William Shakespeare, this theory also had a supernatural component—the deposition of an anointed king, being a violation of divine law, led inexorably to the divine punishment of civil war. Although this view has today fallen out of fashion, some modern historians have partially revived it by arguing that HENRY VI and MARGARET OF ANJOU were much concerned for the future of the house of LANCASTER in the 1450s, and that many of their attitudes and actions were shaped by fear of the dynastic ambitions of Richard PLANTAGENET, duke of York.

In the late nineteenth century, Charles Plummer and William Denton advocated the theory that bastard feudalism was the chief cause of the Wars of the Roses. They argued that a corrupt offshoot of the feudal social system (which Plummer termed bastard feudalism) allowed a small group of wealthy nobles to raise large bodies of armed RETAINERS with which they conducted private quarrels and defied the authority of the Crown. Developing in the fourteenth century during the reign of Edward III (r. 1327–1377), bastard feudalism disrupted English political society in the fifteenth century. Civil war resulted from a collapse of central authority brought on by "overmighty subjects" who used the Crown and the royal government for their own ends.

After 1940, K. B. McFarlane and his students largely demolished the notion that a corrupted form of feudalism caused the Wars of the Roses. They argued that bastard feudalism was the basis of political society from the thirteenth through the sixteenth centuries, and that only the weakness of the Crown under the inept Henry VI allowed the system to be corrupted in the fifteenth century. As McFarlane wrote, "only an undermighty ruler had anything to fear from overmighty subjects" (McFarlane, p. 238). In the last thirty years, the debate has shifted from the belief that the wars arose mainly from the weaknesses of Henry VI to discussion of a general shift in the balance of power between the Crown and its most powerful subjects. This idea salvages some of the Plummer/Denton theory by holding Edward III responsible for altering the king's relationship with his nobles. Instead of standing clearly above and apart from leading noblemen, as Edward I had done, kings after Edward III stood more as first among equals, a consequence that made effective kingship more dependent on the personality of individual monarchs. When a truly ineffective monarch came to power in 1437, royal government ceased to function as it should, and powerful nobles had more scope for making trouble, with bastard feudalism serving as only one of the means by which they did so.

In the 1930s, M. M. Postan suggested that the "political gangsterism" (Postan, p. 48) of the fifteenth century arose from the financial distress of a nobility experiencing declining incomes. In the 1950s, Charles Ross and T. B. Pugh expanded this idea and tied it into the theory of bastard feudalism by arguing that financially strapped nobles became increasingly dependent on Crown patronage and therefore fought each other not because they had the wherewithal to raise private armies but because they needed royal largess to pay the retinues they already had. This theory of noble insolvency as a cause of civil war also embraced the increasing financial woes of the Crown under Henry VI. In the 1390s, Richard II enjoyed an annual revenue of £120,000, while in the 1450s Henry VI's annual income had shrunk to about £40,000. Besides experiencing the same decline in rents that affected the PEERAGE, the Crown also suffered from a European-wide depression that reduced customs revenues and from the king's free-spending tendencies, a point that also reinforces the idea that Henry VI's incompetence was a prime cause of the wars. Although the general financial position of the nobility in the fifteenth century has been much debated, the bankruptcy of the Crown is not in doubt; what is in question is how much of a role royal insolvency played in the coming of the civil wars.

Certainly the Crown's poverty was a factor in the English loss of Normandy in 1450, and the loss of that important province, which was both a psychological blow to England's pride and a financial blow to the incomes of numerous noblemen, helped initiate the quarrel between York and Edmund BEAUFORT, duke of Somerset. This quarrel over standing at COURT and access to patronage is generally accepted as an important immediate cause of the wars. Another immediate cause was the entry into politics of Margaret of Anjou, who worked on behalf of her son, Prince EDWARD OF LANCASTER, to thwart the political ambitions of York. What is less accepted is the effect, if any, of the ending of the HUNDRED YEARS WAR on the coming of the Wars of the Roses. The notion that the internal disorder of the 1450s was the result of returning hordes of unruly soldiers (and magnates), who had earlier directed their aggression toward the French, has been largely abandoned, but the idea that dissatisfaction with the Lancastrian regime's handling of the French war made possible Yorkist opposition to the government is still much debated.

Recently, scholars have pointed out that the theories discussed above apply only to the civil wars before 1471. For the revival of the conflict in the 1480s, a general consensus finds the main cause in the actions of one man— RICHARD III. Some historians suggest that EDWARD IV, by basing his regime too narrowly on a small number of supporters, such as William HASTINGS, Lord Hastings, and the WOODVILLE FAMILY, was responsible for creating conditions that allowed Richard to easily topple his nephew, EDWARD V. Although this may be true, the fact remains that only Richard's usurpation, undertaken in 1483 for any number of reasons, allowed Henry Tudor, earl of Richmond (see HENRY VII), to become a serious contender for the throne and transformed the defunct struggle between the houses of Lancaster and YORK into a struggle between the latter and the house of TUDOR.

See also Richard II, Deposition of; Shakespeare and the Wars of the Roses
Further Reading: Dockray, Keith, "The Origins of the Wars of the Roses," in A. J. Pollard, ed., *The Wars of the Roses* (New York: St. Martin's Press, 1995), pp. 65–88; McFarlane, K. B., "The Wars of the Roses," in *England in the Fifteenth Century: Collected Essays* (London: Hambledon Press, 1981); Pollard, A. J., *The Wars of the Roses* (New York: St. Martin's Press, 1988); Postan, M. M., "The Fifteenth Century," in *Essays in Medieval Agriculture and Economy* (Cambridge: Cambridge University Press, 1973); Pugh, T. B., and Charles Ross, "The English Baronage and the Income Tax of 1436," *Bulletin of the Institute of Historical Research* 20 (1952): 1–22.

Wars of the Roses, Naming of

"Wars of the Roses" is a modern term used to describe the intermittent civil conflicts that occurred in fifteenth-century England between partisans of the houses of LANCASTER and YORK. Sir Walter Scott is usually credited with coining the term in his 1829 novel *Anne of Geierstein,* although Sir John Oglander had published a 1646 pamphlet entitled *The Quarrel of the Warring Roses* and David Hume had written in his 1762 *History of England* about "the Wars of the Two Roses." Although the phrase "Wars of the Roses" was unknown to contemporaries, who referred occasionally to "Cousins' Wars," the idea of a civil conflict symbolized by two competing rose emblems originated in the late fifteenth century.

During the civil war, the white rose was one of the chief BADGES of EDWARD IV and the house of York, but use of the red rose as a symbol for Lancaster or of the idea of competing rose emblems is hard to find before 1485. But after that year, the red rose as a symbol for the TUDOR FAMILY and, by extension, for their Lancastrian relatives, is found scattered throughout English literature, art, and architecture, usually intertwined with the white rose as a representation of the union of Lancaster and York brought about by HENRY VII's 1486 marriage to ELIZABETH OF YORK, daughter of Edward IV. The concept of a union of warring roses became such a commonplace of Tudor PROPAGANDA that the 1509 coronation of Henry VIII, the offspring of this union, was greeted with numerous verses that, like the following lines from John Skelton, extolled the peaceful blending of the two formerly hostile emblems:

Although the term "Wars of the Roses" originated in the nineteenth century, the use of roses to represent the feuding houses of Lancaster and York goes back to the reign of Henry VII, who combined the red and white roses to symbolize the union of the two houses achieved by his marriage to the daughter of Edward IV. Shown here is an unusual reversed Tudor rose, with the white petals outside the red. (Royal MS 20 E III f. 30v, British Library)

The rose both white and red
In one rose now doth grow. (Ross, p. 15)

Some eighty years later, William Shakespeare, following these early Tudor leads, wrote the memorable, if entirely fictional scene that prompted the later coining of the term "Wars of the Roses." In act 2, scene iv of *HENRY VI, PART 1,* Shakespeare has the rival dukes of Somerset and York meet in the Temple gardens, where their followers pick red or white roses as symbols of allegiance to their respective causes. Thus, although less than two centuries old, the term "Wars of the Roses" has today become the widely accepted designation for an English civil conflict fought over five hundred years ago.

> **See also** *Henry VI, Part 2; Henry VI, Part 3;* Shakespeare and the Wars of the Roses
> **Further Reading:** Gillingham, John, *The Wars of the Roses* (Baton Rouge: Louisiana State University Press, 1981); McFarlane, K. B., "The Wars of the Roses," in *England in the Fifteenth Century: Collected Essays* (London: Hambledon Press, 1981); Ross, Charles, *The Wars of the Roses* (London: Thames and Hudson, 1987); Weir, Alison, *The Wars of the Roses* (New York: Ballantine Books, 1995).

Warwick, Earl of. *See* Neville, Richard, Earl of Warwick; Plantagenet, Edward, Earl of Warwick

Warwick the Kingmaker. *See* Neville, Richard, Earl of Warwick

Waurin, Jean de. *See Recueil des Croniques et Anchiennes Istories de la Grant Bretaigne, a present nomme Engleterre* (Waurin)

Weaponry

During the WARS OF THE ROSES, English MEN-AT-ARMS carried various types of weapons into battle, including thrusting and stabbing implements, such as swords and daggers, and powerful battering weapons, such as maces and poleaxes.

For close-quarter combat, the fifteenth-century knight usually carried a sword that could be used for both cutting and thrusting. Such weapons varied greatly in length and width, from a broad, single-handed sword that was about two and a half feet in length to a narrower, two-handed version that was almost three and a half feet long. Swords meant solely for thrusting tended to have longer, narrower blades and longer hilts. When not in use, a sword fit into a scabbard that hung from a hip belt in such a way as to position the point a little to the rear where it could not trip its owner. From the other hip usually hung a rondel dagger, which was used to exploit gaps in an opponent's ARMOR or to pry open the visor of a downed enemy, who was then dispatched by a thrust to the eye or throat. The rondel was characterized by a disk- or cone-shaped guard between hilt and blade and a similarly shaped pommel at the other end of the hilt. Because it was used for stabbing, the rondel had a straight, slender blade that was triangular in shape and up to fifteen inches in length to allow for maximum penetration of an enemy's body.

Because the stronger, fluted armor used in the fifteenth century could deflect sword and spear thrusts, many knights began carrying new types of heavy weapons, often with hooks or spikes, which were designed to crush or puncture plate armor. Perhaps the most deadly of these weapons was the poleax, which consisted of a wooden shaft, four to six feet long, topped by a long spike that was flanked on one side by an ax head and on the other by a spiked hammer or fluke (a curved, beaklike extension for hooking an opponent to the ground). The spike could puncture plate or damage armored joints and rob a man of mobility. The ax and hammer could crush both armor and the flesh it covered. Against unarmored opponents, a skillfully wielded poleax was devastating.

While the poleax was used only for combat on foot, such other battering weapons as the battle-ax, the mace, and the war hammer were carried primarily by horsemen, who swung their weapon with one hand and held their reins with the other. RICHARD III supposedly led his famous cavalry charge at the Battle of Bosworth Field while wielding a battle-ax. Weighing from two to five pounds, the war hammer was serrated and usually carried a fluke opposite the hammerhead. Of a similar weight, the mace had a head composed of six interlocking serrated edges or some similarly formidable configuration of spikes and points. Like the poleax, these weapons were used to deliver crushing blows to armored opponents.

Besides the more formally trained and heavily armored men-at-arms, most civil war armies contained sizable contingents of billmen, foot soldiers who carried any of a wide variety of shafted weapons that could be used to drag enemies to the ground, to cut armor straps, and to frighten horses. Such weapons derived from the billhook, a common agricultural implement used for cutting and pruning that consisted of a blade with a hooked point attached to a long wooden shaft. Characterized by some type of blade, hook, or spike topping a pole that ranged in length from six to ten feet, a bill weapon could be raked, stabbed, or swung at an enemy. Depending on the type of head they employed, such weapons were known by various names, such as the halberd, which carried a spiked ax head and had to be swung at an opponent to be used most effectively. Because they required little training to use and, unlike bows, were easy to maintain, various forms of bills were the weapons usually carried by common soldiers and most often found in rural cottages and houses for protection against intruders.

See also Archers; Artillery; Battles, Nature of
Further Reading: Boardman, Andrew W., *The Medieval Soldier in the Wars of the Roses* (Stroud, Gloucestershire, UK: Sutton Publishing, 1998); DeVries, Kelly, *Medieval Military Technology* (Peterborough, Ontario: Broadview Press, 1992); Goodman, Anthony, *The Wars of the Roses* (New York: Dorset Press, 1981).

Welles Uprising (1470)

Occurring in Lincolnshire in the spring of 1470, the Welles uprising provided Richard

NEVILLE, earl of Warwick, with a second opportunity to overthrow EDWARD IV.

Richard Welles (1431–1470), seventh Lord Welles, was a prominent Lincolnshire nobleman and a former Lancastrian. His father, Lionel, the sixth Lord Welles, had been killed fighting for the house of LANCASTER at the Battle of TOWTON in March 1461. Although Welles was attainted by the first PARLIAMENT of Edward IV, his son Richard, who had himself fought for HENRY VI at the Battle of ST. ALBANS in 1461, submitted to the new king and regained his father's lands. Perhaps because he was related to the NEVILLE FAMILY, Welles was also allowed to assume his father's title in 1468.

Early in 1470, Welles, his son Sir Robert Welles, and his brothers-in-law Sir Thomas Dymmock and Sir Thomas de la Lande attacked the manor house of Sir Thomas Burgh, a Lincolnshire gentleman who was Edward IV's Master of Horse. The attackers destroyed Burgh's house, carried off his goods, and forced him to flee the county. Later official accounts of the incident claimed that Welles was acting on behalf of his kinsman Warwick; the earl was seeking another opportunity to draw the king into the north, where he could be surprised, defeated, and dethroned in favor of George PLANTAGENET, duke of Clarence, who was Edward's brother but Warwick's ally. Some modern historians have dismissed this claim as Yorkist PROPAGANDA and have argued that Welles's attack on Burgh arose from some private feud, a common occurrence in the fifteenth century, and that Warwick simply made use of the incident when the king decided to intervene to support his servant.

Edward summoned Welles and Dymmock to LONDON, but the two men initially refused to comply, pleading illness. Changing their minds, both took SANCTUARY at Westminster, which they were induced to leave by promise of a pardon. Meanwhile, Sir Robert Welles, now likely acting in concert with Warwick and Clarence, issued proclamations throughout Lincolnshire in early March for men to join him in resisting the king, who, it was claimed, was coming north to punish the men of the shire for their support of the ROBIN OF REDESDALE REBELLION in 1469. Already marching north when he learned of Sir Robert's defiance, Edward ordered that Lord Welles and Dymmock be brought up from London. Forced to write to his son, Lord Welles declared that he and Dymmock would die if Sir Robert did not submit. Upon receiving this letter, Sir Robert, who had been maneuvering to trap the king between his rebels and the oncoming forces of Warwick and Clarence, retreated, allowing the royal army to intercept him on 12 March. After summarily executing Lord Welles and Dymmock, the king attacked and destroyed the rebel force at the Battle of LOSECOTE FIELD, where both Sir Robert and documentary evidence of Warwick and Clarence's complicity were captured.

On 14 March, Sir Robert Welles confessed to the king that Warwick and Clarence were the "partners and chief provokers" (Ross, p. 141) of his treason, and that the purpose of the entire enterprise was to make Clarence king. On 19 March, as he prepared to pursue the earl and the duke, Edward had Welles executed before the army. With the Welles uprising crushed and their plans in ruins, Warwick and Clarence fled into the West Country where they took ship for FRANCE. In 1475, a bill of ATTAINDER (later reversed under HENRY VII) was passed against Lord Welles and his son, and the Welles estates were granted to William HASTINGS, Lord Hastings.

Further Reading: Haigh, Philip A., *The Military Campaigns of the Wars of the Roses* (Stroud, Gloucestershire, UK: Sutton Publishing, 1995); Ross, Charles, *Edward IV* (New Haven, CT: Yale University Press, 1998).

Wenlock, John, Lord Wenlock (d. 1471)

Although an early adherent of the house of YORK, and a prominent diplomat under EDWARD IV, John Wenlock, Lord Wenlock, supported the restoration of the house of LANCASTER in 1470.

Born into a Bedfordshire GENTRY family, Wenlock entered the service of Queen MARGARET OF ANJOU in the 1440s, becoming her chamberlain by 1450. In 1455, he fought for HENRY VI at the Battle of ST. ALBANS, but shortly thereafter joined the Yorkists. In 1459, after the Yorkist debacle at the Battle of LUDFORD BRIDGE, Wenlock fled to CALAIS with Richard NEVILLE, earl of Salisbury, and his son Richard NEVILLE, earl of Warwick. Wenlock returned to England with the Nevilles in June 1460 and participated in the successful Yorkist siege of the TOWER OF LONDON. In March 1461, he fought for Edward IV at the Battles of FERRYBRIDGE and TOWTON, and was rewarded later in the year with elevation to the PEERAGE. In 1462, Wenlock took part in Warwick's siege of DUNSTANBURGH CASTLE.

During the 1460s Wenlock served on numerous diplomatic missions with Warwick, including efforts to find a foreign queen for Edward IV. He and Warwick concluded a truce at sea with FRANCE in 1464, and in the following year they were joined by William HASTINGS, Lord Hastings, in a wide-ranging peace mission to various European courts. Although he was implicated in the CORNELIUS PLOT, a shadowy Lancastrian conspiracy uncovered in 1468, Wenlock suffered no serious consequences because he was engaged at the time in conducting the king's sister, MARGARET OF YORK, to BURGUNDY for her marriage to Duke CHARLES. In April 1470, when Warwick fled England after the failure of his second coup attempt, he sailed to Calais, where Wenlock was in command as Warwick's deputy. Although sympathetic, Wenlock knew the garrison was loyal to Edward; he refused admittance to Warwick and his party but privately advised the earl to seek refuge in France. For this action, Edward rewarded Wenlock with the governorship of the town, but he then grew suspicious of Wenlock's loyalty and dismissed him from the post in favor of Anthony WOODVILLE, Earl Rivers.

When Warwick forged his alliance with Margaret of Anjou in the summer of 1470 (see ANGERS AGREEMENT), Wenlock was one of the few Yorkist peers to follow the earl into the Lancastrian camp. Although his exact reasons for this defection are unclear, he may have shared Warwick's dislike for Edward's Burgundian alliance and for the rise of the WOODVILLE FAMILY. Wenlock landed in England with Queen Margaret and Prince EDWARD OF LANCASTER in April 1471 and was a leader of the Lancastrian army at the Battle of TEWKESBURY on 4 May. According to one account, Wenlock was slain by Edmund BEAUFORT, duke of Somerset, the Lancastrian commander, who was enraged at what he considered to be Wenlock's failure to support his attack. However, other sources say that Wenlock was simply killed in battle.

Further Reading: Hicks, Michael, *Warwick the Kingmaker* (Oxford: Blackwell, 1998); Ross, Charles, *Edward IV* (New Haven, CT: Yale University Press, 1998).

Westminster-Ardtornish, Treaty of (1462)

By making EDWARD IV the ally of dissident Scottish noblemen, the 1462 Treaty of Westminster-Ardtornish sought to compel the Scottish government to abandon its support for the house of LANCASTER.

After their defeat at the Battle of TOWTON in March 1461, HENRY VI, Queen MARGARET OF ANJOU, and their chief noble supporters fled into SCOTLAND, where they were given protection by Queen MARY OF GUELDRES, who led the Scottish government as regent for her nine-year-old son, JAMES III. Allowed to use Scotland as a base for raids into England, the Lancastrians kept the northern counties in turmoil. To force the Scots to abandon his opponents, Edward IV allied himself with the Scottish king's opponents. By the Treaty of Westminster-Ardtornish, John, the semi-independent Lord of the Isles, severed his links to the Scottish Crown and declared his allegiance to Edward IV. In return, Edward agreed to pay the Lord of the Isles a pension and to grant him northern Scotland, most of which was already under his influence, when the country was conquered by the

English. The rest of Scotland was pledged to the treaty's other signatory, James Douglas, ninth earl of Douglas, a Scottish rebel who had been resident in England as a pensioner of the Crown since 1455.

No attempt was made to put the treaty into effect, for the agreement was probably meant only to highlight the Scottish Crown's vulnerability in northern Scotland and to convince the Scottish government to come to terms with Edward IV and expel the Lancastrian exiles. A truce was concluded in 1463, and Scotland thereafter ceased to be a safe haven for Lancastrian adventures. However, Edward IV remembered the ploy and resumed negotiations with the Lord of the Isles in 1479 when he was again at odds with the Scottish king.

See also North of England and the Wars of the Roses
Further Reading: Mackie, J. D., *A History of Scotland,* 2d ed. (New York: Dorset Press, 1985); Ross, Charles, *Edward IV* (New Haven, CT: Yale University Press, 1998).

Whethamstede, John, Abbot of St. Albans (c. 1390–1465)

The *Registers* of John Whethamstede (or Wheathampstead), abbot of the important Benedictine monastery at St. Albans, are important sources for the personality and reign of HENRY VI and for the first phase of the WARS OF THE ROSES.

Born in Hertfordshire and educated at Oxford, Whethamstede entered the monastery of St. Albans, where he was elected abbot in 1420. Because St. Albans was an old and wealthy foundation, Whethamstede was frequently involved in litigation to protect the monastery's privileges and properties. Although a shy man in public, Whethamstede tenaciously defended the abbey's interests by cultivating persons of influence. Henry VI visited St. Albans in 1428 and in 1459, and the king's younger uncle, Humphrey, duke of Gloucester, became the abbot's close friend and patron. Whethamstede resigned his abbacy in 1440, ostensibly for ill health, but was reelected to the office in 1451.

Although influenced by Renaissance ideas, Whethamstede was not a humanist. His Latin works of history and classical mythology display much learning, but they were written in the flowery and verbose medieval style. Whethamstede was important in opening England to humanist scholarship, but he was not himself part of the humanist movement. Nonetheless, his *Registers* are important sources for the last years of Henry VI, especially since their author witnessed several key events firsthand. After the Battle of ST. ALBANS in 1455, Whethamstede asked leave of Richard PLANTAGENET, duke of York, to bury the bodies of Edmund BEAUFORT, duke of Somerset; Henry PERCY, earl of Northumberland; and Thomas CLIFFORD, Lord Clifford. During the second Battle of ST. ALBANS in 1461, the abbey was so heavily damaged that Whethamstede and his monks had to disperse to temporary quarters elsewhere.

In about 1457, Whethamstede wrote in his *Register* that Henry VI was "simplex et probus," which, in the context of the passage, would have been translated as "honest and upright." Some later historians used the comment to support the laudatory view of Henry put forward by John Blacman in his "COMPILATION OF THE MEEKNESS AND GOOD LIFE OF KING HENRY VI." However, after the Yorkist triumph in 1461, Whethamstede described Henry as "his mother's stupid offspring, not his father's, a son greatly degenerated from the father, who did not cultivate the art of war . . . a mild-spoken, pious king, but half-witted in affairs of state" (Wolffe, p. 19). Because of this seemingly radical change of heart, Whethamstede was accused by historians of transforming overnight from a staunch partisan of the house of LANCASTER to an ardent supporter of the house of YORK. But the abbott's earlier use of "simplex" may actually have hinted at his Yorkist sympathies; it may have been a veiled allusion to Henry's childish simplicity.

Although too anxious to please the party in power and too ready to accept myth and anecdote—e.g., he attributes the 1461 St. Albans defeat of Richard NEVILLE, earl of Warwick, to the ill effects of too much sun on the blood and resolution of southerners—Whethamstede provided useful accounts of such events as Henry VI's initial illness, the Battle of NORTHAMPTON, and York's attempt to claim the Crown (see HENRY VI, ILLNESS OF). Whethamstede died at St. Albans in January 1465.

Further Reading: Weiss, Roberto, *Humanism in England during the Fifteenth Century* (Oxford: Blackwell, 1967); "John Whetehamstede," in Michael Hicks, *Who's Who in Late Medieval England* (London: Shepheard-Walwyn, 1991), pp. 264–265; Wolffe, Bertram, *Henry VI* (London: Eyre Methuen, 1981).

Wiltshire, Earl of. *See* Butler, James, Earl of Wiltshire and Ormond

Winchester, Bishop of. *See* Courtenay, Peter; Wainfleet, William

Winchester, Earl of. *See* Gruthuyse, Louis de, Seigneur de la Gruthuyse, Earl of Winchester

Woodville, Anthony, Earl Rivers (c. 1442–1483)

Through his control of the person of EDWARD V and his leadership of the politically powerful WOODVILLE FAMILY, Anthony Woodville (or Wydeville), Earl Rivers, may have unwittingly helped convince Richard, duke of Gloucester (see RICHARD III), that it was in his best interest to seize the Crown from his nephew in 1483.

The eldest son of Richard WOODVILLE, Earl Rivers, and of JACQUETTA OF LUXEMBOURG, duchess of Bedford, Woodville, like his father, supported HENRY VI on the outbreak of war in 1459. In January 1460, Woodville and his father were captured at Sandwich by Yorkist raiders, who carried the two men to CALAIS, where they were soundly berated as social upstarts by the Yorkist leaders, Richard NEVILLE, earl of Warwick, and his father Richard NEVILLE, earl of Salisbury. Freed shortly thereafter, Woodville married the daughter of the Lancastrian peer, Thomas SCALES, Lord Scales. After fighting for the Lancastrians at the Battle of TOWTON in March 1461, Woodville transferred his allegiance to EDWARD IV and was recognized as Lord Scales in right of his wife in 1462.

In 1464, the king's marriage to Scales's elder sister, Elizabeth WOODVILLE, led, much to the chagrin of Warwick, to the rapid advancement at COURT of Scales and his numerous siblings. In June 1467, Scales, who was an accomplished knight, fought Anthony, the Bastard of BURGUNDY, the natural son of Duke PHILIP, in a tournament at Smithfield. Scales distinguished himself in the contest, which had been arranged in part to emphasize the Woodville connections, through Duchess Jacquetta, with the highest European nobility. Part of the embassy that negotiated the marriage of Edward's sister, MARGARET OF YORK, to Duke CHARLES of Burgundy, Scales accompanied the princess to her wedding in 1468. When Warwick launched his first coup attempt in July 1469, Edward sent the Woodvilles from his presence, both to protect them and to allay discontent. In August, after the defeat of the king's forces at the Battle of EDGECOTE, Scales's father and brother were executed by Warwick, though Scales—now Earl Rivers—escaped to rejoin the king after the collapse of Warwick's uprising. In April 1470, Rivers foiled Warwick's attempt to retrieve his ship *Trinity* from Southampton harbor and later in the summer defeated Warwick's fleet in the Seine.

When Warwick, now allied with Queen MARGARET OF ANJOU, forced Edward IV to flee the kingdom in October 1470, Rivers was one of the peers who shared the king's exile in Burgundy (see EDWARD IV, OVERTHROW OF). After spending the winter negotiating for shipping, Rivers returned to England with Edward in March 1471. He fought at the Battle of BARNET in April and was instrumental in driving Thomas NEVILLE, the Bastard of Fauconberg, from LONDON in May. In July, Rivers angered the king by asking leave to go abroad; although Edward granted the request, he replaced Rivers as lieutenant of Calais with William HASTINGS, Lord Hastings, an action that later caused ill feelings between Rivers and his successor. Rivers traveled widely during the 1470s. After returning from Portugal in 1472, he undertook pilgrimages to Compostella in Spain in 1473 and to Rome in 1475. In November 1473, Edward appointed Rivers governor of the young Prince of Wales, an important and powerful position that made its holder a political force in WALES and, potentially, in the next reign.

Upon the death of Edward IV in April 1483, Rivers was at Ludlow (on the Welsh border) with Edward V. Ordered by the COUNCIL in London to limit the size of the royal retinue, Rivers and the king left Ludlow on 24 April accompanied by 2,000 men. On 29 April at Stony Stratford, Rivers and his half nephew Richard Grey returned to Northampton to meet the king's uncle, Richard, duke of Gloucester, who was coming south with Henry STAFFORD, duke of Buckingham. Cordially received by the two dukes, Rivers and Grey were next day arrested and sent north in custody. Gloucester's apparent fears that the Woodvilles intended to control the minority government seemed confirmed when large quantities of arms were found in Rivers's baggage and Queen Elizabeth, upon hearing the news of Rivers's arrest, fled with her other children into SANCTUARY. On 25 June, Gloucester's servant Sir Richard RATCLIFFE executed Rivers, Grey, and Thomas VAUGHAN at Pontefract, likely without benefit of trial.

Rivers was the most cultured and popular member of his family. He was an early patron of the printer William CAXTON, whose first productions from his English press were Rivers's translations of *The Dictes and Sayings of the Philosophers* (1477) and the *Moral Proverbs* of Christine de Pisan (1478). Dominic MANCINI, the Italian observer who was present in London in 1483, was critical of the Woodvilles, but described Rivers as "a kind, serious and just man. . . . [who] had injured nobody, though benefiting many" (Ross, p.

98). Although a political realist who safe-guarded his family's interests, Rivers was also something of an ascetic, as evidenced by his many pilgrimages and the hair shirt he wore under his garments. Nonetheless, his influence over Edward V and the political and military resources he wielded as head of the extensive Woodville AFFINITY threatened Gloucester's future and persuaded the duke to strike down Rivers and seize the throne, actions that re-opened the WARS OF THE ROSES in 1483.

See also all other entries under Woodville
Further Reading: "Anthony Woodville," in Michael Hicks, *Who's Who in Late Medieval England* (London: Shepheard-Walwyn, 1991), pp. 346–348; MacGibbon, David, *Elizabeth Woodville: Her Life and Times* (London: A. Barker, 1938); Ross, Charles, *Edward IV* (New Haven, CT: Yale University Press, 1998).

Woodville, Elizabeth, Queen of England (c. 1437–1492)

Through her secret marriage to EDWARD IV, Elizabeth Woodville (or Wydeville), a shrewd and strong-willed woman, brought her large and ambitious family sufficient political power to alienate both Richard NEVILLE, earl of Warwick, and Richard, duke of Gloucester, and thereby helped to bring about the later phases of the WARS OF THE ROSES.

The daughter of Richard WOODVILLE, Lord Rivers, and JACQUETTA OF LUXEM-BOURG, duchess of Bedford, Elizabeth married Sir John Grey in about 1450. After Grey died fighting for HENRY VI at the Battle of ST. ALBANS in 1461, Elizabeth was denied her portion of the Grey estates by her mother-in-law and was forced to make suit to Edward IV for redress. The king was smitten by the attrac-tive widow, but his sexual advances were re-buffed, and he could only attain his desire by marrying Elizabeth secretly on May Day 1464. When revealed later in the year, the marriage, which was the first royal match with an Englishwoman since the thirteenth cen-tury, was immediately unpopular; it brought England no diplomatic advantages and saddled Edward with numerous in-laws seeking politi-cal influence and economic preferment.

Besides her parents, Elizabeth had five brothers, seven sisters, and two sons by her first husband. Because the king felt bound to find titles, lands, or marriages for these relatives, the Woodvilles soon claimed the bulk of royal pa-tronage. Feeling shut out from the king's bounty, and opposed to the pro-BURGUNDY foreign policy espoused by the queen's father and brothers, Warwick and the king's brother, George PLANTAGENET, duke of Clarence, launched a rebellion in 1469 and eventually overthrew Edward with French and Lancas-trian assistance in the autumn of 1470 (see ANGERS AGREEMENT; EDWARD IV, OVERTHROW OF). The queen, who eventu-ally bore Edward three sons and eight daugh-ters, was delivered of her first son, the future EDWARD V, while in SANCTUARY at West-minster in November. After Edward IV's restoration in 1471, the WOODVILLE FAMILY became the center of an increasingly powerful political faction, which was led by Elizabeth and her eldest brother, Anthony WOOD-VILLE, who had succeeded his father as Earl Rivers when the older man was executed by Warwick in 1469 (see EDWARD IV, RES-TORATION OF). The Woodvilles probably pressed for the destruction of Clarence in 1478 and, through Rivers's guardianship of the prince, positioned themselves to exercise a strong influence over the future king (see CLARENCE, EXECUTION OF).

On Edward IV's death in April 1483, Eliza-beth, with the assistance of her eldest son, Thomas GREY, marquis of Dorset, took charge in LONDON while Rivers conveyed Edward V to the capital from Ludlow. Seeking to establish immediate Woodville dominance, the queen attempted to have the twelve-year-old king declared of sufficient age to rule. This device aroused strong opposition and gave Richard, duke of Gloucester, the king's surviv-ing paternal uncle, the initial support he needed to establish a protectorate and eventu-ally usurp the throne (see USURPATION OF 1483). Gloucester seized custody of the king; executed Rivers and the queen's son Richard Grey; and forced Elizabeth to seek sanctuary at Westminster with her remaining children. Although convinced (or compelled) to yield her younger son, Richard PLANTAGENET, duke of York, to Gloucester's custody in June 1483, Elizabeth was soon persuaded that Gloucester (now ruling as RICHARD III) had slain both her sons, for in the following autumn she helped plan BUCKINGHAM'S REBELLION, which aimed at replacing Richard with Henry Tudor, earl of Richmond. Elizabeth joined the uprising on the understanding that Richmond would marry her eldest daughter, ELIZABETH OF YORK, once he had secured the Crown.

In March 1484, several months after the rebellion failed, Elizabeth accepted a pension and her daughters' reception at COURT as the price for leaving sanctuary and abandoning Richmond. Although Richmond (then HENRY VII) married Elizabeth of York in January 1486, five months after winning the Crown at the Battle of BOSWORTH FIELD, he showed little favor to his mother-in-law. In 1487, the ex-queen fell under suspicion of supporting the Yorkist plot then forming around Lambert SIMNEL. Henry deprived Elizabeth of her property and dispatched her to Bermondsey Abbey, where she remained until her death in June 1492.

> **See also** all other entries under Woodville
> **Further Reading:** "Elizabeth Woodville," in Michael Hicks, *Who's Who in Late Medieval England* (London: Shepheard-Walwyn, 1991), pp. 325–327; MacGibbon, David, *Elizabeth Woodville: Her Life and Times* (London: A. Barker, 1938); Ross, Charles, *Edward IV* (New Haven, CT: Yale University Press, 1998).

Woodville Family

Between 1464 and 1483, the Woodvilles, the family of EDWARD IV's queen, comprised the most favored and resented political grouping in England. Jealousy over their rapid rise to power at the Yorkist COURT, coupled with hatred caused by their greed, ambition, and arrogance, made the Woodvilles a disruptive political influence that was partially responsible for the USURPATION OF 1483 and the eventual fall of the house of YORK.

The Woodvilles' social rise was based on two spectacular mésalliances. The first, in

1436, was the secret marriage of Richard WOODVILLE, a Northamptonshire gentleman, to JACQUETTA OF LUXEMBOURG, the widowed duchess of Bedford and a descendent of European nobility. The second, in 1464, was the secret marriage of their eldest daughter, Elizabeth WOODVILLE, to Edward IV. Prior to 1461, Woodville, then Lord Rivers, had been a Lancastrian; he and his eldest son Anthony WOODVILLE, Lord Scales, had fought for HENRY VI at the Battle of TOWTON, while Elizabeth's first husband, Sir John Grey of Groby, died fighting for the house of LANCASTER at the Battle of ST. ALBANS in 1461. After Towton, Rivers submitted, and by 1463 he was a member of Edward IV's COUNCIL. However, the family's political and social advancement became unprecedented in speed and scope after the king's marriage to Elizabeth.

Other than her beauty, the new queen brought her husband no political advantages and a host of problems, not the least of which was providing for her large family, which, besides her parents, included five brothers, seven sisters, and two sons by Grey. Between 1464 and 1466, Edward and the queen obtained numerous highborn spouses for unmarried Woodvilles. Several of these marriages angered Richard NEVILLE, earl of Warwick, the king's chief advisor. For instance, in 1464, Margaret Woodville married Warwick's nephew, the son of the earl of Arundel. In 1465, the court was shocked by the marriage of twenty-year-old John Woodville to Warwick's kinswoman, Katherine Neville, the sixty-five-year-old dowager duchess of Norfolk. The marriages of Anne Woodville to the son of Henry BOURCHIER, earl of Essex; of Eleanor Woodville to the son of Edmund GREY, earl of Kent; and of Katherine Woodville to Henry STAFFORD, duke of Buckingham, deprived Warwick's daughters, Isabel and Anne NEVILLE, of prospective husbands. The marriage of the queen's son, Thomas GREY, to the daughter of Henry HOLLAND, duke of Exeter, claimed the bride who had been promised to the son of Warwick's brother, John NEVILLE, Lord Montagu. Nor was Warwick happy with the marriage of Mary Woodville to the son of William HERBERT, the earl's rival for lands and influence in WALES.

Although Warwick ascribed his declining influence with the king to the Woodvilles, most of the English nobility accepted the family and sought to exploit their favor at court. Nonetheless, the Woodvilles were highly unpopular. With the exception of Scales, who became head of the family as Earl Rivers after Warwick executed his father in 1469, contemporary observers characterized the Woodvilles as greedy, ambitious, overbearing, and a malign influence on the king. For instance, in 1468, the family's ill-treatment of Sir Thomas COOK was said to have cost that LONDON merchant his fortune and turned him into a convinced Lancastrian, and in the 1480s, the Grey brothers and Edward Woodville were condemned for encouraging the king's drinking and womanizing. Although Warwick's desertion of the house of York in 1470 was a result of the king's independence and the earl's ambition, Warwick's hatred for the Woodvilles was a contributing factor. In the 1470s, Woodville influence seemed even more sinister as it increased while the competition disappeared—the NEVILLE FAMILY was destroyed in 1471; the king's one brother, George PLANTAGENET, duke of Clarence, was executed in 1478; and his other brother, Richard, duke of Gloucester (see RICHARD III), withdrew from court to govern the north.

At Edward IV's death in 1483, the reign of EDWARD V seemed likely to open with a Woodville-dominated regency, a prospect that frightened many noblemen, including Gloucester and William HASTINGS, Lord Hastings, a close friend of the late king and a rival of both Rivers and of the queen's son, Thomas Grey, marquis of Dorset. As governor of the prince after 1473, Rivers controlled the person of the new king and exercised great power in Wales, where he could quickly recruit large numbers of men. In London, the queen and Dorset controlled the TOWER OF LONDON, the royal treasure, and the young king's brother, Richard PLANTAGENET, duke of York, while Sir Edward Woodville controlled

the fleet. Gloucester probably had good cause to fear for his future in a Woodville-dominated government. By playing on the family's unpopularity, Gloucester was able to mask his own ambitions and to convince men like Hastings to support his initial moves to control the regency. Unable to generate much support from other nobles, the Woodville influence was in ruins by the end of 1483. Rivers and Sir Richard Grey were executed, Dorset and Bishop Lionel WOODVILLE were in exile, the queen was in SANCTUARY, and Gloucester was king as Richard III. The usurpation of Edward V's throne and the subsequent disappearance and probable murder of the young king and his brother were in some part made possible by the actions and unpopularity of the Woodville family (see PRINCES IN THE TOWER; USURPATION OF 1483).

See also: Appendix 1, "Genealogies"
Further Reading: Hicks, Michael, "The Changing Role of the Wydevilles in Yorkist Politics to 1483," in Charles Ross, ed., *Patronage, Pedigree and Power in Later Medieval England* (Stroud, Gloucestershire, UK: Alan Sutton, 1979), pp. 60–86; MacGibbon, David, *Elizabeth Woodville: Her Life and Times* (London: A. Barker, 1938); Ross, Charles, *Edward IV* (New Haven, CT: Yale University Press, 1998).

Woodville, Lionel, Bishop of Salisbury (c. 1446–1484)

The third son of Richard WOODVILLE, Earl Rivers, and the brother of Elizabeth WOODVILLE, wife of EDWARD IV, Lionel Woodville (or Wydeville), bishop of Salisbury, involved himself in the political turmoil of 1483 by helping to plan BUCKINGHAM'S REBELLION against RICHARD III.

Educated at Oxford in canon (i.e., church) law, Woodville began his ecclesiastical career in 1478 when he was appointed dean of Exeter (i.e., head of a community of clergy residing at Exeter Cathedral). A year later, he was made chancellor of Oxford University, and in 1480 he acquired a prebendary (i.e., an endowment for the support of clerical services) at St. Paul's Cathedral in LONDON. In 1482, he received the wealthy bishopric of Salisbury.

Woodville was in London when Edward IV died in April 1483; the bishop fled into SANCTUARY at Westminster with his sister the queen when they learned of the arrest of their brother Anthony WOODVILLE, earl Rivers, by Richard, duke of Gloucester, as Rivers was escorting his nephew, EDWARD V, to the capital. By June, Woodville had left sanctuary, but in the autumn, after Richard III had usurped the throne and, according to rumor, had ordered the murders of Edward V and his brother, Woodville helped organize a rebellion of Woodville supporters and former servants of Edward IV that aimed at placing Henry Tudor, earl of Richmond (see HENRY VII), on the throne. When the uprising failed, Woodville fled the country to join Richmond in BRITTANY, where the bishop died in June 1484.

See also Richard Plantagenet, Duke of York (d. c. 1483); Henry Stafford, Duke of Buckingham; all other entries under Woodville
Further Reading: MacGibbon, David, *Elizabeth Woodville: Her Life and Times* (London: A. Barker, 1938); Ross, Charles, *Edward IV* (New Haven, CT: Yale University Press, 1998); Ross, Charles, *Richard III* (Berkeley: University of California Press, 1981).

Woodville, Richard, Earl Rivers (c. 1410–1469)

Richard Woodville (or Wydeville), Earl Rivers, was the father-in-law of EDWARD IV and the head of a large and ambitious family whose advancement by the king in the 1460s helped provoke Richard NEVILLE, earl of Warwick, to rebel against the house of YORK.

Born into a minor GENTRY family in Northamptonshire, Woodville was knighted by HENRY VI in 1426 and served in FRANCE in the 1430s. His surreptitious marriage in 1436 to JACQUETTA OF LUXEMBOURG, the young widow of John, duke of Bedford, Henry VI's uncle, transformed Woodville's fortunes and social standing. Although this shocking (for the time) mésalliance cost the bride a £1,000 fine and forced the groom to obtain a royal pardon, it also allowed

Woodville to advance himself by drawing upon his wife's family connections with the highest nobility of Europe. The match also helped Woodville rise into the PEERAGE as Lord Rivers, in 1448, and produced fourteen or fifteen children, a brood that later allowed the Woodvilles to marry into the leading families of England.

In the 1450s, Rivers helped suppress JACK CADE'S REBELLION and served in CALAIS as a lieutenant of Edmund BEAUFORT, duke of Somerset. A partisan of the house of LANCASTER, Rivers was entrusted in 1459 with guarding Sandwich against an invasion from Calais by Warwick. When a Yorkist force swept down on the town in January 1460, it surprised Rivers in his bed and carried him and his eldest son, Anthony WOODVILLE, to Calais, where Warwick castigated them as traitors and parvenus. Having gained his freedom by unknown means, Rivers fought for Lancaster at the Battle of TOWTON in March 1461, but by August had abandoned Henry VI and submitted to Edward IV.

In 1464, a second mésalliance, the secret marriage of his widowed daughter Elizabeth WOODVILLE to Edward IV, once again revived River's fortunes. The king appointed Rivers treasurer, advanced him to an earldom, and married his children into the oldest and wealthiest noble families. The ambition and avarice of Rivers and his large family earned the Woodvilles great unpopularity and the enmity of Warwick, whose own political ambitions were threatened by the growing Woodville influence. When Warwick broke openly with Edward IV in 1469, he gave the king's close association with lowborn counselors like Rivers as a primary reason for his actions. In July 1469, when the king became Warwick's prisoner after the Battle of EDGECOTE, Rivers and his son Sir John Woodville were dragged from hiding and carried to Coventry, where both were executed by Warwick's order on 12 August.

See also all other entries under Woodville
Further Reading: MacGibbon, David, *Elizabeth Woodville: Her Life and Times* (London: A. Barker,

1938); "Richard Woodville," in Michael Hicks, *Who's Who in Late Medieval England* (London: Shepheard-Walwyn, 1991), pp. 328–329; Ross, Charles, *Edward IV* (New Haven, CT: Yale University Press, 1998); Weir, Alison, *The Wars of the Roses* (New York: Ballantine Books, 1995).

Worcester, Earl of. *See* Tiptoft, John, Earl of Worcester

Wydeville. *See* all entries under Woodville

York, Archbishop of. *See* Booth, Lawrence; Neville, George; Rotherham, Thomas

York, Duchess of. *See* Neville, Cecily, Duchess of York

York, Duke of. *See* two entries under Plantagenet, Richard, Duke of York

York, House of (1461–1470, 1471–1485)

A branch of the royal family of Plantagenet, which had ruled England since 1154, the house of York and its partisans comprised one of the parties contending for the throne during the WARS OF THE ROSES.

The family of York descended from Edmund, first duke of York (1341–1402), the fourth son of Edward III (r. 1327–1377). Because Richard II (r. 1377–1399), Edward III's grandson and heir, was childless, the legal succession to the throne came to rest with the Mortimer family, descendants of Richard II's eldest uncle (and Edward III's second son), Lionel, duke of Clarence (1338–1368). However, in 1399, Henry of Bolingbroke, son of John of Gaunt, duke of Lancaster (1340–1399), third son of Edward III, deposed his cousin Richard II and assumed the throne as Henry IV (r. 1399–1413), first king of the Lancastrian branch of the royal family (see RICHARD II, DEPOSITION OF).

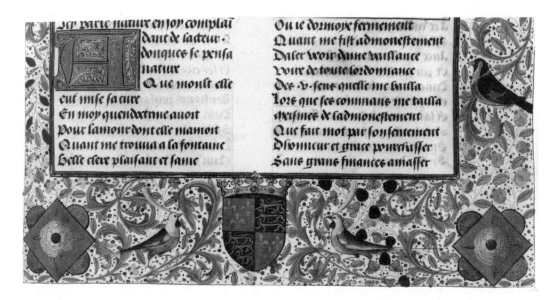

The white rose, shown here decorating the border of a fifteenth-century manuscript, was the best-known badge of the house of York. (Royal MS 14 E II f. 77, British Library)

Because the Lancastrian usurpation of 1399 bypassed the proper heirs, several people had a claim to the Crown that was technically superior to that of the ruling dynasty. When the last direct Mortimer heir died in 1425, the family's claim passed to their Yorkist cousins in the person of Richard PLANTAGENET, third duke of York, the son of Anne Mortimer (1390–1411). By the 1440s, York was informally recognized as heir presumptive to the (then) childless HENRY VI, third king of the house of LANCASTER. Although York made no claim to the throne, he did revive the royal family's ancient surname of Plantagenet, perhaps to emphasize his right to a special position in his Lancastrian cousin's government (see PLANTAGENET, HOUSE OF). The Wars of the Roses emerged in the 1450s from the desire of York to rule on behalf of an incompetent Henry VI, an ambition that was thwarted for much of the decade by Queen MARGARET OF ANJOU and the clique of royal favorites who supported her.

In 1460, when York finally made formal claim to the Crown, the queen's faction coalesced around Henry VI as the core of the Lancastrian party, while the local rivals of Lancastrian courtiers and other nobles who felt excluded from power formed around York as the core of the Yorkist party. Although York failed to achieve his ambition, dying at the Battle of WAKEFIELD in December 1460, his eldest son, proclaimed as EDWARD IV, secured the throne at the Battle of TOWTON in March 1461. The civil wars revived in 1470 when an uneasy alliance between the Lancastrians and the NEVILLE FAMILY, former Yorkist allies led by Richard NEVILLE, earl of Warwick, briefly restored Henry VI (see EDWARD IV, OVERTHROW OF). In the spring of 1471, Edward IV regained the throne at the Battles of BARNET and TEWKESBURY; the death at Tewkesbury of EDWARD OF LANCASTER, Prince of Wales, freed Edward IV to liquidate the direct male line of Lancaster by ordering the murder of the imprisoned Henry VI in May (see HENRY VI, MURDER OF).

After 1471, the Wars of the Roses appeared finished and the house of York seemed secure;

however, the conflict reignited in 1483, and the dynasty fell from power in 1485. The downfall of York flowed from the death of Edward IV at age forty, in 1483, and the subsequent supersession and likely murder of his twelve-year-old son, EDWARD V, by the boy's paternal uncle, who assumed the throne as RICHARD III (see PRINCES IN THE TOWER; USURPATION OF 1483). This usurpation created a coalition of former Lancastrians and dissident Yorkists around Henry Tudor, earl of Richmond, who, through his mother, Margaret BEAUFORT, inherited the Lancastrian claim to the Crown (see BEAUFORT FAMILY). Richard III's death at the Battle of BOSWORTH FIELD in 1485 ended Yorkist rule and enthroned Richmond as HENRY VII, first monarch of the house of TUDOR.

Although Henry sought to unite the royal lines of Lancaster and York by marrying ELIZABETH OF YORK, daughter of Edward IV, the Tudor dynasty was actively menaced for over a decade by plots and invasions aimed at restoring the house of York. Centering on pretenders impersonating either a son of Edward IV or Edward PLANTAGENET, earl of Warwick, the last Yorkist claimant in the direct male line, these attempts were all unsuccessful (see SIMNEL, LAMBERT; WARBECK, PERKIN). Hopes for a Yorkist restoration faded in the sixteenth century as Henry VIII, the second Tudor monarch and a grandson of Edward IV, gradually eliminated the children of Edward IV's sisters and daughters (see YORKIST HEIRS [AFTER 1485]).

See also: Appendix 1, "Genealogies"
Further Reading: Johnson, P. A., *Duke Richard of York* (Oxford: Clarendon Press, 1988); Ross, Charles, *Edward IV* (New Haven, CT: Yale University Press, 1998); Ross, Charles, *Richard III* (Berkeley: University of California Press, 1981).

Yorkist Heirs (after 1485)

When HENRY VII overthrew RICHARD III and the house of YORK at the Battle of BOSWORTH FIELD in 1485, many descendants of Richard PLANTAGENET, duke of

York, remained alive to challenge the house of TUDOR and its possession of the throne.

With continuance of their dynasty threatened by their own failure to produce healthy male heirs, Henry VII and his sole surviving son and successor Henry VIII executed many persons of Yorkist blood to eliminate any possibility of a Yorkist restoration. The most dangerous plots during Henry VII's reign centered on impostors, such as Lambert SIMNEL and Perkin WARBECK, who claimed to be, but in fact were not, members of the house of York. The uncertainty over the fate of EDWARD V and his brother Richard PLANTAGENET, duke of York, the sons of EDWARD IV who disappeared in the TOWER OF LONDON in 1483, made such impostures particularly effective. After 1485, York's last direct descendent in the male line was the duke's grandson, Edward PLANTAGENET, earl of Warwick, the son of George PLANTAGENET, duke of Clarence. One of Henry VII's first acts as king was to secure the person of Warwick and confine him in the Tower, where he remained until his execution for treason in 1499.

With Warwick imprisoned, the leading Yorkist heirs were the sons of Edward IV's sister, Elizabeth, and her husband, John de la POLE, duke of Suffolk. The eldest, John de la POLE, earl of Lincoln, involved himself in the Simnel conspiracy and died at the Battle of STOKE in 1487. In 1499, Lincoln's younger brother, Edmund de la Pole, earl of Suffolk, fled to CALAIS, where he remained for a time with Sir James TYRELL, the governor of one of the Calais fortresses. Suffolk returned to England shortly thereafter and was taken back into favor until 1501, when he and his brother Richard fled to the court of Maximilian I and tried to convince the emperor to fund an attempt on the English throne. Henry arrested a third de la Pole brother, William, and imprisoned him in the Tower, where he stayed until his death in 1539. In 1502, the king also took advantage of Suffolk's connection with Tyrell to make the rise of any future Yorkist impostors more difficult. Tyrell was an ideal instrument for this purpose; a former servant of Richard III now awaiting execution for his involvement with Suffolk, Tyrell confessed to having murdered the sons of Edward IV in 1483 on Richard's orders. With his own eldest son, Prince Arthur, having recently died, Henry VII wanted it made clear that the PRINCES IN THE TOWER were dead. Although the confession could be genuine, the circumstances and timing of Tyrell's revelation cast doubt on the truth of its claims.

Suffolk, meanwhile, was unable to interest a continental monarch in his enterprise and remained safely in the Netherlands until 1506, when Duke Philip of BURGUNDY concluded a treaty with Henry VII that required the duke to cease supporting Henry's enemies. Suffolk was duly surrendered to the English at Calais and remained in the Tower until 1513 when his brother was recognized as "Richard IV" by Louis XII of FRANCE, an act that prompted Henry VIII to execute Suffolk. Richard de la Pole later served as a soldier in Hungary and in France, and died in 1525 fighting for Francis I at the Battle of Pavia.

In the late 1530s, after the birth of his long awaited male heir, Henry VIII resumed the destruction of the house of York with a series of judicial murders. In 1538, he executed Henry Courtenay, marquis of Exeter, the son of Edward IV's daughter Katherine, and, in 1541, he eliminated Warwick's sixty-eight-year-old sister, Margaret Pole, Countess of Salisbury. The Countess's eldest son, Henry Pole, Lord Montague, had also gone to the block in 1538. By his death in 1547, Henry VIII, himself a grandson of Edward IV, had almost fulfilled his openly avowed intention of extinguishing his Yorkist relatives.

Further Reading: Arthurson, Ian, *The Perkin Warbeck Conspiracy, 1491–1499* (Stroud, Gloucestershire, UK: Sutton Publishing, 1997); Bennett, Michael J., *Lambert Simnel and the Battle of Stoke* (New York: St. Martin's Press, 1987); Chrimes, S. B., *Henry VII* (New Haven, CT: Yale University Press, 1999); Chrimes, S. B., *Lancastrians, Yorkists and Henry VII,* 2d ed. (New York: St. Martin's Press, 1966).

Appendix 1
Genealogies

House of Lancaster and Beaufort Family

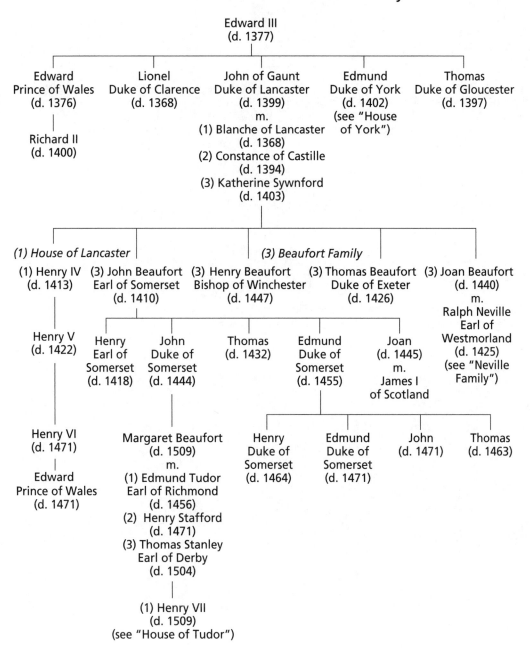

Edward III
(d. 1377)

Edward Prince of Wales (d. 1376)	Lionel Duke of Clarence (d. 1368)	John of Gaunt Duke of Lancaster (d. 1399)	Edmund Duke of York (d. 1402) (see "House of York")	Thomas Duke of Gloucester (d. 1397)

Richard II
(d. 1400)

John of Gaunt m.
(1) Blanche of Lancaster (d. 1368)
(2) Constance of Castille (d. 1394)
(3) Katherine Sywnford (d. 1403)

(1) House of Lancaster　　　　　*(3) Beaufort Family*

(1) Henry IV
(d. 1413)

(3) John Beaufort
Earl of Somerset
(d. 1410)

(3) Henry Beaufort
Bishop of Winchester
(d. 1447)

(3) Thomas Beaufort
Duke of Exeter
(d. 1426)

(3) Joan Beaufort
(d. 1440)
m.
Ralph Neville
Earl of
Westmorland
(d. 1425)
(see "Neville
Family")

Henry V
(d. 1422)

Henry
Earl of
Somerset
(d. 1418)

John
Duke of
Somerset
(d. 1444)

Thomas
(d. 1432)

Edmund
Duke of
Somerset
(d. 1455)

Joan
(d. 1445)
m.
James I
of Scotland

Henry VI
(d. 1471)

Edward
Prince of Wales
(d. 1471)

Margaret Beaufort
(d. 1509)
m.
(1) Edmund Tudor
Earl of Richmond
(d. 1456)
(2) Henry Stafford
(d. 1471)
(3) Thomas Stanley
Earl of Derby
(d. 1504)

Henry
Duke of
Somerset
(d. 1464)

Edmund
Duke of
Somerset
(d. 1471)

John
(d. 1471)

Thomas
(d. 1463)

(1) Henry VII
(d. 1509)
(see "House of Tudor")

Neville Family

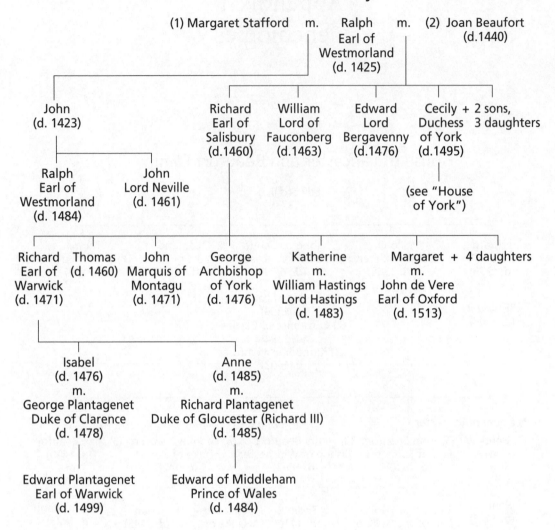

(1) Margaret Stafford   m.   Ralph   m.   (2) Joan Beaufort
Earl of   (d.1440)
Westmorland
(d. 1425)

John
(d. 1423)

Richard   William   Edward   Cecily + 2 sons,
Earl of   Lord of   Lord   Duchess   3 daughters
Salisbury   Fauconberg   Bergavenny   of York
(d.1460)   (d.1463)   (d.1476)   (d.1495)

Ralph   John
Earl of   Lord Neville
Westmorland   (d. 1461)
(d. 1484)

(see "House
of York")

Richard   Thomas   John   George   Katherine   Margaret + 4 daughters
Earl of   (d. 1460)   Marquis of   Archbishop   m.   m.
Warwick   Montagu   of York   William Hastings   John de Vere
(d. 1471)   (d. 1471)   (d. 1476)   Lord Hastings   Earl of Oxford
                                  (d. 1483)   (d. 1513)

Isabel   Anne
(d. 1476)   (d. 1485)
m.   m.
George Plantagenet   Richard Plantagenet
Duke of Clarence   Duke of Gloucester (Richard III)
(d. 1478)   (d. 1485)

Edward Plantagenet   Edward of Middleham
Earl of Warwick   Prince of Wales
(d. 1499)   (d. 1484)

House of Tudor

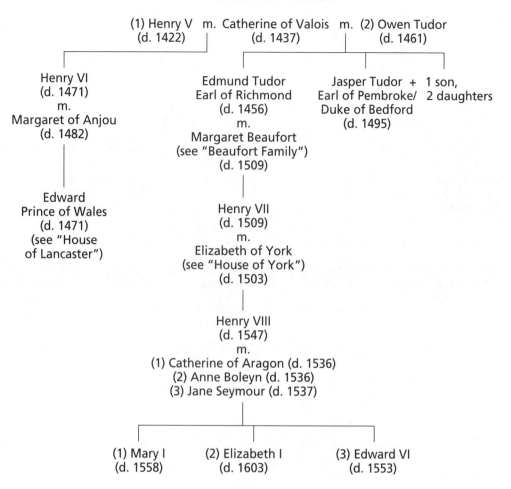

(1) Henry V   m. Catherine of Valois   m. (2) Owen Tudor
(d. 1422)   (d. 1437)   (d. 1461)

Henry VI
(d. 1471)
m.
Margaret of Anjou
(d. 1482)

Edmund Tudor
Earl of Richmond
(d. 1456)
m.
Margaret Beaufort
(see "Beaufort Family")
(d. 1509)

Jasper Tudor + 1 son,
Earl of Pembroke/   2 daughters
Duke of Bedford
(d. 1495)

Edward
Prince of Wales
(d. 1471)
(see "House
of Lancaster")

Henry VII
(d. 1509)
m.
Elizabeth of York
(see "House of York")
(d. 1503)

Henry VIII
(d. 1547)
m.
(1) Catherine of Aragon (d. 1536)
(2) Anne Boleyn (d. 1536)
(3) Jane Seymour (d. 1537)

(1) Mary I
(d. 1558)

(2) Elizabeth I
(d. 1603)

(3) Edward VI
(d. 1553)

Woodville Family

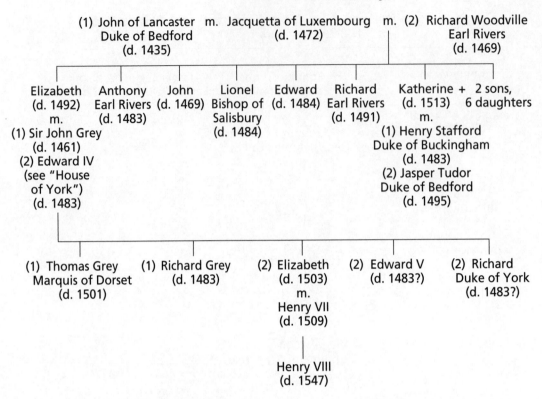

(1) John of Lancaster   m.   Jacquetta of Luxembourg   m.   (2) Richard Woodville
Duke of Bedford   (d. 1472)   Earl Rivers
(d. 1435)   (d. 1469)

Elizabeth (d. 1492) m. (1) Sir John Grey (d. 1461) (2) Edward IV (see "House of York") (d. 1483)

Anthony Earl Rivers (d. 1483)

John (d. 1469)

Lionel Bishop of Salisbury (d. 1484)

Edward (d. 1484)

Richard Earl Rivers (d. 1491)

Katherine (d. 1513) m. (1) Henry Stafford Duke of Buckingham (d. 1483) (2) Jasper Tudor Duke of Bedford (d. 1495)

+ 2 sons, 6 daughters

(1) Thomas Grey Marquis of Dorset (d. 1501)

(1) Richard Grey (d. 1483)

(2) Elizabeth (d. 1503) m. Henry VII (d. 1509)

(2) Edward V (d. 1483?)

(2) Richard Duke of York (d. 1483?)

Henry VIII (d. 1547)

House of York

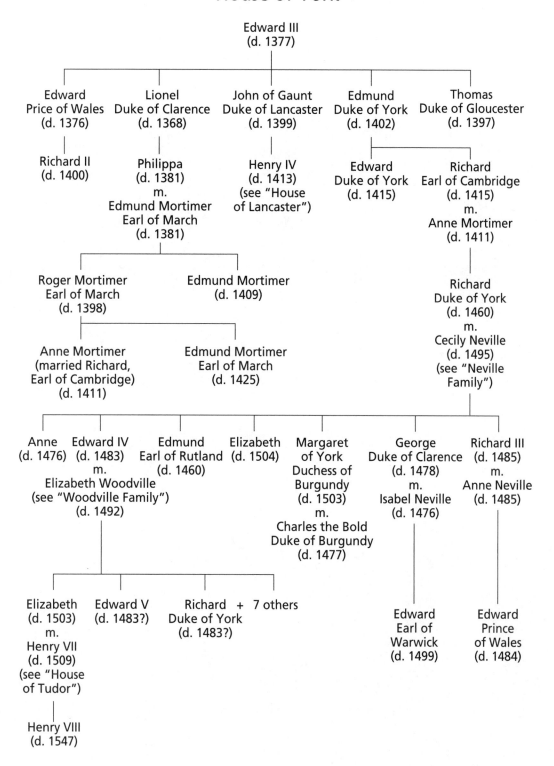

Edward III
(d. 1377)

Edward
Price of Wales
(d. 1376)

Lionel
Duke of Clarence
(d. 1368)

John of Gaunt
Duke of Lancaster
(d. 1399)

Edmund
Duke of York
(d. 1402)

Thomas
Duke of Gloucester
(d. 1397)

Richard II
(d. 1400)

Philippa
(d. 1381)
m.
Edmund Mortimer
Earl of March
(d. 1381)

Henry IV
(d. 1413)
(see "House
of Lancaster")

Edward
Duke of York
(d. 1415)

Richard
Earl of Cambridge
(d. 1415)
m.
Anne Mortimer
(d. 1411)

Roger Mortimer
Earl of March
(d. 1398)

Edmund Mortimer
(d. 1409)

Richard
Duke of York
(d. 1460)
m.
Cecily Neville
(d. 1495)
(see "Neville
Family")

Anne Mortimer
(married Richard,
Earl of Cambridge)
(d. 1411)

Edmund Mortimer
Earl of March
(d. 1425)

Anne
(d. 1476)

Edward IV
(d. 1483)
m.
Elizabeth Woodville
(see "Woodville Family")
(d. 1492)

Edmund
Earl of Rutland
(d. 1460)

Elizabeth
(d. 1504)

Margaret
of York
Duchess of
Burgundy
(d. 1503)
m.
Charles the Bold
Duke of Burgundy
(d. 1477)

George
Duke of Clarence
(d. 1478)
m.
Isabel Neville
(d. 1476)

Richard III
(d. 1485)
m.
Anne Neville
(d. 1485)

Elizabeth
(d. 1503)
m.
Henry VII
(d. 1509)
(see "House
of Tudor")

Edward V
(d. 1483?)

Richard
Duke of York
(d. 1483?)

+ 7 others

Edward
Earl of
Warwick
(d. 1499)

Edward
Prince
of Wales
(d. 1484)

Henry VIII
(d. 1547)

Appendix 2
Map of Wars of the Roses Battle Sites

Appendix 3
Table of Dynastic Affiliations

Name	1455	1459–1461	1469–1471	1483–1485	1485–1499
Beaufort, Edmund, Duke of Somerset (d. 1455)	L★				
Beaufort, Edmund, Duke of Somerset (d. 1471)		L	L★		
Beaufort, Henry, Duke of Somerset	L	L	L★		
Beaufort, Margaret, Countess of Richmond and Derby			L	T	T
Beaumont, William, Lord Beaumont			L		
Blount, Walter, Lord Mountjoy		Y	Y		
Bonville, William, Lord Bonville	L	Y★			
Booth, Lawrence, Archbishop of York		L			
Bourchier, Henry, Earl of Essex		Y	Y		
Bourchier, Thomas, Cardinal Archbishop of Canterbury		Y	Y		
Brackenbury, Sir Robert				R★	
Bray, Sir Reginald				T	T
Brézé, Pierre de, Seneschal of Normandy		L (1462–1463)			
Butler, James, Earl of Wiltshire and Ormond	L	L★			
Catesby, William				R★	
Clifford, John, Lord Clifford	L	L★			
Clifford, Thomas, Lord Clifford	L★				
Cook, Sir Thomas			L		
Courtenay, Henry, Earl of Devon			L★		
Courtenay, John, Earl of Devon		L	L★		
Courtenay, Peter, Bishop of Winchester			W	T	
Courtenay, Thomas, Earl of Devon (d. 1458)	L				
Courtenay, Thomas, Earl of Devon (d. 1461)		L★			
Devereux, Walter, Lord Ferrers of Chartley		Y	Y	R★	
Dinham, John, Lord Dinham		Y	Y	R	T
Edward of Lancaster, Prince of Wales			L★		
Fitzgerald, Gerald, Earl of Kildare				R	Y
Fitzgerald, Thomas, Earl of Desmond		Y			
Fitzgerald, Thomas, Earl of Kildare		Y	Y		
Fortescue, Sir John		L	L		
Grey, Edmund, Earl of Kent		L/Y	Y	R	
Grey, Thomas, Marquis of Dorset				T	T
Hastings, William, Lord Hastings		Y	Y	E★	
Herbert, William, Earl of Pembroke		Y	Y★		
Holland, Henry, Duke of Exeter	L	L	L		

(continues)

Name	1455	1459–1461	1469–1471	1483–1485	1485–1499
Howard, John, Duke of Norfolk		Y	Y	R★	
Howard, Thomas, Earl of Surrey and Duke of Norfolk			Y	R	T
Hungerford, Robert, Lord Hungerford		L★			
Hungerford, Sir Thomas			L★		
Hungerford, Sir Walter				E/T	T
Jacquetta of Luxembourg, Duchess of Bedford		L	Y		
Kennedy, James, Bishop of St. Andrews		L			
Langstrother, Sir John, Prior of the Hospital of St. John of Jerusalem			W/L★		
Lovell, Francis, Viscount Lovell				R★	
Margaret of Anjou, Queen of England	L	L	L		
Margaret of York, Duchess of Burgundy			Y	R	Y
Mary of Gueldres, Queen of Scotland		L			
Morton, John, Cardinal Archbishop of Canterbury		L	L	E/T	T
Mowbray, John, Duke of Norfolk (d. 1461)		Y			
Mowbray, John, Duke of Norfolk (d. 1476)			Y		
Neville, George, Archbishop of York		Y	W/L		
Neville, Sir Humphrey		L	W/L★		
Neville, John, Earl of Northumberland and Marquis of Montagu		Y	W/L★		
Neville, John, Lord Neville		L★			
Neville, Richard, Earl of Salisbury	Y	Y★			
Neville, Richard, Earl of Warwick	Y	Y	W/L★		
Neville, Sir Thomas	Y	Y★			
Neville, Thomas, Bastard of Fauconberg			W/L★		
Neville, William, Lord Fauconberg and Earl of Kent		Y			
Percy, Henry, Earl of Northumberland (d. 1455)	L★				
Percy, Henry, Earl of Northumberland (d. 1461)		L★			
Percy, Henry, Earl of Northumberland (d. 1489)			Y	R	T
Percy, Thomas, Lord Egremont		L★			
Plantagenet, Edmund, Earl of Rutland		Y★			
Plantagenet, George, Duke of Clarence			W/Y		
Plantagenet, Richard, Duke of York (d. 1460)	Y	Y★			
Pole, John de la, Duke of Suffolk		Y	Y	R★	T
Pole, John de la, Earl of Lincoln				R	Y★
Ratcliffe, Sir Richard				R★	
Rhys ap Thomas				T	T
Roos, Thomas, Lord Roos		L★			
Rotherham, Thomas, Archbishop of York			Y	E	
Russell, John, Bishop of Lincoln				R	T
Scales, Thomas, Lord Scales		L★			
Stafford, Henry, Duke of Buckingham				R/T★	
Stafford, Humphrey, Duke of Buckingham	L	L★			
Stafford, Humphrey, Earl of Devon		Y	Y★		
Stanley, Thomas, Earl of Derby		L/Y	Y	T	T

(continues)

Name	1455	1459–1461	1469–1471	1483–1485	1485–1499
Stanley, Sir William		Y	Y	T	Y★
Stillington, Robert, Bishop of Bath and Wells		Y	Y	R	
Tailboys, Sir William		L★			
Thomas ap Gruffydd		L	L★		
Tiptoft, John, Earl of Worster			Y★		
Touchet, James, Lord Audley		L★			
Trollope, Sir Andrew		L★			
Tudor, Edmund, Earl of Richmond	L				
Tudor, Jasper, Earl of Pembroke and Duke of Bedford	L	L	L	T	T
Tudor, Owen		L★			
Tunstall, Sir Richard		L	L	?	T
Tyrell, Sir James			Y	R	T
Urswick, Christopher				T	T
Vaughan, Sir Thomas		Y	Y	E★	
Vere, John de, Earl of Oxford			L	T	T
Wainfleet, William, Bishop of Winchester		L	L		
Warbeck, Perkin					Y★
Wenlock, John, Lord Wenlock		Y	W/L★		
Woodville, Anthony, Earl Rivers		L	Y	E★	
Woodville, Elizabeth, Queen of England			Y	E	
Woodville, Lionel, Bishop of Salisbury			Y	E/T	
Woodville, Richard, Earl Rivers		L	Y★		

L= Lancastrian; Y = Yorkist; T = Tudor; W = Warwick/Clarence, 1469–1471; R = Richard III, 1483–1485; E = Edward V, 1483; ★killed in battle or executed afterward

Appendix 4
Involvement of the Higher Peerage
in the Wars of the Roses

Title/Duke	Outcome of Involvement
Dukes of Bedford	
George Neville	Deprived of title in 1478; died 1483
Jasper Tudor	Fought for houses of Lancaster and Tudor; died 1495
Dukes of Buckingham	
Humphrey Stafford	Slain at the Battle of Northampton in 1460
Henry Stafford	Executed in 1483
Duke of Clarence	
George Plantagenet	Executed in 1478
Duke of Exeter	
Henry Holland	Fought for house of Lancaster; died 1475
Duke of Gloucester	
Richard Plantagenet (became Richard III in 1483)	Slain at Battle of Bosworth Field in 1485
Dukes of Norfolk	
John Mowbray, 3d duke	Fought for house of York; died 1461
John Mowbray, 4th duke	Supported house of York; died 1476
Richard Plantagenet	Disappeared in the Tower of London in 1483
John Howard	Slain at the Battle of Bosworth Field in 1485
Dukes of Somerset	
Edmund Beaufort, 2d duke	Slain at the Battle of St. Albans in 1455
Henry Beaufort, 3d duke	Executed in 1464
Edmund Beaufort, 4th duke	Executed after the Battle of Tewkesbury in 1471
Dukes of Suffolk	
John de la Pole	Supported house of York; died 1491
Edmund de la Pole (surrendered title of duke and became earl of Suffolk in 1493)	Executed in 1513
Dukes of York	
Richard Plantagenet, 3d duke	Slain at the Battle of Wakefield in 1460
Edward Plantagenet (became Edward IV in 1461)	Died 1483
Richard Plantagenet, 5th duke	Disappeared in the Tower of London in 1483

Title/Marquis	Outcome of Involvement
Marquis of Dorset	
Thomas Grey	Opposed Richard III; died 1501
Marquis of Montagu	
John Neville	Slain at the Battle of Barnet in 1471

(continues)

Title/Earl	Outcome of Involvement
Earl of Arundel	
William Fitzalan	Little involvement in the wars; died 1487
Earl of Derby	
Thomas Stanley	Avoided firm commitments, although opposed Richard III; died 1504
Earls of Devon	
Thomas Courtenay, 5th earl	Supported York, then Henry VI; died 1458
Thomas Courtenay, 6th earl	Executed after the Battle of Towton in 1461
Henry Courtenay (Lancastrian 7th earl)	Executed in 1469
Humphrey Stafford (Yorkist earl)	Executed in 1469
John Courtenay (Lancastrian 8th earl)	Slain at the Battle of Tewkesbury in 1471
Earl of Essex	
Henry Bourchier	Supported house of York; died 1483
Earls of Huntingdon	
Thomas Grey (also marquis of Dorset)	Opposed Richard III; died 1501
William Herbert (formerly earl of Pembroke)	Supported house of York; died 1490
Earl of Kent	
Edmund Grey	Supported house of York; died 1489
Earl of Lincoln	
John de la Pole	Slain at the Battle of Stoke in 1487
Earls of Northumberland	
Henry Percy, 2d earl	Slain at the Battle of St. Albans in 1455
Henry Percy, 3d earl	Slain at the Battle of Towton in 1461
John Neville (Yorkist earl)	Forced by Edward IV to surrender title in 1470; slain at the Battle of Barnet in 1471
Henry Percy, 4th earl	Supported house of York; slain by rebels in 1489
Earl of Nottingham	
William Berkeley (later Marquis Berkeley)	Supported house of York; died 1492
Earls of Oxford	
John de Vere, 12th earl	Executed in 1462
John de Vere, 13th earl	Supported houses of Lancaster and Tudor; died 1513
Earls of Pembroke	
Jasper Tudor (Lancastrian earl)	Supported houses of Lancaster and Tudor; died 1495
William Herbert (Yorkist earl)	Executed after the Battle of Edgecote in 1469
William Herbert (2d Yorkist earl; later earl of Huntingdon)	Forced by Edward IV to surrender title in 1479; died 1490
Earls of Richmond	
Edmund Tudor	Supported house of Lancaster; died 1456
Henry Tudor (became Henry VII in 1485)	Died in 1509
Earls of Rivers	
Richard Woodville	Executed in 1469
Anthony Woodville	Executed in 1483
Earls of Salisbury	
Richard Neville	Executed after the Battle of Wakefield in 1460
Richard Neville (also earl of Warwick)	Slain at the Battle of Barnet in 1471
Edward Plantagenet (son of Richard III and Prince of Wales)	Died in 1484

(continues)

Title/Earl	Outcome of Involvement
Earls of Shrewsbury	
John Talbot, 5th earl	Slain at the Battle of Northampton in 1460
John Talbot, 6th earl	Little involvement in the wars; died 1473
George Talbot	Little involvement in the wars; died 1538
Earl of Surrey	
Thomas Howard (later duke of Norfolk)	Attainted after Battle of Bosworth Field for supporting Richard III; restored to lands and titles by Henry VII and Henry VIII; died 1524
Earls of Warwick	
Richard Neville	Slain at the Battle of Barnet in 1471
Edward Plantagenet	Executed in 1499
Earl of Westmorland	
Ralph Neville	Little involvement in the wars; died 1484
Earls of Wiltshire	
James Butler (Lancastrian earl)	Executed in 1461
John Stafford (Yorkist earl)	Supported house of York; died 1473
Earl of Winchester	
Louis de Gruthuyse, seigneur de la Gruthuyse	Burgundian nobleman given title by Edward IV in gratitude for his help during Edward's exile in 1470; died 1492
Earl of Worcester	
John Tiptoft	Executed in 1470

Title/Viscount	Outcome of Involvement
Viscount Berkeley	
William Berkeley (later earl of Nottingham and Marquis Berkeley)	Supported house of York; died 1492
Viscount Lovell	
Francis Lovell	Slain at the Battle of Stoke in 1487

Appendix 5
European Rulers in the Fifteenth Century

English Monarchs	French Monarchs	Scottish Monarchs	Burgundian Rulers
House of Plantagenet	*House of Valois*	*House of Stuart*	*House of Valois*
Edward III (1327–1377)	Charles VI (1380–1422)	Robert III (1390–1406)	John the Fearless
Richard II (1377–1399)	Charles VII (1422–1461)	James I (1406–1437)	(1404–1419)
	Louis XI (1461–1483)	James II (1437–1460)	Philip the Good
House of Lancaster	Charles VIII (1483–1498)	James III (1460–1488)	(1419–1467)
Henry IV (1399–1413)	Louis XII (1498–1515)	James IV (1488–1513)	Charles the Bold
Henry V (1413–1422)			(1467–1477)
Henry VI (1422–1461)			Mary of Burgundy
			(1477–1482)
House of York			
Edward IV (1461–1470)			*House of Habsburg*
			Philip the Handsome
House of Lancaster			(1482–1506)★
Henry VI (1470–1471)			
House of York			
Edward IV (1471–1483)			
Edward V (1483)			
Richard III (1483–1485)			
House of Tudor			
Henry VII (1485–1509)			

★Archduke Maximilian of Austria (Holy Roman Emperor as Maximilian I after 1493) served as regent of Burgundy during the minority of his son Duke Philip the Handsome.

Appendix 6
Popes and English Church Leaders
in the Fifteenth Century

Archbishops of Canterbury	Archbishops of York	Popes
Henry Chichele (1414–1443)	Henry Bower (1407–1423)	Nicholas V (1447–1455)
John Stafford (1443–1452)	John Kempe (1426–1452)	Calixtus III (1455–1458)
John Kempe (1452–1454)	William Booth (1452–1464)	Pius II (1458–1464)
Thomas Bourchier (1454–1486)	George Neville (1465–1476)	Paul II (1464–1471)
John Morton (1486–1500)	Lawrence Booth (1476–1480)	Sixtus IV (1471–1484)
	Thomas Rotherham (1480–1500)	Innocent VIII (1484–1492)
		Alexander VI (1492–1503)

Appendix 7
Selected Historical Fiction with Fifteenth-Century Characters and Settings

For other works of fiction set in fifteenth-century England, see Roxane C. Murph, *The Wars of the Roses in Fiction: An Annotated Bibliography, 1440–1994* (Westport, CT: Greenwood Press, 1995); Lynda G. Adamson, *World Historical Fiction: An Annotated Guide to Novels for Adults and Young Adults* (Phoenix, AZ: Oryx Press, 1999); and Donald K. Hartman and Gregg Sapp, *Historical Figures in Fiction* (Phoenix, AZ: Oryx Press, 1994).

Abbey, Anne Merton. *Katherine in the Court of the Six Queens.* New York: Bantam Books, 1989.

Abbey, Margaret. *The Warwick Heiress.* London: Robert Hale, 1970.

———. *The Crowned Boar.* London: Robert Hale, 1971 [published in the United States in 1973 as *Son of York* by Pinnacle Books].

———. *Brothers-in-Arms.* London: Robert Hale, 1973.

———. *The Heart Is a Traitor.* London: Robert Hale, 1978.

———. *Blood of the Boar.* London: Robert Hale, 1979.

Allison-Williams, Jean. *Cry "God for Richard."* London: Robert Hale, 1981.

———. *Mistress of the Tabard.* London: Robert Hale, 1984.

———. *Simon of the Tabard.* London: Robert Hale, 1984.

Anand, Valerie. *Crown of Roses.* London: Headline Book Publishing, 1989.

———. *Women of Ashdon.* London: Headline Book Publishing, 1993.

Andrew, Prudence. *A Question of Choice.* New York: G. P. Putnam's Sons, 1962.

Appleyard, Susan. *The King's White Rose.* Toronto: Paperjacks, 1988.

Barnes, Margaret Campbell. *The Tudor Rose.* London: Macdonald, 1952 [published in the United States in 1953 by Macrae Smith Company].

———. *The King's Bed.* London: Macdonald, 1961.

Barringer, Leslie. *The Rose in Splendour: A Story of the Wars of Lancaster and York.* London: Phoenix House, 1952.

Belle, Pamela. *The Lodestar.* London: Bodley Head, 1987 [published in the United States in 1987 by St. Martin's Press].

Bennetts, Pamela. *Bright Son of York.* London: Robert Hale, 1971.

———. *The Third Richard.* London: Robert Hale, 1972.

Bentley, Elizabeth. *The York Quest.* London: Robert Hale, 1980.

Bentley, Pauline. *Silk and Sword.* Richmond, Surrey, UK: Mills and Boon, 1993.

Bentley, Phyllis. *Sheep May Safely Graze.* London: Victor Gollancz, 1972.

Bibby, Violet. *The Mirrored Shield.* London: Longman Young Books, 1970.

Blake, Margaret Glaiser. *A Sprig of Broom.* London: Robert Hale, 1979.

Bowden, Susan. *In the Shadow of the Crown.* New York: Bantam Books, 1987.

Brandewyne, Rebecca. *Rose of Rapture.* New York: Warner Books, 1984.

Bridge, S. R. *The Woodville.* London: Robert Hale, 1976.

Brooks, Janice Young. *Forbidden Fires.* New York: Playboy Press Paperbacks, 1980.

Burgess, Mallory. *Passion Rose.* New York: Avon Books, 1987.

Carr, Robyn. *The Everlasting Covenant.* Boston: Little, Brown, 1987.

Carsley, Anne. *This Ravished Rose.* New York: Pocket Books, 1980.

Clynes, Michael [P. C. Doherty]. *The White Rose Murders.* London: Headline Book Publishing, 1991 [published in the United States in 1993 by St. Martin's Press].

Coates, Sheila. *A Crown Usurped.* London: Robert Hale, 1972.

Cummins, Mary. *The Glenorchan Ruby.* London: Robert Hale, 1982.

———. *Fingala, Maid of Rathay.* London: Robert Hale, 1983.

Daniell, David Scott. *The Boy They Made King, a True Story.* New York: Duell, Sloan and Pearce, 1950.

Darby, Catherine. *A Dream of Fair Serpents.* London: Robert Hale, 1979.

Davidson, Margaret. *My Lords Richard.* London: Cassell, 1979.

Davies, Iris. *The Tudor Tapestry.* London: Robert Hale, 1974.

———. *Bride of the Thirteenth Summer.* London: Robert Hale, 1975.

Dewar, Margaret. *Philippa*. London: Robert Hale, 1982.

———. *The Loyalty Game*. London: Robert Hale, 1984.

Dexter, Susan. *The Wizard's Shadow*. New York: Del Rey/Ballantine Books, 1993.

Dodd, Christina. *Outrageous: A Story of the Wars of the Roses*. New York: HarperCollins, 1998.

———. *Dove Amongst the Hawks*. London: Robert Hale, 1990 [see also Michael Clynes and C. L. Grace].

Doherty, P. C. *The Fate of Princes*. London: Robert Hale, 1990 [published in the United States in 1991 by St. Martin's Press; see also Michael Clynes and C. L. Grace].

Drake, Shannon. *Lie Down in Roses*. New York: Berkeley Publishing Group, Charter Books, 1988.

Durst, Paul. *The Florentine Table*. New York: Charles Scribner's Sons, 1980.

———. *The Lord of Greenwich*. London: Dobson Books, 1980.

Dymoke, Juliet. *The Sun in Splendour*. London: Dennis Dobson Books, 1980.

Eckerson, Olive. *The Golden Yoke: A Novel of the War of the Roses*. New York: Coward-McCann, 1961.

———. *Some Touch of Pity*. New York: Doubleday, 1976.

Edwards, Rhoda. *Fortune's Wheel*. London: Hutchinson, 1978.

Evans, Jean. *The Divided Rose*. London: Robert Hale, 1972.

———. *The Rose and Ragged Staff*. London: Robert Hale, 1974.

———. *The White Rose of York*. London: Robert Hale, 1972.

Eyre, Katherine Wigmore. *The Song of a Thrush*. New York: Oxford University Press, 1952.

Fairburn, Eleanor. *The Rose in Spring*. London: Robert Hale, 1971.

———. *White Rose, Dark Summer*. London: Robert Hale, 1972.

———. *The Rose at Harvest End*. London: Robert Hale, 1974.

———. *Winter's Rose*. London: Robert Hale, 1976.

Farrington, Robert. *The Killing of Richard the Third*. New York: Charles Scribner's Sons, 1971.

———. *Tudor Agent*. London: Chatto and Windus, 1974.

———. *The Traitors of Bosworth*. London: Chatto and Windus, 1978.

Few, Mary Dodgen. *Under the White Boar*. Atlanta: Droke House/Hallux, 1971.

Ford, John M. *The Dragon Waiting*. New York: Simon and Schuster, 1983.

Frazer, Margaret. *The Novice's Tale*. New York: Jove Books, 1992.

Garabet, Marilyn. *Dearest of Princes*. London: Robert Hale, 1981.

Gaunt, William. *The Lady in the Castle*. London: W. H. Allen, 1956.

Gellis, Roberta. *The Dragon and the Rose*. Chicago: Playboy Press, 1977.

Gleason, Edwin Putnam. *The Mystery of Boshingham Castle: A Tale Concerning the Wicked King Richard III and the Princes in the Tower*. New York: Pageant Press, 1967.

Gower, Iris. *Destiny's Child*. Thorndike, ME: G. K. Hall, 1999.

Grace, C. L. [P. C. Doherty]. *A Shrine of Murders*. New York: St. Martin's Press, 1993.

———. *The Eye of God*. New York: St. Martin's Press, 1994.

———. *The Merchant of Death*. New York: St. Martin's Press, 1995.

Graham, Alice Walworth. *The Summer Queen*. New York: Doubleday, 1973.

Grey, Belinda. *Proxy Wedding*. London: Mills and Boon, 1982.

Griffith, Kathryn Meyer. *The Heart of the Rose*. New York: Leisure Books, Dorchester Publishing Company, 1985.

Hamilton, Julia. *Son of York: A Novel of Edward IV*. London: Sphere Books, 1973.

Hammand, N. B. *Samaritana*. London: Robert Hale, 1979.

Hammond, Jane. *The Red Queen*. London: Robert Hale, 1976.

Hardwick, Mollie. *I Remember Love*. London: Macdonald, 1982.

Harnett, Cynthia. *The Load of Unicorn*. London: Methuen Children's Books, 1959 [published in the United States as *Caxton's Challenge* by the World Publishing Company and in 1984 as the *Cargo of the Madalena* by Lerner Publications Company].

———. *The Writing on the Hearth*. London: Methuen's Children's Books, 1971.

Harrod-Eagles, Cynthia. *The Founding*. London: Futura Publications, 1980.

Harwood, Alice. *Merchant of the Ruby*. Indianapolis: Bobbs-Merrill Company, 1950.

———. *The Clandestine Queen*. London: Robert Hale, 1979.

———. *The Uncrowned Queen*. London: Robert Hale, 1983.

Henley, Virginia. *The Raven and the Rose*. New York: Dell Publishing, 1987.

Higgins, Paul. *Puzzlebone Wood*. London: Bachman and Turner, 1979.

Hill, Pamela. *The King's Vixen*. New York: G. P. Putnam's Sons, 1954.

Hocking, Mary. *He Who Plays the King*. London: Chatto and Windus, 1980.

Honeyman, Brenda. *Richard, by Grace of God*. London: Robert Hale, 1968.

———. *The Kingmaker*. London: Robert Hale, 1969.

———. *Richmond and Elizabeth*. London: Robert Hale, 1970.

———. *Good Duke Humphrey*. London: Robert Hale, 1973.

Hood, Evelyn. *The Kingmaker's Daughter*. London: Robert Hale, 1974.

Horter, Pamela Jean. *Brief Candles*. New York: Vantage Press, 1983.

Hunt, Wray. *Satan's Daughter*. London: Robert Hale, 1970.

Irwin, Frances. *My Lady of Wycherly*. London: Robert Hale, 1971.

———. *The White Pawn*. London: Robert Hale, 1972.

———. *The White Queen*. London: Robert Hale, 1974.

———. *The Winter Killing*. London: Robert Hale, 1977.

Jarman, Rosemary Hawley. *We Speak No Treason*. Boston: Little, Brown, 1971.

———. *The King's Grey Mare*. London: William Collins Sons, 1973.

———. *Crown in Candlelight*. Boston: Little, Brown, 1978.

———. *The Courts of Illusion*. Boston: Little, Brown, 1983.

Jefferis, Barbara. *Beloved Lady*. New York: W. Sloane Associates, 1955 [published in Great Britain in 1956 by J. M. Dent and Sons].

Jones, Cherry Calvert. *Proud Cis*. London: Robert Hale, 1980.

Kettle, Jocelyn. *Memorial to the Duchess*. London: Herbert Jenkins, 1968.

Kilbourne, Jamet. *Garland of the Realm*. London: Robert Hale, 1972.

———. *Wither One Rose*. London: Robert Hale, 1973.

King, Betty. *The Lady Margaret*. London: Herbert Jenkins, 1965.

———. *The Lord Jasper*. London: Herbert Jenkins, 1967.

———. *The King's Mother*. London: Robert Hale, 1969.

———. *The Beaufort Secretary*. London: Robert Hale, 1970.

———. *The Rose Both Red and White*. London: Robert Hale, 1970 [published in the United States in 1974 as *The Rose, Red and White* by Pinnacle Books].

———. *Margaret of Anjou*. London: Robert Hale, 1974.

———. *Owen Tudor*. London: Robert Hale, 1977.

Kramer, Kathryn. *Desire's Masquerade*. New York: Dell Publishing Company, 1987.

Lamb, Hilda. *The Willing Heart*. London: Hodder and Stoughton, 1958.

Layton, Edith. *The Crimson Crown*. New York: Onyx/New American Library, 1990.

Leary, Francis. *The Swan and the Rose*. New York: A. A. Wyn, 1953.

———. *Fire and Morning*. New York: G. P. Putnam's Sons, 1957.

Lewis, Hilda. *Wife to Henry V*. London: Jarrolds Publishing, 1954.

Lide, Mary. *Command of the King*. London: Grafton Books, 1990 [published in the United States in 1991 by St. Martin's Press].

Lindsay, Philip. *The Merry Mistress*. London: Hutchinson, 1952 [published in the United States in 1953 by Roy Publishing Company].

———. *They Have Their Dreams*. London: Hutchinson, 1956 [published in the United States in 1971 as *A Princely Knave* by Sphere Books].

Lofts, Nora. *The Town House*. New York: Doubleday, 1959.

———. *The Maude Reed Tale*. New York: Thomas Nelson, 1972.

———. *Knight's Acre*. London: Hodder and Stoughton, 1975.

———. *The Homecoming*. New York: Doubleday, 1976.

———. *The Lonely Furrow*. New York: Doubleday, 1976.

Long, Freda M. *The Coveted Crown*. London: Robert Hale, 1966.

———. *Requiem for Richard*. London: Robert Hale, 1975.

Maiden, Cecil. *The Borrowed Crown*. New York: Viking Press, 1968.

Makepeace, Joanna. *Pawns of Power*. London: Hurst and Blackett, 1972.

———. *My Lord Enemy*. London: Macdonald, 1984.

———. *Battlefield of Hearts*. London: Mills and Boon, 1991.

———. *Reluctant Rebel*. London: Mills and Boon, 1993.

———. *Crown Hostage*. London: Mills and Boon, 1994.

Malvern, Gladys. *The Queen's Lady*. Philadelphia: Macrae Smith Company, 1963.

McDonald, Eva. *Cry Treason Thrice*. London: Robert Hale, 1977.

Miall, Wendy. *John of Gloucester*. London: Robert Hale, 1968.

———. *The Playing Card Queen*. London: Robert Hale, 1970.

Morgan, Denise. *Second Son*. London: Robert Hale, 1980.

———. *Kingmaker's Knight*. London: Robert Hale, 1981.

———. *Sons and Roses*. London: Robert Hale, 1981.

Nickell, Leslie J. *The White Queen*. London: Bodley Head, 1978 [published in the United States by St. Martin's Press].

Nicolson, Joan. *Cuckoo Summer*. London: Hurst and Blackett, 1962.

Oldfield, Pamela. *The Rich Earth*. London: Macdonald Futura Publishers, 1980 [Volume 1 of *The Heron Saga*].

Orford, Margaret. *That Beloved Esquire*. Swansea, Wales: Christopher Davies, 1980.

Palmer, Marian. *The White Boar*. New York: Doubleday, 1968.

———. *The Wrong Plantagenet*. New York: Doubleday, 1972.

Penman, Sharon Kay. *The Sunne in Splendour*. New York: Holt, Rinehart and Winston, 1982.

Perot, Ruth S. *The Red Queen: Margaret of Anjou and the Wars of the Roses*. n.p.: FirstBooks Library, 2000.

Peters, Elizabeth. *The Murders of Richard III*. New York: Dodd, Mead, 1974.

Peters, Maureen. *Elizabeth the Beloved*. London: Robert Hale, 1965.

———. *The Woodville Wench*. London: Robert Hale, 1972 [published in the United States as *The Queen Who Never Was* by Pinnacle Books].

———. *Beggarmaid Queen*. London: Robert Hale, 1980.

Pierce, Glenn. *King's Ransom*. Los Angeles: Medallion Books, 1986.

Plaidy, Jean. *The Goldsmith's Wife*. New York: Appleton, 1950 [published in Great Britain by Robert Hale; also published in 1960 as *The King's Mistress* by Pyramid Books].

———. *Epitaph for Three Women*. London: Robert Hale, 1981 [published in the United States in 1983 by G. P. Putnam's Sons].

———. *Red Rose of Anjou*. London: Robert Hale, 1982 [published in the United States in 1983 by G. P. Putnam's Sons].

———. *The Sun in Splendour*. London: Robert Hale, 1982 [published in the United States in 1983 by G. P. Putnam's Sons].

———. *Uneasy Lies the Head*. London: Robert Hale, 1982 [published in the United States in 1984 by G. P. Putnam's Sons].

———. *The Queen's Secret*. London: Severn House, 1988 [published in the United States in 1990 by G. P. Putnam's Sons].

———. *The Reluctant Queen*. London: Robert Hale, 1990 [published in the United States in 1991 by G. P. Putnam's Sons].

Potter, Jeremy. *A Trail of Blood*. London: Constable, 1970 [published in the United States in 1971 by McCall Publishing Company].

Powers, Anne. *The Royal Consorts*. Los Angeles: Pinnacle Books, 1978 [published by Leisure Books in 1978 as *Queen's Ransom*].

Rabinowitz, Ann. *Knight on Horseback*. New York: Macmillan, 1987.

Ragosta, Millie J. *Gerait's Daughter*. Garden City, NY: Doubleday, 1981.

———. *The Winter Rose*. Garden City, NY: Doubleday, 1982.

Reddicliffe, Sheila. *The Cornish Serjeant*. London: William Kimber, 1984.

Ridge, Antonia. *The 13th Child*. London: Faber and Faber, 1962.

Rosenthal, Evelyn B. *Presumed Guilty*. New York: Vantage Press, 1982.

Ross, Barnaby. *The Passionate Queen*. New York: Pocket Books, 1966.

Ross Williamson, Hugh. *The Butt of Malmsey*. London: Michael Joseph, 1967.

———. *The Marriage Made in Blood*. London: Michael Joseph, 1968.

Rowling, Marjorie. *Shadow of the Dragon*. London: Faber and Faber, 1965.

Rush, Philip. *My Brother Lambert*. London: Phoenix House, 1957.

St. James, Scotney. *By Honor Bound*. New York: Avon Books, 1989.

Saunders, Susan. *The Tower of London*. New York: Bantam Books, 1984.

Schoonover, Lawrence. *The Spider King: A Biographical Novel of Louis XI of France*. New York: Macmillan, 1954.

Scott, Amanda. *The Rose at Twilight*. New York: Dell Publishing, 1993.

Sedley, Kate. *Death and the Chapman*. London: HarperCollins, 1991.

———. *The Plymouth Cloak*. New York: St. Martin's Press, 1992.

———. *The Holy Innocents*. New York: St. Martin's Press, 1995.

———. *The Weaver's Tale*. New York: HarperPaperbacks, 1995.

———. *The Eve of Saint Hyacinth*. New York: St. Martin's Press, 1996.

———. *The Wicked Winter*. New York: St. Martin's Press, 1999.

Seibert, Elizabeth. *White Rose and Ragged Staff*. Indianapolis: Bobbs-Merrill, 1968.

Seymour, Arabella. *Maid of Destiny*. London: Robert Hale, 1971.

Simonds, Paula. *Daughter of Violence*. London: Robert Hale, 1981.

Sisson, Rosemary Anne. *The Queen and the Welshman*. London: W. H. Allen, 1979.

Small, Beatrice. *The Spitfire*. New York: Ballantine Books, 1990.

Stanier, Hilda Brookman. *The Kingmaker's Daughter*. London: Robert Hale, 1978.

———. *Plantagenet Princess*. London: Robert Hale, 1981.

Stephens, Peter John. *Battle for Destiny*. New York: Atheneum, 1967.

Stevenson, Robert Louis. *The Black Arrow*. Pensacola, FL: A Beka Book, 1999 [first published in 1888].

Stewart, A. J. *Falcon: The Autobiography of His Grace James the Fourth, King of the Scots*. London: Peter

Davies, 1970 [published in the United States in 1970 by Delacorte Press].

Stoker, M. Brooke. *Prince Perkin*. London: Robert Hale, 1966.

Stubbs, Jean. *An Unknown Welshman*. New York: Stein and Day, 1972.

Sudworth, Gwynedd. *Dragon's Whelp*. London: Robert Hale, 1973.

———. *The King of Destiny*. London: Robert Hale, 1973.

———. *The Game of Power*. London: Robert Hale, 1975.

———. *The Game of Kings*. London: Robert Hale, 1977.

Tey, Josephine. *The Daughter of Time*. New York: Macmillan, 1951.

Townsend, Guy M. *To Prove a Villain*. Menlo Park, CA: Perseverance Press, 1985.

Tranter, Nigel. *Chain of Destiny*. London: Hodder and Stoughton, 1964.

Trevan, Ruth. *Loyalty Binds Me*. London: Robert Hale, 1966.

Viney, Jayne. *The White Rose Dying*. London: Robert Hale, 1973.

———. *King Richard's Friend*. London: Robert Hale, 1975.

Welch, Ronald. *Sun of York*. Oxford: Oxford University Press, 1970.

Wensby-Scott, Carol. *Lion of Alnwick*. London: Michael Joseph, 1980.

———. *Lion Dormant*. London: Michael Joseph, 1983.

———. *Lion Invincible*. London: Michael Joseph, 1984.

Westcott. Jan. *The Hepburn*. New York: Crown Publishers, 1950.

———. *The White Rose*. New York: G. P. Putnam's Sons, 1969.

———. *Set Her on the Throne*. Boston: Little, Brown, 1972.

Whittle, Tyler. *The Last Plantagenet: A Study of Richard the Third, King of England, France and Ireland*. London: William Heinemann, 1968.

Wiat, Philippa. *The Master of Blandeston Hall*. London: Robert Hale, 1973.

———. *Prince of the White Rose*. London: Robert Hale, 1984.

———. *The Kingmaker's Daughter*. London: Robert Hale, 1989.

———. *The Child Bride*. London: Robert Hale, 1990.

Willard, Barbara. *The Lark and the Laurel*. London: Longman Group, 1970 [published in the United States in 1970 by Harcourt, Brace and World].

———. *The Sprig of Broom*. London: Longman Group, 1971.

Williams, Bert. *Master of Ravenspur*. London: Thomas Nelson and Sons, 1970.

Williamson, Joanne S. *To Dream upon a Crown*. New York: Alfred A. Knopf, 1967.

Willman, Marianne. *Rose Red, Rose White*. New York: Harlequin Books, 1989.

Wilson, Sandra. *Less Fortunate than Fair*. New York: St. Martin's Press, 1973.

———. *The Lady Cecily*. New York: St. Martin's Press, 1974.

———. *The Queen's Sister*. New York: St. Martin's Press, 1974.

———. *Wife to the Kingmaker*. New York: St. Martin's Press, 1974.

———. *The Pentrich Dragon*. London: Robert Hale, 1977.

York, Elizabeth. *The Heir of Berkwell*. London: Robert Hale, 1977.

Young, D. V. *The White Boar*. London: Robert Hale, 1963.

Appendix 8
Selected Web Sites for Fifteenth-Century Topics

The Internet offers a large and growing number of sites relating to the Wars of the Roses and to the history of the British Isles in the fifteenth century. Many of these sites provide brief biographical information on important civil war figures, brief narratives of the wars or of particular battles, and discussions of military and political aspects of the conflict. Besides sites that provide access to the latest scholarship on the period or reproduce contemporary documents and source materials, the Internet contains a host of sites developed and maintained by interested individuals and by various Wars of the Roses reenactment groups. Although the quality of these latter sites can be uneven, many provide interesting or unusual information, illustrations, and links that are well worth the time and attention of any student or enthusiast of the Wars of the Roses or the fifteenth century. Many sites, besides the well-known Richard III Society and its many branches (which are listed below in their own section), focus on the life and career of Richard III, who is clearly the most captivating Wars of the Roses figure for modern students of the period. The sites described below are by no means an exhaustive listing of Wars of the Roses materials to be found on the Web; they are simply a selection of a few of the most useful and best-designed sites currently available.

Scholarly Sites

The History of King Richard III by Sir Thomas More
<http://darkwing.uoregon.edu/~rbear/r3.html>
This site by Renascence Editions supplies the full text of More's narrative of Richard III.

The Labyrinth
<http://www.georgetown.edu/labyrinth/labyrinth-home.html>
Located at Georgetown University in Washington, D.C., the Labyrinth is an evolving Web resource for medievalists that offers full texts in the original languages of many works in the medieval canon, medieval Latin word lists, bibliographies, and extensive links to other online resources. Users can match topics of special interest, such as "Armor" or "Art," with particular types of materials, such as bibliographies, course materials, glossaries, or maps, to find the exact information they are seeking.

Medieval Academy of America
<http://www.medievalacademy.org/>
With approximately 4,000 members, the Medieval Academy of America is the preeminent professional association for medievalists in the United States. Located in Cambridge, Massachusetts, the Academy was founded in 1925 for the promotion of research, publication, and instruction in medieval records, art, archaeology, history, law, literature, music, philosophy, science, social and economic institutions, and all other aspects of the Middle Ages. The Web site offers listings of conferences, publications, and prizes, as well as links to related sites. The Academy publishes *Speculum,* which was founded in 1926 as the first scholarly journal in North America devoted exclusively to the Middle Ages. For the journal, the Web site contains an index to articles published since 1975, submission guidelines for authors, and subscriber information.

Medieval Institute
<http://www.wmich.edu/medieval/>
The Medieval Institute at Western Michigan University was established in 1961 as a center for teaching and research in the history and culture of the Middle Ages. The Web site describes the offerings and activities of the institute and provides listings of programs, publications, and conferences, as well as a bulletin board and links to related sites.

ORB: The Online Reference Book for Medieval Studies
<http://orb.rhodes.edu/>
ORB is written and maintained by medieval scholars for the benefit of their fellow instructors and for serious students of medieval history. This extensive site offers a reference shelf with excerpts and full texts of primary and secondary sources found on the ORB server and elsewhere on the Web; resources for teaching, such as syllabi, study questions, writing guides, tips for test-takers, and subject-specific bibliographies; and full-length textbooks written by experienced scholar-teachers and tested both in the classroom and on the Internet. The ORB Encyclopedia page contains

chronological and geographical indexes of essays, bibliographies, images, and documents, as well as links to related sites and other online resources.

WWW Medieval Resources
<http://ebbs.english.vt.edu/medieval/medieval.ebbs.html>
This site provides links to a wide variety of medieval history Web pages. These resources include the texts of medieval literature (both English and continental); sites on medieval history, archaeology, architecture, and science; archives of medieval art and manuscript facsimiles; links to libraries with significant medieval holdings; and links to miscellaneous resources, such as the British Library site, the Louvre site, and a Gregorian chant site.

Richard III Societies

Richard III Society
<http://www.richardiii.net/>
Founded in 1924 as the Fellowship of the White Boar by Liverpool surgeon S. Saxon Barton, the Richard III Society acquired its present name in 1959. The Society's membership now exceeds 4,000, with national branches (see below) in Europe, the United States, Canada, Australia, and New Zealand, and local/regional groups in Australia, the United Kingdom, and the United States. The society's goals are to promote the study of fifteenth-century history, especially research pertaining to the life and reign of Richard III. Believing that the traditional view of Richard is not supported by the evidence, the society seeks to secure a reassessment of Richard's reputation and place in history through its encouragement of scholarly activity.

The society publishes a newsletter and a well-regarded scholarly journal (*The Ricardian*); organizes lectures, conferences, and seminars; collaborates in the publication of relevant books and papers; maintains a library of materials on Richard III and his times; erects memorials to Richard at important sites; participates in the maintenance of such sites; and cooperates with other organizations in the creation and promotion of various programs relevant to the history of the fifteenth century. In 1986, the society established an independent charity known as the Richard III and Yorkist History Trust, which aims to maintain and broaden the Society's publishing program, to raise funds, to support research, and to promote cooperation between the Society and the academic community.

The Society's Web site offers a brief biography of Richard III, a discussion of his reputation, a brief description of the Wars of the Roses, a list of important sites associated with Richard, discussions of Richard's alleged physical deformities and of the bones found in the Tower of London in 1674, and information on

Society projects, publications, and activities in the United Kingdom. Providing links to the Web sites of other branches, the parent society site is a good place to start for the latest research on the life and times of Richard III.

Richard III Society, American Branch
<http://www.r3.org>
This extremely useful Web site by the American Branch of the Richard III Society is an excellent starting point for any online search for information on the Wars of the Roses or fifteenth-century England. Although the site reflects the pro-Richard point of view of the Society, it also offers a wide variety of useful features for the student of the civil wars. Besides an extensive online library providing the full or partial texts of important source materials, such as the *Croyland Chronicle,* Philippe de Commines's *Memoirs,* and Sir Thomas More's *History of King Richard III,* the site also includes all or part of such works of modern scholarship as Sharon D. Michalove's paper on "The Reinvention of Richard III" and Jeremy Potter's chapter on the fate of the Princes in the Tower from his 1983 book, *Good King Richard? An Account of Richard III and His Reputation.*

The site also provides links to sites covering a variety of dramatic renderings of Richard III's life, from the text of William Shakespeare's *Richard III* and a discussion of Maxwell Anderson's unpublished *Richard and Anne* to a radio interview of Laurence Olivier discussing Richard III and a description of Al Pacino's recent film, *Looking for Richard.* The site also offers a variety of aids for teaching and studying Richard III and the fifteenth century and an extensive series of links to a wide range of scholarly and popular Wars of the Roses and Richard III sites.

Richard III Society of Canada
<http://www.cgocable.net/~tbryce/>
The Canadian Branch of the Richard III Society was formed in 1966. Subscribing to all the goals and objectives of the parent society, the Branch's members meet regularly in Toronto for conferences and discussions on Ricardian topics. The highlight of the year is the Annual General Meeting and costumed Medieval Banquet, which are celebrated on or near Richard's birthday on 2 October.

Besides brief biographies of important Wars of the Roses figures, such as Edward IV, Henry VI, and Margaret of Anjou, this Web site also offers biographies of lesser-known people, such as Richard III's two illegitimate children, Katherine and John Plantagenet; his legitimate son, Edward of Middleham; and Edward IV's mistress, Jane Shore. Also provided are a chronology of events in the life of Richard III, a narrative of the Battle of Bosworth Field, a debunking of several crimes ascribed to the king by the traditional view of Richard III, and a discussion of the princes in the

Tower and Richard's possible role in their deaths. The full text is also given for various papers written by members, such as Tracy Bryce's study of Sir James Tyrell and L. Clement-Hobbs's discussion of women, courtship, and marriage in late fifteenth-century England. Links are provided to other branches of the Richard III Society, including local groups in Australia and the United Kingdom, and to such other sites as the Richard III Museum in York <http://www.richardiiimuseum.co.uk/>.

Web Addresses for Other Richard III Society Branches and Groups

(Australian Branch) <http://home.vicnet.net.au/~richard3/welcome.htm>
(New England Branch) <http://www.r3.org/chapter.html>
(New Zealand Branch) <http://www.taheke.co.nz/>
(Nottinghamshire and Derbyshire Group) <http://www.geocities.com/richardiii_2000/>
(Ohio Chapter) <http://www.r3.org/ohio1.html>
(Queensland Branch) <http://www.riiiqld.org.au/>
(Western Australia Branch) <http://members.iinet.net.au/~hardegen/>
(Worcestershire Branch) <http://www.richardiiiworcs.co.uk>
(Yorkshire Branch) <http://members.aol.com/R3Yorks/index.html>

Shakespeare Sites

Complete Works of William Shakespeare
<http://tech-two.mit.edu/Shakespeare/>
This site from MIT provides public domain texts, with a glossary, of each of William Shakespeare's plays, including the entire cycle, from *Richard II* to *Richard III,* that depicts the history of fifteenth-century England. The site allows users to search the entire canon for their favorite words or phrases.

Mr. William Shakespeare and the Internet
<http://daphne.palomar.edu/shakespeare/>
This site is a complete annotated guide to the scholarly Shakespeare resources available on the Internet. It also provides such additional features as a Shakespeare time line and genealogy, a biographical quiz on the playwright, the prefatory material to the 1623 First Folio of Shakespeare's works, and a list of the plays, giving their probable dates of composition and publication. The site is an excellent first stop for an online Shakespeare search.

Shakespeare Bookshelf
<http://www.ipl.org/reading/shakespeare/shakespeare.html>
This site from the Internet Public Library offers the full text of all William Shakespeare's plays, including

the fifteenth-century history cycles, as well as links to sites of Shakespeare criticism and Shakespeare Internet discussion groups.

Popular Sites by Groups, Individuals, or Battlefield Societies

The Battle of Blore Heath 1459
<http://www.bloreheath.co.uk/battle.html>
This site on the Battle of Blore Heath offers information about the battle, photos of the battlefield, a discussion of fifteenth-century combat and tactics, and information on the annual reenactment of the battle. The page also provides links to related sites.

Continuing Battle of Bosworth Field
<http://www2.prestel.co.uk/magor/images/bosworth2.htm>
This site, which relates efforts to develop the site of the Battle of Bosworth Field for tourism, contains some excellent photos of the battlefield and some useful information on the battle itself. For a more detailed discussion of the Battle of Bosworth Field, see the Bosworth page that is part of the Richard III Society (American Branch) Web site at <http://www.r3.org/bosworth/>.

Maps of Medieval England
<http://www1.pitt.edu/~medart/menuengl/mainmaps.html>
Containing an interesting map entitled "Britain in 1455–1494," which depicts the major regions of Lancastrian and Yorkist allegiance, this Web site also offers eleven other maps of Britain prior to 1500, with subjects ranging from the Roman province to the diocesan boundaries of the medieval English Church.

Richard III: Historical Debate
<http://www.geocities.com/Athens/Crete/2918/>
This Web page is dedicated to discussion and study of the Yorkist and early Tudor periods of English history, with a special emphasis on the reign of Richard III. Besides a useful family tree of the house of Plantagenet from Edward III to Henry VII, the site offers an online discussion forum, a series of essays by students and enthusiasts of the period, and a useful bibliography that includes contemporary sources, modern works, historical fiction, and recent films. Links to the main branches of the Richard III Society and to the online resource library of the American Branch are also provided.

Richard III Foundation, Inc.
<http://www.richard111.com/>
The Richard III Foundation, Inc., is a nonprofit educational organization that seeks to authenticate the life and times of King Richard III, his contemporaries,

and his era, and to expand information about the medieval period, especially the years from 1450 to 1485. Besides a description of the services and tours offered by the foundation, the site includes a biography of Richard III, descriptions of Wars of the Roses battles, a map of battle sites, and links to other medieval history Web pages.

Tewkesbury Battlefield Society
<http://www.tewkesbury.org.uk/battlefield/index.html>
This Web page provides information on the Battle of Tewkesbury and on the society's efforts to preserve the battle site, including a recent successful campaign to prevent the construction of housing on a portion of the battlefield.

Towton Battlefield Society
<http://www.oldtykes.co.uk/TowBatSoc.htm>
This site provides information on the Battle of Towton and on the battlefield site, the preservation of which is the main aim of the Society.

Warrwykk's Wars of the Roses Page
<http://www.geocities.com/Area51/Cavern/5123/index.html>
This Web site includes brief biographical sketches of important civil wars figures, such as Henry Stafford, duke of Buckingham (d. 1483), and Edmund Beaufort, duke of Somerset (d. 1455), as well as all the relevant kings and queens. Also included are a map and a dated listing of important battles and a page of basic but helpful answers to Wars of the Roses FAQs. One fun feature is a challenging multiple choice quiz on the Wars of the Roses (I got twenty-three out of twenty-three but had a few tense moments). Warrwykk's page also offers a wide and varied selection of links to other Wars of the Roses sites.

Wars of the Roses
<http://www.warsoftheroses.com/>
This basic site provides a brief but useful time line, biographies of key figures, descriptions of major battles that give casualty figures and lists of notable dead, and links to related sites.

The Wars of the Roses
<http://www.northcoast.com/~ming/roses/roses.html>
This site by Matthew Ingalls is useful for its detailed genealogical charts of the house of Plantagenet and of the most important noble families involved in the Wars of the Roses. It also includes the usual series of biographical sketches, battle accounts, and rather breezy discussions of the causes of the wars. Also provided are useful links to Shakespearean and Richard III Society sites.

The Wars of the Roses
<http://www.fifteenthcentury.net>
This site by Alison Orr offers a brief narrative of the Wars of the Roses, short biographies of key figures involved in the wars, descriptions of major battles, an examination of the debate surrounding Richard III, and general information on life in the fifteenth century. However, it is especially useful for providing detailed family trees of the families of Lancaster, York, Neville, Beaufort, Mortimer, Percy, Woodville, and Tudor.

Wars of the Roses Fiction
<http://uts.cc.utexas.edu/~soon/histfiction/ricardianlist.html>
This Web site lists authors and titles (but no publishers or dates) of twentieth-century historical fiction with Wars of the Roses or fifteenth-century characters and settings. Carol Mitchell of the Richard III Society compiled the list, so Richard and his story are well represented.

Reenactment Groups

The Company Ecorcheur Medieval Society
<http://www.ecorcheur.co.uk/>
The Company Ecorcheur was formed in 1991 by a group of experienced reenactors whose aim is to provide an accurate and entertaining portrayal of military and civilian life in the second half of the fifteenth century. The company specializes in displays of medieval foot combat that employ a wide range of period weaponry, including pollarms and bows. Associated "living history" crafts demonstrated at company encampments include medieval cookery, fletching, calligraphy, and tailoring; also demonstrated are period games, pastimes, dances, and songs. A member of both Livery and Maintenance and the Federation of the Wars of the Roses (see below), umbrella organizations that bring together reenactment groups across Britain to present large-scale battles and sieges for a variety of customers, the Company Ecorcheur portrays the household troops of Richard Plantagenet, duke of Gloucester (Richard III), and also serves as the garrison for Warwick Castle, where it presents a variety of military and craft exhibitions throughout the year. Besides a list of upcoming events and equipment suppliers, the Web site offers brief descriptions of Wars of the Roses battles, a fifteenth-century songbook, and links to related groups.

Federation of the Wars of the Roses
<http://homepages.shu.ac.uk/~conseal/fedindex.htm>
Because the federation is an umbrella organization for fifteenth-century reenactment groups, this site offers links to various groups, descriptions of upcoming reenactments, lists of suppliers of and traders in me-

dieval equipage, photos of groups in action, articles by federation members, and a brief narrative of the Wars of the Roses. This is a good place to start for information on fifteenth-century reenactment groups.

Listings for Medieval Reenactment Societies
<http://www.medievalgarb.com/fav_links.html>
This detailed and extensive listing of reenactment groups provides mailing addresses, phone numbers, brief descriptions, and Web site links. The site is another good starting point for anyone interested in participating in a Wars of the Roses reenactment group.

The Medieval Free Company
<http://www.medievalfreeco.org.uk/>
The Medieval Free Company is a nonprofit living history group specializing in Wars of the Roses period reenactments. The site's most interesting features are a listing of books and music for the medieval enthusiast, links to suppliers of medieval equipage and reenactment support services (such as the Drunken Monk Tavern people who man beer tents), and tips on training with medieval arms and staging medieval combats.

Medieval Re-enactment Society
<http://www.shef.ac.uk/~mr/>
The society comprises enthusiasts of fifteenth-century history who reenact the battles of the Wars of the Roses. Society members have taken part in reenactments at Richmond and Bodiam Castles and on the battlefields at Tewkesbury and Bosworth. The site mainly provides information about the society and its activities, but also includes an extensive set of links to other reenactment groups and organizations.

The Red Company
<http://www.historicenterprises.com/redco/>
This American reenactment group portrays a continental military company in the service of Burgundy in the year 1471. During their annual encampments, the company's members sleep in tents, cook meals over a fire, shoot crossbows, fight with swords and pollarms, drill with pikes, and ride horses in armor. Besides a history of the company and a listing of upcoming events, the Web site offers photos of the Red Company encampments, a discussion of fifteenth-century military life, and links to other reenactment societies.

Society for Creative Anachronism
<http://www.sca.org/>
Headquartered in California, the Society for Creative Anachronism (SCA) is an international organization dedicated to researching and recreating pre–seventeenth-century European history. The Web site is an excellent place to start for anyone interested in getting involved in fifteenth-century reenactments in the United States.

Bibliography

General Works

Carpenter, Christine. *The Wars of the Roses: Politics and the Constitution in England, c.1437–1509.* Cambridge: Cambridge University Press, 1997.

Chrimes, S. B. *Lancastrians, Yorkists and Henry VII.* 2d ed. New York: St. Martin's Press, 1966.

Cole, Hubert. *The Wars of the Roses.* London: Hart-Davis, McGibbon, 1973.

Cook, David R. *Lancastrians and Yorkists: The Wars of the Roses.* London: Longman, 1984.

Gillingham, John. *The Wars of the Roses: Peace and Conflict in Fifteenth-Century England.* Baton Rouge: Louisiana State University Press, 1981.

Goodman, Anthony. *The Wars of the Roses: Military Activity and English Society, 1452–97.* New York: Dorset Press, 1981.

Hallam, Elizabeth, ed. *The Wars of the Roses.* New York: Weidenfeld & Nicolson, 1988.

Jacob, E. F. *The Fifteenth Century, 1399–1485.* Oxford: Oxford University Press, 1993.

Keen, M. H. *England in the Later Middle Ages.* London: Routledge, 1995.

Lander, J. R. *The Wars of the Roses.* New York: Capricorn Books, 1965.

McFarlane, K. B. *The Wars of the Roses.* Annual Raleigh Lecture. London: British Academy, 1964.

McKisack, M. *The Fourteenth Century, 1307–1399.* Oxford: Oxford University Press, 1959.

Neillands, Robin. *The Wars of the Roses.* London: Cassell, 1993.

Pollard, A. J. *The Wars of the Roses.* New York: St. Martin's Press, 1988.

Ross, Charles. *The Wars of the Roses: A Concise History.* New York: Thames and Hudson, 1987.

Seward, Desmond. *The Wars of the Roses: Through the Lives of Five Men and Women of the Fifteenth Century.* New York: Viking, 1995.

Weir, Alison. *The Wars of the Roses.* New York: Ballantine Books, 1995.

Reference Works

Boyce, Charles. *Shakespeare A to Z.* New York: Dell Publishing, 1990.

Connolly, S. J., ed. *The Oxford Companion to Irish History.* Oxford: Oxford University Press, 1998.

Gardiner, Juliet, and Neil Wenborn, eds. *The Columbia Companion to British History.* New York: Columbia University Press, 1997.

Hicks, Michael. *Who's Who in Late Medieval England.* London: Shepheard-Walwyn, 1991.

Keay, John, and Julia Keay, eds. *Collins Encyclopaedia of Scotland.* London: HarperCollins, 1994.

Kenyon, J. P., ed. *A Dictionary of British History.* New York: Stein and Day, 1983.

Murph, Roxane C., comp. *The Wars of the Roses in Fiction: An Annotated Bibliography, 1440–1994.* Westport, CT: Greenwood Press, 1995.

Wedgwood, Josiah C. *History of Parliament: Biographies of the Members of the House of Commons, 1439–1509.* London: His Majesty's Stationery Office, 1936.

Collections of Essays and Articles

Archer, Rowena E., ed. *Crown, Government and People in the Fifteenth Century.* New York: St. Martin's Press, 1995.

Britnell, R. H., and A. J. Pollard, eds. *The McFarlane Legacy: Studies in Late Medieval Politics and Society.* Stroud, Gloucestershire, UK: Alan Sutton, 1995.

Chrimes, S. B., C. D. Ross, and R. A. Griffiths, eds. *Fifteenth-Century England, 1399–1509.* 2d ed. Stroud, Gloucestershire, UK: Alan Sutton, 1995.

Clough, C. H., ed. *Profession, Vocation and Culture in Later Medieval England.* Liverpool: Liverpool University Press, 1982.

Davis, R. H. C., and J. M. Wallace-Hadrill, eds. *The Writing of History in the Middle Ages.* Oxford: Clarendon Press, 1981.

Dobson, R. B., ed. *The Church, Politics and Patronage in the Fifteenth Century.* New York: St. Martin's Press, 1984.

Gillingham, John, ed. *Richard III: A Medieval Kingship.* New York: St. Martin's Press, 1993.

Griffiths, Ralph A., ed. *King and Country: England and Wales in the Fifteenth Century.* London: Hambledon Press, 1991.

———, ed. *Patronage, the Crown and the Provinces in Later Medieval England.* Atlantic Highlands, NJ: Humanities Press, 1981.

Griffiths, Ralph A., and James Sherborne, eds. *Kings and Nobles in the Later Middle Ages.* New York: St. Martin's Press, 1986.

Guy, J. A., and A. Fox, eds. *Reassessing the Henrician Age.* Oxford: Blackwell, 1986.

Hammond, P. W., ed. *Richard III: Loyalty, Lordship and Law.* London: Richard III and Yorkist History Trust, 1986.

Highfield, J. R. L., and R. A. Jeffs, eds. *The Crown and Local Communities in England and France in the Fifteenth Century.* Stroud, Gloucestershire, UK: Alan Sutton, 1981.

Horrox, Rosemary, ed. *Fifteenth-Century Attitudes: Perceptions of Society in Late Medieval England.* Cambridge: Cambridge University Press, 1994.

McFarlane, K. B. *England in the Fifteenth Century: Collected Essays.* London: Hambledon Press, 1981.

Michalove, Sharon D., and A. Compton Reeves, eds. *Estrangement, Enterprise and Education in Fifteenth-Century England.* Stroud, Gloucestershire, UK: Sutton Publishing, 1998.

Pollard, A. J., ed. *The North of England in the Reign of Richard III.* New York: St. Martin's Press, 1995.

———, ed. *Property and Politics: Essays in Later Medieval English History.* Stroud, Gloucestershire, UK: Alan Sutton, 1984.

———, ed. *The Wars of the Roses.* New York: St. Martin's Press, 1995.

Rosenthal, J. T., and C. F. Richmond, eds. *People, Politics and Community in the Later Middle Ages.* Stroud, Gloucestershire, UK: Alan Sutton, 1987.

Ross, Charles, ed. *Patronage, Pedigree and Power in Later Medieval England.* Stroud, Gloucestershire, UK: Alan Sutton, 1979.

Rowe, J. G., ed. *Aspects of Late Medieval Government and Society.* Toronto: University of Toronto Press, 1986.

Thompson, B., ed. *The Reign of Henry VII.* Stamford, 1995.

Primary Sources

Bruce, John, ed. *Historie of the Arrivall of Edward IV in England and the Final Recouerye of His Kingdomes from Henry VI.* In *Three Chronicles of the Reign of Edward IV.* Introduction by Keith Dockray. Stroud, Gloucestershire, UK: Alan Sutton Publishing, 1988, pp. 131–193.

Carpenter, Christine, ed. *Kingsford's Stonor Letters and Papers, 1290–1483.* Cambridge: Cambridge University Press, 1996.

Commines, Philippe de. *The Memoirs of Philippe de Commynes.* Edited by Samuel Kinser. Translated by Isabelle Cazeaux. 2 vols. Columbia: University of South Carolina Press, 1969–1973.

Davis, Norman, ed. *The Paston Letters: A Selection in Modern Spelling.* Oxford: Oxford University Press, 1999.

———, ed. *The Paston Letters and Papers of the Fifteenth Century.* 2 vols. Oxford: Oxford University Press, 1971, 1976.

Ellis, Henry, ed. *The Chronicle of John Hardyng Together with the Continuation of Richard Grafton.* London, 1812.

———, ed. *Hall's Chronicle.* Reprint ed. New York: AMS Press, 1965.

———, ed. *Three Books of Polydore Vergil's English History, Comprising the Reigns of Henry VI, Edward IV, and Richard III.* London: Camden Society, 1844.

Fabyan, Robert. *The Great Chronicle of London.* Edited by A. H. Thomas and I. D. Thornley. Stroud, Gloucestershire, UK: Alan Sutton, 1983.

———. *The New Chronicles of England and France.* Edited by Henry Ellis. London: Printed for F. C. & J. Rivington, 1811.

Fortescue, Sir John. *De Laudibus Legum Anglie.* Edited and translated by S. B. Chrimes. Holmes Beach, FL: William W. Gaunt & Sons, 1986.

———. *Sir John Fortescue: On the Laws and Governance of England.* Edited by Shelley Lockwood. Cambridge: Cambridge University Press, 1997.

Gairdner, James, ed. *The Historical Collections of a Citizen of London in the Fifteenth Century* [Gregory's Chronicle]. New York: Johnson Reprint Corporation, 1965.

———, ed. *The Paston Letters, 1422–1509.* 6 vols. London: Chatto & Windus, 1904; reprint, Stroud, Gloucestershire, UK: Alan Sutton, 1984.

Halliwell, James Orchard, ed. *A Chronicle of the First Thirteen Years of the Reign of King Edward the Fourth, by John Warkworth.* In *Three Chronicles of the Reign of Edward IV.* Introduction by Keith Dockray. Stroud, Gloucestershire, UK: Alan Sutton Publishing, 1988, pp. 1–102.

Hanham, Alison, ed. *The Cely Letters 1472–1488.* Oxford: Oxford University Press, 1975.

Hardyng, John. *The Chronicle of John Hardyng.* Reprint ed. New York: AMS Press, 1974.

James, M. R., ed. *Henry the Sixth: A Reprint of John Blacman's Memoir.* Cambridge: Cambridge University Press, 1919.

Kendall, Paul Murray, ed. *Richard III: The Great Debate.* New York: W. W. Norton, 1992.

Kirby, Joan, ed. *The Plumpton Letters and Papers.* Cambridge: Cambridge University Press, 1996.

Littleton, Taylor, and Robert R. Rea, eds. *To Prove a Villain: The Case of King Richard III.* New York: Macmillan, 1964.

Malory, Sir Thomas. *Le Morte d'Arthur.* Edited by Keith Baines. New York: Bramhall House, 1962.

———. *Le Morte d'Arthur.* Edited by R. M. Lumiansky. London: Collier Macmillan Publishers, 1982.

Mancini, Dominic. *The Usurpation of Richard III.* Edited and translated by C. A. J. Armstrong. Stroud, Gloucestershire, UK: Alan Sutton, 1989.

Matheson, Lister M., ed. *Death and Dissent: Two Fifteenth-Century Chronicles.* Woodbridge, Suffolk: Boydell Press, 1999.

More, Sir Thomas. *History of King Richard III.* In Paul Murray Kendall, ed. *Richard III: The Great Debate.* New York: W. W. Norton, 1992, pp. 31–143.

——. *The History of King Richard III and Selections from the English and Latin Poems.* Edited by Richard S. Sylvester. New Haven, CT: Yale University Press, 1976.

Myers, A. R., ed. *The Household of Edward IV.* Manchester: Manchester University Press, 1959.

Nichols, John Gough, ed. *Chronicle of the Rebellion in Lincolnshire, 1470.* In *Three Chronicles of the Reign of Edward IV.* Introduction by Keith Dockray. Stroud, Gloucestershire, UK: Alan Sutton Publishing, 1988, pp. 103–131.

Pronay, Nicholas, and John Cox, eds. *The Crowland Chronicle Continuations: 1459–1486.* London: Richard III and Yorkist History Trust, 1986.

Rous, John. "The History of the Kings of England," in Alison Hanham, *Richard III and His Early Historians, 1483–1535.* Oxford: Clarendon Press, 1975.

——. *The Rous Roll.* Reprint ed. Stroud, Gloucestershire, UK: Alan Sutton, 1980.

Stapleton, Thomas, ed. *The Plumpton Correspondence.* London: Camden Society, 1839; reprint ed., Stroud, Gloucestershire, UK: Alan Sutton, 1990.

Three Chronicles of the Reign of Edward IV. Introduction by Keith Dockray. Stroud, Gloucestershire, UK: Alan Sutton Publishing, 1988.

Vergil, Polydore. *The Anglica Historia of Polydore Vergil.* London: Royal Historical Society, 1950.

Virgoe, Roger, ed. *Private Life in the Fifteenth Century: Illustrated Letters of the Paston Family.* New York: Weidenfeld and Nicolson, 1989.

Warrington, John, ed. *The Paston Letters.* 2 vols. Revised ed. London: J. M. Dent & Sons, 1956.

Waurin, Jean. *Recueil des Croniques et Anchiennes Istories de la Grant Bretaigne, a present nomme Engleterre.* Edited and translated by Sir William Hardy. 5 vols. London: Longman, Green, and Roberts, 1864–1891.

Ireland, Scotland, and Wales

Brown, Jennifer M., ed. *Scottish Society in the Fifteenth Century.* New York: St. Martin's Press, 1977.

Cosgrove, Art. *Late Medieval Ireland, 1370–1541.* Dublin: Helicon, 1981.

Davies, John. *A History of Wales.* London: The Penguin Group, 1993.

Evans, H. T. *Wales and the Wars of the Roses.* Stroud, Gloucestershire, UK: Alan Sutton Publishing, 1995.

Lydon, James. *Ireland in the Later Middle Ages.* Dublin: Gill and Macmillan, 1973.

Mackie, J. D. *A History of Scotland,* 2d ed. New York: Dorset Press, 1985.

Nicholson, Ranald. *Scotland: The Later Middle Ages.* Vol. 2 of *The Edinburgh History of Scotland.* New York: Barnes and Noble, 1974.

Otway-Ruthven, A. J. *A History of Medieval Ireland.* New York: Barnes and Noble Books, 1980.

Reeves, Albert C. *The Marcher Lords.* Llandybie, Dyfed, UK: C. Davies, 1983.

Williams, Glanmor. *Renewal and Reformation: Wales, c.1415–1642.* Oxford: Oxford University Press, 1993.

Wormald, Jenny. *Court, Kirk, and Community: Scotland, 1470–1625.* Toronto: University of Toronto Press, 1981.

Brittany, Burgundy, France, and Europe

Armstrong, C. A. J. *England, France and Burgundy in the Fifteenth Century.* London: Hambledon Press, 1983.

Calmette, Joseph. *The Golden Age of Burgundy: The Magnificent Dukes and Their Courts.* Translated by Doreen Weightman. New York: W. W. Norton, 1963.

Cope, Christopher. *Phoenix Frustrated: The Lost Kingdom of Burgundy.* London: Constable, 1986.

Galliou, Patrick, and Michael Jones. *The Bretons.* Oxford: Basil Blackwell, 1991.

Harvey, Margaret. *England, Rome and the Papacy, 1417–1464.* Manchester: Manchester University Press, 1993.

Jones, Michael. *The Creation of Brittany: A Late Medieval State.* London: Hambledon, 1988.

Lloyd, T. H., *England and the German Hanse, 1157–1611.* Cambridge: Cambridge University Press, 1991.

Potter, David. *A History of France, 1460–1560: The Emergence of a Nation State.* London: Macmillan, 1995.

Thompson, Guy Llewelyn. *Paris and Its People under English Rule: The Anglo-Burgundian Regime, 1420–1436.* Oxford: Clarendon Press, 1991.

Vale, M. G. A. *English Gascony, 1399–1453: A Study of War, Government and Politics during the Later Stages of the Hundred Years' War.* London: Oxford University Press, 1970.

Vaughan, Richard. *Valois Burgundy.* Hamden, CT: Archon Books, 1975.

Political, Constitutional, and Legal History

Baldwin, James F. *The King's Council in England during the Middle Ages.* Gloucester, MA: P. Smith, 1965.

Bean, J. M. W. *From Lord to Patron: Lordship in Late Medieval England.* Manchester: Manchester University Press, 1989.

Bellamy, J. G. *Bastard Feudalism and the Law.* Portland, OR: Areopagitica Press, 1989.

———. *Crime and Public Order in England in the Later Middle Ages.* London: Routledge and Kegan Paul, 1973.

———. *The Law of Treason in England in the Later Middle Ages.* Cambridge: Cambridge University Press, 1970.

Blatcher, M. *The Court of King's Bench, 1450–1550: A Study in Self-Help.* London: Athlone Press, 1978.

Butt, Ronald. *A History of Parliament: The Middle Ages.* London: Constable, 1989.

Davies, R. G., and J. H. Denton, eds. *The English Parliament in the Middle Ages.* Philadelphia: University of Pennsylvania Press, 1981.

Ferguson, John. *English Diplomacy, 1422–1461.* Oxford: Clarendon Press, 1972.

Harding, Alan. *The Law Courts of Medieval England.* London: Allen & Unwin, 1973.

Lander, J. R. *Conflict and Stability in Fifteenth-Century England.* 2d ed. London: Hutchinson University Library, 1974.

———. *Crown and Nobility, 1450–1509.* Montreal: McGill-Queen's University Press, 1976.

———. *English Justices of the Peace, 1461–1509.* Stroud, Gloucestershire, UK: Alan Sutton, 1989.

———. *Government and Community, England, 1450–1509.* Cambridge, MA: Harvard University Press, 1980.

———. *The Limitations of the English Monarchy in the Later Middle Ages.* Toronto: University of Toronto Press, 1989.

Loades, D. M. *Politics and the Nation, 1450–1660: Obedience, Resistance and Public Order.* London: Fontana Press, 1986.

———. *The Tudor Court.* Totowa, NJ: Barnes and Noble Books, 1987.

Reid, Rachel R. *The King's Council in the North.* Totowa, NJ: Rowman and Littlefield, 1975.

Starkey, David, et al. *The English Court: From the Wars of the Roses to the Civil War.* London: Longman, 1987.

Social, Economic, and Cultural History

Acheson, Eric. *A Gentry Community: Leicestershire in the Fifteenth Century, c.1422–c.1485.* New York: Cambridge University Press, 1992.

Baker, Timothy. *Medieval London.* New York, Praeger, 1970.

Bolton, J. L. *The Medieval English Economy, 1150–1500.* London: J. M. Dent and Sons, 1980.

Carpenter, Christine. *Locality and Polity: A Study of Warwickshire Landed Society, 1401–1499.* Cambridge: Cambridge University Press, 1992.

Coleman, D. C. *The Economy of England, 1450–1750.* Oxford: Oxford University Press, 1977.

Cross, Claire. *Church and People, 1450–1660.* Glasgow, UK: Fontana/Collins, 1976.

Davies, C. S. L. *Peace, Print and Protestantism, 1450–1558.* London: Hart-Davis, MacGibbon, 1976.

Du Boulay, F. R. H. *An Age of Ambition: English Society in the Late Middle Ages.* New York: Viking, 1970.

Given-Wilson, Chris. *The English Nobility in the Later Middle Ages.* London: Routledge and Kegan Paul, 1987.

Gransden, Antonia. *Historical Writing in England.* Vol. 2: *c.1307 to the Early Sixteenth Century.* Ithaca, NY: Cornell University Press, 1982.

Harrison, Frank L. *Music in Medieval Britain.* 4th ed. Buren, Netherlands: F. Knuf, 1980.

Hatcher, John. *Plague, Population and the English Economy, 1348–1530.* London: Macmillan, 1994.

Hicks, Michael. *Bastard Feudalism.* London: Longman, 1995.

Hindley, Geoffrey. *England in the Age of Caxton.* New York: St. Martin's Press, 1979.

Keen, Maurice. *English Society in the Later Middle Ages, 1348–1500.* London: Penguin Books, 1990.

McFarlane, K. B. *The Nobility of Later Medieval England.* Oxford: Clarendon Press, 1973.

Mears, Kenneth J. *The Tower of London: 900 Years of English History.* Oxford: Phaidon, 1988.

Mertes, Kate. *The English Noble Household, 1250 to 1600: Good Governance and Politic Rule.* Oxford: B. Blackwell, 1988.

Munro, J. H. *Wool, Cloth and Gold: The Struggle for Bullion in Anglo-Burgundian Trade, 1340–1478.* Toronto: University of Toronto Press, 1972.

Norwich, John Julius. *Shakespeare's Kings.* New York: Scribner, 1999.

Pollard, A. J. *North-Eastern England during the Wars of Roses: Lay Society, War, and Politics, 1450–1500.* Oxford: Clarendon Press, 1990.

Porter, Roy. *London: A Social History.* Cambridge, MA: Harvard University Press, 1994.

Postan, M. M. *The Medieval Economy and Society: An Economic History of Britain, 1100–1500.* Berkeley: University of California Press, 1972.

Rowse, A. L. *The Tower of London in the History of the Nation.* London: Weidenfeld and Nicolson, 1972.

Saccio, Peter. *Shakespeare's English Kings,* 2d ed. Oxford: Oxford University Press, 2000.

Sheppard, Francis. *London: A History.* Oxford: Oxford University Press, 1998.

Walker, S. *The Lancastrian Affinity, 1361–1399.* Oxford: Oxford University Press, 1989.

Weiss, Roberto. *Humanism in England during the Fifteenth Century.* Oxford: Blackwell, 1967.

Wilson, Derek A. *The Tower of London: A Thousand Years.* London: Allison & Busby, 1998.

Winston, J. E. *English Towns in the Wars of the Roses.* Princeton, NJ: Princeton University Press, 1921.

Woolgar, C. M. *The Great Household in Late Medieval England.* New Haven, CT: Yale University Press, 1999.

Military Issues, Wars, and Battle Accounts

Allmand, Christopher. *The Hundred Years War.* Cambridge: Cambridge University Press, 1988.

Bennett, Michael. *The Battle of Bosworth.* New York: St. Martin's Press, 1985.

———. *Lambert Simnel and the Battle of Stoke.* New York: St. Martin's Press, 1987.

Boardman, Andrew W. *The Battle of Towton.* Stroud, Gloucestershire, UK: Sutton Publishing, 1996.

———. *The Medieval Soldier in the Wars of the Roses.* Stroud, Gloucestershire, UK: Sutton Publishing, 1998.

Bradbury, Jim. *The Medieval Archer.* Woodbridge, Suffolk, UK: Boydell Press, 1985.

Brooke, Richard. *Visits to Fields of Battle in England of the Fifteenth Century.* Dursley, UK: Alan Sutton, 1975.

Burne, Alfred H. *The Battlefields of England.* London: Greenhill Books, 1996.

Curry, Anne. *The Hundred Years War.* Hampshire: Macmillan, 1993.

DeVries, Kelly. *Medieval Military Technology.* Peterborough, Ontario: Broadview Press, 1992.

Fairbairn, Neil. *A Traveller's Guide to the Battlefields of Britain.* London: Evans Brothers, 1983.

Foss, Peter J. *The Field of Redemore: The Battle of Bosworth, 1485.* 2d ed. Newtown Linford, UK: Kairos, 1998.

———. *The Battle of Wakefield, 1460.* Stroud, Gloucestershire, UK: Sutton Publishing, 1996.

Haigh, Philip A. *The Military Campaigns of the Wars of the Roses.* Stroud, Gloucestershire, UK: Sutton Publishing, 1995.

Hammond, P. W. *The Battles of Barnet and Tewkesbury.* New York: St. Martin's Press, 1990.

Hodges, Geoffrey. *Ludford Bridge and Mortimer's Cross.* Herefordshire, UK: Long Aston Press, 1989.

Keen, Maurice, ed. *Medieval Warfare.* Oxford: Oxford University Press, 1999.

Kinross, John. *The Battlefields of Britain.* London: David and Charles, 1979.

Norris, John. *Artillery: An Illustrated History.* Stroud, Gloucestershire, UK: Sutton Publishing, 2000.

Oman, C. W. C. *The Art of War in the Middle Ages.* Rev. ed. Ithaca, NY: Cornell University Press, 1953.

Perroy, Edouard. *The Hundred Years War.* New York: Capricorn Books, 1965.

Prestwich, Michael. *Armies and Warfare in the Middle Ages: The English Experience.* New Haven, CT: Yale University Press, 1996.

Rodger, N. A. M. *The Safeguard of the Sea: A Naval History of Britain.* New York: W. W. Norton, 1998.

Rogers, H. C. B. *Artillery through the Ages.* London: Seeley, 1971.

Rowse, A. L. *Bosworth Field: From Medieval to Tudor England.* Garden City, NY: Doubleday, 1966.

Seward, Desmond. *The Hundred Years War.* New York: Atheneum, 1978.

Swynnerton, Brian, and William Swinnerton. *The Battle of Blore Heath, 1459.* Nuneaton, UK: Paddy Griffith Associates, 1995.

Vale, M. G. A. *War and Chivalry: Warfare and Aristocratic Culture in England, France, and Burgundy at the End of the Middle Ages.* Athens: University of Georgia Press, 1981.

Williams, D. T. *The Battle of Bosworth.* Leicester: Leicester University Press, 1973.

Early Fifteenth Century, 1399–1437

Allmand, C. T. *Lancastrian Normandy, 1415–1450: The History of a Medieval Occupation.* Oxford: Clarendon Press, 1983.

Bennett, Michael. *Richard II and the Revolution of 1399.* Stroud, Gloucestershire, UK: Sutton Publishing, 1999.

Harriss, G. L., ed. *Henry V: The Practice of Kingship.* Oxford: Oxford University Press, 1984.

McFarlane, K. B. *Lancastrian Kings and Lollard Knights.* Oxford: Clarendon Press, 1972.

McNiven, Peter. *Heresy and Politics in the Reign of Henry IV: The Burning of John Badby.* Wolfeboro, NH: Boydell Press, 1987.

Strohm, Paul. *England's Empty Throne: Usurpation and the Language of Legitimation, 1399–1422.* New Haven, CT: Yale University Press, 1998.

Reigns of Henry VI and Edward IV, 1437–1483

Dockray, Keith. *Edward IV: A Source Book.* Stroud, Gloucestershire, UK: Sutton Publishing, 1999.

———. *Henry VI, Margaret of Anjou and the Wars of the Roses: A Source Book.* Stroud, Gloucestershire, UK: Sutton Publishing, 2000.

Griffiths, Ralph A. *The Reign of King Henry VI: The Exercise of Royal Authority, 1422–61.* Berkeley: University of California Press, 1981.

Gross, Anthony. *The Dissolution of the Lancastrian Kingship: Sir John Fortescue and the Crisis of Monarchy in Fifteenth-Century England.* Stamford, UK: Paul Watkins, 1996.

Harvey, I. M. W. *Jack Cade's Rebellion of 1450.* Oxford: Clarendon Press, 1991.

Kendall, Paul Murray. *The Yorkist Age: Daily Life during the Wars of the Roses.* New York: W. W. Norton, 1962.

Storey, R. L. *The End of the House of Lancaster.* 2d ed. Stroud, Gloucestershire, UK: Sutton Publishing, 1999.

Watts, John. *Henry VI and the Politics of Kingship.* Cambridge: Cambridge University Press, 1996.

Wolffe, B. P. *The Crown Lands, 1461–1536: An Aspect of Yorkist and Early Tudor Government.* London: Allen & Unwin, 1970.

Reign of Richard III, 1483–1485

Buck, Sir George. *The History of King Richard III.* Edited by A. N. Kincaid. Stroud, Gloucestershire, UK: Sutton Publishing, 1982.

Dockray, Keith. *Richard III: A Source Book.* Stroud, Gloucestershire, UK: Sutton Publishing, 1997.

Gairdner, James. *History of the Life and Reign of Richard the Third,* 2d ed. Cambridge: Cambridge University Press, 1898.

Gill, Louise. *Richard III and Buckingham's Rebellion.* Stroud, Gloucestershire, UK: Sutton Publishing, 1999.

Halsted, Caroline A. *Richard III as Duke of Gloucester and King of England,* 2 vols. London, 1844; reprint ed., Stroud, Gloucestershire, UK: Sutton Publishing, 1977.

Hanham, Alison. *Richard III and His Early Historians, 1483–1535.* Oxford: Clarendon Press, 1975.

Hicks, Michael. *Richard III and His Rivals: Magnates and Their Motives in the Wars of the Roses.* London: Hambledon Press, 1991.

Lamb, V. B. *The Betrayal of Richard III: An Introduction to the Controversy.* Stroud, Gloucestershire, UK: Alan Sutton Publishing, 1996.

Markham, Sir Clements R. *Richard III: His Life and Character, Reviewed in the Light of Recent Research.* New York: Russell & Russell, 1968.

St. Aubyn, Giles. *The Year of the Three Kings, 1483.* New York: Atheneum, 1983.

Tey, Josephine. *The Daughter of Time.* New York: Berkeley Medallion Books, 1975.

Walpole, Horace. *Historic Doubts on the Life and Reign of Richard III.* Edited by P. W. Hammond. Stroud, Gloucestershire, UK: Sutton Publishing, 1987.

——. *Historic Doubts on the Life and Reign of King Richard III.* In Paul Murray Kendall, ed. *Richard III: The Great Debate.* New York: W. W. Norton, 1992.

Wood, Charles T. *Joan of Arc and Richard III: Sex, Saints and Government in the Middle Ages.* Oxford: Oxford University Press, 1988.

Princes in the Tower

Fields, Bertram. *Royal Blood: Richard III and the Mystery of the Princes.* New York: Regan Books, 1998.

Jenkins, Elizabeth. *The Princes in the Tower.* New York: Coward, McCann & Geoghegan, 1978.

Pollard, A. J. *Richard III and the Princes in the Tower.* New York: St Martin's Press, 1991.

Weir, Alison. *The Princes in the Tower.* New York: Ballantine Books, 1992.

Williamson, Audrey. *The Mystery of the Princes: An Investigation into a Supposed Murder.* Chicago: Academy Chicago Publishers, 1986.

Reign of Henry VII, 1485–1509

Arthurson, Ian. *The Perkin Warbeck Conspiracy, 1491–1499.* Stroud, Gloucestershire, UK: Sutton Publishing, 1997.

Elton, G. R. *England under the Tudors.* 3d ed. London: Routledge, 1991.

Griffiths, Ralph A., and Roger S. Thomas. *The Making of the Tudor Dynasty.* New York: St. Martin's Press, 1985.

Gunn, S. *Early Tudor Government, 1485–1558.* London, 1995.

Levine, Mortimer. *Tudor Dynastic Problems, 1460–1571.* London: George Allen & Unwin, 1973.

Mackie, J. D. *The Earlier Tudors, 1485–1558.* Oxford: Oxford University Press, 1994.

Pugh, T. B. *Henry VII: The Importance of His Reign in English History.* London, 1985.

Storey, R. L. *The Reign of Henry VII.* New York: Walker and Company, 1968.

Biography—Individuals

Allmand, Christopher. *Henry V.* Berkeley: University of California Press, 1992.

Bacon, Francis. *The History of the Reign of King Henry Seventh.* Edited by F. J. Levy. Indianapolis: Bobbs-Merrill, 1972.

Bagley, John J. *Margaret of Anjou.* London: Batsford, 1948.

Blake, N. F. *Caxton: England's First Publisher.* New York: Barnes and Noble, 1976.

——. *William Caxton and English Literary Culture.* London: Hambledon Press, 1991.

Bryan, Donough. *Gerald Fitzgerald, the Great Earl of Kildare, 1456–1513.* Dublin: Talbot Press, 1933.

Chrimes, S. B. *Henry VII.* New Haven, CT; Yale University Press, 1999.

Cleugh, James. *Chant Royal: The Life of King Louis XI of France (1423–1483).* Garden City, NY: Doubleday, 1970.

Clive, Mary. *This Sun of York: A Biography of Edward IV.* New York: Macmillan, 1973.

Deacon, Richard. *A Biography of William Caxton: The First English Editor, Printer, Merchant, and Translator.* London: Muller, 1976.

Dunlop, Annie. *The Life and Times of James Kennedy, Bishop of St. Andrews.* Edinburgh: Oliver and Boyd, 1950.

Erlanger, Philippe. *Margaret of Anjou: Queen of England.* London: Elek Books, 1970.

Falkus, Gila. *The Life and Times of Edward IV.* London: Weidenfeld and Nicolson, 1981.

Field, P. J. C. *The Life and Times of Sir Thomas Malory.* Cambridge: D. S. Brewer, 1993.

Griffiths, Ralph A. *Sir Rhys ap Thomas and His Family: A Study in the Wars of the Roses and Early Tudor Politics.* Cardiff, UK: University of Wales Press, 1993.

Hammond, P. W., and Anne F. Sutton. *Richard III: The Road to Bosworth Field.* London: Constable, 1985.

Harriss, G. L. *Cardinal Beaufort: A Study of the Lancastrian Ascendancy and Decline.* Oxford: Clarendon Press, 1988.

Harvey, Nancy Lenz. *Elizabeth of York: Tudor Queen.* New York: Macmillan, 1973.

Hay, Denys. *Polydore Vergil: Renaissance Historian and Man of Letters.* Oxford: Clarendon Press, 1952.

Head, David. *The Ebbs and Flows of Fortune: The Life of Thomas Howard, Third Duke of Norfolk.* Athens: University of Georgia Press, 1995.

Hicks, Michael. *False, Fleeting, Perjur'd Clarence: George, Duke of Clarence, 1449–78.* Rev. ed. Bangor, UK: Headstart History, 1992.

———. *Richard III: The Man Behind the Myth.* London: Collins & Brown, 1991.

———. *Warwick the Kingmaker.* Oxford: Blackwell Publishers, 1998.

Horrox, Rosemary. *Richard III: A Study in Service.* Cambridge: Cambridge University Press, 1991.

Hutchison, Harold F. *The Hollow Crown: The Life of Richard II.* London: Eyre & Spottiswoode, 1961.

———. *King Henry V: A Biography.* New York: Dorset Press, 1967.

Johnson, P. A. *Duke Richard of York, 1411–1460.* Oxford: Clarendon Press, 1988.

Jones, Michael K., and Malcolm G. Underwood. *The King's Mother: Lady Margaret Beaufort, Countess of Richmond and Derby.* Cambridge: Cambridge University Press, 1992.

Kendall, Paul Murray. *Louis XI: The Universal Spider.* New York: W. W. Norton, 1971.

———. *Richard the Third.* New York: W. W. Norton, 1956.

———. *Warwick the Kingmaker.* New York: W. W. Norton, 1987.

Kirby, John Lavan. *Henry IV of England.* London: Constable, 1970.

Labarge, Margaret Wade. *Henry V: The Cautious Conqueror.* New York: Stein and Day, 1976.

Macdougall, Norman. *James III: A Political Study.* Edinburgh: J. Donald, 1982.

———. *James IV.* East Lothian, UK: Tuckwell Press, 1997.

MacGibbon, David. *Elizabeth Woodville: Her Life and Times.* London: A. Barker, 1938.

McGladdery, Christine. *James II.* Edinburgh: John Donald Publishers, 1990.

Mitchell, R. J. *John Tiptoft: An Italianate Englishman, 1427–1470.* London: Longmans, Green, 1938.

Painter, George D. *William Caxton: A Biography.* New York: Putnam, 1977.

Pollard, A. J. *John Talbot and the War in France, 1427–1453.* London: Royal Historical Society, 1983.

Potter, Jeremy. *Good King Richard? An Account of Richard III and His Reputation.* London: Constable, 1994.

Rees, David. *The Son of Prophecy: Henry Tudor's Road to Bosworth.* 2d ed. Ruthin, UK: John Jones, 1997.

Roskell, John S. *William Catesby, Counselor to Richard III.* Manchester: John Rylands Library, 1959 [reprinted from the *Bulletin of the John Rylands Library,* vol. 42, no. 1, September, 1959].

Ross, Charles. *Edward IV.* New Haven, CT: Yale University Press, 1998.

———. *Richard III.* Berkeley: University of California Press, 1981.

Saul, Nigel. *Richard II.* New Haven, CT: Yale University Press, 1997.

Seward, Desmond. *Henry V: The Scourge of God.* New York: Viking, 1988.

———. *Richard III: England's Black Legend.* New York: Franklin Watts, 1984.

Simon, Linda. *Of Virtue Rare: Margaret Beaufort, Matriarch of the House of Tudor.* Boston: Houghton Mifflin Company, 1982.

Tucker, Melvin J. *The Life of Thomas Howard, Earl of Surrey and Second Duke of Norfolk, 1443–1524.* The Hague, Netherlands: Mouton, 1964.

Tyrrell, Joseph M. *Louis XI.* Boston: Twayne, 1980.

Vale, M.G.A. *Charles VII.* Berkeley: University of California Press, 1974.

Vaughan, Richard. *Charles the Bold: The Last Valois Duke of Burgundy.* London: Longman, 1973.

———. *John the Fearless: The Growth of Burgundian Power.* London: Longman, 1979.

———. *Philip the Bold: The Formation of the Burgundian State.* Cambridge, MA: Harvard University Press, 1962.

———. *Philip the Good: The Apogee of Burgundy.* New York: Barnes and Noble, 1970.

Weightman, Christine. *Margaret of York: Duchess of Burgundy, 1446–1503.* Stroud, Gloucestershire, UK: Alan Sutton, 1993.

Williams, E. C. *My Lord of Bedford, 1389–1435.* London: Longmans, 1963.

Wolffe, Bertram. *Henry VI.* London: Eyre Methuen, 1981.

Biographies—Families

Bagley, John J. *The Earls of Derby, 1485–1985.* London: Sidgwick & Jackson, 1985.

Bennett, H. S. *The Pastons and Their England: Studies in an Age of Transition.* 2d ed. Cambridge: Cambridge University Press, 1990.

Clifford, Hugh. *The House of Clifford.* London: Phillimore, 1987.

Coward, Barry. *The Stanleys, Lords Stanley, and Earls of Derby, 1385–1672: The Origins, Wealth, and Power of a Landowning Family*. Manchester: Manchester University Press, 1983.

Gies, Frances, and Joseph Gies. *A Medieval Family: The Pastons of Fifteenth-Century England*. New York: HarperCollins, 1998.

Hanham, Alison. *The Celys and Their World: An English Merchant Family of the Fifteenth Century*. Cambridge: Cambridge University Press, 1985.

Harvey, John. *The Plantagenets*. 3d ed. London: Severn House, 1976.

Harwood, William R. "The Courtenay Family in the Politics of Region and Nation in the Later Fifteenth and Early Sixteenth Centuries." Ph.D. dissertation, Cambridge University, 1978.

Rawcliffe, Carole. *The Staffords, Earls of Stafford and Dukes of Buckingham, 1394–1521*. Cambridge: Cambridge University Press, 1978.

Richmond, Colin. *The Paston Family in the Fifteenth Century: The First Phase*. Cambridge; Cambridge University Press, 1990.

——. *The Paston Family in the Fifteenth Century: Fastolf's Will*. Cambridge: Cambridge University Press, 1996.

Young, Charles R. *The Making of the Neville Family in England, 1166–1400*. Woodbridge, Suffolk, UK: Boydell & Brewer, 1997.

Articles and Essays

Allan, Alison. "Yorkist Propaganda: Pedigree, Prophecy and the 'British History' in the Reign of Edward IV." In Charles Ross, ed., *Patronage, Pedigree and Power in Later Medieval England*. Stroud, Gloucestershire, UK: Alan Sutton, 1979.

Antonovics, A. V. "Henry VII, King of England, by the Grace of Charles VIII of France." In Ralph A. Griffiths and James Sherborne, eds., *Kings and Nobles in the Later Middle Ages*. New York: St. Martin's Press, 1986.

Ayton, Andrew. "Arms, Armour, and Horses." In Maurice Keen, ed., *Medieval Warfare*. Oxford: Oxford University Press, 1999.

Britnell, R. H. "The Economic Context." In A. J. Pollard, ed.. *The Wars of the Roses*. New York: St. Martin's Press, 1995.

Cherry, Martin. "The Struggle for Power in Mid-Fifteenth-Century Devonshire." In Ralph A. Griffiths, ed., *Patronage, the Crown and the Provinces in Later Medieval England*. Atlantic Highlands, NJ: Humanities Press, 1981.

Crawford, Anne. "The Private Life of John Howard: A Study of a Yorkist Lord, His Family and Household." In P. W. Hammond, ed., *Richard III: Loyalty, Lordship and Law*. London: Richard III and Yorkist History Trust, 1986.

Davies, C. S. L. "The Wars of the Roses in European Context." In A. J. Pollard, ed., *The Wars of the Roses*. New York: St. Martin's Press, 1995.

Davies, Richard G. "The Church and the Wars of the Roses." In A. J. Pollard, ed., *The Wars of the Roses*. New York: St. Martin's Press, 1995.

Davis, V. "William Waynflete and the Educational Revolution of the Fifteenth Century." In J. T. Rosenthal and C. F. Richmond, eds., *People, Politics and Community in the Later Middle Ages*. Stroud, Gloucestershire, UK: Alan Sutton, 1987.

Dockray, Keith. "The Origins of the Wars of the Roses." In A. J. Pollard, ed., *The Wars of the Roses*. New York: St. Martin's Press, 1995.

——. "The Political Legacy of Richard III in Northern England." In Ralph A. Griffiths and James Sherborne, eds., *Kings and Nobles in the Later Middle Ages*. New York: St. Martin's Press, 1986.

Dunn, Diana. "Margaret of Anjou, Queen Consort of Henry VI: A Reassessment of Her Role, 1445–53." In Rowena E. Archer, ed., *Crown, Government and People in the Fifteenth Century*. New York: St. Martin's Press, 1995.

Dunning, Robert W. "Patronage and Promotion in the Late-Medieval Church." In Ralph A. Griffiths, ed., *Patronage, the Crown and the Provinces in Later Medieval England*. Atlantic Highlands, NJ: Humanities Press, 1981.

Griffiths, Ralph A. "The Crown and the Royal Family in Later Medieval England." In Ralph A. Griffiths and James Sherborne, eds., *Kings and Nobles in the Later Middle Ages*. New York: St. Martin's Press, 1986.

——. "The King's Court during the Wars of the Roses." In Ralph A. Griffiths, ed., *King and Country: England and Wales in the Fifteenth Century*. London: Hambledon Press, 1991.

——. "Local Rivalries and National Politics: The Percies, the Nevilles and the Duke of Exeter, 1452–1455." In Ralph A. Griffiths, ed., *King and Country: England and Wales in the Fifteenth Century*. London: Hambledon Press, 1991.

——. "The Sense of Dynasty in the Reign of Henry VI." In Ralph A. Griffiths, ed., *King and Country: England and Wales in the Fifteenth Century*. London: Hambledon Press, 1991.

——. "Wales and the Marches." In S. B., Chrimes, C. D. Ross, and R. A. Griffiths, eds., *Fifteenth-Century England, 1399–1509*. 2d ed. Stroud, Gloucestershire, UK: Alan Sutton, 1995.

Guth, DeLloyd J. "Climbing the Civil-Service Pole during the Civil War: Sir Reynald Bray." In Sharon D. Michalove and A. Compton Reeves, eds., *Estrangement, Enterprise and Education in Fifteenth-Century England*. Stroud, Gloucestershire, UK: Sutton Publishing, 1998.

Guy, John A. "The King's Council and Political Participation." In J. A. Guy and A. Fox, eds., *Reassessing
the Henrician Age.* Oxford: Blackwell, 1986.

Harvey, I. M. W. "Was There Popular Politics in Fifteenth-Century England?" In R. H. Britnell and
A. J. Pollard, eds., *The McFarlane Legacy: Studies in
Late Medieval Politics and Society.* Stroud, Gloucestershire, UK: Alan Sutton, 1995.

Hicks, Michael. "The Case of Sir Thomas Cook,
1468." In Michael Hicks, *Richard III and His Rivals:
Magnates and Their Motives in the Wars of the Roses.*
London: Hambledon Press, 1991.

——. "The Changing Role of the Wydevilles in
Yorkist Politics to 1483." In Charles Ross, ed., *Pa-
tronage, Pedigree and Power in Later Medieval England.*
Stroud, Gloucestershire, UK: Alan Sutton, 1979.

——. "Dynastic Change and Northern Society: The
Career of the Fourth Earl of Northumberland,
1470–89." In Michael Hicks, *Richard III and His
Rivals: Magnates and Their Motives in the Wars of the
Roses.* London: Hambledon Press, 1991.

——. "Lord Hastings' Indentured Retainers?" In
Michael Hicks, *Richard III and His Rivals: Magnates
and Their Motives in the Wars of the Roses.* London:
Hambledon Press, 1991.

——. "Piety and Lineage in the Wars of the Roses: The
Hungerford Experience." In Ralph A. Griffiths and
James Sherborne, eds., *Kings and Nobles in the Later
Middle Ages.* New York: St. Martin's Press, 1986.

Lander, J. R. "The Treason and Death of the Duke of
Clarence." In J. R. Lander, *Crown and Nobility,
1450–1509.* Montreal: McGill-Queen's University
Press, 1976.

——. "A Collector of Apocryphal Anecdotes: John
Blacman Revisited." In A. J. Pollard, ed., *Property
and Politics: Essays in Later Medieval English History.*
Stroud, Gloucestershire, UK: Alan Sutton, 1984.

Lovatt, R. "John Blacman: Biographer of Henry VI."
In R. H. C. Davis and J. M. Wallace-Hadrill, eds.,
The Writing of History in the Middle Ages. Oxford:
Clarendon Press, 1981.

McFarlane, K. B. "Bastard Feudalism." In K. B. McFarlane, *England in the Fifteenth Century: Collected Essays.* London: Hambledon Press, 1981.

——. "The Wars of the Roses." In K. B. McFarlane,
England in the Fifteenth Century: Collected Essays.
London: Hambledon Press, 1981.

Pollard, A. J. "The Richmondshire Community of
Gentry during the Wars of the Roses." In Charles
Ross, ed., *Patronage, Pedigree and Power in Later Me-
dieval England.* Stroud, Gloucestershire, UK: Alan
Sutton, 1979.

Postan, M. M. "The Fifteenth Century." In M. M.
Postan, *Essays in Medieval Agriculture and Economy.*
Cambridge: Cambridge University Press, 1973.

Pugh, T. B. "The Magnates, Knights and Gentry." In
S. B. Chrimes, C. D. Ross, and R. A. Griffiths,
eds., *Fifteenth-Century England, 1399–1509.* 2d
ed. Stroud, Gloucestershire, UK: Alan Sutton,
1995.

——. "Richard Plantagenet (1411–60), Duke of York,
as the King's Lieutenant in France and Ireland." In
J. G. Rowe, ed., *Aspects of Late Medieval Government
and Society.* Toronto: University of Toronto Press,
1986.

Reeves, A. Compton. "Lawrence Booth: Bishop of
Durham (1457–76), Archbishop of York (1476–
80)." In Sharon D. Michalove and A. Compton
Reeves, eds., *Estrangement, Enterprise and Education
in Fifteenth-Century England.* Stroud, Gloucestershire, UK: Sutton Publishing, 1998.

Richmond, Colin. "Bosworth Field and All That." In
P. W. Hammond, ed., *Richard III: Loyalty, Lordship
and Law.* London: Richard III and Yorkist History
Trust, 1986.

Ross, Charles. "Rumour, Propaganda and Popular
Opinion during the Wars of the Roses." In Ralph
A. Griffiths, ed., *Patronage, the Crown and the
Provinces in Later Medieval England.* Atlantic High-
lands, NJ: Humanities Press, 1981.

Rowney, I. "Resources and Retaining in Yorkist En-
gland: William, Lord Hastings and the Honour of
Tutbury." In A. J. Pollard, ed., *Property and Politics:
Essays in Later Medieval English History.* Stroud,
Gloucestershire, UK: Alan Sutton, 1984.

Storey, R. L. "The North of England." In S. B.
Chrimes, C. D. Ross, and R. A. Griffiths, eds., *Fif-
teenth-Century England, 1399–1509.* 2d ed. Stroud,
Gloucestershire, UK: Alan Sutton, 1995.

Wood, Charles T. "Richard III, William, Lord Hastings, and Friday the Thirteenth." In Ralph A. Griffiths and James Sherborne, eds., *Kings and Nobles in
the Later Middle Ages.* New York: St. Martin's Press,
1986.

Index

Boldface page references denote full entries. The abbreviation (illus.) indicates a photograph, table, or other illustration.

About the Author

John A. Wagner has taught U.S. and British history at Phoenix College and at Arizona State University. He is the author of *The Devon Gentleman: The Life of Sir Peter Carew* (1998) and the *Historical Dictionary of the Elizabethan World* (1999). He holds a B.A. from the University of Wisconsin–Oshkosh and an M.A. and Ph.D. from Arizona State University.